WILDERNESS
WAR ON
THE OHIO

Best Regards,

Alan Fitzpatrick

WILDERNESS WAR ON THE OHIO

The Untold Story of the Savage Battle
for British and Indian Control
of the Ohio Country during
the American Revolution

by Alan Fitzpatrick

Edited by Sylvia Rutledge
Illustrations and Maps by Anne Foreman

Table of Contents

Acknowledgments

The idea for this book was conceived nearly 15 years ago as the result of an accidental discovery. At the time, I was visiting the National Archives of Canada located in Ottawa, Ontario, to clear up a mystery surrounding our family's roots. My father had recently found evidence that suggested our ancestors had not come directly from Ireland to Canada in the mid-1800's as family tradition told, but instead, arrived as refugee loyalists or Tories from New York after the close of the American Revolution in 1783. I went to the National Archives hoping to find out if this was true and what had actually happened. While searching through the collections of letters, dispatches, memorials, and muster rolls of loyalists who supported the British during that war, I stumbled upon the names of men who I was familiar with from local history of the Wheeling, West Virginia area dating back to that same time.

I was taken aback by what I read. Here were letters from Simon Girty, Alexander McKee, Matthew Elliott and others. American historians had called these men rogues, renegades, and criminals for siding with the Indians attacking the American frontier of the Ohio River Valley during the American Revolution, however, very little was known about them personally, and less about the exact role they played during the war beyond what was conjecture and rhetoric of the time. Here in the letters of these men were intelligence reports, military communiqués, pay records, and personal petitions that revealed not only the character and temper of the individuals, but more importantly, the concerted effort on the part of Great Britain to militarily control the Ohio Country on a scale not fully known or understood by American historians. These letters from the men who had fought for the British alongside the Indians had been buried for over 225 years in the British Archives. As a result, an account of their conduct in the war had never been told from their point of view and in their own words.

I told my father about it. Being a Canadian and a descendent of a United Empire Loyalist, he suggested that it was important for posterity that the content of the letters of these men be brought to light and their story told, just as light had been shed on the story of our own family and their original roots in America. Consequently, much of the credit for this work is due to him. Without his inspiration and encouragement, the story of the men of the British Indian Department in the Ohio Country would not have come about on my own.

Equally, a great deal of credit for this book is due to Sylvia Rutledge, a Wheeling, West Virginia native now living in Pittsburgh, Pennsylvania. Sylvia gave her time, insight, energy and expertise to the laborious task of editing the book as I was writing it, over a two-year period. In addition, Sylvia helped me through many starts and rewrites of the book as I struggled to define the writing style which would fit the story I wanted to tell. For her unflagging support in helping me find the way to say what it was I wanted to say, I am forever grateful.

My deep gratitude extends to Anne Foreman, Wheeling West Virginia's premier frontier artist, who through her sketches, was able to vividly portray the anguish, hardship and suffering endured by all participants who lived through one of the most dark and troubling times of early American history. Her talented depiction of militiamen, native warriors, Butler's Rangers, and civilians on the frontier of the Ohio Country, as well as her compilation of maps, are some of the first-ever historically accurate drawings to be done.

A number of living history re-enactors and historians, both from the Wheeling, West Virginia area and abroad, provided me with their practical insights into the life and times of the period I was researching and gave me a newfound depth of understanding from their own research and experience into why the individuals of the time period lived the way that they did. A special thanks is in order to the late Joe Bassa, Mike Fitzpatrick, Willie Frankfort, Nathan Gagich, William Hintzen, Robert McCulloch, James Morrison of upstate New York, Greg Park, Joe Roxby, Jeff Shanks, Jerry and Penny Smith, Gavin Watt of Ontario Canada, and Sue Weigand for all the help they provided.

I am grateful to Cindy Consonery of Harrisburg, Pennsylvania for her work to correct the myriad errors I had committed on computer and to put the book into form that would allow it to be printed from the raw chapters I presented her.

And finally, I thank my close personal friend, Cecy Rose, for all her logistical help in making this book happen. She put up with me through the tough times and lent her vital support when I needed it most.

Wilderness War on the Ohio

Introduction

There is an untold side of the American Revolution; a forgotten, lost war fought within the context of that better known war for American independence from Great Britain. It is an untold story surrounded by mystery and misconception to this day because of the very nature of what happened. While Washington's patriot armies were battling British redcoats in set-piece actions across the colonies in the East, a war of a far different nature was being conducted in the West to determine who was to control the frontier and Indian lands of the upper Ohio River Valley, the Ohio Country to its west, and the Kentucky lands to the south. This forgotten, lost war was savage, brutal, bloody and partisan. It was fought without fixed boundaries or large armies, without accepted rules of engagement, or agreed-upon non-combatants.

A British-allied confederation of Indian tribes battled Virginian militiamen and settlers from 1774 until the end of the war, and further, for control of their ancestral lands. In an attempt to halt white encroachment from eastern colonies, the Indian tribes of the Ohio Country were not motivated as the British were to put down a growing colonial rebellion from British rule. White man's politics to the Indians were irrelevant. At the heart of this struggle was a clash of race and culture. The method of war, as in all such wars fought by implacable enemies who view each other from irreconcilable differences was simply the extermination of their opponent by any means. Today we call recent wars that result in unspeakable atrocities, wars of genocide and ethnic cleansing. To the American victors of that forgotten frontier war that moment in history is known simply as the "Indian wars," the "wilderness war," and the "border wars."

History is never kind to the vanquished in what humanity judges to be a "dirty" war. When the guns fall silent, and the victors sit down to give a written account of what transpired, they cannot forget and will never forgive. What we do know of the war on the western frontier has come to us from accounts written entirely from the American patriot or settler perspective. The chronicles of the post-revolution era tell us a terrible story of a largely defenseless frontier population under constant threat of ambush, attack, and siege by savage painted Indian warriors who moved freely through uncharted woods in small war parties, striking down men, women, and children in their isolated cabins, leaving butchered scalped bodies and burnt homes in their wake. The survivors of this kind of frontier war had no need to understand or record anything about the British and Indian character, motivation or point of view. Through the writings of Draper, Withers, Kellogg, Thwaites and De

Hass we gain a perspective of history as seen through the eyes of those who were "inside the walls" of settler's forts and blockhouses. They lived to tell their tale; many of their neighbors and friends did not.

To such frontier settlers, their enemies were the feared faceless savage Indians, who were thoroughly hated and needed to be destroyed if the settlements were to prevail. Survival was paramount for those who lived through those times. It is hard not to judge them for this conviction, having not ourselves lived through that struggle and suffered from that brutal type of warfare. The Greathouses, Wetzels, and other Indian fighters were called heroes of their time for killing Indians, and as is the case in all such ethnic and racial wars of genocide, they could not be called by any other name when that kind of war called upon some men to do extraordinary things that at any other time might appear uncivilized and inhumane. War, we say, is hell, and it is difficult to justify atrocities when it is over. American reprisals for Indian killings, such as the Moravian massacre in early 1782, have been viewed from the settler perspective as justifiable, and at worst, a necessary evil: retaliation on a savage enemy bent upon nothing less than the annihilation of the white man. Accounts of this time in history are regrettably one-sided in both presentation and point of view. And that one-sidedness is our side, for we are the descendents of the victors, and we all understandably sympathize with the brave frontiersmen who battled against such a despised and brutal enemy at such imposing odds. It is our culture and ethnicity that survived, not that of the Indian. It was our ancestors who wrote history, while still fresh in their minds, for the benefit of their descendants, who are none other than us. It is those ancestors, the Zanes, Bradys, Wetzels, and countless others, the victors of that war of attrition, to whom belonged the spoils of that terrible struggle, and with their victory they also won the right to pen history in their words and images. If they had lost their struggle, what would we have known of them?

Undeniably, the frontier people hated Indians for their savagery, depredations, paganism, and primitiveness. Yet another enemy was even more despised by the frontier settler and militiaman during the wilderness war years. Written accounts again and again tell of white men seen fighting alongside Indians, against their own kind. The settlers called them "renegades" and "white Indians." Some were thought to be fugitives from the law, or even outcasts from the rough and tumble frontier society. Others were known to be men who were captured as young children from their frontier homes by Indians during the French and Indian war. Taken into the interior wilderness of the Ohio Country, these children were adopted into Indian families, raised in the Indian culture, and learned a new language. Fully integrated to the Indian way of life, they gradually forgot everything about their former lives. Many of these children, as young adults, were repatriated at the end of the war according to terms of the peace. Many would tearfully refuse to leave their adopted Indian family, and were forcibly taken away by soldiers and returned to the eastern settlements. The younger the child at the time of his capture and the greater number of years spent with the Indians, the more indelible the mark of Indian life was believed to be made upon him.

Another type of white man was believed to be living and fighting with Indians once the rebellion in the eastern provinces turned to open armed revolt. In New York, for instance, the open rebellion of 1775 forced the populace to determine their loyalties. Not everyone had supported the chaotic revolt with open arms. Many citizens and landowners remained loyal to the British Crown, which they felt, despite its shortcomings, was still the lawful government. Under no circumstances would they support the efforts of a minority to overthrow British rule, and jeopardize all they possessed when Great Britain put down the revolt and punished the rebellious, as they were convinced would happen. In actuality, one third of the populace of New York colony were in support of the rebellion; one-third were indifferent to the freedom movement and wished it would all go away; and one-third of the people were outright opposed to revolt. As time progressed, both loyalists and patriots would become polarized and increasingly hardened in attitude. Ultimately loyalists to the Crown and patriots to the cause would resort to arms, when diplomacy with each other failed. Those men and their families, sympathetic and loyal to the Crown, would find themselves forced from their homes and arrested by patriot mobs. Evicted or facing jail, hundreds would be forced to flee to Canada and there joined loyalist regiments composed entirely of other American exiles. Foremost in their mind was the support of the British military effort that would soon move to put down the colonist rebellion by force. These loyalists, commonly called "Tories" by the rebels, were sought out and arrested or expelled by the "Committees for Detecting Conspiracies" that were active in every town and village that supported the rebellion in New York. Families and households were split as fathers opposed sons and brothers opposed brothers for their allegiance to the Crown or to the rebellion. In most cases, the "Tories" were driven into exile.

Upon their arrival in Canada, these men enlisted in provincial loyalist regiments. Their military role changed quickly from support units for British continental troops in the field to fighting forces in their own right, capable of independent offensive action. Unlike their rebel counterpart, the Colonial militia, these loyalist regiments evolved into well organized, highly disciplined military ranging units, who would take the war back to their rebel-held hometowns with a vengeance. These men were motivated by revenge and they knew the lay of the land, which they vacated better than any British officer. Trained and supplied by the British in a way that the rebel government could not match for any militia, these loyalists would operate from their bases along the Canadian frontier and attack the Mohawk, Hudson, and Schoharie Valleys. By mid-1777, they would begin to conduct a series of raids that would last throughout the war years and would gain them a notorious reputation. These loyalist regiments known as Butler's Rangers, the Royal Yorkers, and Jessup's Corps would transform themselves into seasoned ranger fighting units, operating in the manner of Indian war parties—appearing from nowhere and without warning, and using hit-and run tactics again and again from behind the rebel lines. And to bolster their numbers on each raid and institute a reign of terror throughout the northern New York frontier, the loyalist ranger corps used a tried-and-true tactic reminiscent of the French and Indian Wars some twenty years previous. British-allied Iroquois Seneca and Mohawk Indians were employed on the large-scale raids to deliver devastating blows to the rebel populace and militia. A scorched earth policy was the rule. Every rebel home, barn, mill, and crop was burnt in an attempt to both punish and neutralize. White men fighting alongside a terrorizing horde of Indians only added a dimension of incredible fear to those living on the border of the wilderness.

However the war on the western frontier was a different matter concerning British sympathizers. When rebellion broke out in the East and word finally reached the Upper Ohio Valley, the majority of settlers shrugged their shoulders with indifference to political matters and allegiances. The reality of physical survival in a harsh frontier environment plagued by the threat of intermittent Indian raids was far more important. The causes of liberty or loyalism did not touch or affect them directly at first. Besides, the frontier settlements were too far removed from the turmoil hundreds of miles to the east for anyone to really think that red-coated British troops would arrive to enforce British rule even if the frontier people chose to support the cause of liberty, as they would probably do in time. Regardless, if a man did express a certain degree of sympathy for the Crown he could be tolerated on the frontier in a manner unlike that in New York province, where British troops were on the march and loyalists were posing serious threat to the patriot cause. On the frontier, the loyalist or Tory had no British provincial loyalist regiment to enlist in so he was not a problem. Being so far removed from the turmoil and politics in the East, who cared?

However, a white man sympathetic to the Indian cause was another matter entirely. Such views were heinous in every frontier home and settlement. Yet as the war years progressed and the Indian attacks increased in intensity and severity, white men were increasingly seen fighting alongside the Indians though their identity remained, for the most part, a mystery. The settlers and blockhouse defenders along the lands east of the Ohio River did not know who the "white Indians" were or why they would choose to support the Indians and forsake their own white race. New York and the Western Frontier were two vastly different worlds. In New York, the whites fighting with Indians were known to be former friends, family, and neighbors, and now were called "Tories." They fought for the British cause, not really that of the Indian. On the western frontier, far removed from the politics of loyalism in the East, the mystery of these "white renegades" was incomprehensible. The historical accounts bear out the mystery. They reveal frontier attitudes of much deeper hatred towards these "whites" who had "gone over" to the Indians, than hatred commonly held towards Indians. Indians could be understood for who they were: a savage hated enemy who would kill whites until he was killed. They did not fit into the frontier white man's world that espoused only white man's beliefs. But "white Indians" were regarded as renegades from the frontier, from their own white man's world. How could a white man possibly turn against his own people, then? The undying deeper hatred towards such men was because they had betrayed their own race by allying with an implacable enemy, the Indian savage. The accounts and descriptions of these white men portray them as nothing less than "monsters most evil." It was inconceivable that they might be Tories, albeit supporters of the British Crown, and possibly soldiers in service. The western frontiersman bordering the Ohio was ignorant of the partisan war already being fought across the frontier of New York province. So that the historical accounts written from the colonial frontier perspective soon after the border war years tell us virtually nothing about the true identity and motivation of these men. They appear all as "Girtys," after the infamous Simon Girty. By the end of the war, the name Girty became synonymous with "Indian renegade" and "inhuman monster."

Curiously, few of these white men, if any, were ever captured and questioned, or perhaps we would be left with more understanding of the role they played. In accounts that record the sighting of white men fighting alongside the Indians in raiding parties, these whites always manage to slip away. And when the war was over, and the Indians finally expelled from the Ohio lands, Draper and other frontier interviewers did not seek out and interview these white men now in exile in Canada, nor, for that matter, any of their descendents in an attempt to understand more of the unique part they played in conducting the wilderness war against the frontier. Obviously it did not matter to the victors. That terrible long war that cost so many their lives had been won and the Indian enemy was either exterminated or expelled from the border frontier settlements once and for all. But the question about the identity of "white Indians" still remains. Really, who were these men that fought so long and hard with Indians against their former friends, neighbors, and family?

The untold story of the western frontier war of 1774 to 1783 begins here with these men. When rebellion broke out in 1775 in the colonies in the East, war on the frontier with the Indians was already underway. The British found themselves in a tough position in North America. They had underestimated colonial resentment and unrest, and never believed that it would result in open revolt. Militarily, they were stretched far too thin to maintain control over the vast expanse of land that extended from the Atlantic coast north to Canada, west to the Great Lakes and south to the Ohio River Valley and beyond, which they inherited from the French in 1760 with the fall of Quebec. British presence was most lacking along the western frontier with only undermanned posts at Fort Niagara, Oswego, Fort Detroit, and Michilimackinac. Gradually as the war years progressed, British policy would evolve into a military build up at these posts to safeguard their supply routes and the Great Lakes waterway. This would provide the opportunity, through fortifying and strengthening these posts, of not only cementing British hold on the western lands but, more importantly, allowing for a concerted effort to be made to ally the Indian tribes of the Ohio Country already warring against the frontier settlements. Those border settlements, as rebel settlements, now posed a threat to British control of the Ohio lands. As the British could not possibly put an army in the field against those settlements, working with the Indians was strategically the best possibility of securing that frontier by containing its expansion across the Ohio River. The task at hand, to work closely with the Indians, had enormous challenges, and the gap between white and red cultures, a substantial one for the British, would have to be bridged. However it was a method that was already being done on the New York frontier, and it depended upon putting a certain type of white man in the field with the Indians, an Indian liaison, if they were to have any chance of success. In fact it would take white men who knew the Indians intimately, who spoke their language, and who could understand Indian thinking and motivation. Out of necessity, such men would need to live with the Indians in their villages and dress like them if they were to gain the tribe's complete confidence and respect.

In fact, such men could be found. They came from the ranks of the Frenchmen, traders, exiled loyalists, and runaways who had prior dealings with Indians visiting the British posts to trade for goods. There were white men who could be counted on who were already living among the various tribes. They were the white children, captured and raised by the Indians of the Ohio Country in the previous war, who, upon their repatriation to the white man's world, could not fit for one reason or another. Many had returned to the Indians, the only people and only way of life where they felt comfortable. Many dressed as Indians and had taken Indian wives. The British Indian Department at the British posts would need expanded to make room for the influx of new men in the employ of the British cause. Fort Niagara and especially Fort Detroit, already Indian trade centers, would become natural bases of operations for future campaigns. Clearly, the hard lessons studied and learned about wilderness warfare in North America 20 years prior during the French and Indian War and Pontiac's Conspiracy, would provide the British with a blueprint of strategy and tactics in the upcoming military campaign to maintain control of the western lands of the frontier known as the Ohio Country and prevent further encroachment by rebel settlers and troops.

From British command headquarters in Quebec city, a policy for conducting the war on the far western frontier was devised that could make the best use of Indian fighters to further the British interest of protecting the western lands from rebel American expansion while preserving these same lands for the Indian tribes. It was easy to see that British and Indian interests were the same and each could help the other if a concerted effort were made by both to attack the rebel American frontier posts which were hostile to both. Through transportation of supplies, ammunition, and equipment by British ships operating upon the Great Lakes between posts at Niagara and Detroit, the Indians could be given the means to conduct a more methodical war against their enemies, the western frontier settlers, who were now British enemies. Out of necessity, goals would need to be kept simple. Great distances were involved in transporting quantities of war material from Quebec to Detroit an on to Indian villages deep within the Ohio Country that would serve as staging areas for raids against the settlements. From those Indian villages to the actual Ohio River Valley rebel frontier forts and blockhouses added many more miles for the attackers. If they were to make any concerted effort, the obvious limitations of re-supply would be placed upon them. By 1778, the British would ambitiously plan to keep the rebels bottled up on the east side of the Ohio River and prevent their movement south to the Kentucky lands or west into Indian country. Any idea that the American bastion at Fort Pitt could be taken, or the settlers driven back across the Allegheny Mountains, was dismissed.

Recruitment for the Indian Department would provide the British with their own men in the field who would not only see that the Indians received their provisional support for war parties raiding along the frontier, but more importantly, attempt to take gradual command of the Indians and provide structure to this growing British war. They could do essential things that the Indians would not. Intelligence on the enemy and his movements would need to be taken from live prisoners rather than dead, scalped corpses. Those rebel prisoners would need to be questioned by men who could speak English as well as Indian dialects, so that prisoner information, as well as what could be gleaned from returning Indian war parties in the field could be funneled back to Fort Detroit, and sent on to British headquarters in Quebec for assessment of the western war effort. However unsavory a character the men of the Indian Department might appear to be to regular officers, out of necessity they would become the backbone of British war efforts in the west. Often these men were viewed by high command with skepticism, and as another sort of necessary evil to be tolerated in a far-removed wilderness war. To the British, the necessity of using Indians and their savage methods of warfare to attack the American frontier was a decision based upon the exigencies of wilderness fighting and not one based upon conscience. Every British officer posted in the wilderness implicitly knew that once supplied and set loose upon the hapless frontier settlements, the Indians would likely spare no one, not even women and children in their depredations. However, a lot was at stake for the Crown in their struggle to control the Ohio Country, and regular British troops could never be spared for offensive actions in the West.

In any joint effort, compromises are always made, and using Indians in the conduct of the war was only one of them. While many Indian Department officers would fight with the Indians for pay, some would do so for plunder, and in some cases for pleasure. Uncomfortably, the British at Detroit would have no choice but to give these men total command of whatever forces they had at their disposal once they were on the wilderness trail. Whether these "officers" were qualified or capable would be the question. Those men who were made officers would, nonetheless, need to possess special qualities if they were to have a chance of success. Foremost, they would need to be able to cultivate a rapport with their Indian allies and be able to motivate them. Indians were always considered to be temperamental at best, and capable of abandoning any military effort if they so desired for any superstitious reason.

The men of the Indian Department would be entirely dependent upon the Indians once in the field, so they could not risk angering them and possibly face abandonment. Men of the Indian Department needed to be highly resourceful and capable of making wise decisions on the spur of the moment, in addition to being physically fit for the demanding rigors of year round travel on foot through the wilderness in all types of weather. Like the Indians, these men would have to be able to endure conditions of hardship brought on by lack of adequate provisions, for they would be unable to carry enough food on their backs for an extended campaign. Carrying too much would impair their ability to conduct the war parties in quick, successful hit-and run raids which were dependent upon traveling light to increase rapid field mobility. By necessity, they would need to be great woodsmen who could live off the land when returning from raids when supplies ran short. Most importantly, these men had to be able to grasp all the intangibles of utilizing Indians in a wilderness war that British regular officers could not possibly comprehend. How could they keep Indian morale up, while supplicating Indian wishes and weaknesses? How could they keep Indian scouts in the field constantly to better gather quality intelligence, and if so, what method of reward to the Indians for their loyalty? Raiders must be encouraged to take prisoners alive if precious intelligence was to be gained, but it was not the Indian way to take a man prisoner if he resisted or tried to escape. How would one exert some measure of control over the Indians and yet appease the well-known Indian desire for blood, booty, and scalps. Precious food, ammunition, and supplies would be wasted if all Indian war parties returned with scalps alone, or if Indians broke off a pending attack after reaching their objective because of one warrior's disturbing dream which his comrades took as an ill-omen and a sign to go home. All in all, diplomacy with the Indians would be a tall order for any man to fill, and few would be found that could rise to the demands of the position.

This British plan for the defense of the western frontier which devised using Indian war parties from the tribes of the Ohio Country accompanied by white men of the Indian Department to conduct a guerilla type of hit-and-run war to contain the Americans on the western frontier, was found to be lacking by the autumn of 1778, despite early successes. In response to the Indian attacks, George Washington directed his generals at the western posts to take the initiative and stage campaigns of their own against the British-led Indians. With the building of American Fort Laurens on the Tuscarawas River deep within the Indian lands by General Brodhead from Fort Pitt, and the stunning capture of British Fort Vincennes to the west in the spring of 1779 by General George Rogers Clark, it became clear that the Americans had taken the offensive and intended to strike not only the Indians in their villages but British Detroit itself. In conjunction, Washington ordered General Sullivan to strike deeply into the lands of the Six Nations Iroquois in western New York and destroy their villages and homes from where they were constantly raiding American settlements, and to punish them, too, for their part in the destruction of Mohawk,

Wyoming and Cherry Valleys. This campaign would seriously threaten the security of British Fort Niagara, like Fort Detroit. By mid-1779, the momentum of the frontier war was shifting in favor of the Americans. In response to the American moves, the British judged that more material support for their Indian allies was needed, but that alone would not be enough. Headquarters staff in Quebec reasoned that they would need to put more British regulars in the field and into the fight if the Ohio lands were to be held and the reverses caused by the increased American presence be challenged. Red-coated regulars were not the answer. They were neither suited for wilderness warfare, nor could they be spared from the war in the East.

The answer would come from Fort Niagara, the headquarters for a provincial corps of tough, seasoned rangers known as Butler's Rangers who had been actively raiding the New York and Pennsylvania frontier settlements with great success. The rank and file were expelled loyalists from the colonies and they were led by Colonel John Butler, a veteran of the British Indian Department and the French and Indian War. Butler, an Indian Department officer and local magistrate in the Mohawk Valley, had fled his home at Butlersbury in the spring of 1775 to avoid arrest by rebel authorities. He answered the call of the British government to raise a provincial regiment that could serve as a military ranging unit on the New York frontier. It would be modeled much like that of the famed British Roger's Rangers of the French and Indian War, who were able to take the war to the French and their Indian allies by ranging far beyond British bases, enduring physical hardships while in the field, and ruthlessly destroying the enemy whenever encountered.

Known as Butler's Rangers, after their namesake, the ten companies were clothed in green coats, much like the early Rogers' Rangers, to better conceal them in the forest as they ranged far into enemy territory on scouts and raids. It would be these men who would be called on to support the Indian Department officers in the field of the Ohio Country in the latter part of the war. Butler's men could live and fight Indian-style in the wilderness. In addition, while fighting alongside Indians, the rangers possessed qualities that Indian warriors did not. Butler's Rangers were a highly-trained, disciplined military unit that could deliver sustained volley fire when needed, and at the same time, were well versed in all aspects of small group tactics that could be used against pursuing rebel militia which Indians preferred to avoid, once they were detected. Indian raiders alone would hit and run, where rangers could hit again and again, if necessary. Dozens of successful raids along the length of New York and Pennsylvania had proven that Butler's Rangers and Indian allies together were a formidable fighting force to be reckoned with anywhere on the frontier where regular troops, both British and American were at a disadvantage.

The addition of Butler's Rangers to Ft. Detroit and the Ohio Country, late in the conduct of the war, would turn the tide on the frontier temporarily in favor of the Indians and British. In June 1782, two companies of rangers commanded by one of the most able and experienced captains, William

Caldwell, would join an Indian force led by Indian Department officers Alexander McKee, Matthew Elliot, and Simon Girty, and would engage and destroy nearly half of Colonel Crawford's 500 man expedition as he attempted to destroy the hostile Indian villages at upper Sandusky deep in the Ohio Country. Ranger casualties would amount to one man killed and three wounded, with less than a dozen Indians killed or wounded. Two months later and over 100 miles to the south in Kentucky, Caldwell and McKee would lead 30 rangers and over 200 Indians in a successful raid-turned-ambush on a pursuing force of seasoned mounted militiamen at Blue Licks. While claiming to have killed, wounded and taken prisoner 146 Kentuckians and nearly all their officers, not a ranger was lost and only six Indians were killed, ten wounded, and one of the Indian Department officers, a Frenchman, killed. In September, a company of Butler's Rangers and Indians led by Captain Andrew Bradt, nephew of Colonel John Butler, would besiege Fort Henry at Wheeling on the Ohio River with the intent to destroy the fort, all surrounding homes, livestock, and crops, in addition to annihilating its defenders. This attack has become recognized as the last major battle of the American Revolution.

The story I am about to tell is one that has never been adequately documented. It is the story of an untold, unknown war that was never acknowledged by American historians—the British campaign for control of the Ohio Country. It is the story of the forgotten men who fought for the British Crown and the Indian way of life in Ohio, and lost, ultimately not by their lack of effort, but rather by a lack of will of Great Britain to continue the struggle any longer in North America. Called "Tories," "white Indians" and "renegades" by their former friends and family, they turned their backs to the frontier and patriot cause of their fellowmen, and instead, supported the British in a savage war that employed Indians against the frontier. Once the war was over, these men found that they were so strongly hated by their former enemies that they could never return to former homes and family, under penalties of death for their prior service. Exile to Canada would be their choice.

This is the story of the white "Indians" who were seen by the defenders of Ft. Laurens, Bryan's Station, and Ft. Henry and were made mention of later in frontier accounts of the war. Their story in no way diminishes that of the bravery and fortitude of their opponents, the American frontier militiaman and settler. As evidence now shows, these men who fought for the Crown in the western wilderness war were equally as brave in battle as their American counterparts. While admitting among their ranks some men driven to ruthlessness, excess and cowardice, most of the men of the Indian Department and the Ranger Corps obeyed the call of duty with honor. In doing so, they suffered from hardship, hunger, and disease brought about by the great distances involved in campaigning in the wilderness far from adequate re-supply. Their service, much like that of their American counterparts defending their frontier homes and posts, locked them in an intense personal struggle to survive in an inhospitable environment that was unforgiving, in the context of a war that was brutal and savage.

Based upon the pages of war correspondence, official documents, and personal letters written on the battlefield, that have lain undiscovered for more than 215 years in the British Archives and War Office Records in England and Ottawa, Canada, this is their story; the story of the men of the British Indian Department and Butler's Rangers who fought to control the Ohio Country and the Upper Ohio Valley for cause of the King and the Indians during the American Revolution. Finally, now it can be told.

PART ONE

Indian Wilderness Warfare:
Lessons Learned Well

Part One
Introduction

No period of American history brings to the mind of the reader more terrible images of savagery and brutality than that of the Indian wars fought on the 18th century eastern frontier. Shocking accounts of those times reveal a war fought in the wilderness, which was unlike any previously or since recorded. The accounts tell us of native Indian warriors, hideously-painted vermillion and black, with beads and silver ornaments dangling from noses and ear lobes and naked except for breech-clouts and leggings. They would spring from the cover of the forests, screaming their frightening war whoops with bloody hatchets and tomahawks raised high to pounce upon unsuspecting European soldiers, colonial militiamen, and settler families.

The accounts tell us of red-coated British soldiers stumbling in terrified, numbed confusion in forest clearings, unable to see the enemies firing upon them. Dozens of their comrades were dropped by the hail of Indian musket-shot and arrows unleashed from hidden positions. We hear the shrieks and screams of the wounded and dying in the wake of the ambush as the now victorious Indian warriors, methodically move from body to body, pausing to scalp, strip, and mutilate beyond recognition those unfortunate enough to be left alive upon the field. Eyewitness accounts tell of prisoners taken by the Indians and marched to distant Indian villages, where they were flayed and burned alive in day-long ordeals of torture. There are more details in those chronicles, much worse, and too horrific by anyone's standards to be told, yet all of it is true. The incidents of Indian depredations upon frontier settlers and militiamen occurred innumerable times during the course of the Indian wars of 18th century.

The war for control of the Indian lands of the Ohio Country, which continued from 1774 until the turn of the century was possibly the most brutal and bloodiest of all the wars. The accounts of that conflict are filled with the tales of sustained Indian savagery waged against the white frontier settlements which earned for the Indians the undying hatred of settlers, soldiers and scouts. The accounts, with their ghastly descriptions of events, demonstrate the methods used by the Indians in waging frontier warfare. According to white men of the period, the Indians were savages who fought in an uncivilized manner. They ruthlessly attacked from ambush, sparing no men, women, or children that they came upon. The Indians relied upon methods of warfare which were long a part of their culture and tradition. As an example, the slaying of the enemy's wounded in battle was viewed by Indians as one of the spoils of victory. Attacking an enemy in a forest ambush was a tested and true tactic. It provided the attacker with the element of surprise that offered the maximum opportunity for success, against an unsuspecting foe. This was how Indians fought. These were their tactics that worked well in the wilderness where European rules of warfare were ineffective.

But if account after account tells us how the Indians fought, do they tell us fully the reasons why? By and large, nearly all the frontier accounts from that period tell the same story. The Indian tribes fought white settlers and soldiers to simply maintain control of their ancestral lands and keep the white man out. To a great degree this is the truth. It is easy to believe that the Indian tribes collectively battled against the white intruders for the same reason. The wars of the latter half of the 18th century were conflicts of annihilation and attrition between whites and Indians. While the Indian tribes as a whole were motivated to fight for their lands against white intrusion, and used this reason as one of their arguments for war against the whites, it was not the primary and underlying cause.

It is easy to confuse the frontier accounts of Indian raids, the end result of Indian tactics of that time with Indian strategy. To understand Indian nature and culture at the time they came in contact with white men would shed light on their collective limited ability to wage war against the settlers. Such understanding would point to the root cause of the Indian wars and demonstrate that it is not enough to simply say that the tribes fought for their lands. However, many of the Indian raids and campaigns of that era are examples of that belief alone. Pontiac, Logan, Cornstalk, Brant, and Tecumseh, all notable chiefs and warriors of woodland tribes, tried to forge alliances in their efforts to prevent incursion of whites into their lands. While enjoying some success in inflicting casualties upon white soldiers and settlers, Pontiac and Tecumseh were failures. Although they were by far the most dominant Indian leaders of the time, neither realized his dreams of regaining their lands from the whites. It never came to pass. Why then were the frontier Indians wars such a prolonged, terrible struggle, which brought years of unrelenting raids and blood-letting that resulted in the loss of life for hundreds of white scouts, settlers, and soldiers? The true reason is that white men and their governments were as much to blame as the Indians for the conflict.

What we fail to understand is that most of the Indian wars of the 18th century were the result of Indians fighting as allies of white men and their colonial governments, who were waging war against one another. With the advent of the white man into Indian lands, Indian wilderness warfare began. The French and English in North America were European adversaries, who sought alliances with the native tribes in hopes of gaining control of the wilderness lands and undertaking warfare against their rival. They looked upon the hundreds of Indian warriors, who were skilled in the unique tactics of a wilderness battlefield as important potential allies. However the ability of the Indians to wage war in a consistent manner was always in question. On their own, Indians had no resources, weaponry, command structure, or resolve to do anything beyond "hit and run" skirmishing. Although their struggle with the white men lasted nearly 50 years, the intensity and longevity of their struggle could not be attributed to the minor parts played by a handful of noted Indian leaders such as Pontiac. In reality the Indians were drawn into a conflict between European powers for colonial dominance.

The frontiers in the beginning of that struggle were New England and New France. The wilderness separating them was Indian lands. With both French and English arguing that the ultimate goal was preservation of Indian lands, the European war was carried on in a unique form to the edge of white civilization and beyond. The combatants on both sides were armed, provisioned, and led by white men.

At the end of the Seven Years War between France and a victorious Great Britain, relative peace returned the frontier. There no longer was a need to arm the Indian tribes and utilize them in a military strategy. Pontiac's Conspiracy, an Indian rebellion against British rule over land the French ceded to Great Britain, was a continuation of the French and Indian War. The uprising demonstrated that Indians, without the support of white men, were unable to sustain a frontier war against an organized opponent. An inability to manufacture or obtain massive supplies of gunpowder, lead for musket balls, muskets, and campaign provisions combined with the impossibility of forming coalitions between the tribes doomed Pontiac's Indian rebellion against British rule. The conflict was over by 1763.

With no war between the French and English, the Indian warfare against the frontier ended, at least temporarily. At the same time, the frontier shifted steadily to the west of the Allegheny Mountains with settlers crossing over into the lands of the Indians. In spite of rising friction between white settlers and the Indian tribes of the Ohio Country, there was no open warfare because white men were not fighting white men.

In the spring of 1774, that changed. Indian war whoops and the smoke of burning settler cabins again filled the air of the frontier after nearly a decade of peace. In the upper Ohio River valley, Indians under the Mingo chief Logan sought revenge for atrocities committed by whites, and soon Shawnee warriors under Cornstalk would follow. Those events, as well as independent Indian raids, led to a Virginia-sponsored campaign against the Indians known as Lord Dunmore's War. The attempt to quell the hostile Indians was eclipsed by tumultuous events in the eastern colonies as rebellion against the rule of Great Britain turned to revolution and open warfare by the spring of 1775.

As the British sought to put down the colonial rebellion through military means, it became necessary to enlist the aid of the Indian tribes of the wilderness frontier in the effort. To the tribes of the Iroquois Confederacy in New York, and the Wyandot, Delaware, Shawnee and Mingo tribes in the Ohio Country, alliance to the British cause was appealing. With the Indians already embroiled in a struggle against the influx of settlers into their ancestral lands, the British had little difficulty convincing the Indians that they would help in ousting the land-hungry Americans. With few exceptions, the Indians cast their lot with the British and picked up the war hatchet.

As the war for American independence from Great Britain raged on in the eastern colonies between European-styled armies in set-piece battles, a war of a far different type was being fought on the frontiers of New York, Pennsylvania, and Virginia. Indian allies of the British, armed and provisioned from plentiful stocks, were employed in this new "white man's war" in attacks against a new "white enemy" in a manner and scale never seen before in Indian warfare. A campaign of total destruction aimed against the American frontier settlements was undertaken with the goal being devastation of the American settlements and eliminating American efforts to attack British-held Canada. In the process, settlers were killed or driven out, and their homes, livestock and crops destroyed.

The viciousness, intensity, and duration of the Indian attacks along the frontier were part of the plan. Though the British-allied Indian warriors were similar in character to those who fought 20 years earlier, they were better armed and possessed greater experience in fighting wilderness warfare against white men. They were more acquainted with the white man's language, his style of fighting, his weaknesses, and his character. Thus the Indians of this new war were able to fight in a more consistent and effective manner than ever done before.

However, the real difference in the conflict came from white men employed by the British Indian Department and the newly commissioned provincial Ranger Corps, who would do more than advise and supply the Indian raiders. These men were called upon to devise and carry out the devastating raids, live with the Indians on the campaign trail, and fight alongside them in battle. They put into practice all the lessons learned by the British of the strategy and tactics of Indian wilderness warfare. This practical knowledge was not based upon European military thinking or text-book principles. Instead, it was derived from direct experience in the field and learned through tactical trial and error, when all conventional wisdom failed. The valuable lessons learned from fighting the French-allied Indians in the cauldron of wilderness warfare of the Seven Year's War, more than 20 years earlier, were used by the British in taking that war to French Canada and ultimately bringing about its defeat. The price tag those lessons carried was high, dearly paid for with the lives of hundreds of British colonials and soldiers.

Soon the American frontier would come to bear the full brunt of what had been learned of the art of conducting an Indian wilderness war. Nowhere were those lessons put to more use and with more refinement, than with the savage battle for control of the lands of the Ohio Country bordering the western frontier of the Ohio River valley from 1778 to 1783.

Before that story can be told, we must look at the lessons of Indian wilderness warfare, which were learned two decades earlier and put to use during the American war for independence. At the beginning of the Seven Years War, the British knew little about dealing with Indians. Other than some trade with nearby tribes, they possessed scant knowledge of the tribes of the Ohio Country, and little more with the Iroquois nations beyond the Mohawk Valley. As a result, the British had little or no influence among the Indians. On the other hand, their

French counterparts in Canada had spent many years cultivating a close relationship with the many Indian tribes with whom they had contact. Unlike the British, the French were well-experienced and well-versed in the nature, character, language and the ways of Indians. By the outbreak of war in 1754, the French had already forged treaties and trade alliances with many of the tribes living within the sphere of French influence, which extended throughout the Great Lakes region.

For the English, the plunge into the crucible of wilderness warfare at the onset of hostilities with the French forced them to re-evaluate their rigid military thinking, which was based upon European standards, when they were handed a series of military defeats by the French and their Indian allies. Ultimately, the English borrowed a page from the French and their savage allies, and not only learned to fight more like Indians but improved upon those tactics. Englishmen like George Washington, Robert Rogers, and William Johnson were able to survive their own military blunders in wilderness warfare, and put into action new strategies more adapted to the wilderness they found themselves fighting in.

Ultimately, this fundamental change resulting from the lessons of wilderness warfare learned at a high cost paved the way to victory in this first wilderness war, and sealed the fate of French Canada. Those lessons were learned well, and were not to be forgotten. They provided the British with the blueprint for frontier war in the next conflict to come. Here, first, is that story.

Chapter 1

Washington: Inexperience Ignites a War

What did 22-year-old George Washington know about the nature of wilderness warfare? Appointed an officer and emissary of Virginia Governor Dinwiddie in 1753, Washington was the son of a Virginian gentleman and plantation owner from east of the Alleghenies. He had no practical military experience and less understanding of the role that he was about to be thrust into by Dinwiddie that would take him to the wilds of the untamed land to the west of the mountains called the Ohio Country. At the time of his appointment, Washington was largely a product of his upbringing among the Virginia gentry. Like his brothers, he was groomed to take his place in Virginian society and not to traverse the uncharted frontiers as a soldier-ambassador. Indeed, Washington's early years were not spent close to the frontier, unlike others, who had gained at least some knowledge through exposure to frontiersmen and the native Indians who inhabited the lands. Washington knew little about the native tribes and cared little about them.

Far more disturbing was the fact that he did not understand the unique demands for survival which the wilderness dictated for all those who entered it. Skills needed for frontier survival were far different than those needed for life in Williamsburg. In short, the wilderness lands he entered in the fall of 1753 on a mission to the French for Dinwiddie and the Ohio Company were completely alien to Washington. Unskilled and ignorant in the ways of the wilderness Washington was severely challenged to prove that he was fit to command in the upcoming conflict with the French if a unique kind of warfare did erupt.

Nonetheless, it would be the young gentleman from Virginia, George Washington, who was called upon by the Governor to serve as emissary to the French, who were claiming the same wilderness lands as the British for as their own. Washington, who had a thirst for adventure and an ambition for political position found himself with the opportunity of a lifetime with Dinwiddie's commission. Little did he know that in fulfilling his duty he would be placed in the center of the gathering storm between Great Britain and France with the wilderness of the Ohio Country as the arena for that conflict. The result would be global warfare between European powers. But in the beginning, it would be George Washington's lack of experience which would inadvertently light the match that would start a war. The lessons he learned would last him a lifetime and impress upon the seasoned veteran George Washington of a later war the importance of understanding and not underestimating those lessons, which had cost so dearly. There may have been other Englishmen before Washington who through their own experience understood implicitly what Washington was soon to learn about the nature and conduct of Indians and wilderness warfare. However, in the wilderness, mistakes were usually fatal. That Washington survived his education in the Ohio Country made the difference between him and others less fortunate.

Washington's first trip to the Ohio Country

The wilderness in question that a young George Washington entered in 1753 and again in 1754 was known as the Ohio Country by the few whites, both French and English, who penetrated its interior. The Ohio Country was a vast sea of untamed forests and rivers stretching west from the crests of the Allegheny Mountains to the Ohio River and beyond. It was a harsh land inhabited by a myriad of savage Indian tribes who ruled their world. By 1750 Frenchmen from Canada in the north and Englishmen from the east began to enter and explore the wilderness and begin trading with the Indians of the Ohio Country.

In 1749, an expedition led by Celeron de Blainville traveled from New France down the length of the Allegheny and Ohio Rivers, claiming all the lands of those watersheds for France. But English traders had already ventured into the Ohio Country, building posts at Indian villages to secure Indian furs for trade goods. A conflict of interest was in the making between the French and English over ownership of the lands. Although they called the lands their own, the thousands of Indians in a dozen or more tribes living there were not consulted.

In mid-May 1754, 22-year-old George Washington began retracing his steps taken a year earlier along the Indian path called the Nemacolin Trail, which torturously wound its way over the crests of the Allegheny Mountains to the western lands beyond. He left behind the furthermost outpost of Virginian civilization at Will's Creek and for a second time entered the vast wilderness empire of the Indians, which was known as the Ohio Country. Unlike his first journey the previous autumn, Washington was not traveling as an emissary of Virginia's governor. In sending Washington on the mission to the French in the fall of 1753, Dinwiddie had more than the interests of the British Crown in mind. Dinwiddie was a partner and financier in the recently formed Ohio Company, a private enterprise of like-minded Virginia gentlemen who were intent on securing the lands of the distant Ohio Country for themselves as investment and profit. [KC 124] On the initial trip to French Fort LeBoeuf, which was located near French Creek, Washington was accompanied by Christopher Gist, his friend and an experienced scout. With Gist as his guide, Washington accomplished his mission, despite being unaccustomed to the rigors of wilderness travel and the harshness of impending winter weather at that late time of the year. In truth, they had barely survived.

Upon his return, Washington recounted to Dinwiddie how he had been rebuffed by the French commander at Fort LeBoeuf who viewed Washington's orders to vacate the region with indifference. In addition, many of the Indians he and Gist encountered on the expedition treated them with hostility and suspicion. To Washington's surprise, if not chagrin, the Indians of the Ohio wilderness were clearly more sympathetic to Frenchmen than to the English. Now in the spring of 1754, Washington was set to return to that same Ohio Country as a colonel in the newly-formed Virginia militia, with a new assignment from the Governor.

Originally, Washington's mission was to outrace the French to the forks of the Ohio River and reinforce the company of Virginians already there, who were under the command of Second Lieutenant Ward. In April 1754, Captain Trent, Ward's commanding officer, with his men of the Virginia Regiment, left Will's Creek post ahead of Washington with orders to make his way as fast as possible to the forks of the Ohio River. There, they were to erect a rudimentary fort on this strategic point of land, thus securing both Virginia and British Crown's interests in the Ohio Country before the French could do so.

Reliable intelligence on French movements reaching Washington was scant, and dependent upon a handful of Englishmen, who were trading powder, ball, and English goods to the Indians for hides and furs. From those Indians, word about the French to the north could be had. The information was passed along to the men returning east over the mountains to the colonies of Pennsylvania, Maryland, and Virginia. However, the Englishmen were unable to say how reliable the word of the Indians might be. The Indians traded with both French and English, making their professed loyalties and camp gossip questionable at best. Consequently, when Captain Trent returned to Will's Creek post from the forks of the Ohio for more supplies, little intelligence, if any, followed him. Washington was left largely in the dark as to what, if anything, the French might do next, or what he might encounter when he reinforced Ward and attempted to peaceably expel the French from the region.

The French reach the Forks of the Ohio in force

Unfortunately for Washington, events were moving far ahead of him. He was about to learn some hard lessons about the wilderness, the French, and the native American Indian which would expose to him a much greater failure than his simple inability to follow the military maxim "know thy enemy." Washington's naivete, underestimation, and miscalculation of the situation, to his shock and dismay, ignited a war which would spread across the vast frontier and cost the lives of hundreds of English colonials. All this was about to happen when a beleaguered Second Lieutenant Ward and his men stumbled into Washington's camp at Will's Creek on April 20 with the startling news of their surrender of the fort at the forks of the Ohio to a huge invasion force of French and Indians.

The news of Ward's surrender was no doubt astounding to Washington. Beyond the military and political implications of losing such a strategic piece of ground to France, Washington wondered how the French could have managed to transport nearly a thousand men over a great distance so quickly, while also providing them with the supplies and provisions necessary to support them for an extended campaign. The odds must have seemed staggering to him, considering the insurmountable difficulties Washington was facing in attempting to lead men and supplies across the rugged Nemacolin Trail. A road needed to be cut through the vast wilderness and then widened to accommodate wagons if a land route from Will's Creek to the interior of the Ohio Country were to be completed. That work required a large amount of sheer manpower, provisions, and time; none of which Washington had in great supply. Upon questioning Ward, Washington learned how the French were able to beat him to the forks of the Ohio. The French had come so swiftly by boat, and in great numbers. This undoubtedly impressed upon him that the nature of the rugged wilderness in which he found himself did not lend itself well to overland travel. Chagrined, Washington realized he had been out-maneuvered.

The French were veterans of wilderness travel by waterway. They learned that lesson well in New France from the native populace a century earlier. Interior rivers and lakes were the key to travel through wilderness, and the Indian canoe the preferred and more plentiful means of doing so. Contracoeur, the commander of the French force that landed upstream from Ward's at the forks of the Ohio, utilized 300 Indian canoes and 60 French bateaux to ferry his superior force of French and allied Indians, supplies and 18 cannon down the Allegheny River with greater speed than Washington could muster. Facing the threat of complete annihilation, Ward was forced to surrender his 41 men. No shots were fired and there were no casualties. Ward and his men were not taken captive, but instead, allowed to leave with their weapons and baggage. Since no war existed between France and England, the French commander was only intent upon expelling the Englishmen whom he declared to be interlopers upon land claimed by France. The confrontation was decisive, yet bloodless.

If Washington did not grasp fully the implication of Contracoeur's swift arrival at the forks with such a large force, the deeper lesson dealt by the French commander should have be clearly evident. It was not merely that the French had used river rather than land transport to shorten the distance traveled. Nor was it the magnitude of the French invasion by those means. What should have been evident was that the French were successful because of the extensive cooperation and support of the Indian tribes of the Ohio Country. Sixty French bateaux alone could not have served the French purpose. The 300 canoes used were noticeably Indian canoes of the Delaware, Mingo, Shawnee, and Seneca tribes. The Indians accompanying Contracoeur were French allies not British. These native allies were from villages throughout the Ohio Country, which were always in close proximity to natural waterways. The Indians knew that canoes were the only means of traveling quickly through the wilderness with a large force.

Because of New France's long standing policy of developing close relationships with the Indian tribes of the interior wilderness of North America without confiscating their lands for large scale colonial settlement as the English did, when the Indians were called upon to support the French in the conflict of 1754, they did so. As brothers to the French, they provided logistical support in the form of hundreds of canoes, and as warriors, accompanied the French soldiers to assist them if warfare should arise.

Washington underestimates the importance of Indians

Unlike his French counterparts, Washington did not take into account that the wilderness of the Ohio Country was populated by a native people who considered the lands their own, not belonging to either the French or English for their use or settlement. He did not comprehend that if the Indians were forced to abandon their neutrality and choose sides in a struggle between the French and English, they would overwhelmingly ally with New France. Although the Indians preferred the English trade goods, which were of higher quality and at lower cost than that of the French, the English were more feared by the tribes because of their appetite for land. That Washington underestimated the significance of the Indian presence in the Ohio Country and the important role they would play in the coming struggle between the English and French was understandable in light of his inexperience. Others following in his footsteps under the British flag would make the same mistakes. Yet the consequences of these mistakes, once events were set in motion, were inexcusable from men of Washington's stature, and the outcomes disastrous.

By all appearances, Washington did not take the necessary time to study the nature of the Indians closely. He was unfamiliar with the tribes, their languages, customs, as well as likes and dislikes, particularly in relation to the French and English. Rather than consider them a force to be reckoned with or a potential ally to be courted if hostilities developed with the French, Washington's actions betray an attitude of indifference, resulting from ignorance of the wilderness and self-conceit. Washington was a product of colonial Virginia gentry in particular and English society in general. In the world from which Washington hailed, Indians were considered heathen savages of the wilderness beyond the frontier. Thus, they were totally alien to Washington. While this attitude was far less prominent in Washington than in the commanders of British regular regiments in North America, it can be assumed that in the final analysis Washington dismissed totally the importance of Indians in conducting his mission.

Imbued with the fullness of youth, and the status of the Governor's new mission, Washington held the rank of colonel commanding 159 men of the Virginia Regiment. Thus, as Washington prepared to set out upon a course of action to counter the French with all the logistic expertise he could muster, he naively believed himself to be a fit and able commander for the wilderness expedition. In that frame of mind he dismissed the Indians as having little strategic and tactical consequence in the final outcome. Logistically, we can guess that Washington looked upon the panorama of virgin forest which stretched unbroken before him as merely an empty land to be claimed and defended by simply cutting a road through it for troops to follow. Indians, who moved through the forest trails and along the rivers of the wilderness with ease were not adequately considered nor their tactics and style of fighting studied for strategic value. All of this thinking would soon be challenged and proved to be in gross error.

Nowhere were Washington's misconceptions of the Indians more apparent than in his misjudgment of the Iroquois warrior named Tanacharison, called the "Half King" by the English traders. On his expedition the previous autumn with scout Christopher Gist to French Fort LeBoeuf, Washington had met Indians along the way, and was counseled by Gist and others in attendance to try to cultivate their friendship. Good relations with the tribes would benefit the English traders in the area, while proving helpful in cultivating alliances with the Indians. Awkwardly through interpreters, Washington attempted to do so with little success.

"For all the stupid things you have said"

At an Iroquois Mingo Indian village known as Logstown, which was situated several miles below the forks of the Ohio on the north bank of the river, Washington met the Iroquois sachem, Tanacharison. What was the difference between a sachem and a war chief? Apparently Washington did not know. However, he was clearly impressed with this Iroquois Indian, who seemed to speak with great authority of his influence among the Ohio tribes. Tanacharison was called the "Half King" by English traders who knew him, because it was said that he was actually dependent on the Council of the Iroquois Confederacy in the east for his authority. Washington either overlooked or failed to investigate the deeper significance.

What impressed Washington was that here was an Indian of some standing in the Ohio Country, declaring himself and his people to be thoroughly pro-British, and openly outspoken in his anti-French sentiments. Side-stepping the issue that he was not a war chief, Half King said that he spoke for his people as a sachem, or tribal councilor and implied that the Iroquois were solidly friends of the English in any conflict with the French. Washington did not understand that Tanacharison spoke only for his own tribe of Ohio Senecas called Mingoes and not the Iroquois nation as a whole. However, Half King stated his case against the French which is what Washington wanted to hear.

His burning hatred of the French stemmed from an earlier incident in which he was rebuffed and insulted by a French officer named Marin, while attending a meeting at French Fort Presque Isle on the south shore of Lake Erie above Fort LeBoeuf in September 1753. Half King headed a delegation of Iroquois Mingo, who was petitioning the French not to advance further into their country to build forts and settlements, while yet encouraging trade. However, Half King's appeal to Marin was taken as a threat. Marin, having heard scurrilous reports about Half King prior to their meeting, dismissed the Mingo out of hand, chastising him "for all the stupid things you have said." He pointed out that Half King did not in fact speak for the tribes of the Ohio Country. Adding insult to injury, Marin stated, "I know that stupid things come only from you, and that all the warriors and chiefs of the Belle Riviere think better than you, and take pity on their women and children. I am obliged to tell you that I shall continue on my way, and if there are any persons bold enough to set up barriers to hinder my march, I shall knock them over so vigorously that they may crush those who made them." [KD-p.50]

The Half King bears a grudge

Marin, in no mood to put up with the empty-handed threat from Tanacharison, reacted angrily. It was obvious in his response that he intended to brush aside all rules of diplomacy for Tanacharison. It was likely he believed that the Half King was a pretender without the real power of a war chief, who was speaking pompously for himself with a certain amount of bluff which needed called. At any rate, Marin ignored Tanacharison's threat and continued on his way to Fort LeBoeuf with his force. Lacking warriors to forcibly stop the French and support his bluff, the Half King was humiliated. Angry at Marin's insult, from that point on, the Half King determined to seek out the English and ally with them to seek redress against the French indignity burning inside him.

The chance meeting with Washington and Gist at the Half King's village at Logstown a few months later gave Tanacharison the opportunity he desired. Unfortunately, Washington did not comprehend the real nature of Half King's grievance with the French or his underlying motive of petty vengeance. Neither did Washington know what Marin implicitly understood, that Tanacharison did not have the support of the Ohio tribes. After his tirade before Marin, the Shawnees of the Ohio Country disavowed any association with him and even the Council of the Six Nations Iroquois admonished Tanacharison for taking sides and stirring trouble between the French and English, since the Iroquois League sought to remain neutral at that time. The Iroquois Six Nations Confederacy viewed the independent and vocal Mingo as a troublesome and dangerous liability. If not restrained in his words and actions, Half King could start a war.

While Washington thirsted for action, war indeed was something he wished to avoid starting. Yet when word of Ward's surrender reached Washington at his Will's Creek camp, Washington dutifully called a council of war on April 23 to decide on a course of action. Obviously, his force of some 150 men had no chance of challenging more than 1,000 French and their Indian allies. Yet when retreat was considered, Washington ruled it out as being unacceptable. Undoubtedly, the personal embarrassment of facing Dinwiddie would have been reason enough to continue on. But along with Ward's grim news, Washington received a document brought by two of the Half King's young warriors who accompanied Ward on his retreat. The letter from Tanacharison caused

Washington to pay closer attention to the words of this sole Indian ally, and convinced him to push on with his force over the mountains rather than return to Virginia. Retreat would undoubtedly lose Washington the favor and loyalty of the Iroquois in the Ohio Country, as demonstrated in the letter from the Half King. Suddenly Washington showed an interest in Indians such as Half King, if their assistance could benefit him.

"I speak with a heart full of grief"

Where was Tanacharison? The Mingo warrior had accompanied Captain Trent's men to the forks of the Ohio to construct the new English fort. Half King had laid the first log of the stockade, and was present when the French came down the Allegheny to demand surrender. On Half King's advice, Ward unsuccessfully attempted to stall the French but to no avail. [FJ2-p.253] Upon leaving the fort with Ward and his men, Tanacharison shouted to the French that he had ordered the fort built, and he, Half King, laid the first log. His defiance was cleverly calculated. Half King only spoke openly to Contracoeur after the terms of capitulation were agreed upon. He was allowed to leave, but did not follow Ward to Washington at Will's Creek. Ever the savage strategist when it came to playing off white men, Tanacharison now wrote to Washington from his wilderness camp to "have good courage and come as soon as possible; you will find us as ready to fight the French as you are yourselves. If you do not come to our assistance now, we are entirely undone, and I think we shall never meet together again. I speak with a heart full of grief." [LT-p.136]

This was perhaps Washington's weakest moment as he considered all the possibilities but was terribly unsure of the course of action to take. Washington suffered consternation while worrying that although Half King's loyalty to the English appeared firm, it may have been shaken by the French show of force at the Forks. Prior to Ward's surrender, Washington appeared to have little interest in cultivating Indian allies. Perhaps he thought he could do it all. Now that circumstances seemed to have changed everything, Washington was apparently reconsidering the need for Indian assistance. Or was Half King's letter to him only providing superficial reason for Washington to move on the French? Coming to the aid of a petitioning ally would give justification to questions posed by the Governor or from his own men.

Washington worried about the loss of what he thought to be a solid ally. Perhaps, he felt that if Half King abandoned him, it would appear to all in Virginia that Washington acquiesced. Washington was sure of one thing when he called the council of war, bringing together all his officers to decide a course of action. Washington was determined not to fail again. In setting his mind upon this course when nothing about him was for sure, Washington unwittingly was about to play into Half King's hand.

A burning thirst for revenge

Who was this Mingo Indian warrior, the Half King, the man who exerted considerable influence upon Washington, which every French officer and trader knew to be more bluff, deceit, and half-truth than real threat? This boastful and defiant Iroquois, who posed as an unqualified spokesman for his people and talked constantly of the warriors soon to join him on the field of battle, was never closely scrutinized by Washington or his translators and advisors. In a sense, Washington could hear only what he wanted to hear. At this critical juncture, the Half King managed to motivate or goad Washington into action in his favor when the Mingo knew he had only a few followers at hand. Tanacharison may have been subject to moments of bluster and conceit, but he was no fool in his own backyard. He well understood that he had carried his game to the limits and the French and their Indian allies would deal with him harshly if he was ever caught.

Perhaps the Half King believed it was best to let Washington do his bidding for him, thus assisting him indirectly in avenging the personal affront and loss of face Marin caused him. Little did it matter to Tanacharison that Marin was now dead, the result of an illness. The "burning thirst for revenge" that consumed Tanacharison inwardly was a matter of Indian nature that neither Washington nor all but a few white men could understand. The importance Indians placed upon vengeance, for slights both real and imagined, was the one aspect of Indian character that was least comprehensible by white man's standards. Revenge was one of the great motivators in Indian life, no matter how seemingly petty the infraction was, nor how concocted the situation appeared to be by anyone else's view. In Tanacharison's mind, it would take the scalp of a Frenchman, any Frenchman, to avenge what he believed to be a tremendous loss of face in the eyes of his immediate tribe at the hands of the now-dead Frenchman.

Marin's death did not change anything because the insult itself was not avenged by Half King. It did not matter to him in the least that the insult delivered by Marin was viewed by the Frenchmen and English traders as nothing more serious than a slight. In the Half King's own mind, only vengeance mattered at the moment. If Washington could only have seen that his "noble Iroquois Indian ally," the man who sang the praises of the English and wished Washington and his men to assist him in repelling the French from the Ohio Country for their mutual political benefit was really thirsting for an singular French scalp, he might have thought twice about his evaluation of Indians in general and Half King in particular. Thus Washington might have paid closer attention to the options available to him. In reality, Tanacharison was not unlike any other Indian of the Ohio tribes. A thirst for revenge could be as strong a desire for an Indian as tobacco, a successful hunt, or ambushing an enemy and making off with horses, plunder, and prisoners to burn in the village fires for amusement. And he would not rule out a drink of the English trader's rum or whiskey if it could be had in return for skins and pelts. It was just at this moment that Tanacharison was consumed with a wish for revenge. If it had not been for Washington's decision to move his small force into the Ohio Country, the Half King would undoubtedly have grown bored with the whole idea and moved on to some other venture more promising. But that did not happen.

Washington decides to move

When the council of war ended at Will's Creek camp, Washington decided to move his men across the Nemacolin Trail. The new mission, as Washington envisioned it was two-fold. It involved the arduous task of having his men labor with shovels and axes to widen the trail into some semblance of a military road while yet forwarding men and supplies to the Ohio Company storehouse built at the mouth of the Redstone Creek on the Monongahela River, where the Nemacolin ended. Washington reasoned that a strong fortification could be built at Redstone Creek to further forward ammunition, men, supplies and artillery necessary to make an assault upon the French downstream at the Forks of the Ohio. [LT-p.136] Washington's plan was ambitious. In light of the letter recently received from the Half King, all talk of caution and compromise with the French was cast aside in favor of a mood of military preparations for war. This was at a time when no declaration of war had formally been made nor endorsed by either Frenchman or Virginian, much less by their European counterparts. Rather it seems Washington was seized with the urge to act and do something other than remain at Will's Creek, which would lead to eventual retreat. Yet the whole situation facing him seemed overwhelming.

"By mid-May, Washington could no longer contain his frustration. He had seized both rank and opportunity, he was commanding a military force on a historic mission, but instead of the crisp certainties any novice would have expected in such a position, he found himself in a swamp of imponderables. This was more comic opera than an imperial expedition—it did not even resemble his recent mission to French Creek. In that case the objective had been clear, the instructions specific, and his companions as responsible and motivated as he. Now nothing was clear, and whatever he tried to do he found his officers and men sullen and unwilling. Even more vexing, he was not getting the basic support of his government. He was being sent into hostile country with a large force of men without being given the means sufficiently to clothe, feed, equip, arm, or pay them. No amount of trying or complaining had been able to produce the wagons and teams for what should have been a substantial baggage train. Nothing in his thinking about the attractions of a military profession had prepared him for this." [LT-p.138]

Did Washington think that he was seizing the initiative, in a military sense? If so, what were his thoughts concerning French countermoves? Had he really considered what he would do if and when he encountered them, in terms of both strategy and tactics? The French army, with their Indian allies at the forks of the Ohio, greatly outnumbered his small mixed force of Virginia regulars and militia and Washington had no more than a promise of future reinforcements.

The Half King promised Iroquois warriors at some point in the future to help in fighting the French but Washington had the vague idea from the Indian's recent letter that the first move was up to him. In addition, Washington could easily see that he was in great need of more supplies, especially food rations for his men. Greatly burdened with the troublesome task of moving his men over the rugged trail while at the same time spending precious provisions to widen it for wagon travel, did not leave Washington with many resources for strategy if he did not have the necessary supplies to support the effort. And none seemed to be coming from Virginia in any substantial quantity.

Lacking expert daily intelligence on the movements of the French in a land that he knew little of other than the trail before him, Washington could not have reasonably believed that he would be able to use superior tactics upon the French to dislodge them from the Ohio Country. While the French held all the advantage at the moment, Washington appeared determined to put aside any nagging doubts about the sensibility of his actions and move his men out, as he retraced his steps to the Ohio Country. He was clearly reacting. In the wilderness, reacting to adversity could lead to carelessness, and easily seal one's fate.

Leaving Will's Creek Station in early May, [FD-p.360] Washington and his troops reached a halfway point along the trail to Redstone Creek, which was called the Great Meadows. It was so called because of the unusually large, grassy, open expanse in the unbroken forest, which was surrounded by low hills. Attempts to obtain better intelligence and find a quicker route to Redstone Creek both failed. Washington's advance party of 25 men under Captain Adam Stephen returned to Washington with the news that a Mingo Indian had seen Frenchmen at Redstone Creek however Stephen could not verify it as true. In addition, Washington's attempt to find a quicker route for canoes down the Youghiogheny River failed when the river was found impassable due to waterfalls and cliffs.

"Give my services to my brothers the English"

While camped at the Great Meadows, events quickly began to change. First, two Mingo warriors arrived in camp with a message from the Half King, warning Washington that that an advance party of Frenchmen were on their way from the forks of the Ohio to attack Washington. "On acc't of a freech armey to meat Miger Georg Wassiontton therefore My Brotheres I deesir you to be awar of them for deisinid to strike ye forist English they see ten days since they march d I cannot tell what nomber the half-King and the rest of the Chiefs will be with you in five days to consel, no more at present but give my serves (services) to my Brothers the English," signed, "The Half King, and translated by John Davison." [FD-p.367] Washington must have read Half King's message translated from French into English by an English trader John Davidson with true alarm. It appeared that his force at the Great Meadows was in danger, as the French were on the initiative to counter him. Implicit in the warning was the knowledge that the Half King possessed expert intelligence and understood the French motives while Washington did not.

Yet there is a question, which Washington apparently did not ask himself—were the French intent on offensive action, which would commit them to war, as the Half King appeared to be so certain? Or was Tanacharison, understanding Washington's naivete and lack of solid intelligence, making use of French forward reconnaissance patrols to prompt Washington into committing himself to hostilities toward the French? If not plying a deeper motive, then perhaps the movement of any force of white soldiers in the wilderness, as seen through the eyes of a war-like savage Indians, could only mean an attack. In either case, the outcome remained the same. Washington prepared his men for hostilities. Secure in the belief that the Half King would soon join him with many chiefs and warriors to support him, Washington did not closely examine French motives. He also did not question how his native ally with superior intelligence would write to him of a French army on the move yet not know of their approximate numbers.

While Washington was pondering his next move, an Indian trader arrived at the Great Meadows on May 24 and reported seeing two Frenchmen at Christopher Gist's settlement a few days earlier. The trader was certain that French troops were on the march, confirming the Half King's warning. [FD-p.368] Washington became anxious, as Gist's cabin was only 18 miles away. He immediately set his men to clearing the brush around his camp at the Great Meadows and planning for a defense.

Then on the morning of May 27 Gist rode into Washington's camp with startling news. On the previous day, a French officer with 50 soldiers came to his plantation and threatened to destroy it. The Frenchmen had come by canoe from the landing at nearby Redstone Creek and on his way to warn Washington, Gist had come across the tracks of numerous white men no more than five miles from Washington's camp at the Great Meadows, whom Gist took to be French. It seemed clear to Washington that the French were on the offensive and intent on attacking him at any moment. Washington directed Captain Hogg to take 75 men and capture the French troops before they could return to their canoes. At the same time, Gist left for Will's Creek and Virginia. [LT-p.142] The stage was set.

A messenger from Half King with news of the French

Late in the dark evening after Gist's departure, Silverheels, an Indian messenger from Half King arrived with word that the Mingo sachem, while on his journey to join Washington, came across the tracks of Frenchmen about six miles from the Great Meadows. He believed the French had enemy troops camped nearby. In his message, Tanacharison was urging Washington to join him and attack the French first, if they could be found. Without hesitation, Washington assembled 40 armed men and, in utter darkness and a heavy rain, set out following Silverheels to the Half King's camp deep in the woods.

A surprise was awaiting Washington when he and his exhausted force arrived at Tanacharison's camp of crude huts shortly before dawn. There,

Washington discovered the truth about his staunch Indian ally. To his shock and dismay, Half King had only a dozen Indians with him, of which two were mere boys. In addition, six or seven of the warriors were without firearms. No chiefs were present as the Half King had mentioned in his message. The handful of warriors was far smaller than Washington had imagined. It wasn't the large force of which Tanacharison had spoken of, and to which others, such as English trader Robert Callender had eluded earlier, as numbering more than 50 warriors.

Did Washington confront the Half King about this important disparity? Whether Tanacharison sensed a confrontation brewing or was oblivious to Washington's disappointment, if not anger, he either ignored it or brushed it aside. Knowing that once his ruse was exposed, Washington would become angry and his reputation would be damaged, the Half King felt he had to do something to lessen the white man's ire. Finding footprints, which were purportedly those of a Frenchman, was a stroke of luck. The discovery was essential to Tanacharison if he hoped to avoid a disagreeable situation, which might cause Washington to rethink the whole relationship. Soon after Washington's arrival at Half King's camp, two Indian scouts arrived, reporting that the French encampment had been found hidden in a nearby rocky glen. Immediately, the Half King counseled Washington that time was of the essence if they intended to take the Frenchmen by surprise at first light. They must set out at once, the Indian told the young Virginian.

If Washington had any doubts, they gave way to his deep-seated desire for action. The force set out through the woods, "not in column, but one after the other, in the Indian manner" with the Half King's men in the lead. The die apparently was cast. Washington's force, accompanied by Half King's Indians, arrived undetected at the hidden French camp. Washington was able to deploy his men to positions surrounding the French, with Half King and his Indians covering one side of the ambush. He could see Frenchmen rising and dressing in the dim light. Why there were no sentries posted about the French camp, Washington did not find odd. However, a skilled and experienced woodsman or Indian would have undoubtedly wondered that if this French force was on a hostile mission deep within enemy territory and camped in a rocky ravine with high ground on all sides so close to the English camp, why would they have not posted a solitary sentry? The conjecture may have been that the French were either blundering fools in the wilderness, or not on a hostile mission at all. An experienced woodsman, knowing all he did about French soldiers in the wilds of North America, could only conclude that they were not fools, and therefore not at war, but rather on another mission. Was then not the secluded campsite of the French selected for its shelter from the elements rather than as a base of operations for offensive action against the English?

Carrying a message from the French government

If those questions were pondered at all, there was no time for answers. A Frenchman in the rocks below saw movement in the tree line above, and called

A Frenchman's scalp is offered as a present.

out a warning. Seeing French soldiers reaching for their stacked muskets, Washington gave the signal and his men fired a volley into the French party of 32 men, killing ten of them immediately. Another 21 immediately threw down their muskets and surrendered. One Frenchman escaped. Ensign Coulon de Jumonville was killed by the Half King with a tomahawk blow to the head, which shattered the side of his skull. With the skirmish over, the Indians immediately set to scalping and mutilating the dead, according to the Indian custom of fighting.

Although the dead were white men like the English, if Washington and his men felt any remorse at the savage handling of the French corpses, none was expressed on the field of battle. Washington most likely had heard of the Indian style of warfare, but he may have been ill- prepared to witness the scalping of Jumonville by Half King, who throughout the short battle, had fought like a demon possessed. [FD-p.270] The Half King drew his razor sharp knife from its sheath about his neck with one hand, while grabbing a handful of Jumonville's hair to raise the dead man's head. Then deftly, Half King ran the blade of the knife around the head, cutting the flesh above the ears as well as the brow of the forehead. Once finished, he gave the hair a sharp yank and with a distinctive pop sound, the bloody scalp came loose from the skull of the dead man. Flicking the scalp against his knee to remove some of the blood, Half King grunted in approval at his workmanship. Then looking down at the bare, bloody, exposed skull of the head of Jumonville at his feet, Half King gave it a kick, knowing that the insult committed against him by the French was now avenged. The Seneca warrior then presented the scalp to Washington as a gift. Washington accepted the bloody trophy reluctantly, knowing now enough about Indians to understand that rejection would be viewed as an insult by the Indian warrior, who was sincerely proud of his accomplishment.

In the meantime, the French prisoners were rounded up. Speaking in their native tongue, the captives seemed to be trying to tell Washington's men something of importance. While Van Braam was the only man among the Virginians who could understand the language, it took him some time to translate what seemed to be cries of protest. If Washington was not shaken enough by the earlier slaughter and mutilation of the French wounded and Half King's scalping of the commanding French officer, what Van Braam told him must have made his blood chill. The captives said that they were "carrying a message from the government of France" to the English. One of the French soldiers bent over a comrade's corpse, retrieved a packet of papers from a pouch, and gave it to one of Washington's translators. Those papers proved to be diplomatic credentials and instructions for the now dead French officer, Ensign de Jumonville, to find the English and deliver to them the enclosed message. It was a warning for Washington and the English to leave the land belonging to the King of France. Further, the French captives protested that they were encamped in the rocky glen near a source of water to escape the elements, not to secret themselves and prepare for offensive actions, nor to use it as a base for spying upon Washington's force. [KC-143]

"The English have murdered my children"

Washington must have considered at some point the validity of their argument. If what the French said was true, then they were on a diplomatic mission, not a hostile one, and there had been no need for Washington to attack them at all. If the French were correct, then Washington had, in essence, murdered these Frenchmen who were acting as ambassadors. In doing so, the Virginian had violated "every principle of international relations," as recognized by France and England. It seemed likely that the war with France would come in the wake of Washington's firing the first shots. All of this had transpired because he had listened to an Indian. Perhaps Washington now thought himself rash to have listened to Half King's impetuous advice. The Indian had completely misjudged French intentions. Or was it that Washington had completely underestimated the Half King's cunning?

Washington returned the Frenchman's scalp to Half King and urged him to take it to nearby Delaware Indian villages and show it with the warning that "this would soon be the fate of all Frenchmen in this territory now claimed by the English." After avenging Marin's insult, the Half King was more than happy to leave Washington and return to his village, although he was convinced Washington was not about to turn over any French captives for burning in his village fires. The Indians gave the French and their Indian allies, who were somewhere ahead on the trail to the forks, a wide berth to avoid them on their journey north.

After writing letters to Dinwiddie, Washington withdrew his men to the Great Meadows, where he regained his composure and resigned himself to the die that had been cast. He ordered a rudimentary, circular, upright log fort to be built in the center of the open field. He felt confident his smaller number of men could successfully defend the fort against 500 Frenchmen, should they come from the forks of the Ohio River to retaliate for his ambush. [FD-p.93]

Word of the English attack on Jumonville's men reached the newly built French fortification at the forks of the Ohio, called Fort Duquesne, from the lone French soldier who escaped the ambush. Immediately Fort Duquesne's commander, Contracoeur, sent runners to all the nearby Delaware, Shawnee, Mingo, Wyandot, and Seneca Indian villages advising them that the French were now at war with the English. He urged the Indians to come quickly to Fort Duquesne and attend his council fire, to decide who among the Indians would "take up the hatchet" in support of the French cause. Soon hundreds of Indians arrived at Fort Duquesne, including a band of Delawares who brought Jumonville's scalp, which Half King had given them only days before their departure. The Delawares presented the scalp to Contracoeur. Instead of heeding Washington's warning delivered by Half King, the Delawares pledged their support to the French. In a rousing speech to the Indians assembled before him, Contracoeur promised to avenge the death of his countrymen by spilling English blood. If the Indians would accompany him, they too could take part in the revenge and help themselves to English scalps and plunder which would rightfully be theirs. "The English have murdered my children, my heart is sick; tomorrow I shall send my French soldiers to take revenge. And now, I invite you all by this belt of wampum to join your French father and help him to crush the assassins. Take this hatchet, and with it two barrels of wine for a feast." [PF-p.76]

To the Indians, revenge in blood and the taking of scalps and booty were things that they could readily understand. Contracoeur's eloquent words were more than enough to motivate the Indians. "Both hatchet and wine were cheerfully accepted" as gifts. In years to come, white men would borrow heavily upon Contracoeur's persuasive technique but found that it did not always work. Soon though, a sizable force of over 500 French soldiers accompanied by more than 350 Indians set out to the southeast along the forest trail to pursue the English.

"The English behave like fools"

At the Great Meadows, Washington continued making improvements on his fort, while receiving modest reinforcements from Virginia. Washington continued planning for construction of the road through the forest to Redstone Creek which he surmised could serve as an avenue for an attack upon the French at the forks of the Ohio. Washington sent men forward to attempt the work. Meanwhile, he met in council with a few Indian representatives of the Delaware, Shawnee, and Mingo but was unable to persuade them to become allies. Washington even tried lying to the Indians, saying he was the vanguard of a vast English army soon to come to "dispossess the French." The Indians remained unmoved by Washington's speech and left after closely examining his defenses. Washington's attempt at Indian diplomacy looked bleaker than ever.

Then Tanacharison arrived at the Great Meadows with a few warriors, promising once again that more men were on the way. Desperate for support of any Indians who could provide him with intelligence of the French, Washington asked Half King to support him in defense of his circular palisade fort, which he called Fort Necessity. To Washington's surprise, Half King refused after looking over the Virginian's preparations for war. This Indian who had allegedly befriended Washington and alerted him to the presence of Jumonville's patrol, and then urged him to immediately attack the French before considering alternatives, ultimately precipitating the crisis that Washington now found himself in, did not reserve critical judgment of Washington and his fort. First, the Indian pointed out that fighting from behind a log fort was "not the way to fight a war." From the Indian point of view, Washington's defensive preparations were cowardly. To Half King, there was only one way to fight, the Indian way. It was an aggressive style of ambush and hit-and-run. Secondly, Half King noted that Washington had made a poor choice for the fort's location. Once inside the fort in the center of an open field, Washington's force would be completely surrounded by enemy forces, lacking an avenue of escape. In addition, with the field lower than the surrounding wooded slopes, Half King judged that an enemy would have good cover and an open field of fire. Half King advised Washington that if he must make a stand, to move immediately to a nearby wooded hill.

Washington rejected Half King's advice, patiently explaining that the open meadow surrounding the fort would allow his men to pour great musket fire upon the French soldiers when they marched upon the fort from the woods. To this, Half King angrily shook his head, and replied sharply to the provincial interpreter, Conrad Weiser, before turning his back on Washington. "The white chief Washington is a good-natured man, but he has no experience and will by no means take advice from us. He would rather drive us on to fight by his directions; he thinks that the French will come up to him in an open field, [but they will not]. Why should we endanger ourselves and our people when the French behave like cowards and the English like fools?" [FD-p.282]

If Half King were sincere in his disgust with Washington's preparations, it was because he viewed the English as being worse than foolish. It was inherently contrary to any Indian to risk a single warrior needlessly in battle by exposing him to the firepower on an enemy in open ground. Ambush was a favored tactic since it held the opportunity of "inflicting loss without suffering any."[FD-p.101] What Washington was proposing was a European-style battle between opposing lines of men advancing on each other, while giving and taking musket fire. To the Half King, it was pure madness. Tanacharison conferred with his warriors at a distance from Washington. Reaching quick agreement, they left the English and made their way to the edge of the woods. In a moment the Indians were gone, swiftly melting into the forest, leaving Washington and his men without any native allies.

Soon Half King's warnings proved to be true. Contracoeur's French and Indian force under de Villiers arrived at the Great Meadows on the morning of July 3, 1754, and surrounded Fort Necessity on all sides. But rather than advancing upon the crude fort as Washington had hoped, the attackers began to pour heavy musket fire upon the English post from the protection of the woods. After nine hours, the French called a truce and called upon Washington to surrender. With his position hopeless and casualties mounting, Washington capitulated. Under the terms of surrender, Washington and his men would be allowed to leave with their sick and wounded, retreating to Virginia, never to return. In addition, Washington was to sign a document admitting his role in the deaths of Jumonville and his men which the French called assassinations.

Washington is forced to capitulate

On the morning of July 4, 1754, a humbled and humiliated Washington ordered his men to surrender Fort Necessity to the waiting French and Indians. Unable to constrain the Indians any longer, the French commander watched helplessly as a horde of warriors rushed into the fort once the English had left. They plundered everything of value before burning the fort. In addition, all of Washington's horses and cattle, which he was depending upon to carry the wounded and baggage back to Will's Creek, were slaughtered by the Indians, who were angry for not yet wetting their knives and hatchets in the enemy's blood, nor taking a single scalp. Enraged that de Villers had prevented them from killing the English, the Indians grabbed two unguarded prisoners, dragged them away, and tomahawked and scalped them. [PF-p.79] A wholesale slaughter was narrowly averted, but the Indian lust for blood was hardly sated. They complained bitterly to the French commander that Contracoeur's promises made to them at the forks of the Ohio had not been kept.

A dejected Washington and his men made their way back along the trail to Virginia. His mission to secure the wilderness of the Ohio Country for Virginia and Great Britain was a sheer failure. Most of the blame was Washington's to bear, the result of his inexperience, misjudgment, and blunder in the wilderness. That Washington and the bulk of his men escaped their dire circumstances at the Great Meadows was nothing short of a miracle. The whole episode affected Washington profoundly and caused him to reflect on what had gone wrong, and why.

Once he reached the Great Meadows, Washington suffered from a lack of reliable intelligence on the movements and intentions of the French ahead of him. English traders passing through Washington's camp shared with him whatever information they had on their visits. But the Virginian had no men available who were well-adapted to the rigors of the wilderness and able to live off the land undetected for days at a time in the deep forest while seeking intelligence. Washington was unable to recruit and train such scouts from among his own men and none were forthcoming from other sources in great enough numbers.

A glaring lack of adequate scouts

Such men, if they could be found, needed to get close enough to observe the French without being discovered themselves, and then relay an uninterrupted flow of accurate information back to Washington. To be successful in such a delicate mission, such men first needed to elude hostile Indians who were patrolling the country between the French outposts and Washington. The Indians knew intimately every creek, trail and rocky glen that could afford an enemy spy any concealment. Such men also needed to discard their military uniforms and gear in favor of clothing that afforded them maximum camouflage, allowing them to blend into the forest colors rather than standing out.

The French, on the other hand, had at their disposal an unlimited number of individuals uniquely adapted to the survival skills needed for spying missions. The Indians could provide the French with all the necessary intelligence on the English without being detected. To translate the Indian scouts' observations, there were French Canadians, white men who lived with the Indians and often had Indian wives. The French found themselves at a loss for information only once and that came during the Jumonville mission, when no Indians accompanied them. The Indians' conspicuous absence put the two sides on an even playing field. However, it provided Half King with the opportunity to send two of his warriors to find the Frenchmen, who were hidden in a nearby rocky glen. At the time, passing that information on to Washington suited his purposes. When it came to gathering intelligence on an enemy in the wilderness, Indians excelled at it. One needed either reliable Indian allies or white men uniquely trained in the ways of the wilderness who were able to move, live, conceal, track, and spy in the manner of Indians.

Superior tactics will decide the outcome

One of Washington's critical mistakes was in acting too hastily when confronted with Half King's intelligence on the French force hidden near his camp. He had nothing else but the word of the Indian to go on as to the hostile intention of the French. Due to Washington's total lack of corroborating intelligence, he took the word of his Indian companion too quickly and attacked the French. Half King may or may not have known the real mission of the French, but did not disclose it to Washington for fear of foiling his own plans for revenge. The small force of French soldiers was isolated from reinforcements and had none of their own Indians to protect them from ambush. Washington, none the wiser at this critical juncture and with other options open to him other than attacking, had no experienced men to appraise the situation accurately, judging both French intentions and Half King's. Rashly, Washington fired first, and started a war.

When it came to the Indian style of fighting that Washington witnessed at the Jumonville engagement, he was ill-prepared to deal with it. The shocking scalping and mutilation of the dead, the killing of the helpless French wounded, and the demand of Half King's warriors that the French prisoners be turned over to them as booty to be sold, made slaves, or burnt upon their village fires was beyond Washington's comprehension. His lack of understanding went beyond the apparent savageness of the Indians and the inability to control them. Washington, like most of his English contemporaries, did not understand Indians at all. He had not lived with them in their villages, eaten their food, become acquainted with their languages, nor immersed himself in their tribal cultures to know their world view, their beliefs, their religion, and their values. Without having done so, he did not know intimately the real nature and character of Indians to understand the workings of the Indian mind.

Without that understanding, the Indian savagery on the battlefield did not fit into the Virginian view of the world. Likewise, European rules of warfare did not apply to the wilderness. Rather, the wilderness was the domain of the Indians. Washington and his men found themselves in the Indian world, where they fought as their ancestors had for centuries. It was no wonder that Washington totally misunderstood the Indians and did not see their value as allies until it was too late. He was defeated because he did not know how to influence them. His misjudgment of Half King was a case in point that nearly cost Washington and his men their lives. If one was going to survive and succeed in any wilderness venture in the future, the Indians could never again be so overlooked or underestimated.

In the defense of Fort Necessity, Washington discovered to his chagrin that European military tactics were not only ineffective, but a liability. The French adopted quickly the Indian style of fighting and refused to send their men into the open in a linear assault upon the English position. Rather, they chose to attack from the cover of the wooded perimeter surrounding Ft. Necessity, without exposing their men to the English muskets, as Washington naively presumed they would do. Tanacharison's warning to Washington about his poorly made plans proved true. The French and Indians were able to pour heavy fire upon Washington's men, inflicting many casualties, while suffering few themselves. It forced the surrounded English to surrender or face annihilation. Superior tactics had been used against Washington, just as he had used them in his attack upon Jumonville. Those tactics of fighting from a position of ambush and the protection of the cover of the forest were part of the Indian style of fighting that was supremely adapted to difficult, broken terrain, where the massed firepower of conventional armies was neutralized.

In all, Washington's 1754 disastrous defeat in the Ohio Country was not without some merit. Though Englishmen of greater rank would follow in his footsteps and commit the same mistakes, Washington paved the way for others who would ultimately learn the lessons of wilderness warfare gained from costly failures. In the deepening struggle with the French, it would soon become apparent to the British that the Indians were a dominant and dangerous force with which to be reckoned. Before the English could boast of any victory, they would need to find Indian allies and learn to fight more like them in the wilderness. However these were still the early days in the lessons, and the French were far ahead in the game.

Chapter 2

Captain Beaujeu:
An Officer by Another Name

What advantage did the French have in the new war with the English for dominance of the wilderness empire of North America? By 1755, the colony of New France was more than a century and a half old. During that time, Frenchmen had explored the huge wilderness interior to the west of the seigneries of Quebec by traveling the vast network of waterways that connected the great St. Lawrence River to the Great Lakes and the Mississippi flowing to the south. Unimpeded by any great natural barriers such as the Allegheny Mountains that separated the English colonies of the eastern seaboard from the interior lands to the west, the French were able to paddle by bateaux and canoe more than a thousand miles into the wilderness lands to establish a flourishing fur trade with dozens of Indian tribes living there. Over the years, French traders, explorers, missionaries and soldiers built a chain of forts and posts, and extended the influence of New France far beyond the confines of Quebec to the Mississippi River and the Louisiana colony. [AF-p.6]

Yet, the French had by no means colonized those lands that the voyageurs traveled. Indeed, they were incapable of exerting any substantial control over such a huge area of wilderness that was only accessible by paths or water routes. New France had neither the resources nor the population to do so. However, without any European rivals in the interior of the continent, the French were able to gain considerable influence over the Woodland Indian tribes that they came in contact with through trading European goods and arms for furs, which the Indians trapped and hunted. The friendship between the French "couriers' des bois" or "runners of the woods" [AF-p.7] and the Indians was cemented over the course of time by much more than just trade. With great distances to travel to journey to the remote tribes of the Great Lakes, many Frenchmen found themselves increasingly far from their old homes and bases in Montreal. They spent more and more time living and wintering with the Indians; learning the native languages and different tribal cultures. These rough and tumble men of New France's far-flung outposts became more than trading partners to the Indians. Many men were adopted into the village tribes, took Indian wives, and sired children of mixed-race who themselves grew up to live in the burgeoning world of French and Indian co-existence in the wilderness in which racial identities, social values, and cultural boundaries were often blurred.

The distinct advantage that the French held over the English when war came in 1754 over who would control the Ohio Country was that the French already had established firm and unshakable alliances with the myriad Indian tribes who ruled over the lands to the south of the Great Lakes region. The French had 150 years of experience in dealing intimately with the Indians. The English, relative newcomers to the wilderness lands over the Alleghenies and beyond the confines of the Hudson, Mohawk and Delaware River valleys of New York and Pennsylvania colony did not. Having the majority of the Indian tribes within their sphere of influence already firmly allied to their cause at the beginning of the conflict would make all the difference for the French.

There was something else that gave the French an edge over the English on the field of battle when war broke out in the spring of 1755. Out of necessity, the English would be forced to depend heavily upon their British regular regiments to defend their colonies against the French. Unlike the French, they had made little provision over the years to develop any substantial provincial troops raised from the local populations throughout the colonies. This was a result of British military policy and philosophy that regarded colonial-mustered regiments as inferior to the highly-trained professional soldiers of the British Army. Though the individual colonies, like Virginia, were able to muster militiamen in a time of crisis, they possessed scant training at best, and usually had to provide for their own arms and clothing during the duration of their limited service. Provincial regiments raised from the colony and trained as soldiers to do military service was an idea largely in the making by 1754, due to the fact that there had been relative peace on the continent and therefore no need for an established military beyond that of garrison troops from England supplemented with poorly trained and undermanned local militias. However, this was not the case in New France.

The establishment of French colony troops

At the outbreak of war with the English, New France could count on French regular regiments from Europe to help with the fighting. In addition, militia companies composed of the inhabitant farmers of the St. Lawrence Valley and Quebec could be called up to serve in protecting the immediate colony. The large numbers of Canadian courier des bois living and trading with the Indians beyond the immediate confines of New France were always depended upon to accompany Indian war parties, if such were a necessity, but these men were by and large not of military upbringing nor inclined to that type of service. Closer to the Indians than the French military, the Canadians were dispersed and far away in times of crisis, and could be counted upon only when the Indians themselves were drawn into a conflict. New France, on the other hand, had created a colony infantry to fill the gap between the far-away continental regiments who would have to cross the Atlantic Ocean and the Canadian militia and woodsmen who lacked sufficient military training and discipline. War between New France and the Iroquois Confederacy in the 1680's prompted the French to raise and develop a professional military army in Canada to be known as "Les Compagnies Franches de la Marine" commonly French Marines, and known as Canadian colony regiments.

"Les Compagnies Franches de la Marine served throughout New France. Full companies and small detachments garrisoned posts from the Canadian Maritimes to the Great Lakes. There were 28 companies in Canada at the beginning of the 18th century." [GA-p.13] Who were these men of the French Marine? In the beginning, recruits were drawn to fill the rank and file from France and the slums of Europe. The enlistment preferred by the French Crown was for the term of life, and often the man was transported to Canada as a newly paid professional soldier without expectations of returning. [GA-p.135] The offer was lucrative compared to a peasant's life in France and Europe. A soldier of the Marine could expect to retire after a reasonable lifetime of service and receive a reward in a grant of land in Canada and some necessities to go with it. [EC- 95] The only requirement would be to adapt to the harsh environment of New France and "become part of the civilian society they served" upon their discharge. [GA-p.13]

French Marine officers were native born

Unlike the enlisted men who were drawn from recruitment in Europe, the officers of the French Marine in Canada were drawn from those young men born in French Canada to the upper class society. By 1722, more than half of the officer's corps were born in Canada and the number would increase by 1750. [GA-p.13] As native-born cadets, they began their training often as teenagers, learning a military style more adroitly adapted to New France than the regular regimental officers on the Continent. As such, the French Marine officers were thoroughly acquainted with the nature of unconventional warfare on the North American continent that by necessity demanded they understand and work well with the many Indian allies of the colony. Such officers learn a manner of command in the field that relied upon the ability to act independently in the wilderness where they might find themselves far from the support of regular troops.

Where death in battle is preferable to capture

By the outbreak of war with the English in 1755, most of the captains of the companies of French Marines stationed throughout New France had "20 to 30 years of experience" in the field. [GA-p.18] That experience included a close relationship with Indians and an in-depth understanding of the Indian mind. Because these officers were exposed to the nature of living in the wilderness and fighting a war both with and against Indians, they were uniquely prepared for the brutality and savageness of the upcoming struggle and would be able to pass that knowledge along to their French-born soldiers. The war fought against the Iroquois in the late 1600's had left an indelible impression upon the officer corps of the French Marine that was passed on from generation to generation. "The Canadian experience in warfare included a century of small fights where death in battle was preferable to capture and the "slow fire" (of Iroquois torture by burning any captives taken in battle). [GA-p.19] "Half a century earlier the Canadians had experienced the same sort of attacks in the Iroquois war and initially they had suffered heavy casualties, but they had mastered the art of guerrilla warfare and then beat back the Iroquois by using their own tactics of surprise, ambush, and swift assault where least expected. In that cruel war the Canadian military tradition was born.

"Knew how to make bloody war on the English"

With an aggressive spirit and practical training in the field, French Marine officers learned to attack an enemy quick and hard in determined assault that would be decisive, while their European counterparts in regular regiments from the continent were compelled to perform in tradition line formations where taking the initiative in command was forbidden. As such, the Marquis de Vaudreuil, who became the new Governor of New France in 1755, commented on that difference, in saying, that the soldiers of the French Marine "knew how to make bloody war on the British, while French regulars, fought in too gentle and conventional a manner." [GA-p.16]

French Marines had been with Contracoeur when he arrived at the forks of the Ohio the previous year to oust the English already there. The experienced Canadian officer, Sieur de Jumonville, who had been born in Vercheres, Quebec, led the force of men, including marines that had been ambushed by Washington and the Half King on the fateful morning of May 28, 1754. French Marines, too, were with Captain de Villiers on his retaliatory expedition that attacked Washington at Fort Necessity. Marines were part of the mixed force of French regulars, Canadians, militia and Indians that forced the English to surrender. Of the two French casualties during that engagement, both were listed as "Canadians." [BJ-p.63] Undoubtedly, they were French Marines. [GA-p.28]

An English invasion begins

Now in the spring of 1755, rumors of an English invasion reached the veteran French commander Contracoeur at Fort Duquesne in the Ohio Country. A massive English army comprised of recently-arrived British regulars from England, along with large numbers of colonial provincial troops accompanied by siege artillery was being assembled in Virginia commanded by British General Edward Braddock. Evidently, the English intended to march by way of Washington's old route over the Allegheny Mountains to attack the French at the strategic forks of the Ohio River and reduce Fort Duquesne by an overwhelming superiority of men, arms and cannon.

At the same time, a 44-year-old Montreal-born [GA-p.28] career soldier and Captain of the Independent Company of Marine Infantry received his new orders and left Quebec on the long journey west and south to the same French fort on the Ohio, where he was to succeed Contracoeur and take command of the installation there. The native-born officer, Daniel-Hyacinthe-Marie Lienard de Beaujeu would prove he was both a bold leader and an experienced hand at understanding the nature of Indian allies. Like many French Marine infantry officers in the field, Beaujeu's audacity would gain him laurels that would re-shape conventional military thinking of his time, and teach others in the years to come an important maxim in conducting wilderness warfare. For Beaujeu, the price to pay would be high.

Braddock leads the expedition to attack Fort Duquesne

On the morning of June 9, 1755, General Braddock ordered his 2,200-man army to begin their march from Fort Cumberland, Maryland near the head of the trail that would lead them to Fort Duquesne. Ahead of the five-mile long column of men, horses, oxen, wagons and artillery, a large contingent of axe-men and engineers labored to cut and level a road through the dense forest and rocky hills that would follow the course of the existing trail. With Braddock were over 1,000 regular red-coated soldiers of the 44th and 48th Regiments of Foot recently-arrived in America. In addition, Braddock's army included both Independent Companies and provincial soldiers from the colonies, as well as mounted troops, auxiliaries, artillerymen, wagoneers, and camp followers. [AF-p.31] George Washington, who had resigned his commission as colonel of the Virginia Militia in October 1754 after returning from his defeat at Fort Necessity, was invited by Braddock to join his staff on the expedition to the Ohio Country. He did so, though in ill-health, on May 30. [LT-p.173] There, Washington learned of Braddock's meeting with a group of Delaware, Shawnee and Mingo Indians, whom the trader George Croghan had brought to Braddock's camp for Braddock to persuade them to offer their much-needed scouting services to the English.

"He looked upon us as dogs"

Braddock was not amused. At age 60, the British general was a 43-year veteran of the Coldstream Guards Regiment and had held command of Gibraltar in 1753. [LT-p.165] Recently arriving in mid-February to America, Braddock had no time, patience or interest in the Indians, whom he viewed as savages. When he told the Mingoes that "no savage shall inherit the land" which he and his men were about to wrest from the French, the Mingoes recoiled in shock at Braddock's grievous insult, and promptly left to join the French. Of the eight warriors who remained with the English as they left camp, one would recall later of Braddock, and the encounter:

"He was a bad man (Braddock). He looked upon us as dogs, and would never hear anything what was said to him." [LT-p.172] The expedition to the forks of the Ohio was underway. Without experienced and able Indian scouts who would have been able to gain necessary information and intelligence on the French and their Indian allies who were somewhere ahead in the wilderness,

Braddock nonetheless left. Just as Washington had done the previous year Braddock underestimated the value of Indians as allies and scouts. Equally, he discounted their abilities as adversaries who were bound by a different set of rules of warfare particular to the forests. The Indians were mobile and relied upon ambush and surprise rather than standing in rigid lines to attack a foe.

By June 16, the excruciating slow-pace of the lumbering military column caused an irritated General Braddock to call for a council of war with the officers present to discuss what could be done to speed up the movement of the army, which he guessed at the current pace would take more than a month to reach Fort Duquesne, far longer than they had provisions for. Before the meeting, Braddock sought his aide's private opinion, and Washington advised the general to advance with a picked force of 1,200 troops and a few artillery that could dash ahead of the rest of the army to attack the fort before the French received reinforcements. [FJ2-p.124] Reluctantly, Braddock agreed, and a select force was chosen. Staying behind briefly till his health improved, Washington noted with alarm that on June 25, two Englishmen looking for stray horses were ambushed and scalped by hidden hostile Indians. Apparently the French already had their Indian allies in superb position to scout Braddock's force and skirmish with impunity. [LT-p.175]

The French plan a counter move

Unknown to Braddock and his officers, a steady stream of reports from Indian warriors scouting the movement of the English army were being brought back to the French commander Contracoeur at Fort Duquesne, detailing the English position and strength at any given time. Contracoeur was distressed when his Indian spies told him of the overwhelming size of the British army, and the presence of artillery which he knew would be used to reduce the wooden walls of the fort, for which his own small cannon were no match. [PF-p.156-157] On the advice of Chaussegros de Lery who had come from Fort Detroit with a few men, Contracoeur became convinced that the fort would not be able to withstand a siege. [GA-p.28] He reasoned that his only chance in defeating the approaching British lay in successfully intercepting them before they could make to open ground east of the fort, and by inflicting enough casualties upon them to discourage Braddock from pushing the rest of his army forward.

However, Contracoeur was having problems raising a significant force to meet the enemy. By early July, the garrison of the fort consisted of approximately 600 men, made up of a few companies of regular troops and a substantial number of Canadians that included French marine infantry, militia, and couriers' des bois from the outlying wilderness posts. Recently arrived was Captain Daniel Beaujeu, with provisions and a sizable reinforcement of some 300 men from Quebec, but Contracoeur knew he could expect no more help from New France in time. What he desperately needed were more Indians with fighting spirit.

After Washington's surrender of Fort Necessity the previous year, the Indians who had gathered at Fort Duquesne naturally dispersed in all directions to their villages and hunting grounds as autumn approached and the English threat diminished. With them they took many of the gifts that were given to them earlier, as well as any plunder that they had been able to get their hands on at the surrender. They would not be seen again during the winter months. In the spring, when Contracoeur first heard of the rumors of a new English invasion army, he promptly sent runners to the tribes of the Shawnee, Delaware, Mingo, and Wyandots of the Ohio Country, as well to all Indians of the lands encompassing New France. He called them to attend a great council to be held at Fort Duquesne, once the ice had broken up on the rivers and travel permitted. He wisely summoned them with the promise of gifts of goods, food, and ammunition, to be distributed at the council. Unfortunately, he knew he must be draw from the fort's meager supplies to fulfill that promise, a promise that would be hard to keep.

The Indians are in no mood to fight

Nonetheless, by early July 1755, Contracoeur was able to count over 800 warriors camped before the walls of the fort from tribes as far away as the Great Lakes and the St. Lawrence River valleys, including many of the most savage Indians of all ever assembled. There were Miamis, Pottawattamies, Ojibwas, and Chippewas from the Lakes area, along with Ottawas under a fierce new war chief named Pontiac. To the northeast had come the Abenakis, Caughnawagas, Hurons and others, with their French courier des bois brethren. All in all it was one of the greatest assemblages of painted savages Contracoeur had ever seen [PF-p.157] and he would have been pleased beyond belief that they had come so far to support him, if it were not for the troubling fact that collectively they were in no mood to fight.

Each new report on the approach of the English army brought back to Fort Duquesne from Indian runners caused greater ripples of consternation among the Indian throng in the wigwams and shelters built before the fort. Indian spies reported on the great size of the English army and more importantly, that they brought artillery with them, which alarmed the warriors. As a result, Contracoeur was aware that he was helpless to prevent what he knew was about to happen. The chiefs of the many tribes, as best as he could determine, were privately counseling their warriors to remain neutral in the coming fight, in which they could see that the French were badly outnumbered by the approaching English, and in addition, woefully outgunned by superior artillery. No Indian wished to be caught under the range of heavy artillery, and the British were bringing it with them. The situation did not look good for Contracoeur on the morning of July 8, 1755, as he surveyed the multitude of warriors who by their tone were growing more disgruntled and fearful by the hour. To make the situation worse, two of his men, the brothers Normanville, had just returned from their scout of the English, and excitedly reported that the English were only some six leagues distant to the southeast, following the banks of the Monongahela River (French league= apprx. 2 1/2 miles). [BR-p.13] To those who knew, it meant that the English would soon cross the natural fording place of the river, and would be within one day's march of the French fort. [PF-p.158]

Contracoeur speaks to the Indians

This startling news threw the Indian camp and the Frenchmen in the fort into a great state of alarm, filling Contracoeur with deep dread. His attempts to speak with the many chiefs of the multitude of tribes over the last few days to reassure them and request their support to attack the English had been met with aloofness and open disapproval. Dressed in all the finery of his French regular officer's uniform to impress his guests, Contracoeur attempted to entice the chiefs with the promise of more gifts, and all the scalps and plunder of the English they could manage if they would agree to attack, but this had not moved them in the least. Some Indians remembered all too well the false promises made to them the previous summer at the Great Meadows. When Contracoeur's second in command, de Villiers had refused to turn over to them the surrendered Englishmen to do with as they pleased for the scalps, the gauntlet, the fire, or their pots, which the Indians deemed their right in payment for their service. They spoke openly of the insult as the reason they would not fight now, but that was only a pretext to hide their fears and misgivings about supporting the French at this moment.

Judging the ugly mood of the Indians, Contracoeur privately had every reason to believe at this very critical moment, only a day away from a battle with the English, that the Indians were about to desert Fort Duquesne. He heard rumors that a few Indians were preparing to leave by quietly gathering their possessions. [LT-p.177] Personally he felt powerless to dispel their negativity. Claude-Pierre Pecaudy, Sieur de Contracoeur, former commandant of Fort Niagara and second-in-command on Celeron's 1749 expedition to the Ohio Country [KD-p.15] had a wealth of experience in dealing with the Indians of New France over the years. However in spite of that, he did not know at this moment what to say to them to replace their growing fear and uncertainty with the fierce, savage temperament that he knew they were capable of, and which would be necessary if they were to be of help to him if he were to fight the English. Contracoeur had tried to motivate them with the usual bribes he had seen work before, much in the same way that he had done successfully the year before, when he asked them to help the French avenge Jumonville's death. What had effectively moved the Indians to war then, did not have any effect now, and the support of the Indians to attack Braddock was the only realistic hope the French had to win. In light of the Indians' unanimous rebuff to his repeated requests, Contracoeur returned to the fort walls and came to the conclusion that the situation was hopeless and all was lost. Despairingly, he called for a private council with his officers and explained to them the deteriorating situation they found themselves: the Indians could not be counted upon to support any French attack on the numerically superior English. Finally, Contracoeur suggested to his three captains present, Ligneris, Dumas, and Beaujeu that Fort Duquesne be abandoned as soon as possible while there was still time for the garrison to withdraw, rather than face a humiliating surrender to the English. [KD-p.28]

Beaujeu argues for a chance to lead an attack

Of the three captains with Contracoeur, Daniel Beaujeu spoke up opposing the idea that they withdraw without a fight. Having not yet taken over command of the fort officially from Contracoeur, Beaujeu nonetheless asserted himself and put forth to the officers present an idea that had been formulating in his mind for some time on what should be done. Beaujeu agreed with Contracoeur that their only hope in defeating the English lay in attacking them, by ambush or headlong assault, while they were still on the forest trail. [AF-p.34] This could only happen if the Indians would join them, and though at the moment they were not inclined to do so, Beaujeu was confident that if given the chance, that he could do what Contracoeur had been unable to. Implicit in his argument too, was the conviction that Contracoeur, given his ineffectiveness with the Indians, was ready to give up without a fight, something that Beaujeu, having just arrived from Canada, found disagreeable, if not dishonorable. Whether he voiced those opinions or not in that brief meeting, Beaujeu's arguments were persuasive. He would convince the Indians to accompanying him with what men of the fort could be spared to attack the English. He would lead the attack himself, and if nothing else, perhaps could so weaken the English they would either retreat due to lack of provisions or could be withstood if what was left of them did attempt to move on the fort. [WE- 328]

Contracoeur, undoubtedly taken aback by the brashness of his junior officer, could not disapprove of Beaujeu's request without risking a charge of cowardice leveled from the men for failing to let a bolder officer attempt a plan that held a slight chance of success. Nor could his pride allow Beaujeu the opportunity to relieve him of his duties as commandant, as he knew Beaujeu's orders stated, but for the courtesy of rank had been delayed. At this critical moment, when all eyes at Fort Duquesne were turned to Contracoeur, he did not want to lose face, which would certainly happen if he tried to deny Beaujeu the opportunity to try. Acquiescing, Contracoeur reluctantly approved Beaujeu's plan, but reminded him that he had not as yet crossed the first hurdle of convincing the Indians. That problem to Contracoeur seemed insurmountable.

"I am determined to meet the English"

Beaujeu left the meeting at once to speak with the Indians outside the fort. Calling all the chiefs of every tribe together before a council fire on the evening of July 8, Beaujeu made his argument to them that it was paramount to attack the English from the cover of the forests rather than wait for the English to attack them at the fort, which would surely come in a day or two at the most. Many chiefs spoke openly now, disapproving any attack on the English, saying that their scouts had counted the English and there were too many of them for their own men to fight. Undaunted, Beaujeu continued to argue, cajole, plead and coax the growing horde of Indians about him, raising a tomahawk high above his head as he spoke, and asking them to accept it and join him and his men in this fight with the English. Again, many of the chiefs told Beaujeu that they would not fight, but the stubborn French Marine of Canadian birth would not hear it, and continued on into the night, gradually gaining the approval of some of the chiefs present, who admired the singular courage and spirit of the white man before them.

Realizing that any decision to fight on the part of the chiefs must be a unanimous decision by all of them, Beaujeu reasoned he must convince the chiefs who were steadfast against his plan of attack, or all his efforts would be for not. Having spent a great deal of time studying the Indians who lived near the posts where he had served for so many years throughout New France, Beaujeu resorted to a stratagem that he thought might work to convince the chiefs who were refusing to fight the English. To the amazement of the throng of Indian onlookers, Beaujeu removed his leather shoes and putting on a pair of Indian moccasins, began to step and shuffle around the blazing fire, singing what each Indian knew to be "the war song," a dance that had great meaning to all Indians. Intuitively Beaujeu understood that Indians expressed themselves more with "their voices and feet, dancing and chanting their agreement" in the making of war upon an enemy, rather than listening and discussing. [LT-p.177] If he could get enough Indian warriors to dance with him, he might create a mood by which opinion could be swayed and recalcitrant chiefs could reconsider their refusal to attack. Beaujeu's dancing had a catalytic effect upon the Indians, and warriors began to join him. A Frenchmen observing Beaujeu's dance remarked "all the Indian nations immediately joined him except the Pottawattamies of the Narrows, who were silent." Beaujeu had with him a horde of Indian warriors dancing, singing, and chanting the war song as they circled the fire into the night, and nearly had succeeded in winning all of the chiefs over but for a few. [LT-p.177]

Early on the morning of July 9, 1755, Daniel Beaujeu roused himself and at once set out to speak to all of the chiefs. To his disappointment, he found that a few still refused to fight the English, and those few were preventing any of the others from allowing their warriors to accompany his men. Surprisingly, in the face of the adversity, Beaujeu did not despair, though it was becoming apparent to him that time was running out, if he were to succeed. Somehow, he felt that the task could be done, but he did not know how. Out of desperation, Beaujeu tried one more tact as he motioned the chiefs and their warriors to silence, so he could speak. He began to harangue them, in a bold, scathing, sarcastic tone. Personally determined to prove his point and attack the English himself, if need be, Beaujeu now questioned the courage and bravery of the horde of savages assembled before him.

"I am determined to meet the English!" Beaujeu shouted to the Indians. "What?" he raised his arm and pointed to them, "Will you let your father go alone?" [PF-p.159] Then stepping away from the astonished, murmuring warriors and chiefs, Beaujeu motioned for the priest to give him communion, after which he began a ritual of preparation that no Frenchman at Fort Duquesne had ever witnessed. Silencing any further argument with reluctant chiefs, Daniel Beaujeu began stripping off his white linen French Marine uniform until he was naked but for his breeches and leggings. Methodically, he began applying streaks of red and black paint to his bare chest, arms and face, in a manner that was familiar to all Indians watching. They could see he was making his preparations for battle. In a few moments, Beaujeu looked very much like a warrior to them, an Indian warrior, who was brave enough to fight the English alone, without any help. Amazingly, this final desperate appeal had the desired effect.

Beaujeu's appeal to the Indians is successful

First one and then another warrior raised their war hatchet high in the air and let out a shrieking war whoop of approval. Within seconds, dozens of Indians were clamoring for their weapons and issuing similar howls, and when Beaujeu, caught up now in the excitement of what he had begun raised his hatchet and musket in the air over his head and let out a war whoop of his own, the clamoring horde of warriors before him, incited by a shared spirit, screamed in unison as one, and quickly began to paint themselves with their own war paint, sealing their pact with Beaujeu to go and fight with him. When the howling roar of the Indians reached the fort, Contracoeur ordered that kegs of gunpowder and lead ball be brought out beyond the gate and opened so that the warriors and assembling soldiers could fill their powder horns and cartridge boxes. [BR-p.19] Within a short time, final preparations of the soldiers and warriors were made for the attacking force. Beaujeu, painted as frightful as any Indian, tied the strings to a silver officer's gorget about his neck, allowing it to dangle on his chest slightly above his heart. It may have been an afterthought or a premonition—many of the Indians ornamented themselves in a similar manner. Beaujeu was if fact the officer in command of the French soldiers during the upcoming attack, and too, gorgets were a symbolic piece of armor carried over from the middle ages that had been worn by knights in battle to protect them from a mortal sword or lance thrust. Whatever his thought, the gorget only added to Beaujeu's fierce countenance and brought him nods and grunts of approval as he moved through the horde of Indians who at the moment were making their last minute adjustments to musket flints, hatchets and knives. Signaling Contracoeur and the few men on the fort walls that was ready, Beaujeu raised his war-hatchet above his head and let out a hearty war whoop, which was followed by the tumultuous roar of 637 Indian warriors, 36 French officers and cadets of the Marine, 72 regular soldiers, and 146 Canadian militia and woodsmen—in all, a force of about 900 men bent on attacking over 1,300 English regular infantry.

In an instant, the entire attacking force was off at a trot across the open field to the Indian trail at the edge of the woods that led to the southeast along the heights above the river, away from the site of Fort Duquesne and to the southeast. The trail wound over the wooded ridges, angling from the old Delaware Indian village called Shannopin's Town on the east bank of the Allegheny River, a few miles upriver from the French fort [WP-p.144], towards a juncture of trails that led to the east and south towards the mountains and over to the Delaware villages of the Monongahela and Susquehanna Rivers. It was the southern path that generally followed the curve of the Monongahela River and branched towards the natural ford of the river some eight miles upstream from its juncture with the Allegheny near the mouth of Turtle Creek which emptied into it. Here the path met trails that branched in many directions southward intersecting the Old Town path and then on farther to Nemacolin's village at Redstone beyond, and to the paths leading east to the Susquehanna.

Braddock's army has no Indian scouts

Indian scouts knew that Braddock's force had been following one of the branches of Nemacolin's Path that led from the Potomac River Valley and Virginia beyond, and was the same trail that the trader Gist and Washington had used in previous years to enter the Ohio Country. For some unknown reason, spies had reported that the English had left the main path that would have taken them to the ridge trail above the river, and English engineers cut a rough road down the creek valley (Long Run [WP-p.113]) and crossed the Monongahela River near its mouth. After following the west side for several miles to avoid the narrow defile of the river to the south of Turtle Creek, Braddock had his force re-cross the river at the ford in the morning. They did so with methodical precision and caution, fearing that of all places, this ford of the river would be a most likely site for an Indian ambush. None was forthcoming, and Braddock's English scouts out ahead of the vanguard, gave the all clear sign for the men to begin moving along the path that would cross several brushy gullies and ascend the wooded heights, before turning westward towards the forks of the Ohio, less than eight miles distant. Frustrated the day before by Christopher Gist's Virginian scouts who had unfortunately blundered when they had taken a wrong trail and lost precious time for Braddock, he chose instead this shorter route, which held more danger than the other, in that his men would not only be exposed at the two fords of the Monongahela River, but now would have to climb a grade that rose from the river bottom for a stretch.

Without a mass of Indian allies acting as scouts whom he could send ahead in a wide screen to detect any approach of the enemy, Braddock resorted to sending his handful of English scouts ahead, with six mounted Virginians to scout the trail, as they generally were acquainted with it. Lacking confidence in their competence to give him and the main body ample warning in the event of an attack or ambush, Braddock ordered Colonel Gage to follow the scouts with a body of 300 picked men within musket shot range, to act as a vanguard. In all, Braddock's advance column ahead of his main body of men was well armed and sufficient to deter any enemy skirmishers. However, because the forest and

*Captain Beaujeu leads the attack at the front
of the Indian warriors and French marines.*

brush to either side of the path was unusually dense, Gage's men gradually compressed themselves on the trail rather than struggle unnecessarily through the underbrush in order to spread themselves out. They were never more than a few hundred yards ahead; closer than Washington would have liked, thus putting themselves at a disadvantage (something that a group of Indians would never have allowed themselves to do.) Being naturally adapted to the forest, Indians would have chosen to be much farther ahead and deeper on the flanks of the column to intercept ambushers or attackers before they could meet them. After all, it was the Indian way of woods fighting.

The two forces collide and Beaujeu is killed

Having just passed through a small ravine on the path, the forward scouts suddenly ran into Beaujeu and a horde of painted Indians who were coming towards them through the deeper forest at a trot. Beaujeu, himself astonished to see the English so precipitously close, having not yet reached the spot that he had in mind that would make for an ambush close to the crossing at the ford of the river, nonetheless did not hesitate nor lose step with the English, but let out a tremendous war whoop to spur on his French and savage compatriots as he motioned for them to spread out on each flank in a wide arc to bring maximum arms to bear on the English and deliver a quick, devastating blow to their front. As Indians and French alike began to fire their muskets, Gage, reacting to the fusillade, brought his men into line and fired several deliberate volleys in the direction of Beaujeu, who at that moment, was directing his men from the open path. With Gage's third delivery of musket fire, Beaujeu fell dead with several lead balls to the chest; he was among the first to die in the battle. [PF-p.161] The warriors near him were momentarily disheartened, not only by the death of the brave Frenchman, but more so by the ferocity of the English musket fire that appeared to them to be the work of artillery. For a time, it seemed as if the Indians would falter. [LT-p.181]

Dumas rallies the French and Indians

Captain Jean Dumas, a regular army officer and second-in-command to Beaujeu, cursed to himself at what he determined to be Beaujeu's ill-timing which had cost him his life. To Dumas, Beaujeu had allowed the front of his force, which was all Indian warriors, to attack the English before the rest of the Frenchmen could get into position of line, as was to Dumas the rule of war. Thus when Beaujeu's Indians began to fire at the withdrawing English scouts, they were essentially out of range. [KP-p.251] However, Dumas did not understand Beaujeu's thinking, which was the difference between a European-trained officer and a Canadian-born infantry marine. "On the fields of Europe, the game followed the rules; in the forests of North America a quick, determined attack often decided the issue," and Beaujeu had instinctively wanted to hit the English first to knock them off-balance before they could bring their greater fire-power to bear. Dumas watched horrified as the mass of Canadians at once turned and fled the field rather than fire at Gage's line. The Indians had not left, nor were they advancing, but rather had each taken to protective positions of the trees, and thus neutralized the English volleys while still keeping up a constant fire on the English, whom they could see by their red coats. Shaken, but undeterred, Dumas rallied what remained of the Frenchmen who had not fallen back. These men, all French Marines, let loose a volley themselves and then advanced a step or two. Seeing this, the Indians instinctively regained the initiative and began to move through the woods on either side of Gage's force, all the while delivering hot fire.

Paradoxically, what Dumas did not comprehend was that had he been able to persevere in forming up all the French regulars, Canadians, and Marines into classic European line formation, Gage would have been able to bring to bear against the French all the firepower of his men with that of the main force of troops moving to join him at the quick step. That mass of English soldiers, if they had been able to fire their muskets in accordance with their conventional training, would have annihilated the smaller French force as they stood their ground, obeying commands to load, present and fire. But that was not the case. With Beaujeu dead, the Indians were still able to make all the difference in the battle, as they neither obeyed Dumas to fight in a line, nor were they compelled to attack the English by European rules of warfare. Rather, they continued to move from tree to tree, flanking Gage's force while delivering their own musket fire. Amazingly, the Indians were not taking any casualties, and were becoming bolder.

The Indians flank Braddock's army

Within minutes, Gage's men began to give ground. Though he ordered them forward, not a single man advanced. Rather, they began to fall back, as more and more men crumpled from the fire of the Indians, whom they could not see clearly enough into the woods to respond in kind. At length, the tremendous noise and smoke of musketry combined with the constant din of shrieking Indians, caused Gage's men to recoil in confusion, retreating in disarray upon the woodsmen and Braddock's main body. However the Indians at this point had reached far deep onto the sides of the army, and could now deliver witheringly accurate fire upon the masses of English soldiers, so that dozens of men were shot and fell, and order among the ranks of men began to disintegrate. Within minutes, the regulars began to panic, and all their military training geared for conventional battles could not be put to use. They stood in groups, paralyzed, and died by the dozens, until giving way in a rout. No orders could stop them as the Indians having fired and moved from tree to tree with impunity had "worked their way along both sides of the compacted British mob until they had almost closed the circle."

Braddock's force is annihilated

Within a few hours, more than 700 British soldiers were dead or wounded, including Braddock and over 50 of his officers. [GA-p.31] Most of the wounded were left on the field to the merciless Indians. What remained of Braddock's force recrossed the Monongahela and fled by the way they had come, in mortal fear of their lives from the horrible spectacle that they had just witnessed and somehow survived. Washington was one of them. With the remainder of the British army gone, the Indians turned their attention to the hundreds of dead and wounded Englishmen on the field. They descended upon them like a host of demons, moving from man to man, and plunging their tomahawks and war clubs into their victims' skulls. Scalps by the hundreds were cut and torn from mangled heads, and the corpses were stripped of their clothing and the bodies cut to pieces in an unrelenting orgy of bloodletting and butchery until every Indian had had his fill, for their were more than enough victims to go around for each. About a dozen terrified Englishmen had surrendered to the Indians at the height of the battle, hoping that their lives would be spared if they allowed themselves to be made prisoners. These men were now stripped naked by the Indians, and bound with their hands behind their backs. Their faces and bodies were blackened, as they were to be taken back to the Indian camps at the forks where the warriors planned to celebrate their great victory over the English.

Dumas, along with his fellow captain Ligneris and about 100 marines and French regulars, decided not to pursue the fleeing English, fearing that the reserve army of the English was close at hand. Returning from the river to the scene of the battle, he was truly amazed at how light their own casualties had been as he surveyed the field. Only three officers, three Canadians, two marines and 15 Indians had been killed, and a handful more wounded. [GA-p.31] On the battlefield the British had left a tremendous prize to the victors, including, "13 artillery pieces, 500 head of cattle and horses, 30 wagonloads of ammunition and provisions and equipment including Braddock's personal papers and his war chest containing his valuables." [LT-p.189] This of course did not include the hundreds of British Brown Bess muskets, flints, cartridge boxes, bayonets, officer's side arms and thousands of items of personal gear and uniform pieces that the Indians claimed as their own, in addition to the bloody scalps of the dead. It would take a day to bring all the plunder back to camps at Fort Duquesne. The rotting, disfigured corpses of the English dead were left unburied where they fell, as macabre food for the wolves.

The victorious Indians returned to Fort Duquesne late in the afternoon of July 9, many of them completely covered in the blood of their recent victims, with fresh scalps dangling from their belts, and each carrying their own booty taken from the battlefield by the armload. Many of the warriors had dressed themselves in British officers' redcoats. Still others wore upon their heads the tall miter hats of British grenadiers, attesting to the Frenchmen in the fort, including Contracoeur who had remained, the magnitude of the victory that the Indians had won. Near the end of the steady stream of returning men came the

English prisoners, who the Indians hustled to waiting canoes that were readied far from the fort gates, and immediately taken across the Allegheny River to the Indian camp on the opposite shore.

The Indians "yelled like infernal spirits"

Of all men who witnessed this, Contracoeur, more than any other, knew its significance. The Indians were not to be denied this time their right to do with their prisoners as they pleased without interference from any Frenchman. Having denied them once at the Great Meadows the right to the prisoners through the officer de Villiers, the Indians were in no mood to turn the poor unfortunates over this time. Contracoeur, knowing what fate awaited them on the opposite shore, was in no position to bargain for their lives, as the Indians had helped the French defeat the English. This was not the time to interfere, so he did not consider it. In full view of the walls of Fort Duquesne, one by one the English victims were tied to stakes set in the ground and roasted alive with dozens of firebrands and red-hot irons touched to them. Their hideous screams and pitiful cries filled the air long into the night, while the Indians "yelled like infernal spirits," and danced like demons possessed, pleased with their savage handiwork. [PF-p.166]

Within a matter of days, the multitude of warriors from the various tribes that assembled at Fort Duquesne before the battle, packed their possessions and set out for their own distant villages. Each knew that they had won a great victory. They could claim for once that their blood-lust had been thoroughly sated. Every scalping knife and tomahawk had been bathed in English blood; from every belt hung a fresh enemy scalp, taken in battle. For Contracoeur, the immediate ordeal was over but the threat from the English had not passed, at least in his mind. Not knowing that Braddock was mortally wounded, Contracoeur was unsure what Braddock would do once reinforced by his reserves, under the command of Dunbar, who were somewhere behind Braddock's retreating force. Without the Indians, Contracoeur knew that the fort was essentially unprotected, a disagreeable situation that he again would have to deal with, though this time alone.

Captain Jean Dumas took much of the credit for the great victory. He was critical of Beaujeu's impetuous initial attack that could have cost the French the battle. Dumas had rallied the marines when the Canadians had given way, which had made all the difference in his mind. That Beaujeu had hit the English first, and that the Indians had moved to flank the enemy, thus turning Gage's men back, was not seen by Dumas as of greater importance or consequence. Dead men do not speak for themselves, and in the years to come, Dumas would create for himself without contradiction a reputation as a military officer and would return to France in 1760, to continue his military career in the regular army. [GA-p.31]

"Who would have thought of it?"

For Braddock, mortally wounded on the battlefield, the end was nearing. On July 11, the retreating force with Braddock on a litter, reached the former site of Gist's plantation, and rested. After a day of painful silence, Braddock spoke in a whisper to those officers huddled around him. "Who would have thought of it," he questioned without reply. On the evening of the next night, Braddock, in excruciating pain, spoke again, giving orders for the relief of the wounded men. Then, as if summarizing what had happened, he said, "we shall better know how to deal with them (the Indians) another time," and died a few minutes later. [PF-p.168] Washington directed Braddock's burial in an anonymous grave in the wagon road, "to hinder any suspicion of the French Indians...." [KC-189] The Indians, obviously, were on everyone's minds.

Washington had lived through the worst military defeat suffered by the British in America. Writing to his mother a week after the battle, he derided the English regular soldiers whose refusal to follow the orders of their officers precipitated the panicked flight by all. Holding to a conventional view, Washington was not critical of either Braddock or the English officers for their conduct. However, he more than anyone else, would have known that the officers who ordered their men to form up in line and stand at attention, all the while in the face of withering fire from a hidden enemy that was dropping them in heaps, demanded the impossible. Was it not akin to the lesson Washington himself had learned at the battle of the Great Meadows? Publicly, he would not condemn either Braddock or any other in command. [LT-p.90]

Beaujeu, the architect and genius behind the great victory, was dead. In the excitement of days following the battle, he and what he had done to win the Indians over on the night prior to the battle, was all but forgotten. Presumably, Contracoeur had Beaujeu's body brought back to the fort, and at least given decent burial. Yet the lesson that man had taught, an essential maxim of Indian wilderness warfare, had been stunning, and could not be forgotten in the years to come. Never before had a white officer, either French or English, been able to influence the Indians and incite them to war when the odds had been heavily against them. Beaujeu had done so by an unconventional method that would be repeated again in years to come; not by appearing to the Indians as a white man urging them to help him in a white man's war, but speaking to them as a fellow Indian, dressed and painted in a manner they could see was an Indian warrior, challenging them with words of steadfast bravery that they could admire, and dancing around their fires and war posts in songs that could inspire them.

Essentially, Beaujeu appeared to the Indians as one of their own, and not a white man. Added to this, Beaujeu's resolute determination to attack the English first and hard, in order to keep their numerically superior force of regulars off-balance, was key to the victory, and not chance. Beaujeu, a Canadian who had lived close to the Indians and knew their ways well, had a vision that no other Frenchman shared with him: believing that the English could be defeated. His last act in life had been in directing the Indians on either side of him to begin to flank the enemy through the woods. They had done so and succeeded, heeding their white warrior-captain well.

"The British gentlemen were confident they would never be attacked"

The lesson was not entirely lost on some Englishmen, as well. Captain Adam Stephen, who had been with Washington the previous year at the surrender of Fort Necessity and was now in command of the Virginia Provincial Regiment, was openly critical not only the performance of the regulars and their officers, but of Braddock himself, laying much of the blame after the battle at the general's feet. Stephen's orders prior to the battle had been to escort the packhorses bringing provisions up to Braddock from the rear. He had at his disposal 100 men, and during the 50-mile march were "dogged night and day by the Indians" that attacked the column from ambush. Stephen was able to accomplish his mission only by learning to use constant vigilance to detect the Indians, and fight them in the manner that they were using upon him. "We beat them out of their ambushes, and always had the first fire on them."

Successfully using new tactics suited to the wilderness, Stephen fought his way through the Indians to reach Braddock, but found the General and his officers overconfident and ignorant of the situation they faced. "The British gentlemen were confident they would never be attacked" and were ill-prepared for the kind of Indian warfare that Stephen himself had just experienced. Stephen reasoned correctly from what he had seen that the Indians would not defend the fort itself, as it was against their way of making war, but rather would only fight the English before they got to the fort, at some point in the heart of the forests. Thus, if the French did not take the initiative to attack, "(they) must lose the use of their Indians." [LT-p.91]

"Attack them first; fight them in their own way"

Summarizing the reasons for English loss and what should have been done to prevent it, Captain Adam Stephen, criticized Braddock for adhering to only conventional military thinking, which would not work in the wilderness, where new strategy and new tactics were needed. "His Excellency found to his woeful experience, what had been frequently told him, that formal attacks and platoon-firing would never answer against the savages and Canadians. It ought to be laid down as a maxim to attack them first, to fight them in their own way, and go against them light and naked, as they came against us." The lessons on Indian wilderness warfare, taught by Beaujeu and learned by Stephen in the forest battle on the Monongahela, had come at frightful cost. The question was, would other men learn them as well?

Chapter 3

Le Petite Guerre: Indians, Partisans and the Tactics of Terror

Panic and retreat was what happened to the survivors of Braddock's force following the battle, and no effort by any of the officers could stem the disintegration of the remains of the army into a mob of terrified soldiers who dropped their muskets and fled down the trail to the Monongahela River ford to escape the Indians. Though Washington himself tried to organize men for a rearguard, no one would listen to him nor anyone else, but abandoned wounded comrades along the trail to fend for themselves because they were terrified that the Indians would manage to cut them off. Each man could not forget what he had just experienced, seen and heard which drove him on. "The yell of the Indians is fresh on my ear, and the terrific sound will haunt me until the hour of my dissolution."[KC-187] Braddock, himself severely wounded, was left by the retreating soldiers on the battlefield. A few officers, including Washington loaded him into a small cart themselves and saved him from the Indians. One of the officers was, Orme recalled, "trying to bribe some men to help Braddock, but money held no interest for them." [LT-p.187] Escaping the Indians was all that mattered for every man still capable of running, walking, or crawling away.

Dunbar's camp panics and flees

Once past the second ford on the evening of July 9, Braddock was transferred to a litter by the handful of men still with him. Conscious, he commanded Washington "to halt those who had been earlier in the retreat."[FJ2-p.130] However, when the General was told that this was no longer possible as there were no more men behind them to stop, Braddock ordered Washington to move ahead up the trail and attempt to reach Dunbar, some 50 miles away, to bring help. Setting out at once in the darkness with two guides, Washington recalled later, "the shocking scenes which presented themselves in this night's march are not to be described." [LT-p.187] For the first hour, Washington came upon hundreds of wounded men along the trail who were badly in need of help, which was not forthcoming. Panicked flight had taken them a couple of miles along the trail where they had collapsed in exhaustion, unable to go any farther. Washington passed them by, unable to help. He remembered vividly almost 30 years later. "The dead, the dying, the groans, lamentations and cries along the road were enough to pierce a heart of adamant." [FJ2-p.130] Wounded men were left to die because the fear of Indian attack terrorized almost every man remaining alive after the battle. Their one common thought was to escape capture by the Indians, at the expense of all else.

The rout of the defeated English did not stop at Dunbar's camp, although no Indians had been seen or heard in pursuit of the mass of men. When Washington reached Colonel Dunbar, he found to his dismay that word of the great slaughter and defeat of Braddock's force preceded him. Wagon and packhorse men, who were at the rear of Braddock's column during the battle, were the first to flee the battlefield once they were able to see that Braddock's force was being annihilated, and they themselves were in danger of being cut-off by the flanking Indians. The first arrivals to Dunbar's camp brought more than word of the defeat, for their own panic caused pandemonium among Dunbar's troops. By the time Washington reached Dunbar, "many soldiers and teamsters took to flight, in spite of the sentinels, who tried in vain to stop them." [PF-p.167] Just the threat of Indians continued to cause havoc.

Caught in the grip of the terror which was becoming contagious, Colonel Thomas Dunbar acted irrationally at his camp, some six miles southeast of Gist's abandoned plantation. Although he commanded over 1,000 men who had not been involved in the action with Braddock, and who could have been put to work reinforcing their position and reorganizing the shattered remains of Braddock's regiments, Dunbar did not do so. To the contrary, Dunbar gave orders that the huge store of ammunition and provisions with him be destroyed immediately, along with 100 wagons burned, once General Braddock was brought into camp, and Dunbar could assess for himself the magnitude of the Indian threat. Finally he gave commands for an orderly withdrawal of the men across the mountains to the safety of Virginia: but within minutes that order too, degenerated into a rout. The terror of the Indians traveled with the men, and the contagion quickly spread across the frontier of Pennsylvania, Maryland and to Virginia, as the remnants of Braddock's army returned with word of the disaster at the hands of the Indians.

The English frontier is left undefended

By September 1755, terror gripped the English settlers in the isolated cabins and settlements spread across the frontier, as word spread to the outlying areas of Braddock's terrible defeat and the horrible accounts of the Indians scalping and tomahawking the wounded. The stories were spread by surviving provincial soldiers, wagon men and civilians who had since returned to their homes. Realizing that the frontier was now undefended, and with nothing between them and the French at Fort Duquesne to stop the Indians should they attack, everyone in the outlying settlements dreaded what might happen next. George Washington returned to Virginia, and worried, too, about the defenseless frontier which "the consequences this defeat may have upon our back (country) settlers." [AF-p.40] Chillingly, as autumn deepened, what the settlers feared the most was soon to arrive.

At Fort Duquesne, Captain Dumas replaced Contracoeur as commander. His first order of business was to strengthen Fort Duquesne in the only way possible. Realizing that the French had been most fortunate in defeating Braddock's army which had come within only a day's march of attacking it, Dumas fully understood that the fort would have never withstood an assault with artillery. General Montcalm in Quebec, who had never seen Fort Duquesne, nonetheless agreed with de Lery's earlier evaluation that the fort was "not worth a straw," [GA-p.32] as a defensible position. Dumas reasoned that his best defense against a future attack by an English force was to prevent one from happening, and using the only means available to him, took the war to the English by sending out raiding war parties of French and Indians to attack the English frontier east of the Appalachian mountains. With most of the allied Indians of the Great Lakes gone, Dumas turned to the tribes of the Ohio Country closest to Fort Duquesne, including the Shawnee, Delaware, Wyandot and Mingoes, to begin attacks on the border settlements late in 1755. Dumas found the warriors eager to take up the war hatchet against the English and share in the scalps, prisoners, and plunder that many had previously missed. [PF-p.235]

By mid-October 1755, French and Indian raiding parties began to strike with a fury. In the mountains of the western frontier of Pennsylvania colony, many inhabitants living in isolated cabins built along the streams that flowed into the Susquehanna River were the first to be hit. War parties moved quickly along the web of forest paths and reached those settlers undetected, striking suddenly without warning; they slaughtered the scattered settlers, burned their cabins, and disappeared without a trace. Word of dozens of attacks traveled quickly, and as no forts had been built on the previously peaceful frontier to provide refuge from Indian raiders, many of the populace gathered their families and a few possessions and fled their homes to the settlements and towns of the east rather than take a chance of staying and being killed. As word of the Indian raids in Pennsylvania reached Maryland and Virginia, war parties crossed the mountains easily and began to hit there too. "Braddock had opened a road for them by which they could cross the mountains at their ease; and scouts from Fort Cumberland reported that this road was beaten by as many as when the English army passed last summer." [PF-p.236]

As autumn progressed, Indian attacks increased in intensity along the entire length of the colonial frontier; leaving in their wake the scalped and burnt remains of anyone unlucky enough to be caught in the path of the lightning-strike raids. The Indians were becoming bolder and bolder, and there was no way and no one to prevent the attacks. Washington, now in command of the newly raised Virginia Provincial Regiment, wrote from his beleaguered headquarters in Winchester. "Every day, we have accounts of such cruelties and barbarities as are shocking to human nature. It is not possible to conceive the situation and danger of this miserable country. Such numbers of French and Indians are all around that no road is safe." [PF-p.236]

The truth was that as bad as the raids had been, terror from the threat of the Indians was far worse. Reports of raids had been passed word of mouth from farmer to farmer, and each retelling of the ghastly atrocities committed by the Indians against friends and neighbors only served to increase the panic. Captain Waggoner of the Virginia Regiment was on the march with 30 recruits to Winchester when he encountered a mob of refugee settlers headed east that slowed his progress. "Crowds of people were flying as if every moment was death" he wrote, leaving behind everything they owned and running for their lives, because of an unfounded rumor that Winchester had been attacked and was burning. [LT-p.199] The onset of winter brought a brief respite to the frontier settlers as the attacks by Indian war parties lessened. However, the terror of Indians did not abate at all among those people left in their fortified homes or holed up in the nearest settlements of any size. The strain of not knowing when and where the Indians would strike next and who would be the unfortunate victim of a moment's carelessness or lack of vigilance, caused continued terror among those English people remaining on the frontier. Whether the French and Indians knew it or not, the terror of Indian war parties was becoming a tactic in of itself.

"To burn you, by God, and eat you"

With New York colony involved in the war as well, Indian raids on the northern colonial frontiers had similar frightful consequences as French allied Abenaki, Caughnawaga, and Huron warriors struck the Hudson, Mohawk, and Connecticut River valleys, intending to kill, burn, scalp, destroy and spread terror in every direction, with little but ill-equipped colonial militias to attempt to stop them. In April 1755, William Johnson, a prosperous New York landowner of wealth and standing, was appointed Major-General of a provincial army that was to attack the French fort Crown Point on Lake Champlain, north of Albany. Unexpectedly, his provincial troops encountered the French and their Indian allies on the southern shore of Lake George. To Johnson's advantage, he had with him nearly 300 Mohawk warriors of the Iroquois Confederacy supplementing his 2,200-man army of provincial soldiers and levies. Before some of Johnson's troops could walk into a carefully laid Indian and Canadian ambush, Johnson's Mohawks detected the enemy Indians, and alerted the militia before they were totally annihilated. Johnson's Indians had made the difference in the outcome of the Battle of Lake George fought in early September 1755. His Indians were able to force the French Indians and Canadian auxiliaries effectively out of the fight by using Indian tactics of warfare against them, thus forcing French regulars and French marine infantry to attack Johnson's main force on open ground.

Just as Braddock's force had been defeated trying to fight using formal European linear tactics in a wooded setting, so were the French under Baron Dieskau likewise beaten, and their wounded commander captured on the field and his defeated army forced to retreat. [GA-31] Dieskau, a prisoner of William Johnson after the battle, barely escaped death at the hands of Johnson's Mohawks, who demanded that Johnson turn the French commander over to them as their right. After a long heated discussion with the Mohawk warriors in their own tongue, the Indians left. Dieskau, curious at what had transgressed, asked Johnson what the Indians had wanted, to which he replied, "to burn you, by God, eat you, and smoke you in their pipes, in revenge for three or four of their chiefs that were killed." [PF-p.222] Dieskau recoiled in horror. Indian tactics of terror could work both ways.

Indian tactics mirrored hunting techniques

By the spring of 1756, French and Indian war parties resumed raiding across the entire English frontier with renewed vengeance. To the south, Fort Duquesne became a major base for the Indian raids, and there, Captain Dumas was doing everything in his power to see that the Indians were amply supplied. In addition, he ordered French marine cadets and junior officers to accompany the Indians and French Canadians on their raids. This was done not only to bolster numbers, but more importantly, to give the Indians the advantage of one of his own military men in the field, all the while increasing the field experience of those same men, making them more and more effective at fighting an Indian style of warfare on the frontier wilderness. [GA-p.32]

What was the Indian style of warfare and why was it so well suited to the wilderness that they lived in? The tactics of battle of the many Woodland Indian tribes was anything but haphazard, as many whites presumed them to be. The majority of white military men such as Braddock could not comprehend the nature of Indian tactics in warfare because they were so imbued with the invincibility of European rules of warfare that they espoused. Rather than take the time to study the nature of Indian warfare to see its effectiveness in the non-European setting of the North American wilderness, they dismissed it altogether, believing that European tactics could be adapted to any battlefield, including that of the forests. However, Indians had been developing and refining their methods of making war on an enemy for centuries before the coming of the white man, when they fought each other. Consequently, Indian warriors instinctively fought by a unique set of tactics that were proven by trial and error to be highly effective against an enemy, using these same tactics in hunting animals, as well as men. To the warrior, there was little difference.

The English, in particular, were slow to comprehend that the Indian manner of fighting an enemy in the woods was very similar to the way in which they hunted game, and that "Indian tactics on the field of battle exactly mirrored their hunting techniques." [GR-p.101] In fact, from the time an Indian boy was old enough to hunt, his training began. By the time he reached manhood he was skilled in the use of weapons as well as the strategy and tactics of hunting which he and his family depended upon to survive. He was able to hunt alone, but a large part of his training involved working with other hunters. "In these hunts, young men learned to act in concert with one another and maneuver as a unit." The warrior, as an individual, "was familiar with his comrades in arms and could move in perfect harmony with them." Hunters working together learned to "either drive the animal in a given direction or to force the animal into a confined area where their weapons could be used to maximum efficiency." [GR-p.101] The same tactics a warrior learned in training for the hunting of animals were utilized in war to "combat the enemy." With the defeat of Braddock's army, the new enemies of the French-allied Indians were the English settlements along their frontier, and war and scalping parties of warriors mercilessly raided the settlers.

Organizing a war party

Where did the Indian war parties come from and how were they organized? Though French Captain Dumas was taking credit for creating the war parties, the planning for them usually began in the Indian village of a tribe loyal or sympathetic to the French. The Indians may have been allies of Dumas, but they were not under his control or at his beck and call. If the chiefs and warriors of a tribe decided not to make war upon the English at a particular time, then it would not happen in spite of any commands or pleas of the French. However, this was not the case in the weeks following Braddock's defeat. To the north and west of Fort Duquesne along the banks of the many rivers and streams that fed into the Allegheny, Monongahela and Ohio Rivers, there were a number of villages of the Delaware, Shawnee, Mingo, and Wyandot who were eager to take up the war hatchet against the English.

A war party would begin when a particular war chief or a warrior of considerable experience and standing in the village would conceive the idea of leading an attack upon the English frontier. Often, the French officer at the nearest post such as Fort Duquesne would send an Indian runner or French Canadian courier des bois to the village in question with the proposition or request to take up the war hatchet against the English. The warriors would talk about the possibility at length taking into account various matters of importance to the tribe at the moment, such as the need to plant corn, hunt, or visit a neighboring village, and after the matter was weighed for some time, if general agreement on the idea persisted, then a warrior or chief who desired to lead the war party would formally ask his fellow warriors to smoke a tobacco pipe to join him in the upcoming expedition to raid the English.

On occasion, a French officer or cadet of the marine infantry himself would come visit the village to try to solicit support of the warriors for a raid by offering them not only gifts of tobacco and perhaps liquor, but promising them gunpowder and lead, and some provisions of food from the French commander of the fort as inducements to attack the English. If enough warriors were in agreement to take part in the raid, then the warrior or chief leading the party would inform the French officer or French Canadian to take word of the proposed raid to the French fort, signifying acceptance of the offer of ammunition and other essentials. In some cases, depending on the distance of the village from the nearest French post, and the trail by which the raiders intended to take to reach the English frontier, the French officer might tell the Indians that he would make haste for the fort and return with the supplies and other Frenchmen, either marines or Canadians who would lend their support to the Indians on the proposed raid. At this point the warriors, in agreement on the time they would leave and the general area that they intended to strike, would begin their individual preparations not only for the journey but also for battle.

Preparing for war with the English

Each man would tend to his weapons. He would see to it that his scalping knife and war hatchet or tomahawk were strong and sharp. Because of his frequent trade with French merchants at the posts and some previous contact with English traders before the outbreak of war, almost every warrior was armed with a flintlock musket which most commonly was a French fusil trade gun of various caliber or in a few instances, a French Charleville .69 caliber military smoothbore gun. Immediately following Braddock's defeat, hundreds of British Brown Bess .75 caliber smoothbore muskets that lay scattered about the battlefield were picked up by both victorious warriors and the French from Fort Duquesne, along with excess kegs of gunpowder, lead, flints, and musket tools, parts, and spare springs. Virtually all of these weapons eventually fell into the hands of many more Indians who were allied to the French cause but had not been present at the battle on the Monongahela. The warriors obtained the British arms by either trade with other Indians or from the French themselves, who were only too willing to see these weapons fall into the hands of those Indians who were intent on using them against the English. In preparation for battle, each warrior would look over his weapon to see that it was in working order, and pack his shot or ammunition bag that he carried strung over his shoulder and neck with enough lead ball and pieces of flint to last the duration of the campaign. In addition, he would see that his powder horn were filled and stopped with a watertight plug.

As the war party depended upon their ability to travel a great distance in a short matter of time, both on the trail and returning from the raid, it was essential that each man pack only gear that was necessary for survival and that did not interfere with the group's mobility. Each warrior packed light, carrying with them a minimum amount of clothing, food, and other necessaries that they could carry comfortably on their backs for the extended raid to the settlements that might take them days of traveling on forest trails to reach. Predictably, a warrior would keep clothing to a minimum. He would wear leather moccasins, leggings made of wool, leather or any other trade material, a breech cloth held in place at the waist by a belt, and in very cold weather a trade shirt or coat that would provide some warmth. He would carry a wool blanket tied by a strap and hung over a shoulder that he would sleep in. Also he would have with him in a pouch, bag or sack containing a quantity of food such as parched corn and dried meat for provisions, as well as extra material to repair his moccasins which customarily wore out after many days of 10 to 15 mile marches over rugged, damp muddy trails that would take them over the Allegheny mountains.

It was no wonder that the English such as Braddock could not understand the Indian style of fighting when they could not move an army of soldiers any distance in the wilderness without having a battalion of engineers and axe men to cut and level a road wide enough to serve the near mile long baggage train of wagons that carried the food, ammunition, tents and gear necessary for the soldiers to march. The Indian style of wilderness warfare was always based upon taking the war to an enemy and hitting him swiftly where he least expected it. If the object of the war party was to attack the English posts, settlements, and cabins by making its way along the forest trails to attack without warning and subsequently disappear into the wilderness before anyone could stop them, then warriors always needed to travel light to maintain mobility. This was a maxim of wilderness warfare.

The French Marines adopt the Indian style of fighting

As they began to accompany the Indians on their raids, the French realized the need to adopt the Indian methods of fighting and their rugged reliance on Spartan principles. The French Canadians and officers of the Marine infantry quickly styled themselves after the Indians with whom they traveled and fought. In reality, they did so not so much out of choice but out of necessity if they were to keep up with the warriors on the trail. Every Frenchman learned that he needed to carry in his military pack on his back only those things that he absolutely needed; anything extraneous would add extra weight and cause him misery on the trail. He learned that extra clothing was an unnecessary burden for him, as well as tents, heavy cooking utensils, and tools.

French marine cadets and junior officers from Fort Duquesne such as Lieutenant Douville, Ensign Niverville de Montizambert, Captain Francois de Villiers, and cadet Philippe de Rocheblave took on a more partisan or Indian look as time went by, discarding unnecessary heavy uniforms or justacorps woolen coats and heavy wool or canvas leggings in favor of lighter materials, which the Indians and their French Canadian brethren wore in the woods. As French-issued leather shoes were of such poor quality that they rotted and fell apart with any extended use in wet weather, Indian or French Canadian sewn moccasins were worn by the Frenchmen, and in time each man learned to sew and repair his own as the Indians did. As the raids progressed, these French white men who were living, traveling and fighting with the Indians looked more and more like their Indian warrior counterparts in appearance as they adapted to the daily existence and rigors of living in the world of the Indian wilderness empire.

In addition, the French marine officers became adept at new skills their previous service had not required. If they did not know them already, each man needed to learn the many facets of woodsmanship which he would be called upon to use for his own personal survival and that of his comrades in the unique situation he found himself with an Indian war party. He would need to learn everything there was to know about scouting an enemy. Especially he needed to learn what an Indian warrior looked for that told him beyond a doubt that other men were nearby or had passed, and who they were and how many and their direction of travel. He must learn to discern from the trail, the signs of his own scouts who were ahead from that of an enemy who was scouting him or a force that was setting an ambush.

The French officer would have to learn to live off the land literally and find enough food in the forest to sustain him until he returned to French posts or Indian villages when his meager rations ran out along the way. He would by necessity be called upon to fish, trap, and hunt while in enemy territory without firing a musket which would attract attention and give away his position. He must be able to live off a handful of corn when he had it, and cook, if at all, in a lightweight tin cup if he must. The physical rigors alone of learning the style of Indian warfare were daunting for these white men.

Like Indians, the Frenchmen had to be able to travel long distances, sleep in the open or under natural cover without tents and in all kinds of weather, while at times shunning the comfort of a campfire altogether, and when far enough away from the enemy, learn to light a smokeless fire close to dusk to cook over which would be extinguished at dark in case an unseen enemy was following. For warmth against the evening chill and damp, a solitary wool blanket would have to make do. If wounded, or needing to tend a wounded comrade, the French marine had to be able to dress the wound and treat it with herbs found in the forest. Equally so, he had to steel himself for the possibility that he must leave a severely wounded friend to certain death in the wilderness when the man was incapable of traveling, and the officer unable to carry him. His own dead must be left unburied where they fell for there would be no time to tarry when an enemy was close at hand. And in his mind, he must weigh the possibility that it might be him one day who would be abandoned and left for the wolves to tear to pieces if the enemy did not. This was the nature of wilderness warfare in its many ramifications which the French marine did not adapt to overnight and could not take a lead in commanding without first gaining considerable experience.

The French Canadian "Courier de Bois"

Where the French marines were newcomers to living and fighting an Indian style of warfare alongside warriors, the French Canadians was another matter entirely. The couriers des bois or "bush lopers" as the English called them were present in nearly every Indian village in the Ohio Country that was sympathetic to the French cause. These Frenchmen were by their very nature, far different than the French military, in that many lived continuously with the Indians, having taken Indian wives for themselves and bred children of mixed blood. If such a man were himself part Indian, his sympathies lay first with the tribe that he lived with and second to the French interests. With such allegiances firmly rooted in both worlds, the French Canadians were well acquainted with the Indian the methods of fighting, having taken part in Indian tribal warfare for generations, since the first French voyageurs and traders came in contact with the Indians more than a century earlier.

When it came to warfare, French Canadians were more Indian than white, for in battle they dressed themselves as Indians, painted their faces in the same manner, moved through the woods with the same ease, and wielded the scalping knife against their common enemies without hesitation. Canadians were capable of brutality and savagery as well, and were as deadly an adversary in the woods as any warrior. They could resort to Indian techniques of torture, dismemberment and eating an enemy, white or red, which French marine infantry and the regulars abhorred. The partisan half-breed warrior Charles Langlade was a good example of a French Canadian straddling both worlds, and possessing all the skills and techniques of Indian warfare with part of a white man's flair. Born to a French Canadian father and an Ottawa Indian mother, Langlade lived with the Ottawas of his mother's family, and took up the occupation of his father in the area where he was born near Michilimackinac in the great Lakes region, becoming a trader with the Indians.

Langlade, a Canadian partisan leader

In June 1752 Langlade, at the behest of the French commander of Fort Detroit, led a war party along with a young Ottawa war chief named Pontiac and over 200 Ottawa and Chippewa warriors into the Ohio Country to destroy the Miami Indian village known as Pickawillany, situated on the Great Miami River. There the principal Miami chief named Unemakemi, and known by the English as Old Britain, had allowed English traders to build a trading post at the exclusion of all French, thus firmly establishing an English foothold in the Ohio Country under the guidance of the English trader George Croghan. Langlade's motivation was personal. The previous year he had suffered an insult from Unemakemi, which he was compelled to avenge, as was the Indian custom.

On June 21, 1752, Langlade and his warriors attacked the Miami village. Langlade killed Unemakemi himself, and before the Miami chief died, Langlade scalped him, and then cut out the dying man's heart and ate it. It was the Indian belief that one gained the strength of the man who had been an enemy by doing so. [EA-212] Then the bodies of the dead chief, an English trader and two Miami warriors were cut into chunks of meat and boiled and eaten by the victorious war party. Such was the savage nature of Charles Langlade, a typical French Canadian partisan fighter. [PF-p.79]

While these French Canadians were as fierce and savage a fighter as any Indian warrior in the field, they disliked taking orders from French officers, and shunned any form of military discipline that was contrary to the Indian way of fighting. Their way of fighting was the Indian way, and not that of the French marine or regulars, who were versed in linear tactics of standing in a line and delivering massed firepower. Consequently in battle, the Canadians shifted with their Indian brethren, and fought the surprise, hit and run style from tree-to-tree. As fighters, each man fought his own battle largely independent of the others, with little command structure among them. As a fighting group, Canadians were prone to leaving the field of a battle if they perceived the opposition to be stronger or gaining the upper hand, as had occurred at Braddock's defeat, at the moment when Beaujeu was killed. The French Canadians reacted to the massed volley fire of Gage's vanguard, which crashed with considerable noise under the tree canopy but did little damage. Nonetheless, panic ensued among them, and they were heard to exclaim "every man for himself" whereupon, according to Dumas, close to 100 of the Canadians "shamefully turned tail" and fled the battle, leaving the Indians and the French marines to deal with the English.

At the Battle of Lake George, several hundred of the Canadians there refused to leave the protection of the woods to support the French marine and regular troops in their assault on the English defenses. Rather, they left the battle to return to the scene of the morning ambush to plunder and scalp the English dead that lay there. While busy doing so, they fell victim to an English ambush by a scouting party of backwoodsmen, who though greatly outnumbered by the Canadians, nonetheless caused them considerable casualties and forced the Canadians to flee, leaving their packs and food behind. [PF-p.221] All in all, while French Canadians were as fierce and skilled a fighter in the ways of wilderness warfare as any Indian warrior, they left much to be desired in conducting a concerted campaign of attacks against the English, which is what the French military command at Fort Duquesne and other posts desired if they were to defeat the English. It seemed that the nature of the character of the Canadians was much like that of the Indians with few exceptions. A war party led by Canadians could never be counted on with certainty to carry out their mission due to fickleness which might result in the war party changing objectives or retiring prematurely from the raid. Canadian resolve to make war was never greater than that of the Indians themselves. With ammunition and provisions for the raids provided by the French from their own scarce supplies, French commanders needed to be sure that war parties sent to attack the English frontier were effective, and to do so, effective men who could obey orders needed to be with those war parties and able to influence the Indians if not lead them. French marine officers and not Canadians seemed to be the best candidates to fill the role of a new and more effective breed of officer and partisan leaders in the field of the French and Indian war being waged upon the English.

French and Indian war parties set out

Before the war party (numbering between a handful of warriors and 100 men) set out from their village to attack an English settlement, last minute preparations were made. Each man checked his gear again to be sure that everything that he was carrying was in order for the extended raid. Often the warriors would dance around a painted post set in the ground, striking the war post with their raised tomahawks as a final pledge to meet the enemy and destroy him. Many warriors would apply a war paint consisting of charcoal and vermillion mixed with bear grease to their faces and exposed chest and limbs in designs signifying their own bravery in battle, finishing their preparations for war with the addition of feathers and dyed quill hair roaches fastened to their own scalp lock tufts. Bedecked in their finest beads and trade silver hanging from their necks, noses, and split ear lobes, the warriors were finally ready to depart, promising those left in the village that they would return with many scalps of the enemy, prisoners to roast in the communal fires, captives to be adopted into the tribe to replace those that had been lost, and as much plunder as could be safely carried. After saying their farewells to family and friends, the war party set out in single file along the trail at a brisk pace to make the daily 15 mile distance needed to get them over the mountainous paths winding through the tangled wilderness forests of the Allegheny Mountains to the east. With scouts far ahead of the main body, the warriors and Frenchmen with them could concentrate on the arduous trip ahead of them that would fill their daylight hours from the previous evening's camp to the next.

As the war party crossed over the mountains and neared the English frontier settlements, the Indians began to employ a series of tactics that would enable them to attack the enemy with surprise and speed. One of the most basic tactics used by the Indians in the deep forest of the wilderness had been employed from the time the war party was within a few dozen miles of the vicinity that they intended to attack and that was the use of vigilance and stealth in the forest. This was the learned ability of the war party to be able to find the enemy with their own scouts while at the same time never being seen by any enemy sentinels. Scouts from the war party were sent far ahead on the trails to determine where the best place to attack lay, and what numbers of the enemy were there. Scouts studied the habits of the enemy, watching to see what could be used to their advantage in the coming attack, and where the best route was for the war party to set the attack and to leave when it was over.

Then the scouts would return to the main group, and after a brief discussion, would direct the warriors to the enemy's position if it were a settler cabin, a group of farmers working in their fields, English militia on the march, or a settler fort or blockhouse. Each man would take a position near the enemy, by moving slowly and carefully through the forest, always using the cover of trees and brush to conceal their movements. Thus, the warriors would not be spotted by the enemy, and yet, would themselves know the exact number and positions of that enemy at every moment. The use of stealth ensured successful preparations for the surprise attack.

Attacking the English frontier

Simultaneous with the tactic of moving without being seen in the forest to get to the enemy, was the necessity of concealment at all times by the warriors. While moving into a position close to an unsuspecting enemy, the Indian warriors had to blend into their surroundings at all times to avoid detection by any enemy scouts or patrols. In addition, while the warriors were waiting for the precise moment to launch their attack they needed to remain hidden so that the element of surprise would not be lost if an ambush was planned. Consequently, warriors learned all the necessary elements of concealment and camouflage that would make them invisible in the vast screen of foliage, brush, and trees that were the backdrop of the wilderness forest. Usually, they prepared themselves by stripping off clothing to their breechclouts, leggings and moccasins. They painted their bodies and faces with streaks of vermillion and black which were colors of war, but also, in effect, broke up their silhouette in the forest and made each man difficult to detect by an enemy who would be scanning the woods for objects that might stand out. Unlike the English soldiers who were easily seen in the forest due to their red coats and white leather cross-straps of their uniforms, the Indians discarded light or colored trade shirts and match-coats before a battle to make concealment in the forest easier. Then they moved or remained hidden by using the natural surroundings to their maximum advantage; using shadows, tree trunks, deadfalls, and brush to enhance their camouflage while avoiding open areas in the forest and shafts of sunlight that pierced the wooded canopy above them and illuminated spots of the forest floor in which a man would become visible at a distance if he walked through the bright sunbeams.

Ambushing an unsuspecting enemy from a concealed position was always a preferred overall strategy of Indian warfare because it gave the attacking warriors a tremendous advantage in taking an enemy by total surprise. An ambush would begin with all the attacking Indian warriors firing their weapons at once at the exposed enemy, catching him off-guard. Using the element of surprise attack that an ambush afforded insured that the attackers would inflict a maximum number of casualties upon the enemy while exposing the warriors to the least amount of danger during the moment of the first volley. Also, the element of surprise afforded the Indian ambushers a definite tactical edge because of the shock value created by the surprise volley from which the enemy would invariably reel. Caught off guard by the initial Indian assault which had caused the enemy's lead men to fall dead or wounded, the enemy would be put on the defensive from which they often never recovered, as the attackers would press them immediately, and never give up the initiative created by the shock of hitting first by surprise attack. In many cases, an enemy who was ambushed on a wooded trail would be forced to fall back with what remained of their force or face becoming overrun and annihilated once the trap was sprung and new tactics came into play.

If the target of the war party was one of many settler cabins far from the larger settlements and nestled deep in the woods along one of the many creeks that flowed into the tributaries of the Susquehanna River along the English frontier, the Indians would set their ambush for the unsuspecting men of the household along the edges of the cleared field to which they knew he would go to in the morning to hoe his corn or clear brush and trees. Catching him out in the open, the warriors would fire their muskets and then rush in on the startled or wounded settler and his sons or neighbors, instantly tomahawking them with their hatchets and pausing only to rip the victim's scalp from his head before kicking in the door of the cabin and capturing or killing the women and children inside. Flanking warriors would see to it that no one escaped the attack, and swiftly the Indians would pillage the interior of the crude log home of anything of value, while butchering anyone found who was too young or too old to be taken alive on the trail. Loading the plunder on the backs of those unfortunate to be taken prisoner, the cabin would be put to the torch and the raiding party would disappear into the woods to repeat the same attack on the next settlers at their home several miles away.

Ambush: concealment combined with movement

If scouts returned with word that a group of English scouts, hunters, or militia were on the march along a nearby road or trail, an ambush could be used against them as one of many tactics to engage a larger enemy force in the field. If an ambush could be prepared somewhere along the path of the advancing enemy force, it could be used to open a battle with them. Hidden by the cover of the woods, the Indians would fire an opening volley, and then would instantly move from their ambush positions. The tactic of movement was key to every Indian attack. Warriors rarely remained in a fixed place, knowing instinctively that to stay rooted in one spot was to lose any initiative gained by surprise attack, as well as allowing an enemy the opportunity to spot the warrior and fire upon him. The movement of Indian warriors in a battle allowed them to follow up on any initial assault by flanking or enveloping an enemy while he was still recoiling from the shock of the attack. Warriors would move from tree to tree, firing at the enemy and never staying long enough to be clearly spotted or accurately fired upon, while all the time the attackers, by working together in the same manner that they used to drive a herd of deer to a killing zone when hunting, would force an enemy to withdraw or flee rather than become surrounded completely. "Firing from behind the cover of trees, the warrior instantly moved and fired again" while at the same time his fellow warriors were doing the same in what was described as "a kind of running fight." [GR-p.101]

The overall effect of Indian warriors continually moving from tree to tree while firing upon an enemy yet not giving them a distinct target to shoot at was devastating when used upon European soldiers. English militia, like regulars were trained to stand in a fixed line and deliver concentrated musket volley fire upon an enemy line a short distance away. They had no other experience than that of linear tactics, and moving by column or line in slow, precise steps. Consequently, they found themselves at a great disadvantage in fighting Indians, as linear tactics were useless against a constantly moving unseen enemy who was able to see the English soldiers clearly by their redcoats, lack of concealment, and inability to move without orders. Unwittingly, that made them ideal targets. Added to the battle were the constant terrifying sound of Indian war whoops and yells that had an unnerving psychological effect upon European soldiers who were out-maneuvered and out-gunned by superior Indian wilderness tactics. When those tactics were applied, in most cases an enemy was forced to withdraw in defeat, never having at their disposal the means to respond effectively to Indian attack. In Braddock's case, the flanking movement of the Indians caused the forward troops to give ground, and fall back, ultimately, precipitating a retreat that turned into a rout, resulting in predictably high casualties in comparison to the Indians. The French and Indian victory was not due to good fortune or random chance, but rather Indian tactics where "concealment, combined with movement, frustrated and demoralized the whites." [GR-p.101]

Indian tactics included defensive movements as well, designed to break off a battle if needed, and retire from the field when desired. A war chief or warrior in command of the war party during a battle would use vocal signals to do so. "General orders are commonly given in time of battle, either to advance or retreat, and is done by a shout or yell, which is well understood, and then they retreat or advance in concert." [GR-p.102] While the war cry or war whoop or halloo in many cases signaled warriors to open an attack, the signal to retreat was an agreed upon word that would be shouted and only the war chief in command had the authority to initiate. Vocal commands used by the Indians during battle demonstrated a high degree of discipline, contrary to what English officers assumed about the Indians as "undisciplined savages." James Smith, a white man taken captive by the Caughnawagas in Pennsylvania in 1755 and who lived among the Indians for several years told what he had witnessed about Indian battle tactics. Smith reported that Indians have "all the essentials of discipline" in battle. "They are under good command and punctual in obeying orders" [GR-p.101]

The Indian tactic of ambush could be used in a defensive role as well. Where ambushing an enemy in the forest could open a battle against enemy warriors or soldiers who were advancing to attack, sometimes as a war party was setting out on the nearest trail from a completing a raid on a settlement, fort, or settler's cabins, warriors would set an ambush for an enemy force which their rearguard or scouts reported were in pursuit of them, specifically to slow them down or repel them without engaging them in full battle, especially when the enemy following the war party had greater numbers. Often this tactic would be used against a party of white militiamen or scouts who were attempting to intercept or overtake the Indian raiding party to free white captives who were abducted on a raid. As such, the Indian ambushers would chose an opportune spot on their forest trail where they could best lay concealed and yet have an open field of fire overlooking their pursuers. A likely spot for an ambush might be found where the trail crossed a small ravine, and warriors could be hidden on the upper side and use the advantage of the rise of ground to fire upon anyone on the trail as it descended. On a given signal, the warriors would fire on their targets and then quickly melt into the woods and disappear from view before the enemy had any opportunity to get re-organized and scout the ambushing party to determine their numbers, location, and direction of attack.

French Marine officers gain experience

The Indian war parties that Captain Dumas supplied and sent far afield from Fort Duquesne in the spring of 1756 into the border lands of Pennsylvania, Maryland and Virginia had one purpose, and that was to raid and destroy the undefended English frontier settlements comprised of hundreds of settlers' families living in isolated cabins along the entire stretch of the Alleghenies. The aim was to drive the English back across the mountains, thus securing the Ohio Country solidly for the French. The Indians were well aware of the nature of their mission and needed no coaxing or coercion to stage attacks. Though they were motivated by hatred for the English settlers invading their lands, by far of more importance to the warriors was the promise that raids held for the taking of scalps, booty, and prisoners from the English settlers.

English captives, particularly young women and boys, could be spared the hatchet to be taken home and adopted into the tribe to replace dead relatives. [WP-p.49] Occasionally adult men were saved "to provide the Indian village with a sacrifice" which meant torture by burning. [DF-p.8] All other English adult settlers, including the weak, the wounded, and the elderly were killed and mutilated, and their scalps taken as victory trophies. [DF-p.8] Once on the trail home or to the next raid, if any captive, young or old lagged behind, whimpered or fell to exhaustion they were mercilessly slain so as to not impede the movement of the war party that relied on the elements of surprise, hit and run, and quick undetected escape for success. As spring turned to summer on the wilderness frontier of 1756 that success was quickly forthcoming.

At Fort Duquesne, Captain Dumas wrote to Quebec, detailing to his superiors the success of the war parties that he organized and sent against the English settlements. Dumas could boast that he had "six or seven war-parties in the field at once" and that he had "succeeded in ruining the three adjacent provinces, Pennsylvania, Maryland, and Virginia, driving off the inhabitants, and totally destroying the settlements over a tract of country 30 leagues wide, reckoning from the line of Fort Cumberland." [PF-p.235] Judging by the steady stream of prisoners being brought back by the war parties from the raids to the surrounding Delaware and Shawnee villages, Dumas could conclude that "the enemy has lost far more since the battle (Braddock's) than on the day of his defeat." However, Dumas was well aware that many more English settlers were dead than could be counted, and defenseless women and young children were among those slaughtered with disregard. Though he had advised the French officers who were accompanying the Indians on their raids to try to prevent them from doing so, it had little effect overall, prompting a French priest to write about the Indians that "they kill all they meet" sparing few women whom they prefer to "slaughter or burn." [PF-p.235]

Captain Dumas, in command of the French at Fort Duquesne in the spring of 1756, attempted to have those French Marine officers of the infantry who were accompanying every Indian war party leaving the fort for the English frontier to try to persuade the Indian warriors to spare captured women and children from the scalping knife, and prevent them, as much as possible from resorting to torturing prisoners both on the trail and at their villages upon returning. While the Frenchmen did what they could to temper Indian savagery, it did not help much, as they found that once the raiding party left the fort and traveled the deep wilderness trails that wound east, that they were not in command nor control of the warriors, but conversely were, dependent upon the Indians. Nonetheless, Dumas issued each officer orders to prevent Indian atrocities when they left the fort, which they carried with them into the field. In a few cases, where those men were casualties on one of the raids, those orders signed by Dumas were found upon their bodies, as in the case of Lieutenant Alexander Douville from Fort Duquesne who was killed on an Indian raid on a small English fort in Hampshire County, Virginia. [GA-p.32]

While exerting what influence each man personally could, by and large, the French officers who went along on the Indian war-parties were helpless to dissuade the Indians from their depredations, and while having little compassion for their English enemies, they were forced to witness atrocities against unfortunate victims of the Indians, that they could do little for without risking the anger of their Indian allies if they objected too strongly. Only when the victims of Indian torture were well beyond saving, after enduring hours of torment, might an officer dispatch the still-alive half-roasted remains of what had once been a human being with a compassionate musket blast to the head, once the Indians had satisfied themselves with their cruel torments and grew bored. [BC-p.10] In adapting to Indian wilderness warfare, the Frenchmen accompanying the Indians ran a risk of becoming accustomed to Indian brutality, and indifferent to the savagery that was being meted out to English men, women, and children alike in the frontier raids.

As French colony officers quickly gained needed field experience in Indian tactics of warfare from the raids on the English frontier, they moved more and more into leadership roles, filling the gap between the Indians and Canadians, proving that they had the ability to make future raids more devastatingly effective and on a larger scale against the English. By relying upon a more comprehensive strategy of sustaining a series of attacks by splitting war parties off from the main group so that they could operate across a wider area of land in the area that they moved through as a whole, Marine officers were able to hit the English enemy again and again before withdrawing to the northwest. This was a significant improvement in leadership tactics for the French and Indian attackers. Canadian and Indian-led war parties tended in general to hit an enemy and then quickly return to their own village if the plunder and captives were sufficient to sate their appetites, without having maximized their ability to lay waste to more cabins or minor settlements over a larger area. Colony officers were more capable in that respect. Once in command in the field, they were able to demonstrate greater military capability than their counterparts. The raid on Fort Granville in Pennsylvania in the summer of 1756 proved that beyond a doubt.

*A grief-stricken survivor of the French
and Indian reign of terror in 1756.*

French and Indian attack on Fort Granville

In early July 1756, Captain Dumas at Fort Duquesne gave orders for Captain Francois Neyon de Villiers of the French Marine infantry, brother of Captain Louis Coulon de Villiers who forced Washington to surrender at Fort Necessity, to lead a major war party against the English frontier settlements along the Susquehanna River valley to the east with the intent of destroying any remaining posts, forts, cabins, or blockhouses in the general area and either killing, capturing, or routing what populace could be found. De Villiers left with 23 marine infantry from the fort garrison and 32 Indians. Knowing that he needed a much stronger force to be effective, de Villiers headed north up the Allegheny River to seek Indian reinforcements from the Delaware village of Kittanning. [BC-p.5] There, his force was joined by over 70 warriors, including Delaware, Shawnee, and a few Seneca. With little pause, de Villiers set out at once with a large war party of over 120 men along a trail that ran from the east bank of the Allegheny River in a southeast direction across the mountains of Pennsylvania for the English frontier.

After reaching the vicinity of the Susquehanna valley undetected, de Villiers allowed his men to temporarily split into smaller groups and raid a few isolated settler cabins in outlying areas, while he personally scouted a militia stockade and the surrounding cabins of Fort Granville on the Juniata River not far from where it emptied into the Susquehanna some miles above Fort Hunter and Harris' Ferry. De Villiers's aim was to strike a deadly blow at the recently constructed crude stockade which was defended by a sizable group of militia and provincial troops. To accomplish this, he devised a plan based upon deception and executed with terror.

Calling in his war parties, de Villiers assembled his force and attacked Fort Granville on July 22. Knowing from his scouts the size of the garrison of men within the fort, de Villiers wisely hid a part of his force from sight of the fort, and sent a contingent of Indian warriors to fire from a safe distance beyond musket shot, so that the fort defenders were able to see what appeared to be the much smaller war party. De Villiers hoped to convince the defenders that this was a small war party of Indians and possibly draw the English provincials out of the fort to pursue the Indians straight into his ambush. Wisely, Captain Edward Ward in command of Fort Granville would not let any of men out of the fort, even when de Villiers appeared before the fort and challenged the English to battle. Unsuccessful at his ruse, de Villiers switched tactics, and after a day of desultory musket fire on the fort, led the Indians who were in sight of the fort away, in a feint designed to make the defenders believe that the Indians were giving up the fight and withdrawing when they could not take the fort by storm. This was in fact a well-known habit of the Indians when they were unable to breach a fort. However, unknown to Ward, de Villiers had another strategy in mind to reduce Fort Granville.

De Villiers hid the main party of his attackers near the fort, all the while keeping scouts hidden to report on the moves of the English. After a week passed uneventfully and no Indians were seen anywhere, Captain Ward took it for granted that the Indian raid was over and that they had left for their villages. With the threat of the Indian raid passed, the settlers holed up in Fort Granville petitioned Captain Ward to accompany them as protection to tend to their wheat fields on their farms in nearby Sherman Valley that were neglected and needed worked. Seeing no reason to stay, Captain Ward left with the bulk of the men of his company on the morning of July 30. At Fort Granville, Lieutenant Edward Armstrong remained in command of 23 men to guard the fort and a number of women and children. On the day that Ward's company marched, Indian scouts alerted de Villiers, who gathered up his raiders once again to attack on the next morning. The battle opened with a furious assault on the fort by the French and Indians that lasted through the afternoon and into the evening. With the coming darkness, de Villiers was able to send some men undetected along the banks of nearby Juniata Creek where they worked their way up a hidden ravine to close proximity of one of the fort walls and then set it on fire. Through the widening hole caused by the blaze, several of the defenders were killed or wounded, including Armstrong. In a lull during the fighting, de Villiers called out to those remaining in the fort to surrender. He promised them that if they did so, he would see that they were neither harmed nor mistreated by the Indians, as he only wanted to destroy the fort. However, if they chose to continue fighting, he would not be able to restrain the Indians and they would surely massacre everyone, including the women and children. It was a ruse that de Villiers hoped would work, but a promise which he knew he could not keep, as the Indians had suffered a few casualties and they were intent on taking revenge.

Lieutenant Turner, in command since the death of Armstrong, considered de Villiers offer in light of the threat of an Indian massacre if the defenders attempted further resistance. Reluctantly he accepted de Villiers terms, conceding that the welfare of the women, children, and the wounded men was more important than the fort. Turner ordered his surviving men to throw down their weapons and he opened the gates of the fort himself. Immediately, the Indian warriors rushed into the fort, taking the horrified Lieutenant Turner and the women and children prisoner, while slaughtering all but one of the remaining men who escaped in the darkness. De Villiers allowed the Indians to plunder anything of value within the fort and then ordered it burned. He turned the hapless English captives over to the Indians who "loaded them with burdens" of plunder, and sent them back over the rugged trails to the Indian village of Kittanning miles to the northwest, under the guard of about 30 warriors.

The Indians wish to return home

De Villiers, however, was not ready to leave yet. Flushed with the success of destroying Fort Granville, he intended to take the rest of his party and raid more outlying cabins and posts before heading home. Though the force of nearly 100 warriors and Frenchmen at his disposal was still large enough for de Villiers to consider ambushing any English provincial troops whom he knew would attempt to relieve Fort Granville, the Indians with him making up the majority of his troop were in no mood to continue any attacks, in light of the fact that their comrades already left for Kittanning loaded with plunder. The warriors with de Villiers wished to join them rather than risk further engagement with the English, and they argued that they had been in the field long enough.

With the will to fight gone out of the Indians, de Villiers had no choice but to break off further hostilities. He could not order the warriors to follow him or to fight, as he could the Frenchmen with him. Rather, de Villiers had to content himself with the victory that was won, knowing full well that his sizable force was yet capable of launching more attacks on the English if it were not for waning interest on the part of the Indians. After all, with the fall of Fort Granville the Indians and French were the masters of the field. The Indian tactics employed by de Villiers worked to perfection but only because of his cunning, patient, determined strategy. Indians and Canadians alone could not have taken the stockade, nor would they ever have attempted to do so. Attacking a fort, however small and crude, was not their style of hit and run fighting. It had been difficult for de Villiers to convince the Indians to do so, even when the garrison was significantly reduced by Ward's departure.

With the Indians on the verge of deserting him if he pressed the matter of further attacks, de Villiers yielded to their demands and ordered the raiders home. Careful not to outwardly show his displeasure and run the risk of angering the warriors whose cooperation and support he still needed to get the rest of his men back to Fort Duquesne, privately de Villiers was disappointed at what he concluded to be one of the shortcomings of fighting with the Indians, whom he could not manage nor control. Nor would he be the only French officer to complain of the difficulties inherent in working with the Indian allies. From the point of view of officers like de Villiers, the only way in which New France was to defeat the English was by sending out many war parties on a large scale that could strike again and again the forts and settlements along the English frontier through extended coordinated raids to make the most of limited supplies and ammunition. Getting the Indians and the Canadians to do so, against their fiercely independent nature and style of fighting would be a daunting task for any Frenchman in command.

Elevating wilderness warfare to a higher level

French and Indian war parties raiding the English settlements of Pennsylvania from Fort Duquesne and the surrounding Indian villages were not the only men active against the English frontier. To the north, from the southern shore of Lake Ontario extending eastward to the Champlain valley and south to Lake George and the English settlements of the Hudson River valley, partisan warfare initiated by the French was intensifying on a large scale. The sporadic Indian raids of 1756 by Abenaki, Caughnawaga, Huron and Nippising war parties that attacked the English settlements of the Mohawk, Hudson, and Connecticut River valleys were by early 1757 giving way to more organized and much larger raiding parties sent against the English frontier. These partisan forces were led by French colony officers of the marine infantry, and their men numbered not dozens but hundreds of fighters, including Indian warriors, French troops of the marine, French Canadians, and militia. Raiding parties of this size were acting in effect as irregular battalions in the wilderness. They would be needed for what the Governor of New France had in mind.

With the French defeat at the battle at Lac St. Sacrament in 1755 by the English provincial General William Johnson, Fort William Henry was built on the south shore of the lake which Johnson re-named in honor of King George of England. [MW-225] To the south, on the great bend of the Hudson River, Fort Lyman was expanded in size, and when strengthened, was renamed Fort Edward, and connected to Fort William Henry by a military road over a dozen miles long. Both English forts were garrisoned with provincial troops and efforts were planned by the English to use Fort William Henry, their most-northerly fort in the wilderness which separated them from Canada as a base to launch future offensive campaigns against the French forts that lay along Lake Champlain, and ultimately north into Montreal and the heart of New France itself.

To counter this English move, the Governor-General of New France, Vaudreuil, with his newly arrived military commander in chief, the Marquis de Montcalm, planned their own campaign against the English designed to attack and destroy the new English forts before the English could mount an offensive of their own. To accomplish that complicated task, greater emphasis was placed on expanding the use of French irregulars and Indians who could maneuver in the wilderness. War parties needed to do more than just raid outlying civilian settlements and militia posts. These highly-mobile fighting forces needed to be comprised of a sufficient number of men to enable missions of more military nature once they were deep in the wilderness and near to the English frontier. French officers leading those parties were able to use their detachments to scout enemy forts while harassing any English they encountered, as well as intercepting English supply wagons on their way to the forts, and bring in live English captives to provide the French with intelligence on the movements of the English. In addition, it was hoped that the war parties would strike deep behind enemy lines of communication, using the presence of the Indians to strike terror across the frontier populace, while bottling up the English garrisons and effectively severing them from the rest of New York province.

Having properly set the stage for Montcalm and his regular regiments to besiege the English forts, when the time arrived for the assault to begin, the French and Indian forces already in position would serve as flying wings to flank and destroy any English attempts to escape, or for reinforcements to get through. Vaudreuil's bold plan depended upon the success of his partisan forces to operate with impunity along the length of the New York frontier, and sweep English opposition before them. If it were possible, they would elevate wilderness warfare to a higher level than the previous isolated and largely uncoordinated Indian war parties and provide the ways and means for Montcalm and his regular regiments to defeat the English on conventional terms. But therein lay the problem. For these forces to be successful, they would by necessity be operating much of the time at great distances from their bases and behind the lines of the English, thus cut off from communication and supply with Canada. The logistics would be daunting. The makeup of the force would need more troops of the marine infantry along with Canadians to provide stability and balance to the Indian warriors who were less inclined to take orders. And most of all, the men who would lead these partisan armies in the field to conduct their petit guerre, or little wars, would have to be men possessing courage, patience, and leadership, with an ability to command effectively. Vaudreuil would find such men, like Daniel Beaujeu, forthcoming from the cadre of Canadian-born officers of the colony's marine infantry.

The French mount an offensive

In May 1756, Vaudreuil set his sights on attacking the English Fort Oswego built on the southern shore of Lake Ontario at the mouth of the Oswego River. He selected marine officer Coulon de Villiers, the victor of the battle at Fort Necessity, to head a force of nearly 1,100 colony troops, Canadians and Indians to attack and "harass Oswego and cut its communications with Albany." [PF-p.277] Previously in February, Marine officer Lieutenant de Lery led a mixed party 362 men, including 27 marines, to attack either Fort Bull or Fort Williams positioned some four miles apart at the "Great Carrying Place," or portage between the Mohawk River and Wood Creek along the supply route to Fort Oswego. De Lery's force attacked the weaker of the two English posts, Fort Bull, and as a result, nearly all the English defenders were killed and the fort and its supplies destined for Fort Oswego destroyed, while De Lery suffered only light casualties. [LM-33] In May, Coulon de Villier's force attacked a supply convoy of English boats returning upriver from Ft. Oswego to the "Carrying Place." De Villiers men ambushed the English boats, killing over 100 men, and routing the rest. Surprisingly, casualties were light once again. According to Bougainville, "we lost in this affair a colony officer, six Canadians and colony soldiers and one Indian." [HE1-p.61]

"They make war with astounding cruelty"

In August 1756, Montcalm moved his force of over 3,000 men accompanied by artillery by boat on Lake Ontario to attack and reduce Fort Oswego by conventional siege. To cover the landing of his troops and guns, Montcalm sent a force of over 400 marines and Indians to secure the landing site, scout the English, and surround the fortifications. Then with the siege underway, he ordered Rigaud with his French marines, Canadians and Indians to cross the river and cut off any retreat from the fort while making sure that English reinforcements, if any, could not break through to the fort. Consequently, the situation for the English inside Fort Oswego became hopeless.

When a flag of truce was raised and an officer's council called with the English, the French officer Bougainville proposed terms of capitulation, which were accepted. The terror caused by the Indians surrounding the fort was precipitous. "The cries, threats, and hideous howling of our Canadians and Indians made them quickly decide," observed Vaudreuil after the English defeat. [PF-p.289] With the fall of the fort, the Canadians and Indians plundered the stores, became drunken on rum, and began butchering English prisoners out of hand. Rushing to the scene, an exasperated Montcalm immediately intervened and was able only "by unstinted promises to succeed in appeasing his ferocious allies." [PF-p.289] To Montcalm, the Indians were an unfortunate, and at times a regrettable necessity in waging war in the wilderness. "They are villains messieurs," he wrote. "They make war with astounding cruelty, sparing neither men, women, nor children, and take off your scalp very neatly." [PF-p.263] Soon, Montcalm would find all the more reason to regret the Indians and their appetite for unparalleled savagery.

"It is a long job to get them to make up their minds"

After the fall of Fort Oswego, the French renewed their efforts to regain control of the waterway of Lake Champlain south of the French post of Crown Point, and then launch an attack upon the English at Fort William Henry on the southern end of Lac St. Sacrament. The aim was to destroy the English fort and its supply garrisons, and drive the English back to Albany and force an end to the war. First, a new French fort was built upon the strategic neck of land that jutted out into Lake Champlain and commanded the approaches in either direction to the important north-south waterway. Upon the promontory called Ticonderoga by the Indians, a well-constructed French fort was begun in 1756 called Carillon. Soon it became a major staging area for French and Indian raiding parties headed south against Fort William Henry, Fort Edward, and the English frontier settlements. By mid-1756, the size and pace of the French partisan attacks began to quicken.

In late May colony marine officer M. de La Colombiere set out from Fort Carillon with a mixed force of over 400 marines, Canadians and Indians to strike south of Fort William Henry and destroy supplies and boats at Fort Miller on the Hudson River, between Fort Edward and Saratoga. Soon, war parties were ranging far and wide, routinely cutting off English communications with Fort William Henry, and raiding as far south as "toward Albany and into New England, taking prisoners almost within sight of Boston." [GA-p.34] Marine officers like St. Luc de la Corne, Joseph Marin, and Langis de Montegron proved again and again that they were excellent commanders in the field who were by and large able to effectively marshal the Indians who made up a large part of their own unconventional armies in the field.

In the winter of early 1757, a French campaign against Fort William Henry was mounted at Fort Carillon. Rigaud commanded a force of over 1,200 men that included 300 regulars, 896 French marine infantry and Canadians, and more than 300 Indians. The raid was part of Montcalm and Vaudreuil's overall strategy to harass and isolate the English within the fort in preparation for a summer conventional warfare offensive. Rigaud's second-in-command was the experienced marine officer de Longueil and the brigade major was Sieur Dumas. [GA-p.37] The raiders caused considerable destruction before returning north.

By July 1757, Montcalm was ready to attack the English at Fort William Henry. He had assembled near Fort Carillon an immense force of French regular troops, colony marine infantry, and Canadian couriers des bois that numbered over 8,000 men. In addition to the French force, encamped near the fort walls were several thousand Indians from over 41 different tribes; some from as far west as the Mississippi River. After much preparation, the army of French and Indians were ready to move.

Joseph Marin with a large partisan force of Canadians and Indians raided to the south of Fort William Henry in the vicinity of Fort Edward to drive in the English scouts and return with prisoners for intelligence, as Montcalm's force headed south by boat over the waterway while the bulk of the Indians and Canadians traveled by a trail along the west side of the lake. As Montcalm and his French army with siege artillery made for land near the fort, the marine officer St. Luc de la Corne swiftly took his command of hundreds of Indians and Canadians through the woods to surround the fort by a massive flanking movement and not only seal off any escape of the English, but more importantly, guard the military road that approached Fort William Henry from the south and prevent any reinforcements from Fort Edward and Albany from breaking through, once the siege artillery were in place, and the battle begun by Montcalm.

The maneuvers of the large partisan forces were not without their problems. Feeding and supplying the Indians was a constant strain on Montcalm since their arrival at Fort Carillon, as the Indians were uncontrollable, eating all their weekly rations in a few days. Without food on one occasion, "they took the matter into their own hands, and butchered and devoured 18 head of cattle intended for the troops, which no officer dared oppose." [PF-p.331] On the trail, the Indians were equally unpredictable and temperamental, coming and going as they pleased, and ignoring French regular army officers, causing Bougainville to comment about dealing with them, "the caprice of an Indian is, of all possible caprices, the most capricious." Adding further, he commented, "It is a long job to get them to make up their minds. It requires authority, brandy, equipment, food and such. The job never ends and it is very irksome." [EA- 477]

"Kill me, but spare the English"

Observing the Indians cut up, roast and devour three live English prisoners unfortunate to be captured, he recoiled in horror at the shocking sight. However there were many more incidents of Indian savagery to follow that would cause Bougainville to record that the Indians were cruel, insolent, and horrible barbarians without souls. When an English corpse was discovered floating in the water near their camp on July 28, "they crowded around it with loud cries, drank its blood, and put its pieces in the kettle." [HE1-p.150] Nonetheless, in spite of the tremendous difficulties the Indians presented to the French,

Montcalm and his regular officers including Bougainville were aware of the necessity of employing the Indians in wilderness warfare and their reliance upon them to do what regular troops could not. "Here in the forests of America we can no more do without them than without cavalry on the plain." [PF-p.334]

On August 9, 1757, Fort William Henry fell to Montcalm's siege guns and capitulated without receiving help. The next morning, as English soldiers and civilians marched out of the fort with empty muskets a massacre ensued, beginning when a horde of Indian warriors rushed inside the fort and tomahawked all the English wounded inside that were unable to walk. In addition, over 100 women and children were butchered, and dozens of unarmed provincials and English soldiers cut down and scalped on the spot before the eyes of St. Luc de la Corne and other marine officers who some observers said were indifferent to the pleas of the terrified English. Montcalm and his officers attempted to stop the slaughter with little affect. He pleaded with the Indians, saying, "Kill me, but spare the English who are under my protection!" When Montcalm took from an Indian an English officer whom the warrior had taken captive, "several other Indians immediately tomahawked their prisoners." They feared that Montcalm would order that they should likewise give up their prisoners. [PF-p.351]

The massacre continued until the French regained control, when the blood lust of the Indians had finally run its course and order could be restored. The following morning the Indians loaded themselves with their plunder, scalps and prisoners, and left Montcalm en-masse for Montreal, but not before digging up 18 recent English graves outside the fort and even scalping the rotting corpses. As they departed, they left many half-cooked corpses on spits around the previous evening's campfires. In their grasp were over 200 English prisoners destined for ransom, adoption, torture and the spit. [DE-p.93]

Partisans: men of a particular character and force

The fall of Fort William Henry brought a temporary halt to English advances that began with Braddock's disaster two years before and that successively rolled back the English frontier in a string of shocking defeats in the wilderness won largely by partisan forces which the English were unable to adequately counter. The strategy and tactics of partisan warfare had not only come of age, but reached a zenith, proving to both French and English alike that though conventional sieges could reduce fixed fortifications, it was the successful mastery of the style and techniques of Indian wilderness fighting that paved the way for those victories, and accomplished militarily with small detachments of highly mobile skilled woods fighters what regular armies could not do in the depths of the impenetrable forests. However distasteful Montcalm and others found the use of Indians to be in making war upon the English, they learned the valuable lesson that you could not fight a war in the wilderness without Indians on your side. Whatever the difficulties and costs incurred in getting them to fight, Indian wilderness warfare worked. The wave of unparalleled bloody savagery that was unleashed upon the men, women, and children of the English settlements, was the unfortunate price paid in return for that victory. Ironically, Montcalm, possessed with the civility and bearing of an experienced French Continental officer, had to remind himself that the battlefield he fought upon was not Europe but the untamed wild lands of North America; his victorious vanguard was a horde of naked, painted savages with pendants dangling from their noses and scalping knives tucked in their belts; his officers were a handful of colonials who seemed more Indian than French and sometimes appeared in the field as officers in name only, acting autonomously.

Who were these men that elevated the tactics of partisan warfare to a level where critics in France were silenced and Montcalm himself humbled by his reliance upon them to do to the English what he and his regular army could not? Privately, the regular French officers viewed the partisan colony officers with contempt. Montcalm himself shared those feelings, writing to an officer, Levis, "remember that Mercier is a weakling and an ignoramus, St. Luc a garrulous braggart, Montigny admirable, but a looter, Villiers and Lery good, Langy excellent, Marin brave but stupid; the rest are not worth mentioning, not even Rigaud my senior lieutenant general." [GA-p.40] Though his judgment of the partisan officers was made soon after his arrival in Canada before the fall of Fort William Henry, it did not alter much in the months to come when it came to the men that commanded the Indians for which Montcalm's contempt ran deep, due to their constant depredations and uncontrollability.

That partisan warfare was successful was due to the fact that there existed a few French colony officers in Canada who were capable of leading the Indians and getting them to commit themselves to a campaign of systematic warfare, which was largely against their inherent nature to attack, raid, and run with the spoils haphazardly. The partisan leaders were all men born in French Canada, into a lifelong brotherhood that began in their youth when they entered the French troupes de la marine as infantry officer cadets. They shared equally a lifetime of experience in dealing with the Indians during their duties at the many far-flung wilderness posts of New France, and some were naturally more inclined to sympathize with the Indians in a way that no regular French officer could comprehend, due to his European upbringing based on a different set of values.

Those men of the colony marine officer's corps that led the partisan detachments in the field were unique people, who by their own nature, straddled both worlds, that of French Canada and that of the Indian. They were men of a particular character and force of personality that the Indians found charismatic. Already immersed in the lifestyle of a military brotherhood from an early age, the marine officers found the brotherhood of Indian warriors equally attractive and inspiring. They were able to naturally build a rapport with the Indians that became a bond of trust for which they gained the respect and personal loyalty of the Indians. Beaujeu had been able to rally the Indians behind him prior to the battle with Braddock's force, by the same process of building rapport with them which his intuition correctly told him was the only course of action that would work.

The covenant forged between partisan and Indian

These white French military men understood Indians, shared in their feasts, rejoiced at their victories, and suffered their hardships, yet they were more complex than the Canadian couriers-des-bois, for they were military men, and natural leaders too. Their intimate knowledge of Indian nature gave them the insight to understand their behavior. They learned how to motivate the Indians without taking advantage of them, nor interfering with the darker side of Indian nature and its taste for the blood, flesh, and torture of captives. Men like Marin and de Villiers understood that however horrible, the savagery of the Indians was a natural part of the Indian way of life. Other civilized men who were unable to adequately accept or explain the compulsive savagery of the Indians would only arouse the Indians' lasting wrath when they attempted to stop it by imposing a white man's morality. This was the reason why Luc de la Corne was reluctant to prevent the warriors from killing English prisoners, "the horror of the incident hanging over La Corne like a cloud for the rest of his life," in Canada. [BK-p.56]

Nonetheless, the Indians followed the partisan French Canadian marine officers into a white man's war because these few men were beloved by the Indians, who would follow no other French officer into the field with the same trust and regard. It is why the warriors who were with Captain Daniel Beaujeu did not break and run at the fateful moment of his death as Beaujeu was fearlessly motioning them to flank the enemy when he was killed. The Indians hesitated long enough to hide his body, fearing that the English would mutilate it if they found it, and then they attacked the English with a fury, without mercy. The victory was not Dumas's doing. He never dressed as an Indian to speak to them. Nor did he paint himself as a warrior, or dance around their fires as Beaujeu had done. Dumas did not command them because he was not a brother in the eyes of the warriors as Beaujeu had been. Rather, in battle the warriors were already in motion, moving on the flanks of the English when Dumas rallied the marines. The victory over Braddock was Beaujeu's victory, an Indian victory, and vengeance dealt to the English to pay for the death of a beloved brother and leader to them.

Through this covenant of kinship forged between Indian savages and a handful of uniquely qualified leaders like Marin, Luc de la Corne, Langy and Beaujeu, irregular partisan forces well-adapted to the demands of frontier war on a large scale could be put into the field and achieve more than what Indians or a regular army alone could do. This was an important lesson of wilderness warfare learned by the French. The "petit guerre" that these partisan detachments waged had stunned the English army, and struck terror across the entire length of the English colonies. Their success depended upon capable leaders who could meet the task. It remained to be seen if the English had such men who could learn this lesson of wilderness warfare as well.

Chapter 4

Sir William and
the Indian Department

There was an irony in the early English defeats. Due to an arrogant belief in the infallibility of English arms, the military had underestimated the importance that Indians could play in the wilderness campaigns. Men in command like General Braddock brushed aside Indian emissaries when they came offering their services, looking upon the savages as an unnecessary annoyance that need not be tolerated; thus ignoring virtually all advice from colonial woodsmen to the contrary. Braddock's ignorance, along with that of others, cost the English dearly when French-allied Indians cut to pieces British red-coated regulars by the hundreds in the forests from the Monongahela to the Hudson Rivers. Proving they were a force to be reckoned with, it was the Indians who now taught the English the brutal, bloody lesson that the strategy and tactics of European-styled warfare did not work in the wilderness, nor could a battle be successfully won without having Indian warriors fighting on your side as allies. Frenchmen like Beaujeu, Dumas, De Villers and La Corne instinctively grasped and put to use this maxim of wilderness war, but the English had as yet to understand it, as they grappled with the staggering losses and wavered on what course of action to take. Even a reluctant Montcalm who was trained in conventional European military tactics accepted out of necessity the use of Indian warriors as prudent for the French cause once he saw Indian tactics effectively work in the unconventional wilderness war he found himself fighting. The loss of Fort William Henry to French siege guns and savages was a bitter dose of reality to swallow for the English Crown, Parliament and the colonial government. Conceitedly they believed that there was nothing that could be learned from their enemies. Not only did they detest everything that was French, but anything that was Indian as well, considering both uncivilized in North America. The irony was that at the moment, the French and their Indians held the upper hand in the war. Their successes were due to the fact that they had learned the lessons of wilderness warfare well, and that was all that mattered.

In the four years that had passed since Washington traveled to Fort LeBoeuf to deliver to the French an English ultimatum to vacate the lands of the Ohio Country claimed by England, it was ironic that not a single Englishman could be found alive west of the mountains but for a handful of individuals fortunate enough to still call their scalps their own, who lived as captives of the Indian tribes scattered throughout the Ohio Country. An English army had been sent to the forks of the Ohio to enforce the British claim and subdue the French and their savages. Braddock's army never returned. Their bones lay bleaching in the sun along the banks of the river where they had fallen, and a thousand or more settlers' cabins along the length and breadth of the English frontier from Connecticut to the Carolinas lay in smoldering ruins as testament to the fact that the English did not control anything, least of all its own provincial frontiers. However, there was one success that could be spoken of, won by a colonial backwoods landowner named William Johnson who at Williamsburg in 1755 had been appointed to lead a provincial English army against the French fort at Crown Point to the north of Albany. Johnson had no formal military training nor did he have any regular English troops with him when his force unexpectedly met the French on the shores of Lake George. It was ironic that General Edward Braddock considered William Johnson's campaign in the north the least likely to succeed of those planned in 1755, due to what was viewed as Johnson's shortcomings.

Yet at the head of a provincial army made up of levied raw recruits and flanked by 300 Mohawk Indian warriors loyal to Johnson and a handful of seasoned colonial woodsmen and scouts, Johnson was able to turn back the French and their Indian allies at the battle of Lake George in September 1755. How had he done so? Johnson wisely used the Mohawk Indians with him to his best advantage. Once Johnson's scouts warned him of the French, he sent the Indians ahead to seek out the enemy. The Mohawks, who were as skilled at the art of wilderness warfare as their French-allied counterparts, were able to foil a French and Indian ambush, forcing the Caughnawagas, Abenakis and French Canadians to withdraw from the battle, leaving the French regulars to assault Johnson's troops in the open. Johnson's strategy worked. Stripped of their native allies, the French suffered a disastrous defeat just as Braddock had. The white-coated soldiers were cut down by the dozens from the withering fire of Johnson's provincials who fired from behind log barriers rather than trees.

Johnson's victory over the French was heralded throughout the streets of Albany, New York and Philadelphia just as Braddock's defeat had been lamented only a few weeks earlier. This wealthy backwoods Irishman who claimed the sole victory over the French was anything but what an English career officer and a gentleman of his time was supposed to be. Possessing a raw-boned friendly temperament, Johnson was honest, if not generous, by nature in his business dealings with the poor German immigrants to the Mohawk Valley, and was well-liked by most colonial common men. To the staid aristocracy of the province, Johnson had acquired the reputation of a man more at home with the savages on the frontier than the social circles of New York and London for which he was looked down upon. Many of the Dutch burghers in Albany and English gentlemen of New York thought of him to be more like the Frenchmen he as fighting than themselves. Yet it was for this reason alone that William Johnson was in a unique position to understand the true nature of the wilderness war that was being successfully waged against the English frontier and do something about it. Uncluttered by conventional military thinking and unorthodox in his sympathy to the Mohawk Indians of the Iroquois Six Nations, William Johnson would borrow a page from the lessons on wilderness warfare learned by the French and forge an alliance between the Iroquois and the English that would have a lasting effect on the outcome of the war. In the course of doing so, William Johnson, known by his adopted Iroquois name, Warraghiyagey, would come to write a chapter of his own.

Was it simply a twist of fate, some inner sense of his own destiny, or something in the makeup of his character that drove William Johnson onward from his humble beginnings in Ireland to the precipitous position of an unlikely man of the hour who would come to salvage the English cause in 1755 in its northern colonies currently locked in war with the French? In all likelihood, it was Johnson's overriding ability since youth to be able to seize the moment when opportunity knocked and always set a personal course for what appeared to him to be the most sensible and pragmatic, regardless of what others thought of him or expected him to do.

William Johnson's restless youth in an impoverished Ireland did not give any hint that sensibility and pragmatism would lead to great personal opportunity. He was born in County Meath, Ireland, in around 1715 to Christopher and Anna Johnson; one of seven children in a family with too many mouths to feed and too little income to support them. William's father, Christopher Johnson, was a local magistrate and poor tenant farmer who eked out a living on a meager 199 acres of land leased from the Earl of Fingal. William's mother Anna was from the Warren family of nearby Warrenstown and a sister of Admiral Warren, a noted naval military man who had attained stature and rank in the service of Britain. The Warrens could boast an estate with a stone manor house that had been passed down from their English ancestors who had conquered Ireland and were awarded a land grant by the King for their military service. Though the Warren Manor at Killeen was not large by any means, nonetheless, it afforded Anne some wealth and stature that was lacking in Christopher Johnson. When Anne married the Irish tenant of the Earl of Fingal it was not for money or standing but for love. Where other Irish tenant farmer's children might starve and be turned out to fend for themselves in the downward economic spiral of early 18th century Irish society, Anne Warren could ensure that her own children would have food, warmth, and clothing. It was Anne's family, the Warrens, and not Johnsons, who were people of some means in County Meath. It would be a Warren who would bring opportunity to William.

Only later in life would William Johnson come to understand the nature and circumstances of the Ireland he had been born into and through good fortune escaped, unlike his own father. Christopher Johnson was by his own birth an Irishman and a Catholic, and thus a man subject to the harsh, if not cruel laws enacted in England by the parliament to more closely control the Irish populace to curtail any hope of rebellion by the Irish against English rule as was occurring in Scotland. Foremost of the repressive laws, the English forbade Irish Catholics to buy or own land themselves. All the lands of Ireland were owned by English barons and earls, who ruled from England mostly as absentee landlords. They appointed in their place Irish managers who oversaw the day-to-day business of their private estates. Further, an Irish tenant could only rent for no more than 31 years at which time the lease would come up for renewal, as it did in 1728 for Christopher Johnson. [FJ1-p.8] By the 1730's, more and more poor Irish tenants were facing eviction from their plots of ground as overseers tossed them from their farms for their inability to pay rising rents. Sometimes, eviction was simply the wish of the overseer to convert the farmland to pasture for imported sheep that promised higher profits for the earls and barons in England. More and more starving Irish families were clogging the countryside roads with their tattered possessions on their backs, seeking any means of work and sustenance to survive.

Consequently, the world of William Johnson's youth was a time of terrible hardship, poverty, and unending suffering for the majority of Irishmen and their pitiful families, and where increasingly sheep held more value than human beings. All of this was a consequence and culmination of England's dominance of the Irish, and it held out no hope for an Irish commoner growing up into those desperate conditions. To William, now an eighteen-year old young man of unusual height and build who possessed an indomitable restlessness and ambition, the hopelessness of his own situation to be able to build a life for himself began to sink in with growing maturity and began to give him a pragmatic understanding that the best he could hope for his future was to follow in his father's footsteps.

William Johnson would in later years claim that his father had come from a lineage known as "honorable in its alliances" referring to his father's unequal marriage to Anne Warren. William could not help but realize that he, too, was born an Irish Catholic in a land that held out no hope for ambition in which one couldn't, in the words of one of William's brothers, "expect to rise" with "no money, interest nor friends." [FJ1-p.8] Their father had done as well as anyone of his standing could expect. Growing into a young man, William found himself more preoccupied in romances with local maidens from nearby villages and farms who were smitten by his good looks and uncommon charm. However, none were from families of better standing than his own, and perhaps he viewed pragmatically that his chances were poor of repeating the good fortune of his father and marrying into better rank and privilege. Perhaps he dismissed the idea but nonetheless set his sights on a better life for himself by other means. William's parents were able to send him away for some schooling in Dublin where he learned to read and write, but found little opportunity save that of some study with a local barrister before returning home. Schooling, William found, was not to be for him, and he struggled with a growing mood of discontent and frustration at the lack of avenues open to his ambitions. Like most young men who possess the conceit of youth, William could not shake the belief that he was meant for something better in life than which his father counseled lay before the young man. William Johnson dreamt for the day when opportunity and good fortune would come knocking for him. He would never be content becoming a tenant farmer like his father or submitting himself to military service in the English army. William was sure that somehow fate would take him beyond the dismal lot in life that he saw before him. Indeed, by a twist and turn of events that were set in motion by a land exchange in the outermost reaches of the frontier of New York Colony in North America, the 18-year-old William Johnson was soon to have his meeting with destiny.

It would come to him in the form of a letter from Captain Peter Warren, a 30-year-old naval officer in command of an English warship [EA-p.25] and the brother of William's mother, his uncle that he had never met. Peter Warren requested William to join him in North America to help manage his newly won properties in the Mohawk Valley. Without hesitation, William Johnson seized the moment and following his uncle's instructions, set sail. Opportunity finally came knocking.

Peter Warren was, in large part, a stranger to his native Ireland since leaving as a child with his own uncle, Admiral Matthew Lord Aylmer and entering the British navy. [FJ1-p.11] By 1733, the 28-year old Warren had spent all of his life since the age of 12 in military service, rising to the rank of captain of an English warship. Thoughtfully, Peter Warren realized that the time had come for him to marry, and so he did to Susannah De Lancey of New York colony. The De Lancey family was "one of New York's richest merchant families" [FJ1-p.11] and a family that had much influence in New York social and political circles. Peter's wife was sister to none other than the chief justice of the colony, the Honorable James De Lancey, appointed by the Royal Governor of the colony, William Crosby.

Among the many interests of Governor Crosby was the purchase of a sizable tract of land to the interior of the colony along the south banks of the Mohawk River to the west of its confluence with the Hudson at Albany. The land Crosby obtained in 1733 was Indian land belonging to the Mohawk tribe of the Iroquois Confederacy, and it amounted to nearly 14,000 acres of prime river bottom lying east of the Mohawk village of Teantontalogo where Schoharie Creek emptied into the Mohawk River from the south. It was there on the east bank of Schoharie Creek at its mouth on the Mohawk River that the Crown had erected in previous years a rudimentary stockade called Fort Hunter which served as a remote military outpost, giving testament to the Crown's possession. Interested in land speculation and knowing that Indian lands were by far the easiest gain with the least amount of effort, Crosby called upon the captain in command of Fort Hunter, Captain Walter Butler, to help him execute his plan to obtain the Mohawk lands for which Butler, in return, would come to possess some of the land for his part.

The governor instructed Captain Butler to return to Fort Hunter and call together all of the Mohawk sachems from the upper and lower villages to come to the Fort where he was to distribute generous gifts of goods and rum to the Indians. Once the chiefs were drunk, Butler was to have each of them make their mark upon Crosby's legal document ceding the surrounding land to himself. It mattered not to Crosby that the Indians had no idea of what they were signing, nor did it disturb him that much of the land in question had already been purchased by the same surreptitious means by a group of New York merchants called the Corporation of Albany. As Governor of the province, Crosby merely took possession of the previous deed and burned it, thus destroying any evidence and claim. [FJ1-p.11] Dutifully Captain Butler returned to Fort Hunter and carried out Crosby's plan. Within a month the Governor would come to secure 86,000 acres of Mohawk lands on both sides of the river from which he would retain some 14,000 for himself while dividing the rest of the spoils among his friends and paying Captain Butler handsomely for his handiwork a large sum of land on the north side of the river. Ironically, Crosby did not live to enjoy the fruits of his labor of deception, for in the same year that Peter Warren wed Susannah De Lancey, Crosby died coughing from tuberculosis, and his lands passed to Peter Warren who purchased the 14,000 acres in the Mohawk Valley for a paltry sum of 110 Pounds in an agreement arranged by Susannah's brother, James De Lancey, Crosby's Chief Justice.

Peter Warren ambitiously planned to develop his newly acquired wilderness lands. To do so, he reasoned that he would need tenants to work the wooded wilderness lands, and an overseer to manage his estates. A likely candidate came to Peter Warren's mind, and soon he sent a letter to his nephew in Ireland, William Johnson, advising him of the great opportunity that lay before the young man to recruit tenants for him in Ireland and to seek passage as soon as possible to America. It was not long before William Johnson arrived in Boston to join his uncle and by the spring of 1738, was making his way north up the Hudson River to Albany and then west along the Mohawk River trail that disappeared into the virgin wilderness of Warren's Mohawk lands with a load of trade goods in tow and instructions from his uncle to set up a trading post near Fort Hunter. [FJ1-p.14] At his destination William Johnson first came in contact with the Mohawk Indian tribe and established a firm and friendly relationship with them that would last a lifetime.

Heeding the orders of his employer uncle, William Johnson set to work establishing a trading post for Peter Warren's handful of Irish tenants who were beginning to clear lots of leased land for planting at Warrensburg, as well as providing goods for the poor German migrants upriver at the villages of Stone Arabia and German Flats on the Mohawk River. Most importantly, as William became acquainted with the Mohawks coming and going at Fort Hunter, he took a natural liking to these strange native savages, and encouraged them to trade their furs for his essential goods. With the trading post flourishing and progress being made by the tenants at Warrensburg, William Johnson turned his attention to a piece of land on the north side of the Mohawk River that attracted his eye and sharpened his own ambitions to put his own business acumen to work for himself. In 1739, William rode to Albany where he purchased the tract of land in question under his own name from the profits he had earned at his uncle's post at Warrensburg. Proudly writing Peter Warren of his purchase, William was shocked to receive an angry response from his uncle, who viewed William's move as insubordinate.

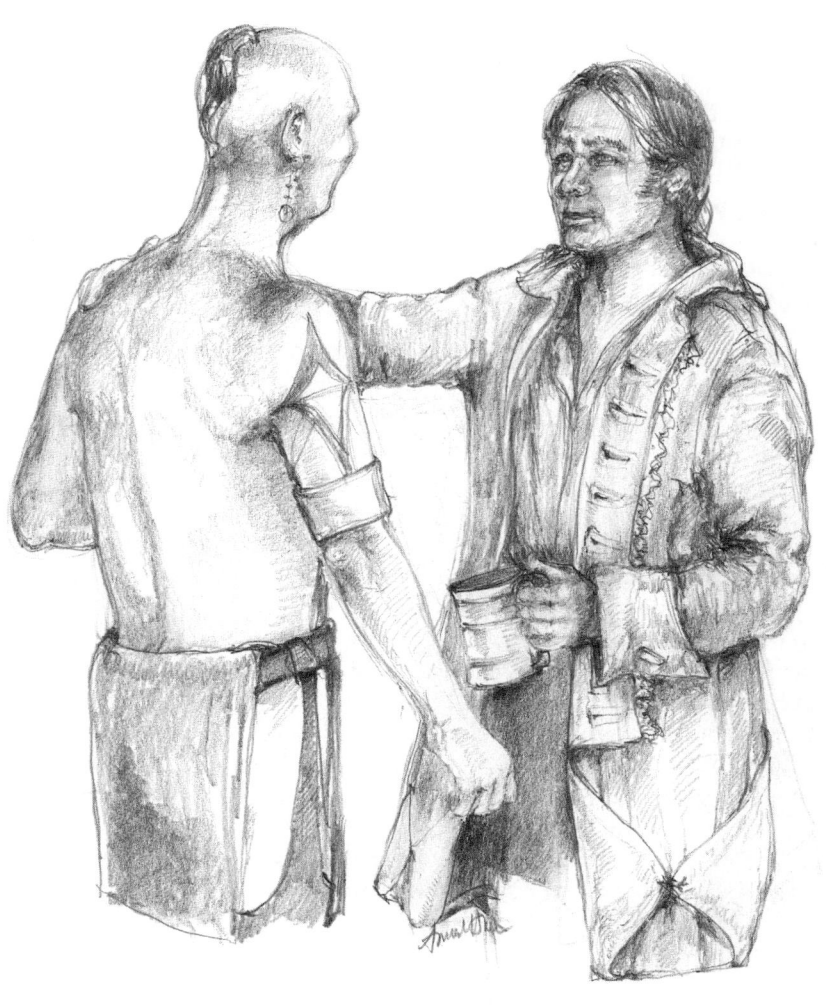

William Johnson gains the friendship and trust of the Mohawks.

William broke from his uncle and moved across the Mohawk in 1740 to his own land where he began building a stone house he would call Mount Johnson in response to his uncle's own Warrensburg. In addition, he set up a store of his own on the north side and resumed trade with his customers from Warrensburg, forcing his uncle's trading post to close. William Johnson in a short time had come a long way in declaring his own independence and establishing himself as a man of considerable means on the frontier wilderness. However it would be Johnson's achievement in dealing with the Mohawk Indians and the tribes of the Iroquois Confederacy which would prove to be most significant in the years of war and crisis yet to come. It would happen all by his natural rapport and affinity toward the Indians whom other white men of his time viewed with nothing less than distain. Did he see in the plight of the Indians losing their land to the intrusion of the whites into the colonies, and the Mohawk Valley in particular, as something akin to the poor Irish? If he observed the similarities, Johnson's writings did not record such thoughts, though the dissolution of the native clans of Ireland and those of the mighty Mohawk tribe had much in common.

William Johnson spent much of his time in the early 1740's working to build a thriving business of trade at his new home at Johnson Hall on the north side of the Mohawk, and though he dealt in all kinds of goods for white man and Indian alike, nonetheless a great deal of his business centered increasingly upon trade with the Mohawks and their Iroquois brothers to the west. Trading furs from the Indians for goods was making Johnson a wealthy man, and at the same time, he was developing a reputation for himself among the Indians as a white man of fairness and honesty whom the Indians could trust in their dealings, as he gave them fair value for their furs and did not get them drunk and then steal from them as other white traders commonly did. To this end, Johnson had more than just an altruistic motive. While he genuinely liked the Indians and formed friendship with them, at the same time, he looked upon the largely dishonest Dutch traders from Albany with growing dislike for they reminded him too much of the absentee landlords and overseers in Ireland who, while being "unconcerned with the welfare of the peasants, sought from them only one thing: profits." [FJ1-p.36]

William Johnson did what no other white trader in the Mohawk Valley was willing to do. Johnson visited the Mohawks in their villages at Teantontlogo and Canajoharie. He sat with the people and learned from interpreters who the prominent Mohawk men and women were. Gradually he learned the difficult Mohawk language so as to be able to converse directly with these people. As Johnson made friends with them, he asked that they teach him all that they knew about the Mohawk tribe, their history and culture, as well as the skills of hunting and woodsmanship in the deep forests all around him. William Johnson made it his business to learn all that he could about the Mohawk Indians. Some could say that he did so because of his mercantile shrewdness, but the Mohawks knew that William Johnson did so because he truly liked them, and unlike most white men, considered the Mohawks friends and brothers. And though Johnson remained firmly ensconced in the white world of Mount Johnson and New York colony, nonetheless he had some heartfelt sympathy for the Mohawks that went well beyond business. Perhaps in the Indians William Johnson saw a part of himself, a man of common simple roots unencumbered by complex thinking and social conventions, much as he found the Mohawks in their own world to be. It was a relationship that he would not compromise in the years to come.

What cemented Johnson's tie to the Mohawks? In the long run it was more complex than Johnson simply just sitting by their fires, smoking their pipes, and listening to their complaints. William Johnson was quick to implement ideas that they both mutually shared in common that would endear him to the Mohawks and demonstrate to them that he understood them and respected them as no white man had previously done, and which naturally stood as cultural barriers between the English and the Indians. No where did these lasting gestures of mutual understanding be put into practice more adeptly than in Johnson's handling of the question of the selling of spirited liquors to the Indians, an idea long opposed by the local clergymen of the Church of England who advocated a wholesale ban on any traders distributing rum to Indians either as gifts or in exchange for goods. Much of their reluctance was based on more than ecclesiastical teaching. Ministers such as Reverend Barclay at the Mohawk chapel at Fort Hunter knew all too well the sufferings that drunkenness had brought to the Mohawks as a result of unscrupulous English and Dutch traders from Albany. It was well known that the Mohawks had been swindled out of vast tracts of their land by signing documents while in a drunken state. Further, once rum was liberally plied upon them, the Indians lost all sensibleness, often trading all the goods they had for paltry sums to obtain more liquor leaving them totally destitute the following day, or finding to their chagrin that bales of their hard-earned furs had been traded away for paltry sums if not outright stolen, sending them back to their lodges "with hangovers, and as poor as rats." [FJ1-p.73] If that were not bad enough, many drunken festivities resulted in unfortunate violence where warriors fought each other and were maimed, disabled, or killed by their fellows. Yet in spite of all this, it seemed to the clergymen such as Barclay that the rum peddling could not be stopped by a pariah of traders intent on making their fortunes at the expense of the Mohawks, who though wary of the influence that liquors had upon them as a whole, nonetheless could not compel themselves to stop indulging in the spirits which they seemed to crave. William Johnson determined, by and large, to solve the problem for the Mohawks in more ways than one, benefitting both himself and them, taking into account that the Indians, much like himself, should be allowed to get as drunk as they wished. To Johnson, it was simply a matter of who would provide the liquor and how fairly would the Indians be treated once drunk.

Reverend Barclay openly advocated to colonial authorities a prohibition of liquor at Fort Hunter and the lower Mohawk castle or village called Teantontalogo, in an attempt to free his Indian parishioners from the evils of rum. While acknowledging the problem, Johnson openly opposed Barclay. To protect the Mohawks, he invited them to drink and trade with him at his home and post on the north side of the river at Mount Johnson or in either of their two villages. Upon accepting Johnson's offer, the Indians were astounded to find when they awoke from the previous night's drunken stupor that Johnson and his agents had protected their pelts and goods through the night. They still had furs to buy the necessary clothing and ammunition they needed to support their families. While they had been able to enjoy Johnson's rum they were neither financially ruined by the night's revelry, nor injured in a melee which Johnson discouraged (contrary to the tactics of other traders who used drunken Indian fights as an opportunity to make off into the night loaded down with Indian furs that they had obtained by every means available.) William Johnson simply drank with them, stripping off his clothes in favor of an Indian breechcloth and dancing and singing with the warriors around a blazing fire into the early hours of the morning before collapsing with them. Unaccustomed to such hospitality, William Johnson quickly made for himself a reputation of friendship with the Mohawks and their Iroquoian brethren to west. Almost as quickly, the Indians ceased to trade with anyone else on either side of the river, and virtually all of their valuable peltry stopped at Mount Johnson for exchange, rather than Albany.

In addition, Johnson endeared himself to the Indians in other ways. As he nurtured trade with the Mohawks, learned their language, and visited them frequently in their own villages, Johnson came in contact with one of their great sachems or chiefs, named Tiyanoga, commonly called King Hendrick by the Dutch. In Johnson, Tiyanoga saw a man who was capable of furthering the Mohawk tribe's interest and could bridge the gap between the white man's English world and that of the Mohawk which Tiyanoga could not. In 1710, Tiyanoga, as a young man, was one of four principal chiefs of the tribe to travel to England at the behest of Queen Anne. Unlike other Mohawk leaders, Tiyanoga was aware of the might of the white man. He knew that the white man was indelibly changing the Mohawks. As more and more white men streamed into their lands, it meant that their ancestral way of life was fading. In his own generation he had seen the once proud and mighty Mohawk nation become dependent upon the white man's goods and weapons, and their once limitless domain eaten up by more and more land grants and purchases to white men. In Johnson, Tiyanoga could see much more than a true friend to his people. William Johnson had the capacity to become what Tiyanoga knew the Mohawks desperately needed, and that was a white man to champion and protect their rights in a world that was becoming increasingly for the Mohawks a white man's world. Not prone to naivete, Tiyanoga no doubt knew that the price to be paid to Johnson would be Mohawk loyalty and he was determined to bring this about. However for Johnson to become the ambassador for the Mohawks, he would need to truly become one of them, one whose word they would implicitly trust because his blood, mind, heart and soul were undeniably Mohawk though his outer skin was white. What he proposed or initiated was unprecedented: William Johnson must be adopted into the Mohawk tribe.

The ceremony for William Johnson's adoption into the Mohawk tribe was held in October of 1742 at the Great Council House or lodge at the upper

Mohawk castle or village called Canajoharie, where Tiyanoga himself lived, some 30 miles west of Teantanologa. After a preliminary preparation where Johnson was stripped of his white clothing, dressed in an Indian breechcloth and designs painted on his face and bare body, Tiyanoga summoned all the members of the tribe as Johnson was taken down into the shallows of the Mohawk River by three young squaws where they ceremoniously washed him with sand and gravel to symbolically wash away his white skin. Then he was led back to the Council House where he was dressed in Indian finery and painted as a warrior. After speeches from Tiyanoga and various sachem followed by silence and the passing of smoking pipes, Tiyanoga again rose from his seat to address Johnson directly, announcing, "My son, you are now flesh of our flesh and bone of our bone." To cement the bond of adoption into the tribe that would bind William Johnson to his new role as emissary for the Mohawks, Tiyanoga likely added, "after what has passed this day, you are now one of us by an old strong law and custom. My son, we are now under the same obligations to love, support and defend you that we are to love and defend one another," implying that Johnson was obliged to likewise fulfill this oath as a Mohawk and defend all of them. [EA-p.59] It was not a ceremony and oath to be taken lightly by any Indian, or any white, most of all by William Johnson. To give meaning in the fullest sense to the adoption that was more than just ceremony, William Johnson was re-named in the Mohawk language. From this time forward he would be known to all Indians of the Iroquois League as not William Johnson, but as "Warraghiyagey" or "The-Man-Who-Undertakes-Great-Things." [EA-p.59]

If the great sachem Tiyanoga thought that adoption into the Mohawk tribe would be the ultimate tie that would bind William Johnson to them, Johnson had thoughts of his own. When he first moved across the Mohawk River years past and built his stone house, William Johnson soon after had found a mate in a young woman of German descent named Catherine Weisenberg, whom he took as a mistress and lover to live with him. Though it was rumored in Albany that Johnson's companion had been bought by him as an indentured servant whom he was smitten with, William Johnson shunned conventional wisdom and did not marry her, though by October 1744, she had borne him two daughters and a son. Acknowledging a weakness for beautiful women, Johnson amiably sent Catherine Weisenberg with the children to New York where they were to be well taken care of by him, though she was "not to return until summoned." [EA-p.93] With the outbreak of war between France and England on the continent finally reaching the Mohawk Valley, Johnson persuaded Tiyanoga to sell to him a beautiful French Canadian prisoner, Angelique Vitry, who had been taken by the Mohawks during a raid into French territory to the north. Not satisfied with his new-found love, Johnson, in his travels that took him to the Mohawk villages to speak to the council of sachems and solicit Mohawk support (rather than neutrality for the English cause) frequently found himself attracted to the young pretty Mohawk squaws from which several half-Mohawk children were sired, including William Johnson or Tagcheunto, also known as "William of Canajoharie" because his mother was from the upper Mohawk village, and Brant

Johnson, called Keghneghtaga, because that mother was a relation to the Brant family of the same village. [FJ1-p.99]

Tactfully consorting with Indian maidens did not at all dampen Johnson's elevated status among the Mohawks. Rather, they viewed Johnson's amorous relationships as Warraghiyagey's taking of a "formal Indian wife" when the first of many children were born to him, as this was considered both normal and appropriate in the Mohawk tribe as a right bestowed upon any warrior of clan, adopted or otherwise. That his children were considered not only illegitimate but also half-breed by other Englishmen of the New York frontier did not bother Johnson in the least. What was important to him was that he had become a man of power and standing in both worlds, Indian and white, where he felt as much at home in the social circles of the gentry of Albany and New York as in the wigwam lodges of the Mohawks. Taking a Mohawk woman as his wife and siring children by her was only another indication to the tribe that William Johnson was living up to his vows of his Mohawk blood and taking them seriously. As the short-lived frontier war between the English and French heated up on the fringes of the Mohawk Valley, the words of the powerful white man, William Johnson, who argued for the Mohawks to support the English Crown and to take up the hatchet against the French and their Indian allies to the north was given all the more weight by the fact that Warraghiyagey's children played among their own, providing the Mohawks with the most visible tie of Johnson to their own people. However, no tie would bond as great as that which would become established between William Johnson and the young Mohawk Joseph Brant who would one day become a great war leader of his people.

Often staying at the Brant family cabin at the Upper Castle of Canajoharie on his many visits to the Mohawks, William Johnson no doubt had come to know the Brant family intimately and watched the sachem's daughter mature into a young woman. Johnson was smitten with her beauty, grace, and poise, and by 1759, during the second series of war years between the French and English, Margaret "Molly" Brant, now in her early twenties, would become the prominent love of Johnson's life. She came to live with him in his home at Mount Johnson and later Johnson Hall, and over the years bore him many children. William Johnson had the innate knack "to feel simultaneous loyalty to both Indian and white institutions, and to move (among the two worlds) with no sense of strain" that would have restricted any other man of similar upbringing. [FJ1-p.38] Molly Brant never gave up nor turned her back on her Mohawk heritage in favor of Johnson's. She, too, like William, was capable of straddling both worlds and serving both well. "Molly Brant brought more than children to the union with Johnson. Sir William once explained that her brother, Joseph, would be useful because of his "connection and residence" at Canajoharie. He must have viewed Molly in a similar light. Sir William did not make a list of suitable heiresses to marry in order to expand his wealth and social standing, as he did for his son, John, years later. But Molly Brant was someone he needed in his world. Personal and professional success depended upon his ability to maintain good relations with the Iroquois, a fact which must have brought considerable tension to his daily life. She helped Johnson maintain these important connections." [HL-p.23]

By those very connections forged by William Johnson and the Mohawks, a new chapter was being written on the frontier of New York colony that was to have great significance. While there were many white men on the frontier who had traded their breeches for breech-cloths and had gone to live and trade among the Indians because they preferred the native way of life to that of the white man's world, William Johnson was unique in his sympathy for the Indians. He was a wealthy gentleman who could live between both worlds red and white without sacrificing one at the expense of the other. Rather, Johnson was able to live in both worlds simultaneously at any given moment and profit from the trust he had gained by both red and white men, while all the while affording himself a degree of protection from those who could be counted as enemies. As he cheated neither Indians nor white men of the valley in his business dealings, Johnson's detractors were found in the gentry of the colony, both English and Dutch, who saw in Johnson a growing threat to their political power and wealth. One thing is sure. While William Johnson did not speak for the Iroquois League nor have a voice in their tribal affairs, he nonetheless had built for himself the friendship, loyalty and trust of the Mohawks and many other Iroquois. Whether William Johnson knew it or not, he had deeply endeared himself to them by simply learning their language, clothing himself in the native way, dancing by their fires and taking part in their revelries, and siring children by their women. To the Indians, Warraghiyagey was a true brother unlike any other white man. William Johnson cared little what the Dutch burghers of Albany or the aristocrats of New York were thinking or saying about his unorthodox relations with the Indians whom they considered nothing more than savages.

Johnson had made a fortune for himself in trade to the Indians and settlers of the Mohawk Valley, and increased his own land holdings astronomically, while forging a personal alliance with the Iroquois League that would soon prove fortuitous for the English colony when war broke out on the wilderness frontier with the French and their own Indian allies in 1745. As war parties of French and their Indians from Canada to the north began to filter south to raid the vulnerable English frontier in what was called King George's War in North America, the English government sounded a call to arms to meet the danger the best way possible.

The governor of New York turned to William Johnson for help. Governor Clinton knew that the French military were extensively using French-led Indian war parties which could quickly maneuver the forest trails from Canada to raid the English frontier with success. However, the English had only poorly equipped militia and some regular soldiers to counter the French and their Indians, and these forces were incapable of fighting the new wilderness style of warfare erupting around the edges of the colony. Clinton called upon Johnson at a conference held at Albany in August 1746 and attended by the Iroquois, to become a "Colonel of the forces to be raised out of the Six Nations" when it became evident to him that his own clumsy oratory and deportment with the

Indians had not personally convinced them that they should side with the English if they should fight the French. The governor knew Johnson's reputation among the Iroquois and saw in Johnson the hope that he could do what Clinton himself could not.

Subsequently, William Johnson was empowered to raise a staff of officers of his own choosing who would assist him in sending out "as many parties of the said Indians as you possibly can against the French and their Indians."[FJ1-p.63] This was the beginning of what would become known officially as the British Indian Department, which would be the liaison led by William Johnson between the Indian allies of the English and the colonial government of New York. Johnson's aim, through the development of the Indian Department was to bring the Iroquois into a firm alliance with the English, supply them adequately with everything they would need to go to war, and send them out into the forests to the north to counter the French threat directly. It was a plan that was drawn up and executed not in London, New York city, or in Albany, but in the drawing room of Johnson's own home far to the west on the Mohawk River. With his usual resourcefulness and ingenuity, it was a plan that would prove to work, with the loyal Mohawks led by Tiyanoga at Johnson's side. As more and more Mohawk war parties returned from their raids to the north with French scalps and captives, the tide of the war turned to favor the English. When the short order-war came to close in October 1748 by the Peace of Aix-la-Chapelle signed between England and France, William Johnson, known as New York colony's "Colonel of the Indians" and his fledgling Indian department would have little time to catch their breath until another war with the French of greater intensity and scope would begin, known as the Seven Years' War in North America.

When word reached New York colony that war had again ignited between the French and English with George Washington's attack upon Jumonville, and his subsequent defeat by the French at Fort Necessity, William Johnson was called upon by the Governor of New York and its legislature to once again take up his position of Superintendent of the Department of Indian Affairs of the colony and Colonel of the Indians of the Six Nations, by which he would be expected to bring the Iroquois into an alliance with the English colonies against the French. For Johnson, this was a more difficult task than it seemed, as the Iroquois were in dissension over the matter. Most of the Mohawks to the east of the League favored supporting the English while many of the Oneidas, Onondagas, and Cayugas in the middle of Iroquois land advocated neutrality in any fight between the white men. In the western lands that were close to the French at Niagara, the fierce Seneca and Tuscaroras tribes favored the French. The League as a whole was split and William Johnson worried that even he would not be able to influence them as a whole, especially with the recent incursion of the French into the Ohio Country and the building of the French fort at the forks of the Ohio River in 1754.

More than anything else, William Johnson understood the Indians well enough to know what no other white man understood the implications of Washington's defeat upon the Indians as a whole. He wrote, "The unlucky defeat," would "animate" the pro-French Indians and "stagger the resolution" of the pro-English. Johnson's own Mohawk emissaries to Washington had been driven away by the brash Virginian. They complained that Washington had treated them "as his slaves." Johnson cringed at the thought of what all Indians would think now that the "prestige of British arms" had been severely damaged by the Virginian who mistakenly underestimated the importance of Indians in wilderness warfare. To Johnson it was clear that the defeat would change the minds of thousands of warriors who were once considering allegiance to the English. William Johnson's new deputy agent in the Indian Department, Daniel Claus who had recently arrived from Pennsylvania and was well acquainted with the tribes of the Ohio Country, those most affected by the rapid change of events, wrote that "there was never the like seen, how quick the nations turned after Colonel Washington's defeat."[FJ1-p.122-23]

Nonetheless, William Johnson persevered. He gathered about him a core of trusted men who could serve as officers or agents in the field, who not only were able to speak the languages of the Iroquois nations fluently but also were Englishmen in Johnson's service who understood the Indians as he did, or in the least, could reliably carry his instructions to the Indians without being compromised by either white or Indian minds contrary to Johnson. Daniel Claus, a recent German emigrant to Pennsylvania colony who was sent by the legislature to study under William Johnson, renounced his allegiance to the Pennsylvania Quakers and joined Johnson's growing Indian Department to serve with him throughout the war with the French. On the frontier of New York colony, William Johnson sought out the allegiance of the aged Captain Walter Butler and his sons, Walter Jr., John, and Thomas. Captain Butler lived a Butlersbury, on the north side of the Mohawk River in a house he built in 1742 on a tract of land obtained earlier from Governor Crosby. His home was a few miles west of William Johnson's home and sat on the heights overlooking the valley. [SH-p.9]

Much of the elder Butler's military service after command of Ft. Hunter took him to the faraway English post at Fort Oswego on the eastern end of Lake Ontario. He took with him his sons, whom he educated as Indian interpreters as he himself, who had "acquired considerable influence among the Indians" [CE-p.11] that gave him the opportunity to school his two sons in the ways of the Indians as well under his own tutelage, rather than send them away to New York or Philadelphia for a formal education. With the outbreak of war with the French, William Johnson, as Colonel in the British Indian Department nominated old Walter's sons, John, Thomas and Walter Jr. as officers in his burgeoning Indian Department in preparation for the coming expedition to seize Crown Point. In May 1755, prior to Johnson's campaign in the north, he sent John Butler, whom he appointed "a Lieutenant over the Indians" [CE-p.13] to meet General Braddock at Williamsburg, Virginia to convince Braddock of the importance of using Indian warriors sympathetic to the British cause to scout and fight alongside his force, accompanied by Englishmen skilled in the ways of Indians and forest warfare. Meanwhile, Thomas Butler remained at Oswego on duty with the Indians, while Walter Jr. led parties of Mohawks on scouts to the north, looking for French troops and their own Indian war parties that were probing the English frontier.

With his growing cadre of trusted men, William Johnson surmised correctly that he would be able to meet the growing French threat from the north on their own terms and counteract the French allied Indian threat that Braddock had not been willing or able to do. The word of Braddock's defeat and death at the hands of the French and their horde of Indian allies reached Johnson in July 1755 when he learned the details of the forest massacre. Implicitly he understood that his officers might be able to accomplish what English officers and regular soldiers could not do—fight an Indian style of wilderness warfare that he knew his French opponents had already mastered with one exception. Where French Marine officers found that mixed war parties of Frenchmen and Indians were far more effective in the field than Indian war parties alone, they nonetheless suffered from a lack of unified command. This was due to the fact that each Indian tribe inadvertently favored their own French officer. Johnson's men in the field were handpicked by him, and in essence, an extension of himself. They answered only to him and no one else. So with warriors and a smaller number of officers than the French, Johnson was confident that he would have at least an advantage in command over them in a fight. He knew that the Mohawks respected and trusted Johnson's officers because each man carried the word and direction of Warraghiyagey. The Iroquois would fight with his men, and follow them, as if he were with them himself.

On his way north to Crown Point in September, William Johnson and his combined English and Indian force encountered the French at the south end of Lake George and a heated battle ensued which resulted in a victory for Johnson's men. However the losses were high for the Indian Department and the Mohawks. Several officers were killed, including Walter Butler Jr. and Farrell Wade, a brother-in-law of William Johnson, who were with the Mohawk Chief Hendrick and his warriors at the front of the English militia column on the road to Fort Edward when it was ambushed by Caughnawaga and Abenaki French-allied Indians. Chief Hendrick himself was killed along with many Mohawk warriors in that initial encounter while John Butler, in spite of his brother's death and that of many of his Indian friends, was said to have "distinguished himself greatly" [CE-p.11] by rallying the remaining Iroquois and withdrawing them from the battlefield to join Johnson on the lake. They bought Johnson the time he needed to regroup his militiamen and face oncoming French regulars who were stripped of their own Indians and Canadian irregulars when they quit the fight to go back and scalp the English dead. Thus the French were defeated and Johnson was victorious.

Furthermore, though his Indian Department had been bloodied, it had proved itself capable in meeting the French threat with Indians led by Englishmen against Frenchmen and Indians whereas Braddock, with regulars alone, had not. William Johnson's policy of drinking and conferring with the Indians to gain their confidence and support, like that of his French counterparts La Corne,

Marin, and Langy had worked for him, but his approach fell on the deaf ears of the English generals, like Braddock, whom William Johnson could not persuade.

William Johnson's victory at the Battle of Lake George brought him knighthood, an extensive land grant, greater recognition of his unorthodox Indian-style military tactics and a larger budget from the English government for Johnson's influential Indian Department which was growing in size and stature. In 1756 Sir William appointed George Croghan of Pennsylvania to serve as the first deputy superintendent in the department, "second only to Johnson as the most powerful white Indian on the continent."[FJ1-p.126] Croghan brought with him years of experience trading with the Delaware, Shawnee and Mingo tribes of the Ohio Country where he was well-liked by the Indians and held great influence with them. By 1759, with the fortunes of war tilting away from the French and decidedly in favor of the English, Sir William Johnson's years of courting the wavering allegiances of the Iroquois tribes and western Indians away from the French to neutrality if support of the English could not be guaranteed, nonetheless began to pay off. It would be the English assault on the French fortress of Niagara which would put into play not only Johnson's successful political strategy that was promoted by the Indian Department, but would turn the tables on the French with tactics once thought to be exclusively French and Indian.

The English planned a traditional set-piece siege of French Fort Niagara to reduce the fortification. Johnson, the Indian Department and those Iroquois loyal to him were to play a secondary, if not minor role in the attack as conceived by English Major General Jeffery Amherst. He appointed Colonel John Prideaux overall commander of the Niagara expedition and ordered Johnson "to go along with his Indians" [MB- 201] as scouts and skirmishers. Johnson accompanied a force of some 600 Indians with Indian Department officers as a vanguard to the British invasion force.

Arriving ahead of the British regulars, Johnson deployed his Mohawks to cut off the fort from any help that might arrive from the trail leading south to the upper French posts, while conferring with many of the Indians already in the area, such as the Seneca of the Iroquois who were known to be sympathetic to the French cause. Johnson urged them to remain neutral in the coming battle if they would not support him and the English. As the British arrived and opened up on the fort with their siege artillery, William Johnson continued his strategy of covert Indian diplomacy, sending his own emissaries to the western tribes. Gradually, more and more of the French Indians were convinced to remain neutral. Meanwhile, the English army at Niagara settled in for a protracted siege. Days of constant bombardment wore on as the English guns were inched closer and closer to the French walls.

Unexpectedly, on the night of July 20 of the siege, General Prideaux was instantly killed when he stepped in front of a British artillery piece that was about to fire, the "gunner not seeing him in the night." [DB-p.71] Without an appointed successor, Sir William Johnson took command of the army and the British siege of the fort. While there was some doubt among the regular officers about Johnson taking command of the army that arose from Amherst's orders that he was to "lead the Indians and assist Prideaux with advice and intelligence," William Johnson, ever confident in his abilities and always the man to seize the initiative when it presented itself "had no doubt about his right to command." [DB-p.74] Johnson's decision would prove fortuitous for the British, considering that a large French relief column from the upper posts was at the same moment making its way to Niagara, intent on lifting the siege and destroying the English by unconventional means.

Advancing quickly from the upper French posts to relieve the French at Niagara was a force of French marines, Canadians and Indians numbering close to 1300 men under the command of the noted French marine partisan officers Marin, Lignery, and Aubrey, who had conducted years of wilderness war successfully against the English. More than half of their force was French-allied Indian warriors, and as the relief column landed at the Niagara portage trail above the falls, Johnson's Iroquois met with the French Indians in an attempt to dissuade them from fighting each other near the fort. With the French column temporarily halted while negotiations went on between the Indians, Sir William Johnson set an Indian-style ambush on the road ahead for the French when they decided to proceed.

At a wooded area of the road leading north to Fort Niagara from the escarpment heights, Johnson hastily deployed British regulars, grenadiers, and light infantrymen in a V-shape ambush with the open end of the ambushers pointed towards the trail to the south from which the French were surely to come. The Englishmen were ordered to get down behind a freshly-cut rampart of logs, limbs, and brush, so that they would not be seen by the French until the last moment. Here, over 400 red-coated regular soldiers, grenadiers, and light infantry of the 46th and 44th Regiments along with New York provincial troops were deployed by Johnson, and ordered, some for the first time in their military lives, to take Indian-style positions laying down or behind trees rather than in perfect standing lines to await the coming French attack. [DB-p.92] Johnson copied the Indian method of concealed ambush and attack that had been used so successfully by the French and their allies time and time again against the English and he hoped it would work this time against the French. When talks between all the French and English-allied tribes ended, the French Indians agreed to remove themselves from the coming fight and that "war-painted horde vanished into the forest, leaving with their French allies only 30 of the most resolute warriors." [FJ1-p.207] On Sir William's side, he could not count on his own Indians to support him initially, but knew that if he could stop the French column for a while, his Iroquois supporters would join him, smelling blood. Angered at the loss of their Indian allies and with time running out to save the fort, the French officers quickly ordered the column to advance at a trot and they ran directly into the English ambush, falling by the dozens in the initial volleys. Immediately the column of Frenchmen were staggered, and as they began to falter, Johnson's Iroquois warriors massed and set upon the Frenchmen with horrific shrieks when the marines and Canadians turned to flee down the road in retreat, and then rout.

"The Iroquois reacted swiftly to the first signs of panic among the French troops who had enjoyed so many successes in five years of wilderness warfare. One British writer believed that the Indians thought them to be invincible. However, "...as soon as they found to the contrary, and that the French gave way, it is said but a Yard of Ground, they fell on them like so many Butchers, with their Tomahawks and long Knives, hooping and shouting, as if Heaven and Earth were coming together, and killed Abundance of the Enemy." [DB-p.97]

Johnson's defeat of the French relief column was complete, and the fate of Fort Niagara sealed. As a post-script to the English ambush which was fought Indian-style by the English under Johnson, it would be the Iroquois who would deliver to the French the lessons of the cruelty of Indian style wilderness warfare. Dozens of the French wounded in the battle were butchered by the Iroquois and scalped while many of the Frenchmen, attempting to escape or surrender to their savage attackers were mercilessly cut down, including the French chaplain of the French expedition, Father Claude-Joseph Virot, a Jesuit, who was cut to pieces by the pursuing Iroquois. While some effort was made on the part of British regular officers to attempt to restrain the Indians, "they also expressed a certain satisfaction that their French enemies had received a taste of their own medicine" [DB-p.98] obviously in light of the atrocities committed by French Indians against Braddock's men as well as the soldiers and civilians who surrendered at Fort William Henry.

Johnson was able to ransom the few French officers and cadets left alive who were captured by the Mohawks and Oneidas, but was unsuccessful in saving the 96 enlisted men whom the Iroquois stripped naked and then beat, before dividing them equally among their tribes, along with 150 fresh French scalps. They hurried the captives off to their own villages for torture, before Johnson was able to further intervene. As at the end of the Battle of Lake George, Johnson's Mohawks had wanted the officers as well, and were angered with him when he interceded in their plans of taking all of the French prisoners. He ransomed and saved what men he could, knowing that he would not be able to save them all. The unfortunate sacrificing of the rank and file French prisoners of the defeated relief force was part of the price to be paid for using Indians as allies. Johnson knew, as well, that the precious French furs, goods, and munitions still held within Fort Niagara would by necessity have to be turned over to the Indians as plunder, if he hoped to keep the remaining warriors with him until the total capitulation of the French. Too, even though he was Warraghiyagey to the Iroquois, Johnson knew that there were limits as to how far he could go before he would fall from their good graces. Some Iroquois had not entirely forgiven him for his grievous insult of not giving them the captured French commander Dieskau at Lake George for their cooking pots. So when word of the fall of the French Fort Niagara reached New York City in the late summer of 1759, and the toast "Johnson forever" became the popular celebration of the great English victory in New York's finest social circles, in the Iroquois villages deep in the forest wilderness from the Genesee River to the Mohawk, another toast was made among the Iroquois tribes to celebrate their great victory. Above the agonizing screams of their tortured victims, the Indian toast was made with French blood and flesh.

By using an Indian-style ambush upon the French relief force, who themselves were superb partisans well-versed in the techniques of Indian-styled wilderness warfare, Johnson was able to turn the tables on the French, ultimately winning the battle for Fort Niagara and contributing to the fall of French Canada. However William Johnson had done far more for the English cause than just win a battle on the wilderness frontier. Throughout the years of war with the French, Johnson had learned in his own way and with no one to teach him the lessons of fighting a wilderness war that no previous Englishman had dared to attempt. These lessons learned were not only used by him with success, but noted by other men, like Major Robert Rogers, who would come to command irregular forces like Johnson. They would pattern their own ideas of raising companies of white men capable of fighting like Indians in an enemy's own countryside on what Johnson had proven possible. Though the official English military thinking of generals like Amherst would remain relatively unchanged throughout the course of the war in regard to the use of Indians, William Johnson had learned well several important lessons in wilderness warfare that would not be forgotten.

First and foremost, Johnson learned the importance of Indians in fighting a wilderness war. He proved that if the English were going to win the war with the French, they needed militarily to secure the help of the Indians of the Iroquois nations on the colonial frontier as allies. Unlike Braddock, Johnson understood that only Indians, skilled in the ways of traversing the impenetrable forests that lay between New England and New France, could pave the way for English victories, in the same manner as the French had done with their own Indian allies. In the tangled wilderness of the frontier, it took Indians to counter Indians, and Indians to take the war to the enemy in their own lands. At the beginning of the war, when Washington surrendered at Fort Necessity and Braddock's men were massacred on the Monongahela at the hands of Indians, the English had no Indian allies of their own that they could count on.

Courting the allegiance of Indians, though, was another matter. The Indian tribes of the Iroquois Confederacy were at times both sympathetic and hostile towards the English. Like all Indians, the Iroquois were fiercely independent and would not take orders from white men, nor allow themselves to be governed nor forced to fight. Rather, they had to be convinced that it was in their interest to support the English against the French and their own Indian allies, for it was their inherent nature not to fight other Indians in what was obviously a white man's war. Thus seeking the allegiance of the Iroquois, and in particular the Mohawks, would prove to be a daunting task that William Johnson seemed uniquely suited for. His charismatic style of mixing business, diplomacy, and pleasure in his dealings with the Indians endeared them to him. When the Mohawks adopted Johnson into their tribe and gave him the name Warraghiyagey, he had gained a great deal of their allegiance, and this would become the English cause when war came. By acquiring the favor of the Mohawks through adoption into their tribe, William Johnson had written a maxim of wilderness warfare. For Indians to fight with a white man and take the risk of dying for him, that white man must first be accepted as one of them, and become an Indian in their own eyes. William Johnson was able to do that, and other white men in the years to come would follow his lead.

In addition, William Johnson created the British Indian Department which served during the war as both a separate military arm of the British war effort and an effective liaison between the English and Johnson's Indian allies. Johnson was able to see the shortcomings of sending Mohawk war parties into the field to reconnoiter and attack the French. In typical Indian fashion, they would hit the enemy from ambush and then return to their villages once they had obtained enough scalps and plunder. Johnson envisioned sending handpicked white men along with the raiding parties to accomplish more militarily while in the field just as the French counterparts to the north were doing. He selected his department officers from other provincial men like himself whom he knew and trusted. They were individual border men like the Butler brothers who were raised on the frontier and therefore capable of dealing with the forest wilderness as well as being familiar with the Mohawks that they accompanied on raids north. Unlike the French partisan leaders, what was unique about Johnson's officers was that they reported only to Johnson's command, and as such, maintained the allegiance of the Indians that they traveled with who instinctively knew that the white men with them could be trusted because they carried the word of Warraghiyagey. In New France, each partisan leader operated independently, and had only the allegiance of those Indians of who were with him, but not any other. Johnson counted that his Indian Department would be more effective than the French because his combined force of white officers and Indians were under his sole command and would operate as one.

On the frontier battlefield, Johnson learned two important things about tactics in conducting wilderness warfare that would have implications for the English in the future. First, he saw that even in the wilderness, the use of heavy artillery was necessary to reduce frontier forts. Nothing less than a sustained bombardment from large guns could batter down gates and walls and force fort defenders to capitulate by neutralizing the tremendous defensive advantage afforded them. Montcalm found this to be true when he assaulted Fort William Henry, and so did Johnson at the siege of Fort Niagara. In breeching the walls of a fort, no matter how he looked at it, Indian-styled tactics did not apply. Indians might frighten a fort's defenders but could they could not penetrate nor scale walls. To force an enemy fort to surrender required artillery and that fact precluded the need for conventional siege tactics conducted with the support of a large regular army. In the future war to come on the frontier of the Ohio Country, this maxim of the use of artillery, or lack of it, would prove itself to be true again and again.

Secondly, though Johnson understood that laying siege to a frontier fort through the use of conventional warfare might be necessary in the overall strategy, the use of Indian tactics applied everywhere else in a frontier wilderness war. Specifically, the Indian style of ambush had its important place in wilderness warfare and could easily change the outcome of a battle when used correctly. Since the only way to move a large body of troops through heavy forested areas was by means of frontier roads, it was possible to destroy such an enemy force with an ambush as long as that enemy force did not have their own Indians scouting ahead or on the flanks of the main body, searching for a likely spot for an ambush or surprise attack.

At the Battle of Lake George, Johnson attempted to move a large party of his own militiamen up the road from Lake George in the direction of Fort Edward in search of the French and Indians. On the advice of the Mohawk Chief Hendrick, Johnson sent a large party of Indians and scouts ahead to reconnoiter. The Mohawks, skilled in the Indian tactics of ambush, were fortunately able to detect the enemy ambush and thwart the Abenaki, Caughnawaga, and Canadian plans to destroy Johnson's men who were following at a distance by sounding the alert and avoiding annihilation of the English such as happened to Braddock's army. However at Niagara, when the French relief force from the upper posts began moving down the road from the portage towards the French fort, they did not have their Indians scouting ahead of the main body looking for the enemy and a possible ambush. Consequently the French partisans and marine troops blundered headlong into Johnson's undetected ambush where they were devastated by the initial volley fire. Most of the French officers in the lead were taken by surprise, and felled. The result was that the rest of the French were never able to recover from the shock.

Ironically, William Johnson experienced a hard truth about using Indians as allies at the Niagara ambush. He learned that no matter how hard one worked over the years to cultivate and maintain Indian allies as he had, native warriors were highly unpredictable and could leave the field at the most critical time and decide to sit a battle out, as the Iroquois did prior to the arrival of the French relief column, or desert and head for home, as the French allied Indians from the Ohio Country chose to do, rather than fight the Iroquois. Now suddenly faced with the prospect of no warriors to ambush the French, Johnson was able to deploy regular troops to fill the gap. While the Indian tactics of a forest ambush of an enemy force were superior, the reliability of the Indians was not. The saving grace for William Johnson was that he was able to use those tactics without using Indians, and did so out of necessity rather than risk losing the battle. Consequently, an all-white force of English regulars were able to set aside their training in linear European tactics and fight from concealed positions. The irony for Johnson was that as "Colonel of the Indians," he was unable to force them to stay and fight, whereas he was able to order English troops to do so without question, proving that white men could fight like Indians when the situation warranted it, an idea that most military men of his time abhorred, and thought not possible since only Indians could fight like Indians.

Lastly, Johnson learned from his experience that when Indians who had sat out a battle finally did join in, as the Iroquois did at the ambush at Niagara, they did so not out of loyalty for the English but because they smelled blood, and then fought with such savageness that even Warraghiyagey was unable to control them. The Iroquois butchered the French wounded with savage excess and ignored Johnson's plea to spare most of the prisoners a worse fate, just as the French-allied Indians had done to the English wounded and captives after the fall of Fort William Henry when Montcalm tried to stop them. It may have been a bitter pill for Johnson to swallow if he thought about it. While he was an adopted Mohawk in their eyes, and a man who all believed could straddle both the white world and that of the Indian, at heart William Johnson was still an Irishman in America, and not a born and bred savage. He could reason, that for the moment, Indian tactics of fighting in the wilderness were superior to that of the white man. However, from the white man's view, Indians were unpredictable, unreliable, and uncontrollable. When they attacked they were utterly ruthless savage fighters, who could rout an enemy and spare not one life. Their unspeakable depredations against a foe made them a necessary evil to contend with, best rationalized as the unavoidable cost of employing Indians as allies, by either side. Bougainville, a French officer of Montcalm, wrote of the nature of the "evil" of employing Indians, when he witnessed the chiefs of the French-allied Indians come to speak to M. de Montcalm at Fort William Henry to protest his orders to spare the English captives, wounded, women and children. A prominent chief argued, "Father, don't expect that we can easily give quarter to the English. We have some young warriors who have not yet drunk of this broth. Raw flesh has led them here from the ends of the earth; they must learn to wield the knife and to bury it in English hearts." [HE2-p.64]

What William Johnson could ponder but never know for sure was what would have happened if the tables had not turned? If the English regulars waiting in ambush had not smashed the French reinforcements rushing to save Fort Niagara, whose blood would the Iroquois have smelled, and who's wounded would their warriors have mercilessly fallen upon like hungry wolves, and whose bloody scalps would have hung from their belts?

Chapter 5

The White Devil: Robert Rogers and His Independent Company of Rangers

At the same time that William Johnson was making his preparations to lead an army of Indians and provincial troops north from Albany in the summer of 1755, another Englishman of more modest means and rank than Johnson was making his own plans to go to war. Robert Rogers was one of hundreds of New England colonials who were recruited by Governor William Shirley of Massachusetts to volunteer for military duty in provincial regiments which would serve in the upcoming campaign planned against the French at Crown Point. Raised in the obscurity of the backwoods of the New Hampshire frontier, the 23 year old had one thing on his mind when he brought in over 50 of his recruits to Portsmouth on April 24. [CJ-p.18] As captain of "Company One" of the regiment under the command of New Hampshire's Colonel Blanchard, Robert Rogers cared little about English military tactics and strategy. The young man wished one thing more than anything else and that was to fight Indians. He had heard the stories of the savage Indian raids told by the veterans of King George's War, and he wanted a chance to fight Indians too.

In a span of five years to come, Rogers would get his wish and more. Through sheer audacity and an ability to command in the most unlikely of circumstances, he would be thrust to the forefront of the war in the north for the English. Risking all, Robert Rogers would come to make his indelible mark upon not only the conduct of the intensely-contested warfare fought in the wilderness, but help seal the fate of the French and their Indian allies once and for all. More so, through innate grasp of the tactics of wilderness fighting, Rogers would change forever the face of warfare on the North American frontier in the years to come, and write a unique chapter of his own from the lessons he and his men had learned so well, and paid for, at the cost of the lives of many of their comrades.

Robert Rogers humble beginnings

Robert Rogers had few things in common with William Johnson. He was born in America in 1731, in Methuen, a small town in Massachusetts Colony. His parents, James and Mary Rogers recently emigrated from Northern Ireland

and with a growing family of four children to feed, the Rogers moved to an area of the colony known as the "Great Meadow," some 35 miles northwest of Methuen, to take up farming. It was here that the restless youth who possessed little desire to apply himself to an education beyond a few rudimentary basics, found his calling. Instinctively he found himself to be more comfortable wandering the wilds of the forested mountains around his home than in sitting in a classroom or hoeing corn. Like William Johnson, Rogers' parents were poor people with little means who struggled to eke out a living from the soil. Unlike Johnson, Rogers did not have the opportunity of good fortune to come knocking for him in the form of a gentleman relative. His future was to be determined by his own efforts that would bring him fame but little fortune. Those wheels of destiny began to turn for him in the summer of 1745, when at the age of 14, he answered a call to arms that would shape the rest of his life. In such men who unknowingly heed what comes to be their call of destiny, Robert Rogers had much in common with William Johnson.

Rogers takes to scouting for Indians

In 1744, word of the declaration of war between England and France reached the colonies, and by mid-1745, Indian war parties from New France in the north were attacking the frontier towns and posts of New England with increasing regularity, striking without warning. The main thrust of the Abenaki Indian raiders was against the closest English settlements in the Merrimack River valley of New Hampshire. The Indians hit settlers' cabins and farms, ambushing militiamen who were called out on the frontier to protect those settlers who refused to flee. When Captain Daniel Ladd's company of militia was attacked and several men killed, Ladd sought out men to replace those men lost at Rumford who would be brave or foolhardy enough to pursue the Indians. One of those who eagerly volunteered for the hazardous duty was the 14 year old lad, Robert Rogers. [CJ-p.8]

Rogers spent the next two years in the militia patrolling the frontier trails of New Hampshire, looking for signs of Abenaki war parties infiltrating from the north. During this time, Rogers spent as little time as possible helping his father with the family farm between alarms. Rather, he found the life of a militia scout compelling. Danger was always present, and the exhilaration that he felt was different than the dread that filled most men at the thoughts of Indian attack. During this period Rogers matured physically, growing to six feet in height with a strong athletic build. The weeks and months of physical hardship that he spent outdoors on active militia duty on the many trails looking for Indians toughened him both mentally and physically, while adding to his knowledge of woodsmanship and the trials of endurance. When King George's War ended in 1748, and the threat of Indian raids momentarily eased, Rogers found himself more adapted to the ways of frontier scouting in the wilderness than to farming. Privately, he may have found himself wishing for the day when the Indian attacks would resume, and he would heed another call to arms. The excitement and danger of scouting for hostile Indians was in his blood and he wanted more of it. Unfortunately for the settlers of the frontier, Rogers' wish would not wait long to be fulfilled.

Rogers joins Johnson's campaign on Lake George

The news of Washington's attack upon Jumonville and his subsequent surrender to the French at Fort Necessity in early July 1754, did not take long to bring about a reaction from French Canada. Within a few weeks, Abenaki Indian war parties from the north began to filter south and raid the settlements sporadically on the New Hampshire frontier. The governor called out the militia and Robert Rogers quickly volunteered, serving with a company that patrolled between the Merrimack and Contoocook Rivers until they were discharged in late September. Then in spring 1755, word reached the settlements of war between England and France. A new call to arms was issued for men with experience to fill provincial regiments earmarked first for a campaign against French Nova Scotia, and then revised for the new campaign to be headed by William Johnson for an attack on the French fort at Crown Point on Lake Champlain. Rogers volunteered immediately and began recruiting others. Because of his previous ranger experience, Rogers was able to gain himself an appointment as captain in the militia company when he reported with his men at Portsmouth. Soon the regiment was on the march overland to join Johnson at Albany. The stage was now set for both Rogers and Johnson.

When William Johnson left Albany on August 8 with his provisional army of provincial soldiers, militiamen and Mohawk Indians, the New Hampshire regiment under Colonel Blanchard had not as yet arrived, and it would take additional time to straggle in to Albany. By mid-August, Johnson ordered the regiment to bring a supply train from Albany to his army. Blanchard chose Rogers and 100 men for the duty, which Rogers accomplished, arriving at the newly built English fort on the east bank of the Hudson River, near the "Great Carrying Place" below the falls. Here, Rogers awaited Colonel Blanchard and the rest of the regiment, noting the large island across from the log fort which sat in the middle of the river. One day it would become his base of operations. When Blanchard arrived on the fourth of September, word had reached the fort that French and Indian war parties had been spotted in the vicinity. Rogers was ordered to scout for the exact location of the enemy at Lac du Sacrament, re-named Lake George. On the eighth, Johnson's army was attacked by the French and their Indian allies. With the help of the Mohawks, an ambush of Johnson's force was thwarted, and the French were forced to attack Johnson's troops in the open, which enabled him to defeat them, thus winning a great victory for England and himself.

When the battle was over, the French withdrew to the north. However, in spite of the fact that Johnson had won the battle, the ability of his army to continue north to Crown Point was deteriorating rapidly. Many were wounded including Johnson himself and needed immediate attention. With orders from

Shirley to proceed north, Johnson turned to his trusted Mohawk scouts to determine where the French were, only to find that they had deserted him. In the confusion after the battle, the Mohawks departed, after falsely telling Johnson they would soon return. The Mohawks in fact were angry with Johnson for several reasons. First, their great sachem, Chief Hendrick had been killed, along with many warriors in the initial foiled ambush on the road, and there was grieving to be done over those losses. Second, the Mohawks had inadvertently been forced to fight against their former blood brothers, the Caughnawagas, who were now allies of the French, and with whom they had no great quarrel. Too, many warriors were livid that while the Mohawks had taken the brunt of the casualties in the road ambush, William Johnson would not turn over to them the captured French general, Baron Dieskau, so they could cook him and eat him. They were disgruntled. As each warrior already had his fill of French scalps, the Mohawks could see no further need for war against the French, so they quietly decided to return to their villages in the Mohawk Valley. Consequently, Johnson was left with no Indian scouts, and did not know where the French were.

Rogers up to the impossible task

In desperation, he turned to Blanchard's New Hampshire regiment for any men with scouting ability. Blanchard reported to William Johnson that he had one man of considerable scouting experience to recommend; Robert Rogers was called to report to William Johnson, whereupon Johnson ordered him to reconnoiter the French position at Crown Point immediately. Rogers set out by whale-boat with four men on the night of September 14, heading north on Lake George into French-held territory where no Englishman had gone before without friendly Indians for guides. [CJ-p.21]

Rogers' small scouting party was the first of many he would lead in autumn 1755 to gain intelligence on the French that William Johnson urgently needed. Where and what were the retreating French forces that he had engaged at Lake George doing? Were French reinforcements moving down Lake Champlain from Crown Point to attack his own stalled army again? How many French-allied Indians were there between himself and Canada, ready to assist the French if they should be preparing for a new offensive? Johnson had no way of knowing these things after the loss of his Mohawk scouts and he could only decide upon a course of action once he knew the true intentions of the French whom he reasoned would soon outnumber his army. Rogers needed to do more than scout a few miles north of Johnson's army. He must find a way of traversing the vast tangled wilderness of lakes, mountains and impenetrable forest of the Champlain Valley that would take him into the heart of French territory to spy on the French. He must accomplish this without being spotted by the enemy at any time. Such a mission would be impossible for any man unacquainted with the wilderness and a tall order to fill for even a talented scout like Rogers.

Once Rogers left the security of the English camp and ventured deep into enemy territory, he would be entirely on his own. Most importantly, Rogers would have to elude the Abenaki and Caughnawaga scouting parties who were themselves masters of those same woodlands. They would be on the lookout for any Englishman foolish enough to enter their wilderness domains and he and his men could expect a slow agonizing death with no mercy if they were caught. Rogers' scouting mission would only be deemed a success if he returned alive to tell what he'd seen. Anything less meant failure and death. Remarkably, Rogers believed he was up to the task.

Rogers scouts deep into Enemy territory

From his previous experience in New Hampshire where he first learned the unwritten principles of scouting and put them into practice, Robert Rogers chose a plan for his future reconnaissance mission that held the greatest likelihood of success, relying upon the use of a small number of hand-picked men best suited for the job, rather than opting for a larger scale operation. His scouting groups in autumn 1755 typically numbered four to five men including himself. He wisely reasoned from his previous wilderness experience tracking Indians that he needed to pattern his small unit of scouts after the highly successful Abenaki war parties that were able to adeptly attack the New Hampshire frontier without being caught. Rogers had hunted them without much success because the Abenaki rarely traveled in large groups which could be more easily spotted. The Abenaki knew large parties left more distinct tracks on the trails, and were forced to move slower due to their larger numbers. The Abenaki chose small war parties that could scout without being seen, and after striking the unsuspecting white settlers, could swiftly melt into the cover of the forests before any retaliatory militia force could stop them. While hating the Abenaki Indians, Rogers could not ignore their superb ability in the woods, and so he adopted their wilderness tactics.

Throughout the remainder of 1755, Rogers scouted into the wilderness and obtained the necessary intelligence for William Johnson. Time and again he returned from his scouting with valuable information on French positions at Crown Point and Ticonderoga, accomplishing the difficult task while eluding the enemy who had many patrols of their own in the field. Many of his excursions began under the blanket of darkness. Rogers preferred to travel much of the great distance separating him from the French in the north by boat on the lakes at night. Rogers devoted time to making maps as the English had none of the area, and he knew that future missions by himself and others would depend upon reliable cartography. On occasions during these scouts he had opportunities to attack enemy soldiers or Indians. Rarely did he do so, knowing that once his men fired their muskets they gave away not only the element of secrecy surrounding their spying mission, but also their position and numbers as well. Rogers instinctively knew his success and survival depended upon stealth. Scouting parties were designed precisely for scouting the enemy, and not for fighting them unless there was no other choice to survive.

There were a lot of questions left unanswered—answers Rogers needed to ensure the success of his scouting mission. He would discover by trial and error the means of surviving in the enemy's woods, if the experience didn't cost him his scalp and his life. How would the bateau be hidden once he and his men reached a point of land along the lake where he wished to set out on foot? The bateau would be needed for the return trip but had to be concealed for an extended period of time so that enemy scouts and war parties did not discover it. Otherwise, they could pursue his small party by backtracking along his trail, or set an ambush for him as he was returning to the boat. Concealment of the boat was paramount for success of the mission.

Cutting inland through the dense forests presented further problems. The French and their Indians knew the trails and he did not. Any twist or turn along a path could bring him into direct contact with a much larger hostile force. He would have to compensate for that possibility. How were he and his men to disguise their own tracks and signs of their passing so hostile Indians would not find them? If he left the few trails through the woods, how was he to find his way without getting lost in the untracked forests and swamps? The trails were the only quick means to travel northward through the woods, but they put him and his men in grave danger of a chance encounter with the enemy. Could he and his men survive on cold rations with no fire? A fire for cooking or warmth could easily give the small party's location away to enemy scouts who had excellent eyes and noses for the careless Englishman's fire. How would he and his men stay warm in wet and cold weather? All the minute details of these wilderness situations had to be taken into account and resolved as they arose in the field without producing lethal results. Robert Rogers was undaunted by the enormity of the challenge ahead.

"To carry the fight to the Enemy"

Again and again Rogers and his men entered enemy territory and returned alive with information on the activities of the French at Crown Point and Ticonderoga. His successes proved that he and his men had learned how to survive in the wilderness and move like the Indians. Rogers methodically conducted his reconnaissance behind enemy lines as no Englishman had done before in North America, and in doing so, perfected tactics that were outside English military doctrine of his time. Other conventional scouting parties made up of men from provincial military units trained by English officers were sent out from Johnson's camp on the south shore of Lake George but were always reluctant to venture more than a few miles north. All of these parties would return in haste once they lost their nerve to advance further, fearing Indian ambush. They lacked more than Rogers' aggressive determination and courage to go farther up the lake into the hostile wilderness. They had not discovered and put into practice the necessary woodland skills to survive in the wilderness along with the physical stamina to endure the rigors of the harsh environment that Rogers and his men had honed and tempered over the months. Buoyed by his success which was bringing Rogers and his small group of men some celebrity in Johnson's camp, Rogers set his sights higher in the early months of 1756 to face a new more demanding challenge of his own device. Now that he knew that he could traverse the wilderness and find the enemy in their camps, he fixed in his mind "to carry the fight to the enemy." [CJ-p.29]

Robert Rogers plan for the winter months was simple. He would do what no French or English military officer thought probable or possible. Rogers knew that the winter months in North America were a time when French, English and Indian alike went into their sheltered winter quarters or wigwams and considered all offensive military action over with for the season, as the cold temperatures, harsh wintry winds and deep snows prohibited any campaigning. Rogers reasoned that if he could master the skills of movement and survival in the winter elements that he would be able to do more than spy upon the French, but actually set out to capture prisoners and attack and harass the enemy who were holed up. To accomplish this he would need more men and more firepower for his raiding parties than his previous scouting parties provided. In essence, Rogers envisioned moving from a defensive role of scouting the enemy to offensive missions. The risks would be greater, but so too would be the rewards. Live French prisoners could provide the English with much more accurate intelligence than previously gleamed. Also, by attacking the enemy where and when they least expected could give the English a tremendous psychological advantage by causing the French to lose face with their Indians. It was a matter of seizing the initiative from the French in the wilderness war, which had not been done as yet with any concerted effort.

Modeling his tactics after the Indians

In January 1756, Rogers led a party of 17 men, a dozen more than his previous scouting party, north over Lake George on skates and then across the mountains to set up an ambush for the French north of Ticonderoga. There he and his men attacked a sleigh and took two French prisoners back to a newly-built English fort on the shore of Lake George at William Johnson's former camp. Another raid soon after by Rogers and 50 men netted more prisoners taken from Crown Point. [CJ-p.31] In February during some of the coldest weather of the winter, Rogers set out with 60 men on a 15 day scout to once again raid the French. Gone for two weeks without any word, Rogers and his men returned from their trip unscathed, again proving that with proper knowledge, gear, preparations and training, his men could overcome the severe conditions of the harsh elements and turn winter to their advantage by scouting and raiding when the enemy thought it impossible to be done.

Rogers modeled his tactics in the field after Indian war parties of both the Abenaki and the Iroquois. His thinking was a great departure from conventional military doctrine of the English, but Rogers knew that those tactics and rules did not apply to the wilderness war the English faced. By using Indian tactics more adapted to the wilderness, he was determined to aggressively take the war to the French by attacking them repeatedly. Rogers reasoned that to successfully conduct such a war on a small scale he needed all the advantages that he and his men could muster. At some point he decided that he would increase the impact of his raids by employing another Indian tactic that the Abenaki used successfully upon his own people on the New Hampshire frontier: he would use ruthlessness and terror tactics against the French.

Rogers knew as no other English captain in the field the shock value of scalped bodies, burnt buildings and slaughtered livestock. He had seen for himself the impression made on the survivors of such Abenaki raids in New Hampshire. That frontier had quickly depopulated once the terror of Indian raids struck. Those same tactics could be used as well upon the French. Ultimately, he would give them a taste of the type of savagery and brutality that they had been employing against the English through the use of the Indians. The French were relatively immune from such attacks upon them since the start of the war, as the English had few Indians allies who would or could attack the French directly. As Rogers had no Indians of his own to terrorize the French, his own men would have to do so. They would not only move in the woods like Indians but fight like them as well. It did not matter to this uneducated homespun woodsman from New Hampshire that by using the tactics of terror against the French, he would further deviate from English doctrine of civility. The war being fought on the frontier was a no-holds-barred war of extinction between the two sides, because of the involvement of the Indians. Unlike his military counterparts in the provincial and regular English army, Rogers would have no qualms about taking French scalps when the situation arose. If ruthlessness worked, then terror and retribution were the lessons he hoped to teach.

"We put an end to him to prevent discovery"

As Rogers' raids in 1756 began to strike deeper into French-held territory and increased in size and scope, the nature of his raids began to change. It was not enough to fire upon a French patrol from ambush or from a distance and then escape. His attacks became more and more ruthless by design. In early January, French sledges were intercepted on the frozen ice of Lake Champlain as they were carrying supplies from Crown Point to the new French post called Carillon at Ticonderoga. The French drivers were taken prisoner for questioning. The sledges with the supplies and horses were destroyed. Many weeks later, when French horses, cattle, and hogs were discovered in the course of a lightning raid near Crown Point, Rogers ordered that the livestock be slain, to further deny the enemy fresh meat and any sense of security. Barns filled with grain were put to the torch. Farmhouses and outbuildings were burned to the ground and anything missed was destroyed later on successive raids. [PF-p.217]

In the course of conducting more raids resulting in more engagements with French patrols and the subsequent taking of more French prisoners, out of necessity Rogers ordered that any Frenchman captured who was too wounded to walk back to Fort William Henry be killed so that a rescue party could not learn from the man the size of Rogers' force and the direction they were taking. Such French wounded were dispatched by Rogers' men using blows to the head from the tomahawk that each carried. A musket shot would have created enough noise in enemy territory to give away their positions. Besides, ball and powder were precious commodities and the limited amount each man carried on the raid could not be replaced until he returned to their base. Ammunition was something not to be needlessly wasted on executing a prisoner. A killing Indian-style blow to the head of the unfortunate victim sufficed. Taking the man's scalp would be done for a grisly trophy and for ruthless effect upon those Frenchmen who would ultimately find the man's scalped corpse. Upon returning from raids, Rogers routinely noted in his reports the ruthless execution of wounded prisoners, one of whom "could not march, therefore we put an end to him, to prevent discovery." [PF-p.218] On one of many forays to the French post at Crown Point, Rogers described what happened when an ambush netted a Frenchman who refused to surrender to him. "He refused to take Quarter so we killed him and took of His Scalp in plain sight of the fort." For Rogers, these tactics were a part of wilderness war. He knew that he and his men could expect no mercy from the French and their Indians if they were captured alive. He was not fighting a gentleman's war, but rather a war of extermination.

Rogers' early raids of 1756 were successful and brought him growing fame in the northern English colonies. Word of Rogers audacious exploits reached William Shirley, the Governor of Massachusetts, and at the moment, the Commander in Chief of the British Army in North America until a replacement from the regular army arrived from England. Shirley summoned Rogers from the Lake George frontier on March 15, 1756, to meet with him in Boston, after the New York General Assembly voted to award Captain Rogers a large amount of money in payment for his "courage, conduct, and diligence." [BB-p.29] Shirley, himself an ardent student of military history and warfare, envisioned a wider role for Rogers in which he wrote, "It is absolutely necessary for His Majesty's Service, that one Company at least of Rangers should be constantly employed in different Parties upon Lake George and Lake Iroquois (Champlain) to make Discoveries of the proper Routes for our own Troops, procure Intelligence of the Enemy's Strength and Motions, destroy their Magazines and Settlements, pick up small Parties of their Battoes (Bateaus) upon the Lakes, and keep them under continual Alarm." [PF-p.33]

Rogers recruits and prepares his company of rangers

In Shirley's decree, Robert Rogers had been given his orders to proceed. In actuality, Shirley officially blessed Rogers own unique style of scouting and fighting that was foreign to the military establishment. To give Rogers added credibility, Shirley commissioned Rogers and his men to be the first recognized ranger company in the British army, and yet not really a part of the regular army. Rogers' company of men were to be a separate provincial unit that though subject to regular army orders, rules, and pay, was able to operate separate from the

Backwoodsmen are recruited for Rogers'
Independent Company of Rangers.

army, and yet had no permanent status beyond that created by the governor and commander in chief. Shirley stated, "I do Hereby Constitute and Appoint you the Said Robert Rogers to be Captain of an Independent Company of Rangers to be forthwith raised and Employed." Rogers was authorized to enlist 60 privates, and six officers besides himself, from men whom Shirley demanded should be "experienced in hunting, tracking and long marches." [CJ-p.33]

Rogers set out for New Hampshire at once to recruit the necessary men and return to the New York frontier as quickly as possible with a full company of men to outfit them, and resume ranging missions. Without a formal uniform, each man in Rogers' company was allowed a choice of his own comfortable clothing which he wore on the frontier. Coats were cut short in the back to make walking through heavy woods easier. Sleeved waistcoats were worn in warmer weather, and many men discarded their boots or shoes for moccasins with wool or leather leggings better suited for long marches. For weapons, each man brought his own smoothbore musket or fowler of different calibers. They carried musket ball and pea shot in waist pouches and cartridge boxes, and would often mix their shot, adding "six or seven smaller shot to a larger ball" to increase the stopping power of each round that they fired at an enemy. [CJ-p.53] Gunpowder was kept in powder horns slung under their right arm and in addition, each man carried a tomahawk or small hatchet of their own design in their belt, along with an all-purpose scalping knife. Dried provisions and a blanket were often tied on a belt slung over their back. Cooking utensils and tents were not brought along on the dangerous scouts. A man had to be able to move long distances and travel quickly with as light a load on him as possible. Only when absolutely necessary would a man use his flint and steel to start a fire to dry out a wet flintlock.

In the winter, additional gear was added to the ranger kit. Iron ice creepers were brought along to be strapped on one's winter moccasins when needed to walk on the frozen lakes. Sometimes skates were added to permit quicker travel on ice, and snowshoes or "rackettes" as the French called them, were constructed for each man and were used to walk through the heavy snows in the valleys surrounding the Lake Champlain area. Woolen mittens, hoods, and capotes or overcoats rounded out each man's gear that would be necessary to deal with the cold and prevent frostbite and hypothermia while on the march. While Rogers' men had a decided hodgepodge look about them, they were unmistakably dressed and armed for function.

It would not be until January 1758 that Rogers' company of rangers would be issued a standard uniform. By this time his Independent Company of Rangers had expanded to several, with two more companies added in February 1757, and more slated to be raised, to fill a Battalion or Corps of Rangers. At his forward base of operations for the rangers on an island in the Hudson River across from Fort Edward, some eight miles away from Fort William Henry, his men received their dark green woolen uniforms consisting of "short sleeveless jacket with wings such as worn by drummers, waistcoat with sleeves, drawers, gaiters, a tricorn hat for parade and a tam for field work." [DE-p.164] Green was chosen over red as the color of the uniform for obvious reasons. Braddock's red-coated regulars had presented easy targets to the French and Indians in the green and brown forest backdrop of the Ohio Country. The French marines were learning the same lesson that their off-white buff coats were easily spotted from a distance. Green allowed Rogers' men to blend into the forest more appropriately for the type of clandestine operations that they were given behind enemy lines, where the ability to camouflage oneself like an Indian might mean the difference between life and death. Aptly dyed or painted brown gaiters made of linen, leather, or canvas, buttoned from the ankle to mid-thigh to protect the legs of each man from thick prickly underbrush when scouting in the wilderness.

Arms changed little with the new uniform. Some men elected to carry the standard .75 caliber British Brown Bess smoothbore musket and set to work in their barracks on Rogers Island to cut off eight inches of the standard issue weapon for two reasons. A shorter barrel meant greater ease in loading the powder and shot down the muzzle because the open end of the cut-down musket was closer now to the loader's hand. In addition, the shorter musket could be loaded easier while laying down in a concealed position and it provided greater ease when moving through thick forest undergrowth as there was eight inches less to get tangled in branches while on the march. By 1758, the standard issue British leather cartridge had replaced the shot pouch. Some men carried bayonets in addition to their sheathed knives and tomahawks. [RR-75] By the end of the war in 1760, Rogers' Ranger companies would be expanded to a total of 12, encompassing hundreds of green-uniformed men.

Learning the rules of ranging from mistakes

By late 1756, the French and their Indian allies were determined more than ever to stop Rogers and his ranging company from continuing his forays into French-held territory. The French partisan leaders who themselves were masters of woodland warfare and ranging, looked for an opportunity to kill or capture Rogers and his men, who had eluded their grasp the previous year. By sending their own patrols and war parties out continually to search for Rogers, they needed only for him and his men to make a mistake giving them the advantage to destroy him. While Rogers had learned a great deal about the rules of ranging in a wilderness war, he had not learned everything, and would consequently make a series of mistakes that would nearly cost him his life and the destruction of his ranger corps. The price of learning the lessons of wilderness war would be the high cost of many of his men's lives.

Rogers' first serious mistake came in the dead of winter in January 1757. After stopping at Fort William Henry for two days to make snowshoes, on January 17 Rogers led a force of more than 70 rangers in winter gear north to attack the French at Crown Point. He wanted to begin by ambushing French supply sledge headed from Fort Carillon to the Fort at Crown Point, and so after arriving unseen at the end of the arduous trip, Rogers picked an ideal spot hidden along the frozen lakeshore. [PF-p.221] Soon a French horse-drawn sledge was seen approaching at a distance, and Rogers sent a party of men under Captain

Stark to intercept it. While Stark was moving into position, to Rogers' surprise 8 or 10 more horse-drawn sleighs were seen moving far behind the first. Rogers sent a man to attempt to warn Stark not to spring the trap on the first sledge, but was unsuccessful. The following French spied the capture of their first comrades ahead, and immediately turned their sleighs around to return to Fort Carillon and warn the garrison there. The French commander quickly sent over 100 men north to find the tracks of Rogers' men, reasoning that in the deep snow, it would be likely, however foolish, for Rogers and his men to return to Fort William Henry by the same way they had come.

The Rangers walk into an enemy ambush

Rogers was correct to reason that the French had been alerted to the presence of his ranger force and that he needed to head south as quickly as possible to avoid a confrontation with the French and Indians who would surely outnumber his men. It was at this point that Rogers underestimated the ability of his enemies to range as far and wide as he could in winter, and that he needed to avoid the area of French activities entirely. For the safety of his men, they needed to take an entirely different route home, regardless of the deep snows. For whatever reasons, Rogers did not. It would be his undoing, and a fateful learning experience. "Ignoring one of the most important rules of forest warfare, Rogers' Rangers returned to the site of the previous night's campfires, rekindled the coals into fire, and again dried out their muskets. After a quick meal, they headed back south by way of their original route for the safety of Fort William Henry. Quite a few would not make it." [BB-p.31]

Rogers and his men walked into a ravine along their previous day's trail and a waiting French ambush. The French had found the ranger trail and following it for a way, picked the ravine as an ambush site to annihilate the Englishmen. On a signal the French let loose a tremendous volley that felled many of the rangers in the front of the column. Rogers and the men in the rear returned fire and then fell back across the hollow to a piece of high ground where they kept up a hot fire on the French and Indians, repelling several attempts to overrun them. The French who outnumbered Rogers' men called upon him by name to surrender his men, or face being cut to pieces by the Indians who would show no mercy. Rogers, himself wounded in the wrist, ignored the French and planned a breakout for his surviving men once night fell. Under the cover of darkness, Rogers and his men who were able to move slipped through the French, leaving those men who were wounded too badly to travel where they lay. [PF-p.222] Rogers and his able bodied men escaped the French and reached Fort William Henry. In the ambush, he had 14 men killed and six believed captured, and most likely dead. The lesson was costly for Rogers and by all rights he was most fortunate to have so narrowly escaped annihilation. Of the dead, Rogers had to live with the knowledge that his carelessness had brought about the loss of men that he had known for a considerable time and had trusted.

The disastrous battle on snowshoes

Another mistake, more destructive and terrible than the first, occurred over a year later in March 1758, after the fall of Fort William Henry to the French. On March 10, 181 rangers under Rogers left Fort Edward on orders from the commander, Colonel Havilland, to scout the area of Ticonderoga surrounding the French at Fort Carillon. Rogers marched his men on the ice up Lake George. When the force reached a point several miles south of Ticonderoga, Rogers had his men don their snowshoes and march overland to keep them from being spotted in their dark uniforms on the ice by any Indian scouts ahead. He picked a route that ran to the northwest along a creek valley, keeping a mountain between him and the French at Carillon. Resting for the night of March 12, Rogers did not allow his men the comfort of fires for fear that they would be spotted by the enemy. What he did not know was that his trail on the ice had been discovered by an Abenaki war party, which followed it until it left the ice for the forested valley. Quickly the Indians returned to Fort Carillon and reported their findings to the French, who made preparations to find the English rangers the next morning.

Early the next morning a force of 96 Indian warriors and French Canadians under the partisan leader Durantaye left Fort Carillon for the west, which they deduced from the previous day's reports was the direction the English rangers may have been headed. About a half-hour later, a much larger force composed of Indians, Canadians, French marines and some regular troops commanded by the able French partisan commander, Langy, set out from Fort Carillon on the heels of Durantaye's force. [BB-p.52]

Breaking camp in late afternoon, Rogers sent three scouts ahead to reconnoiter the creek valley as it wound to the northeast in the general direction of the French fort to which Rogers intended to march. From a vantage point, the three rangers spied Durantaye's force moving down the creek valley in their direction. Staying in position until they felt sure that no other force was coming from the fort, they quickly returned to Rogers, who set a trap for the approaching enemy. Had his scouts stayed longer, or had just one man remained in position, Langy's larger force would have been seen and disaster avoided. Unfortunately for Rogers and his rangers, the scouts did neither.

As Durantaye's party approached, the rangers opened the ambush with a devastating volley that felled dozens of Indians on the spot. Rogers was sure that his men would be able to wipe them entirely out, if they rushed the enemy immediately. The surviving French and Indians immediately fell back upon their own trail with Rogers and his men in hot pursuit. As the rangers rounded a bend in the creek, they suddenly came face to face with Langy's attacking force. "At that instant many of the rangers realized that they had made a terrible mistake, and for most, it would be their last." [BB-p.57]

In a matter of minutes, dozens of rangers were killed, wounded and scalped. Seeing what was happening, Rogers yelled for his men to fall back, but many were unable to do so, having been overrun by the Indians and outflanked by the Canadians who were attempted to cut off Rogers avenue of retreat. The rangers attempted to hold their positions while firing behind trees but the French and Indians were too numerous and the firing too heavy. Dozens of men were wounded, in addition to those rangers killed. A group of Rangers under Phillips became cut off from Rogers and was forced to surrender. The Indians immediately tied them to trees and then stripping them naked, cut them to pieces while they were still alive with knives and hatchets as retribution for the scalps that the rangers had taken earlier from their brothers.

Sensing total disaster as the sun began to set, Rogers gave the order for the surviving rangers to make their own escape back to the frozen lake any way that they could. Without hesitation the remaining men, including Rogers, made a run for it for the frozen lake, without their heavy overcoats and provisions which had to be left behind. Battling the cold, snow, fatigue and hunger, the remnants of the rangers walked for two days to Fort Edward, towing a few of the wounded on sleds. Robert Rogers was the last man in. The ranger captain had left the fort with 181 men. He returned with only 54 rangers, including several wounded, who died shortly after. Rogers and his men had suffered a crushing defeat for which he entirely took the blame, calling it a mistake in judgment, when he wrote in his report," I now imagined the enemy totally defeated." [CJ-p.78]

Searching for answers to explain the costly mistakes

In fact, the disaster that befell the rangers was the result of much more than one mistake alone. Rogers and his veteran officers were responsible for a host of tactical errors that could be laid at the feet of all of them. Piled together, the mistakes sealed the fate of the rangers. First, Rogers had to know that it would be virtually impossible to conceal the tracks of such a large body of men as he had, who were traveling on creepers over the ice, and on snowshoes single-file over land. One hundred and eighty one men made a distinct trail in the winter. It would be a mistake to presume that the French would be idle at Fort Carillon, and not have continuous patrols in the field searching for any signs of Englishmen in the area. With chances heavily favoring that enemy parties would especially scout the most likely avenues of approach to the Ticonderoga area, especially the frozen shores of nearby Lake George, it was paramount that Rogers leave sentries, scouts, or a rearguard of men behind him to deal with any enemy patrol crossing his men's obvious trail and give him this critical intelligence if they got away to the French fort. He had more than enough men to spare from his large force. Why he did not do so is a mystery, considering that Rogers had a premonition before leaving Fort Edward that his rangers were in for trouble.

Second, Rogers did not send but three scouts out ahead of his main body of men. He did not order any scouts out in the direction of the French fort to observe what was going on there, even when he was within a couple miles of Carillon. He had plenty of time to do so, as he did not begin to move his men on the fateful day of the battle until afternoon. By having scouts watching the fort from a distance to give him intelligence of enemy activity, he would have been forewarned that the increased activity within the fort that morning could only mean that the enemy knew of the presence of his rangers and were making preparations to attack. Such scouts would have observed the initial French and Indian force under Durantaye leave the fort in the direction of the rangers. Some of the scouts could have gone back to warn Rogers while the others, observing the fort to see if any reinforcements joined, would undoubtedly have spotted Langy's larger group leave about a half hour later.

As it was, Rogers had only three scouts a short distance away to rely upon, and from their position they were only able to spot Durantaye's approaching force. Confident after a few moments that no other French and Indians were coming, they left to inform Rogers, ruining any chance of detecting the larger force of Langy's closing the gap behind Durantaye. [BB-p.55] Thus the fate of the rangers was sealed. When Rogers gave the order to open the ambush with an initial volley of musket fire on Durantaye's force and then let his men abandon all caution and rush in on the escaping Indians, he did so with no scouts on his flanks to tell him that overwhelming enemy numbers were approaching to the sound of gunfire from just around the bend in the creek. Those pursuing rangers in the forefront would come face-to-face with this new threat with no chance to escape but to die to a man on the spot. When such mistakes were made in wilderness warfare against such implacable foes as the French and their Indian allies, the outcome was inevitable. Rogers lost over 130 men in the engagement. Many of them were irreplaceable seasoned veterans of ranging, and capable officers like Phillips. Some were personal friends. For Rogers, the debacle was part of the high cost of learning.

Deadly consequences when Rogers lets his guard down

One of the most important lessons that Rogers learned in the conduct of wilderness warfare was the need for rangers to keep a constant vigilance while in the field. Because of the total concealment that the heavy forest provided, the enemy could be anywhere. To protect against a surprise ambush or attack, the rangers had to be on the highest alert at all times and not let their guard down. In August 1758, while on a scout, Rogers broke this important rule himself and the consequences were deadly. The rangers had been called out to sweep the area east of Lake George to Wood Creek and South Bay of Lake Champlain to attempt to intercept a large party of French and Indian raiders. Rogers commanded a sizable force of rangers, Connecticut provincials, and regular light infantry numbering about 700 men. After scouring the area for a few days and finding no sign of the enemy, Rogers received orders to return to Fort Edward by the way that he came to search for another possible enemy force lurking in the area. He headed his force southward and reached the ruins of old Fort Anne, where he ordered camp to be made for the night. Observing his usual caution, sentries were posted and fires forbidden. [PF-p.319]

Having seen no sign of the enemy in days, Rogers relaxed his guard on the morning of August 8 and engaged in a target contest with an officer of the light infantry before setting out for Fort Edward. The shots that could be heard for miles reached the ears of a sizable French and Indian force of nearly 500 men under the marine Captain Marin. Immediately Marin sent out his scouts to reconnoiter the English, and then chose an ambush site along the trail headed south which the rangers were sure to follow. The shooting done, Rogers' force took up their packs and began marching south along the trail, with the Connecticut men in the lead. On a signal from Marin, the French and Indians let loose a terrible volley into the provincials, killing and wounding dozens of men. A battle ensued for an hour, with heavy casualties on both sides until Rogers was able to bring to bear all of his muskets and the French and their Indian allies broke into small parties and fled the field. Rogers remained on the battlefield to bury 49 rangers who died in the fight, not withstanding the provincial and regular casualties. Nearly an equal number of wounded rangers were carried to Fort Edward the next day on litters. As for Rogers' judgment, the Connecticut survivors are said to have questioned it at length when they reached Fort Edward. As they bore the brunt of the initial ambush, Rogers' carelessness had cost an exorbitant number of Connecticut lives needlessly. [BB-p.34]

Rules for surviving wilderness warfare

The lesson was ironic for Robert Rogers, for he had made the mistake of breaking one of his own rules of ranging which he wrote in the fall 1757 at Fort Edward. Rogers called his ranger's rules a "Plan of Discipline" which he presented to the British commander Lord Loudoun, William Shirley's successor. Loudoun was a military man who could appreciate the effectiveness of Rogers' ranger companies in the much different wilderness war that the British army was fighting in North America. Loudoun requested Rogers formally write down on paper his carefully thought-out ranging tactics so that regular army officers could be taught Rogers' unique methods of scouting. In writing down what he had learned at a high price about wilderness warfare from experience, Rogers' rules could "be claimed to be the first written manual of warfare in the New World," upon which fighting units in future wars would come to rely. [CJ-p.55]

Robert Rogers wrote 28 rules of ranging on paper, drawn from his knowledge of Indian tactics and scouting experiences. The rules were comprehensive. They covered nearly every situation that rangers could encounter in the field, operating against an enemy well versed in the same woodland tactics. The rules explained how to execute the tactics and for what reasons, in the hope that the rangers would be able to effectively maximize their advantages, minimize their own weaknesses, complete their mission and come back alive. They were rules for survival in wilderness war.

"March in a single file"

Rogers' first rule was that all rangers were to appear at every evening roll-call equipped with their musket, 60 rounds of ammunition, hatchet and gear for inspection. This was instituted so that rangers could march at a moment's notice "to be ready on any emergency" that might arise. Before dismissing the men, the officers were to appoint the guards and scouts chosen for the next day. Next, Rogers stated that when a small patrol was on a scout in enemy territory, they were to "march in a single file, keeping at such a distance from each other as to prevent one shot from killing two men." Further a scout was to be sent well ahead of the patrol with flanking rangers on either side at a distance, to be able to signal the patrol if an enemy was approaching. This tactic was a necessity when following a trail that wound its way through forest and brush where an advancing enemy on the trail would likely not be seen until the last moment. [CJ-p.54-59]]

Rogers worried that rangers would be easily detected by an enemy when they marched over soft or marshy ground where they would leave distinct footprints in the soil. He advised that rangers should march abreast across such ground "to prevent an Enemy from tracking us," due to the negligible prints that each man's singular steps would make when he was not in a column or file with other rangers. When deep in enemy territory, Rogers felt that it was imperative for rangers to march until dark before camping for the night so as to not give away their camp during the light of dusk to any lurking enemy scout. Further, they should chose the camp "on a piece of ground that afford your sentries the advantage of seeing or hearing the enemy" at a distance before they reached the camp. One half of the ranger force must alternatively stay awake during the night to protect against a night attack by the enemy against undefended sleeping men. [CJ-p.54-59]]

Before reaching the appointed place where the rangers were to scout or attack an enemy, it was important to stop the men some distance from that point and send one or two of the best men ahead, carefully, to "look out the best ground for making your observations" and for taking action. This was done so as to avoid blundering into any enemy sentries or ambushes which would compromise the entire mission. Another rule of Rogers stated that prisoners taken by the rangers were to be kept separate until they could be questioned at length, so that they could not corroborate between them any false stories or intelligence. Unwritten in the rules was a maxim that was nonetheless strictly followed. If the rangers were attacked and forced to retreat, all enemy prisoners in their possession were to be immediately executed with hatchets so that they could not give their comrades any intelligence on the Rangers if they escaped or were freed in the course of the retreat.

"Let your front fire, and then fall down"

Rogers strongly felt that it was important for rangers to return from a ranging mission by "a different route from that which you went out." This prevented an enemy who had discovered the ranger's line of march to prepare an ambush for any rangers foolish enough to retrace their steps on their return. By taking a different route a ranger had a better chance of knowing if he was being pursued, since the enemy would not know his intended route, but could only follow his trail. A pursuing enemy who was moving through the woods and making some degree of noise could be detected easier by one's rearguard than stationary hidden ambushers ahead. [CJ-p.54-59]

Large bodies of 300 to 400 rangers presented the need for special tactics when moving through the woods. When the ground permitted it, the men were to be divided into three columns marching single file, with flanking parties to the sides, rear, and far out front to prevent any opportunity of a surprise enemy attack. If the ranger force was attacked from the front, it was important to keep strong flanking parties of men out, "to prevent the enemy from pressing hard on either of your wings, or surrounding you." This tactic was designed to counter the Indian method of attacking hard on the flanks of the main body, as was done against Braddock, with the intent of "surrounding you, which is the usual method the savages, if their number will admit of it." Braddock's force was enveloped and decimated when his small, weak flanking parties were easily driven in by the Indians. [CJ-p.54-59]

Rogers devised rules for attacking an enemy force. His innovative tactics were suited to wilderness warfare, and far different from conventional European linear tactics. Contrary to regulars who stood in a line when delivering and receiving fire, Rogers advised that when a group of the enemy was about to fire on the rangers that his men should "fall or squat down till it is over, and then rise up and discharge your weapons at them." Since the enemy had just fired over the ranger heads without inflicting any casualties, they would be caught in the act of reloading empty weapons when the rangers fired. If an enemy force attempted to push forward with an attack, Rogers devised countermoves. "Let your front fire and fall down, and then let your rear advance thro" them and do the like, by which time those who before were in the front will be ready to discharge again." By repeating this tactic over and over, the enemy would be faced with a continuous constant face of musket fire from advancing rangers which would force them to fall back or be killed. If the enemy fled under pressure, as the French and Indians did during the initial phase of the Battle on Snowshoes, Rogers added that it was of utmost importance to "be careful in your pursuit of them, to keep out your flanking parties" to prevent the arrival of undetected enemy reinforcements. When Rogers did not heed this rule at that fateful battle, the consequences were disastrous. [CJ-p.54-59]]

"At first dawn of day, awake your whole detachment"

Another rule covered organized retreat. Falling back before an advancing enemy could be done in the reverse manner as the fighting ranger advance. Two lines of rangers several yards apart could alternate their fire and leave the field of battle. Each line would cover the withdrawal of the previous with loaded weapons to prevent the enemy from rushing by presenting them with a constant face of line of fire which they would not be able to overwhelm. Such a controlled systematic retreat could continue for a great distance if need be until a tired or frustrated enemy disengaged. However, in the case of overwhelming enemy odds that threatened to surround a ranger force, Rogers determined to "let the whole body disperse, and every one take a different road to the place of rendevous" that was predetermined, and altered on a daily basis to prevent a captured ranger confessing under torture the appointed location, which would doom everyone. If the rangers became surrounded Rogers advised everyone to "form yourselves into a square in the woods, a circle is best, and if possible, make a stand till the darkness of night favors your escape." It went without saying that all enemy prisoners should be killed before breaking out. [CJ-p.54-59]]

Rogers had more rules on battlefield tactics to deal with any maneuver needed to attack an enemy or receive an attack from any direction under different conditions, depending on how an enemy faced the ranger force. If the rangers were advancing, and suddenly attacked from the rear, "the main body and flankers must face about to the right or left, as occasion shall require, and form themselves to oppose the enemy," Rogers stated. His reasoning was simple. If you turned your men quickly to face an advancing enemy and then engaged them, you could move other men to the offensive and develop countering tactics of your own while those facing the enemy held them in check. Other battlefield tactics were equally simple. If an enemy was rushing to attack, hold your fire and then volley for maximum effect when they were close, and immediately rush them then with hatchets while they were still reeling from the devastating fire. Likewise, if the rangers needed to rally after falling back to face a pursuing enemy, "endeavor to do it on the most rising ground you can come at," which would give the men the advantage of firing on an enemy below them. [CJ-p.54-59]]

Further rules covered the placement and duties of sentries around camp, and procedures for them in case they detected an enemy approaching. Other rules dealt with the use of boats and the particular situations that could arise for rangers when traveling on waterways. Rogers wrote rules on how to bring a ranger force out of enemy territory intact. First, vigilance by all rangers was a necessity. They were to constantly look for signs that the enemy had anticipated the ranger's return route and were ahead of them, planning to intercept them when they least expected, and often close to the ranger's fort or base. Early morning was a particular dangerous time for rangers as they arose from the night camp. Rogers wrote, "At first dawn of day, awake your whole detachment; that being the time when the savages chose to fall upon their enemies." Rogers wanted his men to always be ready for such an attack. Before leaving camp, he advised that small parties of men should be sent out to scout around the camp, to "see if there be any appearance or track of an enemy that might have been near you during the night." If tracks were found, scouts could alert the main force that the camp had been discovered by the enemy and an attack or ambush was imminent. [CJ-p.54-59]

"To preserve a firmness and presence of mind on all occasions"

When returning on a trail, Rogers knew that it was human nature for rangers to let their guard down the closer that they got to home. Consequently, he wrote that rangers should avoid the usual fords across rivers which would be a likely place for an enemy ambush. If passing by lakes, rangers were to keep "at some distance from the edge of the water" where they either could be spotted from the other shore, or attacked with their backs to the water with no avenue of escape. Finally, when the rangers were within a couple miles of their fort, it was necessary to "avoid the usual roads and avenues thereto," in case the enemy had circled around and headed off the rangers, preparing an ambush along the main trail to the fort that the rangers were most likely to take when they were "almost exhausted with fatigues." The same held true if the rangers were following an enemy scouting party that were discovered to be near a fort or camp. Danger lay in following the enemy's tracks because their rearguard would be on their highest alert for pursuing rangers, and likely to set an ambush. Rogers cautioned his men to study the direction of the enemy's tracks, and then "endeavor, by a different route, to head and meet the enemy in some narrow pass, or lay in ambush to receive them when and where they least expect it." [CJ-p.54-59]

All of Rogers' rules were tactics based on moves and countermoves against an enemy, designed to gain military initiative and advantage over that foe. He did not derive them from either French or English conventional tactics, but rather, intensely studied the movements of Indian war parties in battle in the wilderness, and took from them their own tactical strengths while keeping in mind a way of countering those same strengths with specific moves. Thus the rangers could use tactical moves against an enemy that they knew how to counter when used against them. Rogers reasoned that he could out-think and out-maneuver Indians in battle every time through superior command of his men tactically. Musket for musket may be equal, but to Rogers, the grasp of tactics was not, and he felt that tactical advantages made the difference on the battlefield. However as his own experience demonstrated, one wrong decision, hesitation or error in judgment could have deadly consequences against a ruthless determined enemy who allowed no room for a second chance, nor any quarter for those whom they defeated.

In summing up his rules for ranging, Rogers believed that while knowing the rules was important, the ability of his men to grasp and implement them as a situation called for was more significant. He said, "Such in general are the rules to be observed in the ranging service; there are however, a thousand occurrences and circumstances which may happen that will make it necessary in some measure to depart from them and to put other arts and stratagems in practice; in which case every man's reason and judgment must be his guide, according to the particular situation and nature of things; and that he may do this to advantage, he should keep in mind a maxim…to preserve a firmness and presence of mind on every occasion." The men had to be better than the written rules. Each ranger had to do more that simply know the tactics of ranging in Rogers' manual. Many regular officers from the British army might try to emulate the rangers by studying Rogers' tactics, but something was always missing. In essence, the rules of ranging had to be instilled in a ranger's head and become a part of him. In understanding the tactics of the Indians he must become, by second nature like an Indian. How else would a Ranger be able to "get that feeling" that he was being watched by the unseen eyes on an enemy, "smell" an ambush ahead of him on the trail, or "feel" that an enemy force would break and run if pressure were immediately applied to their left, by flanking them? Essentially, Rogers knew that a good ranger needed to develop an "instinct" for ranging, as he believed Indians possessed. Without that instinct a Ranger might misread or overlook an important sign along a trail, pause too long at a stream for a drink, doze off during sentry duty while deep in enemy territory, or light a fire to keep from freezing when to do so meant certain death. Instinct would keep him alive. To Rogers, the quintessential ranger could be described as the man who had become the rules, instilling them in his very being rather than learning them. The proof of a Ranger possessing this instinct would be simple. He would be one of the men who lived to tell about the wilderness war when it was over. [CJ-p.54-59]

The St. Francis Expedition

Rogers had yet to prove to the British army the offensive capability of his ranger corps on a large scale, which he believed they could accomplish. He was sure that his rangers could go and do what no regulars or light infantry battalions were capable of in a wilderness war. In early September 1759, Rogers received orders from General Amherst, commander in chief of British forces in North America, to mount a daring, punitive raid against the Abenaki Indian tribe at their village of St. Francis in French Canada. The problem lay in the fact that St. Francis lay nearly 200 miles north of Ticonderoga very deep in enemy territory. To reach it, Rogers and his men would have to tackle some of the roughest, most inhospitable terrain that lay between them. Amherst directed Rogers to attack St. Francis if he could, and teach the Abenaki a lesson for capturing and torturing two envoys that Amherst had sent to the French under a flag of truce. Rogers was eager to attempt the mission, for added reasons.

The Abenaki were considered by him to be the fiercest and most savage Indian allies of the French, who had been raiding the northern New England frontier with impunity for years. These Indians, though nominally Christianized by French Jesuit missionaries, nonetheless burned, tortured and killed countless English men, women, and children without distinction or mercy. The scalps of over 600 victims hung from poles among the 40-odd huts at St. Francis. Amherst gave Rogers instructions to gather over 200 of his best men along with a handful of Mohawk scouts and Stockbridge Mohicans and set out against St. Francis, reminding him to "take your revenge, but don't forget that those dastardly villains have promiscuously murdered women and children of all ages, it is my order that no women or children be killed or hurt." [PF-p.385] Rogers would have no trouble remembering the deeds of the Abenaki, having seen for himself the pitiable scalped and mutilated corpses of his New Hampshire neighbors since he was a boy. Rogers was not an educated European gentleman officer like Amherst. As Amherst ordered, he would take the war directly to the Abenaki when and where they least expected it. However Rogers intended to do more than simply punish the Abenaki if he got to St. Francis. If it were in his power, Rogers would see to it that these inhuman savages, the pariahs of the English frontier, were completely destroyed. If his raid were successful, it would be a testament to the character, courage, training, and perseverance of the men of his ranger corps, who were able to go and do what no other British military unit was capable of accomplishing anywhere in the wilderness.

"The surprise was complete"

On the night of September 13, Rogers set out with his force by boat on the first leg of the journey. The rangers carried 30 days' rations and a quantity of powder and lead in their packs. For days they rowed, carefully bypassing French sentries on Lake Champlain until they neared the northern end of the lake. Along the way, Rogers lost almost a fifth of his men to sickness and accidents that he was forced to send back in small parties. At Missisquoi Bay, Rogers carefully hid the boats and set out with his remaining men on foot for the northeast, leaving Stockbridge Indian scouts behind to watch the boats. On the evening of the second day of his overland march through swamps and thick forests, the Stockbridge scouts came into the ranger camp with the startling news that a force of over 400 French and Indians had discovered and burned the boats, and were now making their way towards the rangers, intent on destroying them. With his avenue of retreat cut off, Rogers considered the situation and wrote, "Being so far advanced in their country, where no reinforcements could possibly relieve me, our boats being taken, cut off all hope of retreat by them, besides the loss of our provisions left with them." [CJ-p.104] Conferring with his officers, Rogers determined to push on to St. Francis and complete the mission, and then return by a different route to the southeast through virgin wilderness to Lake Memphremagog and then south to the reaches of the Connecticut River. By doing so he could possibly outwit the French and avoid them entirely. It was a plan that might work if his men could cover the great distance.

On the evening of October 5, 22 days after setting out on the mission, Rogers and his 141 effective rangers arrived undetected at St. Francis and lay in wait for a dawn attack. Rogers scouted the Indian town of over 40 houses, four stone buildings under construction, a Jesuit church, and an assortment of huts and outbuildings. He observed that Indians were preoccupied with dancing and drunken revelry and no sentries were posted around the village. Rogers deployed his men and waited for the first light of dawn. At 6 a.m. Rogers gave the signal for the attack to commence, and as the rangers struck the village, they found the Abenaki still asleep in their beds. "The surprise was complete." [PF-p.107]

"Fell victim to the fury of the Indian women"

Seeing dozens upon dozens of fair-haired English scalps dangling from poles in front of the huts, the rangers struck the Indians with fury and vengeance. The Abenaki were shot down, bayoneted, tomahawked and burned alive in their huts in the merciless slaughter. Rogers estimated over 200 Abenaki men, women, and children were killed before all resistance ceased. The rangers put the entire village to the torch and destroyed the Jesuit church as well. By 7 a.m., in less than an hour's time, the work was done and St. Francis and its Abenaki inhabitants ceased to exist. Rogers took account of his men. One Stockbridge Indian scout had been killed. One ranger was seriously wounded and six others lightly. He ordered the rangers to fill their packs with Abenaki corn and prepare to march. Rogers had little time to waste. Information gathered from a handful of prisoners and freed white captives confirmed that a sizable force of French and Indians were less than a day's march away at a nearby village called Wigwam Martinique. Rogers knew that their scouts would see the high plume of black smoke curling in the air from the St. Francis inferno and would come running. Greatly outnumbered, the rangers had no time to lose. Shortly after 7 a.m. Rogers ordered his men to begin moving.

The arduous trip back was one filled with incredible hardship and suffering. The provisions of corn gave out, and the Rangers began to starve. When the men split up into smaller parties to try to hunt for game, several were overtaken by French and Indian pursuers and cut to pieces. Others who were able to elude the enemy, continued on the march, eating what nuts, berries, roots, and leaves they could find. Some hungry rangers resorted to eating their leather cartridge boxes and straps. A few men who were starving came upon the mangled, scalped remains of their comrades, and resorted to eating human flesh to survive. [CJ-p.110] Eventually, the small bands of rangers straggled into the English posts along the Vermont and New Hampshire frontier and were saved, though some died there, "miserably of the effects of famine and exhaustion," from the return trip. [PF-p.387] The rangers who came in had "suffered every hardship which men could endure" having traveled over 230 miles through the wilderness from St. Francis. Rogers and his rangers had successfully completed their mission, at a cost of a number of men killed, wounded, or captured by the enemy, as well as a few who were missing in the wilderness.

French accounts of the raid differed from that told by Robert Rogers. They claimed that the rangers killed only 30 Indians at St. Francis and not "the 200 of which Rogers claimed." [CC-p.178] After the attack, the Abenakis tracked down the rangers and killed over 40 of them. Ten prisoners were captured whom the Indians carried back to their village where they "Fell victim to the fury of the Indian women, nothwithstanding the efforts the Canadians could make to save them." [CC-p.178] The numbers did not matter. The raid had been a success. St. Francis was obliterated and many Abenaki killed. Though they could easily rebuild the village, the Abenaki would never recover from the shock of the raid. Since the Abenaki for decades "were accustomed to sustaining minimal casualties in battle and eluding pursuit by their enemies," [CC-p.179] the psychological effect of the ranger raid on the heart of the Abenaki homeland constituted a disaster for them. Though Abenaki warriors were still capable of fighting, they no longer had the heart for it after Rogers' raid. The fall of St. Francis ultimately contributed to the fall of French Canada which could no longer count on the protection of the Abenaki.

The "White Devil" creates an elite fighting force

The St. Francis raid was the proof that the rangers were up to any task that could be conceived in fighting a wilderness war which previously was thought impossible. This was due to Major Robert Rogers' effort and commitment to promote his corps of rangers within the British military establishment and prove their worth. Regular officers within the British army in North America who studied Rogers' tactics and advocated the development of regular light infantry companies, as opposed to rangers, were disgusted to find that regular light infantry who were trained in ranger tactics, failed when put to task. At Ticonderoga in 1758, it was General Thomas Gage's Light Infantry who were to replace the rangers and lead the way through the dense forest for General Abercrombie's invasion army after the initial landing. They failed miserably in the woods, losing their way, and blundering into a French scouting party, during which General Howe was killed. [RR-85] On the return trip from St. Francis, it was a group of 18 men under Lieutenant Dunbar of Gage's Light Infantry accompanying the rangers who were attacked by pursuing French and Abenaki. Dunbar and 11 of the men were killed. [CJ-p.110] Rogers' success and the dismal performance of Light Infantry units in general elevated the ranger corps to permanent status, in spite of Gage's negative attitude.

In the course of the war, Rogers had done far more than lead a stunning large-scale raid deep into French territory. In creating the concept of provincial Englishmen organized into companies of rangers and trained to fight like Indians and the French partisans, Rogers had gone beyond merely writing a manual of tactics pertinent to wilderness warfare. He elevated the concept of rangers from scouting parties into an elite fighting force capable of out-thinking, out-fighting, out-pacing and out-maneuvering any Indians or partisan troops that the enemy could field. Though the road had been rocky for the development of rangers, and not without setbacks along the way, Robert Rogers had brought the ranger corps into its own element, and earned for him personally the name "Wabo Madohondo, the White Devil" by his Indian adversaries, for his exploits. [LB-p.132] Through the rangers, Rogers had come to write his own chapter in lessons of wilderness warfare that in years to come, would once again raise the specter of green-coated men of the British Crown traversing the wilderness far beyond their own lines to lay waste to a new unsuspecting enemy on the frontier.

Chapter 6

Caught Between Two Worlds: The White Indians of the Wilderness

Had the English provincial rangers won the wilderness war with the French? While the rangers had played decisive roles in the outcome of fighting along the French frontier, as the battleground shifted from the forested wilderness separating New France from New England to the farmlands of French Canada, so did the tactical advantage of rangers acting against French partisans and Indians diminish. A Corps of several hundred rangers had been created by Rogers to counter the French partisans and their Indian allies in the unique irregular style of Indian warfare in the wilderness of the English colonial frontier. However, when Quebec fell to Wolfe's British army assault in late 1759 and French Canada was defeated, neither Rangers, Indians nor partisans had much impact. The French and Indian War which had begun in the wilderness, ended on a conventional battlefield, fought between opposing armies of regular troops. An uneasy peace settled over the colonial frontier abutting the wilderness of the Indians, broken once briefly by Pontiac's Indian uprising against British rule. It would take more than a decade before a new wilderness war would erupt.

In the coming war, more devastating than the previous, provincial English rangers would be called upon again, this time to fight with Indians under the same flag against the common enemy, the rebellious American colonials. This new breed of rangers, equally of scant numbers, would by necessity, need to work hand-in-glove with large parties of Indian warriors from many tribes to mount offensives in a wilderness war far different from that which Rogers and his men had faced. To do so effectively, they would need the help of a class of Englishmen not seen before on the colonial frontier, to bridge the gap, just as the French Canadians and their partisan brothers had done, between the world of the red man and that of the white. Without the pivotal role of capable go-betweens, the wilderness war could not have been fought with such ruthless effectiveness by the British.

Though English rangers had made an important impact during the conflict with the French, still, at the heart of wilderness warfare in North America in the latter half of the 18th century were the feared denizens of the deep forest. Hideous-painted Indian warriors could attack without warning and disappear quickly without a trace on their hit and run raids. These fighting men of the Native

American woodland tribes from the St. Lawrence River to the Great Lakes, from the Mohawk Valley to the western Seneca, and from the lands to the west in the Ohio Country were still intact, despite disease and war casualties. While at peace, they opposed any colonial expansion into their lands, and held the potent threat to attack frontier interlopers as effectively as they had raided the frontiers of New England and New France in the by-gone war, just as they had, as ancestral enemies, waged war against each other prior to the arrival of the white men.

For generations, Iroquois and Huron warriors raided each other across the woodland wilderness with regularity in countless campaigns seeking blood vengeance, hunting grounds, plunder, and captives from their enemies. [TE-p.28] With the influx of Europeans to the continent, the face of Indian warfare changed forever as contact with the white men widened, and Indians traded furs for guns, powder, and lead. Tribal allegiances shifted, and became more complex, as Indians jockeyed for trade with the white man. In exchange for weapons and goods, Indians were willing to support the whites in their conflicts, beginning as early as 1609. The Europeans and Indians, however different, could never be separate. War was the tie that would bind them.

Learning to fight as the French had done

During that summer of 1609, the French explorer Champlain accompanied a war party of Huron from his fort at Quebec, who were headed south on a raid into Iroquois territory. Encountering a large party of Mohawks at Ticonderoga at the south end of the great lake later named after him, Champlain and his men fired their muskets at the advancing warriors, [HE2-p.21] killing several of the Huron's hated blood enemies, and forcing them to retreat. Subsequently, the Iroquois were forced to seek support from the Dutch, and then the English in years to come, to obtain the white man's weapons, used to retaliate against both the Huron and the French in the widening wilderness war, fought for revenge. White men who could understand the Indians were needed as liaisons and advisers.

In turn, as the French, Dutch, and English hungered for more land to expand their colonial empires and more furs to fuel their own lucrative trade ambitions, war between the wilderness colonies became an inevitability as these European rivals fought for supremacy. While looking upon the Indians contemptuously as savages, the French and English were compelled nonetheless to seek Indian allies from the Huron and Iroquois Leagues to their own interests, including ultimate sovereignty and control of North America. Indians would be the means to bring about victory over colonial rivals on the frontier of the wilderness. While new weapons changed the face of wilderness warfare, the methods did not. The impassable forests, valleys and streams did not lend themselves well to the movement of conventional European armies. This dictated that only Indians and white men who could fight like Indians would be able to navigate the impassable roadless lands to wage war.

However, key to maximizing the effectiveness of Indians in their particular tactical style of wilderness warfare lay not directly with the Indians, but with a special breed of white men who acted as go-betweens. They would need to be more than Rangers who could fight like Indians. To fight as the French partisans had done, these Englishmen had to be able to speak the native languages, understand tribal beliefs, and know implicitly the Indian mind to effectively motivate and direct them in a war which many Indians needed to be convinced was in their best interests to fight. This Rogers and his men had not done. He had no need to fight alongside large Indian forces. Though Rogers had a handful of Stockbridge Indian scouts under his command in the field, he generally despised Indians too much to work in any greater capacity with the Indian allies at his disposal, preferring instead to develop his corps of rangers from colonial backwoods men like himself. Looking only at the limitations of Indians, Rogers and his rangers did not see their intrinsic value in wilderness war.

However, the French were to accomplish this task. Extensive trade with the native tribes within the greater realm of New France cultivated a class of Frenchmen and their mixed-blood children known as French Canadians, or "couriers des bois," who lived with the Indians in their villages, and traveled to the French posts to buy and sell goods and furs between the red and white worlds. The nature of French colonial expansion and the Roman Catholic Church allowed culturally for intermarriage with the Indians, as did their tribal societies, who saw little difference in the color and breed of those adopted into the tribe. In battle, the French Canadians would fight with their Indian brethren rather than with French regulars or marines. Being of French and mixed-blood allowed them to effectively play the role of both interpreter and liaison between Frenchmen and warriors on the battlefield when the occasion arose. French officers could know what their Indian allies were thinking and wanting to do, through the words of the French Canadians who acted as betweens. In warfare in the wilderness, this was an advantage and convenience of extreme importance.

For the English, the situation was far different. Only a handful of men, mostly traders on the frontier with the Indians of the Ohio Country, New York, Pennsylvania, and the Hampshire colonies, lived with the Indians and intermarried. By the time that the first Englishmen ventured into Indian lands to the north in the 1730s and 40s and west of the Allegheny Mountains in the early 1750s, the Indians they encountered were already allied to the French and in no mood to allow English expansion into their lands jointly claimed under the protection of New France. When wilderness warfare with the French became a reality, the English were greatly disadvantaged. They had virtually no Indian allies. While William Johnson was instrumental in paving the way for the Mohawks and Iroquois Confederacy to align themselves with the English against the French, it would take seven years of wilderness war for a new breed of Englishmen to emerge on the frontier that shared Johnson's empathetic vision of Indians, and understood his methods.

English prisoners of the Indians

Why did it take so long for the English when the need was so pressing to have white men, specifically Englishmen, who were able to bridge the world of the Indian and the English colonial with the blessing of both? This group of men in question was not from the same mold of William Johnson, nor the "courier des bois" of French Canada. Rather than being the bridges between the world of the Indians and the white men, this new group of Englishmen to emerge on the frontier in the early 1770s had been the victims of the previous wilderness war. Caught between both worlds, red and white, ultimately they found they belonged to neither. Disenfranchised and scorned by white frontier society for what had befallen them as children, these white men would come to play pivotal roles for the British in the future wilderness war yet to be fought. They were some of the hundreds of English children who were captured by the Indians in the French and Indian War, who spent many of their formative years growing up adopted into the tribes and immersed in their culture. When repatriation forced them back to an English frontier society they had all but forgotten, they had great difficulty making the adjustment. Though their skin was white, their hearts remained Indian, and their minds dwelt somewhere in between.

How and why had these colonial English children been captured by the Indians? Taking enemy prisoners was an essential and natural part of Woodland Indian warfare, practiced before the arrival of the white man to North America. Early Europeans found that all of the tribes waging war with each other routinely took prisoners of their enemy when the opportunity arose. Sometimes, taking prisoners was the sole purpose of the raiding the enemy. The Huron were observed by the French explorers to set out every year in the spring and summer for enemy Iroquois country, where they would break up into small groups of five or six warriors and "lay flat on their bellies in the fields and woods and along the main paths and at night prowled about and even entered the villages to capture a man, woman, or child. [TE-p.29]

In some instances, captives were taken specifically to avenge the death or capture of one of the tribe's members at the hands of the enemy. The warriors would take their prisoners back to their village and give them to the family that was grieving the loss of a loved one. When this was done the declared vow of vengeance against the enemy could be fulfilled. "These captives were either adopted into the family or were tortured to death" [TE-p.28] by that family as retribution for their loss. It mattered not to them that the prisoner who was about to die a terrible death was not the one who had been personally responsible for the previous murder, torture, or capture of their loved one. The cause of the wars between Indian tribes may have been complex and many, but the desire for vengeance to correct a grievance was as strong as any motivation. Therefore the need for taking enemy prisoners in war was shared equally by all Indians whether they were Abenaki, Huron, or Iroquois.

Europeans who came in contact with the Woodland tribes were horrified to find that more often than not, prisoners were taken in war simply for savage enjoyment, to "put them to death over a slow fire." [HU-29] Champlain first discovered this to be true in 1609 after his encounter with the Iroquois. About a dozen Iroquois prisoners were seized by the Huron when the battle was over. After traveling some distance to safety, the Hurons lit a fire and selected a prisoner, whom they began to burn slowly. "After listening for a while to the shrieks of the unhappy victim he (Champlain) begged the tormentors to put the wretch out of his misery," [TE-p.23] Unfazed, the Hurons continued, until a Frenchman who could stand it no longer put an end to the prisoner's agonies. The Hurons promptly cut the victim's heart out.

Torturing prisoners to death by burning was ritual sport for every tribe. Prisoners usually were brought back to the village where they were slowly burned alive in a most deliberate ritualistic manner that "might last five or six days." [TE-p.33] Such village burning of enemy prisoners was done as much for the enjoyment of the tribe as retribution against their enemy. By burning their victim slowly so he would not die quickly, it was hoped that the victim would cry out in pain and anguish before he expired, which would please the members of the village. When a prisoner shrieked out as he was burned, "the whole crowd imitated his cries, or rather smothered them with shouts." [HU-37] After a pause in the burning of a particular victim in order to revive him, the youth of the village assembled to begin torturing him again, taking turns "to devise other methods to make him feel the fire more keenly," [TE-p.37] thus involving all members of the tribe. If the prisoner were brave and did not cry out much, then a great feast would be held after his death, whereupon the Indians would drink his blood and cook and eat his dismembered flesh with relish, "in order to be courageous also." [TE-p.39] The Mohawks after the Battle of Lake George in 1755 wished William Johnson to deliver the wounded French commander Baron Dieskau to them as a gift. The Mohawks wished to burn Dieskau in revenge for the death of their comrades and then cut him up for their cooking pots to eat him in respect for the man's courage, as was their custom, but Johnson could not acquiesce. [FJ1-p.151]

Who was to be adopted and who was not

Early French, Dutch, and English explorers to the interior lands of the most populous Woodland Indian tribes of the Huron and Iroquois nations, found them alike in this respect. They all indulged in taking and killing of prisoners to torture and eat. Many men besides Champlain observed these Indian raids against Indians for the purpose of taking captives. On one Huron raid, observed by the Jesuit Sagard, "they captured about 60 of the enemy, most of who were killed on the spot, and rest brought back alive, put to death, and then eaten at a feast." [TE-p.29] Another Jesuit priest recorded the words of an Huron torturer to his Iroquois victim, during the course of burning him. Taunting the victim, the Huron asked, "But let us see, were you not very cruel to prisoners? Now just tell us, did you not enjoy burning them?" [TE-p.38] When the victim had almost expired from the cruelest burning, he was dismembered alive and eaten, for the Hurons feared that he "would die other than by the knife." [TE-p.38]

The Iroquois nations were equally cruel in their treatment of prisoners taken in war from the Hurons, and practiced the same methods. When the Huron tribes accepted the French Jesuit priests into their country in the 1630's, the Jesuits themselves became victims of Iroquois torture when they were captured with the Huron and brought back to Iroquois villages in the Mohawk River valley and beyond. Jesuits like Brebeuf and Lallemant were burned alive by the Mohawks during this period. Father Isaac Jogues, himself made prisoner by the Mohawks in 1642, was forced to watch the slow burning to death of his Huron companions while enduring initial tortures and then captivity as a slave, until his release to the Dutch at Albany. Jogues recounted his initial capture and torture. He was beaten by the Mohawks and then endured having "most of his fingernails torn out by the roots, ripped off by Indian teeth." Then a Mohawk "chewed one of the priest's forefingers until the bone was crushed and splinters of it protruded." [FT-27] In addition to the torture, many times he was forced along with the other captives to run the gauntlet when arriving at a village of his captors.

The running of the gauntlet by prisoners was a universal practice among the Woodland tribes. Typically, when a war party arrived at a camp of their fellow warriors or returned to their own village, the newcomers would alert everyone by screaming the "sharp, high-pitched war whoop to indicate the number of scalps and prisoners they had taken." [WP2-p.49] The entire village, including women and children, would rush to cut clubs and switches, "and then run out to meet them, placing themselves in two rows," [WP2-p.49] to prepare for the running of the gauntlet by the prisoners. Commonly, in preparation for the prisoner to run, he or she would be stripped of all clothes, and sometimes had their arms bound tightly behind them. [TE-p.32] Then a warrior would point out to them a house or post at the end of the two opposing lines of Indians that they must pass through to end their ordeal. He would give them the order to run, and if they did not do so, were likely kicked or thrown ahead into the gauntlet of waiting Indians. Typically, "as soon as they set out, the people begin to strike at them with switches, clubs, hatchets or their fists. If they gain the house or post, though ever so bruised and bloody, they are perfectly safe"[WP2-p.50] for the moment. If a prisoner fell, or was knocked unconscious, he risked being condemned to torture, or killed on the spot, depending on the mood of the villagers.

Father Jogues suffered more torture when forced to run the Mohawk gauntlet. As he could make it only half way, he "fell to the ground beneath the blows. Then he was further mishandled, a fingertip burned, another crunched by Indian teeth, and threatening gestures made of cutting off his nose," [HE2-p.27] before his angry captors spared his life. However, once the prisoner ran the village gauntlet, a final decision was made by the chief concerning the victim's ultimate fate. Most male warriors were condemned to die by slow burning for the edification of the village, or to repay a bereaving family desiring retribution.

An enemy warrior would be painted black [WP2-p.50], and be told to prepare to die a terrible death, by singing to himself his "war song" taught to him in childhood to bolster his courage.

Generally, an enemy warrior was not adopted into the tribe. Women and children captives were most often treated differently by the Woodland tribes, and were seldom put to death or tortured by fire. These prisoners might be given away as gifts to families or other tribes, but more often than not, adoption into the tribe was the likely outcome. While many enemy warriors were killed or tortured before the raiding party returned to their village, women and children captives had to endure the hardships of the trip back. Sometimes it was not possible, and if the raiding warriors "were unable to carry off the women and children they had captured, they put them to death and carried off the heads or the scalp." [TE-p.31] If the captured made it back to their captor's village, their chances of adoption increased if they could run the gauntlet. If they were successful, their faces were painted red to mark them as likely candidates for adoption, if a family was willing to take them.

For the most part, adult women were considered less valuable than children, and so they quite often were designated slaves to either the family group or the tribe. Young, healthy women captives could be spared slavery by marriage to a warrior, with the hope of producing children for the tribe, to replace members lost to incessant warfare and disease. Of course, children of both sexes were prized. Adopted children were treated kindly by the family, "as if they were actually their own children" [HU-31] in every way and brought up in the tribe as a member of that tribe, foregoing all vestiges of their former lives. Adopted child captives often became greatly attached to those Indians who raised them. Young captured boys would grow up as warriors of their new adopted tribe and, without hesitation, would fight their birth tribe now their new enemy.

As France and England began to war with each other by the end of the 1600s, many Woodland Indian tribes in close proximity to New France, such as the Abenaki, Huron, Nippising, Algonquin, and Caughnawaga found it in their best interest to ally themselves to the French, in an attempt to stem the growing influence and presence of the English to the south. As war with the Iroquois lessened and conflict with the English increased, the Woodland tribes allied to the French, focused their raids on the English frontier in an attempt to devastate their settlements and drive the English back out of ancestral lands, thus maintaining the lucrative fur trade for themselves and the French. King Philip's War, which broke out in 1675, heralded the attacks by Abenaki and others against New England settlers. During dozens of raids against the English frontier, English men, women and children were taken captive by the Indians. One such raid in the fall of 1677 occurred when a party of 20 Abenaki warriors attacked the town of Hatfield in Massachusetts. The Abenaki took 17 white captives and three more from nearby Deerfield before hastily leaving for their villages in the north for fear that Mohawk war parties were nearby. [CC-p.84] Those English prisoners were but a few of dozens that trudged along mountain trails to a new life with the Indians, creating an unending stream of English captives during the latter years of the 1600s as war smoldered on.

During February 1704, a French force of 200 marines and Canadians with nearly 150 Abenaki and Caughnawaga warriors traveled over 200 miles through heavy snow to attack the Massachusetts town of Deerfield. On the morning of February 29, while Deerfield residents were still sleeping, the French and Indians assaulted the town, killing 50 people and burning it to the ground. As they retreated to Canada, they "carried off 109 captives," putting the numerous English children in sleighs, and tomahawking those prisoners "unable to keep up" on the hurried, grueling march to Montreal. [CC-p.103] Some of the prisoners were sold or "ransomed" to the French, however the vast majority of the English captives were taken back to the Abenaki villages for adoption.

"To Dry His Tears in the Fires"

Though ransoming a white prisoner, or selling them to the French for trade goods, weapons, and ammunition was a choice for the Indians, ransoming English prisoners was usually reserved for notable adult captives, such as military officers who had value to the French. As the French began to pay a bounty for English scalps, it became easier for the Indians to dispose of the adult captives without losing the bounty. "If too much encumbered with these (captives), they (the Indians) took the scalps with the hair on them and tanned them," stretching the skin over a wooden hoop to deliver for a bounty reward, or to keep as a trophy. [TE-p.29] For the dozens of English women and children who were not scalped, and who were not ransomed to the French, a new life with the Indians was beginning in earnest, as they were sent to the many Indian villages doting the forested landscape of the wilderness.

The fate of English captives was decided on their return with the Indian raiding party. As the Indians kept a grueling pace to outdistance any pursuers, many prisoners found themselves at some point, unable to keep up. Often, adult prisoners were loaded down with plunder from the previous raid, which they were forced to carry all the way back to the Indian villages. Any prisoner lagging behind or slowing the progress of the group due to wounds, sickness, infirmity of old age, complaining, or crying (as in the case of babies), was immediately killed with a tomahawk blow to the head, and then scalped. Prisoners were not shot as a musket shot was a waste of powder and lead, and more importantly, could give away the Indians' position if an English scouting party were nearby. The bloody corpses of friends, family, and children of the living prisoners would be left on the trail where they fell, adding to the misery of the captives. As the war party returned to the villages in the wilderness, surviving prisoners were divided equally among the tribes present in the raid, some to Abenaki warriors, and some to Huron or Caughnawaga if they had participated. Then each group of warriors took their respective captives back to their own separate villages to do with as they pleased, whether that be adopting, ransoming, enslaving, or burning the English.

The prisoners were given over to the old men of one of the villages who decided how the spoils of the war party should be distributed and held council "on which villages the prisoners should be bestowed" and to whom should be given a prisoner for adoption to replace a dead loved one, or "to dry his tears" in the fires of slow burning. [TE-p.34] Most often the English women and children were adopted and assimilated into the tribe.

Warriors among them who had once been white children

A French-allied Indian village, such as one of the many Abenaki villages on the wilderness frontier of the early 1700s was typically a heterogeneous mix of many people. Traditional Abenaki families lived in a community that was becoming "intertribal and interracial" as time went on. "In any village could be found traders, captives, spouses, refugees, and visitors from other groups." [CC-p.11] French Canadians and their mixed-blood children would mingle in the village and would trade goods obtained in Montreal for furs from the Indians. Equally present in the village were Indians adopted from enemy tribes as well as those enslaved by the Abenaki, as well as Indians from friendly tribes visiting the village, and many who had fled their home villages as refugees from the English, and decided to stay with the Abenaki. Into this mix were brought the English captives to be absorbed in the greater tribe as adopted sons or daughters, adult slaves to work the fields, or spouses for returning warriors. The assimilation of captives into the Woodland tribe "helped offset losses caused by disease and war," thus becoming a vital strategy for defense and survival. [CC-p.11]

As the English had few Indian allies until the entry of the Iroquois Mohawks in King George's War in 1745, they took few French or allied Indians captive during the many prior years of constant warfare across the frontier borders. The Iroquois were reluctant to adopt either French or Huron prisoners when they captured them, preferring to put them to death by slow fire, as in the case of the Jesuits. English settlers, scouts and militia who attempted to stem the Indian raids on their frontier were in no mood to take Indian captives, when that rare situation provided them an opportunity. They were enraged at the Indian depredations against their settlements which left homes in smoking ruins and the bodies of friends and family mutilated beyond recognition. When they could, the English retaliated and killed Indians immediately and without distinction.

In the years following the Deerfield Raid of 1704, some of those Indians killed were actually white captives adopted into the tribes. When a militia captain with a dozen men from Deerfield tracked some Abenaki Indians to the shores of Lake Champlain in the spring of 1707, they fired upon the group and "shot an Indian woman in the back. But when the soldier ran over to cut off her head with his hatchet, he found that he had killed a white captive, which very much startled him." [CC-p.105] The "captives trails" traveled frequently by French and Indian war parties in the first half of the 1700's became known simply "as the Indian Road" through Vermont from New England, over which more than 1,600 English were taken from New England, and by which most "disappeared without a trace, many into Abenaki villages" [CC-p.27] where they remained for the rest of their lives adopted by the Indians.

King George's War 1745-1748, the Seven Years War or French and Indian War fought from 1754 till 1760, and Pontiac's Conspiracy or Rebellion ending in 1763 saw a relentless cavalcade of innumerable white prisoners taken captive by the Indians from their English settlements and brought to several hundred native villages from the Ohio Country to the Great Lakes region and east across the wilderness bordering former New France to Quebec. Equally uncounted were the hundreds of Englishmen made up of soldiers, militia and scouts who were taken prisoner on the field of battle and slain, ransomed, or burned in village fires, for the Englishmen in military service were equal in this respect. The French-allied Indians had no desire to spare them for adoption, as they considered their English enemies not worth adopting. Of the more than 1400 men of Braddock's expeditionary force that was attacked on the banks of the Monongahela River in the Ohio Country in 1755, hundreds were killed or wounded during the battle and left by the retreating army. None of the wounded left on the field were claimed as prisoners, the Indians preferring only their scalps. About a dozen English soldiers who surrendered to the Indians on the battlefield were spared immediate death, only later to be stripped naked, bound and painted black. "These prisoners they burned to death on the banks of the Allegheny River opposite the fort (Duquesne)"[SJ-p.26] as part of the Indian victory celebration.

Such prisoners were valuable only for their ability to haul English goods plundered from raids back to villages, and to serve as a source of savage enjoyment or the object of retribution when they were slowly roasted in fires; or have a worth equal to an amount of trade goods when they were ransomed alive to French; or their scalp redeemed from their lifeless corpse for a bounty. In almost all cases, the Indians considered male English prisoners only a commodity in some form for their pleasure or commerce.

"Only five children, four girls and a boy were at home"

English women and children held better potential as valuable prisoners who could and would become adoptees. Though women and children were sometimes killed in raids during the French and Indian wars against the English, hundreds more were taken alive as captives, such as in the raid on Saratoga. In November 1745, 400 Frenchmen and over 200 Indians attacked the English settlement of Saratoga, only 30 miles north of Albany on the Hudson River. The town was burned and many residents killed, but the raiders took over 100 English captives with them. [FJ1-p.49] Some were destined for Montreal for ransom or exchange; some were taken by the Indians for torture but most were destined for adoption, not to be seen again even when the war ended in 1748, though most of those women and children taken by the Indians were still alive. Interestingly, in the course of fighting the Indians, English militia and scouts skirmished with Abenaki war parties that had warriors among them who had once been white children captured by the Indians years previous, such as in the

Deerfield Raid of 1704, or who were believed to be the descendents of English captives taken much earlier.

In June 1748 a militia company en route to Fort Shirley in Massachusetts was ambushed by Abenaki. "The Indian leader was said to be a chief named Sackett, reputedly the descendant of a white captive." [CC-p.156] An Abenaki Indian serving with the French in 1747 was "Joseph Louis Gill, the white chief of St. Francis Abenaki," [AB-156] an English child captive of the Indians, now grown into manhood. So when peace returned to the frontier, many white captives, now totally assimilated into life as Indians, did not make their way back to white civilization.

The brief respite between wilderness wars ended when war broke out again between France and England in 1754. New waves of English captives began filtering into the Indian villages to the north and west of the colonies as Indian war parties set out for the English frontier following Braddock's defeat in 1755. A floodgate of new white captives taken by the Indians was opened when the Pennsylvania frontier, particularly, east of the Allegheny Mountains came under intense attack by French and Indian raiding parties, both large and small, from Fort Duquesne. French Captain Coulon de Villiers's raid was a good example. With 23 men and over 100 Indians attacking, he forced English Fort Granville to surrender on July 22, 1756. The Indians with him killed the wounded and most of the men inside, while taking captive more than a dozen women and children who were destined for the Delaware Indian village of Kittanning for adoption. [BC-p.8] The French militiaman Chauvigniere, along with an Indian scalping party, described the taking of white captives on a raid on an English settler's cabin. "Only five children, four girls and a boy were at home…we took some clothes for the children and some provisions." Fortunately for the children, their parents were not at home at the time of the attack, or the adults would have likely died struggling with the Indians, along with any of the children who resisted. While it was apparent that the Indians placed value upon white women and children captives by sparing them in countless attacks against frontier settlements and homes, the Indians could be brutal when a situation arose that warranted it, in their minds.

"Take Leave of my Son for I would never see him again"

As the French and Indian wilderness war intensified across the frontier, Indian encounters with larger groups of English increased as did Indian casualties. Consequently, the number of white captives taken by the Indians grew from a few people to dozens upon dozens. In large battles, the Indians could become unpredictable and worse, uncontrollable, if taken to pillaging an enemy's supplies that included rum. Becoming captive was not always a guarantee of survival for women and children at the hands of drunken, bloodthirsty Indian warriors. After the fall of Fort William Henry to the French, the English garrison, which included over 100 women and an unknown number of children, was subjected to the uncontrollable butchery of the French Indian

Captured by the Indians!

allies following their killing frenzy of the English wounded. "All of the women and children, with the exception of one unidentified woman and child, were killed." [DE-p.95] They perished in a most terrible manner, "the throats of most, if not all, the women were cut, their bellies ripped open and the children were taken by the heels and their brains beat out against the trees and stones." [DE-p.90]

The French and Indian war against the Pennsylvania frontier settlements brought dozens of English prisoners to the tribes of the Ohio Country, that included the Shawnee, Mingo, Wyandot, Seneca, and Delaware whose villages stretched across the wilderness lands to the west and north of the Pennsylvania frontier. These Woodland tribes, allied to the French in the beginning of the war, had not undergone an influx of white captives prior to 1754, as had their Woodland brothers to the northeast, the Huron, Abenaki and Caughnawaga tribes, who had been fighting the English nearly 100 years prior. The tribes of the Ohio Country to the west of the Allegheny Mountains had simply not come in contact with white settlers, nor experienced war with the English until Washington's arrival. However, that changed abruptly after Braddock's defeat. Shawnee and Delaware war parties raiding the Pennsylvania frontier brought back with them English women and children to their villages along the dozens of rivers and creeks that fed into the Ohio, and west to the wilderness lands beyond.

The tribes of the Ohio Country took women and children captives primarily for adoption or marriage into the tribe, as did tribes of the Great Lakes region, and the Northeast. Adult white males were reserved for ransom to the French or slavery, which in both cases was better than death by scalping or the slow fire. Accounts of white captives taken by the Indians bear this out. However a few white adult males were captured and survived, such as Charles Stuart who was taken with his young son and daughter at the beginning of the war. A war party surprised Stuart, who was "captured by the Indians on October 29, 1755" at his home in Cumberland County, Pennsylvania with his young children and taken to Fort Duquesne and then across the Ohio River to Indian villages on the Muskingum River, where he met a party of Indians with other white captives. At a Shawnee town on one of the branches of the Scioto, he was told by the Indians that he would be their slave, and he was forced to part with his children and told by a chief "To Take Leave of My Son for that I would never see him again". [BR-p.24]

"Spent the next eight years with the Delaware"

Marie Le Roy was captured with her younger brother and a little neighbor girl when their cabin was attacked by Indians near the Susquehanna River in October 1755. The men of her family were killed outright; then the Indians moved on with their captives to a nearby cabin and slaughtered the adult men there, taking two more women prisoners, Barbara and Regina Leininger. The group was taken to the Delaware village of Kittanning in December 1755, and then on to Fort Duquesne months later. The women were used as slaves by the Delaware while the young children were separated and eventually taken to villages on the Muskingum River in the Ohio Country for adoption. [BR-p.30]

Hugh Gibson was a 15-year-old boy when captured by an Indian war party in 1756 near Carlisle, Pennsylvania, when his family was attacked and he witnessed his mother killed and another woman tomahawked. Taken to the village of Kittanning, and then on to Fort Duquesne, he resided at a Delaware village on the Mahoning River across the Ohio. There he encountered a 12-year-old captive taken from the Tuscaroras Valley in Pennsylvania, who lived as an adopted child of the Delaware. Gibson was adopted by a Delaware minor chief named Bisquittam, who took a Dutch captive as his wife. Later in 1758, at a village on the branch of the Muskingum River, Gibson encountered a captive German woman named Grove, who was awaiting marriage to a warrior. [BR-p.32]

John McCullough was an 8-year-old boy when he was captured in 1756 by Indians at his home near Fort Loudon in Pennsylvania. After his parents were killed the boy was taken prisoner with his younger brother, and "spent the next 8 years with the Delawares, wandering from place to place" in the Ohio Country from the Beaver River to the Cuyahoga, Walhonding, and Scioto rivers. During his repatriation in 1764, many white captives were delivered up by the Indians to General Bouquet's army as terms of the peace, including McCullough. On their way under guard to Fort Pitt, two white women, Rhoda Boyd and Elizabeth Studebaker made their escape, and "went back to the Indians." [BR-p.39]

How did the Indians determine if a captured white male was to be adopted or a candidate to be tortured to death, scalped, ransomed, or enslaved? Sometimes the fate of white males was determined at the time of capture, depending upon whether they attempted to fight off the Indians' war party. Warriors considered their enemy to be white Englishmen, armed or not. A farmer hoeing corn in a field was no less the enemy than a militiaman patrolling a trail. To the Indians, the enemy was to be attacked and killed; his scalp taken as a trophy of war fit for a bounty upon the warrior's return. The farmer in his field or cabin and any adult men of his family were considered by the Indians to be the enemy. If they did not surrender to the Indians but put up a fight or attempted to run away, they could expect to be killed on the spot by the warrior who happened to be closest to the victim. Rarely was an adult male spared unless the warriors needed a white man to carry a heavy load of plunder. The prisoner could expect no mercy once he reached the war party's destination with the heap of goods.

"I did not doubt that they were about to put me to death"

What was more important than anything else in determining whether a white male would be taken captive for adoption was the relative age of the prisoner and whether or not he was wounded at the time of his capture or if he put up a fight. Young boys and youths were prized as captives. The Indians knew instinctively that a white male up to the close of his teen years had the greatest potential for adoption into the tribe upon their return to the village. The older they were, the less pliable was their nature, or the more "white" the captive was, having thus less potential. If a warrior deemed the white teen male "too old" he was dispatched with a tomahawk on the spot, as were any younger males that were wounded or causing difficulty for their captors. Two cases of white male captives serve to illustrate the distinction.

James Smith, aged 18 was captured by a Delaware and Caughnawaga war party in May 1755 while cutting a road in the Pennsylvania wilderness near Bedford to supply Braddock's troops. Smith's companion was killed, but Smith offered no resistance to the Indians. He was then taken to Fort Duquesne and because of his age, forced to run the gauntlet. Halfway through it, he was knocked unconscious and taken into the French barracks to be treated by a doctor. Upon recovering, he asked a Delaware Indian the reason for his unmerciful treatment by the Indians and was told, "It was only an old custom, like saying how do you do." [SJ-p.24]

Smith witnessed from the fort walls the torture of a dozen English prisoners from Braddock's defeated army who were slowly burned to death during the Indian's victory celebration. A few days later the Indians took Smith from the fort up the Allegheny River to a village where he was adopted into the tribe. First his hair was plucked out except for a scalp lock, then his ears and nose pierced for rings, his clothes were stripped from him and his head, face, and body painted in various colors. Says Smith, "I knew nothing of their mode of adoption, and had seen them put to death all they had taken. As I never could find that they saved a man alive at Braddock's defeat, I made no doubt but they were about putting me to death in some cruel manner." [SJ-p.29]

Smith, in the company of the Caughnawagas went to a village deep in the Ohio Country near Lake Erie. In the spring of 1756, the warriors left to raid the English frontier of Pennsylvania and Virginia, taking with them all Indian males as young as age 12, but leaving him with the women, and a lame old man, as he was old enough that the Indians did not trust him not to attempt to escape. Throughout his captivity, Smith encountered Indian war parties returning with scalps, horses, other white captives, and plunder. Never did he forget who he was, or that he wished at an opportune time, to escape his captors, who kept a watchful eye on him. Finally, in April 1759, while with a group of Indians visiting a Caughnawaga Indian town close to Montreal, Smith made his escape to the French, and eventually was exchanged in November and returned to his home in Pennsylvania. [DF-p.60] While James Smith was willing to please the Indians during his captivity to ensure his survival after they adopted him, he nonetheless was old enough to maintain his white English mentality, with which he eventually made his way to freedom.

"To deliver to Fort Pitt all prisoners held by them"

The capture of the four Girty brothers tells a different story. The young brothers, Thomas aged 17, Simon aged 15, James aged 13, and George aged 11, were taken prisoner at the fall of Fort Granville in Pennsylvania to French, Shawnee and Delaware Indians in July 1756, along with their mother, Mary Girty Turner, their militia step-father John Turner, and their baby step-brother John. Loaded with plunder, they were taken along with other captives to the Delaware village of Kittanning, on the Allegheny River. There the boys and their mother witnessed the torture and burning of John Turner, who suffered terribly before dying. Then their mother and baby brother were separated from the boys and taken to Fort Duquesne by Delaware Indians, and then across the Ohio River. The four brothers believed that they would never see her alive again.

The Girty brothers were still at the village of Kittanning when it was attacked on the morning of September 3, 1756, by a force of Pennsylvania provincial troops under the command of John Armstrong. The eldest of the four Girty brothers was rescued by the militiamen during the intense fighting, along with 10 other white prisoners. Simon, George, and James were hurriedly taken across the Allegheny River into the woods by Indians. Later after the fighting, the boys were brought back to the village and witnessed the cruel burning death of a white woman captive who tried to run away and was brought back. The boys were forced to watch as the woman was slowly burned and mutilated, "from nine in the morning until sunset, when a French officer took compassion on her and put her out of her misery" with a musket shot. [BC-p.10] Three days later, "an Englishman was brought in, who had likewise attempted to escape with Colonel Armstrong and burned alive in the same village," while the three remaining Girty brothers watched.

Late in September, the Indians decided to abandon the village. The Girty boys were told that they were going to be split up for adoption among different tribes, and they would never see each other again. Simon was given to the Senecas of the Iroquois and taken to their village of Cattaraugus near the shores of Lake Ontario. George was adopted by the Delawares, and taken with a party of them to a village on the Scioto River in the Ohio Country. [EA-p.485] James, the youngest, was taken with the Shawnee to their principal village of Goschachgunk to the west, across the Ohio River. For the next four years, the three brothers became totally immersed in the Indian culture of each tribe, "speedily mastering the languages," adopting Indian dress, and learning the ways of living in the wilderness, as taught by the Indians. Unlike James Smith who was older than they were, the Girty brothers, once separated, soon gave up all thoughts of rescue, escape, or of their previous lives in Pennsylvania, as days turned into weeks, months, and years. For all practical purposes, their young ages and defenselessness signaled for each a true conversion to the Indian way of life that encompassed an understanding of all the accepted daily aspects of Indian culture from religion to the torture of prisoners. In reality, the Girty brothers became assimilated as Indians, in a degree relative to their youth. Simon was the least Indian of the three because he was the eldest, while George, the youngest was more Indian in identity than his two brothers, having the most pliable, culturally unencumbered mind of the three at age 11. Practically, their actions, moods, and very thoughts gradually dwelled no longer in the white world that they were born into, as the Indian language replaced English, and interior thinking was shaped by the Indian tongue that integrated their character into an Indian identity. The Girtys, like other young white male captives kept by the Indians over a period of time, discovered in the years of manhood to come, that the Indian psyche became more a part of them than they could ever have imagined—nor would it be easily lost even when they were repatriated. In essence, they became Indians—white Indians. In the wilderness war to come to the Ohio Country, they would play a leading role from the lessons learned by becoming, rather than knowing. To the frontier, they would earn the reputation not as white Indians but white savages.

With the fall of French-held Quebec City on September 13, 1759 and Montreal soon after, hostilities on the frontier ceased and an uneasy peace settled over the wilderness, as France ceded its former lands to British control. The former Indian allies of the French in the Ohio Country buried their war hatchets and during that autumn, many tribes sent delegations to talks with the English at Easton, Pennsylvania and to Fort Pitt, built on the former site of Fort Duquesne. A treaty between the Shawnee, Delaware, Wyandot, and Seneca tribes was concluded, and in return for the British prohibiting further settlement into Indian lands west of the Allegheny Mountains, the Indians agreed to stop all attacks against their former white enemies, and deliver to Fort Pitt "all prisoners held by them" regardless of age and sex. [BC-p.11]. Among those white captives brought in by the Indians to Fort Pitt were the three Girty brothers, Simon, George, and James, where they were reunited with their mother Mary and their young half-brother John. While Mary felt that they were all fortunate to survive Indian captivity, the three brothers had mixed feelings about leaving the Indians.

A continued liking for the Indians

The thoroughly Indianized Girty brothers returned to the rough frontier settlement called Pittsburgh that was sprouting up in a jumble of settler cabins and crude buildings on the ground adjacent the fort. However the Girty boys, like many other former white captives, faced an immediate problem on repatriation. They were no longer fluent in the English language, naturally having forgotten it during their captivity when they learned to speak the dialects of the Indians who adopted them. In their look, manner, dress, and speech they no longer looked like Englishmen but more like Indians. When the time came for the three brothers to leave with their mother for the east, they refused to go, as their attachment to her had been severed by their captivity and "the gap that had formed between them and their mother was unbridgeable." [EA-p.639] With Simon, now 18, leading the way, the brothers stayed to "shift for themselves" among the traders, frontier scouts, hunters, trappers and former prisoners like themselves who are unable to "give up, to a great extent, the habits and manners which had been acquired by them during their captivity." [BC-p.14] Whether they understood it or not, the Girtys, like so many other child captives of the Indians, would never be able to make the transition to civilized society. Only their eldest brother Thomas would be able to do so. His captivity by the Indians had been the shortest.

Unable to return to the Indians, the Girty boys could not find a means of regular employment to survive. The rough and tumble world of the white frontier society, while better than civilization to the east, nonetheless did not unequivocally accept the Girtys. Many of the settlers and frontiersmen had lost family and friends fighting the Indians in the previous war. Though the Girtys were recognized to be former white captives, the frontier people did not readily accept the three whose looks, actions, and speech were no longer white, but Indian. Reluctantly, the three accepted repatriation, and changed clothes for a more frontier look to stay. In time, the Girtys gravitated to those men on the frontier who were most like them, the white traders at the settlement of Pittsburgh who arrived with goods destined for trade with the Indians, to be "resumed immediately with the restoration of peace." [BC-p.13] Here the Girty boys found a home. They took jobs as interpreters, hunters, and assistants for the traders to the various tribes. Improving upon their English as well as learning to speak fluently all the languages of the Indians of the Ohio Country, the brothers, each with their own particular understanding of the Delaware, Shawnee, Wyandot, and Ohio Seneca, made themselves indispensable to traders crossing the Ohio River, and entering Indian lands to visit their villages and acquire furs. As for the Girtys, the intervening years since their return to the English frontier did neither dim nor damper their "continued liking for the Indians, enjoying heartily, whenever the occasion offered, visits to their camps, which were frequently to be seen in the vicinity." [BC-p.14]

Alexander McKee's mother a captive of the Shawnee

Pontiac's Indian rebellion to oust the English from the wilderness frontier was an interlude for the Indian traders, which ended in 1764 with a new peace treaty. Again, the Indians were forced to release their white captives who numbered nearly 300 men, women and children. Trade resumed with the Indians and the Girtys, along with other former captives who sympathized with the Indians, found work employed by those men who were licensed by the British Indian Department to engage in the lucrative trade. George Croghan, Sir William Johnson's Deputy Agent for Indian Affairs at Pittsburgh, recently returned from England in the autumn of 1764, wrote to his assistant deputy agent at Fort Pitt, Alexander McKee, asking him "to inform the tribes around Fort Pitt that he would soon return to the military post to re-establish the fur trade in the region." [NL-p.55] McKee, himself an interpreter and former Indian trader from eastern Pennsylvania when he became Croghan's assistant in the fall of 1759 at the end of hostilities with the French, was well acquainted with the Indians of the tribes of the Ohio Country, and knew that the Indian Department would need men like himself who could act as interpreters, scouts, and liaisons to the Indians once the flow of goods was sent to the tribal villages and exchanged for furs. The Girtys could also fill that need as only former white captives were able. McKee needed men who knew the trails to the villages, and were sympathetic, not antagonistic to the Indians. The ability to favorably parley with the Indians and strike fair, compromising deals was what counted, and in that respect, McKee and his charges were alike in their empathy for the Indians. However, McKee was not a former Indian captive as the Girtys, but the son of a captive.

Alexander McKee was born "about 1735 in the Pennsylvania backwoods of the Susquehanna Valley." His father Thomas had come from Ireland as a boy with his father sometime after 1707, and settled in Lancaster County, Pennsylvania to farm. Averse to farming, Thomas took to trading with the western Indians prior to the war with the French and Indians, and by 1740 established several posts along the tributaries of the Susquehanna River. [NL-p.25] Alexander's father was well acquainted with the "flamboyant land speculator and trader" George Croghan during the ensuing years, and helped Croghan in many of his dealings with the Pennsylvania Delaware.

Sometime in 1743, Thomas McKee met Alexander's mother while visiting a village of mixed Shawnee, Delaware and Iroquois Indians on the Susquehanna River. Mary, as she was later called, was "a white woman who had been captured as an infant in North Carolina and later adopted by the tribe" of the Shawnee. She was raised as an Indian squaw and could speak little English when she chose to leave with McKee and become his wife, although never relinquishing her close ties to the tribe in favor of the white man's world. As a young man, Alexander was raised by his mother and consequently, he was able to speak the Shawnee language, "follow their customs and observe their rituals" while taking a place next to his father in their trading enterprise which existed on the frontier between the Indian world and that of the whites.

When war came to the frontier, Alexander, like his father, enlisted in the local militia near their trading post where their regiment spent much of 1756 constructing Fort Augusta on the upper Susquehanna River to protect settlers from Indian raids. Supporting the English cause to attack French Fort Duquesne, Alexander, as a scout, accompanied General Forbes army in 1758, as it slowly pushed its way west through the Pennsylvania wilderness. He was wounded with the militia during Grant's failed assault on the French fort, though lived to see its fall, and subsequent replacement with Fort Pitt, where McKee would eventually come to reside, working as assistant to George Croghan in the affairs of the Crown's Indian Department. During Pontiac's Indian uprising in 1763, McKee served as Indian interpreter to the military at Fort Pitt in the absence of George Croghan and provided them with badly needed intelligence during the attacks and siege of June and July when Fort Pitt was surrounded and cut off. Now that the war was over, and Croghan returned to the frontier to council with the Indians, McKee, as deputy agent of the Indian Department, was advised directly by Sir William Johnson, Superintendent, to use his "best endeavors to conciliate and fix to the British Interest all the Several Nations and Tribes of Indians who may fall within the reach of your Influence." [NL-p.48]

Though McKee's sympathies lay with the Indians, like the Girtys, McKee by his employment to Johnson and the British Crown in the role as "Gentleman

and Assistant Deputy" was clearly encouraged, and ordered to "identify himself
with the broader social values of the British Realm" [NL-p.48] at the expense
of personal prejudice. McKee, though raised by a white Indian mother and
subsequently more sympathetic to the causes and concerns of the Indians than
most white men, was by occupation and social standing a long way off from the
Girtys, and those like them, in many respects. When wilderness war would come
once again to the frontier, it would be their similarities, and not differences that
would bind each of them to the others, out of survival against their common
enemy, and that of the Indian brotherhood that none of them could turn upon.

Matthew Elliott's affection for the Shawnee

Arriving on the frontier of the Ohio Country at the same was a man who
shared many similarities with McKee, the Girtys, and the Indian traders of the
wilderness frontier. Matthew Elliott, born in Ireland in 1739, came to America
in 1761 and made his way to the Pennsylvania frontier to seek a living. Finding
the frontier aflame with Indian attacks due to Pontiac's rebellion, Elliott
volunteered for Colonel Bouquet's army that was making its way westward to
end the siege at Fort Pitt. At Fort Ligonier, Elliott became acquainted with
Alexander Blaine, who was to become a trader partner once the war was over.
Elliott accompanied Bouquet's 1764 expedition into the Ohio Country to the
Muskingum River, and soon after Bouquet's return to Fort Pitt, Elliott was
engaged in a modest business venture that would lead to trade with the Indians.
[HR-p.5]

The next fall of 1765, Matthew Elliott headed west from Fort Pitt across
the Ohio River to the Shawnee villages on the Scioto River deep in the wilderness
of the Ohio Country where he intended to trade with them. At a Shawnee village
on the Scioto Elliott decided to winter with the Indians for whom he had respect
and affection. Here he learned to master the Shawnee dialect, and acquaint
himself with their customs and way of life. "Throughout the long winter he
gathered furs and skins, and in the spring brought them east of the back of his
packhorses" to Fort Pitt, for shipment and sale in Philadelphia. [HR-p.4] Like
other accomplished traders of his time, Matthew Elliott found that living with
the Indians a part of the year was more than just good business sense. As he
gained the trust of the Shawnee, he found greater acceptance into their world
where he felt much more comfortable than living at Fort Pitt or much worse,
Pennsylvania society at Carlisle to the east. Elliott had never fit in there, where
by the marks of colonial society of the time, he was nobody—just one more
poor, illiterate Irish immigrant without the means of becoming a gentleman.
Elliott, as so many other men like him, was drawn to the colonial frontier at Fort
Pitt because of its remoteness from the formalities and stratification of colonial
society in which he could neither fit, nor wish to do so. Elliott found his first
friends in the people living on the edge of the frontier at Fort Pitt and then the
Shawnee in the wilderness beyond. Like William Johnson in this respect,
Matthew Elliott found the company of Indians ultimately more pleasing than

that of whites. As evidence of his affection for the Shawnee, Elliott would take a Shawnee wife and raise a family, while traveling to and from Fort Pitt engaged in his trading venture. [HR-p.xii]

During these years of relative peace before a new wilderness war would erupt, white men like Elliott, McKee and the Girtys crisscrossed the Indian trails of the Ohio Country leading from the growing settlement at Pittsburgh on the Ohio River to the dozens of Shawnee, Delaware, Mingo, and Wyandot Indian villages beyond. Trade, diplomacy, friends, and family would take each man there to live off and on with the Indians and return to Pittsburgh when the need or occasion arose. Elliott built a trading house during the 1760's at Pecaweca, north of the large Shawnee village of Chillicothe on the Scioto River, and spent a great deal of his time living and trading among the Shawnee villages scattered along Paint Creek to the west. [HR-p.4] At the village of Wockachaalli, three miles north of Chillicothe, Alexander McKee lived part of his time while not in Pittsburgh engaged in Indian Department diplomacy with the Shawnee for George Croghan, as well as conducting the daily affairs of his own private trading business. McKee and Elliott became friends, due to their mutual interests in trade and their close relationship to the Shawnee which each shared. [HR-p.4]

The indelible mark on the Girty brothers

James Girty, a captive of the Shawnee as a youth, gravitated back to them during the period preceding war, working as "a laborer and interpreter for the traders" to the Shawnee, who by the dozens, were entering the Indian lands to trade at their numerous villages. A missionary from New Jersey named Rev. David Jones traveled to the Shawnee villages on Paint Creek in 1772 to attempt to minister Christianity to the Indians. There, he employed James Girty as an interpreter but gave up in his enterprise due to Girty's complete lack of interest in religion which was "contrary to the tenor of his life." Further, Girty refused Jones' instructions to proceed with the Indians until Girty was sure that some Shawnee "head men" or chiefs had returned to the village, whom Girty did not wish to offend without first obtaining their permission. While waiting for the Shawnee chiefs, Jones changed his mind and promptly left. [BC-p.15]

Meanwhile, George Girty, once a captive of the Delaware, found working for other men engaged in the Indian trade to be too confining for him. Starting a modest business of his own George "became a trader with the Indians on his own account," moving along the trails leading west from Pittsburgh to the Delaware villages on the Muskingum River. He knew the trails by heart and the Delaware people even better. Simon Girty, the eldest of the three brothers, adjusted better to life at the frontier settlement of Pittsburgh, and consequently spent more time there. Although he worked a number of jobs over the years that took him to the wilderness lands of the Ohio Country as hunter, trader, and Indian interpreter, Simon also found time to "make many friends among the white people of Pittsburgh" and was considered both "a man of talents" and of "great influence in the garrison and with the Indians" who came to Fort Pitt to trade their furs for goods. In addition, Simon showed a growing interest in public affairs, including the first election held at Pittsburgh in 1771, and the growing political dispute between Virginia and Pennsylvania over colonial boundary lines. [BC-p.14-15] Though obviously at ease at the frontier settlement, Simon had not given up his previous associations with the Indians as his elder brother Thomas had done upon returning to white society. For Simon, like his younger brothers, had an unmistakable tie to the wilderness and the Indians; a call inside himself that beckoned him, and could never adequately be explained or fathomed in the white world.

What was the lure of the wilderness and the Indians to these men like the Girtys, Elliott, McKee, and others? While never breaking their ties to the white frontier society that spawned them, they nevertheless were as much a part of Indian life and the ways of the wilderness as a white man could be, and still live in both worlds. That part of them that tied them to the Indians was the part of their lives that had made its impression upon their minds and bodies at a young age, and forever bonded them to the Indian mentality. As captives, the infusion of Indian language at the expense of English had opened the door to their swift assimilation, as in the case of the Girtys. McKee's mother, raised from childhood herself as an adopted Indian, brought her son up in the Shawnee culture where he learned the language as simply, if not more quickly, than English. Elliott, as a grown man discovered that marriage to a Shawnee woman would have much the same effect, introducing him to Indian culture and way of life that would make a lasting impression on him. Elliott did not take her from her people into a segregated white frontier society, but rather, he stayed with her at her Shawnee village beyond the reach of the frontier. In marrying her, Elliott wedded a part of himself to Indian life as well.

The impression made upon these men by the Indians was unmistakable, and lasting. What touched them by living with the Indians made an indelible mark upon their character. It was what drew them back again and again, and caused them to seek a means of employment that maintained their personal contact to the Indians, which each man unconsciously could not give up. Each in his own way found that the time they spent living with the Indians appealed more to them than living solely in Pittsburgh. In the same breath, none could bring themselves to sever their ties to their identity in the white world and turn their backs on the frontier settlements. They found that they could co-exist in a world inclusive of and between that of the Indian and the white frontier, only in the space of time that peace provided between the wilderness wars waged between two hardened antagonists. For the moment, life for the Girtys, Elliott and McKee in the 1760's before the Proclamation of 1768 opened the floodgates of white settlers into the Indian lands of the Ohio Country, was a time in which they could live between both worlds that beckoned them equally. In essence, these men were white Indians, with a part of them Delaware, Shawnee, and Seneca and a part of them English. To what degree did their blood run true, no man knew what, in those days before war, would force them to choose to fight against one blood line over the other. For the time, McKee, Elliott, and the Girtys prospered in their different endeavors at Pittsburgh while enjoying the simpler, richer, and more meaningful life around the native campfires smoking pipes and telling stories, a place where each man maintained an identity in a far different community.

The pivotal role of the white Indians in the coming war

A new wilderness war would come to change all of this for the white Indians of the western colonial frontier. The coming war in the east between the colonists and Great Britain would reach the western frontier fully by 1778, a frontier already stricken with bloody raids and battle between Indian war parties seeking revenge and white settlers seeking more land. Lord Dunmore's War would barely be over before the entire frontier from New York to the Virginian settlements in Kentucky would become engulfed in a battle for ultimate control of the lands of the Indians in the Ohio Country. In this vicious war of extermination to be fought between the Indians and the colonist Americans, the British would convince the Indians that their cause was a mutual interest and would support them with military effort. As in the previous wilderness war of 1755, white men would be needed by the British who could understand and work with the Indians in order to win the war which could not be won by Indians alone, nor by British rangers or regular troops. The western frontier of the Ohio Country in particular, was too far flung from British garrisons to provide the men and war materiel necessary to decisively campaign hundreds of miles from their posts at Fort Detroit and Fort Niagara. The British would need the Indians to do the job if the Ohio Country were to be held for Great Britain. In utilizing the Indians, white men such as the French possessed in the Canadian partisans of the previous war who acted as go-betweens linking the military to the Indians would be needed if the wilderness war were to be won by turning the Indians into effective fighting forces in the field.

Who would come to play the pivotal role of "go-betweens" in the coming wilderness war? Fate and circumstances would bring those white men of the frontier who in peacetime were the "cultural mediators" [NL-p.2] tying the Indians of the Ohio Country to the whites of the colonial frontier through the common bond of the fur trade existing between the two, to the forefront of the wilderness war that allowed no man neutral ground in a conflict that was more deeply rooted in antagonism and hatred between opposing races red and white, more so than political differences between British and patriot, loyalist and rebel. The white men living between two worlds on the edge of the frontier would be forced to eventually choose one side or the other. Their choice would lead them to turn their backs forever upon their roots in frontier society and gain them the undying hatred of the Americans who would call them white savages, renegades, devils, and monsters. In the end, men like McKee, Elliott, and the Girtys would find that the choice made to side with the Indians was never theirs to make for these men who would come to lead large Indian war parties against the Virginian frontier with utter ruthlessness and devastating effectiveness had already committed their hearts and minds to the Indian cause years before.

As partisan leaders in the wilderness war to come, the British would find, a generation later, their equals to La Corne, Beaujeu, Langy and Marin in these men of the Ohio Country who had become blood brothers of the Shawnee and Delaware, and officers of the British Indian Department at Fort Detroit. The white Indians had learned their lessons well, and came to teach some twists of their own in wilderness warfare that the American frontier would never forget nor forgive its wayward sons, those lessons written in blood.

Chapter 7

Under One Flag: Indians and Loyalists with Scores to Settle

The Treaty of Stanwix

The Treaty of Stanwix that Johnson brokered in October 1768 between the Iroquois, the Crown, and colonial representatives backed by land speculators, was deeply flawed. On the surface the Stanwix treaty proposed to re-define, once and for all, what was to be a lasting geographical boundary between Indian lands and the frontiers of the northern colonies, thereby permanently limiting by Crown law colonial expansion into Indian lands. The agreed upon line extended south from Ft. Stanwix on the upper reaches of the Mohawk River into the Delaware lands abutting the colony of Pennsylvania, lopping off for the colonists the fertile Wyoming Valley. The demarcation line then proceeded westward to the Allegheny River above its confluence with the Monongahela where the mighty Ohio River formed and then southward along the east bank of the Ohio River to the mouth of the Tennessee River some 30 miles above the spot where the Ohio emptied into the Mississippi. All the former Indian lands between the Ohio River and the crest of the Alleghenies was irrevocably ceded by the Indians to the colonies for settlement, including the vast rich, fertile lands (called "Kantuckee" by the Shawnee,) south of the Ohio River between the Kanawha and Tennessee Rivers. [FJ1-p.325]

The flaw in the treaty was that Sir William had failed to consult the Indians who lived on the lands which were about to be given to the whites. This omission had not been an oversight on his part, but rather an intentional policy decision. The real threat of an Indian uprising in the Ohio Country that he faced now, six years later, was the direct result of his wish to strike a deal exclusively with the Iroquois, whose fraudulent claim to all those lands in question Johnson had supported, at the expense of the tribes he had never met nor negotiated with. It was a moment of weakness on Johnson's part to allow his partiality for the Iroquois to get the best of him. Since the end of the war with the French, the greatly weakened Iroquois League could not in actuality consider themselves to be masters over the Woodland tribes of the Ohio Country, even if their own tribal history and treaty suggested it. Yet Sir William Johnson justified the patent unfairness of the Stanwix treaty with a handsome sum of money awarded to the Iroquois for their selling the wilderness lands they did not own. He rationalized that the other tribes in question would give their approval to the deal by privately stating that they "should be grateful to be loaded down with presents to which they have no right."[FJ1-p.326] If Johnson had meant his words to be prophetic, he had sorely misjudged the temper of hundreds of warriors from a dozen or more tribes to the west, who were neither in the mood in the spring of 1774 to listen to more words from Sir William Johnson nor to consider new treaties to rectify an already deplorable, deteriorating situation.

The problem for Sir William Johnson was that everything which was unfair about the Treaty of Stanwix was now coming back to haunt him. Aside from the fact he had not taken the western tribes into account when framing the treaty and had ignored their valid claims to the lands they lived and hunted upon, Johnson had substantially fueled growing resentment against himself and the Iroquois by the Shawnee, Delaware, Mingo, and Wyandot tribes as he favored the Iroquois at their expense. Now when Johnson needed more than ever to unify all the Indian tribes to a mutually held peace on the frontier, he found that the tribes of the Ohio Country were alienated from him, as Superintendent of Indian Affairs, because of his actions. They were angry with him, and out of his reach. One of the main reasons they no longer listened to him lay in the question of the rightful ownership of the Kantuckee lands.

The Shawnee tribes of the Ohio Country, in particular, considered the vast wilderness lands to the south of the Ohio River, which were rich in game, to be their own exclusive hunting grounds, and not owned by the Iroquois who claimed the Shawnee were a servant nation to the League. Sir William had not taken any of these details into consideration. While his insult to the Shawnee had been a grievous mistake, it paled in comparison to the heart of Shawnee and Delaware complaints reaching Johnson's deputy agent, Alexander McKee, at Fort Pitt.

The White Invasion

It was one thing for Johnson to promise to give all the Indian lands stretching from the Alleghenies to the Ohio River and southward to Kantuckee to the English colonies in the east to open up for expansion and settlement. Adding injury to the insult was the fact that by 1774 the floodgates were opened and settlers were streaming into those lands as never before. The Ohio tribes were angry for good cause. They did not understand the treaty, and would not have agreed to it even if they did. There was no way to stop the white invasion by peaceable means. William Johnson had brought the confrontation upon himself. Now it seemed chaos was about to reign.

The paradox, for Johnson, was the fact that the Stanwix Treaty had been necessary to cover a previous but equally corrupt and unenforceable treaty aimed at legalizing the seizure of Indian lands for westward expansion. The Proclamation of 1763 had formally set as the boundary between Indian lands and the English colonies the crest of the Allegheny Mountains, and forbade western colonial expansion beyond that point. However within a few short years, the illegal flow of white settlers into Indian lands along the Mohawk, Susquehanna and Monongahela Rivers west to the Ohio which began as a trickle, had swiftly become a torrent. With few British troops at a handful of posts scattered along the frontier, every Indian and white man across the breadth of the wilderness knew one truth beyond all else: There was no way that William Johnson, the Indian Department, the colonial governments, or the Crown itself could stop the inflow of settlers.

Rumors of an Indian uprising in the west to stem the flow of white intruders into the Ohio Country had forced Johnson to find a solution, albeit an unfair stop-gap measure in 1768 which was nothing more than a formality to legalize the seizure of those lands for white settlements. With the Treaty of Stanwix Johnson had bought himself some time, and by using the Iroquois as his front piece, kept to his policy of partiality for the Iroquois while "protecting the Colonies by keeping the Indians divided."[FJ1-p.326] It was a policy of his own that worked in the past but could work no longer. His inability to enforce the boundaries of the Treaty of Stanwix through the powers of the Crown, which he represented to all tribes, had proven the treaty to be nothing more than a sham. That fact diminished Johnson's prestige and influence with all the tribes, including the Iroquois, who were facing problems of their own.

While perennial animosities remained between the Iroquois and the western tribes in the spring of 1774, they were united in several respects. Besides their universal complaints of increasing numbers of white settlers illegally entering their lands, (including that of the Iroquois) supposedly restricted by the previous treaty, the tribes brought to Johnson their lists of growing incidences of maltreatment of the Indians at the hands of white traders and settlers. Tribes from the Mohawk to the Ohio Rivers grumbled to Johnson and his agents of unscrupulous "traders carrying into the forests little but rum, with debauched Indians, their guns sold, starved to death amidst plenty of game."[FJ1-p.339] Increasingly along the fluid Indian frontier with the whites, Indians were murdered by white traders, hunters, and trappers with or without reason, with impunity, as no one could arrest these men, try them, and convict them in a colonial court.

Indian and Settler Relations

The case of David Ramsay, an unscrupulous and ruthless trader was brought to William Johnson's attention in 1772. Ramsay had killed three drunken Indians in a quarrel near Fort Niagara. Ramsay then moved along the shore of Lake Erie some distance where it was claimed he attacked some Mississauga Indians and succeeded in "killing three men, one woman, and an infant." Unable to convict him by a jury of frontiersmen peers, Johnson lamented that "had Ramsay killed 100 Indians, no white jury would convict him" even for a man that had "put an infant to death."[FJ1-p.340] Incidences of atrocities committed against the Indians of all tribes only served to heighten their growing anger and the sentiment that a wilderness war would be the only way to right the wrongs committed against them. As he heard the reports, Johnson realized that he would have much to do to convince them otherwise. He knew he neither had a way to stem the outrages nor a way to bring the Indians justice.

McKee - Johnson's Agent in the West

To the west at Fort Pitt in the Ohio Country, Alexander McKee had become Sir William's sole deputy agent in charge of Indian Affairs for the Crown by default since the resignation of George Croghan in November 1771. Croghan left office to pursue more profitable interests that no longer conflicted with his role as deputy agent. [NL-p.64] Sir William recommended McKee for Croghan's position, believing him to be the best man, if not the only man in the area suited to handle the affairs of the Indian Department. [NL-p.67] The problem for Sir William was that, in these trying times for the Indian Department in the west since the diminished presence of the Crown at Fort Pitt, Alexander McKee was nowhere to be found at Pittsburgh, as he had gone to live with his Indian relatives on the Scioto River for an extended time. McKee put himself completely out of touch with Johnson when he was needed most.

Unknown to Johnson was the fact that McKee was disillusioned with him and the Indian Department, and had grown "distant, apathetic, and indifferent" over the previous year to the administration of Indian affairs within the Ohio Country. In the face of growing adversity, it had been easier for McKee to go live with the Shawnee. McKee had the growing realization that the British had no intention of protecting the Indians from the depredations of more and more white traders, hunters, and trappers entering Indian lands. The withdrawal of British soldiers from Fort Pitt in December 1772 had guaranteed that lawlessness perpetrated against the Indians would prevail, [NL-p.67] and with it, the increasing possibility of an Indian war of retaliation.

The planned reduction of Fort Pitt was ordered by British General Gage in the east to help ease the burgeoning financial crisis for the British government. By closing a number of military garrisons throughout the colonies and the frontier, Parliament would save money. Fort Pitt was to be dismantled on August 31, 1772. The post commander was instructed to transport all military guns and supplies to Philadelphia, and anything that could not be sent was to be destroyed, along with the fort walls, buildings and earthworks "in such a manner as it shall afford no defense for an Enemy," though there were none to be concerned with at that time. [NL-p.66] The work was completed by December and the British garrison pulled out, leaving no British governmental authority at Pittsburgh that could enforce the law.

For McKee, the collapse of the Crown's authority brought a predictable reaction from him, considering that he still held a nominal position in the British Indian Department, or what was left of it after the withdrawal of any official military presence. "Unaddressed grievances over uncontrolled white settlement on Indian lands, unrestricted trading practices, and escalating inter-colonial competition fostered by rekindled political aspiration and territorial ambition in the Ohio Country combined to create a climate of suspicion and violence." [NL-p.66] With characteristic sympathy for the plight of the Indians, McKee was understandably despondent that Indian rights would never properly be addressed, and concluded that a wilderness war, at some point, was inevitable.

Without British troops, McKee had no possible way to physically stop the torrent of white settlers entering Indian lands, especially those of Kantuckee which was at the heart of rapidly growing Indian disaffection. Virginians and Pennsylvanians were reaching those lands by a variety of routes in 1774. The old Forbes trail from Carlisle was a common means, in addition to the hard-packed well-used Braddock road that wound its way northwestward from Fort Cumberland in Maryland. Arriving at Pittsburgh, many of these settlers were building flat-bottomed boats to navigate down the Ohio River for points along the south shores of the Ohio from Pittsburgh to the mouth of the Kanawha River and beyond. Other Virginians were arriving at the Kantuckee lands by crossing the Allegheny Mountains along trails blazed through the forests by Daniel Boone and others.

The total influx of settlers was staggering and did not go unnoticed by the Shawnee, who were increasingly encountering white men hunting and trapping in their own hunting grounds and were forcibly driving the whites off threatening harm if they returned. No one had told the Shawnee that those lands had been sold from beneath them to Virginia by the Treaty of Ft. Stanwix. A crisis was culminating on the frontier. McKee, when he returned to Pittsburgh in the spring of 1773, wrote to William Johnson that the threats of an Indian war were looming larger on the horizon, as the Indians were convinced the only way to stop the white men intruding upon their lands was with violence. On one hand, living with the Shawnee, McKee could understand their point of view, and sympathize with their complaints. However, as deputy agent of Indian affairs at Pittsburgh, though powerless to act either on the behalf of the Indians or the Department, McKee was obligated to Sir William Johnson to attempt to restrain the Indians as long as possible. Not only was it his job, but he also had a vested interest in keeping the peace. It did not take much for him to envision what would happen to his trading enterprise, and that of his friend, Matthew Elliott, if Indian war broke out on the frontier.

Dispute Over Land in Pennsylvania and Virginia

Another problem was rearing its ugly head for Alexander McKee at Pittsburgh that was making his task of acting as Sir William Johnson's agent even more difficult. With the British military presence at Pittsburgh gone, the colonial governments of Pennsylvania and Virginia were attempting to claim rights to Pittsburgh by taking "advantage of the region's political vacuum." [NL-p.74] Though the colony of Pennsylvania had long laid claim to the western lands abutting the Ohio River, in January 1774, John Murray, known as Lord

Dunmore, the royal governor of Virginia Colony ordered John Connolly, his agent at Pittsburgh, to physically take possession of what was left of the fortifications and claim to the populace there that the "surrounding area was under Virginia's jurisdiction." [NL-p.75] Connolly did so, and renamed the scant fort ruins Fort Dunmore, in the Governor's name. The uproar not only alarmed the local community but disturbed the local Indians who viewed with distrust the presence of Virginians all the more so because of their incursions into Kantuckee. McKee, allied with Pennsylvania in the dispute, found that what few powers he had in the administration of Indian affairs through Sir William's Crown appointment had been taken away by Connolly and the Virginians who had no need for him. Connolly was firmly in charge of not only the government at Pittsburgh, but also Indian affairs as well. Both to back up his authority as Dunmore's executive, and demonstrate his style of managing the Indians, Connolly drilled the Virginia militia at Fort Dunmore on the cold winter morning of January 25, 1774, in full view of the Mingo and Delaware Indians who lived across the Allegheny River from the fort. When Connolly was done drilling the militia, some of the men fired their muskets at the Indians with Connolly's blessings. Though no one was hurt, Connolly had sent a clear message to the Indians and to McKee of what could be expected from him in the future, so far as Indians' rights were concerned. [NL-p.75]

McKee and Johnson Estranged

Learning of this at Johnson Hall in the Mohawk Valley in late January, Sir William reacted angrily at the loss of his deputy's position at Pittsburgh but placed much of the blame on McKee himself. Writing a reprimand to McKee, Johnson accused his assistant agent of "slow and incomplete reports" which he felt revealed McKee's lack of initiative in the face of growing frustration and adversity at Pittsburgh. Surprisingly, McKee responded to Sir William with an "impertinent letter" of his own, complaining "of Sir William's seeming lack of interest in western affairs," [NL-p.76] that contributed to the dilemma at Pittsburgh. If that were not enough for Sir William Johnson to rail about, a letter which arrived from his old friend and agent, George Croghan, who had recently returned to Pittsburgh from the Ohio Country due to abounding threats of Indian retaliation, described McKee as "indolent and not looking after his duties in a manner consistent with the honor of the Department and the General good of his Country." [NL-p.76] Sir William was livid. Nothing could stop the spiraling deterioration of Indian affairs in the west now that his own agent was openly at odds with him. A communication from McKee in early spring of 1774 reiterated to Johnson the continued threat of Indian war, and the underlying and unaddressed cause for Shawnee unrest which was, "The Expeditious Settlement of this Country gives all the Indian Nations this way Uneasiness and is the Subject of their constant Complaints."[NL-p.76]

23333323

Trying to Avert Indian War in the West

Without saying it, McKee was laying the blame for Indian unrest at the feet of Sir William Johnson, who had caused the current predicament. How could Sir William deny that McKee was right? Nonetheless, Johnson knew that something had to be done in spite of the impossible situation facing him that early spring of 1774. Conferring with his Mohawk wife, Molly Brant, on ways to avert the pending destruction of the peace he had worked so hard for over the years since the end of Pontiac's Indian rebellion in 1763, William Johnson realized that he must send out runners as soon as the snows melted and the ice broke to all the Indian nations along the Indian frontier with invitations to come to Johnson Hall by summer for a council to address and resolve their grievances. It was what Johnson knew best to do—he would use all his remaining persuasive powers to somehow pull Indian relations together into his camp once again.

Of all the problems facing him at the moment, the crisis with the Indians was the most pressing and the one which caused him the most despair. More than anyone else he realized what was at stake. The lives of countless men, women and children settlers along the frontier from the Mohawk River to the Ohio would be lost if an Indian wilderness war erupted, as well as the loss of his own prestige. However, the threat of pending Indian war was not the only problem facing Sir William Johnson that needed his attention. Something equally threatening was happening in the colonies in the east, which caused him considerable trouble.

The Rumors of Rebellion Cause Further Complications

A storm of political protest was gathering wind in the east. Along the colonies of the Atlantic seaboard, a new wave of colonial unrest against the rule of Great Britain was rising in response to the hated Townsend Acts passed by English Parliament to tax the colonies. In spite of the successful howls of citizen protest which had forced Parliament to repeal all taxes but the one on imported tea, the protests had only intensified. In particular, a gang of political firebrands from the Massachusetts colony calling themselves the "Sons of Liberty", had caused considerable trouble for the authorities there. Dressing themselves as Indians, they boarded a recently arrived English trader ship in Boston Harbor, seized the crew, and dumped the entire tea cargo of the ship into the bay in December 1773. When word of this outrageous act reached Parliament in England, they immediately ordered the military to close Boston Harbor indefinitely, and sent troops to the colony to strengthen the government there and put down the unrest. Although Boston was far away from Johnson Hall, William Johnson was relieved to hear that the government had acted quickly to curb the unrest. Well aware that the repercussions of the actions at Boston were rippling everywhere, including New York, Johnson worried that the unrest might lead to mob rule. Equally upsetting to him was the fact that L18,000 of British tea which had been dumped into the harbor was about equal to what he "had spent in a year on presents for His Majesty's Indian subjects." [SH-p.33]

Accustomed to holding to tightened Crown budgets, the loss was inexcusable to William Johnson.

Yet by the early spring of 1774, constant word of the unrest in the colonies reaching the Mohawk Valley gave no reason for him to believe the protests were subsiding. Rather, the blockade of the port of Boston seemed to Johnson to be on everyone's tongue, with sentiment among many of his neighbors increasingly being against the King. Johnson heard that in the east, a movement was afoot in a handful of the colonies to hold a colonial continental congress of protesting representatives to consider the next move to be taken against Britain's increasingly Intolerable Acts. [MB-p.29-30] While the New York colony was more moderate than the radicals of Massachusetts and Virginia, Johnson worried that the whole affair could get out of hand. There was talk already in some social circles of Tryon County that men needed to take a stand on the issues of great importance in the east, and that the matter would be brought before the Quarter Sessions of the Provincial Assembly of New York in June. [CE-p.13]

The news of such unrest against the Crown reaching Tryon County disturbed William Johnson as much as the Indian problem, for he had much at stake that spring. As Superintendent of the Indian Department, Johnson managed the affairs and interests of the Crown's Indian allies, and had divided the duties of the office among his family and friends. As General of the Tryon County militia, Johnson had overseen the recruitment and training of more than 1,400 men under his command whom he reviewed before Governor Tryon during his 1772 visit to the valley. [FJ1-p.342] He had the interests of his family to deal with as well as the management of his own household at Johnson Hall and the surrounding vast properties totaling nearly 170,000 acres of land, including nearly 1,000 tenants to support. He had more than enough to deal with, without a crisis with the Indians and the unrest in the east, if he were a healthy man. The problem in the spring of 1774 was that Sir William Johnson realized that his health was failing him, and the thought depressed him constantly, for his health problems would not go away.

Johnson's Health Problems

Johnson's war wound from the battle of Lake George in 1756 was causing continual pain. The French .62 caliber musket ball in his hip had never been removed. The discomfort flared with intensity from time to time, but recently had forced him to give up riding his horse, for he wrote that he "could rarely attempt to sit on a horse or take my usual exercise." [FJ1-p.336] Recurrent fevers troubled him more and more, which Molly, his Mohawk Indian wife tended to with regular treatments of herbs and with trips to the invigorating healing waters at the springs of Saratoga. Yet the paroxysms continued on and off, and with each new period of fevered illness, Johnson felt himself slip into the spell that he feared a "most excruciating torture," the nature of which Molly and the doctors could find little relief. Johnson wrote, "As the cause remains fixed, I must expect severe returns, which I fear can only be palliated." [FJ1-p.337]

Johnson's declining health forced him to divide the duties of the Indian Department among others, beginning with his son-in-law and nephew, Guy Johnson. Guy Johnson had arrived in America from Ireland during the war with the French, and had worked for his uncle from that time. By the 1770's Guy married Sir William Johnson's daughter, Mary, and built a manor mansion much like his uncle's home. He called their home Guy Park. It was located close to the Mohawk River, several miles east of Fort Johnson, on land purchased from his uncle abutting that of Daniel Claus, Sir William Johnson's other son-in-law and officer in the Indian Department. Here Guy Johnson and his wife, Mary, took up farming and purchased property from the Mohawks adjoining Kayaderosseras Creek for the partitioning and settlement of tenants, much as his uncle had done. Guy Johnson was nominated as an assemblyman to the Provincial Assembly, and filled the position of Adjutant General under his uncle in the county militia where he commanded one of the three regiments along with John Johnson, William's son, and Daniel Claus, each gaining the rank of Colonels. [FJ1-p.336]

Relinquishing Control

Though William Johnson's Indian wife, Molly Brant, was the unofficial diplomat to the Indians in the stead of her husband, Guy Johnson gradually assumed more and more of the daily duties of the Department. In the spring of 1774 Sir William Johnson had his will officially drawn up wherein he named Guy Johnson to succeed him as the Superintendent of the Indian Department in the event of his death. The will recognized what everyone already knew: Guy Johnson was already handling the daily affairs of the Department.

With so many problems facing Sir William Johnson that spring, he inwardly flinched at the thought of his nephew and son-in-law assuming the mantle of the department which seemed to him and the Indians to be ill-fitting at best. For one, Sir William Johnson did not trust his nephew with the Department accounts, and so he gave them to Molly. For Johnson it was more than simply a lack of trust in his nephew that made him uneasy. He could easily see that Guy did not have the personal charisma and character that he did. Portly and at times overbearing, Guy Johnson was neither comfortable around the Indians, nor did he possess the rapport with them that William Johnson had. It was easy for William to see that the Iroquois privately echoed similar sentiments. They, too, had little rapport with the younger Johnson.

John Johnson, Sir William's son by Catherine Weisenberg, had recently arrived from England and had wed Polly Watts in New York City. John returned to the valley with his new wife and settled in to live at Fort Johnson where he assumed more and more of his father's duties in the management of the family lands and tenants. In 1773, William Johnson brought from the Highlands of Scotland almost 600 Roman Catholic Scots to live and work as tenant farmers on the Johnson lands, which John was given substantial responsibilities in managing. [CE-p.15] John had no position in his father's Indian Department.

His age and lack of experience dictated that John help his father with their properties, which he knew one day he was to inherit.

A Constant and Loyal Friend

On a large tract of land several miles south of Johnson Hall overlooking the Mohawk River, John Butler, one of Sir William Johnson's deputy agents in the Indian Department in the late war with the French resided on his estate called Butlersbury and raised his family. John Butler was a constant and loyal friend over the years to Sir William, and the two men had seen considerable service together in both war and peace, since the heady days of the victory at Niagara over the French. John Butler had no title officially in the Indian Department and that bothered William Johnson to some degree. While he liked the stern-looking Connecticut Scotsman, he was aware that his son John and both sons-in-law did not. John Butler was content serving as a Lieutenant Colonel of a regiment of militia under Guy Johnson; however Guy chaffed at the thought of the elder Butler taking any thunder away from him. Considerably older at age 49 than Daniel Claus or Guy Johnson, he was more qualified than either man to head the Indian Department as Sir William Johnson's likely successor. Next to them in rank, John Butler "far surpassed both in natural ability, courage, and experience" and had acquired considerable influence among the Indians. [CE-p.11] A great deal of Butler's influence came from the fact that, unlike Claus or Guy, John Butler, who intimately knew several Indian languages, was a skilled translator for Sir William Johnson, and was constantly in contact with the headmen of various tribes at all of Sir William Johnson's councils with them. [CE-p.12] Already rumors were circulating among the Iroquois concerning Guy Johnson's animosity towards John Butler. If Guy, in his expanding role in the Indian Department were to take it upon himself to dismiss John Butler as their interpreter the Indians would appeal to Sir William Johnson directly and desert Guy Johnson. The problem for Sir William was that he had made John Butler the executor of his will in January 1774. With so much at stake in the looming crisis he faced with the Indians, Johnson knew that he would need the talents of both men more than ever and hoped that his son-in-law would see beyond the pettiness of the moment.

That fateful spring of 1774, Sir William Johnson put the wheels of his simple plan into motion to summon the tribes of the Iroquois and the Western Indians to Johnson Hall to council with him, in a final attempt to mediate their grievances and to try to find answers that mutually benefited them, the colonial settlers, and the Crown in the hope that a wilderness war which he believed was in the making, could be averted. As soon as the deep snows of winter began to melt, and the ice broke on the Mohawk River, Johnson sent his Mohawk runners, on the advice of Molly and her younger brother Joseph, with messages to each of the many villages near and far, with his own personal request that they come to Johnson Hall by early summer. Not only because Molly was Sir William's trusted wife and confident, but more so, because she, as Mary Brant, was a respected matriarchal leader of her Mohawk clan where women held village power, Molly was more than influential in Sir William's decisions with the Indians and the Department, demonstrating on a daily basis the ability to conduct the affairs of her husband with the intimate knowledge that she possessed living in both worlds. Belaying her political power was the fact that she brought to live with her at Johnson Hall not only her grown half-bred children, but invited her brother Joseph, his Mohawk wife Peggy, and their two children to live close to her.

Joseph Brant, like Peter Johnson the half-breed son of Sir William and Molly, and Sir William Johnson's other two half-breed sons William and Brant Johnson, had been sent east at adolescence to learn how to read and write English. In July 1761, at the age of 18, Joseph left home to attend Reverend Eleazar Wheelock's school for Indians in Lebanon, Connecticut to get a white man's education. [KI-p.70] Joseph returned to the Mohawk Valley in July 1763 after the start of Pontiac's Indian uprising against the British. He had learned how to read and write while at Wheelock's, and had shown enough interest in the Bible that Sir William noted him to be "very zealously and devoutly inclined" to a life as a missionary to the Indians. [KI-p.104] However, Joseph had thoughts of his own to the contrary, and in July 1765, married at the Mohawk village of Canajoharie.

Upon the death of his wife Peggy in March 1771 from consumption, [KI-p.133] Joseph became friends with the new Anglican missionary to Fort Hunter, the Reverend John Stuart. In the spring of 1772, Joseph agreed to help Stuart translate portions of the Bible and the church liturgy into the Mohawk language, so that Stuart could learn the Mohawk tongue, and begin preaching to the Indians on a regular basis. Joseph was a great help to Rev. Stuart. By 1774, the two of them had accomplished the near impossible, and sent to press "the Gospel of St. Mark, an explanation of the catechism, and a short history of the Bible, all in Mohawk." [KI-p.134] Stuart was pleased with Joseph's invaluable aid, later recalling that he was "probably the only person in America equal to such a task."[KI-p.134] Dividing his time between Stuart's parsonage, and Johnson Hall, Joseph prepared to help his sister and Sir William with the coming Indian council in the summer of 1774.

Word of the outbreak of Indian war in the Ohio Country reached Sir William Johnson in early June before he could meet with the Indians at the appointed council at Johnson Hall. He was stunned that events had moved more quickly than he. For several weeks Johnson had been forced to lay low due to a new wave of fever which struck him, and he blamed himself for avoiding all activities related to Indian affairs which he believed "in my present low state would exhaust my spirits." [FJ1-p.346] Open Indian warfare in the west could only mean that his deputy agent, Alexander McKee, had been unsuccessful in keeping the tribes from taking up the hatchet. In reality, the truth lay somewhere between.

Chief Logan's Complaint

An incident on the Ohio River in which several peaceful Indians were murdered by whites had triggered the war by inspiring Indians to retaliate against settlers on the frontier to avenge the killings. A Mingo Indian chief named Logan had taken up the hatchet against the whites to avenge the killing of his blood family relatives while he was away hunting. Logan was the eldest son of the Cayuga Iroquois chief Johnny Shikellamy, who had been one of the few Indians to remain loyal to the British during the Seven Year's war, during which he and his family sought refuge at the trading post of Alexander McKee's father. [NL-p.80] Logan had grown up in the Ohio Country at peace with the whites and was one of the few Indians to promote friendship with the incoming settlers. All that had dramatically changed for Logan when he came home to find his brother and sister brutally butchered. He swore to avenge their deaths with the lives of dozens of white settlers.

The Tides of War

McKee had urged the Shawnee to remain calm and not enter into the fray, and by late May he could report that only Logan and his warriors were at war. Hearing that the local Virginia militia was called out on Connolly's orders, McKee wrote to Sir William Johnson, advising him of the deteriorating situation and urging him to reimpose the rule of the Crown in the region in an attempt to halt the violence before Lord Dunmore and Virginia declared war on all the Indians which would plunge the entire frontier into a bloodbath. Without Johnson's direct involvement, McKee believed that "thousands of the inhabitants must be involved in misery and distress," and that a declaration of war on the part of Dunmore and Virginia would bring about "the destruction of this country." [NL-p.81] Johnson read the letter of appeal from his deputy in the west with incredulousness. If McKee had been able to see the Superintendent of Indians Affairs prostrate with fever and debilitating weakness he would have understood that Sir William Johnson's inaction was not due to indifference. Unfortunately for McKee and Johnson, events were unfolding quicker than either man could imagine.

While Sir William Johnson prepared himself for the July Indian council at Johnson Hall, the Shawnee Indians of the Ohio Country went to war with the whites. A prominent Shawnee chief named Silverheels had been seriously wounded by Connolly's militia, when he and a group of Shawnee envoys, who had come peacefully to Pittsburgh at McKee's request to discuss continued peace with the whites, were attacked on Connolly's orders. The Shawnee took their wounded and quickly scattered across the Ohio River. It did not take long for word of the treachery of the whites to spread from village to village, inciting the young hot-blooded warriors to put on war paint. Soon Shawnee war parties were fanning out across the white frontier on the east side of the Ohio, attacking isolated settler cabins and putting the settler's families to the scalping knife and the torch.

As a result, the entire western frontier region around Pittsburgh was put into a state of panic as the Indian attacks increased. To add further worry for Sir William Johnson as he prepared for the Great Council, as the first delegations from the Six Nations of the Iroquois were arriving at Johnson Hall in late June, Molly and her brother Joseph were able to learn that the Shawnee were appealing directly to the Iroquois for military help in their war in the Ohio Country. Everything involving Indian relations was at stake for Sir William Johnson as the Great Indian Council began on July 9, 1774, on the grounds before Johnson Hall. As he patiently listened to the speeches of Indian orators detailing their long list of grievances with the white men, Sir William Johnson knew that he would need to summon all the powers of his personal persuasion and charisma which he relied upon in the past if he were to convince over 600 Indians sitting before him to keep his faith, and not resort to war. Summing up his thoughts on his ability to influence the Indians, which had always worked for him in the past, a mainstay of his own policy with them, Johnson wrote "I shall never be without hopes till I find myself without that influence which has never yet forsaken me." [FJ1-p.347]

The Unexpected

Then something unexpected happened that neither the Indian assemblage nor Sir William Johnson, with so much on his mind, could have anticipated. On the blistering hot afternoon of July 11, Johnson rose to address the sachems of Indian Council in the shade under the arbor behind his house. Needing no interpreter, he began his reply to the speeches of the Indians, as an eyewitness noted; "with all the spirit, activity and energy" that Sir William Johnson was known to muster. [FJ1-p.347] Fervently, Johnson appealed to the Indians to keep the peace and allow the King to administer justice for the recent outrages committed against them by whites. Then hesitating, he felt a wave of malady come over him, which made him feel weak and light-headed. Johnson teetered for a moment, and then steadied himself. Motioning to Molly for help, he ordered "pipes, tobacco, and some liquor for the Indians" and asked to be taken inside to rest. Sir William Johnson, with Molly at his side, eased himself down into his chair, laid his head back, and taking a sip of wine, closed his eyes and quietly died, [FJ1-p.347] leaving the world of the Indians and whites alike who knew him and loved him shocked and turned upside down.

In the months that followed Sir William Johnson's unforeseen and ill-timed death, confusion and uncertainty was the tie that bound his family and friends in the Indian Department together, as they attempted to pick up the pieces that he left, which appeared to them to be increasingly more confused and uncertain with each passing day. In the western lands of the Ohio Country, the war with the Indians known as Cresap's War, had taken on a new face with Lord Dunmore's arrival in Pittsburgh in September at the head of a small Virginia army bent on stopping the Shawnee from further attacks against the settlers. Guy Johnson, as the new Superintendent of the Indian Department, had successfully convinced the Iroquois Confederacy to maintain their neutrality with the frontier, and deny help to the Shawnee. Meanwhile, Alexander McKee at Pittsburgh was able to court the neutrality of the Delaware tribes with promises that Dunmore would administer justice to the guilty whites. Consequently the hostile Shawnee found themselves alone, facing two Virginian armies invading the Ohio Country by late September 1774.

Battle of Point Pleasant

To the southeast, an army of nearly 1,500 men from the Virginia counties of Botetourt, Fincastle and Augusta assembled in late August 1774 at Camp Union on the Greenbrier River just west of the crest of the Alleghenies. [NL-p.83] Placed under the command of Colonel Andrew Lewis, the expedition set out on September 11, with orders from Lord Dunmore to march through the wilderness to the Kanawha River and follow it to its mouth on the Ohio River. There, Lewis was to wait for Dunmore and his army which would be coming down the Ohio River from Pittsburgh by boat. Once the two wings of his army were together, Dunmore planned to invade the Shawnee lands and destroy their villages to end Indian raids.

Lord Dunmore reached Pittsburgh in September at the head of 1200 men comprising the northern division of the army. Strengthening Fort Pitt, he set out with his flotilla down the Ohio River, stopping at the Zane settlement at the mouth of Wheeling Creek on the east side of the Ohio River to review Fort Fincastle which he ordered built in June by Major William Crawford. At nearly the same time in early October, General Lewis and his army arrived at the Ohio River and encamped on the east bank of the mouth of the Kanawha to await Dunmore.

In the early morning of October 9, a large force of Shawnee and Mingo Indian warriors, who had secretly crossed the Ohio River during the previous night and taken up hidden positions around the camp, attacked the Virginians who were just beginning to awake. A stiff battle quickly ensued. Repeated Indian assaults were thrown back by the militiamen with heavy casualties on both sides. Scores of Lewis' men were wounded in the hand-to-hand combat with the Indians. Some of the Virginians were experienced woodsmen and hunters. Others were men like William Caldwell, who had recently emigrated from Ireland in 1773 and had little frontier experience when he volunteered for Lewis' expedition. Many of these men were killed outright in the first Indian volleys from their concealed positions. The emigrants did not take cover nor keep their heads down due to a lack of wilderness warfare experience in fighting Indians. In that respect, William Caldwell was one of the lucky men who were only wounded. [WM-p.2] By late afternoon the battle was over, and though undefeated, the Indians withdrew across the Ohio River, taking their dead and wounded with them. Though mauled and exhausted, Lewis' army could claim victory as they remained on the battlefield known as Point Pleasant. [NL-p.84]

Meanwhile, Dunmore with his army in tow, continued down the Ohio River to the mouth of the Hockhocking River, from where he decided to march into Shawnee country to destroy their villages, without Lewis' aid. Dunmore employed several Pittsburgh men as scouts and interpreters. One was Simon Girty. [BC-p.19] Girty was entrusted by Dunmore to carry messages to Lewis down river, as well as take part in the negotiations with the Indians, when the Shawnee sued for peace. After the battle with Lewis' army that inflicted dozens of casualties, the Indians reluctantly decided they could not defeat Dunmore as he approached with his army. They decided to negotiate with Dunmore and chose to send Matthew Elliott, who had been living among them, to Dunmore with a message detailing their conciliatory wishes. Elliott agreed to act for the Indians and approached Dunmore under a flag of truce, whereupon negotiations opened and peace was re-established. [HR-p.6] Simon Girty worked on behalf of Dunmore to coax the aloof Mingo chief Logan, to take part in the talks. As a result, Logan dictated to Girty his "famous speech" to Dunmore, which Girty translated into English and a man named John Gibson wrote down, in which Logan "lamented" the death of his loved ones at the hands of the whites whom he had always shown friendship. Absent from Dunmore's occupation of the Ohio Country and treaty making with the Indians was Alexander McKee, deputy Indian agent. Sir William Johnson was dead, and the Indian Department was in disarray, and had no direction or orders for McKee in the Ohio Country. Dunmore, like the Virginians he led, had no use for a man like McKee whose sympathies were known to lay with Pennsylvania politics and the Indians. McKee's view that, by re-imposing Crown rule over the western lands through the governmental authority of Pennsylvania the flood of Virginian settlers into the region could be stemmed, ran counter to Dunmore and all Virginians who sought to expand their colony all the way to Kantuckee. In disfavor, McKee had all power stripped from him, and his effectiveness in dealing with Indian affairs was finished.

The onset of winter in late 1774 brought a shaky peace between the Indians and the Virginians along the frontier of the Ohio Country. The militia disbanded and Lord Dunmore returned to Williamsburg having successfully chastised the Indians without dealing with their discontent over settlers from Virginia streaming into their lands, and the threat of many more arriving in the spring. Consequently, the situation between whites and Indians along the border of the Ohio River remained volatile, with both sides poised for renewed hostilities.

Guy Johnson Becomes Superintendent

In the Mohawk Valley to the east, much had changed with Sir William Johnson's family and the Indian Department since his death. Molly Brant, his Indian wife moved back to her Mohawk village at Canajoharie with her children. Sir William's son, John Johnson, as "principal heir and successor" to the vast Johnson empire, inherited his father's title as well, becoming the second baronet of New York. [TE-p.66] He moved his family into Johnson Hall and set up housekeeping to be able to better tend to the vast estate holdings and tenants from the seat of his father's power. As a leading landowner in the valley, he became a major general of the militia that his father formerly commanded. [FJ1-p.349]

Guy Johnson, appointed Sir William Johnson's heir to the Superintendence of the Indian Department in his will, assumed the position with the Crown's official sanction and set up the headquarters for his office in his home at Guy Park Manor where the business of the department could be conducted with confidentiality. Daniel Claus became First Deputy of the Department with the added duties of governing the affairs of the Canadian tribes to the north. The Mohawk Joseph Brant, brother of Molly, was appointed by Guy Johnson as his secretary and liaison between himself and Molly at Canajoharie, whom he sorely needed for her wisdom and advice that he, himself, was woefully lacking. At the last minute however, Guy Johnson realized that Joseph Brant was unable to read or write well enough to be able to fill the important position that required meticulous record keeping. Reluctantly, Guy Johnson appointed Joseph Chew to the position of secretary, but keeping an eye open to Joseph Brant and his important tie to Molly, Guy "continued him as one of his interpreters, and his duties were expanded to include all treaties and negotiations" which satisfied Brant. [KI-p.140]

Dealing with John Butler was another problem for Guy Johnson. He had never liked the elder Butler who had had close ties to his uncle Sir William Johnson. It mattered little to Guy Johnson that John Butler had campaigned with his uncle in the war with the French, or that the man was one of William Johnson's true friends. Guy Johnson did not like John Butler because he was jealous of the high esteem and respect that the Iroquois headmen held for the man. Guy Johnson misperceived John Butler to be a threat to his power as Superintendent. He reluctantly kept John Butler on the staff as an interpreter for the Indians because the Indians demanded he do so. Guy Johnson could not bring himself to challenge their wishes and dismiss the man. John Butler, on the other hand, was content to ignore both John Johnson and Guy Johnson for the moment, even though he knew that the two men "constantly intrigued against" him openly, now that Sir William Johnson was no longer alive to keep the ill-will of the two younger Johnsons in check. [SH-p.36]

However, John Butler's eldest son, Walter, had different thoughts on the matter of his father's standing in the Indian Department. Walter had recently returned from studying law in Albany when he attended his first Indian congress held by Guy Johnson in September 1774 on the grounds of Johnson Hall. Walter's father was there, acting as Guy's interpreter for the Indian Department, but it was apparent to Walter that his father did not have the same favor of either Guy or John Johnson that had been to him accorded by Sir William, and it angered Walter. Above all else, John Butler had always been loyal to the Johnsons and unwavering in his friendship to them, [SH-p.38] and that, in Walter's eyes, should have been reciprocated by Guy Johnson, when in fact it was not.

All of the petty intrigue in the Indian Department that was inadvertently inspired by Guy Johnson was temporarily put aside on September 18 when the delegation of more than 230 Iroquois assembled before Guy Johnson at Johnson Hall to officially accept him as their new superintendent, giving him the fine Indian name, "Uraghquadirha, or Rays of the Sun Enlightening the Earth."[KI-p.142] Guy Johnson was flattered, and regardless of his own private misgivings of his ability to fill his uncle's shoes, pleased himself with the Indian name which he believed rivaled that of Warraghiyagey given to Sir William Johnson. Whether he truly had the confidence and support of the Iroquois Guy Johnson did not know, nor care to ponder at the moment.

"Resolve to Bear Faith and True Allegiance to their Lawful Sovereign"

Unfortunately for Guy Johnson, the renewed spirit of political discontent brewing in the eastern colonies would not allow him time to bask in the glory of his new office. Growing dissent against the British government in New England was spreading throughout the entire colonies as the year 1774 came to a close, and already that discontent arrived in the Mohawk Valley, first as tavern talk and a plethora of rumors. Then late in the year, the first Patriot Committee of Safety formed in the valley, and soon others began to spring up. [FJ1-p.349] Guy Johnson sneered when he heard self-appointed Committee of Safety members explain in spring 1775 to anyone who would listen in the valley that the reason for the late formation of the Committee was due to the fact that "Tryon County has for a series of years been ruled by one family," implying that the Johnsons were staunchly Royalist, and had prevented attempts to dissent against the Crown in the valley. The innuendo that Guy Johnson thwarted them from meeting was hardly the truth. He was too busy a man to give them any notice, and as a prominent man in the valley, he had no patience for committees of dissent and talk about liberty in tavern circles. However, one thing about Guy Johnson was clear. The fact was that he was a loyal government officer in service to the Crown, as appointed by Sir William Johnson. In all Crown matters he would remain a loyalist committed to his duties without question regardless of what he felt was irresponsible talk against the King.

Although somewhat pompous, arrogant, and overweight, Guy Johnson was not a man who had forgotten where he came from, or how he had gotten to be in the position he found himself. All his positions in government, from Superintendent of Indian Affairs, to Tryon county judge, Lieutenant Colonel and Adjutant General of the Tryon County Militia, and representative of the New York Provincial Assembly had come as largest from his famous uncle, Sir William Johnson, and not a result of his own efforts. Even his manor home at Guy Park and the lands that surrounded it, were largely a gift from his father-in-law. How could he possibly approve of rumors of refusal to pay taxes, a Continental Congress dissenting against the legal government, and the repeated threats by New Englanders of open rebellion if concessions were not made to the dissenters calling themselves Patriots and Whigs? Guy Johnson embodied the government in the Mohawk Valley. More than anyone else, he was the Crown's visible representative, and the one man charged with preserving the affairs, trust, and loyalty of the Iroquois nations. As dissent grew in the valley, Guy Johnson became more and more determined to stop it, and prevent a disruption to his power just when life was beginning to look good for him. Instinctively he turned to those people he needed to count on.

Already John Butler had been approached by a letter written early in the year by a Mr. James Duane, a member of the Continental Congress, requesting that he take part in the upcoming Congress. Always loyal in the service to the Crown that his father had raised him in and that his brother had given his life for fighting the French, John Butler promptly refused the offer. [SH-p.38] In response to formation of Committees of Correspondence in the valley, the Grand Jury of Magistrates at Johnstown signed a declaration of their own, stating "they did therefore resolve to bear faith and true allegiance in their lawful sovereign, King George III." [SH-p.40] John and Walter Butler, along with Joseph Chew were but a few of the local men to sign it, though no outward signs of patriot protest and dissent had as yet to be seen in the valley. But when the Reverend Samuel Kirkland, a Presbyterian minister to the Oneida Indians attempted to explain to the assembled Indian Confederacy at a council at Guy Park in January the intentions of the Continental Congress, Guy Johnson denounced Kirkland openly before the assembled Indians. At his side were Joseph Brant and John Butler to support him. [KI-p.146]

"We are informed that Johnson Hall is fortifying"

On April 19, 1775, dissent in New England broke into open rebellion at Lexington and Concord in Massachusetts colony, as Rebel Minutemen opposed British soldiers marching from Boston with orders to seize suspected stores of illegal ammunition at Concord. Seeing the British red-coated soldiers advancing at Lexington commons, Captain Parker told his 70-plus Minutemen to "Stand your ground; don't fire unless fired upon; but if they mean to have a war, let it begin here." [FA-p.99] A shot rang out, and then volleys from both sides, with casualties.

Open rebellion against the mother country, Great Britain, had begun. Rebellion would soon turn to revolution and revolution to war, as the British would attempt to put down the revolt by conventional military means. In the months ahead, families and friends would be torn apart as the citizens of the Mohawk Valley were inevitably forced to choose sides in the conflict either as Patriots or Tories. There would be no middle ground for anyone who wished to remain neutral. The conflict that was about to engulf all the citizens of the frontier of New York would be nothing less than a vicious civil war fought in their own towns and villages.

Word of the New England open conflict reached the Mohawk Valley very early in May just as the Tryon County Committee of Correspondence, the local patriot organization, was meeting with the intent to send a letter to the Committee of Safety in Albany detailing Guy Johnson's attempts to "dissuade the people from coming into Congressional measures" [BC-p.14] and asking for help in the form of arms and ammunition. "We are informed that Johnson Hall is fortifying by placing a parcel of swivel guns around the same; and that Colonel (Guy) Johnson has had parts of his regiment of militia under arms…we recommend it strongly and seriously to you to take it in your consideration whether any powder and ammunition ought to be permitted to be sent up this way." [CW-p.22] Clearly the situation in the valley was tensing as people reacted to the shocking news of the outbreak of war in the east. While attempting to keep peace and order in the valley, for the first time ever were the Johnsons, their families, and the officers of the Indian Department beginning to feel citizen opposition to their control.

Guy Johnson's Call to Arms

Then on May 11, 1775, the Committees of Correspondence in the Mohawk Valley called for a meeting of patriots at the village of Caughnawaga on the Mohawk River, a few miles below Butlersbury, to deliberate the cause of liberty in sympathy with the Bostonians and to organize open resistance to Crown authority locally. Over 300 unarmed settlers attended the meeting. As it was concluding with the erecting of a "Liberty Pole," Guy Johnson, Sir John Johnson, Daniel Claus, and a force of John Johnson's Highland retainers suddenly arrived on horseback, armed with swords and pistols with which they menaced the startled crowd.

Guy Johnson, as Colonel of the militia, ordered his men to cut down the pole and stop the meeting. Then he spoke to the angry crowd, ordering them to leave, and haranguing them by saying, "Listen to me you fools! You talk about taking up arms against the King? Do you know the strength of that King? Do you realize that he can put down any insurrection you start?" [FA-p.100] A local man in the crowd, Jacob Sammons responded, calling Johnson a "liar and a villain" whereupon Guy Johnson lunged out and beat Sammons, knocking him down. Witnessing the violent confrontation in which Guy Johnson had made good on his threat, the crowd quickly dispersed. Talk of rebellion was quelled for the moment but hardly forgotten.

Quietly, the Rebels, calling themselves patriots and Whigs, began searching for and buying up scarce gunpowder, fearing a more deadly confrontation to come from the Johnsons, as they planned their next move. In the meantime, Guy Johnson was agitated, if not fearful of what might happen in the valley if open rebellion should occur, as it had in the east. He had no one to turn to for advice, as all correspondence with Boston, New York, Canada, and London had been interrupted by Whig patrols on the post roads that were seizing any letters to and from him to gain intelligence on the British. Rumors which spread daily like wildfire were denied by both sides in the increasingly polarized climate that was causing those called Tories or loyalists to the King to speak less and less frequently to those who were Patriots, Whigs and Rebels. The atmosphere in late May was highly charged and uncertain, as both sides bristled increasingly with hostility.

On May 14, Guy Johnson received a letter smuggled through to him from a friend in Philadelphia who was spying on the Continental Congress meeting there. The man warned Johnson that soon a force of Rebels would be sent from New England to arrest him and take him to prison because he was suspected by the Congress to be stirring up the Iroquois Confederacy to side with the British. At word of this, Guy Johnson was seized with panic, and though the local Whigs denied such a plot, he remained unconvinced. Sounding the alarm, Guy Johnson called in all his friends and tenants to Guy Park Manor to fortify the house and prepare to fight. From their lots of land adjoining Guy Park where they were preparing for spring planting, tenants like John Waters, John Phillips, and Peter Fitzpatrick put down their implements, grabbed their firelocks, and left their fields and families to heed Johnson's call to arms, regardless of their own sympathies, for each man was indebted to Guy Johnson and could not disobey his summons.

"We Cannot Spare Colonel Johnson"

As a body of armed Mohawk warriors arrived at Guy Park to guard their superintendent, runners were sent out to the other tribes, calling for their support. One letter to the Oneidas was lost on the King's road by a scout heading up the Mohawk River, and fell into the hands of the Committee of Correspondence. Translated from Mohawk, the letter laid before the Committee on May 21 disclosed that Joseph Brant had written to the Oneidas asking them to come to Guy Park to assist the Mohawks. The Committee was alarmed at this news, fearing that Johnson was calling upon the Indians to attack them. Again, patriot leaders sent word to the Committee of Safety in Albany, begging for help. While sending a letter to Guy Johnson imploring him as Superintendent of the Indians to "use all possible means in your power to restore peace and tranquility among the Indians," [CW-p.29] the Committee also sent four members to Albany to buy ammunition. They had no doubt that a violent confrontation with the Johnsons was coming soon when the Iroquois arrived.

On May 25, Guy Johnson convened a Mohawk council at his home at Guy Park to discuss the grave situation, despite of the fact that neither New Englanders nor Oneidas had been seen anywhere. Gripped with indecision, he finally relented and invited Whig delegates from Albany, Schenectady and Caughnawaga to meet with him and the Indians. Though Guy Johnson loathed their presence and considered them rebels in violation of the King's law, he asked them to come to the council with the hope that he could dispel the rumors that he and his Indian allies were conspiring to attack the Whigs. Graciously, the Mohawks spoke for him, saying, "We cannot spare Colonel Johnson. The love we have for the memory of Sir William Johnson and the obligations the whole Six Nations are under to him, must make us regard and protect every branch of his family." [CW-p.31] Little Abraham, principal Mohawk sachem at their village at Fort Hunter, promised the delegates that the Mohawks would remain neutral so long as Guy Johnson was not harmed. [KI-p.148] The council ended with all sides convinced for the moment that peace could be restored but tensions remained high.

Flight from the Mohawk Valley

A full council of the Six Nations was to commence at Guy Park in June. Fearing that the Rebels would attempt to stop the Indians from coming to his home, and in effect, strip him of his power as Superintendent, Guy Johnson decided he had to go upriver to hold the conference with the Indians where the Whigs would not be able to influence the meeting in any way. Guy Johnson then sent word to the Committee of his intentions to leave the valley briefly for a routine meeting with the Indians to put their minds at rest that he was not up to something else. The members collectively breathed a sign of relief when they heard hundreds of Indians would not be descending into the valley at Johnson's request, a thought which frightened them.

As Johnson notified his department agents and made preparations to go, he unexpectedly received a secret letter from British General Gage in New England, written in code, giving him the first orders he had received from the British government since the crisis in the spring had began. Gage directed Johnson to "take as many Indians as he could gather together" and proceed immediately for Canada to join the forces of General Carleton there for a joint attack upon the Rebels of New England. [KI-p.149] Realizing that the Crown was moving to put down the rebellion with force, Guy Johnson altered his plans to be able to carry out his new orders. Quietly he sent word to the Mohawks and his tenants that they were to accompany him on his trip to the Six Nations council. He did not reveal his true intentions to them for fear of someone disclosing his mission to the Rebels, whom Johnson had no doubts would move to arrest him.

Guy Johnson agonized over abandoning his family and property, as well as that of his tenants, who had worked so hard for to improve their lots. But he knew they must go with him to protect him, and he must go now, before his real intent was discovered. At the last moment he decided to take his pregnant wife Mary and three young children with him, but told no one else other than Daniel Claus of their final destination, so that Claus could take his family as well and all his own valuables. Guy Johnson's tenants, on constant duty guarding Guy Park, said goodbye to their families, believing they would be back home as soon as the council was over. John Butler was accompanied by his son Walter but he left his wife and other children at home at Butlersbury. Joseph Brant as secretary and interpreter packed the records of the Indian Department to take on the trip, but left his family at Canajoharie, including his sister Molly who was determined to stay. Provisions, ammunition, and presents for the Six Nations were packed away in a flotilla of bateaux that left on the morning of May 31, 1775, for the trip up the Mohawk River. All else was kept secret.

More than 120 whites and 90 Indians left with Guy Johnson that day, including all of the members of the Indian Department and 30 of John Johnson's Catholic Highlanders. John Johnson decided not to go along, fearing that he had much more to lose if he left the vast estate of Johnson Hall unguarded. He had his small army of Highlander retainers to protect him if needed, and as he held no public office in the valley John Johnson had not borne the brunt of Whig attacks as Guy Johnson had during the previous month. With public sentiment focused away from him he felt that he could remain on his estate until the rebellion was quelled by the Crown government and order restored. Behind all of these considerations was the fear that his wife would not be able to endure the arduous trip to Canada, which Guy and Daniel Claus revealed to him at the last moment as their real destination.

The momentous die was cast as family and friends said goodbye on the last day of May 1775 and set off on what was believed by most to be a short trip up the Mohawk River to Oneida and Onondaga Indian villages. Many of the men who left with Guy Johnson would not see their beautiful valley and their homes again for more than two years, and then under vastly different circumstances: they would return on a war mission of vengeance, and not for a homecoming. For many, it would be the last they would ever see of their homes, land, and property, for when the winds of war blew into the valley, everyone and everything would be swept up in it, never to be the same.

Joseph Brant on a mission to the King

Guy Johnson took one last look at the stone manor home he called "Guy Park" and wistfully wondered if he were making a mistake in leaving without a fight. Little would he know that he would never see his home on the Mohawk again, and lose all that he had strived for, and much more, since joining his uncle Sir William Johnson in America. Misfortune would strike him deeply, and his life would never be the same once the flotilla of bateaux headed west on the Mohawk River for the Oneida council house deep in the wilderness.

At the Oneida villages, the tribe of the Six Nations vowed neutrality, against Guy Johnson's wishes. At Oswego on the shores of Lake Ontario, his pregnant wife Mary, youngest daughter of Sir William Johnson, died in childbirth "succumbing to the rigors of the long journey in the open boats" just as John Johnson feared would happen to his own wife if he left. [KI-p.153]. Guy Johnson mourned her, and blamed the Rebels, swearing vengeance. But vengeance was not to be his.

On July 17, Guy Johnson arrived in Montreal and found that General Carleton had no soldiers to spare to return to the Mohawk Valley to put down the rebellion. Canada was about to be invaded by the Rebels and every man was needed for its defense. Then word came from England that a new Superintendent of the Indians had been commissioned, and Guy Johnson had no authority to command the Indians in Canada. Carleton ordered him west to Fort Niagara to "take charge of Indian affairs there" [KI-p.158] but Johnson had other ideas.

Against Carleton's orders he decided to take Daniel Claus with him and go to England to petition the Crown for redress. Carleton was furious. At this critical moment when Guy Johnson was needed most, leaving for England was nothing less in Carleton's eyes as a dereliction of duty.

With Guy Johnson gone and the Rebel army defeated, by the spring of 1776, some of his tenants, friends, and Mohawks who had not joined with Carleton to defeat the Rebel army, began drifting back to the Mohawk Valley to their homes and families. There they found the rebellion in full swing. Guy Park Manor and all of Johnson's surrounding lands had been confiscated by the Committee for Safety to be sold to finance Congress's war effort. Any remaining loyalists still living in the valley who were trying to hold onto their homes and land were being arrested or forced to flee to Canada.

Joseph Brant accompanied Guy Johnson to England where he was courted by the Crown to return to America to convince the Six Nations to take up the hatchet against the Rebels. Lord Germain promised Brant that all Indian lands taken by the Rebels would be returned to the Indians by the King once the rebellion was put down, but Brant would need to return to America and go to the villages to tell the warriors of the King's promise and remind them to uphold their commitment to serve the King as they had done so under Sir William Johnson. Joseph Brant agreed to report Lord Germain's promise to the Six Nations, and by 1776 he was back in America, landing at New York, and secretly making his way through Rebel lines to the Indian frontier, preparing warriors along the way for war, even though he was not officially a war chief of the Mohawks.

John Johnson escapes to Canada

Peter Johnson, Molly Brant's youngest son by Sir William Johnson, went to Montreal with Guy Johnson. During the American attack on the British, Canadian and Indian defenders of Montreal on September 25, 1775, he captured Ethan Allen at the gates of the city, thwarting Allen's attack and forcing the Americans to retreat. William Brant Johnson, Peter's brother (another one of Sir William's half-breed sons) decided to remain at his home in the Mohawk Valley rather than join Guy Johnson in Canada. He would stay until fall 1776 when Rebel pressure forced him to leave his home and considerable property in the valley with his family, whereupon his holdings were confiscated. William Johnson of Canajoharie, the other of Sir William's Indian sons did leave for Canada in late May 1775 but returned unexpectedly to Canajoharie and the valley near the end of the year, "much to the indignation of local patriots." Soon he was bragging openly about the many rebels he had killed at Montreal. It did not take long for an arrest warrant to be issued for him by the Committee of Safety. As swiftly as he had come, William of Canajoharie fled the valley forever rather than face imprisonment. [KI-p.177]

Sir John Johnson held out as long as he could at his beloved family estate, Johnson Hall. Finally, in early 1776, he was forced to abandon everything and escape to Canada by way of the Adirondacks. A message reached him from Albany that a large force of Rebels was on its way to Johnson Hall to arrest him. In fact, General Schuyler ordered Colonel Elias Dayton and his Third New Jersey Regiment to march from Albany and arrest John Johnson for breaking the terms of the parole that he and Allan MacDonell of Johnson's Scotch retainers had signed on January 20 when they were forced to turn over to Schuyler and his army their military arms at Johnson Hall. [MJ-p.2] Sir John Johnson hastily buried his valuable papers and left with 170 of his loyal Highlander tenants, unfortunately leaving his wife and children behind. Dayton immediately put them under guard and sent them to Albany as prisoners. Johnson Hall was gutted of its possessions and turned into a barracks for the local patriot militia. Sir John Johnson, with a heavy heart, made the arduous journey through the wilderness to Montreal, guided by a few faithful Mohawks. [CE-p.31]

"Thoroughly Trustworthy and Efficient Servants"

There, Sir John Johnson was given orders from General Carleton on June 19, 1776, to begin recruiting men from the hundreds of refugees from the northern colonies gathering in camps along the St. Lawrence River and to train and arm them for a loyalist regiment that would help the Crown in the coming campaign of 1777 to put down the rebellion. Vengeance burned in his heart as never before. He would return to the valley soon as a Lieutenant Colonel of a provincial regiment named the King's Royal Regiment of New York, to carry out his orders to devastate the Mohawk Valley in the name of duty and honor. [TE-p.70]

Upon reaching Montreal, John Butler wished nothing more in the summer of 1775 than to return to his home of Butlersbury in the Mohawk Valley with his son Walter. He, too, had left his family and property to the mercy of the Rebels in May. When Guy Johnson refused Carleton's request to go to Niagara, Carleton desperately turned to John Butler as his only hope to secure that post and the Indians there for the Crown. Butler was promoted to the position of deputy Indian agent and Colonel of the Indians. [BR-27] Reluctant to go, he was finally persuaded to do so when he received a letter informing him that the Rebels had posted signs on the roads leading into the Mohawk Valley calling for his arrest on sight. In addition, he learned his wife and children had been taken to Albany under guard as prisoner hostages.

Seeing that he could not go home under these conditions, John Butler headed for Fort Niagara, arriving there on November 17, 1775. Under Carleton's orders, Butler dutifully began to council the Six Nations Indians there for their allegiance, as well as to organize the loyalist refugees into a company of men that could serve the Indian Department. A steady stream of fugitives was arriving at Fort Niagara from the border settlements in New York and Pennsylvania whom John Butler viewed as able men skilled in the languages of the Indians and the ways of the wilderness, whom he believed could be employed as scouts and rangers for the Department in the west.

John Butler knew many of those men from New York and considered them to be "thoroughly trustworthy and efficient assistants" when he enlisted them. [BR-29] One man who impressed John Butler was William Caldwell who arrived from Philadelphia escorting a number of British officers whom he had assisted in escaping from prison there [CE-p.29] while eluding arrest by the Rebel authorities who discovered his loyalist activities. At Niagara Caldwell joined John Butler's service and began recruiting men from the colonies. Impressed with Caldwell's ability, Butler would come to find that William Caldwell would prove himself to be one of his ablest officers in the future. [WM-p.3]

The cold winter wind blowing off the Great Lakes made the old stone house in the fort garrison inhospitable for John Butler during the winter of 1775, in comparison to the home he left in the Mohawk Valley. Dread for the safety of his family and anger over the loss of his property kindled in Butler a desire for revenge against the Rebels at whose hands he had suffered. At the moment, there was nothing he could do. However, John Butler was a patient and disciplined man who knew that he must wait for the moment he was convinced would surely come, when the Crown would move to put down the rebellion, to settle scores, and even accounts. Until then, he would see to his duties as he had always done in the past, in service of the Crown.

Committees for Detecting Conspiracies

For the hundreds of men across the frontier of New York and Pennsylvania who faced arrest and imprisonment for their allegiance to the King, Canada was their only refuge. They left their homes and fled in small parties following the wilderness trails north to the promise of safe haven and relief that Canada offered. Many of them had barely escaped capture by the local Committees for Detecting Conspiracies that continued to root out suspected Tories and bring charges of treason against anyone not swearing allegiance to Congress and the revolution. The allegations brought against these loyalists to the Crown were true, for they believed that the King's law was the rightful legitimate government, and that those who supported the rebellion were treasonous.

Yet there were many men driven out of their homes to Canada who had not taken sides in the rebellion. Many people on the frontier knew little about the nature of the rebellion brewing around them, nor did they care. They had wished only to remain neutral and be left alone to tend their farms. However no one could remain neutral for long in the social upheaval of the revolution that swept across the colonies and into the frontier, and eventually touched everyone. The threat that Great Britain would attempt to put down the rebellion by force made everyone who was not actively involved in the patriot cause suspect as to where their loyalties lay. Remaining neutral in the conflict would not be possible, for at the heart of the matter, the patriots believed if you were not for the rebellion then you were against it, even if you had not taken sides. To deal with the real or imagined threat of Tories living among them, the Committees for Detecting

An officer enlisted in the loyalist King's Royal Regiment of New York.

Conspiracies decided that anyone suspected of harboring sympathies to the Crown must be arrested.

Often over-zealous militia officers acted on nothing more than a rumor or an opinion brought against a man. Civil disputes were routinely settled by one man publicly accusing another of being a Tory or spy, when in fact there was no evidence. The accused suddenly faced arrest, imprisonment, or the threat of hanging on hearsay alone, without the benefit of a trial. Without recourse, he became a fugitive overnight, leaving everything, including his family and all his property behind as he made his escape.

Motivated to fight by hatred and revenge

Such beleaguered men made their way north to the numerous refugee camps dotting the St. Lawrence River Valley with little more than the shirts on their backs, arriving embittered and destitute. The fugitives were hungry and in desperate need of clothing and shelter. Adding to their misery was the unpleasant thought of the wives and children that they left behind. Their families were unprotected and had little means of supporting themselves. They did not know if the Rebels would confiscate their property and arrest or drive out their women and children who were left to the mercies of unsympathetic authorities. The rapid turn of events caused by their precipitous flight from their homes and the arduous trip north to safety left many loyalists and others in shock, for their world, as they knew it, had been turned upside down.

By 1776 these men were enlisting by the score into provincial loyalist regiments that were being raised in the camps along the St. Lawrence River to take part in the coming British campaign of 1777 to retake the northern colonies by military force. They would form the rank and file of the large provincial units of Sir John Johnson's Royal Regiment of New York, Jessup's Corps of King's Loyal Americans, Peter's Corps of Queen's Loyal Rangers, MacLean's Loyal Highland Emigrants, Joseph Brant's Volunteers, and John Butler's Corps of Indian Department scouts and rangers, as well as a half dozen smaller units led by loyalist officers like Captains Leake, Adams, McAlpine, Pfister and McKay. [FM-p.179] Unlike the British red-coated regular troops who were paid professional soldiers sent from Great Britain, the loyalists clad in their green uniforms had a private and personal stake in the outcome of the looming war, which they would come to fight in earnest.

These men who fought for the British considered themselves to be Americans like the Rebels. While some were native-born in the colonies, most were Irish, Scot and Welsh emigrants to America just as the men who sided with the rebellion were. They came from the same towns and villages dotting the valleys of the frontier of New York and Pennsylvania. And in many instances, the loyalists were from the families that found themselves split apart as one brother remained loyal to the Crown while a father or younger brother might side with the patriots and the rebellion. Unlike the professional soldiers of the British Army brought to America to fight in an impersonal war, the loyalists personally knew the men who had attempted to arrest them, and in the process, drove them from their families and homes. They could name the hated Rebels whom they were about to take arms against, and in turn, could be named by them, who equally despised them for siding with the King. For both sides, this would be a war fought on an intimate personal level for values beyond loyalism to the Crown or patriotism to the revolution. What motivated the loyalists more than all else was hatred and revenge.

Vengeance burned intensely in their hearts. Getting even with those who had tormented them and turned their world upside down was what drove them to fight, more than the Crown's need to put the rebellion down by force and re-establish British rule. In that respect the loyalists flocking to Canada had much in common with the western Indian tribes of the Ohio Country and the Iroquois of the New York and Pennsylvania wilderness, who were by 1776 increasingly disenfranchised of their lands and way of life by those responsible for the revolt against the King. As allies in vengeance, the provincial loyalists and the Indians would fight the Rebels to attempt to regain their lost homes and property, and when that was not possible, seek revenge against the Rebels. They would bring to the frontier a new wilderness war starkly different than that waged in the east between conventional armies. All of the terrible lessons learned over the past 30 years of wilderness fighting would be brought to bear against the unprotected Rebel frontier settlements that would leave in its wake burned cabins, scorched earth and mutilated bodies. No quarter would be asked nor given by either side for this war would be one of vicious, bloody, savage extermination of the Enemy.

Under the flag of vengeance, the Indians and loyalists were poised by spring 1777 to embark on a determined campaign to settle scores and even accounts with their hated Enemy. All that was left to know was the time and place that the lessons of wilderness war would be carried out.

Chapter 8

The Terrible Lessons of Wilderness Warfare Well-Learned

As the third year of the war for independence in America opened in 1777 and the winter months gave way to spring, the promise of a new British offensive in North America to reclaim the rebellious colonies by military force was put in motion. That military plan, conceived by British Major General John Burgoyne and approved by British parliament and the King, was designed to bring the full might of the British military to bear against the Rebels by a conventional battle in the north. If successful, the northern colonies would be cut in two. Key to Burgoyne's planned offensive was the need for a diversionary force made up of light infantry, loyalists, and Indians to move upon the Rebel frontier through the wilderness. As the architect of the campaign that would utilize Indians and provincial troops, Burgoyne was about to unleash upon the American colonial frontier a new Indian wilderness war that would bring terror, death and destruction more terrible than ever seen before in American history. His diversionary force would put to use all the tactics of Indian warfare learned since the 1750's, and demonstrate those lessons well-learned with deadly effectiveness by the summer of 1777.

The wilderness war about to be unleashed by British-allied Indians and loyalists would be terrible because the King's men and their red allies would fight the Rebels out of hatred and revenge, as much as for King and country. What began on the frontier in 1777 as an adjunct to Burgoyne's conventional battle plan, would with passing months and years, evolve into a full-scale all-encompassing war within a war, as the British attempted to hold the Indian lands of the Ohio Country from Kentucky to the Mohawk Valley for the King, by sending irregular military forces to where few redcoats could go and to depopulate the Rebel frontier by a relentless onslaught. The ensuing atrocities that were committed and the scorched earth left in the wake of wilderness battle would attest to the intensity and savageness of the wilderness war that would last until the guns fell silent with an armistice in the spring of 1783. But in the spring of 1777, the wilderness war of unparalleled proportions was about to begin. The first blow would be struck at Oriska Creek in the Mohawk Valley.

"Blows Must Decide the Outcome"

The military plan that Major General Burgoyne presented to Lord Germain and the Crown in London on February 28, 1777, was bold if not brilliant in theory. Recently returned to England from duty in the American colonies, "Gentleman Johnny" Burgoyne was considered by those who knew him to be more than a military officer, politician, and socialite. [KR-p.74-75] Burgoyne had a reputation as a military strategist and thinker. After taking time to reflect upon the mixed results of Britain's year and half of fighting in America to subdue the rebellion, Burgoyne came up with an idea of his own in which he envisioned a dramatic bold stroke for ending the war. In a written work that he titled "Thoughts for Conducting the War from the Side of Canada," [FA-p.120] Burgoyne proposed a British invasion of the New York colony by a two-pronged attack from Canada designed to sever rebellious New England from the middle colonies. Once New England was isolated, rebel forces could be effectively destroyed piecemeal and a swift end to the war would result, ending the rebellion once and for all.

The idea of an invasion from Canada was not Burgoyne's entirely, nor unfamiliar to Lord George Germain, Secretary of State for the Colonies, and the man in charge of conducting the war in America. [KR-p.65] The idea of a Canadian invasion of the colonies from the north had been touted by Generals Gage, Howe, and Carleton in the past without success. However, by the time Burgoyne presented the idea to Germain, circumstances had changed considerably, and Lord Germain was much more receptive to the idea. The American invasion of Canada by the rebels the previous year, though thwarted, had shaken the Crown. With Canada now secure, King George was pushing for a quick end to the colonial crisis before Canada could be jeopardized again. At the start of the rebellion in 1775, King George had concluded that "blows must decide" the outcome of the growing colonial conflict. The British military had not done so by 1777. Now the King advised Germain that the only course of action to take militarily was to strike deep and hard at the heart of the rebellion, and in doing so, bring his "unhappy people" into line, whom he felt were unfortunately "suffering from delusion, and oppressed by daring desperate leaders." [KR-p.67] It was clear to Germain that as Colonial Secretary responsible for military strategy in the war, he must abandon the road of prudence and caution taken by ministers and generals in the past year and a half, and correct the situation in America in 1777. "Never anything but a hawk on the question of how to deal with the colonies," Lord Germain knew that the rebellion must be crushed, and crushed hard. [KR-p.68]

When Burgoyne presented his strategic plan to Lord Germain in London on February 28, 1777, Germain gave it more than a cursory glance. Looking it over in detail, Germain decided that Burgoyne's plan was militarily sound, and his timing for such an invasion correct. Furthermore, Germain advised King George that not only had Burgoyne presented a bold military plan to stamp out the rebellion, but also, Burgoyne, as the architect of the plan, was the best man to carry out the job.

Germain believed Burgoyne was not like several of his fellow officers in command who had displayed a reluctance to dispatch the rebels with wholehearted ruthlessness in the campaigns of the last year and a half. He viewed Burgoyne as a commander who would wage an aggressive campaign and possessed the best talents for making it succeed. If Burgoyne were not clearly a serious military tactician, Germain reasoned that he was an ambitious military officer and veteran politician who would not tolerate failure. The King agreed, and Lord Germain gave Burgoyne the nod to proceed, as preparations got under way to send reinforcements and war materiel to Canada for the coming campaign. By the end of March, Burgoyne and the regiments were making ready to sail. [KR-p.88]

"Need for a Diversion"

Burgoyne's plan had some complexity. First, he planned to move an army of over 7000 men south from Canada, deep into rebel-held territory over rough terrain, no easy task in itself. Burgoyne proposed to Lord Germain that he would lead this main thrust south through the Lake Champlain and Hudson River valleys of New York colony with the aim of taking Albany. If all went according to plan, Burgoyne would unite at Albany with a British army led by General Howe coming north from New York City that would attack the Rebels defending Albany. With the fall of Albany, a clear road from British-held New York City to Quebec and Canada would be opened, and New England severed from New York and the middle colonies. However, to ensure success, Burgoyne's army would not be the only one to attack the Rebels from Canada. Burgoyne knew that the farther he moved from his base in Canada, the deeper his army would penetrate into Rebel-held territory where sizable militias could be counted on to support the Continental regiments opposing him. He needed a diversion to prevent those Rebel reinforcements from arriving to block his entry into Albany. The diversion Burgoyne envisioned needed to be something that would effectively draw the Rebels off and hold their attention, at the precise time Burgoyne attacked Albany. What better way to do so than to use Indians and provincial troops to attack the Rebels without warning from the wilderness west of Albany, by way of Canada and the Mohawk Valley. It was a plan that Burgoyne believed would work.

The diversionary force that Burgoyne envisioned would be much smaller than his own army, due to the need to move select troops swiftly along difficult wilderness waterways and trails between Canada and the New York frontier. It would be comprised of companies of British light infantry, German mercenary light infantry, provincial loyalist rangers, and a sizable contingent of allied Iroquois Indian warriors. This western prong of the campaign from Canada would travel by boat to Oswego on Lake Ontario and then move southeast to the headwaters of the Mohawk River, destroying Rebel frontier posts in their way and then sweeping east down the river valley, brushing aside opposition, and joining Burgoyne's army somewhere near Albany at the same time.

A Two-Front Campaign

The real purpose of the western prong of Burgoyne's plan of attack from Canada was to effectively distract the Rebels from Burgoyne's approaching army more than to strategically support him. What Burgoyne hoped the diversionary force would accomplish was to force the Rebels to divide their own forces, especially the militia, to deal with the threat from the west. He surmised that the Rebel militias of the Mohawk Valley and surrounding areas would heed the call to defend their own homes, families and property from the threat of Indians, before leaving them undefended, if the militias were called on to oppose Burgoyne's army coming down the Champlain Valley. The diversion was necessary to draw off supplies and support for the Rebel army that Burgoyne would face as he came close to Albany. Here the Rebels would have the logistical advantage over Burgoyne of close reinforcements and good roads to move them over. Burgoyne realized, at this point in his campaign, his army had no chance of reinforcement and re-supply until he joined Howe's army. The diversionary force would simply have to take the Rebel pressure off of him until his juncture with Howe occurred. Burgoyne counted on the threat of Indian attack to cause panic and alarm along the frontier to draw off the Rebels, and crumble some of the resistance he would face. Instinctively he knew that no matter what assurances the Indians gave to the British to refrain from their usual depredations, once they began to scalp, loot and burn the Rebel frontier, the Indians could be counted on to wreck enough havoc that the Rebel militia would have no choice but to meet the approaching Indian threat. The threat of Indian attack on the defenseless frontier itself was all the strategic diversion Burgoyne calculated he would need to keep the Enemy before him divided and off-balance, thus insuring the success of his own army. The diversionary force would be more of a feint in the two-front campaign than anything else.

Lt. Col. Barry St. Leger

Leaving England in late March 1777, Burgoyne arrived at Quebec on May 5 to take command of the grand army which he was to prepare for the coming campaign. Burgoyne notified Lt. Col. Barry St. Leger, the commander of the 34th Regiment of Foot already posted in Canada, of his new appointment as the commanding officer of the diversionary force. St. Leger, born in Ireland in 1739, was a career officer of Huguenot descent serving in the British army, and the man chosen by Lord Germain and Burgoyne to lead the important second prong of the coming invasion. St. Leger, who had seen service in the British army during the Seven Years War in America, had entered the army as an Ensign in the 28th Regiment in 1756, and in 1757 St. Leger went with the regiment for service in America. He had been made a captain at the siege of Louisburg, as was the case with Wolfe at the fall of Quebec when the 48th was ordered out of reserve by a dying Wolfe to cut off the French retreat. [WG2-p.15] By May 1772, St. Leger was promoted to Lt. Colonel in the army and in 1775 he was transferred to take command of the 34th Regiment serving in Canada.

St. Leger was chosen to lead the "light expedition" because of his lengthy service and leadership experience in America. While he was an experienced officer of merit in the regular British army stationed in America, he had "little experience in the American wilderness" [WG2-p.15] and even less when it came to dealing with native Indian allies. In actuality, St. Leger had not served on the American frontier in the Seven Years War against the French and their Indian allies. He had not taken part in the campaigns of that war that were fought in the wilderness. Consequently, St. Leger had neither practical experience in navigating an army through the wilderness or fighting a military campaign in it, which was quite different than service in a regular regiment.

Most importantly of all, St. Leger had not dealt with Indians on a personal or professional level, a prerequisite that one might have expected of the man chosen to lead a military expedition into the wilderness with a force that was to be made up of nearly as many native warriors as light infantry. It would be upon the Indians and their superb scouts that the commander of the light expedition would need to rely for intelligence, direction, and fighting ability once his force entered the forbidding, hostile territory of the Rebel frontier. Surprisingly, St. Leger, as the officer in command of the diversionary force, did not possess the skills or ability to understand and communicate with Indians. It was simply an attribute lacking in St. Leger. "That he had no personal experience with natives was ignored" by Burgoyne when he chose his commander [WG2-p.15]

It may have been an oversight on Burgoyne's part, or he may have believed that this shortcoming in St. Leger's experience could be remediated by including on St. Leger's staff provincial officers who were competent and experienced in dealing and working with the Indian allies. Such men could act as intermediaries between the Indians and St. Leger when he needed to rely upon the Indians to scout the enemy during the campaign. These men, who knew the Indian war captains and could speak their languages, would be able to coordinate the Indian efforts in the field and aid in carrying out St Leger's orders during the expedition.

What were St. Leger's orders? As St. Leger assembled his force in the camps at Lachine surrounding Montreal, he knew that his overall force would be much smaller in size than Burgoyne's massive army. His objective was to invade the Rebel territory of the Mohawk Valley from the western wilderness by way of Canada and Oswego on Lake Ontario with great speed. Once his expeditionary force was completed, he was to make his way up the St. Lawrence River from Montreal by bateaux, until he reached Lake Ontario. This leg of the trip would be arduous for his little army would have to "battle up the 14 major cataracts of the St. Lawrence" before reaching the open water of Lake Ontario. [BC-3] Once there, his force would row in a southward direction, following the shoreline until they reached the post called Oswego at the mouth of Oswego River that flowed north from Lake Oneida deep in Iroquois country. At Oswego, St. Leger was to wait to rendevous with the balance of the provincial troops coming east across the lake from Fort Niagara under the command of Colonel John Butler. In addition, a sizable contingent of Iroquois warriors would meet him there, as had been promised by the agents of the British Indian Department, to join his force to invade the Rebel frontier. Timing would be of the essence in gathering the many-varied units together, but if all went well, St. Leger would be able to set out on his mission to proceed to the headwaters of the Mohawk River, reduce the Rebel fortifications there at the "Carrying Place" called Fort Stanwix, then proceed downriver into the Mohawk Valley and thus devastate the Rebels, while bringing his western prong of Burgoyne's attack from Canada closer to a juncture with the General's army somewhere near Albany. In spite of the greater distances St. Leger would have to travel, the difficult wilderness terrain his force would need to maneuver through, and the large amount of time that his little army would be out of contact with Canada or Burgoyne, St. Leger believed that the plan was one that would work, and work with great success.

The Light Infantry and Regulars

For regular troops, St. Leger had at his disposal two of the ten companies of men from his own regiment, the 34th of Foot. The Grenadier and Light infantry companies had already been assigned to Burgoyne's expeditionary army, and six companies were destined to remain at Montreal for its defense. Two "hat" or regular companies allotted to St. Leger, with their officers, amounted to 132 men. [WG1-p.17] These two infantry companies would retain their red woolen uniforms trimmed with yellow facings for the campaign. [LM-120]

In addition to the men of the 34th, St. Leger was to draw upon nearly two complete companies from the 8th Regiment of Foot or King's Regiment that had been garrisoned throughout the upper posts of the St. Lawrence River and the Great Lakes since its arrival in Canada in 1768. With officers, St. Leger would have 99 men of the King's 8th "hat" and light infantry companies for the expedition who were ordered to meet him at Oswego from their posts at Niagara and Oswegatchie. Likewise, the 8th's wool coats were scarlet red like the 34th's, however their facings were blue trim, and their hats black tricorn like the 34th's. [FA-p.121]

St. Leger also had the use of part of a German mercenary regiment that arrived piecemeal late in the spring at Quebec from the German state of Hesse-Hanau. St. Leger acquired one company of approximately 90 men with officers from the battalion company called the "jager" or light infantry rifleman company. The Hesse Hanau Jager company joined St. Leger after he left Montreal at Buck Island at the mouth of the St. Lawrence River on Lake Ontario, their blue wool uniforms trimmed and faced in red. [MR-p.28]

For artillery in the event that St. Leger faced unforeseen determined Rebel opposition, St. Leger had little option but to travel light and make use of a few mobile fieldpieces available to him. A Royal Artillery detachment would accompany his force, bringing with them two 6-pounder field pieces, two 3-pounder guns, and four co-horns or light fieldpieces. The long distance and rough terrain to the objective dictated that heavier guns could not be taken. Forty-two artillerymen would handle the lighter pieces in the field as well as moving them into position, arming them, and firing them if the situation should arise. [WG1-p.17]

The Loyalist Regiment King's Royal Yorkers

The bulk of the soldiers accompanying St. Leger's regulars as he left Montreal in June for Lake Ontario were the men and officers of a newly-created provincial regiment called the King's Royal Regiment of New York, commanded by Lieutenant Colonel Sir John Johnson, son of Sir William Johnson, and landowner from the Mohawk Valley. Sir John had escaped Rebel prosecution in the valley in 1776 when a warrant was issued for his arrest. His properties were subsequently confiscated and his family arrested by the Rebels and sent to Albany. After recovering from his arduous trip through the Adirondacks to Canada in 1776, Sir John Johnson and the loyalists arriving in Canada to join him assisted General Carleton, the governor of Canada, in ousting the rebels from Quebec by force.

Sir John was awarded the opportunity to raise two battalions of provincial infantry from the disenfranchised men in the camps around Montreal, and by the spring of 1777, Johnson convinced Carleton to let his men of the 1st Battalion join St. Leger's small army in invading the Mohawk Valley, as most of Johnson's recruits were from that area. Most of the loyalist refugees from New York and Pennsylvania had arrived in the camps in Canada without their families. They not only had a burning desire to seek revenge on those Rebels who had persecuted them, but had an even stronger urge to rescue their families and property. Sir John Johnson knew that his loyalist recruits in the battalion of the King's Royal Regiment of New York, or Royal Yorker's, were the best candidates for soldiering in the Mohawk Valley that St. Leger could come by.

By the time St. Leger's force began to move up the St. Lawrence River on June 26, 1777, Johnson had assembled and outfitted for the expedition seven companies totaling 246 men and officers. Six companies were "hat" or regular infantry companies uniformed in green wool with white facings and the seventh was a light infantry company commanded by Colonel Johnson's brother-in-law Captain Stephen Watts. Most of Sir John Johnson's men were refugee loyalists from the Mohawk Valley. Many of them were his former tenants at Johnson Hall. They were provincial loyalist troops in the British military establishment in Canada and were not regular British soldiers. To delineate that difference, the Yorker uniforms were colored green (not red) because green was the color chosen to represent provincial regiments raised in America. However, the difference between a provincial regiment and a regular British regiment went beyond where the unit was raised, or how much the men were paid, or whether their uniforms were red or green.

In the eyes of the officers of the British military, Canada and the greater British colonial empire, provincial troops were not considered to be of the same caliber as regular soldiers. Consequently, however valuable Sir John estimated his men's worth to be in the coming campaign due to their unique personal motivation to fight, and to their familiarity with the land that they were about to invade, in the eyes of General Carleton and his staff, provincial troops raised from the colonies were viewed with some skepticism as non-regulars. Provincials, no matter how loyal to the Crown, were considered better than militia, but far less valuable than regular troops due to lack of training and, therefore, fighting ability on the conventional battlefield. The diversionary wing of Burgoyne's campaign of 1777 would test that premise on the non-conventional wilderness battlefield.

Loyalist of the British Indian Department

In addition to the force that St. Leger assembled at Montreal in early June 1777, he sent orders to the upper British posts of the Great Lakes at Detroit and Niagara for the officers of the British Indian Department at those forts to bring their ranger companies and Canadian militiamen to meet his force at or near Oswego where they would rendevous with the Indian warriors of the Iroquois Six Nations whom St. Leger previously requested to join him on his expedition. Major John Butler of the Indian Department received his orders for the coming campaign as early as June 6 at his post at Fort Niagara, whereupon he began to outfit the men of his ranging company for the planned attack on the Mohawk Valley. While Colonel Guy Johnson was the senior officer of the Indian Department, he had left Canada for England in 1775, only returning to America in 1776, where he remained at British Army headquarters in New York City. [BC-76] John Butler was the senior officer of the Six Nations Indian Department that both Carleton and St. Leger could count on, as he had made himself indispensable in securing Fort Niagara for the British. In the spring of 1777, Butler had been ordered by Carleton to urge the Six Nations to remain neutral for the moment. By and large he had been successful, though the Oneidas were strongly favoring the Rebel cause due to the persuasion of Reverend Kirkland, an ardent Rebel supporter who lived among them, who was a thorn in Butler's side. John Butler had been working unceasingly since arriving at Niagara to gain influential support among the Iroquois, in the hopes that when the moment was ripe, he would be able to persuade them to join St. Leger, even without the Oneidas.

Major John Butler knew he could count on slightly over 100 of his own men at Fort Niagara to accompany him in the St. Leger campaign. Each man was a member of the Indian Department, and handpicked or personally endorsed by Butler himself. Most of the men had made their way through the wilderness to Ft. Niagara in the past year as refugees from Rebel oppression in the Mohawk Valley and parts of Pennsylvania colony. Many of them were former friends and neighbors of the Butler family before he had left the valley in the spring of 1775 with Guy Johnson. All of the men now under his command were seasoned scouts and adept woodsmen who were on duty at the fort recruiting loyalists to the Crown's cause, and working with the various parties of Six Nations Indians who frequently visited the fort seeking trade goods and powder. Many of these men of the Indian Department could speak the languages of the tribes and were respected by the Indians. Among the men that John Butler had come to know and trust was William Caldwell who he would rely upon as an officer in the future.

Joseph Brant's Mission to the Iroquois

Where the allegiances of the Iroquois Six Nations were concerned, Major John Butler knew that the Mohawk Indian Joseph Brant could be counted on to support the cause of the Crown, but for different reasons than the particular duty that Butler served. Brant, who was once the secretary of the Indian Department under Guy Johnson, had gone to England in 1775 with Daniel Claus and Guy Johnson, to petition the Crown on behalf of the Mohawks and their Iroquois brothers. He had a list of grievances of the Six Nations which he wished to put before the King to seek some sort of redress. Instead, Joseph Brant was dined and feted before King George and Lord Germain as an unofficial emissary of the Six Nations, where he was assured that the Iroquois would receive their just rewards once the Rebels were defeated on the coming battlefields. King George and Germain impressed upon Brant that he must secure the allegiance of the Iroquois Confederacy in the coming campaign of 1777, which was to finish the rebellion once and for all. For the Iroquois support of the British military effort, the Crown would see to it that the Iroquois were well compensated. Emissary or not, Joseph Brant now had a mission to fulfill.

Burning with desire to return home, Joseph Brant sailed for America in 1776 with Lord Howe's army, which was sent to attack and secure New York City. While Guy Johnson decided to stay in New York, Brant, and Gilbert Tice, a trusted friend and fellow officer of the Indian Department, traveled in disguise through Rebel-held territory to reach the villages of the Mohawk Indians, where Brant immediately began to urge the Mohawks to support the King and abandon their neutrality. He met with disappointment.

Moving from village to village, Brant encountered little support. Unfortunately, he held no official status as a chieftain or leader of his own people, so they largely ignored him when he spoke. In addition, Brant was not recognized as an appointed war captain among the Mohawk warriors who looked to others for leadership in battle. Those men were advocating neutrality and would not join Brant. Neither did the other tribes of the Iroquois Confederacy view Brant as anything more than a common Mohawk without standing. The Iroquois leadership of the various tribes, especially the Oneidas, was preaching neutrality in the war between the white men. Contrary to Brant's exhortations, the Iroquois chiefs advocated that their people attempt to live in peace with both loyalists to the Crown and Rebels, while choosing neither side.

However, Brant was not bound by the suggestions of the chiefs, and wanted the Iroquois to back the British. It was only in the service of the British

Six Nations Indian Department that Brant had any official presence, and at the moment, what was left of the Department was headquartered at Fort Niagara, under the command of John Butler. Butler's orders from General Carleton in Quebec ran contrary to Joseph Brant's desires, for Carleton was urging Butler to keep the Iroquois neutral at this point. Butler had no choice but to rebuff Brant when he arrived at Fort Niagara late in 1776, urging Butler to support his efforts to rouse the Six Nations to action.

Disappointed and humiliated, Joseph Brant returned home to his family at the village of Oquaga on the upper branch of the Susquehanna River in the mountainous lands south of the Mohawk Valley. Defiant by the lack of Indian support, in the early spring of 1777 Joseph Brant raised the King's standard in the center of the village of Oquaga, and declared he was ready to make war upon the Rebels even if he had no Indian warriors who would follow him into battle. To his surprise, not Indians but white men came by the dozens to Oquaga to rally around Joseph Brant's British flag.

Brant's Corps of Irregular Volunteers

Over 100 white loyalists of English, Irish and Scotch descent joined Brant from their lands in the surrounding mountains where many of them had been threatened and harassed by local Rebels for their loyalist views during the months following the war in New England. In Brant they saw not only an educated man who had been favorably received by the King, but also a leader as well who was ready to take action against the Rebels. For their part, the white loyalists pledged to fight under Brant's leadership as an appointed war captain. For his part, Brant promised the fledgling irregulars, who began calling themselves "Brant's Volunteers," that he would let them fight Indian style, foregoing the strict regimen of regular white troops. The agreement was unanimous.

This "wild and undisciplined" group of disaffected loyalists who "refused to take arms or be under any command" [KI-p.192] other than that of Joseph Brant prepared for military action against the Rebels by dressing and painting themselves like Indians, the irony of Joseph Brant and his volunteer corps was not lost upon Brant. He found himself an English-speaking, white-educated Mohawk Indian with no military rank among the Iroquois League nor the British provincial regiments, who had, nonetheless, raised a corps of white men eager to fight like the Indians (whom he had tried and failed to rouse to war) all in support of the King's cause. The men serving with Brant would come to risk all, including hanging without trial if captured by the Rebels. Of all the loyalist units serving the King's cause, Brant's Volunteers would remain in the field more than any other force, in "almost unremitting actual Service" for the duration of the war on the frontier. [KI-p.192]

On June 13, 1777, Burgoyne's army of over 7000 fighting men began the planned invasion of the rebellious colonies by moving south from Fort St. John's on the Richelieu River towards Lake Champlain. At the same time, St. Leger was putting the finishing touches on his preparations to embark up the St.

Lawrence from his camps at Lachine near Montreal. He dispatched his own Superintendent of the Indians of the Western Expedition ahead of his force to prepare the way for the departure of his light division. Lt. Colonel Daniel Claus had thoughts of his own when he set out on June 23, 1777, with a handful of trusted men and native warriors for the Iroquois Indian village of Akwesasne upriver on the St. Lawrence from Lachine. [WG1-p.3] Claus did not believe that the information floating about St. Leger's staff concerning the poor condition of the rebel forces in the Mohawk Valley was necessarily true, and he wanted to find out for himself.

While St. Leger's entire force of regular troops and Johnson's Royal Yorkers began moving up the St. Lawrence on the morning of June 26, Claus dispatched a party of rangers and Indians to head across country and scout the rebel-held Fort Stanwix located at the portage between the headwaters of the upper Mohawk River and Wood Creek that emptied into Oneida Lake deep in the wilderness of Iroquois country. The aim of Claus's scouts was to reconnoiter Fort Stanwix, count Rebel heads, and capture a few prisoners who could be brought back to Claus for fresh intelligence on the strength of the fort that St. Leger would ultimately attack.

Claus Seeks Fresh Intelligence

While St. Leger's force was struggling through the 14 major cataracts of the St. Lawrence to reach Lake Ontario, Claus's Indian scouts reached Fort Stanwix and attacked a sod-cutting crew of Continental soldiers working outside the fort and took several prisoners back to Claus who personally interrogated them. Daniel Claus was amazed to find out that, contrary to St. Leger's information, not only was "Stanwix in good repair and well garrisoned, but, more alarming, that the Rebels were alerted to the (St. Leger's) expedition." [WG1-p.3] As St. Leger's force neared Buck Island by bateaux near the juncture of the St. Lawrence and Lake Ontario, Claus intercepted St. Leger and presented him with the startling intelligence. Unimpressed, St. Leger dismissed it out of hand.

On July 9, St. Leger's force was joined by a late Hesse Hanau Jager company coming from Lachine along with nearly 50 Quebec militia. On July 19, St. Leger and his army left Buck Island for the old British military post of Oswego at the mouth of the Oswego River. Daniel Claus had left St. Leger several days earlier with his Indian scouts and rangers. Soon after Claus reached the abandoned ruins of Oswego, the former fort of French and Indian war fame, he was surprised by the arrival of his old friend Joseph Brant and his Volunteers on July 23. Brant had received instructions from John Butler at Fort Niagara to head at once for Oswego to meet him and St. Leger for the coming campaign. Brant had brought with him nearly 300 fighting men, consisting of his own Volunteers and "small bands of dissident (Iroquois) warriors who could see no sense in neutrality" as the Iroquois League as a whole had been advising. [KI-

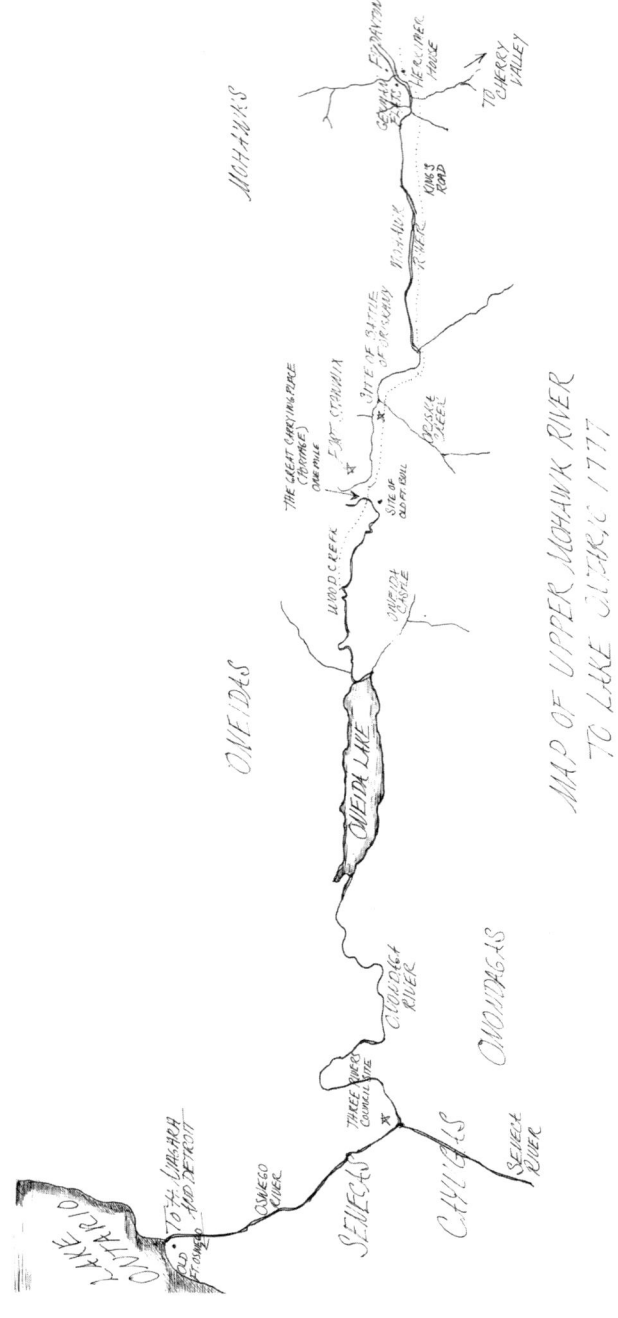

Map of the upper Mohawk River to Lake Ontario, 1777

p.196-198] Impatiently waiting to strike the Rebels at the first possible moment, everyone hoped to see action soon.

Rendevous at Oswego

John Butler and his force arrived at Oswego on July 25, a few days after St. Leger's expedition reached the appointed meeting place. Soon soldiers in green and red uniforms bustled about a newly raised camp. Butler had brought with him a sizable contingent of fighting men, including over 100 rangers of the Six Nations Indian Department, a mixed group of Iroquois warriors from the Fort Niagara area, a company and a half of the King's 8th Regiment stationed at Niagara, and a party of Lake or Huron native warriors and French Canadians from the upper British post of Fort Detroit. All these men were added to St. Leger's command, including Joseph Brant's Volunteers. At last, St. Leger had his entire force massed for the attack on the Mohawk Valley but for one important group who had not yet arrived. The leadership of the Six Nations Indians, primarily the Seneca and the bulk of their numerous warriors was still undecided whether to fight with the British, or sit the battle out. Privately, St. Leger acknowledged that he needed the Iroquois to join him more than ever, as he was deep in the wilderness and far from reinforcement or re-supply.

A Grand Council with all of the Six Nations had been planned for some time. Butler had sent word to the Iroquois far ahead of St. Leger's arrival, and hundreds of uncommitted warriors and their chiefs were awaiting a meeting with St. Leger upstream at the appointed council ground called Three Rivers, where the Oneida and Seneca Rivers joined to form the Oswego, several miles up river from St. Leger's camp. As St. Leger and his army departed Oswego on July 27 for the fateful meeting with the Indians, he dispatched an advanced patrol to range far ahead of him to reconnoiter the Rebels at Fort Stanwix while he conferred with the Iroquois.

St. Leger picked Lieutenant Henry Bird, an enterprising Light infantry officer of the King's 8th Regiment to command the advanced force of 30 soldiers from the 8th and 34th regiments for the mission. In addition, two rangers of the Indian Department were chosen to accompany Bird, along with several sizable parties of Seneca and Mississauga warriors to assist. Bird's orders were threefold. Claus's Indians had come into St. Leger's camp reporting that some Rebel militia from the Mohawk Valley were attempting to block Wood Creek which flowed from the Carrying Place near Fort Stanwix into Lake Oneida; Bird was to prevent the Rebels from doing so with his force. Further, he was to cut off Rebel communication between Fort Stanwix and the Mohawk Valley, as well as intercept any Rebel reinforcements and supplies rumored to be coming up the Mohawk River by bateaux. Gathering his men, Lt. Bird set out at once on the morning of July 29.

The Three Rivers Council Hits a Snag

On July 30, the native Grand Council was held at Three Rivers where St. Leger found all of the tribes present, including the Oneida who were known to be supporting the Rebels and were suspected of alerting Fort Stanwix and the Mohawk Valley of St. Leger's presence. Most of the hundreds of natives gathered were low on food, powder, clothing, and trade goods. St. Leger, on Butler's advice, had the Indian Department officers distribute goods and rum to the Indians as presents of the King while St. Leger, Butler, Claus and Joseph Brant counseled with the chiefs trying to persuade them to join the British cause who would surely win the war. When the numerous Senecas who remained unconvinced talked openly of returning to their villages at the end of the council, Daniel Claus, a veteran officer in dealing with the Indians, cleverly took a different tact with them. Claus spoke to them saying, "Go with us, and see us whip the Rebels. Just sit down and smoke your pipes and see what a great show we shall provide. We shall not need your help!" The ploy worked, and the Seneca decided to come along, as "there was nothing they liked better than to watch a good fight." [KI-p.199]

St. Leger's small army now consisted of more than 750 soldiers [WG1-p.17] and 800 native warriors, of whom more than 50 were principal tribal chiefs and war captains. Of the Six Nations, the Seneca were the most numerous, counting 15 chiefs and over 200 warriors still uncommitted. Before the entire force set off for Ft. Stanwix on August 1, St. Leger dispatched Joseph Brant, his Volunteers, and some 200 Indians to move quickly ahead of the main body to reinforce Bird's advance party. Wilderness warfare had begun.

Attack Begins at Fort Stanwix

As early as June 25, scouting parties of British-allied Indians had not only reconnoitered rebel-held Fort Stanwix to count heads, but also began ambushing anyone who was foolish enough to venture far from the fort, despite the repeated warnings from friendly Oneida Indian scouts that a British army was approaching from the direction of old Oswego with hostile Indians in their employ. Two hunters were ambushed a mile and a quarter from Fort Stanwix by a party of Iroquois who tomahawked and scalped them. On July 3, Ensign Sporr with six men from the fort was detailed to cut sod for construction of the fort defenses. They strayed too far from the protection of the fort walls and were surprised by a party of Daniel Claus's St. Regis Mohawks from Akwesasne who unceremoniously captured the entire squad, clubbed to death and scalped one of the captured men in the presence of the others, and then scalped another who was wounded. The ensign and four others survived to be whisked away for interrogation by Claus under the threat of Indian torture. [WG1-p.195] The Indian depredations continued, to the horror of those inside the fort.

On July 27, three young girls from the fort slipped through the sentinel gate to pick berries some 200 yards from the fort walls in plain view of the sentries. The girls were fired upon by hidden Indians, who scalped the hapless children before any soldiers could save them. When their lifeless, mangled bodies were recovered and brought to their weeping families in the fort, all remaining doubts among the garrison as to if and when the Indians would strike were put to rest. Each within the fort realized that "the terror and bitterness of war had come to the Mohawk Valley" [FA-p.127] at last, against a defenseless frontier by a merciless opponent who would spare no one from the war axe.

The next day, July 28, 1777, the fort commander, Colonel Gansevoort, sent the women and children of the garrison down the Mohawk River to safety with a military escort, as word of the Indian attacks panicked the terror-stricken population below Ft. Stanwix. Gansevoort wrote to his superiors of the Indian attacks, "These mercenaries of Britain come not to fight, but to lie in wait to murder; and it is equally the same to them, if they can get a scalp, whether it is from a soldier or an innocent babe." [FA-p.127] Gansevoort, an easterner with limited military experience gathered from the ill-fated Rebel invasion of Canada and command of the Albany militia had yet to understand the nature of Indian warfare. In the days to come, he would witness firsthand the Indians' effective style of fighting superbly suited for unconventional wilderness warfare, which only fort walls could provide some measure of protection.

On August 3, Lieutenant Bird, with the help of Joseph Brant, his volunteers and a horde of Indians surrounded Fort Stanwix and cut off all communications with the Mohawk Valley. St. Leger sent a dispatch to Bird on August 2, that if Bird found, when the fort was surrounded, that the Enemy, "observing the discretion and judgment with which it is made, should offer to capitulate, you are to tell that you are sure that I am well disposed to listen to them." [JJ-p.96] St. Leger believed, contrary to Brant's intelligence from the field, that the Rebels would surrender the fort rather than fight. What Bird was finding out for himself was the fort appeared ready to fight. Brant sent parties of Indians and his rangers scouting through the woods on both sides of the Mohawk River for miles below the fort silently searching for signs of any militia reinforcements on the move.

Meanwhile, St. Leger arrived at the fort ahead of the bulk of his force, and sent Captain Gilbert Tice of the Indian Department under a flag of truce to call for the fort's surrender. Tice was chosen because, "as a veteran of the Seven Years' War…he was well known to the New York Continentals." [WG1-p.75] Tice delivered St. Leger's surrender ultimatum which threatened the officers that if they should resist, he would have no choice but to unleash upon them "every concomitant horror that a reluctant but indispensable prosecution of military must occasion," [FA-p.128] in the form of hundreds of Indian warriors whooping, yelling, and firing at a distance outside the fort walls, who St. Leger referred to as his "extensive Corps of Indian Allies." [KI-p.203] However Gansevoort, a stubborn and dedicated man to the patriot cause, took quick stock of his 750-man strong garrison, his ample stores of provisions and ammunition, and the sturdiness of the fort walls and decided to fight. He rejected St. Leger's demands and dismissed Tice. Thus began the siege of Fort Stanwix.

Rebels on the March

In the early evening of August 5, just as St. Leger was putting the finishing touches on his preparations for an assault on the fort, an Indian runner came into Joseph Brant's camp from the direction of the Mohawk Valley with an important message for him and St. Leger. The Mohawk youth had come from the Mohawk village of Canajoharie, some 40 miles downriver, where Molly Brant, former wife to Sir William Johnson and sister to Joseph Brant now resided. Living quietly amid the Rebels in the valley while keeping her decidedly loyalist allegiance quietly to herself, she silently watched the activities of the Rebel militia, and sent that intelligence by trusted Mohawks to awaiting scouts who took the information to Canada. Molly was aware of St. Leger's campaign, his movement to Oswego, and the approach of his force to Fort Stanwix long before the Rebel militia of the valley under the command of General Herkimer was informed of the British and loyalist presence from Oneida scouts returning downriver with dispatches from Gansevoort.

Molly sent word to her brother that the entire Rebel militia of Tryon County numbering nearly 1,000 men, was on the march for Fort Stanwix to drive off St. Leger's force and lift the British siege of the fort. Joseph Brant quickly informed St. Leger of this new startling development, and in the same breath, sent out his own trusted scouts to confirm the exact size and location of the militia force moving against them. In the meantime, St. Leger hastily called a meeting of his officers, Sir John Johnson of the King's Royal Yorkers, John Butler of the Indian Department, and Joseph Brant along with the appointed war chiefs of the Iroquois to decide what to do in light of the alarming news of a Rebel militia brigade moving against them. St. Leger surmised that Gansevoort knew of the march of the militia, due to the fact that a party of four men had slipped through the Indian lines earlier in the day and were spotted entering Fort Stanwix "by a path through the swamp believed to be impassable" [CE2-p.17] on the southwest side of the fort. [FA-p.139]

St. Leger was in a quandary as to what action to take. He had underestimated the resolve of Ft. Stanwix's commander and the garrison which refused to surrender as he had convinced himself they would do. Now he was faced with a strong Rebel force moving against him which he had never imagined would happen. St. Leger reasoned that if he allowed the large militia brigade to meet his outnumbered force in the open ground before the fort, the Indians would desert him, preferring not to fight by such conventional tactics. The strong fort garrison could sally out and support the advancing militia, crushing his own troops under the weight of their tremendous combined firepower. His men could not defeat the Rebels if they stood their ground and met the Enemy on the field. St. Leger correctly reasoned that something else needed to be done.

St. Leger turned to his loyalist officers and Joseph Brant for direction at this critical hour. Quickly a decision was made by the officers to attack the Rebel militia before they could advance to the fort, while keeping the fort garrison bottled up inside. Sir John Johnson supported the idea, as did John Butler, but both men had reservations. Both men knew that the advancing militia was composed of their former friends, neighbors, and families, as well as many men whom they believed were apathetic to the Rebel cause, and would join the loyalists if just given the chance. Blood had not as yet been openly shed in the Mohawk Valley and Butler voiced the opinion that he "still hoped to avert a collision and that their adversaries might be induced to disperse without coming to blows." [CE2-p.17] Joseph Brant spoke up, interrupting Butler, to dismiss the idea of some sort of diplomacy with the Rebels at this hour.

"The time for a decisive military resolution was now at hand" [FA-p.148] to deal with those who were his avowed enemies, Brant averred. Brant was speaking for himself at St. Leger's meeting. He was a self-appointed war captain of the Mohawks from Oquaga, but was not recognized as an official war captain by the other Iroquois chiefs present nor was he accepted as a captain of the Mohawks from Canajoharie village. [WG1-p.100] That mattered little to Joseph Brant as he strongly argued for an attack and he declared that an Indian-styled ambush would be the kind of attack that would work, if it could be sprung upon the Rebels while they marched towards Stanwix and were unsuspecting. The Indians present at the meeting agreed with Brant. It would require St. Leger to split his force, and commit the bulk of men to attacking the approaching militia while keeping enough forces around Fort Stanwix to maintain the siege and prevent the garrison from supporting the relief column.

A plan was laid for a substantial force of loyalists and Indians composed of Royal Yorkers, Indian Department Rangers, Brant's Volunteers and a large body of Six Nations and allied Indians numbering some 750 fighting men [WG1-p.19, 34] under the command of Sir John Johnson, Joseph Brant, and John Butler to set out to attack the militia. In the middle of St. Leger's conference, one of Brant's scouts arrived in camp with news that the militia was much closer than first thought. The Rebel army was camped only a few miles away at the deserted Oneida Indian village of Oriska, and when it moved in the morning, it would be within striking distance of St. Leger's camp by midday, having only to cover about eight miles from Oriska to Fort Stanwix. [FA-p.145] With that news, a degree of confusion reigned momentarily among those in St. Leger's attendance, but confidence in what to do and how to do it was restored by Joseph Brant, "the charismatic Mohawk chieftain, (due to) his natural leadership capabilities" [FA-p.148] when he spoke up among the officers and Iroquois chiefs, declaring that he was well acquainted with the lay of the land between them and the Rebel militia, and he knew, from memory, a perfect spot to execute an ambush on the Rebel militia brigade. Time was of the essence if his plan was to be carried out, and Brant set the officers in motion to prepare their men for a midnight march to the ambush site.

An Ambush is Set

St. Leger agreed to commit all of Joseph Brant's white and red volunteers, 150 men, Sir John Johnson and Watt's Royal Yorker Light Infantry company of over 50 soldiers, John Butler and 20 Indian Department rangers, and "a large body of Six Nations and allied Indians," [WG1-p.34] nearly 500 warriors, primarily Mohawk and Seneca fighting men who decided on the spur of the moment to join the fight rather than watch. Late in the evening of August 5, Brant, Johnson, and Butler's force of over 700 men slipped off into the darkness down the trail called the King's road that led towards the militia camp in the distance. With a plan in mind, Joseph Brant led the way to the ambush site, with a fan of scouts far ahead, to scout the Rebel position and to be on the lookout for militia scouting parties. Brant had not forgotten that fateful day of July 24, 1759, at La Belle-Famille before the gates of the French Fort of Niagara. An ambush was sprung then with great success by Sir William Johnson and the Iroquois and a hated enemy cut to pieces within it. Joseph Brant was 16 then, but the memory of the crash of muskets, the smell of gunpowder and the war whoops of the warriors still made his "heart beat quick." [KI-p.65]

Unfortunately for the 760 sleeping men of the Tryon County militia brigade, General Herkimer and his officers had not thought to scout the whereabouts of the British and Indians known to be somewhere ahead, except for the four men General Herkimer sent to the fort to inform the garrison of the relief column. Other than a handful of sentinels posted around the perimeter of the rebel camp at Oriska field, the militia had no men farther in the field gathering intelligence, and thus, Herkimer knew nothing of the approach of the loyalist and Indian force. Joseph Brant, on the contrary, had obtained good intelligence on the Rebel force, and planned to use that knowledge to destroy the hated Enemy.

Joseph Brant chose the ambush site well. He recalled from memory the precise lay of the land about two miles west of Oriska, where the King's road descended a steep heavily-wooded ravine that was bordered on both sides for a distance by soft swampy ground where the trail crossed Oriska creek, rose again steeply for a stretch, and then descended a second ravine, much the same nature as the first, before rising to a wooded ridge to the west and on to Fort Stanwix. Instinctively knowing that the steep slopes and soft, heavily-wooded ground would force any flanking militia scouts or Oneidas onto the firmer road and away from any ambushers hidden in the dense underbrush bordering both sides, Brant picked a site for the ambush which was ideal to trap the entire militia force once they entered the ravines, where they could be cut to pieces by enfilade fire from both sides of the road.

Joseph Brant, conferring with Johnson, Butler and the Seneca war chiefs, posted the warriors and loyalist troops in a classic Indian Vee-shaped ambush. Addressing them in either English, Mohawk, or the Seneca tongue, Brant deployed the loyalist soldiers, rangers, and Indian warriors where he knew they would be best suited for the ambush, according to their own nature and style of fighting. At the mouth or open end of the ambush, Brant and his force of volunteers and Mohawks would occupy the farthest point east on the rising south slope above the road. From here he personally would be able to see the militia enter the mouth of the ambush, and be able to control when the signal was given to begin firing on the militia, once the rearguard of the Enemy had begun to descend into the ravine. Brant trusted no one else to time the ambush. Although Johnson and Butler were loyalist comrades in arms with him, to Brant they were still white men more acquainted with the white man's style of fighting than that of his own people.

There was more to Joseph Brant's decision to place himself and his volunteers and Mohawk warriors at the mouth of the ambush than timing alone. The men and warriors with him would have the most critical role to play in the ambush. Once the signal was given, Brant's men would have to close the mouth or rear door of the ambush so that the Rebels would be surrounded and trapped. None of the Enemy could be allowed to escape, and his volunteers and Mohawks had a lot of ground to cover quickly, as only an Indian could do. Brant knew it would take determined and ruthless men to fire upon the rear troops of the militia as they descended the hillside, and then to engage the stunned Enemy by rushing in and finishing them off in quick hand-to-hand fighting with knives and hatchets. Joseph Brant doubted that either Johnson's or Butler's men would have the stomach to do what needed done—the slaughter of the Rebel rearguard.

Cannily, Brant placed John Butler and his loyalist rangers with the Seneca chiefs Old Smoke and Cornplanter and a sizable number of Seneca warriors on both sides of the road to the west of his own men where the King's road descended to the creek bottom and up the rise on the other side. West of Butler and the Senecas, Brant positioned Johnson and his Royal Yorkers at the head or closed end of the ambush slightly over the next rise and the following ravine, where they would be able to deliver concentrated musket fire into the advancing militia once the ambush was sprung. Brant had another reason to place the Yorkers at the farthest point from the advancing militia. He looked at their green uniforms with buff facings and waistcoats and knew that it would take only one poorly hidden Yorker to give away the ambush, as the white color could be easily seen in the dark underbrush on the forest floor, a chance he could not take.

In addition, 50 men of the Hesse Hanau rifle company arrived in the early dawn hours along with more Indians to support John Johnson's troops, while the rest of the Yorkers still in St. Leger's camp, numbering close to 70 men, prepared to march as a reinforcement of fresh troops for the ambushers once the battle had begun. Joseph Brant made one last tour of the ambush site, making sure that all the men were well hidden from view in the first light of the morning before taking his position on the hillside. A last Indian scout of Brant's who "had been carefully hidden in a causeway to the east" [FA-p.149] came running in to report that the militia were on the march towards Brant's hidden force, and the Rebel brigade numbered fewer than 800 men, roughly equal to the British and Indian ambushers. All was set.

"The Impetuosity of the Indians"

The light of dawn ushered in a hot, humid, overcast morning on August 6, 1777, at the ravine of Oriska creek. A few hours passed uneventfully until mid-morning, when the hidden Iroquois warriors noticed that the birds in the forest canopy above them became silent. Soon, the lead elements of the Tryon County Militia brigade marching towards Fort Stanwix reached the east heights of the ravine road. From his nearby hidden position overlooking the ravine, Joseph Brant could see the vanguard of men begin to descend the sloping road. As he correctly guessed, the steep soft ground on either side of the road was forcing what flankers there were in the woods to seek firmer footing on the road that in places was reinforced with corduroy logs placed side by side to span the soft, swampy soil cut by stream rivulets. The vanguard of 20 or so men made their way to the ravine bottom just as the 1st Battalion of the militia appeared on the heights above, and began their march into the mouth of the ambush.

Onward the militia came with the 1st Regiment from Canajoharie district commanded by Ebenezer Cox, followed by the 2nd Palatine Regiment led by Jacob Klock. More and more men came into Brant's view. The 4th Regiment from Kingsland and German Flats descended into the ravine, just as the vanguard and 1st Battalion were climbing the rise to the second. Still, Brant would not give the signal to begin the ambush. He had not seen the 15 supply wagons pulled by oxen that his scouts had told him were with the militia. Brant knew that the sight of those wagons would mean that the militia rearguard, most likely the men of the 3rd Regiment from the Mohawk district under Colonel Frederick Visscher, was approaching. As soon as they entered the ravine, the trap could be sprung at last, and Brant would see to it that the door was closed. [FA-p.150]

The militia column that was strung out for more than a quarter mile slowed to a crawl as men from the 2nd and 4th Regiments fell out to get a drink from the stream at the bottom of the ravine. On the heights of the King's road to the east, the 3rd Regiment with the supply wagons and the rearguard of troops were finally spotted. Joseph Brant tensed himself in readiness as he waited for the column to move on, and the wagons to enter the ravine. It was then that the unexpected happened.

"Suddenly Brant was startled by the sound of musket fire from the recess of the western ravine beyond his vision," [FA-p.150] and in a second Joseph Brant realized when he heard Seneca war whoops that the ambush had been prematurely sprung. Quickly he motioned to his men by hand signals to remain hidden while he determined what was happening. Word came to him that a group of young Seneca warriors and their chiefs hidden close to the militiamen of the vanguard, found them too tempting a target when they stopped and put their weapons down to drink from a rivulet. The Seneca rose up at once from their hidden positions and fired their weapons at point-blank range; then rushed in upon the wounded and dying men of the vanguard. St. Leger, who was not present, reported to Canada that "the impetuosity of the Indians is not to be described" as they prematurely sprung the ambush, and "rushed in, hatchet in hand" [CE2-p.18] upon the falling militia in the front of them.

In a matter of seconds, the lead men of the column were all slain, but for one man. Their bodies were hacked to pieces, their skulls were crushed by war clubs, and their scalps were torn from their bloody heads by the Seneca warriors. Immediately up and down the length of the alarmed and shaken militia, the hidden ambushers on both sides of the road commenced firing on the hapless men, who fell by the dozens in the initial volleys.

Buoyed by their trophy scalps taken from the fallen vanguard and incited by the sights and smells of battle, the large body of young and inexperienced Seneca warriors and newly appointed chiefs ran up the open road towards the 1st Battalion, in a "bold frontal assault" [FA-p.151]. For the new Seneca chiefs, Axe Carrier, Things on the Stump, Black Feather Tail, Branch of a Tree, Fish Lapper, and Little Billy, this battle was their very first opportunity to wash their war hatchets in an opponent's blood.

Chanting their war cries, and defying all tried-and-true Indian tactics of fighting from cover, the warriors closed in on the men of the 1st Battalion on the road, who had recovered from the initial shock of the ambush. "At about 100 paces the order was given and a solid sheet of flame erupted in the direction of the Indians," as the 1st Battalion of the militia delivered a volley of fire [FA-p.152] that slaughtered the foolish Seneca on the road. Those that could escape melted into the brush of the forest to regroup, before the militia could fire again.

The Rearguard Overwhelmed

Meanwhile, the hail of musket fire from the bulk of the Iroquois warriors and loyalists still in the woods forced General Herkimer to call for the battalions on the road to the east of the 1st Regiment to attempt to move forward and join up with him or risk total annihilation. Already Herkimer could see that dozens upon dozens of militiamen lay dead, dying, and wounded on the road, for they were being easily slaughtered by the British and Indians from the cover of the woods because they could be clearly seen as targets on the road. Many militia officers like himself were mounted on horses, and were especially vulnerable to loyalist marksmen, like Colonel Cox who was shot through the head and killed. Herkimer rallied the remnants of 1st, 2nd, and 4th militia battalions to a rough defensive position on higher ground slightly above the road, before he himself was shot from his horse and grievously injured, taking two musket balls in the leg. Carried to a large beech tree, Herkimer was placed sitting up against the trunk where he could continue to direct his men.

As the remaining men of the first three battalions struggled through the underbrush and gunfire to join with Herkimer, many others, mostly young men and boys, panicked at the initial onslaught of the loyalists and Indians, and ran in confusion towards the 3rd Tryon Battalion on the eastern slope of the ravine. Their panicked flight was understandable. Most of the Mohawk Valley men who heeded the order for the militia to form at Fort Dayton were farmers by trade. The militia call was for all able-bodied men from age 16 to 60, and many men brought with them their sons in their early teens.

"The screams of the wounded, the stench of death, and the roar of gunfire which swirled all around" [FA-p.153] was too much for many of the youth, combined with the horrific sight of their dead and dying brothers, fathers and uncles who had already fallen. Dozens of these frightened boys ran up the road

Militiamen of the Third Tryon Regiment break and run in confusion and terror.

and into the approaching men of the 3rd Battalion, who had not entered the battle as yet. They spread terror and hysteria among the men of the rearguard on the road. Joseph Brant, who still held his sizable force hidden in the woods above, was waiting for the right moment to attack. Brant noticed the growing confusion among the men guarding the supply wagons, and gave the signal to attack.

In an instant the woods surrounding the men of the 3rd Tryon militia battalion erupted in a roar of gunfire as Brant's force, shrieking war whoops and firing their muskets point-blank, descended quickly upon the stunned militiamen. Brant's force swiftly reached the wagons and hacked the defenders to the ground with hatchets, knives, and war clubs, finishing them off to a man. In the process, Colonel Visscher and his forward party of some 50 men were severed from the rest of his battalion. Seeing the horde of Indians fall upon the unfortunate men at the wagons, all that Visscher could do was attempt to fight his way to Herkimer's perimeter. The remainder of the troops in the rearguard of the 3rd Battalion was still on the heights above the ravine. Finding themselves to the rear of the wagons and in the path of the attacking Indians, they turned and ran for their lives. They were pursued by Mohawk warriors who ran more than half of the escapees down and killed them. For the survivors of Herkimer's militia who remained caught in the cauldron to the west, the mouth of the ambush had effectively been sealed by Joseph Brant and his force. Now all that remained was for the loyalists and Indians to press in and wipe out those militiamen with Herkimer who were still alive.

What was left of the Tryon County militia brigade was now completely surrounded, though the wounded Herkimer had been able to get his men off the road and into the forest. There they consolidated a defensive perimeter among the standing trees and fallen trunks, to better stave off the pressing Indians, rangers, and Johnson's loyalists. The battle raged on, with more and more of the combat now confined to close quarter fighting "with the clubbed butt of a musket, the thrust of a knife or spear, or the deadly swinging of a tomahawk blade." [FA-p.154] Since many of the adversaries from both sides recognized opponents and knew them as former friends or acquaintances turned enemies, the fighting became more furious between these foes that fought to the death rather than offer quarter or spare a life. All the pent up hostility and anger of the preceding years since the loyalists had been driven out of the valley came into play as loyalists and Rebels settled scores with bloodletting.

A Ruse de Guerre

Particularly vicious was the fighting between Johnson's Yorkers and the militia. About an hour after the ambush had been sprung, a deluge of rain poured over the battlefield, just as the Yorkers were pressing the militia line in an attempt to break it. The storm brought several moments of respite for both sides before the fighting could continue, and it allowed the combatants a chance to reorganize, though most found their powder dampened and fouled muskets useless. As the storm subsided about noon, Johnson arrived back from St. Leger's camp with a

70-man reinforcement of Royal Yorkers. He ordered Captain-Lieutenant John MacDonell to attack the militia at bayonet point, and break their line. [WG1-p.34]

As MacDonell was forming up the Yorkers for the attack, three cannon booms were heard in the distance of Fort Stanwix, an obvious signal from Gansevoort, the fort commander, for the militia to take heart "with the faint hope of relief on the way," from Fort Stanwix. John Johnson took notice of the signal, as well as Major John Butler, who was inspired to devise a "ruse de guerre" that could be used to defeat the militia. Butler explained the plan to Captain Watts of the Light Yorker Company that "if the militia expected reinforcements, why not provide them with the same in the form of our own men in disguise?" [FA-p.163]

With Johnson's agreement, Watts halted MacDonell and his fresh troops and ordered them to "remove their equipment, doff their (green) regimental coats, and turn them inside out. The reversed coats resembled the natural linen frocks worn by many Continental troops of the Stanwix garrison. That done, the men put on their accoutrements and hats, took up their muskets, formed a column of threes and marched up to the militia's defensive perimeter." [CE-p.34] The ruse was set.

Most of the militia was deceived by the Yorker column marching towards them, overjoyed at the thought that reinforcements from Fort Stanwix had finally come to their aid. However just as the Yorkers were a few paces from the militia line, Captain Gardiner of the 3rd Battalion, who had made his way through the woods to Herkimer's position, recognized that the approaching troops were not Continentals and attacked MacDonell of the Yorkers, killing him. Quickly, the fight was on once again. As the Yorkers crashed into the militia, both sides met each other with hand weapons swinging. Men were bayoneted, stabbed, clubbed, brained, and knifed in the melee as the Yorker column penetrated the militia position.

Meanwhile Watts and his light infantry company with many Iroquois warriors attacked another side of the militia perimeter, engaging them in mortal hand-to-hand combat, during which Watts was severely wounded. Although the Yorker assault was furious and deadly, the Rebel line would not break, though dozens of militiamen involved in the perimeter defense lay dead and wounded amongst the trees, and the number of Yorker wounded continued to mount. Finally, the fighting ebbed in intensity. Johnson's men were spent and momentarily gave up their assault of the Rebel line and melted into the woods to regroup at a distance.

Enough Horror for a Lifetime

While both sides were preparing for more combat, the sound of gunfire was heard in the distance, coming from the direction of Fort Stanwix. Unknown to the combatants in the ravine, a contingent of the fort's garrison had sallied out to raid the Iroquois and loyalist camp that appeared from the fort walls to be deserted. The sudden sound of distant gunfire caused consternation among the Iroquois, who did not know what was happening. Some had already taken the earlier rainstorm as a favorable omen for the militia, which had given them a needed respite. The effect of the rain was disheartening.

However by this time, the Seneca had already lost heart in further battle with the militia. They were largely preoccupied with the staggering loss of their young chiefs and warriors in the early fighting. Several of the older Seneca chiefs had lost relatives of their own in the ill-advised frontal attack on the militia, and the fighting spirit had gone out of them. It was plain to Major Butler who knew them well that the Seneca were done fighting. By the time that the Yorkers had reassembled, the Seneca warriors supporting them were rapidly dwindling. Many were leaving the battlefield for their camp to grieve. Others talked openly in bitterness at how their previous wish to remain neutral had been compromised with this battle that cost them so much in loss of life, when they were "supposed to have been only spectators" of any battle between the British and the Rebels. [FA-p.163] After nearly five hours of continuous battle, the Seneca had had enough, and left the battlefield for their camp to the west, taking with them their dead and wounded, as well as any plunder and scalps that could be taken from the dead.

To the east of the militia position, Joseph Brant could see the Yorkers disengage and the Seneca begin to leave. He knew that there was nothing more that he could do. The Rebels were soundly defeated, but could not be totally destroyed. The element of surprise was gone and what was left of the militia was committed to a defensive posture that Johnson's Royal Yorkers had not been able to break. The Rebels were no longer out in the open and easy prey for the warriors. Only senseless casualties would result from trying to attack them now, where they would make his men come to them, under their guns. Cupping his hands Joseph Brant gave the Iroquois call, "Oonah, Oonah, Oonah" to signal his volunteers and the remaining Mohawks who were spread throughout the surrounding woods to withdraw as the battle was over. [FA-p.164]

Behind them, the Iroquois and loyalists left a scene of horrific carnage. The corpses of over 400 militiamen lay strewn over the battlefield where they had fallen. About 150 of the Tryon County militiamen were left alive with 50 more wounded, including General Herkimer, who would die within days from the amputation of his seriously wounded leg. With the Indians and loyalist troops gone, the militia survivors held the field, but were "incapable of moving westward to the relief of Fort Stanwix," [FA-p.175] and those alive feared another attack imminent. In the eerie silence that descended over the ravine of Oriska creek in the late afternoon, the shattered remains of the militia gathered up their wounded and retreated east to their homes in the Mohawk Valley. Behind them they left their dead comrades and relatives where they lay.

Among the 400 dead were five of the original men of the Tryon County Committee of Safety [KI-p.206] as well as nine others serving the patriot cause in the valley. [WG1-p.193] Nine more committeemen were wounded additionally adding to the loss which Lt. Col. Daniel Claus wrote jubilantly after the battle was "the Ringleaders and principal men of the rebels" in the Mohawk Valley. [WG1-p.157] Eight militia field officers and 17 junior officers were killed, including two colonels, five majors, and nine captains of the militia. [WG1-p.193] Twelve others were wounded.

Of the rank and file of the militia, the loss was staggering. There was scarcely a family living in the Mohawk Valley after the battle that had not lost a father, son, brother, or uncle. Entire families perished on the field, leaving no one alive to return to their home, such as the Snell family of the 2nd Palatine Regiment that lost seven men on the same day, down to the youngest sons. [WG1-p.177] Major Isaac Paris of the 2nd Regiment lived long enough to see his eldest son Peter killed, before he himself was captured and tortured to death in the Seneca camp. The family tragedies among the militia dead were countless and terrible, made all the worse for the survivors by the knowledge that more than 400 bodies of their kin were left unburied at the battlefield. Those few who risked their lives attempting to find relatives among the dead were shocked to find that most of the corpses were scalped and mutilated beyond recognition. [FA-p.177] It would be enough horror to last a lifetime for those surviving the battle.

Many militiamen were missing too. Some men in the rearguard of the 3rd Regiment had managed to escape the ambush and outrun Brant's pursuers. However, those men that had been unlucky enough to surrender or be captured by the Indians and not killed on the spot were taken back to the Seneca camp. There, they were set upon by the mourning, vengeful warriors who were grieving the loss of so many comrades. Neither St. Leger, Butler, nor Brant dared interfere with the Seneca as they tortured the prisoners to death. [KI-p.207]

On the loyalist side, of Major Butler's men of the Indian Department, two of his captains, James Wilson and Gilbert Tice, had been killed in the battle, as well as one or two of the rangers with them. [WG1-p.75] Sir John Johnson had lost his brother-in-law Stephen Watts, captain of the light infantry company, who was severely wounded and left behind on the field. Captain-Lieutenant John MacDonell was one of the six Yorker casualties at Oriskany. [WG1-p.39] Of Joseph Brant's Volunteers, none were known to be killed, though Brant remarked that his "poor Mohawks" had suffered heavily [KI-p.206] with the loss of the young William Johnson, the half-breed son of Sir William Johnson and Caroline, the niece of the great Mohawk sachem Hendrick. William Johnson of the Mohawk village of Canajoharie, who had accompanied Joseph Brant to Oquaga, lay dead on the battlefield.

The Iroquois as a whole had suffered the heaviest losses in the battle. Thirty-three warriors and chiefs were killed; 29 more warriors were wounded. [KI-p.206] More than half of these casualties were among the Seneca, who "lost 17 men, among whom were several of their chief warriors and had 16 wounded." [CE2-p.18] Six newly-appointed Seneca war chiefs had been killed in the frontal attack on the militia on the road. One of these chiefs was Tocenando, the eldest son of the revered Seneca chief Old Smoke. [WG1-p.99] The loss of so many warriors enraged the Seneca and they vowed future revenge upon the Americans. They were by no means satisfied with torturing and killing the prisoners in camp.

Nor did the Seneca find satisfaction in the knowledge that over 400 of the Rebel militia lay dead on the day's battlefield. Nothing would allay their sorrow until more blood was spilled and many more scalps taken to alleviate their pain.

As August 6, 1777, came to a close with nightfall, new Indian wilderness war had been unleashed upon the American colonial frontier with terrible, deadly results. During the previous Seven Year's War with the French and their Indian allies, the combination of highly mobile French Marines, couriers des bois, and native warriors had proven to be an effective fighting force when they worked together in the wilderness. The lessons of that wilderness war had not been forgotten. At Oriskany, the British had fielded a mix of Iroquois Indian warriors with "loyalist infantry and Rangers who were equally effective white elements" [WG1-p.92]. Johnson, Butler, and Brant put to use the tactics of Indian warfare well-learned and with new improvements since the lessons of the 1750's. However, it would not be the only lesson at Oriskany that the Indians and loyalists would come to teach with lethal consequences for the unsuspecting.

Wyoming Valley Campaign

By the spring of 1778, a new campaign was planned in Canada against the Americans in their own heartland of eastern Pennsylvania and New York. After returning to Fort Niagara after a trip to Quebec in September 1777, Major John Butler set about fulfilling the orders he had been given to raise a battalion of eight companies of rangers. He and his newly raised rangers were to "act in the field with the Indians" for the purposes of attacking the Rebel frontier to devastate their settlements. [KI-p.211] Late in June 1778, Major John Butler with the Seneca chief Old Smoke and Cornplanter led a mixed force of 200 rangers and over 300 warriors over a great distance from their base at Fort Niagara and the Seneca villages to the Wyoming Valley in eastern Pennsylvania. They traveled light on the Indian trails that led to the reaches of the upper Susquehanna River, carrying nothing more than food and ammunition on their backs, with no tents, artillery, or regular troops to impede their progress. Once reaching the Iroquois village of Unadilla, Butler was able to float his force "down the Susquehanna River in boats and rafts" from their forward camp with Joseph Brant's Volunteers at Tioga. [CE-p.46]

Neither Joseph Brant and his Volunteers nor Johnson and his Royal Yorkers were with Butler's force when it slipped into the Wyoming Valley on the night of July 1, 1778, far from their base of operations at Fort Niagara to the northwest. The local militia had some advanced warning that a force of British rangers and Indians intended to strike the inhabitants of the 20 mile-long fertile valley of the Susquehanna River that was firmly in support of the patriot cause, but they did not know the size and scope of the invaders headed their way. The Wyoming Valley was defended by eight forts and nearly 500 militia spread out on both sides of the river. Butler attacked on the morning of July 2, forcing several of the smaller Rebel forts to surrender without a fight. He repeatedly exposed only a small portion of his Rangers to the Americans and held the Indians back hoping that the Rebel militia would attempt to attack him, thinking his small force outnumbered.

On the morning of July 3, while parties of his men were scouring the valley to gather up livestock, scouts brought word to Butler that "the militia was assembling in great numbers near Forty Fort, and were apparently preparing for an attack." [CE-p.46] Butler recalled Captain William Caldwell and his other scattered forces while the Seneca rejoiced at the news and prepared for battle. Butler hoped he could lure the bulk of the militia out of their stronghold at Forty Fort, and with the approval of Cornplanter and Old Smoke, planned a ruse on the afternoon of July 3 that he hoped would fool the militia into thinking that he and his men were only a small raiding party. If the ruse worked, the militia might fall into an ambush like the trap at Oriskany the previous year where it could be destroyed.

Butler sent a small force of rangers and Indians forward towards Forty Fort to make contact with the militia, and act as if they were the entire body of Rangers and Indians in the valley. They were to engage the militia and then purposely fall back along the river road to Butler's man force. In the meantime, Butler deployed the rest of his rangers and all of the Seneca in a Vee-shaped ambush, at a site picked along the river road several miles from Forty Fort. When he heard the sound of gunfire from the direction of Forty Fort, Butler ordered Fort Wintemute to his rear to be set on fire, so that the militia would be able to clearly see the smoke, and think that the small force of Rangers and Indians whom their own scouts had just skirmished with, were retreating out of the valley to the north, letting the Indians customarily plunder and burn settler homes as they pulled out.

In a short time, Butler had reason to believe that the ruse was working, when scouts came in with word that the militia was indeed on the march. Sentries at Forty Fort had seen the smoke in the distance and the militia officers agreed to give chase to what was believed by now to be a small party of retreating Tories and Indians. Their goal was to try to intercept the raiders and wipe them out. Late in the afternoon, the rebel militia of some 400 men, some as young as 14, marched briskly from Forty Fort to pursue the retreating Tories and Indians. They had no knowledge of the horror that awaited them ahead on the road.

Colonel Butler's Rangers and the Seneca were hidden in ambush, waiting for the militia to march into the trap. While laying flat on the ground the Rangers and Indians primed and loaded their muskets, while allowing the militia to advance up the road without detecting any sign of pending trouble. This time, the Seneca chiefs Cornplanter and Old Smoke made sure that none of their warriors prematurely attacked. All went according to plan. The vanguard of the militia exchanged shots with a small band of about 40 warriors who had been told to show themselves to the militia and then immediately fall back along the road and into the mouth of the ambush site. Distracted by the appearance of retreating Indians, and firing at some rangers who exposed themselves ahead on the road, the militia took the bait and cast all caution aside in hot pursuit of the Enemy.

At the precise moment when the militia forces had passed the foremost hidden Seneca warriors and were now completely within the trap, Cornplanter "gave a shrill war whoop, which was repeated by each band of Indians in succession and prolonged by the rangers. This was succeeded by a deliberate and deadly volley." [CE-p.47] The ambush was sprung and in the initial firing by the rangers and Indians, well over 150 of the militia were killed and wounded on the spot. The Seneca warriors quickly flanked the rear of the militia and closed the trap, cutting off any chance of retreat back down the road to Forty Fort for the militiamen. As the militia column reeled, melted and fell to the terrible onslaught of musket fire, the ranks crumbled in the ensuing confusion, and resistance turned to panic as the vengeful Seneca warriors rushed upon the remaining militiamen with hatchets and knives in hand. Those militiamen who were still standing dropped their weapons and fled for the river which was their only hope to escape death.

Devastation beyond Belief

The ensuing slaughter was horrific. Over 300 militiamen were slain in the matter of a few minutes. "Our fire was so close and well-directed," wrote Butler, "that the affair was soon over, not lasting above half an hour." [CE-p.47] Filled with anger and rage, the Seneca warriors spared no one on the field. They mercilessly hunted the few escaping militiamen, and cut to pieces not only the wounded, but also any young boys or elderly men who had marched in the column with the militia, and cowered on the road, begging to be spared.

With the battle over and the militia defeated, the Seneca turned their attention from scalping and mutilating the corpses of the militiamen to a large scale rampage of the valley, as all threat of retaliation from the Rebel militia was now gone. The warriors looted and burned the settler homes they came across and killed anyone they found, including women and children who had not managed to flee. Butler estimated that "about 1,000 dwellings were burned, and about 1,000 cattle, sheep and swine killed in the course of the next day. His rangers demolished the eight forts, the grist mills and barns of the valley till not a building was left standing. [KI-p.220] As to the depredations of the Indians, Butler later wrote "that it was with difficulty I could save the lives of these few," referring to only five prisoners that were taken by the Indians that he was able to save. [CE-p.46]

The Wyoming Valley was utterly destroyed when Butler, his Rangers, and the Seneca left to the northwest. On the battlefield, over 300 militia corpses lay rotting where they had fallen. The militia had lost one colonel, two majors, seven captains, 13 lieutenants, 11 ensigns and 268 privates. Only 60 men of the militia column were believed to have escaped the wholesale slaughter. What remained of the civilian population fled east over the mountains to safety, leaving their homes and forts in smoking ruins.

Butler and his force of Rangers and Indians had suffered casualties as well. He wrote after the battle, "On our side we lost one Indian killed, two rangers and eight Indians wounded." [CE-p.44] The raid into the Wyoming Valley had been an unqualified success for John Butler as he reported the utter destruction of the Rebel stronghold. As to his Ranger Corps, Butler heaped praise, writing to Colonel Bolton, the officer in command at Fort Niagara, that "the officers and men of the rangers have supported themselves through hunger and fatigue with great cheerfulness." [CE-p.49]

The horror of a newfound wilderness war that began at Oriskany had been perfected on the road leading from Forty Fort. A lot of things had come together to make the new form of wilderness war more perfect. First, a large force of loyalist Rangers and allied Indians were able to work closer together in the field than ever before to achieve a specific military objective for the campaign. Second, the allied force of Rangers and Seneca were able to travel a great distance through the wilderness in a short period of time to reach that objective on the colonial frontier. They accomplished this feat by marching with only their provisions and ammunition on their backs, unencumbered by wagons, tents, artillery and camp followers who would have slowed their advance. They traveled quick and light so as to be able to reach their objective undetected by the Enemy and thus denying them the opportunity to make defensive preparations for the attack, including sending out a call for reinforcements.

Once the Rangers and Indians began their assault, they did so using indirect, yet decisive tactics that employed decoy and deception to lure an unsuspecting enemy into the trap of an ambush. Their officers and war captains led their men and warriors with courage from the front, and by example. The strategy of employing an ambush of the enemy force was used to obtain the element of surprise, whereby the ambushers were able to subject their enemy to an initial massed volley of musket-fire, in which a large number of the enemy were killed or wounded, and the remaining men of the enemy force were thrown into confusion and panic by the shock of the surprise attack, and unable to respond.

Simultaneous flanking movements by mobile parties of Indian warriors sealed the rear of the ambush, preventing the escape of the remaining militia, which enabled close-quarter Indian-style fighting tactics of the Rangers and Indians to quickly annihilate those militiamen who did not run, before they had an chance to form up and present the ambushers with conventional line firing. In the face of these rapid, fluid, and deadly tactics of fighting, the militia could not make a stand. They were effectively eliminated as a fighting force, due to the maximum number of casualties quickly inflicted upon them by the Rangers and Indians, who concurrently exposed themselves to taking as few casualties as possible of their own.

With the militia out of the way, no quarter was given to their wounded by the Indians, and few prisoners were taken by Rangers or Indians, who did not want to be slowed down in completing the new task at hand, now that the battle was over. The raiders were free to fulfill Butler's military objective in the Wyoming Valley, the real purpose of the raid, which was to destroy the property, livestock and crops of the Rebels which were being cultivated to support the patriot cause in the east. That destruction was done in a methodical manner by the Rangers as there were no Rebel defenders or reinforcements to interrupt their work of putting every building to the torch, one by one.

Those civilians and militia survivors who managed to escape the onslaught and flee the valley quickly spread a tale to neighboring frontier communities of atrocities and horror suffered at the hands of the loyalist Rangers and bloodthirsty Indians the likes of which had never been seen before on the frontier. Survivors would call the attack nothing less than a massacre. Yet this new style of Indian wilderness war that descended upon the Wyoming valley and left it utterly devastated and depopulated, was not accomplished by chance, but rather by design. The lessons of Indian warfare learned decades before in previous frontier wars had now reached a new level of perfection. Those lessons were executed with deadly precision by loyalists and Indians who were better trained, supplied, coordinated, and motivated to fight.

It would be these lessons of wilderness war that would be taught by loyalists and Indians of the Ohio Country to the Rebels on the Virginian frontier bordering the Ohio River. The ensuing wilderness war would become a savage battle waged for years by Great Britain to control the Indian lands of the Ohio Country. Here now is that untold story.

Part Two

The Untold Story of the Savage Battle for British and Indian Control of the Ohio Country during the American Revolution

Part Two
Introduction

The story of Great Britain's battle for control of the Ohio Country from 1778 to 1783 is a hidden story buried within Great Britain's larger struggle to suppress the rebellious colonies in America during their war for independence. We know more about the conventional war fought between the British and Americans on the battlefields in the East because it was chronicled by both sides, through extensive military communiqués, newspapers, officer's reports from the field, and journals of the common soldiers. Accounts detailing the western frontier war from the American militia and settler perspective exist because their stories were recorded from interviews after the war was over.

Accounts of the conduct of the wilderness war from the Indian and British perspective do not exist. The story of the people who supported the British cause in a war that was lost has remained untold to this day because none of the participants in that struggle wrote an account of the role they played for control of the Ohio Country. With a cessation of hostilities in 1783, the guns fell silent and the white men and Indians who had fought to prevent the loss of the Indian lands were defeated by the terms of the new peace treaty which gave those lands away to the Americans, forcing them to move westward or into permanent exile in Canada.

The Americans who fought the British and Indians in the savage, partisan war against the American frontier were not about to forgive and forget their former opponents for the terrible brutality and suffering inflicted upon them. Because hatred for the Indians and the white men who fought with them ran deep, in subsequent years, Americans collectively remained in no mood to hear their opponent's side of the story. Reconciliation with their former enemies, the Indians, was out of the question, and many Americans vowed revenge upon the white men they felt were responsible for inciting Indian depredations against the frontier, if those men were to set foot upon American soil again. Therefore, chroniclers felt no impetus to go to Canada to interview the men who remained vilified by their American contemporaries. "These bastards have been the leading men or war captains that have done us so much mischief," [MD-xii] an American frontier writer wrote of the white mercenaries, characterizing them as sub-humans, more savage than the Indians.

From the point of view of the Indians, no concise or comprehensive account of the western wilderness war was recorded by the tribes of the western Confederacy of the Ohio Country, which included the Shawnee, Wyandot, Mingo, Delaware, and Miami who fought against the Americans. Defiant, many of them kept up the struggle against the white invasion of their ancestral lands after the peace was made between the United States and Great Britain in 1783. Their fight was a hopeless cause, for the Indians could not stem the flood of white settlers streaming across the Allegheny Mountains from the East into the Ohio Country, nor could they adequately fight the American military who were sent to protect those newly-acquired lands, as the Indians themselves were deprived of substantial support by the British in Canada. By the turn of the 18th century, the Indians were driven out of the Ohio Country as their former lands were opened up to settlement by the new United States. Without a written language of their own, and with so few Indians capable of reading and writing the English language, no account of the struggle from the Indian point of view was recorded documenting the events of the war for the Ohio Country. Consequently, we know little of the Indian story, which involved the violent upheaval and ejection of their people from their lands. We do not know what the Indians thought or felt. They had no means to convey it, and those who vanquished them, continued to scorn and spurn the Indians as reviled savages for more than a century.

Of the handful of white men who fought along side of the Indians against the whites of the American frontier, few were able to read and write, for they possessed little, if any, education as children. Most of these men had been born and bred on the wilderness frontier where formal schooling was all but lacking prior to 1770. In most cases, these men were not the children of colonial gentry, but rather the surviving offspring of frontier parents who lost more than 50 percent of all children born on the frontier, who died before the age of ten from disease, accidents, and malnutrition, and other causes. A premium was placed on physical survival, not schooling. Growing to adulthood on the frontier was a struggle against many odds, and those who survived were physically hardy and mentally keen, but not necessarily well -educated.

Sometimes frontier children spent their formative years as captives of the Indians, immersed in the language and culture of the Indian tribe in which they were adopted, as was the case of the three Girty brothers. With little or no education before their captivity, by the time they were repatriated to the white man's world after years of living with the Indians, they had, in most cases, forgotten the spoken English language of their childhood and spoke the native tongue of the Indian tribe that adopted them. Years after returning to Pittsburgh, the Girtys were still fluent in several Indian dialects. If the younger Girty brothers, George and James, had to re-learn English, we do not know if their thoughts were formulated in Indian words, and English was just a new language to be learned. Simon, the eldest brother of the three, spoke fluent English in addition to the Indian dialects he learned during captivity. He apparently had enough grasp of the English language before his capture as a youth by the Indians to be able to dictate his thoughts in a comprehensive manner in letters, although he possessed no writing skills.

Simon Girty's letters from the wilderness of the Ohio Country during the war were dictated to someone with him who could write, as Girty could not.

Girty's dispatches to Major DePeyster, the Fort Detroit commander, detailed his movements in the field, gave accounts of attacks against the Rebels, and passed on intelligence taken from interviews with Enemy prisoners captured by the Indians, often just before he was required to turn them over to their captors for torture and execution. However, with written language an unnecessary encumbrance for the Girtys all through their lives, they dismissed as irrelevant any opportunity, if it in fact arose, to leave a written account of the part they played in the war for the Ohio Country. Without a doubt, they did not sense the historical significance of what had happened.

Men like Matthew Elliott of the Indian Department were no different. Like many frontiersmen on both sides of the armed struggle, Elliott had emigrated from the British Isles to the colonial frontier prior to the war. With no money or means of support, Elliott, a poor, uneducated young Irishman gravitated to the Pennsylvania frontier near Carlisle in the 1760s, where he took up the occupation of a trader to the Indians, to support himself. On the frontier, schooling was neither accessible to him nor a skill he needed to rely upon in the world of a trader. Though lacking education, by the time of the outbreak of war in the Ohio Country, Elliott was given the task of accompanying Indian war parties into the wilderness against the American frontier where he found it necessary to communicate importance events and intelligence to the British at Detroit. While some researchers believe that Elliott could not write, he either found someone with him to whom he could dictate a letter, or Elliott had learned enough writing skills to be able to pen his own letters to Major DePeyster while living and fighting with the Indians. The crudely written letters signed by him betray a rough education. Elliott's sentences were fragmented, and awkward: he phonetically spelled words, writing them as best he could obviously from sounding out the word, and he, or his secretary in the field, had a limited vocabulary. From the infrequency of his letters, one could infer that he did not like to write. However well-versed in the Indian dialects of the Ohio Country, Matthew Elliott found writing English to be a difficult exercise that he shied away from, writing only when he felt it absolutely necessary to communicate to Detroit, or to his friend Alexander McKee, about something of importance in regard to the conduct of the war.

Two British officers in the field fighting alongside the Indian allies in the Ohio Country could and did write fluently and frequently during the war years. Both Alexander McKee, Deputy Agent in charge of the British Indian Department at Fort Detroit, and Captain William Caldwell, commanding Butler's Rangers from Fort Niagara wrote extensive letters, including military dispatches, after-action reports, muster rolls of men under their command, and personal petitions to the British government for themselves and their comrades. The bulk of the military correspondence eventually collected at Detroit from the Indian country and sent on to headquarters at Quebec came from these two men, who were literate before the war, prior to their military service.

Growing up as a child in the backwoods of the Susquehanna Valley in eastern Pennsylvania, Alexander McKee learned to read and write under the direction of his Irish father who saw to that his son had a rudimentary English education in spite of his frontier surroundings. William Caldwell, on the other hand, came from a family of Irish emigrants of modest wealth which enabled him to obtain a formal education in eastern Pennsylvania. By 1760, both McKee and Caldwell became part of a small minority of men living on the edge of colonial society who were literate. By the outbreak of the war, as both men found themselves gravitating towards the British loyalist cause, their ability to read and write, among other qualities, set them apart from many of their contemporaries, and helped them rise to positions of rank because they were able to communicate by writing, something relatively few men on the frontier were able to do.

As officers for the British serving in the wilderness of the Ohio Country, McKee and Caldwell wrote numerous military dispatches to Major DePeyster at Detroit, and to officers at Niagara and in the field. Their letters were as detailed as circumstances would allow under the conditions they found themselves. Often with no roof over their heads to protect them from the elements, McKee and Caldwell implicitly understood and never forgot that writing to British authorities at Detroit and Niagara to keep them informed of developments in the wilderness war was an essential part of their duty as officers. Writing about a particular event that had just transpired or the movement of their own force of Indians and Rangers who were about to attack the Enemy added a degree of cohesiveness and stability to the British war effort in the west, which was pinned on a handful of men strung out over vast distances fighting in an inhospitable wilderness.

Embroiled as McKee and Caldwell were in the day-to-day conduct of their irregular troops in the wilderness war against the Americans, they found little opportunity to write while constantly on the move with the Indians over long distances during campaigns designed to attack the American frontier or to intercept American troops believed to be moving against them. Neither man found that the exigencies of fighting a war allowed them more time than what was absolutely necessary to convey a message with what scarce supply of paper, quill and ink they had at their disposal. Consequently, both men disclosed no more than what needed to be told in their dispatches. They were not writing about their own experiences, but about the military facts that were relevant to the limited audience of officers at Detroit and Niagara. Rarely did they reveal their own personal thoughts and feelings, for duty compelled them to write only what needed to be said. Always on the move in the wilderness, neither McKee nor Caldwell had time or the opportunity to keep a journal documenting his movements, activities, and thoughts about what was happening during the military campaigns. What we do know is limited to the brief dispatches and communiqués that McKee and Caldwell wrote at different times and places during the war.

Once the war was officially over in 1783, McKee and Caldwell found that they could not return to their former homes in Pennsylvania, because of their service and allegiance to Britain during the Revolutionary War. Former Butler's Rangers and men of British Indian Department were not welcome in the new United States, and both McKee and Caldwell risked arrest, imprisonment, or death if they were recognized and captured by former enemies eager to exact revenge upon these men they held responsible for the Indian raids against the American frontier. After years of relentless campaigning in the wilderness, McKee and Caldwell, with what few possessions they could carry, were forced to seek permanent exile in British Canada, where they faced the challenge of establishing themselves in the Detroit area with what scant means they had at their disposal. During those post-war years, preoccupied with survival neither McKee nor Caldwell found the opportunity or time to write an account of the war for the Ohio Country which they had participated in, to record the pivotal part each of them had played in the conduct of the war. Unlike their American counterparts, who either were interviewed by American historians prior to their deaths, or who gave their accounts of the frontier war to family members who years later related these accounts to historians, the story of the savage battle for control of the Ohio Country by the Indians and British passed into obscurity with the subsequent deaths of McKee and Caldwell by the early 1800's. The two key men who conducted that war from the battlefield of the wilderness never wrote an account of the war from the side of the British and Indians, and apparently never spoke to anyone about it.

The untold story of the war from the British and Indian perspective would have remained a mystery if it had not been for one man, Frederick Haldimand, who was Commander-in-Chief and Governor General of Canada, during the war years. Haldimand had a penchant for order in his administration of the war effort. With regard to the massive amount of written paperwork that he had to deal with on a daily basis at British headquarters at Quebec City, Haldimand insisted that all military correspondence sent to him pertaining to his officers at the posts in Canada and the Great Lakes be organized in an orderly fashion. The job of Haldimand's secretary, Captain Matthews was to catalog the letters as they arrived and methodically transcribe each one of them into a ledger book to record chronologically for Haldimand the military intelligence, for his analysis and appropriate reaction. Thus, as McKee and Caldwell sent letters to Detroit by Indian courier, Major DePeyster, the commander there, digested the information, and then passed the letters on to his commanding officer at Niagara, at the time—Major Bolton in the beginning, and Brigadier General Powell or Major General Maclean near the end of the war. From Niagara, the letters were sent to General Haldimand at Quebec for his review and analysis.

With the large volume of correspondence eventually reaching Haldimand on a daily basis from officers at posts throughout Canada and on campaigns against the Enemy, Haldimand needed to devise a way he could expediently access the material which contained reports of military developments, muster rolls of regiments, pay records, and inventories of everything at outlying posts from food to artillery, munitions, clothing, prisoners, and petitions. Rather than perusing indiscriminate stacks of letters, Haldimand found that the use of different ledger books allowed him to read not only what specifically had been sent to him from a particular area of interest, but also to record his thoughts and orders which he sent in response to the men writing him. Specifically, in relation to the war fought in the western wilderness of the Ohio Country, Haldimand's ledger books amply served the purpose to both record what his officers in the Ohio Country and the upper posts of the Great Lakes wrote to him, and as an archive of Haldimand's written orders to those men, which Matthews dutifully recorded in a separate ledger of directives to his officers. Consequently, within Haldimand's ledger containing the correspondence of his officers at the western posts can be found the letters of Captain Alexander McKee, Captain William Caldwell, Matthew Elliott, Simon Girty, and Joseph Brant of the Indian Department.

At the end of the war and with the close of his military service in America soon after, Frederick Haldimand eventually returned to England for knighthood and retirement, taking with him his voluminous papers, including the correspondence from the western wilderness war. At his death, Haldimand's personal papers were inherited by his family, who in the middle of the 19th century donated their ancestor's papers to the British government. The papers were deposited in the British War Library to be preserved for reference and posterity. Much later, a copy of the entire collection of the Haldimand Papers was made available to the National Archives of Canada in Ottawa, Canada, where researchers are able to access the microfilm collection.

It is here, in the Haldimand Papers, that the story of the conduct of the wilderness war for British and Indian control of the Ohio Country from 1778 to 1783 has remained untold for over 220 years. Lost in the pages of this massive collection are letters from men responsible for the conduct of the western war: the officers of the British Indian Department; Butler's Rangers; the commanders of the western posts; and General Haldimand himself. Few historians know of the existence of these chronicles of the western wilderness war. Fewer yet over the years have troubled themselves to investigate the Haldimand Papers in depth to research the story of the wilderness war that lies hidden within its pages. Ernest Cruikshank, in his 1893 book, *The Story of Butler's Rangers* delved into the Haldimand Papers for much of his research material. Likewise, Consul Butterfield used extensive material found in the transcripts of the Haldimand Papers to write the *History of the Girtys*, published in 1890. And recently, Larry Nelson, who has written an exhaustive biography on the life of Alexander McKee, *A Man of Distinction Among Them*, relied upon source letters in the Haldimand Papers for reference in detailing McKee's activities during the war years from 1778-1783. Yet beyond this handful of authors writing about specific participants, no one has told the story of the fight for the Ohio Country in its entirety.

The purpose in telling the whole story of the savage battle for control of the Ohio Country from the British and Indian perspective is neither to dispute the facts previously recorded in the American annals of the frontier border war, nor to set the historical record straight with new information brought to light from Haldimand's archives of primary documents. The reader can weigh the evidence and draw his or her own conclusions. Neither is it the intent of this writer to denigrate in any way the American side of the story that has been told for 220 years, of the heroic, determined, and courageous men and women who fought and died defending their homes and families against a ruthless and savage enemy, the Indians, for the cause of liberty from Great Britain's stifling and repressive control.

Further, the telling of this story is not an attempt to champion the Indian cause and glorify the white men who fought with them. While it is true that the Indians and the white men who fought with them believed that it was their right to defend the lands in the Ohio Country by forcing out the white settlers encroaching on their lands, too many years have passed for us to look upon this chapter of American history with anything less than a dispassionate, objective eye that should not measure either side in the conflict 220 years ago as more just or more right in waging that war. The Indians attacked the American frontier as a means to achieve their aim. Waging a brutal, savage war against the frontier civilian population in which women and children were considered combatants was the only way Indians knew how fight, and the only method readily at their disposal. We may condemn the Indians by our standards of "civilized" warfare but not condemn them for their right to fight, nor for the fact that their tactics of wilderness warfare were largely successful. In the words of James Smith, held captive by the Indians from 1755 to 1759, "when we reflect on the Indian war, we may readily conclude that they (the Indians) are not an ignorant or stupid sort of people, or they would not have been such fatal enemies. When they came into our country they outwitted us—and when we sent armies into their country, they outgeneraled, and beat us with inferior force." [SC-109]

It is as absurd to exalt the Indian cause as it is to condemn them for the war they initiated against the white frontier which quickly evolved into ferocious ethnic cleansing and racial extermination between whites and Indians. Both sides attempted to annihilate the other without mercy, and both settler and Indian resorted to inflicting atrocities upon their opponent when it suited to further their cause. Compromise and diplomacy were not remotely possible, until one side or the other had effectively gained the upper hand. In understanding the story of the savage battle for control of the Ohio Country, we must be careful not to champion either Indian or frontiersman, for both have their place in American history, regardless of the acts of brutality that both sides committed during the course of the war.

The purpose in revealing the untold story of the savage battle for control of the Ohio Country during the American Revolution is threefold. First, is to acquaint the reader with that part of the story that has remained much a mystery to the reader of American history for 220 years. To date, we know only one part of the story of the western wilderness war and that is the story told from the American perspective. We know of the exploits of Major Sam McColloch, Lewis Wetzel, Betty Zane, Sam Brady and other militiamen and settlers living on the frontier during that period, but little is known of the people who were opposing them, due to a lack of information from the British and Indian side. To possess a complete historical understanding of the war for the Ohio Country, we need to know that part of the story that deals with the British and Indians who lost the war fighting the Americans. Knowing their side of the story will give us a complete historical perspective of what happened, just as reading and understanding the point of view from the German soldier during World War II has given us a greater insight and perspective into why and how that war was fought.

Secondly, the story of the battle for the Ohio Country from the British and Indian side reveals, for the first time, that a concerted strategic effort was made on the part of the British to conduct a methodical war for control of the Ohio Country by using irregular forces of native Indian warriors and British Rangers against the western American frontier in an attempt to stem the tide of western colonial expansion. The strategy involved securing the Ohio Country by depopulating the frontier settlements through coordinated attacks designed to force the colonial population supporting the rebellion to retreat or withdraw east across the Allegheny Mountains. In the process, possibly Washington and Congress would be forced to siphon off critical troops needed in the eastern theatres of war to help defend the western frontier posts, or abandon the West altogether to the British and Indians. That the war was planned by the British as a part of their overall strategy, and not merely as an attempt to aid the Indians in their bid to drive out the white settlers invading their ancestral lands is evident in the quotes taken from the letters of Lord Germain, General Haldimand, Governor Hamilton, Major DePeyster, Lt. Col. Butler, Major Bolton, and Captain Bird.

Finally, through the words taken from letters written by the white men who fought with the Indians such as Alexander McKee, Matthew Elliott, Simon Girty and William Caldwell, we can discover, for the first time in 220 years that these men were not monsters and fiends which post-war, polarized American chroniclers portrayed them to be in their writings. In choosing to support Great Britain in its attempt to put down the rebellion in its American colonies by force, loyalists were forced to flee for their lives and abandon their family, friends, property, and the former society in which they had once lived. On the western American frontier of Virginia and Pennsylvania, the loyalists there fled to the security of the Indian lands of the Ohio Country where they eventually supported the British war effort by fighting alongside the Indians. In doing so, they attracted the enmity of the American frontier population which branded them renegades and men more savage than the Indians. In telling their story, we are able to see these men in a true and more human light as we read their thoughts they wrote. They were men not driven by burning hatred, lust for blood, or homicidal pleasure, but men who were as committed to what they were doing as were their American counterparts, in upholding their sense of duty to their cause in a vicious wilderness war fought without rules or convention, other than the maxim of kill or be killed.

Here, now, is the untold story of the wilderness war on the Ohio River from the British and Indian perspective—their savage battle for control of the

Ohio Country during the American Revolution, told in it's entirety for the first time.

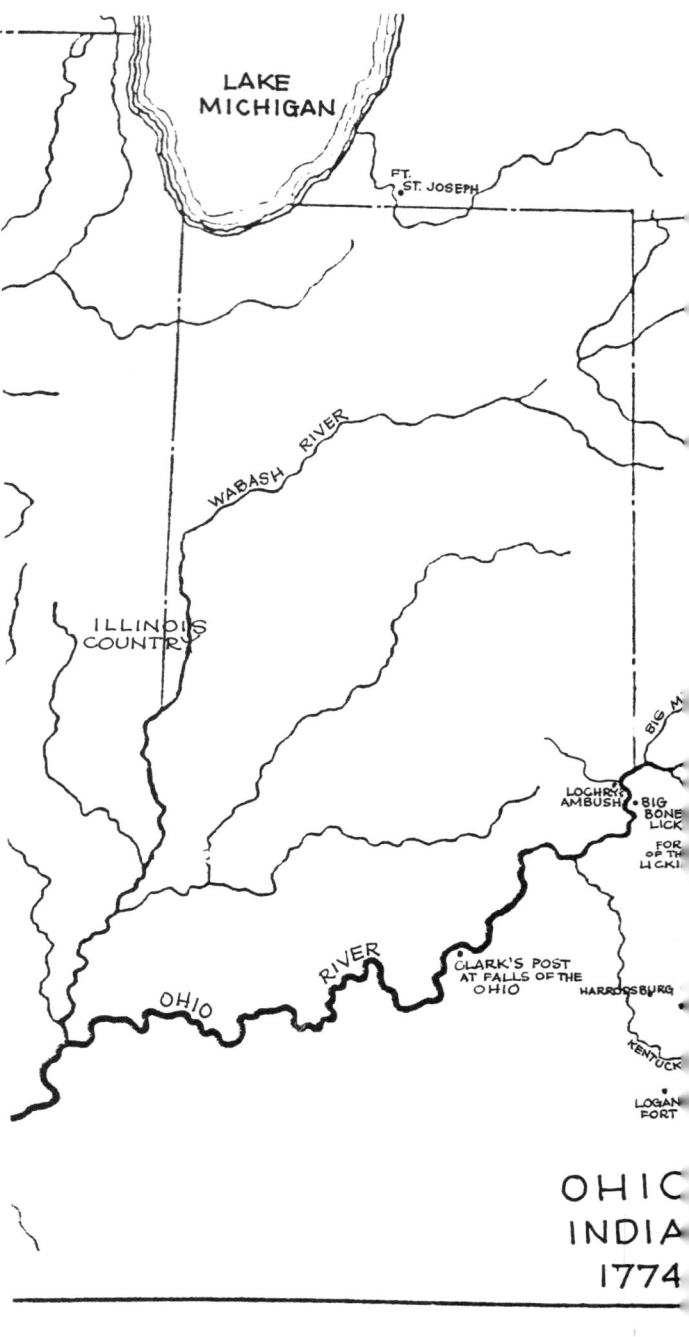

MAP OF OHIO COUNTRY INDIAN LANDS 1774-1782

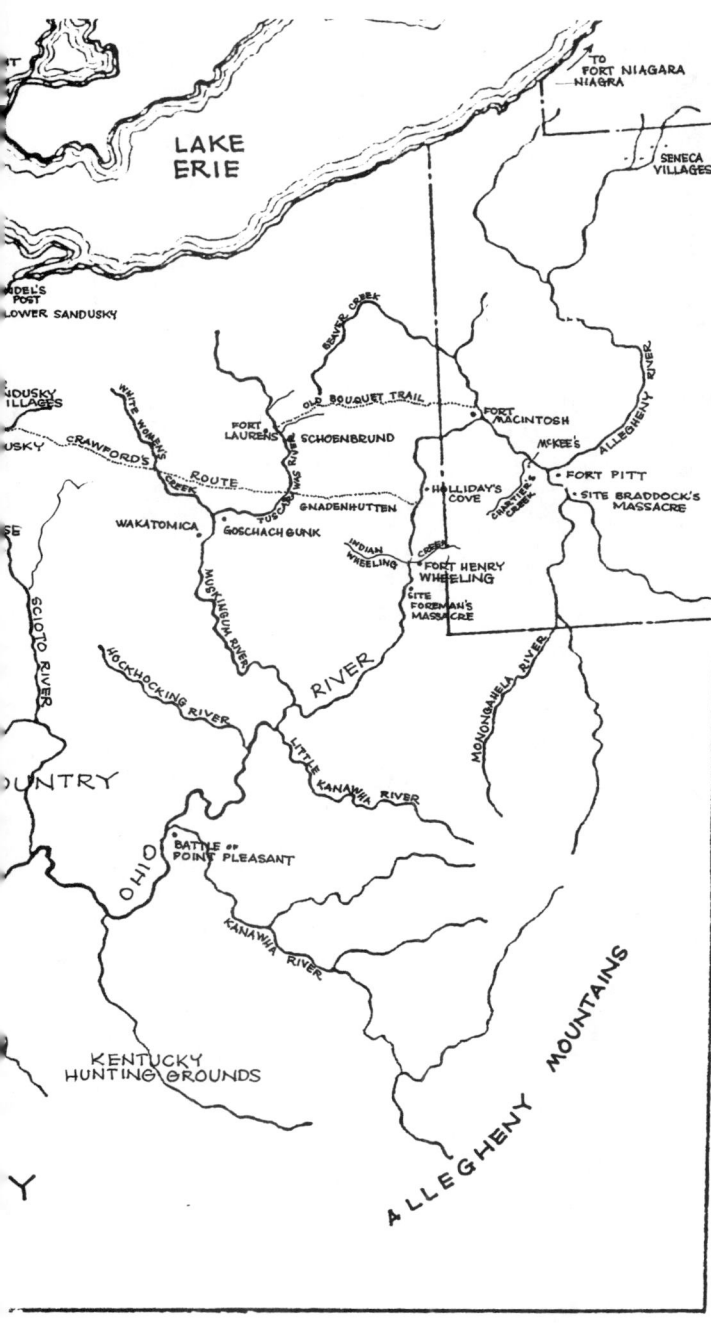

LAKE
ERIE

TO
FORT NIAGARA
NIAGRA

SENECA
VILLAGES

IDEL'S
POST
LOWER SANDUSKY

NDUSKY
ILLAGES

WHITE WOMBUS

OLD BOUQUET TRAIL

FORT
LAURENS

SCHOENBRUND

FORT
MACINTOSH

McKEE'S

ALLEGHENY RIVER

USKY

CRAWFORD'S

ROUTE

BEAVER CREEK

HALLIDAY'S
COVE

FORT PITT

SITE BRADDOCK'S
MASSACRE

WAKATOMICA

GOSCHACH GUNK

GNADENHUTTEN

INDIAN
WHEELING

FORT HENRY
WHEELING

SITE
FOREMAN'S
MASSACRE

CHARTER
CREEK

SCIOTO RIVER

HOCKHOCKING RIVER

MUSKINGUM RIVER

RIVER

MONONGAHELA RIVER

OHIO

UNTRY

LITTLE
KANAWHA RIVER

BATTLE OF
POINT PLEASANT

KANAWHA RIVER

KENTUCKY
HUNTING GROUNDS

ALLEGHENY MOUNTAINS

Y

MAP OF OHIO COUNTRY INDIAN LANDS 1774-1782

Captain Daniel Beaujeu (Portrait by Henri Beau; Courtesy of National Archives of Canada)

Major General Edward Braddock (Engraving by William Sartain; Courtesy Library of Congress)

Major Robert Rogers (Engraving by J. Martin Will after engraving published in London by Thomas Hart)

Sir William Johnson by Thomas McIlworth (Courtesy of the New York Historical Society, New York City)

*Photograph of restored Johnson Hall with blockhouses, Johnstown, New York
(From author's collection)*

*Joseph Brant of Brant's Volunteers, by Gilbert Stuart
(Courtesy of New York State Historical Association, Cooperstown, N.Y.)*

An aerial view of restored Fort Niagara
(Courtesy of Old Fort Niagara Association)

British headquarters during the wilderness war, Stone Castle, Fort Niagara
(From author's collection)

Sir Frederick Haldimand, Governor of Quebec
(Courtesy National Archives of Canada)

Lt. Col. John Butler, Butler's Rangers   (Photo by author, courtesy of Niagara
Historical Society, Niagara-on-the-Lake, Ontario, Canada)

*Butler's Rangers preparing to deliver volley fire as at Battle of Blue Licks
(From author's collection, re-enactment of Caldwell Co., Butler's Rangers)*

*Shawnee warriors rush Kentucky militiamen with hatchets at Battle of Blue Licks
(From author's collection, re-enactment of Battle for the Ohio Country)*

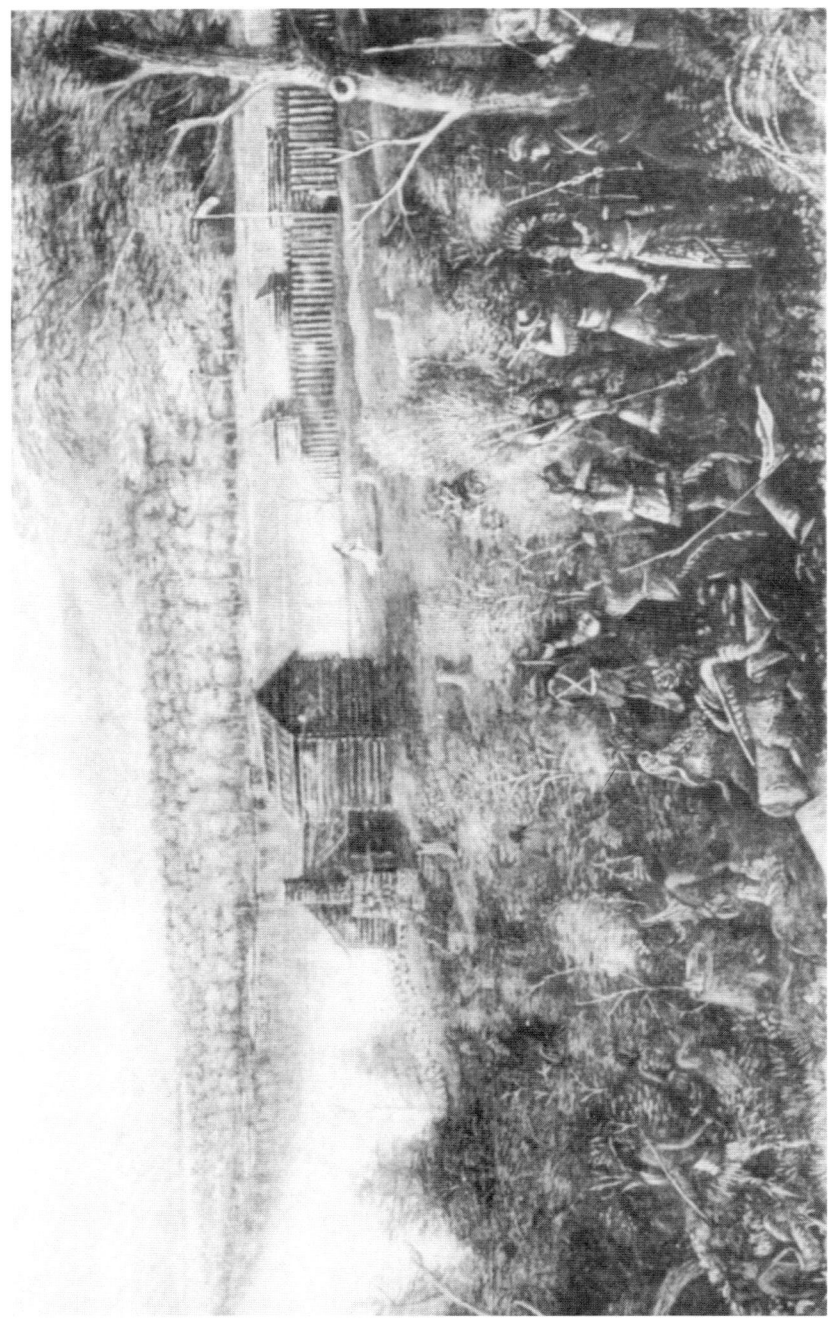

Defense of Fort Henry" 1782 Siege by J.A. Faris, Courtesy of "The Fort Henry Story" by Klein and Cooper

"The Battle of Fort Henry" by Walt Courtney, taken from 12x20 foot Mural Wesbanco Arena, Wheeling WV, courtesy Cress Studios, Wheeling WV

Shawnee and Delaware warriors assault Fort Henry during 1782 siege (From author's collection, re-enactment of Battle of Ft. Henry, 1999)

Bradt's Company, Butler's Rangers provide covering fire during assault on the fort (From author's collection, re-enactment of Battle of Fort Henry, 1999)

An attempt is made to burn Zane's blockhouse with a flaming hay cart (From author's collection, re-enactment of the Battle of Fort Henry 1999)

Alexander McKee, Matthew Elliott, the Girty brothers and other men on the payroll

Chapter 9

1777: Divided Loyalties

By the early summer 1777, word of a new war between the white men reached the countless villages of the many native Indian tribes of the Ohio Country west of the New York frontier, and, to the lands of the Seneca of the Iroquois Confederacy. By runner and by kinsmen returning from trade at the British posts at Detroit and Niagara, the word was carried to the Shawnee, the Mingo, the Delaware and the Wyandot that the British King was sending two armies from Canada, one large and one small, to invade his own colonies and put down by force the rebellious children of the King who were making war on the King's redcoats. Stories were repeated in each village of the preparations being made at Fort Niagara for the departure of over 100 loyalist rangers of the Indian Department under Major John Butler. Butler had sent word to the western tribes to join him and the Iroquois warriors at the rendevous point of Oswego on Lake Ontario, where the British commander, St. Leger would meet them. The plan was to march to the head of the Mohawk River and attack the Rebel stronghold of the Mohawk Valley all the way to Albany on the Hudson River. The talk of a new war to the east of the Ohio Indian lands made those tribes living closest to the white men of the Virginia and Pennsylvania frontier more than a little nervous. They had buried the hatchet with the colonials only two years ago. Now another war threatened to erupt around them.

The headmen and war captains of the tribes discussed and debated this new development around their campfires without reaching any consensus. That the British had asked them to join in their war against the Rebels east of the Alleghenies was disconcerting. Having as recently as 1774 felt the sting of war and the loss of many warriors at the battle with the Virginians where the Kanawha River empties into the Ohio River, many wondered aloud what the consequences might be if they supported the British when so many of the Virginians whom they previously fought were siding against the King. Would their warriors fight again, and for whom?

One thing that the tribes near the Virginian frontier could agree on was that, in spite of the uneasy peace on the frontier and their official stance of neutrality in the white man's affairs, all was not well for the Delaware, Shawnee, and Mingo when it came to the white man's appetite for their land. Nothing had been resolved in the past conflict with the Virginians in this regard, as a steady stream of settlers continued to come across the mountains from the east, looking for more land. This was a major unresolved grievance of the Shawnee, Delaware and Mingo which Lord Dunmore had promised to ameliorate for them. The reality was, however, that every month the situation became a little worse with settlers claiming more and more land on the east bank of the Ohio River, as well as invading and trespassing into the Kentucky lands, the hunting grounds of the Shawnee. This was an open sore that would not heal, and looked to only get much worse.

The war between the whites in the east had brought troubling changes to the frontier which was clearly unfavorable for the tribes of the Ohio Country. The rebellion in the spring of 1775 had deposed Lord Dunmore in Virginia. The Shawnee remembered Dunmore as the man who had forced them to make peace when he marched with his army to their towns deep in the Ohio Country in October 1774. While Dunmore had chastised the Shawnee in particular for making war on the frontier, he had also promised to stem the tide of white immigration of settlers into their lands, one of their greatest complaints with the Virginians. Unfortunately, Dunmore had been forced to flee his office in Williamsburg or face arrest by the Virginian Rebels. Now Lord Dunmore was gone, and the promises made to the Shawnee and all the tribes of the Ohio Country were in jeopardy. Delaware and Shawnee visiting Fort Pitt could see that confusion among the white men reigned supreme, as a new Rebel legislature replaced the King's in Virginia, as well as in Pennsylvania. At Fort Pitt, the men who now represented the new government were the same men whom the Indians had fought in Dunmore's War, and those men were openly antagonistic to the Indians, turning a deaf ear to their complaints. While many of the Ohio Country chiefs counseled for neutrality with the whites in their war, some Indians favored support for the British. They thought the British would help them expel the hated Virginians from their lands, if the time should come when the King would genuinely support them to fight.

"A Modest Man Who Has Shown Great Zeal"

As the western tribes debated the war, the British command in Canada was pre-occupied with the massive preparations necessary for Burgoyne and St. Leger's expeditionary armies. However, Sir Guy Carleton, the Governor General of Canada and commander of all British forces in the north had not overlooked the importance of the Ohio Country, with an eye to the many native tribes that lived there. Carleton had a tireless ally working for him in the region, Lieutenant Governor Henry Hamilton of Detroit, who kept him informed of the activities of the natives of the Ohio Country from his wilderness post at Detroit at the head of Lake Erie. As British sloops plied the waters of the lake from Fort Detroit to Niagara and from Montreal to British headquarters at Quebec, a steady stream of troops, provisions, ammunition, trade goods, and letters flowed to Governor Hamilton from Carleton, who kept Hamilton well-informed of the growing rebellion in the eastern colonies, and of the Crown's campaign planned for 1777 to put an end to it by military force. The Crown's coming campaign to invade the rebellious colonies to put an end to the revolt was an action that Hamilton, a career soldier and diplomat, could heartily endorse.

As early as September 2, 1776, Hamilton wrote to Carleton from his new posting at Detroit to suggest to Carleton that the Indians of the Ohio Country might play an important role in the coming counter offense of the Crown forces if they were actively sought out as allies, and courted with gifts, provisions, and ammunition. Hamilton believed that many of the tribes would fight the Virginians, if counseled and led by officers from Detroit, creating a new front and diversion against the Rebels. General Mason Bolton, commander of Fort Niagara, was aware of Hamilton's many military suggestions put to Carleton, which had prompted Bolton to call Hamilton "a modest man and one who has shown Great Zeal for the King's Service." [HP-126] However, Carleton and Bolton had no guidance from the English Crown as to what specifically Hamilton, at his outpost in Detroit, should or should not do in regard to his suggestions for engaging the Indians in the British cause.

"It is His Majesty's Resolution"

That ambiguity changed in the spring of 1777 when orders arrived in Canada with Burgoyne, from Lord George Germain, the Secretary of the Foreign Office charged by the King with planning and conducting the war in America from England. Germain outlined the conduct of the coming campaigns of Burgoyne and St. Leger. In addition, he detailed to Carleton his policy towards the Indian tribes of the Ohio Country and his plan to recruit them to play a supporting role for the major military activities in the east. What Hamilton had been unaware of was that his request for active service on the western frontier had been forwarded by Carleton directly to Lord Germain and the King, and now a response from Germain had finally arrived in Canada.

Carleton read Germain's orders for Hamilton, written March 26, 1777, from Whitehall, England. Germain directed Carleton to inform Hamilton as soon as possible of what he needed to do at Fort Detroit with regard to the Indians of the Ohio Country. Carleton re-read Germain's instructions carefully before writing to Hamilton at Detroit on May 21, 1777. "You have herewith enclosed the Copy of a Letter from Lord George Germain, which is sent to you at full Length, for your Instruction and Guidance." [HP-211] Carleton added his own comments to the letter, before sealing the packet and forwarding it with the mail destined for Montreal and the head of the St. Lawrence River for the next supply ship leaving for the western posts of the Great Lakes. Carleton knew it would take time for Hamilton to receive it, and he hoped that his officer at Detroit had not acted alone without his advice. Hamilton received that important mail in mid June 1777, on a British sloop coming from Fort Niagara.

Governor Hamilton nodded with satisfaction as he read the letter, realizing that Lord Germain had considered his proposal. Germain wrote, "in the consideration of measures proper to be pursued in the next campaign (Burgoyne and St. Leger), the making a Diversion on the Frontiers of Virginia and Pennsylvania by Parties of Indians conducted by proper Leaders, as proposed by Lieut. Governor Hamilton has been maturely weighed." Germain further added, "It is His Majesty's Resolution that the most vigorous Efforts should be made, and every means employed that Providence has into His Majesty's Hands for crushing the Rebellion." Hamilton read on with great interest. "It is the King's Command that you should direct Lieut. Governor Hamilton to Assemble as many of the Indians of his District as he conveniently can, and placing proper Persons at their Head, to whom he is to make suitable Allowances, to conduct their Parties and restrain them from committing violence on the well affected and inoffensive Inhabitants, employ them in making a Diversion and exciting an alarm upon the frontiers of Virginia and Pennsylvania." [HP-211]

Hamilton felt a sense of pride for having had the courage to send his earlier recommendations to Carleton, in spite of being relegated to the obscurity of service at the far-away post of Detroit. Lord Germain had seen the soundness of his suggestions, and was in total agreement, whereas Carleton, his commanding officer, had been unsure of what course to take. In Germain's orders to Hamilton he added that since "there are considerable numbers of loyal Subjects in those Parts, who would gladly embrace an opportunity of delivering themselves from the Tyranny and Oppression of the Rebel Committees," that Hamilton should "invite all such loyal subjects to join him and to assure them of the same pay and allowances as are given to His Majesty's other Corps raised in America," so that these men could help Hamilton extend his operations, so as to divide the attention of the Rebels" and in Germain's mind, thus weaken the main Continental army in the east.

Hamilton noted that Sir Guy Carleton had included his own instructions cautioning him not to prematurely divert any warriors intent on leaving the Ohio Country to join the Six Nations and St. Leger. "You will therefore be careful not to attempt to draw off any destined for his command," Carleton wrote, knowing Hamilton's inclination to begin calling in the tribes immediately, once he read Germain's directive, which could prove to be divisive. Hamilton knew what his commander, Sir Guy Carleton did not. Few warriors, if any from the Ohio Country, were willing to accompany St. Leger, because of their long standing animosity to the Iroquois who had never missed an opportunity to treat the Ohio tribes as subjects rather than equals.

"Their Extensive Influence among the Inhabitants"

Governor Hamilton noted with interest the appendage to Germain's orders. Germain added to his letter "a list of the names of several persons, residing on the frontiers of Virginia, recommended by Lord Dunmore for their loyalty and attachment to government," who Germain thought could provide Hamilton with assistance in his upcoming campaign in the Ohio Country. Dunmore had evidently provided Germain with the list of influential loyalists on the Virginian frontier after he was deposed by the Rebels in Williamsburg. Hamilton looked over the names and wondered how these men could be contacted and if they could find some way of extricating themselves from the Virginia frontier without arousing suspicions and risking arrest. Hamilton knew that the proposition would be difficult. Dunmore's information to Germain was far too old to be valid as current as Germain stated that most of the men "who his Lordship thinks will be able to give great assistance to Lieut. Gov. Hamilton through their extensive Influence among the Inhabitants." Hamilton was already aware from the coming and going of Indians and traders traveling between Detroit and the Ohio and the Rebel Committee of Safety at Fort Pitt had already detained several of the men mentioned by Dunmore, suspecting them of supporting the Loyalist cause.

Hamilton put the letter down and pondered the situation of the men on Dunmore's list. A more practical man than Dunmore, Hamilton came to the conclusion that Dunmore's loyalists could be no help to him if they stayed where they now were at the frontier settlements firmly in Rebel hands. There were more important matters at hand for him to attend to if he were to set in motion Germain's plans and provisions for Indian war parties to attack the Virginian frontier, as Germain advised. The fate of men like Alexander McKee at Pittsburgh would have to wait for the moment, or take care of itself, Hamilton thought.

Hamilton's assessment of Dunmore's loyalists in spring 1777 was entirely correct, as far as Alexander McKee of Pittsburgh was concerned. As early as the previous January 1776, the former deputy agent of British Indian Affairs for the Western tribes was implicated in a plot formulated by one of Dunmore's loyal aides as Pittsburgh, John Connolly. On the orders of Lord Dunmore, Connolly had met with British General Thomas Gage in Boston to endorse a plan for Connolly to raise two companies of loyalist militia on the Virginia frontier and then, combining with British troops, to attack and destroy Fort Pitt. [NL-p.93]

"The Clamor against McKee Was Wrong-founded"

Connolly's plan implicated McKee and when it was accidentally uncovered by local Rebel authorities, the Lancaster Pennsylvania Committee of Safety issued a warrant for McKee's arrest in Pittsburgh for his role in the conspiracy. At the same time, McKee received a secret letter written on February 29, 1776, from Colonel John Butler at Fort Niagara, ordering McKee, as deputy agent in the Indian Department to meet Butler at Fort Niagara as soon as the weather broke. Butler wrote, "Your knowledge in Indian affairs, your hitherto undoubted zeal for His Majesty's service, and the duty you owe to your government," made it imperative that the two men meet to discuss Crown strategy on the western frontier. [NL-p.95] Somehow, the Rebels at Fort Pitt learned of Butler's dispatch to McKee before it arrived, and the Committee of Safety demanded to see it. McKee was forced to comply or face arrest, and he "denied knowing anything of Butler's intentions." [NL-p.95] The damage was however done to McKee's reputation. He was put on parole by the local Rebels with the promise that he would not communicate with any British official nor conduct any business with the Indians coming and going to Fort Pitt. Worst of all, McKee was forced by the Committee to agree that while on parole, he would not leave Pittsburgh without their consent. The Rebels had effectively put McKee under house arrest.

By mid summer 1777, McKee's situation had improved somewhat. No further evidence linking him to the loyalist cause had surfaced since his parole at Pittsburgh had been instituted. Unfortunately for McKee, more bad news was on the way. General Edward Hand, the newly-arrived commander of Fort Pitt was informed by the Rebel Committee of Safety that a number of men at the nearby settlement of Redstone were engaged in loyalist activities. Hand moved quickly to arrest the conspirators who implicated Alexander McKee and Simon Girty at Pittsburgh. Hand arrested both men for questioning, however further investigation could not produce any hard evidence, and Hand was forced to release McKee and Girty, "concluding once again that the "clamor against…McKee was wrong-founded." [NL-p.99] McKee was forced to sign a second written parole to gain his release late in the summer. McKee was angered by the unnecessary restrictions, and for the first time, worried about his future.

McKee was aware that since his service to the British Indian Department as deputy agent under William Johnson, he had made some enemies over the years. These people were now taking the opportunity to spread rumors and accusations about his character and to question his loyalty to the patriot cause, a situation fueled by the fact that McKee had a Shawnee Indian wife whose people lived across the Ohio River deep in Indian Country. McKee had been free to come and go with his wife to her family's village on the Scioto River, but now the parole to Pittsburgh meant that he could not accompany her. As rumors of a new Indian war formulated by the British at Fort Detroit began to circulate in the late summer, so, too, was McKee's wife treated with suspicion. McKee had heard rumors that his wife was suspected by locals of carrying military intelligence and letters from her husband for Indians to courier to Fort Detroit. Alexander McKee became concerned for her safety, as well as his own, by early September.

The real problem for Alexander McKee was that his private thoughts and feelings concerning his private sympathies to the King and Crown, the Indian Department, and the Shawnee people of his wife, seemed to be in direct contradiction to all that he had built for himself and acquired in the form of property at the forks of the Ohio, since his arrival nearly 15 years earlier. McKee had amassed three substantial parcels of land totaling more than 6,000 acres of prime real estate, buildings, and livestock, much of which lay a mile downriver from Fort Pitt near the mouth of Chartier's Creek on the east side of the Ohio River. [NL-p.101] McKee was determined not to lose without a fight what he had worked so hard to gain over the years. The thought now began to cross his mind that, either the revolutionary government would eventually throw him in prison and seize his lands on the charges of treason, or he would be injured or killed defending his property by those intent on robbing and destroying him to take his property under the guise of eliminating a suspected loyalist and Indian sympathizer.

McKee felt the growing pressure from local officials, and began to wonder if he was running out of time to implement alternate plans extricating him from what appeared to be a trap closing around him. McKee realized that he had misjudged the Rebels. Revolutionary fervor on the frontier was neither subsiding, nor about to be quelled by a British army any time soon, leaving him isolated and alone. McKee mulled over his deteriorating situation, finally reasoning after signing the second parole that he would never be free of suspicion. McKee reached the conclusion that he was condemned by his past, by his association with his wife and her people, by his enemies intent on destroying him, and by the wealth that he had worked hard to accumulate at Pittsburgh. The worst part was that in his conscience he could not deny to himself that he favored both the loyalist and Shawnee cause. This fact alone put him increasingly at odds with nearly everyone around him at Pittsburgh. With this realization, McKee began quietly liquidating his extensive holdings, converting them to cash in the event he would need to make a quick escape. By summer's end he had discreetly sold much of his property to his younger brother, James, for "1,500 pounds, Pennsylvania currency." [NL-p.100]

Tensions only heightened more for McKee when word reached Pittsburgh of the massive, savage Indian attack on Fort Henry at Wheeling, some 40 miles downriver from Pittsburgh, on September 1, 1777. Hamilton at Fort Detroit had been successful enlisting the war chiefs of many of the increasingly hostile tribes of the Ohio Country, to attack the Virginians. With the necessary provisions and ammunition from Carleton to outfit small war parties, the Indians began attacking the frontier along the Ohio River and began hit-and-run raids on isolated settler cabins in mid-July. The isolated successes led to more and more warriors taking the offensive against the Virginian frontier, so that by late summer, General Hand at Fort Pitt was receiving increased reports of Indian attacks occurring from the upper Allegheny River to Fort Randolph downriver at the mouth of the Kanawha. [HW1-p.87] The growing number of Indian raids and their effectiveness to alarm the frontier was largely due to the tireless efforts of Governor Hamilton, who kept them supplied and in the field.

However, Hamilton was not without his own problems. To him, the Indian raids seemed far too haphazard to make any serious impact on the Virginians in proportion to the high cost in provisions and ammunition to keep the war parties on the offensive. Simply, the Indians were consuming large quantities of supplies and not showing much headway for their efforts. Hamilton knew where the fault lay, but was largely powerless to change the fact that he had no able officers among his own corps at Fort Detroit with the experience to accompany the Indians and direct them in a more efficient manner. Dunmore's list of able men with loyalist sympathies on the frontier had come back to haunt Hamilton, as he realized he needed Englishmen who were acquainted with Indians and their style of fighting more so than his conventionally trained officers. Begrudging, Hamilton had to settle for a handful of French Canadians from the Detroit area to accompany the first large-scale war party that was preparing to attack Fort

Henry, and the small settlement at Wheeling on the east bank of the Ohio River, late in the summer.

"No Sign of Indians in the Vicinity"

All that Hamilton was able to do himself was arm and supply the mixed band of more than 200 Delawares, Mingoes, Shawnee and Wyandot warriors as they set out from the Upper Sandusky villages to the east and the Ohio frontier. He could only hope that the war chiefs and the Canadians would wisely concentrate their attack on a major Virginian settlement rather than waste their efforts on more scattered raiding. What Hamilton did not know was that word of the coming attack had already reached the frontier, neutralizing some of the element of surprise. McKee's Shawnee wife had heard from her own people that a major Indian attack was imminent, most probably against Fort Henry, but with all the problems that preoccupied her husband, she kept the information to herself, realizing when word of the attack reached Pittsburgh, Alexander might be accused of complicity if he admitted to prior knowledge.

Unknown to her, a Delaware chief named White Eyes, who was a friend to the Virginians, had informed General Hand at Fort Pitt in mid-August that a large war party of hostile Indians from the upper villages near Sandusky were on their way to attack Fort Henry. Hand immediately sent word to Colonel David Shepherd, commander at Wheeling, warning him of the pending attack. Hand sent three companies of militia downriver to reinforce the small garrison at Fort Henry, but Shepherd dismissed them soon after, writing to General Hand on August 28 that "there had been no sign of Indians in the vicinity." Privately Shepherd complained that the militiamen had consumed much of his precious provisions at the fort during their brief stay. [HW1-p.88] Four days later the Indians struck Fort Henry from ambush.

Although General Hand was able to alert the small garrison at Fort Henry, the large Indian war party was successful in arriving at the Wheeling area undetected, as the fort had no scouts on the west side of the Ohio River watching the many Indian trails for signs of an approaching war party. The warriors crossed the Ohio River on the night of August 31 and took up hidden positions in the cultivated fields surrounding the fort. The next morning, a small party of warriors fired upon some settlers outside the walls, and the garrison sent out a company of militia to chase off the handful of Indians, whom they believed to be a small raiding party.

The militiamen of Captain Samuel Mason's company stumbled into a classic Vee-shaped Indian ambush on the trail leading east of the fort, and were caught in a fusillade of Indian musket fire. "Mason had blundered into a well-designed Indian ambush," and his men "were completely surrounded and cut off" when the ambush was sprung, felling most of his men in the initial volley. [HW1-p.89] Captain Mason and one other man of the 14-man contingent were the only survivors. [HW1-p.89] Unable to know what was happening in the early morning fog, Captain Ogle "led out a relief party of another dozen or so men," to come to Mason's rescue. Ogle's militiamen were likewise ambushed, with only a few able to make their way back to the safety of the fort. Although the Indians were not able to breach the walls, nor lure any more of the defenders out into the open, they did satisfy themselves with scalping and mutilating the dead as well as "burning buildings...killing all the livestock...and rounding up all the horses they could find," before quietly withdrawing during the night. [HW1-p.91] In all, their attack had been largely successful.

A little more than three weeks later, General Hand received another warning of a pending Indian attack at Wheeling from a letter sent to him by David Zeisberger, a Moravian missionary living in the Ohio Country at the Delaware Indian village of Goschachgunk. [HW2-p.32] A militia company stationed at Fort Henry under the command of Captain William Foreman was ordered to go on a short scout along the Ohio River some 12 miles south of Fort Henry, to look for Indian sign and determine what had caused the smoke seen several days before, coming from the direction of an abandoned settler cabin. Foreman and the 46 men with him reached the cabin by noon on September 26 and found it burned to the ground, but little fresh sign of Indians.

On the return trip to Fort Henry the next morning, the militia company walked into an Indian Vee-shaped ambush where the trail emerged into the woods from a narrow defile along the cliffs bordering the river at a particular spot. As the men stopped to examine some Indian articles deliberately left on the trail in front of them, a large party of hidden Wyandot warriors led by their war captain, Half King, opened fire on the militiamen. Quickly the warriors rushed the staggered and seriously wounded men in the vanguard, killing 21 of the militiamen, including Foreman himself. Survivors who were able to escape the ambush and return to Fort Henry led a burial party to the badly mutilated bodies a few days after. [HW2-p.35]

Word of the Indian attack on Fort Henry and the ambush of Foreman's militia company spread quickly up and down the scattered settlements and outlying cabins of the Virginia frontier, causing panic and flight among the inhabitants. The road east from Pittsburgh was clogged with a steady stream of frightened settlers and their families, who had decided it was better to abandon their homes and flee for their lives than risk being the next victims of the Indians in this renewed full-scale Indian wilderness war. General Hand at Fort Pitt attempted to restore order by calling out the local militia to stand in preparedness, but he found that so many able-bodied men had already gone east to support the patriot defense of Philadelphia from British attack, he did not have the manpower to pursue the Indians offensively, and could only hope to consolidate the defenses of the frontier to stave off further attack until colder weather arrived when the Indian war parties returned to their villages for the winter. Minor hit-and-run Indian raids continued into late autumn, undermining General Hand's credibility with the local populace at Pittsburgh, and frustrating him further.

Sorrow for the loss of those men from Fort Henry
who were slain in the Indian ambush.

"Every Person You Have Reason to Suspect"

By December 1777, renewed rumors of McKee's clandestine involvement with the Indians and the British resurfaced, forcing Hand to take some sort of action against McKee to quell the fervor mounting against both men. Capitulating to growing local pressure to restrict McKee, General Hand decided to order Alexander McKee to "present himself before the Continental Congress's Board of War in York, (Pennsylvania) to give an account of his activities." [NL-p.101] McKee was shocked and angered by Hand's orders. McKee knew the accusations made against him were groundless rumors spread by people whom he believed to be working against him. Yet McKee was unsure what to do, so he delayed his response to Hand and the officials at York. McKee wished more than ever that his close friend Matthew Elliott was available to give him advice during this trying time of his life.

Unfortunately for him, Elliott was nowhere to be found. McKee's closest personal friend since his arrival at Pittsburgh had left on a trading mission deep in the Ohio Country the previous year, and had not been heard of since. All that McKee knew about Elliott was rumor that his wife's people had heard from visitors to their Shawnee village on the Scioto, that Elliott had been captured by a Mingo Indian party. McKee did not know whether Elliott was dead or alive, and consequently, the possible loss of his friend was one more issue that added to his own frustration and feeling of helplessness.

What had happened to Matthew Elliott? Ironically, the one man who knew more about Elliott's whereabouts than McKee was asking himself the same question. Governor Hamilton at Detroit had puzzled about Mathew Elliott ever since he received Carleton's letter in early June 1777, which contained Lord Germain's instructions. Hamilton remembered then that Mathew Elliott was the man whom he arrested at Detroit on charges of spying for the Rebels. Soon after he sent Elliott to Quebec for further questioning, Germain's letter arrived from England, which included Dunmore's list of loyalists on the Virginia frontier. When Hamilton read the roster of loyalist names, he was surprised to find that Matthew Elliott's was not on that list. This would have confirmed Hamilton's suspicions that Elliott was indeed a Rebel spy, if it had not been for several other names that Lord Dunmore listed. Hamilton had heard the names of these men from Elliott before he received Dunmore's list.

During Hamilton's questioning of Matthew Elliott at Detroit, Elliott had revealed many things in an attempt to prove his innocence of the charges brought against him. Elliott told Hamilton of his close friendship with Alexander McKee at Pittsburgh, the former British Deputy Agent for Indian Affairs at Pittsburgh. Elliott explained how he and McKee shared a great empathy for the Indians of the Ohio Country, as both men having taken Shawnee women as wives. Elliott tried to further his case by telling Hamilton about his close acquaintance with Simon Girty at Fort Pitt, who had been the interpreter to the Indians for Lord Dunmore during his campaign to quell the Shawnee uprising during 1774. In fact, Elliott claimed to have met Dunmore when he "agreed to carry a conciliatory message to Dunmore's advancing army" as an appointed negotiator for the Shawnee. [HR-p.5-6] He and Girty had conversed with Lord Dunmore over the terms of the peace to be conveyed to the Shawnee. Hamilton was shocked to see Alexander McKee and Simon Girty on Dunmore's list. [BC-p.23-24]

Now Elliott was gone, and Hamilton wondered what had become of him, the man who had protested his innocence, yet whom Hamilton believed to be in league with the Rebels at Fort Pitt. Had Dunmore been wrong in his initial assessment of Elliott? What bothered Hamilton more than anything else was the nagging possibility that he had totally misjudged the man, and in doing so, missed the opportunity to which Germain had alluded in advising him to seek out loyalists who knew the Virginian frontier and were capable of leading the Indians against it. Hamilton reflected on the overall ineffectiveness of the past fall's Indian raiding parties to devastate the frontier with any consistent determined effort. To Hamilton, the fault clearly lay with a lack of men capable to lead the Indians. Neither Canadians nor his own regular officers could do the job. Loyalists were needed, as Dunmore and Germain proposed. Hamilton shuddered at the thought that regularly crossed his mind. What if Governor Carleton at Quebec determined that Elliott was not a spy and the Hamilton should not have arrested the man? Would Carleton inform Lord Germain?

The fact that Hamilton received a letter from Carleton approving his actions concerning Elliott did not provide Hamilton with much solace. Carleton wrote then, "you acted properly in seizing and sending down Elliott and you will treat in the same manner every Person you have reason to suspect of corresponding with, or favoring the cause of the Rebels." Of course Hamilton knew that Carleton had written to him before having a chance to examine Elliott directly. Upon doing so, would Carleton come to doubt the charges against Elliott, and in turn, doubt Hamilton too? [HP-211]

Governor Hamilton put the thought of Elliott out of his mind for the moment. Fortunately, the last supply sloop for the upper posts arrived at Detroit on December 1, just ahead of bad weather. Hamilton was relieved to find that vessel had brought him much needed provisions and reinforcements for the garrison. In addition, Carleton had agreed to send an officer, Captain Lernoult from Quebec, to tend to the needs of the fort, thus freeing Hamilton to spend more time organizing the Canadians and Indians for the planned campaign against the Rebels in the spring. [HP-225]

One of the last large war parties of Canadians and Indians returned to Fort Detroit on December 4, just as the snow was beginning to fly. La Mothe, the Frenchman, had left Detroit on September 20, 1777 with a party of 57 Canadians and 45 Lake Indians. Along the way to the Virginian frontier, he picked up more than 60 Delaware at the Upper Sandusky villages, and gathered a few more warriors returning from the recent raid on Fort Henry at Wheeling. Most of those Indians, La Mothe related to Hamilton, were reluctant to accompany him. They were loaded down with captured horses, scalps, and plunder, wanting only to return to the own villages and family with their loot. Unfortunately, La Mothe could not keep the large war party together. When they reached the Ohio

River, they split up. Hamilton detailed this information in his last letter to Carleton leaving by sloop by way of Lake Erie before it froze. "After some time La Mothe remained with only 12 Indians and a few Canadians, the former having separated into small war parties in their own way," Hamilton wrote that La Mothe's inability to hold the Indians together to strike the Rebels from strength only showed what Germain and Dunmore had alluded to all along. Small war parties of Indians would accomplish little. [HP-225] Again, Hamilton's thoughts turned to Elliott, and the others named on Dunmore's list.

"Well Disposed to His Majesty"

If Hamilton had only known that the list of Dunmore's frontier loyalists was not written by Dunmore at all. How could Lord Dunmore have known so many of the minor personalities at Pittsburgh, like Simon Girty, when Dunmore visited the settlement only once in 1774 while on his march to the Shawnee Indian villages to make war? Dunmore had paid scant attention to the rough and tumble likes of so many of the men on the frontier whom he looked down upon for their lack of breeding and culture. Since Lord Dunmore's military and government official at Fort Pitt before the start of the rebellion had been John Connolly, it had been Connolly who had had the time to acquaint himself with "most of the officers in the militia or magistrates of the county" at Pittsburgh prior to Dunmore's ousting by the Rebels. "Dunmore's list was doubtless made by Connolly" [BC-p.24] who most likely embellished the roster of loyalists with the names of men of some importance at Pittsburgh whom he could recall.

Whether Connolly knew for sure that the men were of loyalist character and suitable for Dunmore's recommendation to Lord Germain was inconsequential. Connolly had too much on his mind when he wrote it. Under suspicion of supporting Dunmore and the Crown, Connolly would soon find himself arrested and imprisoned by the Rebels after Dunmore was forced to flee. Neither man would have further opportunity to evaluate whether those men named were indeed "Well-disposed to His Majesty's Government." How could Hamilton have known that with one or two exceptions, "all of those of the whites on Dunmore's list…had quickly and patriotically rallied with the Whigs." [BC-p.25] Alexander McKee, Elliott's friend, was not one of them. Unfortunately, the bulk of Connolly's list was nothing more than a list of officers at Fort Pitt who had served John Connolly when he was Dunmore's agent prior to the opening of the rebellion. Hamilton would have been truly shocked to know that the list he attached so much importance to was, by and large, fictitious.

"Again Locked Up"

However, not all of the names on the Connolly/Dunmore list were ardent patriots either, nor had they all "rallied with the Whigs" at Pittsburgh. Simon Girty, for one, was the type of man who had never seen the sense of putting too much value on oaths and allegiances, unless he could see some profit in it for himself. Girty had made his living on the Virginian frontier by working all sides in the shifting alliances of the continuing conflict between the white men and the Indians. Since his repatriation as a captive of the Seneca at the end of Pontiac's uprising, Girty was content to find employment at Fort Pitt as an Indian interpreter, scout, and hunter, occasionally supplementing his meager income by trading goods for furs with the Indians across the Ohio River in times of peace, much like Matthew Elliott and other men. As of late fall 1777, Simon Girty had tried his hand as a second lieutenant in the local militia. There was not much else that he could do, since the wave of Indian war parties hitting the frontier had forced General Hand into a defensive posture at Fort Pitt, effectively putting Girty out of business as an interpreter. Most of the Indians, except for a few Christian Delaware, were in no mood to talk or bargain with the whites. For the moment, scalping, burning and bloodletting were all that was on their minds.

Simon Girty was disgruntled with the turn of events in the past months for many reasons. When the patriot government in Virginia sent Captain John Neville to take possession of Fort Pitt late in 1775, Girty lost his position of second lieutenant in the former militia formed by John Connolly prior to the rebellion. Out of work, Girty applied for and was "appointed on the first day of May" 1776 to be an interpreter for the Six Nations Seneca by the new agent of Indian Affairs at Pittsburgh, George Morgan. Only three months later, after a "journey to the Indian Country" for Morgan, Girty was surprised to be "relieved from his duties" because of what Morgan called Girty's "ill behavior," relating to a spate of public drunkenness. [BC-p.28] At odds with his boss, Simon Girty reacted bitterly to the dismissal.

Finding himself out of work again, Simon Girty got the idea of enlisting men he knew at the settlement into a company of patriot militia in the spring of 1777, presuming he would be awarded command of with captain's commission and pay. Unfortunately for Girty, the militia at Fort Pitt had other ideas, and appointed John Stephenson as captain, relegating Girty to second lieutenant. Simon Girty was clearly disappointed that he was passed over, and early in August 1777, he resigned his subaltern commission, staying in Pittsburgh and resuming some "intercourse with the Indians" that were still friendly with the whites on the Virginia frontier. [BC-p.31]

By late August, Simon Girty found himself in trouble again, this time with local officials who accused him of being part of a loyalist conspiracy at Redstone settlement near Pittsburgh. When Alexander McKee was arrested by General Hand, Girty was jailed as well in "the common guardhouse" at Fort Pitt. [BC-p.33] Defiant, Simon escaped from the jail, "however, the next day he returned of his own accord and was again locked up." [BC-p.34] After being questioned by a magistrate from Pittsburgh, Girty was acquitted of all charges and released, whereupon General Hand restored Girty to his former position as interpreter to the Seneca, and soon after, sent him north to the Seneca villages on the upper Allegheny River to find out if the Six Nations were hostile to the Americans, as General Hand believed. Girty was briefly captured by some Seneca who intended to take him to Fort Niagara as their prisoner, but Girty escaped and returned to Pittsburgh with the news that most of the tribes of the

Six Nations were now at war with the Americans, and Fort Pitt was in danger of imminent attack.

Word of the War in the East

At the same time in late fall of 1777, word of the startling developments in the eastern colonies reached Pittsburgh. The inhabitants learned that, while St. Leger and the Indians had given up on the siege of Fort Stanwix and returned to Canada, the Indian and loyalist attack on the patriot militia in the Mohawk Valley had been disastrous for the Americans with hundreds of men killed. The patriots on the frontier could take heart in the news that British General Burgoyne's army had surrendered to American General Gates at Saratoga in New York in October after a series of defeats, but that hardly tempered the more shocking news that the city of New York was in British hands, and in spite of the tremendous number of men who had marched east from the Virginia and Pennsylvania frontier to fight for the patriot cause, Philadelphia, too, had fallen to the British after the American army was routed at Brandywine, barely escaping total destruction. What was left of Washington's army was suffering intolerable conditions at Valley Forge in Pennsylvania with the coming of winter. The cold weather and hostile Indians had everyone holed up at Fort Pitt, including Simon Girty, who now held out little hope of finding useful occupation within the confines of the frontier post.

Events galvanized on their own in early February 1778 in Pittsburgh. First, General Hand had reached a point of desperation at Fort Pitt as a result of the Indian raids up and down the frontier, the continuing threats of loyalist plots plaguing the settlement population, and the military setbacks and bad news reaching the frontier from across the mountains. At the heart of Hand's vexation was that he felt nearly everyone at Pittsburgh blamed him for the sad state of affairs at his post. General Hand came up with the idea to take the military initiative and strike a blow against the hostile Indians in the Ohio Country with a winter expedition against a British-allied Indian village on the Cuyahoga River to the northwest near Lake Erie. [BC-p.35]

"Four Women and a Boy"

Before setting out from Fort Pitt in February with the 500 man force that he had assembled, General Hand took another initiative before he departed, and sent Alexander McKee an ultimatum to report to the authorities in York, as had been requested of him in late December. McKee reported personally to Hand as he prepared to march, promising him that he would leave immediately for York, as Hand desired. As soon as General Hand and his force left the fort, McKee once again reneged, and did not go. [NL-p.101]

Hand's expedition quickly met with disaster due to the inclement weather encountered on the trail to the northwest in mid-February. His army slogged through heavy rain, snow, ice and mud that quickly slowed his force down to a crawl. Most of Hand's men were raw recruits from Westmoreland County who were unprepared for a winter march. By the time the column reached halfway to their destination, it became apparent to Hand that the men could go no further, and his little army would have to turn back. Simon Girty accompanied Hand's expedition as an interpreter and scout, since Girty was well acquainted with the particular area of the Ohio Country, having spent time there while a captive of the Seneca as a youth. Girty shook his head with disgust when a small party of Indian women and children were attacked, and one squaw killed and the rest taken captive. General Hand was disgusted, too, as his exhausted column of shivering, hungry men made their way dejectedly back to Pittsburgh without striking a blow at the enemy. The only Indians encountered, Hand reported, was "four women and a boy," of which one Indian woman, a squaw, was killed. [BC-p.36] Within a few weeks of what would become known as Hand's "Squaw campaign," General Hand would resign his commission as commander of Fort Pitt in humiliation. [BC-p.38]

However, adding to the General's chagrin when he returned to Pittsburgh was the discovery that Alexander McKee was still at the settlement, and "had not reported to York as promised." [MD-101] General Hand was furious at McKee's insubordination, and ordered McKee to report to him at once at Fort Pitt. Face to face with General Hand, McKee apologized. He explained to Hand that he had been too sick to travel which was the cause of his delay. General Hand was not convinced. He dismissed McKee for the moment but privately "Hand suspected that he (McKee) was 'pretending indisposition' in order to delay his appearance before Congress." [NL-p.101] If Hand had only known that McKee was purposely delaying for an entirely different reason. McKee had no intention of ever going to York. An old friend had returned to Pittsburgh while General Hand was gone, and he brought with him startling news.

"Nothing but Peas and Oatmeal"

Meanwhile, at Fort Niagara the commander of the post, Lieutenant Colonel Mason Bolton of the King's Eighth Regiment mulled over the military reports and inventory lists scattered over the table in his quarters in the old stone house within the fort. As he peered out the icy window that overlooked Lake Ontario, Bolton could see the high drifts of snow piled over the thick ice covering the wide expanse of the lake, and silently he shook his head. No supply ships would cross the lake until spring, and that could be more than three months away, Bolton thought. The provisions on hand at Fort Niagara would have to last to feed the 532 souls housed under the King's flag, but that number did not include several hundred Indians with their families huddled in huts around the fort grounds. What did Carleton propose he feed them? [HP-372]

Bolton dwelled on the huge stock of provisions sent to Fort Detroit the previous year, as he wrote to Carleton a "Return of Provisions in Store at Niagara 24th January, 1778 And Also how long it will Last - 532 Men." It seemed to him to be a waste of supplies for Carleton to send so much to Hamilton to feed so few, while the men of the Niagara garrison including regular troops, seamen, and Rangers would be forced onto a restricted diet. The fort's stocks had flour, peas, and oatmeal to last till spring, but that could hardly be considered a soldier's meal. Bolton noted that salted beef would run out in only five days and there was only enough salted pork to last to mid-March. He knew that he had not allowed in his report for any spoilage which was sure to be found in some of the kegs when they were opened. [HP-372]

Bolton signed his name to the letter to Carleton in Quebec and sent it on with the post couriers who would be setting out in the morning by sled for the posts to the east. Privately, he wondered how Carleton intended to conduct a war in the wilderness in the coming spring, with men weakened by the half-rations he had on hand. The questions continued to plague him, as they would any man who was in command of a King's post. Bolton wondered how he would feed the hungry Indians, who would be needed as allies in the spring campaigns. Had not Carleton considered the Iroquois at all? Did he not know that they would not fight if they were not fed and provided for?

"By the Accounts of Prisoners"

At Detroit, Governor Hamilton paced the floor of his quarters as the winter winds howled outside. He thought long and hard about his assessment of the efforts of the Indians attacks of the previous year upon the Virginian frontier, which he had orchestrated from Detroit. Hamilton thought it paramount to convey to Carleton in Quebec the importance of the intelligence that had been gleamed from the Rebel prisoners he and Captain Lernoult had interrogated thoroughly. Most of the men had been taken by the Indians from the vicinity of Fort Pitt during their raids the previous fall. It was not hard for Hamilton to get them to talk. All he needed to do was intimate to them individually that if they did not cooperate with him he would have no choice but to turn them over to the warriors who asked him daily for possession of the men. Hamilton advised the prisoners that once he returned them to the Indians, that he would no longer be responsible for their actions. Consequently, each of the prisoners talked profusely under Hamilton's advice. [HP-222]

Hamilton picked up his quill and began to write a letter to Carleton on February 1, 1778, first conveying to the General his thoughts on the information from the prisoners that he would use to support his proposal. "By the accounts of Prisoners brought in from Fort Pitt, there is room to believe that Place is by no means capable of resisting an inconsiderable force sent against it," Hamilton wrote. He explained why Fort Pitt could be easily taken, in his estimation, because the garrison "does not exceed 120 men," the soldiers are "undisciplined or ill affected," the artillery pieces are "out of condition for Service," and that it could be presumed, Hamilton stated, that "the Rebels will not give much attention to a frontier post, since the taking of Philadelphia must have called for all their people to the southward, and they would scarcely send from that Quarter a good officer, staunch men, and serviceable Artillery." [HP-222]

Hamilton thought for a moment about the returning Indian war parties. He was pleased that General Carleton had seen fit to send a plentiful supply of provisions and ammunition to Fort Detroit the past summer, much of which he distributed to the Indian war parties sent out against the Virginian frontier with success. Returning parties had came to Detroit without any remaining food, having eaten all that they carried with them on the raid, and having not stopped to hunt for game, for fear of pursuit by the Rebels. The daunting task of feeding them through the winter would not sit well with Carleton, Hamilton thought, as the General had made clear to him in his directives that everything given to the Indians had to be strictly accounted for, so that, as Carleton wrote, "the Quantity of Arms, and Ammunition they carry" could be accounted for and sent monthly "in order to be compared with those taken out of the office here." [HP-211] Hamilton wondered if Lt. Colonel Bolton at Niagara was burdened with the same paperwork that took up so much of his own time.

In regard to what Hamilton viewed as the Indians' haphazard manner of attacking the Rebel frontier, he summarized to Carleton that "the parties sent from hence have been in general successful…they have brought in 23 men Prisoners alive, 20 of which they presented to me, and a 129 scalps." [HP-222] Hamilton remembered the unfortunate fate of three men whom the Lake Indians refused to give to him. He recalled their pitiful pleas to him for mercy to spare them from the Indians. He regrettably was unable to do so, knowing that any attempt risked angering the Indian chiefs and war captains to whom the captives now belonged.

Equally disturbing to him was the shocking display of the hair of those whites the Indians killed and scalped for trophies. Hamilton could not help but notice that some of the bloodied scalps dangling from the belts of the warriors were small in size and fair in color. Undoubtedly, Hamilton knew that those scalps were taken from the heads of children. The longer, groomed hair obviously came from the heads of slaughtered white women and Hamilton was revolted at the depredations of the Indians for which he admonished them in the past, but only in the form of a mild warning.

The sight of the scalps disgusted him at the time. Now the memory of it was one that he preferred to purposely turn his mind away from, and not think of again. As an officer and gentleman, Hamilton abhorred the use of Indians in wilderness warfare against the white frontier. Privately he deplored their manner of fighting and the savageness by which they conducted themselves in battle. Yet Hamilton realized that he needed the Indians. For all their shortcomings, the Indians were able to traverse the wilderness and attack the Rebels on the Virginian frontier, a feat impossible for British regulars. If he were to fulfill Germain's orders, Hamilton knew that he must overlook Indian depredations so they could be employed on the Ohio Country frontier to aid in defeating the Rebels and ending the rebellion. In war, nothing else mattered but winning, and the means, however deplorable in a wilderness war, justified the ends, as far as Hamilton was concerned.

Hamilton came to the point of his letter to Carleton. "I beg leave to make a humble offer of my service, whether to act with a body of Militia and Indians," Hamilton began, "or under the direction of a regular officer appointed by your Excellency, to conduct an enterprise," he continued, "for the purpose of distressing the Enemy to attempt Fort Pitt." Hamilton added that the venture against the Rebel fort at Pittsburgh could be conducted in the spring with "150 picked men of the Militia and the Light (Infantry) company," and that the Fort Detroit garrison "might spare an officer plus 30 or 40 men," as well as three to 400 Indian warriors from the Ohio Country. Hamilton sealed the letter and sent it to Carleton with the next post, hoping that the General would look upon his proposal favorably. While Hamilton could take pride in what had been accomplished with the Indians the previous year, he knew that much more needed to be done in 1778 if he were to fulfill Lord Germain and the Crown's orders which he felt was his duty. [HP-222]

"Two Shillings a Day"

In his own quarters at Fort Niagara, Major John Butler labored over the document before him that he had just completed on the night of February 3, 1778. Butler reflected for a moment on the events that had transpired since the defeat of the Rebels at Oriskany, and the subsequent withdrawal of St. Leger's force to Canada, once the Iroquois had abandoned the siege of Fort Stanwix. Butler recalled the arduous trip in September to meet with Sir Guy Carleton to "settle his accounts" and "renew his proposal to raise a battalion of rangers to serve with the Indians." [CE1-p.37] At Quebec, Carleton readily agreed with Butler's proposal to enlist recruits for eight companies, "each composed of a captain, a lieutenant, three sergeants, three corporals, and 50 privates. As to matter of pay, Carleton decided that the men of Butler's Corps would receive the pay of two shillings a day for their service, which was considerably higher than what Butler had imagined, and would be estimated to cost the government "as much as 20 companies of regular infantry." [CE1-p.38] Of course, Butler knew that what Carleton had in mind for his Rangers would be extremely hazardous duty, with every man earning his wages and more.

Now as Major Butler completed his letter to Carleton titled the "Return of a Corps of Rangers to Serve with the Indians, Commanded by Major John Butler" he paused to reflect on the scant numbers. Almost half a year had passed since his "beating orders" from Carleton, and Butler could only report to Carleton that he had two companies completed to date, totaling 112 effective men. Butler hoped that once the winter weather broke, more displaced loyalists from the frontier would arrive at Niagara from whom he would be able to draw upon to complete the additional companies. For now he would have to wait. Major Butler paused for a moment, deep in thought, and added a postscript to the report before signing and sealing it. Butler wanted General Carleton to know that one of his captains was a "Prisoner with the Rebels." Captain Walter Butler had been captured while recruiting in the Mohawk Valley after Oriskany and taken to

Albany in irons. The fate of Captain Walter Butler was unknown. Major Butler swallowed hard and wondered if he would see his eldest son alive again. [HP-349]

"These Assertions Will Not Prejudice You Against Me"

It was early in the cold morning of one of the first days of March that Alexander McKee heard the pounding at the door of his house at the mouth of Chartier's Creek a short distance from Fort Pitt on the south side of the Ohio River. McKee, who had been awake for just a short time wondered who would be calling on him this early in the morning. Quietly he reached for his loaded pistol as he unbarred the door and opened it. To McKee's great surprise, his old and loyal friend Matthew Elliott greeted him with a hearty handshake and a warm embrace. It had been nearly a year and half since the two men had seen each other. There was much to catch up on, though Elliott found himself doing much of the talking, explaining to McKee all that had happened to him, and much more.

Elliott retraced for his friend the fateful trip of early November 1776 when he ventured into the Ohio Country to trade with the Shawnee despite the warnings of several recently returned traders at Pittsburgh who advised against it because of reports of increasing Indian hostility and murder of whites. Elliott had been undeterred, as McKee remembered. Too, he ignored the hostility of many people at the Pittsburgh settlement who were alarmed that Elliott was taking goods to the very Indians who were threatening the Virginian settlements up and down the Ohio. Before leaving, Elliott wrote to fellow trading partner, Alexander Blaine, a response to local critics, saying, "I am sorry the Public makes so free with my character, but as I am convinced that all these assertions will not prejudice you against me," knowing Blaine would understand Elliott's motives of risking trade with the Indians because the price of furs was at an all time high. [HR-p.14] Elliott informed Blaine that he was leaving 26 horses at Pittsburgh and had stored 12 horse-loads of furs in Speer's cellar for safekeeping, until he could return before Christmas with additional pelts he hoped to obtain from the Indians. [HR-p.15]

After obtaining permission on October 14 from George Morgan, the Indian agent at Fort Pitt, Elliott made his final preparations. He left Pittsburgh in early November with "a string of packhorses, a Negro slave, an indentured servant, an a female Indian companion," and by November 12, 1776, Elliott had reached the Christian Delaware Indian villages on the Tuscarawas River in the Ohio Country, he told McKee. There the Delaware warned him of hostile Wyandot and Mingo warriors who might intercept him on his way to the Shawnee towns on the Scioto. But with so much at stake on this trading trip, Elliott again ignored the warnings and continued on his trip westward.

However, the following day Elliott was overtaken by a party of hostile Ohio Seneca warriors who plundered his horses, trade goods, and his Negro for their own. Elliott and his servant were tied up by the Mingo, who prepared to take them to their own village to kill them. Two Christian Delawares had interceded on Elliott's behalf with the Mingoes and were able to obtain freedom for Elliott and his servant, though not his horses or trade goods. Since the Mingo told Elliott that they were acting on the orders of the new chief named Hamilton at Detroit, Elliott made up his mind to winter with his Shawnee friends on the Scioto and then to make his way to Detroit in the spring to recover his lost property. [HR-p.16] His situation being complicated by the arrival of winter weather, Elliott explained that he had not been able to send word to McKee, or anyone else at Pittsburgh, for that matter, concerning his misadventure.

The following March of 1777, Elliott arrived at Detroit to seek an audience with the British Lt. Governor Hamilton to petition the man for his property taken by the Indians. Elliott was shocked when Hamilton instead had him arrested as an American Rebel spy, after Hamilton had read a number of letters that Elliott had kept in a trunk, which were discovered during a routine investigation of the new visitor. Two letters were from George Morgan and William Wilson, both Rebel Indian agents on the Virginian frontier whom Hamilton was acquainted with. [HR-p.16] Elliott told McKee that he strongly protested his innocence to Hamilton, explaining that he was a close friend to former British Indian agent Alexander McKee, but Hamilton remained unconvinced, and sent him to Quebec in irons on the next British ship headed to Fort Niagara. At Niagara, Elliott had seen with his own eyes the preparations of Major John Butler and his Six Nations Indian Department rangers to join the expected British offensive against the Rebels in New York colony.

Once at Quebec, an investigator for General Sir Guy Carleton had questioned Elliott extensively on his activities in the Ohio Country and at Pittsburgh, but reported to Carleton that he could find no direct evidence that Elliott was in fact a spy for the Rebels, and it was decided to release him on parole to return to Pittsburgh. However, the British would only agree to free him by sending him by ship to New York City, which had fallen into British hands, and then overland to Philadelphia which General Howe had taken in the fall of 1777. From there, Elliott explained, he had made his way west through York to Carlisle to stay with old family friends through the harsh winter months before crossing the Alleghenies to Pittsburgh when warmer weather made the old Forbes road passable for a man on a horse. It was during that recent leg of his trip to Pittsburgh through the mountains from Carlisle that Elliott had overheard a number of men in a tavern talking about a scoundrel at Pittsburgh whom they intended to settle scores with. The name they mentioned, Alexander McKee, immediately caught Elliott's attention, whom they accused of being a Tory and Indian lover. Elliott remembered that the tone of their conversation concerning McKee was hostile and threatening.

To report this to McKee was the real reason Elliott was at McKee's doorstep after arriving in Pittsburgh settlement late the previous evening. Elliott was aware of McKee's problems with General Hand and the General's orders for McKee to report to the Board of Inquiry at York. He had heard it from the men in the tavern, who knew that when Hand arrived back at Pittsburgh from his aborted campaign to the Ohio Country, Hand was sure to send McKee to York this time. Elliott was sure that the men in the tavern would be waiting for McKee, who would have had to travel to York by the same trail that Elliott was traveling. From the way the men talked, Elliott knew they considered themselves Patriots from Pittsburgh who were going to take matters into their own hands as they saw it. They intended to follow McKee when he headed to York and further, they planned to ambush him and kill him. [NL-p.102]

McKee shook his head in profound shock and dismay at Elliot's disclosure. He confided to his friend of long-standing that he never thought his situation would come to this, that his enemies were plotting to kill him. McKee realized that the delicate balancing act that he had been walking at Pittsburgh to attempt to protect his financial interests was all for naught. Hand and his expedition were due back at the settlement in a day or two and McKee was sure that the General would demand that he leave immediately for York without any more excuses or delays. McKee realized that his life was now in danger, and if the conspirators didn't kill him on the way to York, if he were released by the Congress at York after questioning, he surely would be slain on the return trip to Pittsburgh, if not killed outright in his own home.

McKee related to Elliott how their mutual friend the Shawnee leader Cornstalk and his son Elinipsico had been murdered at Fort Randolph on the Ohio at the mouth of the Kanawha River, when they had attempted to speak with the commander of the fort. [MD-99] More and more, McKee was hearing cases of vigilante vengeance against anyone on the frontier whom the settlers thought were responsible for aiding the Indians who struck the frontier the previous months. McKee now knew that he was the next target. Elliott added that if those men had known whom he (Elliott) was and that he had recently returned from the British at Quebec, New York City, and Philadelphia, they would have undoubtedly killed him on the spot as a spy for the British, which he in fact was not. Elliott told his friend that he had been careful to make his way through the settlement without being recognized, and had met with no one else, nor confided with anyone but McKee as to where he had been. It was a different Pittsburgh from the one he left a year and a half ago, a Pittsburgh that he no longer had a connection to, nor one in which he knew he would be welcome, if his presence was made known.

McKee asked Elliott to lay low for a couple of days while he considered all the options as to what to do. Elliott agreed to stay close. He intended on discreetly looking up Alexander Blaine, his old partner in the trading business, to have Blaine settle up accounts with him as Blaine owed him a considered sum of money. That was all that held Elliott to Pittsburgh, as everything that he previously owned had been lost to the Mingoes. More than anything else, Elliott wanted to see his son and wife again who were living at the Shawnee village on the Scioto. Perhaps, Elliott thought, he would be able to get back from the British at Detroit the fortune that he had lost to the Mingoes, now that he had been cleared of the charges of spying. Further, Elliott told McKee that he intended to leave Pittsburgh for the Ohio Country as soon as possible to make a new life there for himself. He posed the question to his troubled friend. Would McKee consider joining him to go to the Scioto?

McKee was silent. He waved to Elliott from his doorway as his friend of many years left on the river road for the Pittsburgh settlement. Then McKee reached for the muskets on the mantel and primed and loaded each of them, leaning them against the wall near the door where they would be handy if needed. Deep in thought, he considered what Elliott had said, turning it over and over in his mind. While McKee could admit to himself that he had courted the idea for some time of leaving Pittsburgh as a way of solving his problems with the authorities, he had never seriously considered the prospect until now. Even with his brother's help, what McKee would leave behind in Pittsburgh would be too high a price for him to pay if it were lost in the process. Each time he had considered leaving, McKee could not bring himself to the point of letting go of everything for which he had worked so hard.

Was it Elliott's timely offer that tempted him, or the dire situation that he found himself in that prompted his thinking to consider leaving? McKee intuitively knew that he had only a few days at most to make a decision as to what to do, before General Hand, or others, would decide his fate for him. Late into the night McKee lay awake, carefully weighing and re-weighing all the possible courses of action that he could take to alleviate the situation. His practical Scotch mind was searching for a scheme that would buy him more time; that would allow him to squeeze through this crisis, as he had always been able to do in the past, and protect his property. But this time was different. After several hours, McKee collapsed exhausted on his bed. He could find no sure way out of his predicament that did not jeopardize his freedom, or worse except for one path. With resignation, McKee went to sleep, knowing that he had much to do in the few short days ahead. He had made up his mind. The time had now come to flee.

Chapter 10

1778: The Coming Storm

Alexander McKee was becoming increasingly anxious as the late afternoon sun of March 28, 1778, set behind the hills to the west of his home, quickly bringing a chill to the air by which he could see his breath. McKee and his two Negro slaves checked the loads packed on the string of seven horses that stood behind McKee's cabin where they were out of sight from the river trail. McKee nervously rechecked all his worldly possessions. He was worried for several reasons at the moment. For one, Simon Girty had not arrived yet. He had promised to meet McKee and Elliott before sundown. To make matters worse, McKee's cousin, Robert Surphlit, who had arrived only moments ago in the company of man named Higgins, brought alarming news. [BC-p.37]

Surphlit was sure that the two men who had stopped by McKee's home just before midday asking for directions were either spies for the Patriots at Pittsburgh or informers for General Hand at Fort Pitt. Either way, it became evident to McKee during their brief conversation, the two men had taken special notice of his packhorses. No doubt they had concluded that McKee appeared to be preparing for a long trip, because he was packing a considerable amount of property. If they were spies for General Hand, McKee was sure that word had gotten to the General about McKee's imminent departure. Knowing Hand, McKee realized the he could expect a swift reaction if the General figured from the number of packhorses at McKee's home that McKee's destination was not, if fact, to York in the east. The possibility of Hand sending a squad of soldiers from the fort worried McKee, as well as the whereabouts of both Simon Girty and Matthew Elliott. McKee wondered if the two had been unexpectedly detained or arrested by Hand. Knowing that his plan to discreetly leave Pittsburgh was probably compromised by the two spies, McKee asked himself how long he could afford to wait for Girty and Elliott, risking his own arrest, which would come soon if General Hand was informed of his surreptitious preparations. [BC-p.38] The dilemma gnawed at McKee as he waited for his two friends in the growing darkness.

Finally, nearly an hour after sunset, McKee could make out the forms of two riders approaching his cabin from the river road in the fading light. McKee knew from a prearranged signal that it was Matthew Elliott and Simon Girty, each with an extra packhorse of his own. The seven men gathered together in front of McKee's cabin and quickly exchanged information. Girty verified from

McKee's description of the two morning visitors to his home that he had spotted the two making their way into Fort Pitt. Girty lingered long enough to see them disappear into the officers' quarters of the fort. It was Girty's opinion that Hand would probably send a patrol to arrest McKee in the morning, as he was sure that there were no available scouts at Fort Pitt who could lead soldiers along the river trail in the dark, and Girty knew that Hand's men would not attempt to do so on their own.

Further, when Girty had met up with Matthew Elliott, the two left separately from the settlement so as to not arouse any suspicion from anyone purposely watching the trail leading south from Pittsburgh along the Ohio River. To be sure they were not being followed, Girty doubled back along the river trail after he and Elliott had gone some distance together. Soon Girty caught up with Elliott, positive that they were alone on the trail. The former scout for General Hand told McKee that the cover of darkness would provide them with the opportunity to make their escape, if they did not waste it.

Girty knew the trails well and wanted to get going as soon as possible. Unlike most men, he could travel in darkness, an ability he had learned during his years of captivity with the Seneca. The clear night would provide ample light from the starry sky and the quarter moon to be able to follow the trails into the Ohio Country so they could travel all night to elude any pursuers, who might quickly follow their tracks in the morning unimpeded by packhorses as they were.

All was set. The five men and two Negroes belonging to McKee mounted their horses and headed down the path. Alexander McKee took one long last look at his home. He could faintly see the outline of the cabin and the smoke curling upwards into the sky from his chimney, and wondered if he would ever see again the home which he had worked so many years to acquire, and which he was now about to leave in the care of his brother in Pittsburgh. The thought was troubling, but at the moment, McKee knew that he had no choice but to go, or face certain arrest, or even death if he stayed. He turned his head to the west and tried to put the thoughts of all that he was leaving behind out of his mind. McKee knew there were more important matters at the moment, for if his cousin and Girty were right, even with a large head start, they would be hard-pressed to make it across the river and towards the Muskingum before they could rest assured that they would not be caught by any of General Hand's men. [HR-p.20]

Simon Girty led the way in the dark for the party of men and packhorses. McKee put his implicit trust in Girty for he knew Girty's abilities as a scout and his knowledge of the Indian trails in the wilderness were unsurpassed by anyone at Pittsburgh. McKee reflected on the conversation he had with Girty only a few days before. McKee had decided to approach his old friend and reveal his plans to him, in the hopes that he could persuade Girty to join him and Elliott. Surprisingly, it had not taken much argument to convince Simon Girty to come along.

McKee found Girty to be a man of few words on the subject. His friend was unencumbered with the complexity of mental arguments with which McKee belabored himself in making a decision. While Girty did not have the same ties to the Pittsburgh settlement that McKee did in terms of any property or business ventures, McKee knew that Simon Girty could have just as easily declined to go along, as he had no real reason leave. Girty had just returned from Hand's campaign to the upper Ohio Country, and unlike McKee, Girty was in the good graces of the General. Nonetheless, McKee decided to take a chance in revealing his plans to Girty hoping that he might go with them. And if Girty did not, McKee knew there was little risk that Girty would inform Hand of his departure; for all that was said about Simon Girty in Pittsburgh, McKee knew that he was not called an informer or a spy.

Why did McKee want Girty to join him and Elliott? To begin, Girty was considered one of the best scouts on the frontier, familiar with the Indian trails leading to the Ohio Country, and McKee needed a good scout to help him flee. Secondly, Girty was known personally to most of the Indian tribes from his days with Lord Dunmore. Girty commanded their respect, and they were unlikely to harm him. McKee knew that his party would have to pass close to Mingo or Ohio Seneca towns to get to the Scioto, and the Mingo warriors had already declared war on the whites of the Virginian frontier. Girty was known to all the Mingo as an adopted son of the Iroquois Seneca, and he could secure their passage from any danger from Mingo war parties they might encounter. Girty could speak most of the languages, particularly the Mingo and Seneca dialect, so he would be especially valuable in any hostile encounter.

Finally, McKee knew something about Girty's character that most men at Pittsburgh did not understand. McKee and Girty shared the same private sympathy for the plight of the Indians as they saw it, even though they considered themselves both white men. For McKee, his empathy for the Indians lay in the fact that his mother was Shawnee and he had taken a Shawnee woman for his wife. Girty's compassion for the Indians could be traced to his childhood years of captivity by the Seneca which left an indelible mark on his character, a fondness for the people he had lived with for many years. One thing that both McKee and Girty could agree on was that the Indians of the Ohio Country were justified in their hostility to the Virginians and Pennsylvanians on the frontier. They knew that if their white brethren at Pittsburgh had their way, the Indians would be exterminated.

"His ability to speak the Shawanese language"

Disregarding McKee's personal appeal, Girty threw in his lot with McKee and Elliott for a reason not related to politics or fear. Girty simply decided to go along because he could not stand to sit still at Pittsburgh behind the stockade walls and inside the taverns that he found himself idle in. McKee knew that Girty was perpetually restless when he was at the settlement and most at home when he was on the forest trail. Girty had gained a reputation for discontent and trouble when he was at the settlement and not on a scout. McKee knew that his friend had a flair for frequent drunken brawls in the gritty taverns outside Fort Pitt. And when he was not fighting, Girty was often involved in "a series of heated squabbles with persons in authority at the American outpost" that cost him not only his reputation, but his usefulness for duty. [NL-p.107]

Still, McKee knew that Simon Girty cared little about what people thought of him. It was easy for McKee to see that his friend was just not cut out for sedate civilized living. Consequently, Girty viewed McKee's journey to the Shawnee on the Scioto as just another venture that would get him out of town and out of trouble. Girty wasn't concerned with what the consequences of his leaving Pittsburgh with McKee and Elliott might be. He knew that he had few friends and little standing within the settlement. Further, Girty's youngest brother James had already left for the Shawnee villages on the Scioto about March 1. James was chosen by Patriot government commissioners to take presents and an invitation for the Shawnee to attend an upcoming peace conference in the summer, because of James "ability to speak the Shawanese language with great ease and accuracy." [BC-p.36] James was known to many in the tribe because he had been raised by the Shawnee after his capture and had been adopted by them. If no other reason, Simon Girty decided to go with McKee and Elliott to the Scioto to see his younger brother. All in all, he had little reason to stay in Pittsburgh.

Simon Girty led the way for McKee and the others to the river trail in the dark. After crossing Chartier's Creek near McKee's cabin and continuing on for a short distance, Girty found the shallow ford across the Ohio River below the island named for Brunot. [BR-p.301] Continuing along the river trail on the north bank of the Ohio, Girty knew that they were about halfway from Pittsburgh to the mouth of the Big Beaver River when they crossed a series of small streams entering the Ohio River from the north. Finally arriving at the mouth of the Big Beaver, Girty led the men and horses across the swift current to the far bank of the river, and then turning away from the Ohio and following the west bank of the Big Beaver for a short distance, Girty turned west at the head of the well-worn Indian trail called the "Great Path" [WP-p.62] which he knew would take them to the Muskingum villages of the Ohio Country. The party of men was now 30 miles from Pittsburgh and with a couple of more hours of travel before daybreak, they would be out of reach of any pursuers that General Hand might send in the morning.

By the first light of dawn on March 29, Girty had estimated that they had traveled another 30 miles from the Big Beaver River after crossing the Little Beaver Creek and reached the ford of the Yellow Creek. Almost a mile from the ford, Girty found what he had been scanning the thicketed woods for. Here the Great Path forked equally to both the left and the right. From memory, Girty knew that the right fork of the trail would lead them westward about 70 more miles to the upper reaches of the Muskingum River above the forks and near the Christian Delaware towns. [BR-p.298] This well-used fork of the Great Path was the trail that Colonel Henry Bouquet had taken with his little army during the expedition in 1764 to chastise the Indians of the Ohio Country for supporting Pontiac in his Indian rebellion.

"Our Hearts are Good Towards You"

Bouquet had not only forced the Indians to agree to a new lasting peace on the frontier, but also he demanded that they give up all of their white captives who were living with the various tribes throughout the Ohio Country, some as adopted children since the war with the French. [BR-p.66] Though more than 14 years had passed since Bouquet's expedition, Girty could make out the wide-rutted trail to the Muskingum over which so many of Bouquet's soldiers, horses and oxen had traversed to the Muskingum and back, packing the ground hard and making the trail highly visible years later.

Girty reminded himself that McKee wished to go directly to the Delaware village of Goschachgunk at the forks of the Muskingum [NL-p.106] and avoid the Christianized Delawares under Chief White Eyes and the white Moravian preachers whom McKee knew to be closely associated with General Hand and the Virginians back at Pittsburgh. Instinctively Girty chose the left fork of the trail. He knew that the lesser-used path would take them in a more direct manner to the lower Delaware towns. Soon after leaving the little valley of Yellow Creek, the party headed into the undulating small hills of the interior of the Ohio Country, where Girty chose a camp for the night. [BR-p.298]

Girty knew exactly where they were and how far that the group had yet to go. He reflected on the last trip that he had made on this same trail in mid-July 1775, when he accompanied Captain James Wood of the Fort Pitt militia as an Indian interpreter. Wood was given a mission from the newly-appointed Virginian commissioners to the Indians to inform the tribes of the Ohio Country of a peace conference to be held in Pittsburgh. The two men had traveled deep into the Indian wilderness, making 40 to 45 miles a day to the Indian council at Goschachgunk when the weather was good. At the Delaware council, Girty had listened to Wood and translated into the Delaware tongue the less-than-eloquent speech that Wood had prepared for the assembled chiefs and warriors. While Wood assured the Indian assemblage that the Virginian "hearts are good towards you," and are "desiring of brightening the Ancient Chain of Friendship between us" [BR-p.167], Girty remembered clearly that the Delaware were unconvinced of the sincerity of the message coming from the whites who were interloping on their land, killing their game, and shooting at their people with disregard. On the return trip from Goschachgunk it had taken him and Wood about three days to return to Pittsburgh, which meant to Girty that he and McKee's party had only two more days of hard travel ahead before reaching the Delaware village at the forks of the Muskingum.

Back at Pittsburgh, General Hand sent a lieutenant with a squad of men at first light March 29 to set out for Alexander McKee's home downriver from the settlement and arrest him, but "just before the detachment began to march, information was received at Pittsburgh of their (McKee's) flight." [BC-p.38]

General Hand was enraged at the news of McKee's escape and defection to the Indians, which could not be kept a secret. Within two days the entire community at Pittsburgh was in an uproar over McKee's flight, which many assumed now meant that the former British Indian agent "would immediately encourage the Indians to attack the settlements along the frontier." [NL-p.105] As the word of McKee's escape spread throughout the frontier, more and more settlers, wary of renewed Indian attack with the coming of warmer weather, found reason in McKee's desertion to the Indian Country to pack up their belongings in the early weeks of April 1778 and flee to safety in the east while they believed they still had a chance. [NL-p.105] At Fort Pitt, there was nothing that General Hand could do now that McKee had eluded arrest. In disgrace, and facing a congressional investigation in the days ahead into his past actions, Hand resigned his command of the Fort by the end of the month. [NL-p.106]

"I Cannot Give You any Directions"

At Detroit, Lieutenant Governor Hamilton was unaware of the recent developments on the Virginian frontier. Isolated at Detroit, his only sources of information were by military post from Quebec and from the information brought into Detroit from the Indians and traders who plied the trails of the Ohio Country. In early January 1778, Hamilton conceived a plan to enlist the help of the Moravian missions to the Delaware Indians on the Muskingum River in the Ohio Country, while he waited for Governor General Carleton to approve his plan to attack Fort Pitt by summer. Hamilton sent Edward Hazle, an officer in the British Indian Department at Fort Detroit with a letter to the Delaware missionary with a request for David Zeisberger to arm the Indians with weapons Hamilton could send from Detroit and to advise them to attack the Rebel frontier as soon as the weather broke. Hazle left with a Wyandot party of Indians on January 11 for the villages on the Upper Sandusky River, and Hamilton detailed his plan to General Carleton on the 15th of the month. BC-p.50]

By early April, Hamilton finally received a response from Sir Guy Carleton at Montreal, written on March 14, 1778. Hamilton was surprised to learn that Carleton's tenure as Governor of Canada was coming to an end, as he was awaiting the arrival of General Haldimand to take command so that he could return to England. However that surprise turned to shock when Hamilton read that Carleton refused to take any action on Hamilton's request to attack Fort Pitt by the summer of 1778. Carleton rationalized his reluctance to direct Hamilton to attack Fort Pitt with the reason that "the Instructions sent out last summer by Lord George Germain were so pointed, taking the management of the War on all sides out of my hands." [HP-212] Apparently Carleton had had enough of being caught in the middle. Hamilton knew that when Carleton petitioned Lord Germain to invade the colonies from Canada, that Germain picked Burgoyne to lead the invasion, relegating Carleton to a garrison role in Canada. Carleton was offended by the blow to his pride. Now that Carleton's request to leave for England had been approved, Hamilton believed that Carleton was acquiescing on any action that supported Germain's orders. Apparently washing his hands of the matter, Carleton wrote, further adding, "That I cannot give you any directions, relative to the offensive measures you agitate." Carleton chose to leave the matter in the hands of the new commander, General Haldimand. Until Haldimand arrived from Britain, Hamilton was ordered by Carleton to wait for further instructions. [HP-212]

Hamilton was more than disappointed. Privately he worried that if he was forced to give up the military initiative he had seized the previous fall with the Indian attacks on the Virginian frontier, then the Rebels might be persuaded to go on the offensive themselves and strike at Detroit, Niagara, or elsewhere if they thought that the British and their Indian allies were no longer a threat. Hamilton reflected on the turn of events which caused alarm at Detroit in January after Hazle's departure for the Delawares. The Wyandots, or Lake Indians, had brought to Detroit prisoners from the Virginia frontier taken during their raids in late 1777. However there were men who arrived at Detroit late in the year who called themselves loyalists and traders from the frontier whose loyalty Hamilton had began to suspect. Then in mid-January, several prisoners escaped confinement with outside help.

Hamilton ordered a pursuit to recapture them, which was done. The arrest of the Virginian spies aroused his suspicions that the Rebels had agents at Detroit assessing its defensive capabilities and sending intelligence to the Rebels in the east to prepare for a strike at Detroit. The fact that the prisoners were aided in their attempt to escape to Fort Pitt was all the evidence that Hamilton needed to confirm Detroit was not beyond the reach of Rebel incursion. Luckily, a party of volunteers from the garrison with an officer of the Indians and a handful of warriors had been able to overtake the escapees and bring them back to Detroit. [HP-223]

By mid-afternoon of April 1, 1778, Simon Girty with McKee, Elliott and the others reached a point in the trail where it descended to the flatter bottom land of the Muskingum River valley that led them to the Delaware Indian village called "Mowheysinck Town" or commonly "Bullet's Town," only three miles south of the main Delaware village of Goschachgunk. [BR-pp.266, 299] McKee's party was met by several warriors who immediately recognized McKee, Elliott and Girty and greeted them, and stopped to talk with the three in the Delaware tongue. Within an hour, McKee's party arrived in the larger village of Goschachgunk and were met by several of the local chiefs and headmen of the nearby Delaware villages who happened to be there attending a Delaware council.

The chiefs were acquainted with McKee, Elliott, and Girty. They knew the three men from many encounters with them involving both trade and peace conferences held at Fort Pitt and in their own respective villages over the years. The Delaware were eager to know why the white men had risked coming to their village at this time when so many warriors in the Ohio Country were taking up the hatchet against the hated whites along the eastern frontier. They were surprised and pleased to hear from McKee that he and his friends had escaped the Virginians at Pittsburgh and were on their way to the Shawnee villages on the Scioto to visit friends and kin while deciding what to do. But first and foremost, McKee told the Delaware headmen, he had come to their main village to inform the Delaware people of the hostile intentions of the Americans at Pittsburgh towards all the people of the Delaware nation. McKee asked the chiefs if he could speak at their council the next day about the matter and they agreed. What was on his mind was not only General Hand's abortive "Squaw expedition" but also the rumor that Girty had heard in Pittsburgh before leaving, that Hand intended to wipe out the Delaware and Seneca villages to the north of Pittsburgh on the upper reaches of the Allegheny River known as French Creek. [HR-p.23]

"No Longer a Single Friend among the Americans"

Captain Pipe, a Delaware chief from the village on White Woman's Creek who desired to go to war against the Americans, motioned to McKee that he wanted him to meet an important white man from Detroit who was visiting the Delaware and had brought them news from the British. The friend of Captain Pipe introduced himself to McKee, Elliott, and Girty as Edward Hazle, an officer of the British Indian Department at British Fort Detroit. Hazle explained to McKee that he had been sent by Lieutenant Governor Hamilton on a secret mission to deliver a letter to the Moravian preacher at the Delaware villages on the Muskingum River. Hazle revealed to McKee that Hamilton wanted the preacher to "disperse some papers signed by several of the prisoners taken and brought in by the Indians" to show the preacher that anyone on the frontier with the Indians who wanted to join the British cause could be sure of obtaining a safe conduct to Detroit through the Indian villages with the help of an Indian Department officer to escort them. Hazle detailed for McKee his meeting with the Moravian preacher, Zeisberger, at the village he called Lictenau, upriver. It was obvious to Hazle at once that Hamilton had misjudged the preacher, for Zeisberger was an ardent Rebel, and would not listen to Hamilton's request that he help him to arm the Delaware to "march against the Rebels" on the frontier. [BC-p.50] With that out of the way, Hazle told McKee that he was preparing to return to Detroit in a few days.

McKee met privately with Hazle in a Delaware lodge and the two talked about the war in the east and the British attempt to put down the rebellion. McKee did not know of the events of late 1777, Hazle told McKee everything he knew from information coming to Fort Detroit. The rumors circulating at the post before he left led the British garrison there to believe that, in spite of the setback of Burgoyne's surrender to the Rebel general Gates at Saratoga, the Americans had suffered several major defeats, including the fall of Philadelphia to the British, and the flight of the Congress to York. In addition, Hazle believed the reports to be true that General Washington of the Rebels had been killed and his army largely destroyed defending Philadelphia, and that it was only a matter of time before the Americans surrendered to General Howe's pursuing army. In his estimation from what he had heard, Hazle impressed upon McKee that General Howe would crush the rebellion within the month. [BR-pp.188-191]

Hazle considered it important that McKee know of Hamilton's efforts to thwart the Americans on the frontier of the Ohio Country as well as Hamilton's desire to influence the Indians to support the British. Hazle impressed upon McKee the importance of the role McKee and his friends could play in aiding the British cause to hold the Ohio Country for the Crown, which would guarantee the safety and security of all the Indian tribes whose homes and lives were at stake if the Americans invaded and claimed their lands. McKee listened intently, and considered everything that Hazle had to say.

McKee knew that if he decided to actively support the British effort, he would need to speak directly to the Delaware the next day, and ask them to take up the war hatchet against the Virginians as the Mingo and Wyandot had done. After meeting with Hazle, McKee sat alone to think about everything that had been said. McKee pondered what course of action to take, and how his decision would shape what he would say to the Delaware chiefs in council. As McKee gathered his thoughts, he reflected again upon his underlying affinity for the Indians and their plight which always tugged at his sentiments and swayed his decision making. At the moment he felt much closer to them than the white people he left at Pittsburgh, and those thoughts made him think wistfully of his mother who was dead, and his wife who was with her people on the Scioto.

The next day, McKee met with the chiefs in their council lodge at the appointed hour and addressed the headmen of the Delaware tribes present. McKee explained to them that the Americans on the frontier were intent on destroying all the Indians of the Ohio Country to take their land. The Delaware, who lived closest to the whites, would be the first to face the large army that was assembling at Pittsburgh to invade the Delaware country soon. McKee reiterated over and over to the Delawares that they "no longer had a single friend among the American people," now that he, Elliott and Girty had left. In the future, the Delawares could count on the Americans killing any Indian they met on the trail, either friend or foe, in retaliation for the previous attacks by war parties in 1777. McKee advised the chiefs to both prepare their warriors to fight the Americans or take their families and flee for their lives, for the Americans would spare no Indian, hostile or friendly to their cause. [NL-p.206]

When the council broke, Delaware runners left immediately for the surrounding villages to tell the people the alarming news brought by McKee. At Goschachgunk, many Delaware warriors began shaving their heads to prepare themselves to "turn out for war." Satisfied with the results of his speech, McKee wrote a letter on April 4 to Governor Hamilton at Detroit which Edward Hazle promised to deliver at the first possible moment. McKee informed the Governor of his recent flight from the Rebels at Pittsburgh whom he believed intended to arrest and imprison him for his loyalist sympathies in support of the King. McKee detailed what little intelligence he could offer Hamilton on General Hand's plans to attack the tribes of the Ohio Country, including his opinion that "the Virginians were unprepared to launch any expedition of consequence against Detroit." With

Hazle on his way to Detroit, and the majority of the Delawares making preparations to attack the Virginian frontier, McKee, with Girty and Elliott left Goschachgunk on April 5 on the trail west along White Woman's Creek to one leading them to the Shawnee villages on the Scioto River and to the families that McKee and Elliott longed to see.

"Is a Man of Good Character"

On April 20, 1778, Edward Hazle arrived in Detroit from his return trip to the Delaware villages in the Ohio Country. Within an hour, he met with an anxious Governor Hamilton to report not only on the recalcitrance of the missionary Zeisberger to help the British in any manner, but also more importantly, on his unanticipated meeting with Alexander McKee and his friends. Hamilton listened intently to Hazle's recount, amazed that his agent had stumbled upon the one man that Hamilton most wanted to contact. McKee, the very man at the top of Germain's list of loyalists on the frontier who could be of help to him in conducting a war against the Virginian Rebels. Hamilton was delighted to hear that McKee had escaped the Rebels at Pittsburgh and had spoken to the Delaware to take up the hatchet against the Virginians. Hamilton complimented Hazle on his own efforts to persuade McKee to support the British cause of the Indians in the Ohio Country, and was pleased to hear from the information in McKee's letter that McKee was of the opinion that the Rebels were not planning any immediate attack on Detroit, as Hamilton feared. [HP-224]

Equally astounding to Hamilton was Hazle's mention of Matthew Elliott, who along with Simon Girty was accompanying McKee on his escape from Pittsburgh. Hamilton had not thought he would hear of Elliott again after sending him to Quebec the previous year for interrogation as a suspected Rebel spy. Now Elliott was not only back in the Ohio Country, but traveling with McKee and Girty who were both on Germain's list. Hamilton reflected for a moment upon the dilemma that Elliott presented in his own mind. Apparently his suspicions about Elliott's loyalty had been unfounded. Now that Hazle revealed that the three men in question were going to make their way to Detroit after visiting the Shawnee on the Scioto River, the thought of Elliott made Hamilton uncomfortable. He had been wrong about Elliott, and Hamilton knew he soon would come face to face again with the man he had arrested and imprisoned falsely.

After digesting Hazle's report, Hamilton worried that McKee, Elliott, and Girty would get waylaid on their trip to Detroit by either a Rebel pursuit party sent from Fort Pitt to apprehend them, or by one of the many hostile Wyandot or Mingo war parties that were setting out from Detroit and their Upper Sandusky villages for the frontier. They might not know McKee or his significance to Hamilton, and could capture or harm him by accident. Hamilton realized that he dare not take a chance on jeopardizing McKee's arrival in Detroit, now that Hamilton had an opportunity to meet the one man who might be able to put in motion the orders that he had been given from the Crown. As a result,

Hamilton ordered Hazle to set off at once for the Scioto, to make contact with McKee, and bring him and his friends safely to Detroit. Hazle left Detroit with a Wyandot war party on April 23. In his possession Hazle carried a letter of safe conduct from Hamilton and wampum that would suffice to convince any of the hostile Indians that McKee was personally protected by Hamilton himself. [HP-224]

In addition, Hamilton included with the Hazle note congratulations for McKee, urging McKee that "the sooner your convenience can admit of your coming to this place, the better, as I wish to confer with you on several points it is impossible to touch upon in a letter." A plan was formulating in Hamilton's mind, but he was not about to discuss it with McKee until they met. Adding thanks to McKee for sending several newspapers that McKee brought with him from Pittsburgh and sent to Detroit with Hazle, Hamilton said that "they shall be forwarded to Sir Guy Carleton." Unknown to Hamilton or McKee, the newspapers sent were many months old and the events of the war described were out of date. The sagging fortunes of the Rebels had in fact, began to turn around.

With Hazle gone, Hamilton sat down at once to write Governor General Carleton. Hamilton recounted the recent events, informing Carleton of McKee's recent escape from the Rebels at Pittsburgh along with Matthew Elliott, "the young man who was last summer sent down from this Place a Prisoner." Telling Carleton of McKee's intelligence on the Rebel activities on the Virginian frontier, Hamilton added a personal note on McKee, commenting to Carleton that he believed "Alexander McKee is a man of good character and has a great influence with the Shawanese, is well acquainted with the Country, and can probably give some useful intelligence," noting to Carleton that McKee "will probably reach this place in a few days." [HP-224] Then setting Carleton's letter aside, Hamilton wrote a letter to Colonel Bolton, commander at Fort Niagara and Colonel Butler of the Rangers at the same post, relating to them all of the information concerning McKee that Hamilton thought prudent the two officers be made aware. [HP-224]

"A Flock of Birds Has Come from the East"

Upon reaching the Shawnee villages on the lower Scioto River in mid-May after several uneventful days of travel, McKee, Elliott, and Girty were surprised to meet Simon Girty's younger brother James, who was still visiting with the Shawnee since his departure from Pittsburgh earlier in the year. The two Girty brothers were reunited and it took little persuasion on the part of McKee to convince James Girty to join them in supporting the British. James also shared a common interest and sympathy for the Indians, having spent several years in captivity as an adopted son of the Shawnee in his early youth. The younger Girty "appropriated the presents that had been entrusted to him for the Indians" by Morgan at Fort Pitt, and agreed to counsel with any Shawnee still uncommitted to war with the Virginians, while McKee and Elliott had an extended joyful reunion with their wives and children whom they had not seen in many months. [BC-p.45]

Soon after McKee arrived at his wife's village on the Scioto, a Delaware Indian brought a message to the Shawnee from the Delaware chief named White Eyes at Goschachgunk. White Eyes, with the Moravian preacher John Heckewelder who had reached the Delaware villages from Pittsburgh two days after McKee and his party left Goschachgunk [BR-p.190], had delivered a message to the Shawnee, criticizing McKee, Elliott, and Girty. "Grandchildren, ye Shawanese! Some days ago, a flock of birds that had come on from the East alit at Goschachgunk, imposing a song of theirs upon us, which song had nigh proved our ruin," White Eyes' dispatch began. The Delaware warned the Shawnee that "should these birds, which, on leaving us, took their flight toward the Scioto, endeavor to impose a song on you likewise, do not listen to them, for they lie." [BC-p.45] The Delaware chief was challenging McKee directly, because McKee had urged the Delaware warriors to make war on the Virginians. McKee scoffed at the message, and derided White Eyes as a woman of the white preachers because he had remained silent when McKee had spoken to the Delaware at their council.

However, McKee had no reason to fear that the Delaware chief's message carried any weight with the Shawnee. The Shawnee chiefs spat on the ground in their disapproval and sent the runner home. Since Dunmore's War, the Shawnee "harbored little love toward either the Pennsylvanians or the Virginians" and had been biding their time until a new opportunity came to settle scores with their old foes on the frontier. The Shawnee were "extremely pleased to see McKee" and pledged their support to him and the British cause, which Edward Hazle, as Hamilton's agent in the field, affirmed to them when he reached the Shawnee villages on the Scioto, to guide McKee to Detroit. What McKee did not know as he dismissed White Eyes' message out-of-hand was that there was some truth to the Delaware's claim that McKee was lying. Heckewelder had brought with him recent newspapers from the east to show the Delaware that Washington was not dead, Congress had not yet been destroyed, and the war not won by the British east of the mountains, contradicting the outdated information Hazle had given to McKee. [BR-p.191]

I Shall Place Great Dependencies on His Knowledge"

Towards the end of May, McKee, Elliott, and Girty departed the Shawnee towns on the Scioto for Detroit, with Edward Hazle and a Wyandot war chief from the Scioto Valley named Snipe leading their party. [NL-p.108] They traveled north to the Upper Sandusky River villages of the Wyandots already allied with the British, and from there, made their way to the Maumee River and on to Detroit. Hamilton eagerly awaited news of their arrival, for upon hearing of McKee's defection from the Rebels at Pittsburgh and his subsequent speech to the Delaware urging them to take up the hatchet against the Virginians, had begun to lay plans in his own mind for how he could use McKee in conducting the war effort from Detroit.

Hamilton wrote directly to Lord George Germain on June 7, after Edward Hazle left Detroit to guide McKee to the post, stating "I shall place great dependencies on his knowledge of the Country, and of these people employed for its defense." [NL-p.109] What the Governor had in mind for McKee was to use him at the head of a force of Indians and Rangers supplied from Detroit to attack the Rebel frontier, beginning with the Virginian settlements in Kentucky, which Hamilton perceived as a growing threat to the security of Detroit. Much, as yet, needed to be done before those plans could be put into action. That depended upon McKee, Hamilton thought, and his disposition and degree of commitment to the British cause. Hamilton would have to wait and see. In the meantime, the Lieutenant Governor of Detroit busied himself with the endless paperwork before him. Hamilton completed his return letter to Carleton, detailing the events at Detroit, but sparing himself and the General any further argument on the subject of offensive action against Fort Pitt, which Carleton forbade. As Carleton had requested, Hamilton listed the current state of the settlement at Detroit, and dated it April 26, 1778. Hamilton reflected on the 2144 souls under his charge, detailing for Carleton the 564 men, 274 women, 530 young boys and 438 young girls, with 172 male servants, 39 female servants, and 127 slaves. Even with the nearly 4000 head of livestock within the confines of the settlement, Hamilton sighed at the thought of the enormous amount of provisions that would be needed to feed everyone at Detroit. [HP-226]

Because Carleton had not asked for a tally of the Indians, Hamilton had not included one, though they were always on his mind. If he could not feed the savages and provide them with guns and ammunition, then they would not fight for the British, and worse yet, would not defend Detroit if the Virginians attacked. Without the support of the Indians, Hamilton knew that Detroit would surely fall. Hamilton sealed the letter, and called into his quarters the young man waiting in the hallway. The recently appointed Second Lieutenant John Turney of Major Butler's Ranger Corps had arrived from Niagara only days before with the post express for Detroit. [HP-127] Hamilton was going to give him the letter destined for Carleton in Montreal, but not before he had a chance to speak to the Ranger officer about the events in the east and the conduct of the war from Niagara. In the back of his mind Hamilton hoped that the new General of Canada, Haldimand, could be persuaded to not only bolster the defenses of Detroit but also see to it that some of these Rangers of Butler's Corps be sent west to help him carry out Germain's orders to take the war to the Rebel frontier.

"Children! Let Us Return Thanks to the Master of Life"

McKee, Elliott, and Girty finally arrived at Detroit in the first days of June, at the head of an entourage of supportive Indians from the Scioto and Upper Sandusky towns they passed through. It was a momentous occasion for everyone involved, but more so for McKee and Hamilton who had heard a great deal of each other, but as yet, had not met in person. The meeting of the two men was a success. In the days of meetings that followed, Hamilton discussed his strategy with McKee, and received McKee's commitment to help the British cause. Hamilton revealed to McKee his increasing apprehension that the Virginians intended to strike the Ohio Country, particularly Detroit, before he would be able to mount an offensive of his own against the frontier. McKee assured Hamilton that he would be able to lead a force against the frontier as soon as it could be prepared, and as a result, Hamilton commissioned McKee a captain in the British Indian Department at Fort Detroit, with Simon Girty appointed as an Indian Department interpreter to the Indians. Elliott, on the other hand, was less favorably received by the Governor. While acknowledging Elliott as "the young man who was last summer sent down from this Place a Prisoner" [HP-224] Hamilton was not entirely comfortable with him, as he was a reminder of the embarrassing false accusation on Hamilton's part. For Hamilton, rapprochement with Elliott would take time.

On June 14 a Grand Council with the Indians of the Ohio Country and the Great Lakes tribes was set to begin at Detroit. Governor Hamilton had sent invitations to the Indians more than a month before McKee's arrival. More than 1680 Indians were in attendance the first day with representatives from the "Ottawas, Chippoweys, Hurons, Pottawattamies, Delawares, Shawanese, Miamis, Mingoes, Mohawks, the tribes of Ousashtanon, Saginaws, and Senecas." [HP-238] Hamilton had present with him at the council Lieutenant Governor Abbott from Vincennes in the western Illinois Country, Jehu Hay, Indian Department officer at Fort Detroit, as well as Captain Lernoult of the King's Eighth and commander of Fort Detroit. Hamilton introduced Alexander McKee to them as a newly-appointed Captain and officer of the Indian Department, and then took McKee to personally meet the chiefs of each of the various tribes before the council got started.

McKee looked out in amazement at the hundreds of Indians patiently sitting before the group of officers on the council field outside Fort Detroit, waiting for Lieutenant Governor Hamilton to speak on the clear warm morning of June 14. McKee was acquainted with most of the tribes present, but some of the Indians were from the faraway nations of the upper Great Lakes of whom McKee had only heard. In the near distance surrounding the assemblage, smoke from a thousand campfires curled upward in the still air. Before the makeshift lodges, women busied themselves tending to the cooking for their respective chiefs and warriors. In all, McKee believed there were more Indians present at this Grand Council than he had ever seen gathered before to hear a white man urge them on to war.

Finally, Governor Hamilton made his official entrance to the Grand Council with an honor guard of red-coated King's Eighth soldiers preceding him, so that the Indians would notice him. A quiet descended over the natives as Hamilton mounted the small platform and prepared to speak. "Children! Let us return thanks to the Master of Life for having brought us together here," Hamilton began, resplendent in his red British officer's coat trimmed in white lace and silver buttons. For a half an hour Hamilton addressed the village chiefs and their counterparts, the war leaders of the various tribes, thanking them for traveling so far to come to Detroit for the very important Council that he, as the representative of the King, had called them to attend. McKee knew that the first day's talk would be brief, as many of the Indians were not as yet situated in their camps, and as most of them had brought little food with them, it was important that provisions be distributed on the first day to demonstrate to the tribes that they were the guests of the British, and that the King was powerful enough to feed them all. Hamilton ended his speech to the Indians saying, "As this is the first day of our meeting, I will not fatigue you by keeping you too long, therefore I shall order some fresh provisions for you, and meet you again tomorrow." [HP-239] There was a great murmur of satisfaction from the Indians with Hamilton's words, as he descended the platform and motioned to the sutlers to begin distributing the salt pork and beef to the camps.

"He Has Not As Yet Told Me to Bury It"

Over the next several days, Hamilton spoke to the assembled Indians, urging them to take up the hatchet and make war upon the rebel Americans and Virginians on the frontier. Hamilton had several men with him to serve as interpreters to the various tribes, including "William Tucker, Joseph Druilliard, Isidore Chesne, Duperon Baby, Charles Beaubin" to translate Hamilton's words into the native tongue of each tribe present. The next day, Hamilton addressed the Indian nations gathered in the morning with the words, "Children! Let us return thanks to the Master of Life for having preserved us and given us so clear a sky this day for continuing our business." [HP-239] Then Hamilton motioned for Simon Girty to come forward and Hamilton declared to all of the Indians that Girty had become an Interpreter "as having escaped the Virginians and put himself under the protection of His Majesty after giving satisfaction assurances of his fidelity." [HP-239] Girty's appointment met with the approval of the Indians who nodded in agreement, as they had done when McKee was introduced to them earlier.

Hamilton's council with the Indians lasted nearly three weeks, during which time, Hamilton distributed to the tribes gifts of trade goods, food, provisions, weapons, and ammunition for those about to leave the council for their respective villages and then, he hoped, head to the Virginian frontier in war parties. Over and over, Hamilton encouraged the Indians with the King's words that the "the axe to be put into the hands of his Indian children in order to drive the Rebels from their Land." [NL-p.109] "The King has ordered me to give you an Axe, he has not as yet told me to bury it, whenever he does, my Children shall know it immediately." [HP-240]

One by one, the tribes assured Hamilton that they "would take hold of their father's hatchet and promised not to bury it until the King, their father, ordered peace." [NL-p.109] Hamilton's combination of presents from the King and his request that the Indians attack the frontier had its desired effect. More than ever before, Hamilton could take heart in the numbers of warriors embracing the cause of the Crown, and vowing to ready themselves to make war on the Americans.

With the mood of the Indians more warlike, Hamilton needed to tie up one loose end before he discharged the tribes at the close of the Great Council. Hamilton turned to McKee to exert his influence upon a select group of chiefs that Hamilton invited to a private meeting held on July 3. A target was needed for McKee and the Indians to attack, and Hamilton had been intrigued by the thought of a proposed attack upon Fort Pitt ever since McKee had told him of the fort's extensive weaknesses. Although Hamilton had received Carleton's earlier letter advising him to wait for his replacement, General Haldimand, to decide on such a move, Hamilton convinced himself that, in light of all the information he had forwarded concerning the deteriorated state of Fort Pitt, neither Carleton nor the new Governor General would be able to deny Hamilton such an opportunity. Adding to Hamilton's confidence for an attack was the fact that McKee was successful in consulting with the chiefs. On McKee's persuasion they decided to move against the American fort as soon as preparations could be made to mount the offensive. Unfortunately, an unexpected development on the frontier was about to interrupt everyone's plans.

While Hamilton and McKee had been counseling with the Indians, the Virginians had not been sitting by idly. In fact, preparations had been made many months earlier for the Americans to take the military initiative against the British and their Indian allies in the Ohio Country, beginning with the request of a Kentucky militia captain, George Rogers Clark in the fall of 1777, for permission and support from the governor of the state of Virginia, Patrick Henry, to lead an expeditionary force to seize the Illinois Country for the United States. Clark argued that by seizing the village of Kaskaskia on the Mississippi River at the mouth of the Kaskaskia River, the Americans could secure not only the Ohio and Mississippi rivers as control "would fling the command of the two great rivers into our hands" but also by doing so, the Indian tribes of the Illinois country could be subdued, and could be prevented from further incursions into the Kentucky settlements. [WGA-p.45]

"With the Salvation of Kentucky Almost in Reach"

While preparations were underway to authorize Clark's expedition in the west, on June 11 the Continental Congress mandated a separate campaign to be mounted against Hamilton at Detroit. General Washington put General Lachlan McIntosh in command of the western venture, and ordered the General to put together a sizable force of Continental troops and militia with the necessary ammunition, provisions and artillery for the planned assault on Detroit. [BR-p.192] The staging area for the attack was decided by Washington to be the dilapidated Fort Pitt on the Ohio River. Washington knew it would take time to make the necessary preparations. In the meantime, Washington ordered McIntosh immediately to Fort Pitt to relieve General Hand of his duties, and appointed, as second in command, the militia officer Major William Crawford to the rank of colonel.

By the end of June, George Rogers Clark, feeling that his small force was as ready as it could possibly be, set out from his base camp at the falls of the Ohio River near the Kentucky settlements. However, there was little way that he could overcome the feeling of desperation that faced him as he prepared to set out on the expedition to Kaskaskia. He had only 175 militiamen to accompany him. Though he had been able to stop the trickle of desertions by moving his men to a fortified position on Corn Island in the middle of the river, the reinforcements he expected from the Kentucky settlements did not materialize. Few men wanted to leave their families in their own lightly garrisoned stations and forts across Kentucky in the face of what was likely to be more forthcoming Indian raids. Clark could not blame those young men from the frontier who went east to join Washington's army being recruited for the coming summer campaign. All in all, George Rogers Clark was disappointed with the outlook for success of his small wilderness battalion. Yet Clark was not about to quit, with "the salvation of Kentucky almost in their reach," and made his last-minute preparations to depart. [WGA-pp.53-55]

Setting out by boat on the morning of June 24, 1778, Clark's force quickly reached the site of the abandoned French Fort of Massac, "on the north bank of the Ohio about ten miles below" the mouth of the Tennessee River. Here, the Virginians hid the boats and began the overland march that would take them to Kaskaskia. After six days, Clark's force reached the outskirts of the town on the evening of July 4, and captured the fort and its French commander, Rocheblave, without firing a shot. Within weeks, the remaining French villages on the east bank of the Mississippi River surrendered peacefully to Clark's men, securing for Virginia a new frontier on the Mississippi and Wabash Rivers, and winning over the Indian tribes of the area from the sphere of British influence to the American cause. By July 20, the British fort at Vincennes was taken by Clark's men and, with the escape of British Governor Abbott and his small company of men retreating in haste to Detroit, the population declared their loyalty to the Americans.

Sweating in his quarters in the stifling summer heat on the late morning of August 8, Governor Hamilton put down his quill and ink, as the commotion in the parade yard of Fort Detroit grew louder and louder. Wondering what had so many people upset, Hamilton got up from his writing desk just as Captain Lernoult, with Alexander McKee and Jehu Hay at his side knocked on Hamilton's door, and entered. They brought with them terrible news for Hamilton. An Indian runner from the Miami villages on the Maumee River had just arrived at the fort to tell the Indian Department officers that the Long Knives under their Captain Clark had successfully attacked Kaskaskia in the Illinois Country from the posts in Kentucky, and taken Vincennes without a fight on July 20. Governor Abbott, his family, and a small contingent of loyal men were due to arrive at Detroit in a few days after escaping the Virginian army. All of the French posts of the Illinois Country had fallen to Clark and the French Captain Rocheblave had been made

Clark's prisoner. The western Indians of the Illinois Country had made their peace with the Rebels at a conference called by Clark. Many of those who attended Hamilton's Council, including tribesmen from the Ottawa, Pottawatomie, Chippewa, and the Wabash renounced their support of the British, and it was feared that Clark would soon march with a stronger, reinforced army to take Detroit. [NL-p.109]

"About 400 Indians Assembled to Attack Kentucke"

Hamilton listened in stunned silence, his mind reeling at the shocking news. What he had feared most, an American military initiative on the frontier had happened when and where he least expected it. All that he had accomplished, all that he had worked for to fulfill Germain's orders had effectively come undone as the Rebels seized the initiative in the apparent vacuum created by Carleton's refusal to allow a more aggressive pursuit of the war on Hamilton's part. Angrily, Hamilton quietly cursed his commanding officer whom he blamed for allowing an attack by the Americans to happen. Collecting himself, Hamilton called a meeting of his officers to see what might be done in light of this unexpected turn of events that was nothing less than a calamity. He needed a plan of action before writing to Quebec.

In the meetings that followed in early August, Hamilton weighed possible alternatives to counter Clark's move. Everyone, including McKee, was in agreement on one point—the proposed move to attack and seize Fort Pitt would be abandoned in light of the fall of the Illinois Country to the Virginians. Foremost in Hamilton's mind was the pressing need to mount an expedition to retake Vincennes and expel the Rebels, and Hamilton would not hear of any move on the part of the Indians by his own officers that did not include a counterattack. [WGA-p.64] Hamilton was adamant in leading a planned expedition to Vincennes himself, despite Captain Lernoult's disapproval. [WGA-p.64]

It was an idea that Hamilton had formulated in his mind when he first heard of Clark's move, and one he stubbornly clung to as the days progressed and the shock of the news wore off. It appeared to everyone around Hamilton that he had taken the matter of Clark as a personal affront, one in which Hamilton felt that he must counter and correct himself by leading an attack to dislodge Clark. Although the notion of a counterattack was fraught with risks and danger, Hamilton argued with his officers that it was a sound military decision to retake the Illinois Country before Clark could attack Detroit. Hamilton's rationale appeared sensible, but those who knew Hamilton speculated that the Governor's pride was more at stake than Detroit.

As Hamilton's strategy evolved in those early sessions, he realized that he needed to shut the door on Clark once he set out from Detroit. He wanted to be sure that the supply line of reinforcements, provisions, and ammunition sent to Clark's army by way of the Ohio River from Fort Pitt to Kentucky and beyond be effectively severed. Hamilton needed to assure himself that the force he met would likely be suffering from reduced rations and a shortage of gunpowder.

In the crisis of early August, Hamilton turned to Alexander McKee and Simon Girty for their critical help in the matter of intercepting Rebel aid to Clark's army. With McKee, Elliott and Girty now working for the British Crown, Hamilton ordered McKee to leave immediately for the Shawnee villages on the Scioto River to raise a force of warriors for support of Hamilton's strike against Clark and his posts in Kentucky, and also to distribute ammunition and send out parties of warriors to intercept and strike any Virginians coming down the river in boats with supplies destined for Clark's army.

McKee weighed his words before replying to Hamilton, giving himself time to formulate a response that would not offend the Governor. McKee explained that while agreeing with Hamilton's request, he did not control or give orders to the Shawnee. Rather, McKee would need to consult with the Shawnee war captains and village chiefs to be able to fathom their intentions in the matter of taking up the hatchet against the Long Knives. True, McKee would exert as much of his own influence among the Shawnee as he possibly could with all the persuasion he could muster, but in the end, it would be an Indian decision, not his, to send Shawnee warriors to war. To attempt to command them with orders, as Hamilton was implicitly ordering him to do would be a grievous insult that McKee dared not risk with his wife's people.

McKee assured Hamilton that he would immediately consult with his Shawnee friends presently at Detroit and bring the matter of Hamilton's request up to them. Further, McKee would ask them to send a runner to the Scioto villages to inform the Shawnee of his intentions of returning to live with them and to personally take up the war hatchet against the Virginians. He would ask the Shawnee headmen to discuss these matters in their council lodges, and request them to consider sending warriors to take up the hatchet with him. That was the best McKee could promise Hamilton as the Shawnee would take their time making a decision and they would take offense if he tried to rush them.

McKee was confident the Shawnee would send their warriors against the Rebels because he knew that they had a deep hatred for the Virginians ever since their chief Cornstalk had been slain by the whites at Fort Randolph. The Shawnee desired more than all else to avenge Cornstalk's death, McKee related, and that was why some of the septs or sub-tribes already had war parties attacking the Virginians in Kentucky. But Hamilton had to realize that it would take time for all of the Shawnee to accept the war belts and prepare their warriors. McKee would do the best he could to counsel with them, distribute provisions and ammunition to the warriors, and arrange for any field intelligence gathered on Clark's activities to be sent directly to Hamilton wherever he may be. McKee would meet Hamilton's force on the way to Vincennes with whatever Indians he could muster. Matthew Elliott would accompany McKee, as the two men worked well together with the Shawnee and McKee would need help. Hamilton agreed to McKee's plan and gave McKee orders to outfit packhorses with ammunition and provisions for the Shawnee on the Scioto. [NL-p.109]

Hamilton turned to Simon Girty and his brother James, who had arrived in early August at Detroit from the Ohio Country. James Girty reported to

Hamilton that many of the neutral Delawares of the Muskingum River valley "still go to Fort Pitt but its only till their corn be ripe enough to allow their moving to the head of the Scioto, a place pointed out for them by the Six Nations." [HP-228] James added that he knew that there were "about 400 Indians assembled to attack the fort of Kentucke" referring to the Virginian settlement where Captain Daniel Boone had been captured in the Shawnee raids of early 1778. [HP-228] As far as the younger Girty could tell, many large Shawnee war parties "range the banks of the Ohio" looking for enemy bateaux going either up or down the river in support of Clark, as word had already reached the Shawnee from the western tribes as to the advance of the Virginians.

"Give the Savages All the Lands They Should Conquer"

Hamilton asked the two Girty brothers to help rally the Indians and lead them to go on the offensive and attack the frontier, keeping parties of Mingo and Shawnee warriors active from the falls of the Ohio upriver to Fort Pitt, so that the Rebels would be forced on the defensive there, and unable to support Clark. Both Girty brothers responded to Hamilton in the same manner as McKee, reiterating that it would take time to counsel with the tribes and request their support. Regardless, Simon Girty prepared to set off for the Upper Sandusky Wyandot villages with supplies and ammunition to seek the approval of the Indians there to accompany him to the Mingoes and begin to send out large war parties to hit the frontier. James wanted to accompany his brother by the same route before he would split off to go to the Shawnee villages that he was acquainted with, to bring a war party and join his brother in the field, and Hamilton agreed. [BC-p.54]

With his key men of the Indian Department gathering men and supplies to prepare to set out for the Indian country, Hamilton took time to write to Sir Guy Carleton several letters in the first weeks of August, detailing for the General the recent turn of events of the past week, with his comments and recommendations to the General. Hamilton expressed to his commander the urgency of his taking action to counter the Rebel threat which Hamilton ultimately believed would bring the Rebel Clark with a force against Detroit itself unless he were ousted from the Illinois Country.

By the middle of the month, as Hamilton was engrossed in massive preparations for mounting his own expedition against Clark, Governor Abbott's party came in from their flight from Vincennes with intelligence on the movements of the Virginians and an approximate idea of the strength of Clark's army. Hamilton related this information to McKee and Girty, who immediately sent Indian scouts again from Detroit to the Scioto to inform the tribes there of the great and pressing need to arm their warriors and guard the Ohio River against any movements of the Rebels. Writing to Quebec on the matter, Hamilton reported that "I have taken every step in my power to intercept the Bateaux from the Mississippi or their return parties," referring to his wish that the Indians would respond to the request to attack the Virginians. [HP-228] All Hamilton could do for the moment, with McKee and Girty still at Detroit, was hope.

A British supply ship arrived in Detroit by the third week in August and Hamilton received a reply from Quebec. Upon opening the letter, Hamilton was surprised to find that it was not written by Carleton, but by the new commanding officer of the forces in Canada, General Frederick Haldimand, who had just arrived from England. [HP-213] It was immediately apparent to Hamilton that the new commander had no knowledge of Clark's incursion into the western lands. Haldimand's letter of August 6, written at Quebec, dealt primarily with Hamilton's prior request to lead an attack against Fort Pitt. Haldimand, ever the cautious Swiss tactician, thought it imprudent to assault the fort directly, as "it is at such a distance as to make it very difficult in not impossible to be maintained by us" if it were taken. Hamilton raised his eyebrows at Haldimand's assessment. It was a point he had not considered, and he thought it to be well taken by the new commander of Canada. [HA-213]

However, Haldimand recommended to Hamilton that "if you learn that any considerable magazines of provisions or stores are laid up there, the destroying of these would certainly be a very useful service." But primary to Haldimand's thinking was the importance of using the Indians to devastate the Rebel frontier along the Ohio River. "The destroying of crops and the habitation of all the advanced settlers" by the Indian war parties should be a necessary and vital step in the western war, Haldimand expounded. "I am of the opinion that the driving these settlers back upon their Brethren whom they would distress by an additional consumption of goods would prove a better measure" Haldimand wrote. Hamilton pondered Haldimand's words, knowing that the Governor General's advice did not apply now that the enemy had taken the offensive and Detroit was in jeopardy. Countering George Rogers Clark would have to come first, Hamilton thought. Picking up Haldimand's letter, he read on.

The Indians could be motivated in a unique way, Haldimand proposed. "I think therefore proper to observe to you that it would certainly be good policy to give the Savages the entire property of all lands they should conquer from the Rebels." It was a novel idea that Hamilton believed might work, for the Mingo in particular, as part of the Six Nations Seneca living in the Ohio Country, laid partial claim to lands of the upper Ohio from which the Virginians had already dispossessed them. [HP-213] The rest of Haldimand's letter concerned the transport and accounting of precious provisions sent to Detroit, and the drawing of moneys to pay for expenses incurred by both officers and the men at Detroit. Haldimand was requesting routine reports on the state of Detroit, which meant additional paperwork for Hamilton to complete at a time when he felt he needed to be taking military action. Hamilton's frustration was mounting.

A warrior keeps a watchful eye on the movements of the Americans.

"To Chastise and Terrify the Savages"

Hamilton was not the only stymied commander in the western wilderness. Although George Rogers Clark could bask in the glory of his recent accomplishments in subduing the Illinois Country for Virginia, he too felt a growing helplessness in his attempt to obtain enough reinforcements and supplies from Virginia to allow him to move on Detroit while he still held the initiative. In late August 1778, Clark received word from Kentucky that Daniel Boone had recently escaped Shawnee captivity in the Ohio Country and had made his way back to the settlement of Boones Borough warning the settlers of an impending Shawnee attack. On September 7, Chiefs Blackfish and Black Hoof with several French Canadians of the Indian Department at Detroit led nearly 400 warriors on an attack against the fort that lasted nine days. While the fort defenders were able to hold out against the Indians until the siege was over, the Shawnee moved at will through Kentucky as the large attacking force broke up into smaller war parties. [WGA-p.81] Clark, from his post at Kaskaskia, was disappointed that he was unable to help defend the Kentucky settlements. While he had secured the far western frontier, he had been unable to stop the Indian raids from the Ohio Country.

At Fort Pitt, General McIntosh took over command of the post from General Hand in late August and continued his preparations for an offensive aimed at taking Detroit from the British, as mandated by the Congress. However, those orders issued on June 11 by the Congress in session at York, Pennsylvania, stated "that an expedition be immediately undertaken whose object shall be to reduce, if practicable, the garrison of Detroit," [PT-p.19] were altered by July 25. McIntosh received word soon after the Congress met, that his orders had been changed in light of the fact that the state of Virginia voted to oppose supporting the expedition into the Ohio Country while it was attempting not only to reinforce and provision George Rogers Clark at Kaskaskia, but provide for the defense of its own settlements in Kentucky that were coming under increasing Indian attack by the late summer.

Consequently, General McIntosh was issued new orders from York to scale back his invasion of the Ohio Country, and that "the expedition against the fortress of Detroit be for the present deferred" in favor of an attack against the hostile Wyandot and Delaware Indian villages on the Upper Sandusky River to "chastise and terrify the savages, and to check their ravages on the frontiers of these states." [PT-p.21] The change in plans hardly mattered to McIntosh at Fort Pitt. With the autumn season coming on, he could only lament at the fact that he was yet to see the necessary supplies arrive at Pittsburgh or the Continental troops that he had been promised.

With each passing day, General McIntosh felt increasingly frustrated with his stalled campaign which he was forced to delay later and later in the season against the Indians. The planned council with the Delaware Indian tribes scheduled to take place on July 23 was postponed until September 17. Regrettably for McIntosh and his expedition, he had to gain permission from the friendly Delaware tribe to let his army pass through their lands. Additionally, the Delaware had been requested by the American Congress to openly side with the Americans in the coming campaign, and send their warriors with McIntosh's army. The Delaware at the council refused the request, and further time was lost as the Indian representatives accompanied by the Moravian preacher David Zeisberger protested to McIntosh that the friendly Delaware would not take sides in the coming war against their British-allied brethren. McIntosh was irritated with the whole situation. [PT-p.25]

"Secret and Confidential"

At Detroit, Lieutenant Governor Hamilton finally received what he wanted from headquarters in Quebec by early September. A series of letters arrived from General Haldimand from his new post at Montreal, acknowledging the precarious situation at Detroit and the Ohio Country that Hamilton had previously described to him. Haldimand wrote to Hamilton on August 26 "in the present circumstances of the affairs you relate, it becomes highly necessary to employ every means which offer, if not to retrieve the injury done, at least to stop its further progress." [HP-214] Haldimand went further and detailed his immediate suggestions to Hamilton as to how to employ the Indians to carry out that aim. "All the parties you send out from Detroit, might together fill all the lower parts of the Ohio with bodies of savages that should constantly succeed each other, and at no time leave the river without a force which would be ready to fall upon all the Rebels that appear there."

In light of Clark's success in the west, Haldimand had given up, for the moment, on sending the Indians to ravage the upper Ohio in and around Pittsburgh, and Hamilton reluctantly had to agree that dealing with Clark was more important, as the safety of Detroit was clearly a priority. Haldimand assured Hamilton that he would do what was in his power to secure that aim, adding in his letter, "I shall reinforce the garrison of Detroit from Niagara by as many men as, after a party which I am sending to strengthen that place arrives can possibly be spared." [HP-214]

To Hamilton's surprise, another letter from Haldimand titled "Secret and Confidential" was enclosed in the same post packet delivered to him from the newly arrived sloop at Detroit. Haldimand had written it on August 27, a day later than the first letter. Governor Hamilton opened it cautiously, unsure of what he expected to find in the private directive. Hamilton scanned the short note, and stopped at the last paragraph, which contained Haldimand's confidential orders to him. The Governor of Canada wrote, "in short, with all the resources to be made use of and all the obstacles to be met, I must therefore desire that you will immediately and by the safest and most expeditious conveyance, acquaint me with your Idea of the practicableness of recovering the possession of the Illinois, and with the means you should advise to be employed for that purpose." [HP-215] Hamilton slowly put the letter down on his desk, allowing the import of what he had just read to sink in as he walked over to the window in his quarters that faced to the south. He gazed at the horizon at length, deep in thoughts of planning what he must do. With renewed confidence, Hamilton knew that the time had come to strike the Enemy.

On September 24, Hamilton's advance force of his expedition to Vincennes was ready to move. Captain Norman MacLeod of the King's Eighth Regiment set out from Detroit by boat down the Detroit River and across Lake Erie to the mouth of the Maumee with a vanguard of militia scouts and Indians in the lead. Hamilton hurried the last-minute preparations of his main force, which included two other officers from Fort Detroit along with 30 regulars of the King's Eighth, a large number of Indian Department officers and French militia totaling over 100 men, and accompanied by a body of Indian warriors from various tribes in the Detroit area that would be augmented with anticipated additions from McKee's recruiting efforts. The Governor's plan was simple. He would strike at Vincennes first, and once that post was taken, Hamilton planned to attack Kaskaskia directly and destroy Clark and his army before they could escape. With everything in readiness, Hamilton set his expeditionary force in motion for Vincennes on October 7. [NL-p.110] For Hamilton, the campaign that he wished for had now begun, as the heavily laden bateaux were maneuvered from the wharf into the waters of the Detroit River. In the lead boat, Hamilton felt a momentary twinge of his destiny in the making, as he glanced over his shoulder at the long line of bateaux carrying the men of his little army.

In the meantime, while General McIntosh was belaboring himself with the Indian negotiations at Fort Pitt, he sent a force of militia and Continental troops under Colonel Brodhead in late September down the north shore trail of the Ohio River to the mouth of the Beaver River some 20 miles from Pittsburgh to build a fort. A site was chosen on the west side of the Beaver River and close to the head of the Indian trail to the Ohio Country, from which McIntosh intended to march. Soon a small army of axe men erected a palisade stockade, enclosing nearly two acres of ground, and fortified with bastions on each of the corners of the fort, and armed with six pieces of artillery for added protection against Indian or British attack. The fort was named after General McIntosh, and it gave the General some satisfaction as he prepared to leave Pittsburgh in October, that in the least an essential part in the campaign to gain the Ohio Country for the Americans had finally got underway.

McIntosh left Fort Pitt on the morning of October 23 with the rest of his army, heading for Fort MacIntosh and then on to the Upper Sandusky Indian villages. The thought of the lateness of the season for setting out on an extended military campaign into the wilderness irked MacIntosh to no end. He knew that he could have set out much sooner if the provisions and reinforcements from the east had not taken so long to get to Pittsburgh, faulting Congress, the politicians, the army commissary, and the wagon men, all whom served to handicap him. Now with the column moving westward, MacIntosh resigned himself to the inevitability of ill weather. He was glad, at least, to be finally on the march with some sense of purpose. [PT-p.25]

"Where They Propose Building a Fort"

Alexander McKee, too, was finally on the move by early October, in the company of a party of Shawnee returning from Detroit by way of the Upper Sandusky villages. McKee impatiently led the string of packhorses loaded with supplies and ammunition destined for the war parties at the Shawnee towns on the Scioto. Despite the fact that traveling in the chilly early morning caused some complaints from his Indian companions who would have been quite content to wait in camp until the late morning sun burned off the thick fog clinging to the lowland trail, Alexander McKee felt a compelling sense of urgency to get to the Shawnee towns, now that he knew that Hamilton had left Detroit with his detachment. McKee remembered he had given his word to the Governor that he would raise as many warriors as possible on the Scioto and meet Hamilton somewhere on the trail to Vincennes. There was much for McKee yet to do, and he was in no mood to loiter on the trail.

By the middle of October, McKee and his party reached the upper streams of the Scioto and soon arrived in the largest of the Shawnee towns. With little rest, McKee called the chiefs to attend a series of councils to discuss Hamilton's impending attack upon the Virginians at Vincennes post to the southwest. Within a couple of days he was able to get a commitment from several Shawnee headmen to have warriors go with him to join Hamilton's army. However, the arrival of several runners from the Delaware in the east brought reports of a Rebel army moving towards the Muskingum villages from Fort Pitt, and McKee questioned the scouts at length. He asked them what they had seen, how many men were marching, what they looked like, and what trail the Rebel army was taking. One of the Indians who had seen the American troops for himself described them as wearing uniform coats of deep indigo color, with yellow facings, and tricorn hats on their heads. McKee realized that if the description just given to him was true, it meant that the American army was composed of Continental troops sent from Virginia in the east. [PT-p.22] McKee concluded that the new intelligence was accurate, and was a disturbing new development, for it could only mean that the Rebels had their sights set on attacking Detroit in force with regular troops.

On October 25, McKee sat down and wrote a letter to Captain Lernoult at Fort Detroit, detailing to him the intelligence that had made its way to the Shawnee by way of the Delaware runners. As he was informing Lernoult that he intended to set out the next morning to join Hamilton at the Miami Indian village, a new scout came into the Shawnee town in the early evening with startling news from the Delaware. McKee appended his letter to Lernoult, which he would send at once in the morning to Detroit, adding, "I am informed by an Indian from the Rebel army, that they have three pieces of cannon with them, and that they will take post the 26th of the month at Tuscarawas where they propose building a Fort." [HP-59] As he sealed the post packet to send to Lernoult at Detroit, McKee could only hope that Simon Girty had been likewise informed of the latest news and would be able to do something to stop to Rebels, if they were marching into the wilderness of the Ohio Country for the first time.

"I Expect Hourly to Hear From Him"

In his military quarters at Montreal, Governor General Haldimand at least felt that he was closer to Niagara and Detroit than he had been at Quebec, regardless of the fact that Montreal was still a great distance removed from either post in the western wilderness. Haldimand had taken his succinct secretary with him, Captain Matthews who busied himself day after day sorting and transcribing into Haldimand's official orderly books the endless stream of communications coming and going from Haldimand's office, for th commander to receive, read, and react to with his own hand or by dictation.

In his inner office, Haldimand looked over the recent stack of letters that Matthews had just brought to his attention. Picking up the letter written by Alexander McKee on September 6 while the Indian Department officer was still at Detroit, Haldimand wondered to himself where the energetic officer might be at this moment on October 5, before setting himself down to formulate a response to McKee's request. Much of McKee's letter was old news to Haldimand, an account of McKee's flight from Pittsburgh and subsequent intelligence on the Rebels there. Getting to the crux of McKee's letter Haldimand read McKee's request that "should Your Excellency find it consistent to order my Salary to be paid thro' some channel which will be of infinite Service to me at the present time." [HP-332] Putting the letter down, Haldimand chuckled to himself. Apparently his over-zealous officer in charge of Detroit had taken his warning to control expenses at the post a little too seriously in excluding McKee's salary. Haldimand would enjoy chastising Hamilton for his oversight once his Lieutenant Governor was safely back at Detroit.

Haldimand perused another letter written by Major John Butler at Niagara on September 24, which Mathews had placed on the corner of his writing desk, implying that Haldimand would find it of immediate interest. Butler was reporting the attack of Captain Caldwell with his Rangers and over 160 Iroquois upon the Mohawk Valley settlement of German Flatts. Haldimand found the news encouraging in light of Butler's successes in the Wyoming Valley of late summer. Beneath that letter, Mathews had included a second communication from Butler, written more recently. A smile crossed Haldimand's face as he read Major Butler's words, "Captain Butler has joined the Rangers and Indians, I expect hourly to hear from him." [HP-204] So the news was true that the eldest son of Major Butler, Walter, had escaped the Rebels in Albany. Soon father and son would be reunited.

"Hunting in Defiance of Orders"

Lastly, Haldimand picked up again the report from Colonel Major Bolton at Fort Niagara written on October 3. Colonel Bolton had just received word from Captain Lernoult at Fort Detroit that Governor Hamilton was about to set off on his expedition to Vincennes "with as many volunteers, militia, and Indians as can be assembled at Detroit." Further, Lernoult reported to Bolton that he had received word from the Shawnee towns that more than "400 Shawanese have been sent forward" to rendevous with Hamilton. Haldimand settled back in his chair, digesting the information, and reasoning that piece of information received by Lernoult could only have come from McKee, who had been successful in his attempt to stir the Indians to action, and was now on his way to join Hamilton's force. Curious as to where that juncture might take place, General Haldimand turned his attention to the map of the Ohio Country laid out on the table next to him for study.

Deep in the wilderness of the Ohio Country, General MacIntosh shook his head in disgust at the poor progress his strung out army of 1,200 men had made on November 6. He scolded his officers at their morning call of November 7 for having made only four and one half miles from their previous camp and only slightly more than 18 miles from Fort MacIntosh on the Beaver River. He ordered his field officers to hasten the packhorse and cattle drivers who were habitually lagging behind the army, and admonished his company captains to see that the rank and file picked up the pace of the march. Soon after the army left camp on the trail, two gunshots rang out in the distance. Within a short while, General MacIntosh was notified that two soldiers of the Thirteenth Virginia Regiment had been found dead on the trail, their bodies scalped by Indians while they were "hunting in defiance of orders." It was the first indication that MacIntosh's army was being watched by hostile Indians. MacIntosh feared that there would be more encounters. [PT-p.32]

"They in the Future Would Give No Quarter"

On the stormy night of November 10, far to the northeast near the frontier settlement of Cherry Valley, a strong party of over 200 Rangers and more than 300 Seneca warriors under the command of Captain Walter Butler and several Seneca war chiefs reached a pine forest some six miles from the Rebel settlement south of the Mohawk River undetected. Rebel prisoners taken the previous day stated to the son of Major John Butler that the Continental garrison of nearly 300 men with 150 militia had been alerted by an Oneida Indian that a British force was in the vicinity, however few precautions had been taken. Walter Butler conferred with the war chiefs and then ordered his men to get some rest in the shelter of some pines which afforded some protection from the rain, mud, sleet and snow, because the men had no blankets, tents, or camp fires to warm themselves. [CE-p.55]

On the morning of November 11th, the Rangers and Indians opened a surprise attack upon the small fort, killing or capturing most of the Continental officers who were billeted in civilian homes outside the fort walls. The Indians in a large body detached themselves from the Ranger assault on the fort, and attacked anyone outside the fort walls, including civilian men, women, and children. A wholesale slaughter ensued as residents were cut down by the warriors and scalped. Homes were plundered and burned indiscriminately, as the Rebel fort defenders looked on helplessly as Butler's Rangers defied them to open the gates and save the town they were ordered to defend.

With the settlement reduced to ruins and dozens of corpses littering the ground in the shocking slaughter that occurred around the fort, Walter Butler ordered the Rangers to begin their return march to Fort Niagara the next day, noting that only two Rangers and three Indians were wounded, with none killed. Butler had been unable to control the fury of the Indians, who having sated their blood lust, were now loaded down with scalps, plunder and prisoners they hoped to barter, adopt, or burn alive. In recounting the attack to Colonel Bolton, the younger Butler blamed the Rebels for previously inciting the Seneca with false accusations that served to convince the Indians that "they in future would give no quarter."

Realizing, however, the enormity of the slaughter of the defenseless civilians at Cherry Valley, Butler wrote, "I have much to lament, that notwithstanding my utmost precautions to save the women and children, I could not prevent some of them falling victims to the fury of the savages." [CE-p.56] The news of the destruction of the community of Cherry Valley by Walter Butler and the Rangers and Indians spread quickly down the Mohawk Valley to Albany and beyond to General Washington's headquarters, where the appalling attack would become known as a massacre. [CE-p.56]

To the west in the Ohio Country, McKee and Elliott had reached the forks of the Wabash River with the sizable force of Shawnee warriors a few days in advance of Hamilton's detachment. On November 11, Hamilton's bateaux reached the rendevous spot, and made a brief camp. His men were exhausted and hungry. Their clothing was wet, and they needed to start fires to dry their muskets. Hamilton could boast over 550 Indians with his regulars and militia, poised to set out the next morning for Vincennes. [NL-p.110] However, the ensuing trip to Vincennes was more difficult than expected by Hamilton. Heavy storms and increasingly bad weather delayed his advance by many days, and it was not until December 17 that Hamilton's little army reached the post at Vincennes.

Before preparing to assault the Virginian post commanded by Captain Edward Helm of Clark's brigade, Hamilton turned command of the Indians over to McKee and the officers of the Indian Department with orders to send the warriors ahead to flank the American post and cut off any possibility of retreat along the trail to Kaskaskia. When this was done, Hamilton displayed the red-coated regulars and the militia in view of the defenders of Vincennes, while the Indians let out a chorus of war whoops signifying to the Virginians their overwhelming numbers and that all hope of defense of the post was doomed and any escape was blocked.

Captain Helm took a hard look at the large number of Indians massed against his tiny militia force and realized that if his men fired upon the savages, a massacre of his little garrison would result. Wisely Helm decided that he must surrender to the British while he still could before their red allies were set loose upon his untenable position and his luckless men. In a matter of minutes, Captain Edward Helm and his men became Hamilton's prisoners. [WGA-p.67]

Hamilton was elated at the fall of Vincennes to him without a fight. With the Indians equally disappointed and soon restless, Hamilton dismissed them to "prowl upon the frontiers or return to their homes, with the purpose in the early spring of re-assembling them.' [BC-p.64] Hamilton realized that winter was upon him and nothing more could be done to assault Clark at Kaskaskia. As Hamilton set his own regulars to work re-building the dilapidated Fort Sackville at Vincennes, many Detroit militia decided to risk returning to Detroit. [NL-p.110] McKee and Elliott remained at Vincennes until Hamilton ordered the two near the end of January 1779 to return to the Shawnee villages on the Scioto to help the Indians there prepare to send war parties against the American army now in the Ohio Country. Further if they could, McKee and Elliott were to link up with Simon Girty and his Mingoes. [BC-p.65]

"Make It Home As Best You Can"

On November 18, General McIntosh's army reached the banks of the Tuscarawas River above the mouth of Sandy Creek and crossed the ford to the grassy plain on the west bank of the river. Here his army met a party of friendly Moravian Delaware Indians from the nearby mission at Lictenau who cheered his men. Assessing his situation, McIntosh could take heart in the fact that his army had arrived intact at the halfway point to the Upper Sandusky Indian towns without encountering any hostile resistance. However this was the only positive aspect of his whole campaign of which MacIntosh was certain. At the moment, all else seemed more tentative to him than ever.

Food provisions for the men were running low by the time the army reached the Tuscarawas. The weather had turned much colder, and many men were underdressed for the increased severity, which added to their overall misery. Discipline among the rank and file had become harder for the officers to maintain as the troops complained constantly of the cold and food rationing. In addition, friendly Delaware Indians were non-committal on MacIntosh's request for them to sell him food for his army, yet were quick to report to him that they had seen hostile Indians lurking in the woods, watching the Americans. In the face of all the adversity and with his own reputation at stake, MacIntosh had his officers put the men to work constructing a fort on the site of the camp while the General planned his next move. Publicly, MacIntosh still talked openly to his officers of continuing his expedition to the Upper Sandusky once the fort construction was completed.

MacIntosh planned to name the fort after his friend and benefactor, Henry Laurens, the first president of the Continental Congress. While some men cut down nearby trees and shaped the logs for the walls, other men erected the palisade stockade by placing the poles upright into hastily dug wall trenches. The work was difficult and exhausting for the soldiers. By November 29, with rations reduced again and the fort still uncompleted, morale among the soldiers reached a new low with the men openly grumbling about the harsh conditions and their unanimous desire to return to Fort Pitt. MacIntosh realized that he would be unable to march the army further and decided to call his officers together to see what could and could not be done under the circumstances, which were getting bleaker by the day. [PT-p.40]

On December 1, MacIntosh's officers reached a decision "to return the bulk of the army to Fort MacIntosh as soon as Fort Laurens" was completed. MacIntosh too was in low spirits. With the new fort nearing completion, MacIntosh planned to leave a garrison of 150 men on the Tuscarawas under the command of Colonel Gibson, and MacIntosh consoled himself with the idea that by returning the rest of the army to Fort Pitt for the winter, the new fort that he left behind in the Ohio Country would provide an opportune jumping off point for a renewed campaign to take Detroit in the spring. [PT-p.41]

On December 9, General MacIntosh bid farewell to Gibson and the fort garrison and ordered the bulk of the army to begin its return march to the Ohio River. Each man was given two days' rations in advance, which many men devoured on the spot, with no further source of food until they reached Fort MacIntosh. Discipline disintegrated among the militia once they left the Tuscarawas valley, and an attitude of "make it home as best you can" dominated the hungry, cold and tired men. The returning army fell apart under MacIntosh's gaze, and by the second day, the men were "spread over nearly half the distance between the two forts," Fort Laurens and Fort MacIntosh. [PT-p.41] Dispirited, General MacIntosh and most of the men reached the safety of the Ohio River by December 13, half-starved.

"Scarce Give Any Credit to It"

General Haldimand poured over the letters that arrived from his officers in the field prior to the furious storm that hit Montreal during the third week of December, heralding the arrival of winter. With great interest he read the report from Governor Hamilton, written on December 4 from the Indian village of Ouiatton to the southwest of Detroit. Hamilton wrote, "Since my leaving Detroit, I have been joined on the way by Savages from different quarters," detailing to Haldimand the tribes and numbers that were now with him. As to the disposition of the Rebels at Vincennes, Hamilton remarked that "we are told they are in a miserable condition, for want of provisions," adding, that "the account of the strength of the Rebels varies so much that I am at a loss to form a judgment of it. I do not however believe it to be such as we have the least cause to dread." [HP-227] The news from Hamilton was encouraging, Haldimand thought to himself. With any luck, his western Governor would have taken Vincennes by this time, a first step in reversing the loss of the Illinois Country.

Turning to another matter of growing concern, General Haldimand reviewed again the intelligence sent by Colonel Mason Bolton, the commandant of Fort Niagara. Among the many reports sent by Bolton were the contents of the letter from Captain Lernoult at Fort Detroit, written after Governor Hamilton had left for Vincennes. Lernoult had received disturbing reports on the movements of a sizable Rebel army from Fort Pitt into the Ohio Country, as had Bolton. The news was troubling, and Haldimand read Bolton's words once more. "Captain Lernoult informs me that the Hurons at Sanduski are much alarmed having lately had a message from Captain Pipe and the Delawares that they are in great danger from the Virginians encroachment on their lands." [HP-72]

Haldimand pondered the developing situation in the Ohio Country, as he studied the maps laid out on the table before him. If the Rebels had moved an army to the Muskingum, it could only mean they intended to attack Detroit, Haldimand reasoned. With Detroit weakened considerably by Hamilton's campaign to the Illinois Country and the winter weather slowing the movement of the ships on the Lakes, Detroit was in great jeopardy if the Rebel army moved to take that post. However, as Haldimand gazed at the maps and measured the estimated distances from the Muskingum River to Detroit, he could not help but puzzle over the intention of the Rebels. Their movement so late in the year through increasingly hostile Indian territory defied all common sense, in Haldimand's mind. How could the Rebels move and re-supply themselves in such extreme weather, so far from Fort Pitt and without reinforcements? In his mind, they yet had a considerable distance yet to traverse. It just did not make sense to Haldimand.

The Governor General picked up the letters from the Ohio Country again. All the reports from the Indians indicated to Haldimand that the Rebel army was a mix of militia and Continental soldiers, not of the quality of the rangers such as Major Butler possessed. Regardless, Fort Detroit would have to prepare for the worse, and Haldimand could take some satisfaction in the fact that Bolton had reacted quickly to the situation. "In consequence of your orders for a reinforcement to be sent to Captain Lernoult, I ordered a Captain, two subalterns, and 59 men to Detroit—as many if not more as this post ought to be able to spare considering the present state of the garrison particularly too at this time of year, for soon it will be impossible for the vessels to navigate the Lakes and of course we shall be deprived of all hopes of assistance from Canada this winter." Haldimand sighed, and hoped that Bolton's reinforcement would get to the western post before the ice formed on the Lakes and interrupted any travel.

Bolton's last piece of news caught Haldimand's eye. Bolton had enclosed a letter written by an ensign, reporting on news heard from Rebel sympathizers of a planned assault on Fort Niagara by three Rebel armies coming by different routes, two through Seneca Country. Bolton remarked that he could "scarce give any credit to it" yet thought it important enough to pass along. Haldimand mulled over it for some time. While the report seemed no more valuable than rumor or hearsay, he stopped short of dismissing the possibility. No one had thought it possible that the Rebels would move in the west and take the Illinois Country. At least he could settle his mind that Hamilton had likely reversed that Rebel move by now. [HP-72]

"Showed No Apprehension of Being Hanged"

At the British post of Vincennes, Governor Hamilton had accomplished a great deal in a short period of time since capturing Clark's men. The fortifications at the post had been improved considerably, in preparation of the highly unlikely event that the Rebels would attempt to attack Vincennes in the spring from Kentucky. Hamilton was able to use McKee and Elliott to meet with the tribes of Indians of the Illinois Country and work out treaties with them that neutralized Clark's previous meetings at Kaskaskia, proposing that they accompany Hamilton in the spring in his campaign to seize Kaskaskia from the Rebel Clark and reunite the Illinois Country under the British flag.

In mid-January while waiting for the end of winter to renew his campaign, Hamilton turned his attention once again to the Ohio Country, when news reached him of the Rebel Fort Laurens built the previous November on the Tuscarawas River. Hamilton desperately needed more intelligence on the military situation there, and so on January 20, he sent Matthew Elliott with a party of Shawnee to the Shawnee towns on the Scioto River to obtain enough warriors to proceed "eastward towards Fort Pitt in an effort to secure information regarding American movements." [HR-p.25]

McKee, who had been on the move in the Ohio Country since the first of the year, set out again for the Scioto with dispatches for Detroit, as well as orders from Hamilton for McKee to gather warriors for a spring campaign against Fort Laurens and Fort MacIntosh. [MD-110] Hamilton had already sent a letter to Simon Girty near the end of December instructing him to "watch the movements of the enemy near Fort Pitt." [BC-p.65]. Girty set out from the Mingo villages on the upper Scioto on January 6 with only 17 Mingo warriors, first to reconnoiter the Americans at Fort Laurens, than to continue east. In Hamilton's mind, he had taken the initiative away from the Rebels, and as soon as the spring weather arrived, he could reverse the setbacks he had suffered in the west and he would be able to continue with his ultimate campaign as ordered by Lord Germain.

What pleased Hamilton the most as he wrote to Haldimand from Vincennes late in December giving his commander the details of his successful taking of the post, was the knowledge that he now had George Rogers Clark where he wanted him, boxed in and isolated at Kaskaskia, unable to attack Fort Detroit due to lack of men and provisions, and unable to retreat to Kentucky without giving up his hold on the Illinois Country. Clark and his men were as good as finished in Hamilton's mind and would surely give up without a fight, much like the Rebel Lieutenant captured near Vincennes, who had "two commissions, one from Lieut. Gov. Abbott, the other from the Commandant for the Congress" in his possession, to present to whatever side as the situation demanded. Hamilton related that the captured officer, in being able to swear allegiance to either side, "showed no apprehension of being hanged on the next tree, which he certainly deserved." [HP-229]

That I Shall Be Able to Trepan Him"

At Fort Laurens, matters had gone from bad to worse for Colonel Gibson in command. A mutiny among the men was barely averted in the last weeks of December due to the shortage of food and warm clothing promised to them by General MacIntosh at Fort Pitt. The winter weather was exceedingly cold, and the construction of shelters for the men inside the fort was largely unfinished, leaving the soldiers exposed to the harsh elements, which weakened them considerably. In all, the tiny garrison at the post in the wilderness felt isolated and abandoned, and Gibson could hardly disagree with them. While Gibson was able to obtain some food from the friendly Moravian Delawares, it was not nearly enough to alleviate the starvation facing his garrison if relief were not sent to Fort Laurens soon. Then, on January 21, 1779, a relief party from Fort MacIntosh led by Captain John Clark of the Eighth Pennsylvania Regiment arrived at Fort Laurens with a modest supply of provisions, and left the next morning, carrying several letters from Gibson to MacIntosh, explaining his extreme condition and the necessity of immediate aid.

Unknown to Colonel Gibson and his garrison, Simon Girty had arrived undetected at Fort Laurens the previous day with a war party of almost two dozen Mingo warriors, having laboriously traveled along snow-covered trails by snowshoes at times. Gibson had been informed by a friendly Moravian Delaware Indian John Killbuck that word reached him of the movements of Simon Girty in the company of a Mingo war party with the intent of attacking Gibson at Fort Laurens. In particular, Killbuck reported that Girty was coming to personally take Gibson's scalp.

Gibson scoffed when he heard that piece of news from Killbuck's messenger, writing to Colonel Morgan at Fort Pitt that "Mr. Girty has not yet made his appearance; I hope, if he does, to prevent his taking my scalp...and that I shall be able to trepan him." [BC-p.66] With no sign of Girty or hostile Indians anywhere, Gibson dismissed Killbuck's warning as another rumor of the Moravian Delawares, who were susceptible to hearsay and unfounded rumor, due to their precarious position caught between the Americans and their British-allied brethren. [PT-p.53]

However, Girty observed the fort undetected from a distance, and when by chance, Clark's small supply column was spotted entering the fort, Girty set up an ambush about three miles from the fort to the east along the trail to Fort MacIntosh on the Ohio River. He picked a spot where a sentinel could observe the trail from a distance and alert the rest of Girty's party who were sheltered nearby in a hollow, trying to keep warm. It was a gamble for Girty and the Mingoes, for they could not last but a day or two at the most exposed to the cold weather while they waited. Luckily for Girty, the next morning of January 22, the scout spotted Clark's returning party, and alerted his comrades who took up positions on a snow-covered hillock overlooking the trail. In a matter of minutes, Clark's party walked directly into the ambush along the trail leading to the east. [BC-p.66]

The Mingoes rose up from their hidden positions and fired into the surprised Americans, killing two men and wounding four others. One man was immediately taken prisoner by the Indians, however, Clark and the survivors were able to fight their way back to the safety of Fort Laurens. Girty's ambush had been successful. The Indians scalped the dead and dying, and stripped the prisoner to his underclothes and bound his hands. In searching his woolen coat, the Indians found the prisoner was carrying Gibson's dispatches to MacIntosh, which were read at the Upper Sandusky Indian villages upon Girty's return from the raid, and later carried to Detroit to Captain Lernoult. Lernoult was able to learn, on February 4, for the first time, the details of MacIntosh's march to the Tuscarawas, the building of Fort Laurens on the banks of the river, and the actual deplorable condition of the Rebels at Fort Laurens. [PT-p.52]

General Haldimand read the good news from Colonel Bolton at Niagara, dated February 12, 1779, with a sigh of relief in his quarters at Montreal on the morning of February 23. It was the first dispatch he had received informing him of Governor Hamilton's successful capture of the Rebel post of Vincennes in the Illinois Country. "This day an Indian arrived with letters from Governor Hamilton and Capt. Lernoult with the agreeable news that Post Vincent was in our possession," Bolton wrote. In addition, Lernoult informed Bolton that "having no hopes of any reinforcement, he resolved with the advice of his officers to throw up a strong breastwork on the high ground which commands his weak Fort," meaning, that Lernoult had determined to strengthen the defenses of Fort Detroit, in the event that the Rebels attempted to attack in the spring. The news was encouraging to the commander of Canada. For the first time in awhile General Haldimand could feel satisfied that the Rebel advances of the previous fall had been reversed, so he thought to himself, as he turned towards his bed for a restful night's sleep.

"It Saves the Americans Some Expenses in Building"

With darkness falling, Governor Hamilton at Vincennes turned in early to his bed in the makeshift officer's quarters within the walls of Fort Sackville, and fell quickly into a deep sleep, due to the day's exhaustive work. No more than an hour had passed before Hamilton was abruptly wakened from his stupor by the sound of musket shots outside the fort, and as he raised himself from his bed in an attempt to clear his head and find his boots, Captain MacLeod burst through the door of his room, shouting that the Rebels were outside the walls, attacking in force. Hamilton could hardly believe what he was hearing. In fact, the tiny Virginian army of 170 men under George Rogers Clark had reached the outskirts of Vincennes at dusk after an arduous forced march across swampy land from Kaskaskia in extreme conditions of winter weather. Clark left on February 5, after deciding to boldly attack Hamilton and attempt to take him and his force at Vincennes before Hamilton would defeat him in the spring. Clark sent word to the townspeople of Vincennes to either go to the fort to fight with the British or stay out of his way, for he was determined to fight. Surrounding the British fort, Clark positioned his best riflemen to keep up a constant fire upon the fort, and to attempt to pick off any British soldiers returning fire from the walls or gunners preparing to fire the cannon from the open ports. Clark's strategy worked. Soon, several British soldiers inside the fort were wounded. [WGA-p.72]

Governor Hamilton was extremely apprehensive. At first he "assumed that the shots were only those of a few drunken Indians" but as the night battle wore on and the casualties within his fort mounted from the tremendous fusillade striking the fort. Hamilton realized, in shock, that the attackers were Clark's Virginians, and he was aghast that they appeared to number in the hundreds. His French militia deserted the fort through a sally port in the darkness, which left Hamilton with less than 30 regulars fit for battle, a staggering few, though the men vowed to fight with Hamilton to the end. As to his Indian allies camped outside the fort walls, Hamilton could find none, as Clark had already convinced the Indians to remain neutral when he had a party of pro-British Shawnee returning to Vincennes after accompanying McKee and Elliott, captured as they made their way to the fort. "On Clark's orders, four of them were crudely tomahawked and scalped right before the gate of the fort in full view of the horrified defenders" as well as the Indians camped before the fort, whereupon they gathered their things and immediately left Vincennes. [WGA-p.74] Hamilton was alone; he had no one he could count on save his handful of troops, and time and ammunition were running out.

On the morning of February 24, under a white flag of truce, Clark called for Hamilton to surrender the fort unconditionally. The Governor refused until better terms were negotiated, and the next morning Hamilton and his men marched out of the fort and surrendered their arms. Captain Helm was freed and sent immediately by Clark with a company of men to intercept several boatloads of supplies from Fort Detroit that were coming downriver destined for Vincennes. Clark set free the remaining French militia captured with Hamilton inside the fort and allowed them to return to Detroit, where Clark knew they would terrify the British post with the accounts of his successful capture of Vincennes and Hamilton. To Captain Lernoult, Clark sent a message with the returning French, writing, "I learn... that you were very busy making new works. I am glad to hear it, as it saves the Americans some expenses in building," alluding to Lernoult that Clark would soon be upon Detroit and capture it as well.

Lieutenant Governor Henry Hamilton was made a prisoner, as was Jehu Hay, Captain of the British Indian Department at Detroit, as well as the red-coated soldiers of the King's Eighth. In defeat, Hamilton was chagrined, angry, and humbled, for he had gambled on destroying George Rogers Clark's Virginians, and in attempting to do so, had severely underestimated the daring, determination, and courage of his opponent who bested him. On March 7, Hamilton and his men began the long trip to captivity in Virginia, where Hamilton and Hay would face charges of inciting the Indians against the Virginian frontier populace. For Hamilton, far worse for him than his hostile Rebel captors, was the raw, undeniable fact he had failed in his duty to protect the Ohio Country, as Lord Germain and the Crown had relied upon him to do.

Hamilton bowed his head in silence as the Virginian batteaumen worked the oars of the boat. Beyond a shadow of a doubt he fully realized that whatever happened in Virginia, his own capture had effectively ended his career, dashed it to pieces, and with the fall of that miserable frontier post in the wilderness, his personal ambitions as well.

Chapter 11

1779: Advances, Setbacks, and Stalemate in the Wilderness

The news of the capture of Lieutenant Governor Hamilton and his men at Vincennes by George Rogers Clark in February 1779 did not become immediately known to the combatants in the wilderness of the Ohio Country and the American frontier to the east. The great distances involved and the severity of the winter weather prevented the rapid movement of scouts carrying important intelligence through the wilderness. Word of the disaster that befell Hamilton would travel slowly to Detroit and take weeks to reach the tribes of the Ohio Country allied with the British. Governor General Haldimand and his staff in Canada were still digesting the recently arrived information of Hamilton's success over the Rebels at Vincennes in late December when word would reach Haldimand of Hamilton's untimely defeat and capture. And Haldimand would come to realize that time, distance, and weather would prove to be almost insurmountable obstacles for British forces to counter Clark.

On the western frontier, the American troops at the military posts of Fort Laurens, Fort MacIntosh, and Fort Pitt were equally ignorant of the amazing turn of events in which Clark had wrested Vincennes from Hamilton. Word of Hamilton's capture was only making its way up the Ohio River to Fort Pitt by returning scouts in the latter weeks of February 1779. It would be another month before the startling report of Clark's victory would arrive from Kentucky and be the cause for celebration along the frontier settlements who were bracing themselves for the renewal of Indian wilderness warfare with the coming warmer weather.

However slow the news of Hamilton's surrender traveled, by word of mouth and by letter, the collapse of Hamilton and his forces at Vincennes would have far-reaching implications for everyone involved in the growing struggle for control of the wilderness of the Ohio Country. The Indian tribes allied to the British cause would be the first to feel the consequence of Clark's victory over Hamilton. As word spread to Shawnee, Wyandot, Seneca and Delaware villages, the Indians began to comprehend that the one man who had spoken to them as the representative of the King was gone forever. Hamilton had been defeated in battle by an opponent, Clark, who suddenly gained the recognition and respect of the warriors for his strength, cunning and determination, which they previously held only Hamilton.

Their hatred and hostility for the Virginians which drove them into battle with the Long Knives would diminish rapidly in the face of uncertainty and fear. If Clark could lead an army to Vincennes and defeat Hamilton himself, Clark could attack anywhere and at anytime with his Virginians. For the first time, the Indians of the Ohio Country would come to fully realize that they were not safe in their villages scattered from the Muskingum to the Scioto and the Upper Sandusky Rivers, for George Rogers Clark could strike them in their own lands and destroy them where they once felt invincible. Clark, by attacking Hamilton at Vincennes, struck the Indians of the Ohio Country where they were most vulnerable—their morale and sense of security. Their martial spirit and will to fight the Virginians began to waver as their fear of George Rogers Clark took hold, and many Indians began to consider taking a position of neutrality between the British and Americans.

At British Detroit, the news of Hamilton's defeat would be received by Captain Lernoult and the British garrison with shock. Not only would the loss of Hamilton create a vacuum of leadership at the frontier post, but the capture of the 25 officers and men of the King's Eighth Regiment effectively stripped the fort of key officers and seasoned regular troops at a critical time. In addition, the loss of Jehu Hay, the head of the British Indian Department at Detroit, diminished the number of effective men able to liaison with the Indians at a time when that skill would be needed most. At this critical juncture, Captain Lernoult, however capable a British officer in command of the defense of Detroit, had neither the experience nor the force of personality to deal effectively with either the savages or their French comrades. Lernoult, simply, was no Hamilton. Lernoult was unable to fill Hamilton's shoes as a diplomat to the Indians no matter how hard he tried.

Not only would the news of Hamilton's surrender have an undesirable effect upon the French inhabitants of Detroit, but Clark's message of conciliation, carried with the returning French Canadian militia from Vincennes to Detroit, would undermine their previous loyalty to the British, now with Hamilton gone, and Clark intimating an attack upon Detroit. Clark's request for the French inhabitants to desert the British cause only added to Lernoult's expanding list of worries, as rumors of growing French disenchantment circulated through the settlement, causing him to seriously question French loyalty.

Perhaps more than anything else, Lernoult would come to find in the loss of Hamilton the loss of British military initiative in the western wilderness, which Hamilton's defeat inevitably brought to a precipitous halt. Lernoult would come to dread the dire situation created at Detroit in the late winter and would find that he was without means to take any initiative other than defense. George Rogers Clark and his army at Vincennes along with the Americans at their forts in the Ohio Country now possessed the military upper hand over the British in the west. The Americans held the initiative to take the offensive against Detroit, and the only question in Lernoult's mind would be "when would the Americans attack?"

Lernoult would be faced with problems. The breastwork defenses of Fort Lernoult were still largely uncompleted, and the garrison was unable to be reinforced until the weather allowed resupply from Niagara. The ambivalence of the Indians was growing and their allegiance increasingly in doubt, while the hostility of the French became more evident by the day. Lernoult would come to the conclusion in the late winter that his hold on Detroit was tenuous at best, and in grave doubt if the Rebels should attempt to strike a blow against Detroit from either direction with Clark's Virginians on the Wabash or the Americans at Fort Pitt. Without a doubt, Lernoult, more than anyone else, would come to view the news of the loss of Hamilton and his men as nothing less than a catastrophe. But for now, in early March, time moved ever so slowly in the western wilderness still cloaked in the grip of winter. The events of 1779 had yet to unfold, and would be shaped by what had occurred at Vincennes, and would carry sweeping repercussions for everyone involved.

The year of 1779 began at British Fort Niagara with a measure of severity as harsh winter weather and a scarcity of rations plagued Lieut. Colonel Mason Bolton, commander of the post. Particularly vexing to him were the comings and goings of the multitude of Indians from nearly two dozen tribes that camped near the fort in assorted lodges, each tribe petitioning him constantly for food, ammunition, and provisions to sustain them. While he noted in his "Return of the Indians" that he prepared for General Haldimand, that there were 1,581 souls present at Niagara on January 26, Bolton knew that many more, probably over a 1,000, were in their villages near and far from Niagara, and he could count on all of them to return before the winter weather broke to ask him for food. Never before had the Indians been so dependent upon the British for all their needs, which unfortunately came at a time when the fort had barely enough to feed its own garrison, Bolton lamented to himself, as he sealed the letter destined for Haldimand. [HP-39]

One shining spot for both Bolton and Haldimand was Major John Butler's Ranger Corps which Butler had not only expanded from loyalist recruits arriving at Niagara, but which enabled him to keep parties scouting constantly in the field against the Rebels, even in the depths of winter. John Butler completed his official account of the Corps in early January 1779 showing a return amounting to six companies and over 350 officers and rank and file. [HP-362] In spite of a few losses due to illness, wounds, desertion, and discharge, by March 26 Butler would be able to boast of over 300 effective Rangers under arms. [HP-12] Butler's successes of 1778 and his scouts' ability to provide Bolton with the intelligence he desperately needed on Rebel movements provided Bolton with the impetus to do all that he could to help Butler supply his Ranger Corps.

"To Enable Him to Make Such a Defense"

On February 12, Bolton wrote "Major Butler's Corps having extreme bad arms, I have lent him 100 Firelocks out of the Garrison Stores." Bolton knew the aid was justified. If the Rebels attempted to attack Fort Niagara, the only able defenders would be Butler's men, not the regulars, nor the horde of Indians. To support the war in the Ohio Country, Bolton noted that Butler had sent two parties of Rangers with Indians "towards Fort Pitt, and the places adjacent, to observe the motions of the Enemy," and help Lernoult at Fort Detroit ascertain what was happening east of him as far as the Rebels were concerned. Butler ordered several Rangers to temporarily reside with the Indians in those areas, "in order to have scouts constantly out, and to send the earliest Intelligence to this Place." [HP-206]

At Detroit, in the absence of Governor Hamilton, Captain Lernoult labored to keep Detroit's garrison busy in the spite of the detestable weather. On the advice of his remaining officers, and especially Captain Henry Bird of the King's Eighth (who arrived in October with a company of 50 men sent by Bolton from the garrison of Fort Niagara as reinforcements on orders from General Haldimand) Lernoult resolved "to throw up a strong breastwork on the high ground" above the military barracks, improving the uncompleted fortifications "to enable him to make such a defense" as possible. [HP-128] With Captain Bird now second in command, Lernoult was able to turn over some of his daily workload regarding the construction to him. Work parties of men were needed to dig the breastworks of the fort's redoubts, while other work details were given the arduous task of cutting logs and putting them in place as Lernoult's engineer designated. Bird was able to organize the daily work parties of soldiers assigned to the fort construction, which freed Lernoult from those tasks, thus allowing him to concentrate on the developing situation to the southeast at the Rebel fort in the Ohio Country. Just as Lernoult was learning of the news of Hamilton's success at Post Vincent from an Indian who arrived with the letters from the Governor Hamilton, Simon Girty came into Detroit on February 3 with a startling report about the Rebels at their fort in the Ohio Country. [HP-129]

"No One to Advice with in This Critical Time"

Girty had recently left the Upper Sandusky Indian villages after returning from a successful scout of the Americans. With him he brought "strings of wampum from the Mingoes, Wyandots, Shawnees and Delawares" that Girty related had "7 to 800 men assembled at the Upper Town determined to strike the fort at the Tuscarawas…and to attack them in the night and distress them as much as possible." [HP-129] Girty had several chiefs with him who wanted to meet with Captain Lernoult to ask him to support the proposed attack not only with ammunition and provisions, but with regular troops as well.

The impertinent request by Girty caught Lernoult completely off guard. He presumed that Girty implicitly understood his undermanned position at Detroit and the necessity to marshal all his strength in the construction of the new fortifications, but Lernoult was mortified when Girty pressed the issue with him in a meeting in the presence of the Indians, who expressed their displeasure to Lernoult that Governor Hamilton had gone to Vincennes instead of coming to their aid in the Ohio Country where the Virginians were encroaching on their land and threatening their villages. Girty was quick to add that all the letters taken from the captured American prisoners recently revealed "the main body was to move towards Detroit the latter end of March." The Indian chiefs nodded in approval of Girty's remarks as he translated to them what he had just spoken to Lernoult.

Captain Lernoult had no doubt in his mind that the Girty had some hand in shaping the ill-tempered mood of the Indian chiefs flanking Girty, who sullenly glared at Lernoult, waiting for his response to Girty's request which sounded more like a demand. How Lernoult wished at this moment that he had Hamilton and Hay with him as he had "no one to advise with in this critical time when it requires great caution and attention to keep the Indians in good humor and preserve their friendship." [HP-129] However Lernoult had to make a decision, and he knew that he had no choice but to give in to their demands or have them call him a liar for reneging on Hamilton's past promises. [PT-P.54] Lernoult turned to Captain Henry Bird and ordered him to prepare a force to accompany Girty back to the Upper Sandusky Indian towns.

"Murdered at a Most Horrid Rate"

Captain Bird called for volunteers from the King's Eighth to accompany him to serve with Girty and the large body of warriors assembling at the villages preparing to attack Fort Laurens. Bird's party, with Girty and a large body of Indians in tow, set off from Detroit at once for the Indian villages with ammunition, provisions, and clothing that Lernoult could hardly spare. However, once Bird arrived at the large Wyandot Indian town, he was shocked to find that the situation there was not as Girty had described. The Indians were less than enthusiastic about attacking the Virginians at Fort Laurens. Their numbers were less than 200, not the 800 as Girty had said. To Bird's disgust, when he came into the village he found that the warriors were preoccupied with "enjoying the immediate prospect of torturing a prisoner at the stake to the exclusion, in their minds, of all else." [BC-p.69]

The prisoner was a Virginian captured from the vicinity of Fort Laurens. Captain Bird attempted to reason with the Wyandot headmen to prevent the killing of the prisoner, but to no avail. When he tried to buy the life of the poor wretch, the Indians ignored Bird and dragged the prisoner away from him for some distance whereupon they cut his throat and "murdered him at a most horrid rate." [BC-p.69] Captain Bird, who had witnessed the torturing of Seneca prisoners taken at the battle of Oriskany the previous year, had never reconciled himself to this barbaric custom of the savages, regardless of their allegiance to the Crown. Watching the prisoner die, Bird was aghast. [BC-p.69]

When the Wyandots were finished dismembering the corpse, Captain Bird had some of his men bury the body only to find that the Indians soon dug it up and put the scalped head upon a pole and raised it in the center of the village. In disgust, Bird had the body and head reburied while he fumed at the savagery of his Wyandot allies, finally denouncing them publicly, telling the Indians to "Get away from me; never will I have nothing more to do with you." [BC-p.69] The Wyandots were more puzzled than outraged by Bird's behavior, wondering to themselves why the redcoat officer did not understand their need for entertainment with the unfortunate prisoner, culturally one of the prerequisites of warfare. Bird went into seclusion to cool off and decide what to do in light of the incident.

"The Whole of the Besieging Force Then Showed Themselves"

By February 22, Simon Girty had patched things up between Captain Bird and the Wyandots and was able to finally get a war party together and ready to move in the direction of the Virginians at Fort Laurens. More than 100 Mingo and Wyandot warriors accompanied Bird and his men as they left the Upper Sandusky River and followed the headwaters of White Woman's Creek to its confluence with the Tuscarawas near the Delaware village of Goschachgunk. [PT-p.58] While the mixed British and Indians force was of one mind to attack the Virginians, Captain Bird, in spite of his reconciliation with the Indians, had mixed feelings about who should be in charge.

Captain Bird felt, as the ranking officer, he should be in command of the expedition to Fort Laurens, but in reality he did not lead anyone but his own men. Uncomfortably, Bird was forced to accept the fact that the Indians paid little attention to him. Rather, Simon Girty held the confidence of the Indians, particularly the Mingo or Ohio Seneca warriors who regarded him as a trusted adopted brother. Yet, in Bird's eyes, Girty had no authority to lead, as he was neither an officer in the military nor the Indian Department, but only an interpreter to the Indians. The tension between the two white men was palpable and the Indians sensed it, though Girty paid little attention to Bird. The British officer, for his part, was forced to swallow his pride and stifle his resentment, knowing that while on the trail, Bird needed Girty to assuage the Wyandots, who were still smarting from his unfortunate outburst at Upper Sandusky. It was a delicate situation for Bird to relinquish command to a man whom he considered his subordinate, if not an inferior.

On the evening of February 22, the mixed force of redcoats and Indians arrived at Fort Laurens undetected, due in part to Girty's successful intimdation of the pro-American Moravian Delawares encountered at Goschachgunk. Girty called a meeting of the war captains of the Wyandots and Senecas, and with Bird's consent, laid out a plan of attack during the evening. Knowing the lay of the land and the trails surrounding the fort, Girty had the warriors take up hidden positions in a semi-circle surrounding the fort to wait and see who might walk into the ambush he had set. Unfortunately for the Virginians, Girty did not have long to wait.

The next morning, February 23, an unsuspecting Colonel Gibson ordered a work detail of 19 men from the fort to proceed to bring in a wagonload of firewood. Girty alerted Bird and the Indians and once the work party of Virginians had ventured far enough from the safety of the fort, Girty gave the signal, and the hidden Indians and British regulars fired a volley simultaneously into the Americans, killing or wounding all but two men in the initial firing. Instantly the warriors rushed the dead, dying, and wounded with tomahawks and scalping knives in hand, and proceeded to hack to death all but two men who were immediately taken prisoner.

To the horror of Gibson's men watching the spectacle from the walls of Fort Laurens, the bodies of their hapless comrades were stripped, scalped, and butchered before their eyes by the painted savages, while the rest of "the whole of the besieging force then showed themselves." [BC-p.60] Gibson's defenders were thrown into a state of panic as they realized that Fort Laurens was completely surrounded by Indians leaving them with no hope of escape or relief. As the vengeful Wyandots and Seneca howled derisively and shook the bloody, fresh scalps in victory at the fort, Gibson realized that the large number of Indians with the handful of redcoats was more than an isolated war party, but rather a full-scale expedition. The siege of Fort Laurens had begun.

"Only a Small Amount Was Recovered"

After a few days of desultory fire from the Indians, the attacking force settled into a disquieting standoff as Gibson's 100 or so men still fit for duty were content to man the walls and not come out of the fort to challenge the Indians for the Indians appeared to have an overwhelming advantage of numbers. [PT-p.59] Ammunition was running low as well, and most of Gibson's men were in a weakened state due to the weeks of strictly rationed food. Gibson's overriding problem was not how to defeat the attacking force, but rather how to get word to Fort MacIntosh for help in lifting the siege and getting food for the men before the garrison was reduced to starvation, which was near at hand. Gibson counted on one thing: the impatience of the Indians. From years of experience in fighting them, he knew that laying siege to a white man's fort was not their manner of fighting, now that the initial ambush had been sprung. All Gibson needed was to wait and do nothing, except keep his men defending the fort walls. He was soon to be proven right.

By March 19, provisions began to run low for the Indians and British as well. After more than three weeks of watching and waiting, the Indians had naturally lost interest in the protracted stalemate before the walls of Fort Laurens. They began talking openly among themselves of giving up the attack and returning to their villages on the Upper Sandusky, so when food ran out, the Indians began to leave in small parties for home. Captain Bird had no cannon with him to batter down the gates of the Rebel fort, and with the increasing desertion of the Indians, he, too, was forced to gather his men and break off the attack. While Bird accompanied the Wyandots on the trail to the northwest, Girty elected to remain with the war parties of the Ohio Senecas in their own country, to scout as far east as the Ohio River and prey upon any of the Enemy supply trains or relief parties leaving from the vicinity of Fort Pitt. [BC-p.70] The two men parted ways on good terms.

Unknown to either Girty or Gibson was the fact at the same time that the two men were preparing to leave the vicinity of Fort Laurens, General McIntosh at Fort Pitt was sending a relief expedition to Fort Laurens of approximately 150 men and a train of packhorses loaded with fresh food and provisions for the starving garrison, along with stores for the planned spring campaign to the hostile Upper Sandusky Indian villages. The relief party stopped at Fort McIntosh on the Beaver River and then headed west to the Tuscarawas River, arriving uneventfully in sight of the fort in only four days, to the joy of Gibson's men cooped up inside the walls. Unfortunately for the Americans, the unexpected now happened, wrecking more havoc for the survivors of Fort Laurens than three weeks of Indian siege had been able to do. [PT-p.62]

As McIntosh's supply party from the Ohio came in sight of the fort, Gibson's men, overwhelmed by emotion, excitedly fired their muskets into the air from the fort walls, expressing their joy. The sudden volley of musketry startled the packhorses who stampeded into the surrounding woods, carrying their precious loads of food and ammunition with them before the men handling the horses could stop them. Throughout the rest of the day, the men of Fort Laurens helped the relief party comb the woods for the lost horses and supplies, but "only a small amount was recovered" to the dismay of everyone involved. [PT-p.62]

General McIntosh was livid. The loss of the valuable supplies meant that he would be unable to mount a campaign anytime soon against the Indians of the Upper Sandusky, where he had planned to build a fort from which to launch his final attack upon Detroit. Unwittingly, his own men within Fort Laurens had ensured this would not happen by their outburst of indiscipline, a behavior McIntosh had constantly railed against since his appointment to the Western Department. The General could only shake his head in seething frustration at the situation he now faced. A spring campaign was all but impossible until a new relief party could bring additional supplies to Fort Laurens from Fort Pitt.

Undeterred by this most recent setback, McIntosh called his officers together at Fort Laurens to discuss the possibility of an attack on Sandusky, but found their sentiment strongly against his proposal. To a man, the officers objected to a spring campaign because the trails to the northwest were still too wet in March, there was no forage yet for the packhorses to feed upon, and the remaining provisions at Fort Laurens would only be able to feed everyone for less than two weeks. General McIntosh reluctantly agreed with their opposition, which appeared to him as plausible. As he prepared to set out for Fort Pitt with the returning relief column, McIntosh knew that his dream of taking British

Fort Detroit was over for good. In his heart, Lachlan McIntosh knew that he would never be back. [PT-p.65]

"I Will Do My Best However"

Many miles to the northwest at Fort Detroit, Captain Lernoult found himself mired in a series of unsolvable dilemmas that vexed him to no end. For one, he had not received word from either Governor Hamilton, Alexander McKee, Simon Girty or Captain Bird. The lack of critical information from those sources left him in the dark as what to do next at the isolated upper post. An early thaw had turned the unfinished fortifications into a morass of mud, making completion of the earthworks by the exhausted troops impossible. Provisions were dangerously low due to lack of resupply combined with the needs of hundreds of the settlement's inhabitants and the horde of Indians around the fort, none of whom would lift a finger to assist in the fort construction.

Too, "a great number of cattle furnished for Governor Hamilton's expedition" had left little source of fresh meat at the post, and Lernoult had just learned that some of the garrison's barrels of salt pork were spoiled. [HP-129] The Indians continued to press him to supply them with ammunition and food under the guise of attacking the Virginians, but with little to spare until a supply ship arrived from Niagara, Lernoult had to content them with waiting, just as he was forced to do. Lernoult detailed these circumstances in a letter written to Bolton at Niagara on March 24. Lernoult wanted to inform his senior commander of the situation at Detroit as well as to alleviate his own mounting personal anxiety. Two days later the bottom unexpectedly fell out for Lernoult, bringing him to the breaking point.

On the morning of March 26, Isidore Chesne, one of the French interpreters in the Indian Department arrived at Detroit with two Huron warriors from Post St. Vincent with the shocking news that George Rogers Clark and an army of Virginians had attacked Governor Hamilton and his force and defeated them, taking them all prisoner. Although Clark had released most of the French militia to return on parole to Detroit, Chesne had been lucky to escape the Virginians who were searching for any of Jehu Hay's Indian Department deputy agents as those men responsible for setting the Indians against the Kentucky settlements. Clark had brutally executed five pro-British warriors before the walls of Hamilton's fort, and sent messages to all the Indians and the Frenchmen at Detroit to remain neutral in Clark's soon-to-come attack on Detroit, or face similar consequences.

Lernoult listened in stunned silence as Chesne read Clark's defiant letter written to the commander of Detroit and his officers who were present. Clark complimented Lernoult on his new fort which Clark said would soon suit him and his men, once they attacked Detroit and took possession of the post. [WGA-p.76] By all indications, Lernoult reasoned that Clark's attack on Detroit was sure to come within the next few weeks, and no help could be expected from any of the other posts of the Great Lakes to face this new grave danger. Knowing that the word of Hamilton's defeat and capture would soon become known to all the Frenchmen and Indians at Detroit whose loyalty to the British cause would be questionable once they realized Clark's intention of attacking Detroit, Lernoult finally excused himself from Chesne, the Hurons, and his staff after several hours of discussion. He wanted to retire to his quarters to rest, think things over, and plan a course of action.

Once alone, Lernoult was overcome with despair. His thoughts first turned to his mentor and personal friend, Governor Hamilton, who was now a prisoner with the Rebels. Lost, along with Hamilton, were all the men with Jehu Hay of the Indian Department who were responsible for the allegiance and care of the Indians. Lernoult had no one at this critical moment who could replace them just when they were needed the most to encourage the Lake tribes and the Ohio Country Indians to remain steadfast to the British cause. With the French poised to defect to the Americans when Clark attacked, and with no reinforcements from the upper posts expected any time soon, everything suddenly seemed to Lernoult to be falling apart at Detroit.

Lernoult did not know where to begin to address his dire situation as officer in command. At the moment he could not think clearly. Lernoult was accustomed to following orders, not giving them, or for that matter of fact, creating them. In the face of the multitude of problems confronting him from all sides, Lernoult did not know what to do. His thoughts drifted to the unfinished fort. Not even the gate had been raised as yet to enclose the new fortifications still under construction. How would he defend a fort without a gate against Clark, Lernoult asked himself. No answer was forthcoming from the silence of his quarters. Distressed, an outburst of emotion overwhelmed the British officer. Lernoult put his head down on the writing table where he sat, and began to weep.

In the morning of April 2, 1779, the British sloop "Felicity" arrived at Fort Erie from Detroit and a rider was immediately sent in haste via the post road to Fort Niagara, miles to the north with an important packet of mail for Lt. Col. Bolton, commander of the garrison. Bolton soon had Lernoult's letter in hand written on March 26, detailing the events which had transpired on the fateful day of Isidore Chesne's arrival at Detroit with news of Hamilton's defeat. Bolton was stunned at the developments, knowing that General Haldimand, now at Quebec, was unaware of this startling news. Bolton read and re-read a particular passage of Lernoult's letter that was as disturbing to him. "The loss of Governor Hamilton is a most feeling one to me," Lernoult wrote, "I find the burden heavy without assistance. It requires, I confess, superior abilities and a better constitution. I will do my best however." [HP-76]

"That a Strong Reinforcement May Be Sent"

Bolton wondered if Lernoult was capable of doing his best. He was alarmed at the junior officer's personal remarks which signaled to Bolton Lernoult's inability to handle the situation at Detroit. Clearly, Lernoult was coming apart under the weight of the crisis and needed help. Bolton wasted no time in writing a dispatch to General Haldimand on April 2, filling him in on the recent developments in the west. He included a copy of Lernoult's letter of March 26. "I have received an express from Captain Lernoult by the "Felicity," a copy of his letter I beg leave to lay before Your Excellency." [HP-76]

Bolton hoped that General Haldimand would see for himself the state of mind of Detroit's commander and decide what needed to be done about Lernoult. As far as the military crisis at Detroit, Bolton could see that quick action on his part was needed to avert the disaster of Detroit falling into Clark's hands. Bolton was not about to waste precious time requesting permission from his Commander in Chief when he knew positively what he could do to alleviate the situation in the short term. However, time was of the essence, and Bolton knew he needed to act at once.

Appending his thoughts to General Haldimand on Lernoult's letter, Bolton wrote, "As the Service absolutely requires an immediate reinforcement be sent to Detroit, I have ordered 100 men from this Garrison with officers in proportion, 50 from the King's (Eighth) and the same number of the best men from the Rangers which I hope Your Excellency will approve of." In regards to the condition of Fort Niagara, Bolton added, "this Fort is equally in a ruinous state," recommending to Haldimand that "I therefore hope…that a strong reinforcement may be sent at the same time, otherwise, I am afraid, the Indians will be obliged to observe at least a neutrality." [HP-129] Bolton sealed the letter and within the hour, the post was on its way to Quebec. Then turning his attention to the reinforcements for Detroit, Bolton issued orders to Major Butler of the Ranger Corps and the subordinate officers of the King's Eighth to prepare the necessary men and supplies destined to leave as soon as possible for the upper post of Fort Erie, where the sloop "Angelica" was preparing for departure to Detroit in a few days. With this done, Lt. Col. Bolton was satisfied that he had done all that he could. He thought again of Lernoult's comments, and sincerely hoped that the man would be able to pull himself together, if not for the sake of his duty to British Detroit, then for the sake of his own honor and reputation which were now equally at stake as well.

"My Anxiety for the Safety of Niagara and Detroit"

Frederick Haldimand was disturbed and he did not know why. As the General in command at Quebec of all British forces in Canada, he had not yet received correspondence from his officers at the upper posts in the west indicating any disturbing developments with the Rebels that should give him cause to be worried. Yet he could not shake a nagging doubt over the last several weeks that something was wrong, or something had happened that should give him concern. A thorough man who prided himself on making decisions based upon knowledge and evidence, it was not like him to worry needlessly when he could find no reasonable cause.

Finally giving in to the thought that had been stewing in his mind for some time, Haldimand sat down with Captain Matthews and dictated a letter to his personal aide-de-camp, Captain Brehm on April 8, formulating in words the exact action he wished to take to privately satisfy his mounting feeling of foreboding, while fulfilling his need to know more about the conditions of the far-flung British posts to the west which he could not personally visit. Captain Brehm was a man Haldimand could trust. Brehm would find the facts for Haldimand, in spite of his confidence that the officers commanding those posts were, in fact, doing a good job. Brehm would be detached from it all. He had a knack for seeing those things which officers living there might be apt to miss.

Haldimand explained in his letter to Brehm the nature of his orders. "As it is necessary, I should be exactly informed of the actual state of the Posts we occupy, from La Chine to Detroit, I have judged it right to Dispatch You thither, that you may Examine them upon the spot with the most Critical Attention, as well as with Regard to their Fortifications, as to all that may Contribute towards their future Success." Haldimand added the details of how he wished Brehm to communicate with him, and then closed his orders, "Wishing You a prosperous Journey, and a speedy Return." [HP-60]

Haldimand next wrote to the officers in command of each of the posts that Brehm would visit in the upcoming weeks, informing them of the nature of Brehm's visit and fact-finding mission. Haldimand did not want his commanders to feel that he had lost confidence in their ability to command and that he was sending Brehm to spy on them. To that end, Haldimand knew that he would need to write them in advance of Brehm's arrival, to assuage any doubts on their minds as to his motives. Diplomacy with a pinch of flattery should suffice to quell any misgivings on their parts.

To Captain Lernoult at Detroit, Haldimand wrote, "It is happy for the King's Service, a Post of such importance as that of Detroit should be entrusted to so careful and diligent an officer." Haldimand paused for a moment, as he spied the slight grin that had crept across Captain Matthews' face. "I hope, I doubt not, that you will continue to exert your best endeavors for the security and preservation of that settlement." Haldimand continued to Lernoult, on the subject of Brehm. "Anxious to be exactly informed as soon as practicable, of the state of things in the Upper Country, I send Captain Brehm, my Aid-de-Camp, as far as Detroit, and it is my request, you would open yourself to Him with the utmost freedom, as to a Person in whom you may safely confide, upon all matters which concern the King's Service." If Lernoult had misunderstood Haldimand's directive to him, the General added officially, "Captain Brehm is directed to give you my orders respecting your Post." [HP-241]

In addition, Haldimand enclosed a sealed letter to Governor Hamilton, which he instructed Captain Lernoult to forward by courier from Detroit to the post at St. Vincent, once Lernoult received Haldimand's packet. To his old friend, Henry Hamilton, Haldimand could speak plainly. "Long before this reaches you, you will have been satisfied whether the Rebels seriously intended an attack upon Detroit and acted in consequence, or seen what further could be done for the King's Service in those parts, with the force at present with you." Haldimand thought it necessary to reveal to Hamilton his greatest concern. "My Anxiety for the safety of Niagara and Detroit has induced me to send there Captain Brehm, my Aid-de-Camp, who has my directions to consult Captain Lernoult, and forward you from thence, an exact view of the state of things in those parts, his opinion upon the further measures most proper to be taken by you." [HP-216]

"To Do Their Duty as He Knew They Would"

Captain William Caldwell picked up his musket and full knapsack and strode across the parade grounds in front of the log buildings of the new Ranger barracks. The previous autumn of 1778, Major John Butler had the men construct the new quarters on the west side of the Niagara River opposite Fort Niagara [CE-p.58]. Awaiting Caldwell was a double file of 50 Rangers in full battle gear, ready to march. In Caldwell's left hand were the orders from Major John Butler to assemble at once 50 of the best Rangers of the Corps and make ready to leave for Detroit to reinforce the garrison there and prevent George Rogers Clark and his Rebel army from taking that post. [WM-p.9] Caldwell halted in front of the Ranger Company and called out the roll of the troops from the list of scrawled names that he and Major Butler had agreed upon. Finding that all the men were present, Caldwell ordered the Rangers to shoulder their firelocks as Major Butler approached from his quarters in the barracks to speak to them.

Major John Butler was a man of few words. He told the fully armed and provisioned green-coated Rangers of his own Corps that all eyes in Canada would be upon them to fulfill their duty to destroy the Rebels at all costs before Detroit could be attacked and captured. He reminded them that, although a company of 50 men of the King's Eighth Regiment would accompany them as a complement of the reinforcements promised by Lt. Colonel Bolton for Detroit, he had no illusions that it would be up to the Rangers, themselves, without the help of the Indians, French, or Regular troops at Detroit to defeat the Rebels if they should attack, and thus avert the disastrous fall of the western posts and Canada itself. Nothing less than success would suffice, since the critical moment at Detroit was now at hand. It would be up to the Rangers to do their duty, as he knew they would. Without another word he saluted his men and then turning to Caldwell, bade him farewell. Within minutes, the Ranger Company with Caldwell in the lead, set out on the march up the river road to Fort Erie at the head of the Niagara River on Lake Erie, where the garrison company of the King's Eighth was awaiting their arrival, to depart on the sloop "Angelica" for Detroit, planned for April 15. The race to beat George Rogers Clark to Detroit was now on and the fate of the west of Canada was hanging in the balance. [HP-77]

"While It is Still Ripe for the Taking"

At Vincennes, George Rogers Clark found himself again pacing the floor of his crude officer barracks in Fort Sackville. What was troubling him at the moment was what had troubled him since he took Vincennes from Hamilton and the British in late February. Now it was early April and he still had not set out for Detroit as he had promised the Indians he would, and as he had told himself he must do. However, circumstances beyond his control were forcing him to delay and waiting was something that Clark found especially difficult to do.

Clark appraised his situation again and took count of all the factors involved in his decision to remain at Vincennes. His army of Virginians amounted to few more than 100 men, not nearly enough to attack Fort Detroit, with its sizable garrison, despite the capture of 25 regulars with Hamilton. True, he had succeeded in convincing the Indian tribes of the Wabash to give up their alliance to the British, but Clark was not foolish enough to underestimate the Indians. He reminded himself that the savages were the same ones that raided into Kentucky, causing havoc with the settlers there, and that the best that he could expect from them was that they would remain neutral when he attacked Detroit. Clark reasoned, too, that the closer he got to Detroit and the British, the more that he could expect to encounter Lake Indian tribes who would still be allied to the British cause, and likely give him trouble. Knowing the situation of the Indians, he needed reinforcements to attack Detroit, and as yet he had not received word from Virginia or Kentucky of any men forthcoming. Also, the men with him now at Vincennes were homesick after so many months in the Illinois Country and it would be difficult to convince them to set out on a new campaign without the infusion of considerable reinforcements to Vincennes.

Another problem bothered Clark to no end. He and his small army were nearly out of ammunition and provisions. His men had eaten nearly all of the food that they had captured from Hamilton over the winter. The difficulty was that supplies had to be transported a great distance from Kentucky and Virginia to reach him, and little had found its way to him on the Wabash. Considerable effort was needed to ferry such a huge amount of food and supplies for a large army by boat and packhorse to Vincennes. Even if reinforcements arrived soon, there was little forage to sustain packhorses, adding further delay in setting out for Detroit.

George Rogers Clark gazed out the small window of the barracks room to the trees he could see in the distance over the fort wall. Clark knew that he had the will and the initiative to march on Detroit. Unfortunately, he had neither the men nor the provisions to do so, and as far as he could tell from his scouts on the trails to the southeast towards the Ohio River, none were forthcoming in the near future from Virginia. Clark kicked the toe of his boot against the wall and continued to pace. How could Washington and the Virginia Legislature in the east not see the importance of sending him the men and supplies to take Fort Detroit, the western gateway to Canada, while it was still ripe for the taking? [WGA-p.89]

"Dissuade the Senecas and Mingoes"

At Fort Pitt, the American Continental and militia army was in a much better position to advance on Detroit than was Clark at Vincennes. More troops, ammunition, provisions and packhorses were at the disposal of General McIntosh to send forward to Forts McIntosh and Laurens than during the previous lean months. In addition the trails that an army would need to follow opened up in late April to the Upper Sandusky Indian villages and further on to Detroit, much sooner than McIntosh had envisioned. There was only one major stumbling block. General Lachlan McIntosh was no longer in command of the troops of the Western Department, for in late March, upon his return to Fort Pitt from resupplying Fort Laurens, McIntosh forwarded his resignation to General Washington who accepted it, and by early April 1779, had appointed Colonel Daniel Brodhead to fill McIntosh's position at Fort Pitt. [PT-69]

Colonel Brodhead, who had served under McIntosh, was at odds with his former commander over the question of Fort Laurens. After receiving Washington's orders to take command, Brodhead wrote to Washington on April 17 detailing the difficulties of maintaining the far-flung post on the Tuscarawas River, which was under constant harassment from the Indians and most troublesome to re-supply due to the attacks on the relief columns sent by land. Brodhead advised Washington that "Fort Laurens and other smaller posts were merely symbolic" as they could provide no real security for the settlers on the frontier from Indian attacks. Brodhead suggested that Fort Laurens be abandoned at the first possible moment, and another, more favorable route, be found to attack Detroit. [PT-pp.69-70]

Washington was in agreement with Brodhead in theory to abandon Ft. Laurens but told him he did not want it evacuated at the moment. Washington revealed to Brodhead that a major campaign to invade the lands of the Iroquois Six Nations who supported the British was planned for the summer, aimed at destroying their villages on a large scale, possibly culminating in an attack on Fort Niagara. For that purpose, Washington was going to send two armies under Generals Sullivan and Clinton to attack the Seneca lands in particular, by way of the Mohawk and Susquehanna Rivers. Washington planned to order Brodhead to march north following the Allegheny River with as many men as possible from Fort Pitt to "dissuade the Senecas and Mingoes on the branches of the Allegheny from aiding the Iroquois." Brodhead's diversionary force would serve to dissuade those Indians from joining the bulk of the Iroquois who would be fighting Sullivan and Clinton coming from the east. Key to Washington's strategy was to keep the British and Indians of the Ohio Country occupied with the presence of Brodhead's able Colonel Gibson and his troops at Fort Laurens, deceiving them into believing that Fort Laurens would still be the staging area for a strike against Detroit, when in fact, Washington would have Ft. Laurens abandoned at the last moment and the troops there join Brodhead in his campaign to the north. For the moment, Fort Laurens would have to be garrisoned, and Brodhead would have to keep Washington's plans a secret. [PT-pp.72-73]

"Our Friends Were All Elated"

On the morning of May 7, the British sloop "Angelica" glided through the morning mist on the Detroit River and into view of the British sentries on the parapets of Fort Lernoult, who sounded the alert. Since leaving on April 15, the voyage from Fort Erie had been tumultuous for the men and crew aboard, as several late spring storms beset the ship enroute. As the crew eased the sloop to its mooring, a horde of Indians camping nearby accompanied by French men, women, and children and a smattering of off-duty British troops from the Detroit garrison gathered at the wharf to watch with great curiosity the arrival of the first British ship from the east in many days.

Suddenly a cheer arose from the British in the crowd as Captain Caldwell and his company of Rangers from Niagara smartly marched in single file down the gangplank, followed closely by the men of the King's Eighth Regiment. The applause of the British citizens at Detroit followed the Rangers all the way to the garrison barracks, as more and more soldiers and staff within Fort Lernoult and from the old garrison quarters joined the procession of the new soldiers arriving at Detroit. Everyone except those disaffected Frenchmen who had privately wished and waited for the arrival of Clark and his American army, was elated with the reinforcements, provisions, and stocks of goods that had finally arrived at Detroit. Captain Parke wrote to Colonel Bolton at Detroit, "the arrival of the Detachment changed the face of Affairs. Our friends were all elated, and others as much Depressed." [HP-77]

Captain Lernoult lay prostrate on his bed in his quarters, stricken with the Gout and unable to meet the arrival of the "Angelica." In his place, Captain Parke greeted the reinforcements and briefed Captain Caldwell of the Rangers and the officer of the company of the King's Eighth on the state of affairs at Detroit. Within a matter of days, the combined British garrison was hard at work with renewed vigor, putting the finishing touches on the fortifications of Fort Lernoult, which included raising the structure of the gate and securing it to the framework of the log walls along the parapets on each side.

"Detroit "Would Never Fall"

At the same time, Captain Caldwell met with the Huron and Ottawa headmen camped about Detroit, and reassured them of the King's desire to secure Detroit, the Ohio Country and all the Indian dwelling lands from incursion by the Rebels. While promising them that additional British reinforcement with provisions and ammunition would soon arrive at Detroit, he asked them to reinstill in their warriors the spirit to fight with him when Clark and his Rebel army attacked. Caldwell did not cajole them. That was not his style. The hardened Ranger Captain, who was Major Butler's second in command in the field, left the Indians with no doubt that he would lead the Rangers in the forefront of the fighting. Caldwell gave his word to the chiefs that Clark would be soundly defeated when he came to Detroit. He told them that the Rangers were undefeated on the field of battle against the Rebels in the east, and Caldwell would see to it that the Rebels were destroyed here too, with plenty of Rebel scalps and booty to go around for every warrior who helped him.

True to his word, Captain William Caldwell made plans for the coming battle. First, he determined to take the military initiative to meet the enemy on ground of his own choice, and not wait for Clark behind fort walls. He would not make the same mistake that Hamilton had unfortunately made which was to think that staying behind fort walls was protection enough from the enemy. In Caldwell's estimation, the only true protection was to take offensive action, hitting the enemy first and hard, and not letting up until that enemy was defeated and destroyed. Soon small Ranger scouting parties were in the field along every trail leading to Detroit from the Wabash River and the Illinois Country. Caldwell sent his men further and further to the south, to seek out and spy upon the Rebels.

Caldwell wanted to know everything there was to know about Clark and his army, from the number of men under arms, to the time and direction of the Rebel advance. At the same time, Caldwell instructed his parties to look for ambush sites along the trails and the fords of streams from where they could harass the advancing Rebels and wear them down, create havoc with their rearguard, cut off their supplies, and then cut them up piecemeal when the time was right. On thing William Caldwell was sure of now that he had Rangers in the field: he would gain the initiative over Clark and never give it up. In Caldwell's mind, Detroit would never fall. [HP-77]

Word finally reached General Frederick Haldimand at headquarters in Quebec of the capture of Governor Hamilton and his garrison at the post of St. Vincent on the Wabash River. While shocked at the startling news, Haldimand was not altogether stunned. His nagging intuition that something had gone wrong in the field had been entirely correct. The staff at headquarters was abuzz with speculation concerning the latest developments in the west. However Haldimand's outward quiet, calculating demeanor reflected his inner unshakable composure, an attribute of his character that allowed him to assess the changing military situation from a detached perspective, devoid of emotional coloring. In the case of what Haldimand interpreted from Bolton's express mail, Haldimand had good reason to be confident that, although Hamilton and his garrison were lost to Clark, Bolton had correctly evaluated Lernoult's situation at Detroit, and made the right decision in sending immediate reinforcements to Detroit, rather than wasting precious time requesting orders from Quebec.

"I Flatter Myself that there are Orders to Go"

In Bolton, Haldimand had a fine, capable officer in charge of the post at Niagara who could act on his own initiative when the situation called for it. Looking over the roster of available troops in Canada, General Haldimand ordered the closest companies of the 47th Regiment of Foot under Captain Aubrey to proceed to Niagara at the first possible moment to reinforce the garrison there. If Bolton thought they were needed at Detroit, Haldimand was sure that he would know what to do upon their arrival, based on the fresh intelligence from the officers in the field. As to the matter of the Captain Lernoult's ability to command the garrison at Detroit, Haldimand was not so sure that any action need be taken at the moment to replace Lernoult. Always one to err on the side of caution, Haldimand knew that Lernoult would have a better grasp of who the various chiefs and Frenchmen at Detroit were, more so, than any immediate replacement. With reinforcements on the way, and Captain Brehm soon to arrive to personally assess Detroit for Haldimand, the best course of action was to wait, and allow Lernoult the opportunity to redeem himself, if in fact the officer had lapsed momentarily from the intense pressure.

With that in mind, Haldimand picked up the recently arrived letter on his desk from Major Arent DePeyster, the commander at the western post of Michilimackinac, who had written on May 2, requesting appointment as senior officer over Lernoult, to take command of Detroit now that Hamilton was gone. "I flatter myself that there are orders for me to go and take the command there, for which purpose I hold myself ready at a moment's notice," DePeyster wrote. [HP-117] Haldimand would wait, and DePeyster would have to stay at Michilimackinac for the time being.

"To Observe the Motions of the Enemy"

Not too far to the north of Pittsburgh, on one of the tributaries of the Allegheny River, Lieutenant John Dockstader of Major Butler's Indian Department out of Fort Niagara received word from one of his Seneca scouts on an early mid-April morning that a company of Rebel militia were headed up the trail towards Dockstader's hidden camp, no more than five miles away. Quickly the Indian Dept. officer issued orders to his subordinate officers to call in all scouting parties as quickly as possible and urged the more than 100 warriors to prepare to ambush the Rebels at the spot Dockstader had picked several days ago for just that purpose. Within an hour his entire force lay hidden and waiting on both sides of the trail.

As the sizable militia contingent from Fort Pitt came into view and followed the trail into the ambush Indians, one of the chiefs with Dockstader gave a high-pitched war whoop signaling the ambush to be sprung. Most of the lead men of the militia were felled by the sudden volley into their flanks and fell where they were hit, while the rearguard of the Rebels panicked in fear, barely firing one volley from their own muskets before fleeing in haste at the sound of the Indian war whoops and screams of the wounded. Within minutes the encounter was over, and although Dockstader was himself lightly wounded in three places, he was able to count with satisfaction 21 of the Enemy killed, and nine taken prisoner, with the loss of only one warrior killed and three wounded. [HP-77]

Dockstader had the terrified prisoners brought to him for interrogation. While the Seneca warriors near them methodically plundered, stripped, butchered and scalped the dead comrades of the captured militiamen until they were no longer recognizable as human, Dockstader questioned his captives about the conditions at Fort Pitt to pass any relevant information to Butler at Fort Niagara before the warriors sought revenge upon the unfortunate men for the loss of one of the own people.

True to his orders from Major Butler, Dockstader was keeping the pressure on the Rebels about Fort Pitt, while "observing the motions of the Enemy... and to send the earliest intelligence," to Fort Niagara.[CE-p.61] Little did the Indian Dept. officer know that his offensive actions of the past few weeks had eliminated any remaining doubt in the mind of the new commander at Fort Pitt, General Brodhead, that a punitive expedition against the hostile Indian villages to the north of Fort Pitt was more important in securing the frontier from Indian raids than marching on Detroit, as his predecessor, McIntosh, had advised. In Brodhead's mind, Fort Laurens must be abandoned as soon as possible to support the coming campaign to the north.

"Grasshoppers to Fire Round Shot or Ball"

Simon Girty, his brother James, Matthew Elliott and Alexander McKee were on the move in the Ohio Country, traveling to and from Shawnee and Mingo Indian villages along the tributaries of the Scioto River, mustering support for the coming spring offensive to expel the Rebels from the Tuscarawas, and cut off their flow of supplies down the Ohio River destined for the Kentucky settlements and for George Rogers Clark and his army at Vincennes waiting to march on Detroit. McKee and Elliott traveled together, meeting primarily with the sub-tribes of the Shawnee. Runners from the tribes of the Illinois Country to the west had spread the word of Hamilton's defeat on the Wabash, which considerably cooled the sentiment of the Indians whom McKee and Elliott attempted to counsel to go to war.

Not only had Clark's victory had an effect upon the Shawnee, but the continued presence of the Americans at their fort on the Tuscarawas, combined with word of a new Virginian army assembling at Fort Pitt to march on Detroit had a disconcerting affect upon the Indians as a whole. Some chiefs spoke out against supporting the British around the Shawnee campfires where McKee and Elliott sat; advising their people to remain neutral and wait to see what the British King across the water would do, if anything. McKee recognized that the tribes living along the Wabash were under the influence of Clark, and while "they had determined to set still" and had counseled the Shawnee to do likewise, McKee was, nonetheless, determined to "reinvigorate the western war effort" for the British and gather enough warriors willing to support him to attack Fort Laurens in May, and with the help of the Girty brothers and their Mingo allies, eliminate the Rebels on the Tuscarawas once and for all. [NL-p.111]

To that end, both Girty and McKee had requested that Captain Bird, still at the Upper Sandusky villages, bring troops, supplies, and cannon, if available, to assist them in a concerted attack upon Fort Laurens. On the question of artillery, Major Butler at Fort Niagara had suggested to Lt. Col. Bolton that light cannon could be easily sent to Sandusky for use by Captain Bird against the Rebel's stockade forts in the Ohio Country and Kentucky, if he or General Haldimand agreed. Bolton wrote that Butler advised that two light three-pounder cannons called "grasshoppers" could be transported on the trails by using their portable gun carriages to fire either "round shot or ball", [HP-63] and that two men who were acquainted with their use sent along to operate them. Captain Bird was notified of the possibility. From his previous disappointing attack and siege on the Rebel fort, he knew that without artillery, he would not possess the means to overwhelm Fort Laurens, any more than St. Leger was able to take Fort Stanwix on the upper Mohawk River without artillery two years prior. Optimistic that he would be reinforced and supplied eventually with artillery, Captain Bird sent word by mid-May to both Alexander McKee and Simon Girty to prepare for a renewed campaign against Fort Laurens in the near future. However, Bird's plans for an offensive against the Rebel fort by early June was about to drastically change with a new, unexpected development in the Ohio Country. Unfortunately for McKee, Girty, Bird and their Indian allies, the Rebels were likewise on the move, and they were able to attack first.

"Able to Harass Bowman's Retreat Most of the Way"

Many people in the Kentucky settlements considered Colonel John Bowman of the militia to be downright foolhardy when he spread the word in the early spring of 1779 that he intended on raising an army of mounted men to cross the Ohio River and attack the Shawnee Indians in their own villages in an attempt to stop the Indian raids that promised to increase in intensity as the season progressed. Some of George Rogers Clark's men in Kentucky wanted Bowman to join Clark at Vincennes for an attack on Detroit. Other settlers attempted to dissuade him from leaving the settlements at all, for if his men were defeated and destroyed, Kentucky would be left defenseless to an Indian onslaught. Yet Colonel Bowman dismissed all contrary arguments in favor of his own plan, which he calculated that if he was lucky, held a good chance of success in destroying the Indians when and where they least expected it.

Bowman had good reason to believe that an attack could be successful. For one, he was able to muster a large number of mounted militiamen to join him at Harrodsburg in Kentucky. Two hundred and sixty-two men were prepared to cross the Ohio River in late May. And Bowman was no fool when it came to fighting Indians. Wisely, he had sent a handful of his best scouts ahead across the river to reconnoiter the Indian villages situated on the Little Miami River, particularly one Shawnee village named Chillicothe, to determine whether his army would be able to come close enough to attack the Indian village by surprise and utterly destroy it. As luck would have it, Bowman's scouts returned on the night of May 28 to his camp on the south side of the Ohio with encouraging news that they had not encountered any Indian war parties or scouts on the trail to Chillicothe, as it appeared that the bulk of the warriors from the village were away to the Scioto. Colonel Bowman took the news as a fortuitous sign, and gave orders for raiding party to prepare to leave in the morning.

True to his scout's information, Bowman and his army were able to travel all day on May 29 into the Ohio Indian country undetected by the Indians. Bowman took pains to pick a hidden camp for his sizable force within striking distance of Chillicothe, and yet far enough away that the smell and sound of his horses would not give his force away to the enemy. Before dawn on the next morning, Bowman's men saddled up and made their way up the trail to the Indian village, surrounding it for an attack at first light to destroy all the inhabitants. It was when Bowman gave the order for his men to attack, that things began to break down. [BC-p.71]

As startled Indian villagers raced from their log homes and began to flee at the sound of gunfire, some of Bowman's men broke their orderly ranks and forgot about pursuing the Indians in favor of searching for plunder. Some men broke off the attack to capture as many Indian horses for themselves as they could. Others dismounted and entered Indian cabins looking for valuables. In a matter of moments, Bowman's force had effectively disintegrated before his eyes, allowing a large number of villagers to escape while a few warriors put up a fight against the Kentuckians. In the end, Bowman counted nine of his men dead and several more wounded, with a roughly equal number of Indians slain. [NL-p.111] With the bulk of his men loaded down with plunder and eager to return to Kentucky as soon as possible, Bowman's plan of advancing upon the nearby Indian town of Piqua fell on the deaf ears of his men who could think of nothing but heading back. Reluctantly, Bowman had to satisfy himself with putting the rest of the village to the torch and absconding with over 180 Indian horses. However, he was soon to find that the raid had had little lasting impact on the Indians, who were far from devastated. On the same day, small parties of enraged Shawnee warriors caught up with the militiamen and were "able to harass Bowman's retreat most of the way back to the Ohio River," [NL-p.111] where his men crossed and quickly dispersed to their own homes. Luckily for them, the Shawnee did not follow.

Meanwhile, George Rogers Clark awaited the arrival of Colonel Bowman's reinforcements to join him at Vincennes for an expected campaign against Detroit in early July. Instead, only 30 men reached Clark after Bowman's raid on the Shawnee, and to his dismay, Clark learned of Bowman's diversion against the Indians, instead of fulfilling his promise to march the bulk of his 300 men to Vincennes. The 30 mounted militia that reached Clark hung their heads in shame as they described how the volunteers refused further service and disbanded once they reached the safety of Kentucky, taking their Indian horses and plunder with them, in spite of Bowman's plea to accompany him to Vincennes. [WGA-p.92] The unfortunate turn of events left no doubt in Clark's mind that he had any chance to mount an attack upon Detroit. Clark looked at the odds and shook his head. With only 350 men at Vincennes, he could not risk an advance without substantial reinforcements. Clark was dismayed at the lost opportunity to attack Detroit. He was bitter that he and his men had risked so much and suffered so greatly to take Vincennes, only to lose the initiative in the long run.

"All the Towns Were to be Attacked"

However, Bowman had no way of knowing that the news of his attack upon the Shawnee created more havoc among the tribes of the Ohio Country than his own men had been able to accomplish. Bowman's surprise attack on the Shawnee village of Chillicothe could not have come at a worse time for McKee, Girty, Elliott, and Captain Bird who were counseling with Shawnee, Mingo, Wyandot and Delaware warriors at Indian villages to the north and east, preparing them to revive their efforts to attack and eliminate the Virginians at Fort Laurens. Bird was at the Upper Sandusky villages on June 9 when word of the attack arrived by runner which immediately disrupted Bird's plans, just as he had doled out precious ammunition and provisions to the warriors.

The young Shawnee runner gave "an account of a party of the Rebels had attacked the Shawanese villages nearest the Grand River (Miami) and had drove all their horses off, that 50 Warriors fought manfully, killed 10 or 20 and repulsed the Rebels with only the loss of 4 of their own people killed, one of whom was a great Chief called Black Fish," whom the runner explained was the adopted father of the Virginian named Captain Boone. [HP-79] The throng of warriors was immediately thrown into pandemonium, and began to disperse for their own villages, as the runner added to his story that he thought "all the Towns were to be attacked." Through a white interpreter named McCarty, Bird attempted to reason with the chiefs and headmen but to no avail. They would not listen to his request to restrain the warriors from leaving Upper Sandusky. What was on every Shawnee's mind was his own home and family. Within an hour, Captain Bird found himself alone in the village with his handful of men from the King's Eighth, and a few elderly villagers who hurried about him, packing their possessions. [BD-243]

Disgusted with the impulsive behavior of the Indians, Captain Bird sat down and wrote a letter to Captain Lernoult at Detroit, informing the officer of the unfortunate turn of events that had suddenly enveloped him, upsetting his plans of attacking the Rebels on the Tuscarawas. "News flew that all the towns were to be attacked, and our little body separated in an Instant and past reassembling. Confusion still prevails. Many Indians are removing," Bird added. [HP-243] Bird was dejected. Two months of work in preparing what he modestly believed were upwards of 200 mixed warriors to attack Fort Laurens had been erased by the Rebel attack upon the Shawnee, and there was nothing he could do to prevent their leaving in their state of panic. When Simon Girty came into Bird's camp later in the day with his band of Mingo warriors, Bird and Girty conferred for an hour. Then Bird finished his letter to Lernoult, adding to it "Girty is flying about," before sending the note with two of his own men returning to Detroit who were ill with ague. [HP-243]

As an Ottawa warrior was about to leave in the morning for Niagara, Captain Bird thought it wise to write to Colonel Bolton there about what had happened at Upper Sandusky. Bird related the turn of events that disrupted his plans of a coordinated attack with McKee and Girty against the Rebels at Fort

Laurens. Bird told Bolton that there were several Delawares hanging about the village who were waiting to return to the Tuscarawas. Bird commented that their loyalty to the British cause was in question. These Delaware "make it dangerous traveling," Bird noted, declaring they were "either Rascals or Cowards, they tell me their Heads are down. You may depend upon it Sir that they have made Peace on a belt with the Rebels," Bird wrote, suspecting treachery on the parts of his so-called allies.

However, there was a bright note that Captain Bird detailed as well. "Not a man will turn out to war except a little band of Senecas called Mingoes consisting of 20 or 30, led absolutely by Girty." Bird had the utmost confidence in Girty's abilities. Bird related to Bolton the incident that occurred on his return march from the previous attack on Fort Laurens. "The Rebels offered 800 Dollars for Girty's scalp and five Delawares thinking he marched with me, waylaid us on the Road, Girty was a day forward of us. They did not attack us" implying that these Delaware were some of those friendly to the Rebels on the Tuscarawas. "Girty, I assure you Sir, is one of the most useful disinterested Friends in his Department," was Captain Henry Bird's assessment of the white man fighting with the Indians. [HP-78]

On June 12, Captain Bird wrote to Captain Lernoult again from "Upper St. Duski," telling the officer that "Courier after Courier arrives with accounts of the Rebels advancing to destroy the Savage Villages, now all their corn is planted." Bird was exasperated. Nothing had changed whatsoever with the Indians that would allow him to make any headway in convincing them to mount an attack against the Rebels at Fort Laurens rather than continue to disperse to protect their own villages from what they perceived to be further imminent attack by the Virginians from Kentucky. While angry, Bird was forced to concede that the Shawnee were frightened by the retaliatory raid from Kentucky and were not in any mood to leave their villages undefended to attack the Virginians elsewhere.

If the Rebels were able to strike unexpectedly deep into the Ohio Country, then no place for the moment was out of their reach. Bird had heard the reports from Indians coming in to his post that the Rebels were intent on destroying the Indian villages and their corn crops by raising small armies of armed men very quickly to take action. "I am credibly informed by various means, that the Rebels can raise, in that manner, 3000 or 4000 in a few days for such excursions," Bird wrote to Captain Lernoult. [HP-243] As Alexander McKee and Matthew Elliott had sent word to Bird that they would stay with the Shawnee at their villages on the Scioto, Bird decided to return to Detroit in a few days, once Simon Girty and the Mingoes left Upper Sandusky for the Ohio River.

Simon Girty told Bird that he had no intention of posting himself around Rebel Fort Laurens for the moment. Something more important was brewing. Girty had received word from the Indians that a packet of important papers had been hidden in a hollow tree near the settlement of Holliday's Cove on the Virginian side of the Ohio River several miles above Fort Henry. Those papers were from clandestine loyalists interested in passing information to the British at Fort Detroit on the movement of the Rebels. [BC-p.74] Girty was determined to find those important papers and bring them back to Detroit as soon as possible, for he knew if the Rebels became aware of these papers and seized them before he got there, the identities of those men still loyal to the King living near Fort Pitt would be exposed to the Rebels. Girty and a party of seven Mingoes left Bird's camp toward the end of June by following the trail that led to the Delaware village of Goschachgunk, and then directly east to the Ohio River.

"Had Certainly Been Killed by Them"

What Girty did not know was that a Delaware in the Upper Sandusky villages had gotten wind of Girty's intention, and had left by a different route to the preacher Heckewelder's home above Fort Laurens where he informed Heckewelder of Girty's mission. Heckewelder immediately sent a letter to Colonel Brodhead at Fort Pitt, written on June 29, telling the American commander "that Simon Girty, with eight Mingoes, is gone to the inhabitants (American settlements) to fetch a packet of letters out of a hollow tree, I understand, somewhere about Fort Pitt." [BC-p.72] Armed with this latest intelligence, Brodhead quickly dispatched two of his best scouts, Captain Samuel Brady and John Montour, to try to capture Girty and his party of Mingoes. In addition, Brodhead sent a letter directly to the friendly Delawares at the village of Goschachgunk on July 1 advising them to "seize Girty and his party should he return there, and they are to be brought to me." [BC-p.72] Brodhead made his orders to his scouts and the Delawares sound so simple, as if Simon Girty and his party of warriors were unarmed, and would give themselves up without a fight. In reality, nothing could have been farther from the truth.

Simon Girty was well aware of the Christian Delaware perfidy and prepared himself well. On his first trip east of the Tuscarawas to cross the Ohio River, Girty and the Mingoes successfully eluded detection by those parties of Americans and Delaware searching for him. He was able to retrieve the papers without incident, and re-crossed the Ohio and making his way westward along the trail to Goschachgunk. With them on the return trip was an unfortunate Virginian whom the Mingoes had taken prisoner on the east side of the Ohio who had unsuspectingly fallen into their grasp. Girty had interrogated the man at length to learn all that he could about the intention of the Rebels at Fort Pitt before turning him back over to the Mingoes. It was evident that the prisoner, a settler and not a soldier, possessed little information of value that might justify to Girty the necessity of attempting to bargain with the warriors to spare the man's life. Since the Mingoes owned the poor wretch, they had decided to burn him once they returned to their Mingo village at Upper Sandusky. There was nothing Girty could do about the condemned man's fate without insulting his companions.

On the trail to the Delaware villages, the unexpected happened. Rounding a turn in the path, Girty and the Mingoes met David Zeisberger, one of the Moravian missionaries to the Delawares and an associate of Heckewelder, who was "on his way from a small Moravian Indian village called Lictenau" after visiting Heckewelder. Zeisberger was accompanied by a bodyguard of a few Delaware Christian Indians led by a warrior named Caleb, a friend of Zeisberger's. Both parties were equally startled by the chance encounter, and squared off immediately to prepare to fight, until Girty and Zeisberger recognized each other. Clearly, the two men were antagonists. Girty knew that Zeisberger, like Heckewelder, was friendly to the American cause, and suspected the preacher of passing information on his movements to Brodhead at Fort Pitt.

In the few moments that Girty spoke to Zeisberger, he intimated to the preacher in no uncertain terms his hostility towards him. As Girty could not write, he did not record the conversation that ensued, nor did Zeisberger who could write, though he did inform Heckewelder of the meeting on the trail. Heckewelder immediately wrote to Brodhead of the chance meeting with Girty, noting, "Mr. Zeisberger, who had been here to see us, and who, on his way home, met with those fellows, had certainly been killed by them if not accidentally Caleb, and some more of the Delawares had met together." [BC-p.72] Perhaps what remained in Zeisberger's mind more than all else of his encounter with Girty was the smirk on Girty's face when he proposed to Zeisberger that if he truly was a man of God, he would exchange places with the prisoner of the Mingoes to save the poor wretch from burning. Stunned, Zeisberger had no answer to Girty's jibe. Warily, the two parties left in opposite directions, Zeisberger to the Delaware villages and Girty with his bundle of letters to Captain Lernoult at Detroit. [BC-p.77]

"The Absolute Necessity of an Indian Agent"

At Quebec, General Haldimand opened the letter from his Aid-de-Camp, Captain Brehm, with great interest. Haldimand had been waiting for Brehm's correspondence to arrive from Detroit for some time. Now, with the arrival of the dispatches from the western posts to Quebec on the morning of June 9, Haldimand was about to learn the details of what happened at Detroit since Hamilton was captured. Haldimand gave a nod of satisfaction at Brehm's attention to detail that sometimes bordered on fastidiousness as he read Brehm's opening remarks. Written at Detroit, May 28, 1779, Brehm wrote, "Sir, I arrived the 25th Instant in 34 hours from Fort Erie to the mouth of this River, and later in the night with a Boat to the Fort." [HP-64]

Soon Haldimand found himself immersed in Brehm's lengthy and accurate account of the events at Detroit. Haldimand learned from the latest intelligence at Captain Brehm's disposal the disposition of the five Rebel posts in the Ohio Country, the current condition of the new fort at Detroit, the furtive mood of the various Indians at the post, and the effect that the recent reinforcements had had on the local French populace. Quoting Lernoult, Brehm noted that "the arrival of the 200 men he was reinforced with has made a great alteration in the Inhabitants and even among some of the Indians, the former before that became insolent, and almost daring in their behavior," which Brehm concluded, had now changed for the better. [HP-64]

Of all the intelligence Brehm sent in his lengthy letter, most important in Haldimand's mind was whether Brehm had concluded that Captain Lernoult was capable of commanding Detroit. While the overall state of affairs at the post seemed by Brehm's comments to have stabilized with the arrival of reinforcements and the lack of any sign of the advance of Clark's army from the south, the condition of Haldimand's commanding officer at Detroit was not so promising, for a number of reasons that Brehm particularly wrote of. First, Brehm noted that "Captain Lernoult's constitution is materially weak, and is at present laid up with the Gout and not able to walk about" even though Brehm thought Lernoult to be a very able officer to command the post.

Secondly, Brehm noted a more serious problem for Lernoult, assessing that while the officer was "not Idle in Conducting the designs of the Hurons," Lernoult himself admitted to Captain Brehm "the Absolute Necessity of an Indian Agent being sent up" to Detroit as soon as possible. In Brehm's estimation, Lernoult clearly did not have the expertise to deal with the Indians at this critical moment when their allegiance to the British was in question. Rather, Brehm noted, Lernoult "thinks that all the Western Indians will be lost." [HP-64] With those comments, Haldimand put Brehm's letter down, digesting the information, before coming to the conclusion that had already been formulating in his mind. The time had come to find a new Deputy Agent for the Indian Department at Detroit to deal with the Indians there, as well as a new officer to command the garrison at Detroit. Never one to be caught unprepared, Haldimand had already considered the possibility for some time, and had had a man in mind for each position, if he needed to act, as was now the case.

"Now Uncles, We Once More Speak to You"

At Detroit, the hot humid weather of July brought with it a storm of new troubles for Captain Lernoult to deal with, in between his spells of agonizing gout which incapacitated him for days at a time. Captain Bird returned from the Upper Sandusky villages late in June with news that the Hurons and Shawnee there would not agree to set out against the Rebel fort on the Tuscarawas on any terms so long as the threat persisted of Virginian incursion against their villages. Simon Girty and his party of Mingoes arrived in a few days later with the packet of important loyalist letters from across the Ohio River and with new news that the Rebels at Fort Pitt under Brodhead appeared to be mobilizing for some sort of campaign against Detroit in the coming month. On July 3, Alexander McKee arrived to tell Lernoult that the "Shawnee, Delaware, and Sandusky Indians were so much frightened by the encroachment of the Rebels," that he doubted they would be able to resist much longer if Lernoult was unable to send troops to help them, which Lernoult explained to the Indian agent, was not possible with Detroit threatened by Clark. [HP-65] If that were not enough, to add to Lernoult's physical and mental discomfort was the daily, never-ending parade of Frenchmen and Indians bringing to him the rumors that George Rogers Clark's army at Vincennes was on the move to attack Detroit, though Captain Caldwell of the Rangers declared to Lernoult that he had no solid information from his reliable scouts to indicate so.

Captain Brehm felt compelled to stay on at Detroit to assist Lernoult in his time of need, writing to Haldimand that "Captain Lernoult seems desirous of me not quitting this Post, just now, as affairs here are very critical of what may be expected from being attacked or what can or will be proposed by him to defend during which I may then fully acquaint Your Excellency with." [HP-64] Lernoult's problems, for the moment, were more than just an expected attack from Clark, as Brehm saw it. Trouble seemed to be brewing everywhere. While Lernoult appointed a Frenchman from the Indian Department, a Mr. Baby, to assist in attempting to deal with the Hurons, both he and Brehm were uneasy about Jacques Baby's true allegiance and intentions, judging that he "keeps such company that he makes himself suspicious." [HP-64] Lernoult suspected Baby of a certain degree of duplicity, knowing that Baby was French first, and never trusted what the man said to the Indians in their own tongue that could serve other aims than that of the King's service.

Word arrived at Detroit from Major DePeyster, commander of the upper post at Michilimackinac, sent on July 6 to Lernoult that new intelligence was received at the post from French traders and Indians that "the Rebels were forming an Expedition against Detroit from the Illinois, composed of 700 men with 200 horses."[HP-83] On the heels of that express to Lernoult, word came to him that certain traders at Detroit, a William Boslick and James Cassidy, were conspiring to undermine his authority, advising Henrick Iago that "the Virginians would be at Detroit in a short time" and that they "would make a great deal of money by it." The allegations were made by "Iago, a recruit in Captain Caldwell's Company of Rangers," who gave sworn testimony before Lernoult and Captain Parke on July 20. [HP-246] Lernoult promptly sent a squad of men to Cassidy's house to arrest the two men.

Then, in early August, Lernoult received a secret letter sent from William Arundel at the Lower St. Duski village on the lake detailing a letter circulated among the Wyandots at the Upper villages by a visiting delegation of Delaware from Fort Pitt, who had met privately in council with the Wyandots and the Delawares still hostile to the Rebels, requesting them to desert the British and meet with them at Goschachgunk to council. These Delaware had recently returned from meeting with Congress in Philadelphia. Lernoult read the translated text of their speech, which Arundel had sent sealed to him, as he had heard it from the Delaware chief, the Half King. "Now Uncles, We once more speak to you to inform you, if you have a mind to take hold of the chain of Friendship, you must come without delay, we are still waiting for you, therefore when you hear this, get up and immediately run, if you do not embrace this opportunity, we cannot tell what will become of you, or what may happen to you, you know that trouble will come on you." [HP-247] Arundel noted to Lernoult that the Delaware named Half King wisely told the Delaware delegation that he needed time to think about the import of what they had said, so that his answer he would give to them would be to" send them (the messages) to the chiefs at Detroit, and what they thought fit to do" would be his response. Lernoult could see that the Half King was going to wait and see what the British would do, while putting the Delawares off for the moment, before committing to anything.

The overture of the Delaware delegation from the Tuscarawas to the Delaware and Wyandot of the Upper Sandusky villages angered Lernoult. As though he did not have enough troubles at Detroit, the minute that Captain Bird and his men turned their backs on the Indians there to go to Detroit, the Rebels, through their Christian Delaware friends, attempted to persuade the Indians there to desert the British. This would not have happened if Bird and his men had been present in the villages. Simon Girty had already counseled Lernoult on the danger posed by those Indians living on the Tuscarawas near the Rebel post. Lernoult believed, as did Girty, that the two Moravian missionaries, Zeisberger and Heckewelder living with the Christian Delaware were playing an active role in helping the Rebels divide and conquer the Indians of the Ohio Country. For the moment, Lernoult knew that there was nothing more that he could do. With daily rumors that Clark was moving against Detroit from the west and an army was assembling at Fort Pitt for an attack from the east, Lernoult could ill afford to send any further troops to the Ohio Country, weakening Detroit's position. All Lernoult was sure of was that he must sit and wait until an attack came, or the crisis somehow passed.

"I Mean As I Said Before, Fort Laurens Must Be Evacuated"

At Fort Pitt, General Brodhead reviewed his last minute preparations at the end of July for his long-awaited campaign against the hostile Seneca, Delaware, and Mingo Indians of the upper Allegheny River to the north in support of General Sullivan's major campaign already underway against the tribes of the Iroquois Confederacy allied to the British. While General Washington had written to Brodhead earlier on May 21 advising him that the time had come to abandon both Fort Laurens and Fort Randolph, Brodhead had delayed the issue of Fort Laurens through the month of June as part of his overall strategy to deceive the British at Fort Detroit as to the true intentions of the army he was assembling at Fort Pitt. [PT-p.76]

However, by July 1, Brodhead ordered Lt. Col. Richard Campbell with 75 men of the 13th Continental Regiment to set out for Fort Laurens to relieve the garrison there, and prepare to retrieve any valuable material that could be salvaged from the fort, vacating it only after the necessary horses were sent for a returning pack train. With a substantial number of packhorses and men reaching Fort Laurens within a couple of weeks after Campbell, Brodhead was surprised when no one returned to Fort Pitt. Irritated, General Brodhead wrote to Campbell on July 30, reiterating in no uncertain terms his intention that Campbell was to abandon Fort Laurens and return to Fort Pitt at the first possible moment to join the coming Allegheny expedition. "I mean as I said before," wrote Brodhead, "that Fort Laurens must be evacuated, and...the packhorses are not to be slaughtered." [PT-p.77] With the arrival of Brodhead's ultimatum, Campbell prepared the garrison to move out.

A few days later Brodhead received word from friendly Delawares that two war parties of hostile Mingoes had been spotted "moving from the Ohio in the direction of the Tuscarawas." Brodhead immediately sent a dispatch to Fort Laurens warning Campbell of the Indians, and advising him to intercept and destroy the war parties if possible. His letter arrived too late, and two soldiers were killed by the Indians "within sight of their comrades" as the men moved out of the fort towards the trail to Fort McIntosh. On August 2, Fort Laurens was finally abandoned, the garrison arriving at Fort Pitt on August 7. [PT-p.77]

On the morning of August 11, Brodhead, with his combined force of over 500 men, began his march northward along the Allegheny River to attack the hostile Indian villages as part of Washington's overall strategy to support General Sullivan. Days later, Mingo Indian warriors scouting Fort Laurens found the gates of the fort open and the interior empty. Soon they would be on their way to the Upper Sandusky villages with the startling news to be sent on to Detroit that the Americans at Fort Laurens had mysteriously gone back across the Ohio River.

"As I Wish to Discharge My Expenses"

Unaware of the recent developments on the Tuscarawas, Alexander McKee used his brief stay at Fort Detroit to meet with Captain Lernoult, and petition the officer for necessary provisions and ammunition that could be spared for the Shawnee on the Scioto. With Simon Girty present, the three discussed the possibility of another concerted attempt to rally the Indians of the Ohio Country to fight the Rebels on the Tuscarawas and the Kentucky settlements while the season still held out the possibility of good weather for sending war parties. The problem, as both McKee and Girty saw it, was that the Indians everywhere were still reluctant to fight, fearing further attacks from either Kentucky militia under Bowman or a surprise strike by Clark. McKee wrote on August 16 from Detroit that Hamilton's unfortunate fate had "not only discouraged many tribes well disposed, but inclined others who were wavering to stand neuter." [HP-245] What was needed, both McKee and Girty advised Lernoult, was for soldiers to be sent from Detroit "to act in conjunction with the Indians to engage them again to act with vigor against the Enemy." [HP-245] Lernoult informed the two men that such reinforcements were unfortunately not available. The two men would have to make do with what they had, for in spite of the dire situation facing the Indians, Detroit had to be defended at all costs, and not a man could be spared at the moment.

As McKee prepared his packhorses to leave for the Scioto, he had one last piece of business to take care of at Detroit. McKee sat down in the officers' quarters at Fort Lernoult and wrote a letter he had been meaning to write since joining the Shawnee on the Scioto. Dipping the quill in ink, McKee wrote to the one man he knew who was capable of hearing his petition and doing something about it. Dating it July 16, McKee began his letter to General Haldimand with, "Sir, upon my arrival at Detroit last year I did myself the Honor then to acquaint Your Excellency with the manner of my release from the Enemy." He then refreshed Haldimand's memory with the details of his Service to the Crown since that time. McKee paused for a moment and reflected upon his main reason for writing Haldimand, searching for the right words to come to the point of his letter and express to Haldimand in a modest manner his pressing need to secure for himself some sort of compensation.

Using the personal valuables that he had taken with him on his flight from Pittsburgh, McKee now found himself more than a year later nearly destitute, and without any means of securing payment for what he seen as his service among the Shawnee. Upon hearing that Guy Johnson had recently returned from New York to Fort Niagara to command the Indian Department, McKee, a former deputy agent in the Department thought it best to approach Haldimand first, knowing that Guy Johnson did not consider him (McKee) a friend in any sense of the word, and that he must secure for himself a paid position as agent to the Indians of the Ohio Country. "My affairs make it requisite for me to see him [Col. Johnson], which I have thought my Duty to acquaint Your Excellency of and I have to pray Your Excellency in what manner to draw my Salary, as I wish to discharge my Expenses in the Service I have been on." McKee thought it best not to press Haldimand with the personal details. It was enough for McKee to know that his own financial situation was more dire than Haldimand could imagine: neither the traders at Detroit nor the commissary on the post would extend McKee any more credit until overdue payments were made. [HP-245]

"This Detachment of Men Ordered Up to Go Against Detroit"

Meanwhile, at Fort Niagara, Lt. Col. Mason Bolton, commander of the post, poured over the steady stream of troubling reports arriving daily from Indian scouts and Rangers in the field from the Susquehanna River to the Mohawk Valley and west to Fort Pitt. It was apparent to him that something big was afoot among the Rebels who were massing an army of several thousand men under Rebel Generals Sullivan and Clinton in preparation for a campaign apparently designed to attack the Iroquois Six Nations in retaliation for their devastating raids along the entire Rebel frontier. Writing to Haldimand on August 11, "the Rebels certainly intend an expedition against the Six Nations, and are collecting a strong body of troops for that purpose." Bolton was beginning to feel the pressure from the Indians, as they increasingly realized that an attack by the Rebels into their own lands was imminent, and they petitioned Bolton at Niagara for assistance. "The Indians are a good deal alarmed," wrote Bolton to Haldimand," and are continually requesting a Reinforcement from this Garrison, when we have scarce men to carry on the works." Bolton, like Lernoult at Detroit, knew that there was little he could do for the moment with the men he had on hand. [HP-85] What puzzled Bolton more than anything else was the activity of the Rebels in the Ohio Country. Reports from scouts and interrogations of prisoners brought in by the Indians from that quarter indicated that General Brodhead at Fort Pitt was preparing to mount a campaign soon against Detroit. Apparently a large stock of cattle had been gathered by the Rebel army at Fort McIntosh, [HP-84] and a prisoner brought in on August 2, taken near Fort Ligonier to the east of Fort Pitt informed Bolton that "200 Rebels marched by that post on their way to Fort Pitt a considerable time ago, and were followed lately by 500 men with 25 wagons, …this detachment of men ordered up to go against Detroit." [HP-82]

What did not make sense to Bolton was that while the Rebel General Brodhead was assembling a sizable army at Fort Pitt, as yet he had made no attempt to strengthen the garrison of Fort Laurens and send men, cattle, provisions, and ammunition there for a campaign on Detroit so late in the season. Had not Brodhead learned the lessons of his predecessor McIntosh, when he needed to advance to the Tuscarawas by mid-summer if he was to attack Detroit? The interrogated prisoner brought in by the Indians had said that the men and wagons had passed Ligonier weeks before he was taken. Why had Bolton and Lernoult's scouts on the Ohio not spied these men and provisions on their way to Fort Laurens? Why had the stock of cattle been lost at Fort McIntosh and not sent with a vanguard to the Tuscarawas to graze on the lush fodder while Brodhead's army marched?

Something did not make sense to Bolton. He shuddered for a moment at the thought that if Brodhead was not marching on Detroit, then where was he, in fact, about to head with his army. Silently, Bolton answered his own question, as he deduced what was happening. With the bulk of his reinforcements already stationed at Detroit, Bolton realized that he had overlooked the possibility that Fort Niagara could be an inviting target to the Rebels. Brodhead, on Washington's orders, could feign an attack on Detroit in order to actually move his army north to attack Niagara from the west, while Sullivan attacked from the east. If that was the case, Bolton could only guess the predicament he soon found himself in, outmanned and outgunned as he was at Niagara.

"Destitute of Almost Every Necessary Requisite"

No one was more surprised to see George Girty alive than his own brother, Simon, who had long ago given him up for dead. The two men heartily embraced. They had not seen each other since February 12, 1778, when George was forced to enlist in Captain James Willing's company of marines of the Continental Army that left Pittsburgh by boat "on a predatory mission against the British planters" on the Mississippi River. [BC-pp.35,38] In the year and a half since the brothers had said goodbye, George Girty had completed an odyssey of tremendous proportions that had taken him to New Orleans as a prisoner of Willing's, and then back up the Mississippi River to the Illinois Country, where he escaped to the Spanish side of the river, only to be recaptured. Girty escaped again, and this time travelled across country to Detroit in the company of four British soldiers of the King's Eighth Regiment who had been taken prisoner with Hamilton, plus three Virginian deserters and Captain La Motte's fifer. George Girty and his party had set out from the Illinois Country "on the 19th of June," [HP-86] and, after enduring temporary captivity "by a party of Weatanon Indians under the influence of one Gamblier, a French trader," [BC-p.79] were able to successfully make their way to Detroit, arriving on August 8.

George Girty brought valuable information for Lernoult about George Rogers Clark and his army at Vincennes, which Captain Lernoult quickly passed on to Bolton at Niagara. Lernoult wrote, "the Rebels, he says, were preparing to carry on an expedition against Detroit; but that their credit was hurt by their <u>Bills</u> being returned protested from New Orleans." Apparently Clark had not been able to procure the necessary provisions and ammunition from Fort Pitt, Kentucky or Virginia, and his credit was worthless with the Spanish, forcing him to attempt to "purchase provisions and pack-horses with merchandise taken from Governor Hamilton." [HP-86] Further, Girty stated, "the number of Virginians that could be raised to come this way (to Detroit) from that quarter would not exceed 200, and perhaps 250 or 300 Canadians, the whole to make 500 men, destitute of almost every necessary requisite for such an undertaking."[HP-86]

In all, George Girty believed from what he had seen and heard that Clark would not be able to attack Detroit. This supported other intelligence Captain Caldwell of the Rangers had gathered in the preceding months. Detroit would not be attacked unless Clark was dramatically reinforced and supplied from either Kentucky or Virginia, which, by necessity and speed, would have to reach him by boat on the Ohio River. Control of that river was the key to cutting off Clark once and for all, Simon advised Lernoult. Without hesitation, Lernoult enlisted George Girty as an interpreter in the Indian Department at Detroit at the same pay as his two brothers and Matthew Elliott. Soon, the two Girtys were preparing to lead a string of pack-horses with provisions and ammunition destined for the warriors at Shawnee towns where they planned, along with McKee and Elliott, to make their headquarters at the Shawnee town of Wapatomika, at the headwaters of the Mad River to the south of the Upper Sandusky Indian towns.

"You Are to Deliver Up to Him the Command"

At Quebec, Haldimand perused the pile of letters before him on his writing desk from his officers in the field. While the reports from Col. Bolton at Niagara detailing the movements of the Rebels towards the lands of the Iroquois Six Nations were the most troubling, Haldimand realized the necessity of taking action to resolve the situation at Detroit to be the most pressing. Having taken several weeks to reach conclusions, the General picked up his quill and issued a series of orders to the officers of the western posts. The changes Haldimand were instituting would best serve his ability to command those posts in the months and years to come until the Rebellion was successfully ended and Canada no longer at risk from invasion by the Americans.

Haldimand wrote on July 3 to Major DePeyster of the King's Eighth Regiment in command of the post at Michilimackinac, "it is with pleasure I acquaint you that I have now a prospect of having it in my power to comply with your request…to be removed from Michilimackinac."[HP-119] With the arrival of Captain Sinclair, Haldimand immediately sent him with orders to take command of that post as Lieutenant Governor and Superintendent. [HP-120] General Haldimand then ordered Major Arent DePeyster on August 29 "to repair to Detroit without loss of time and take upon you the Command of that Post, Captain Lernoult having my orders to give it up to you" [HP-120] adding to DePeyster in a note written on the 30, "from Captain Lernoult you will receive my instructions and every information relative to the inspection and management…of the different departments under your command at Detroit."[HP-120] All that was left for Haldimand to do concerning the changes at Detroit was for him to write Captain Lernoult, first on July 29 with a copy of his most recent orders, and then on July 30, with the details of the transition. Sparing the officer a lengthy explanation, Haldimand told Lernoult, "upon Major DePeyster's arrival at Detroit you are to deliver up to him the Command of that Post, and after having made him fully acquainted with every particular relative to the command of it, the management of the settlement and Indian resorting to it, you will repair, without loss of time to Niagara." [HP-248] With the business of Detroit completed, Haldimand was ready to put his writing quill aside, when he remembered that he had one last affair to conduct with the Indian Department at Detroit before he could turn his attention to discerning what the Rebels were up to, east of Fort Niagara. Reports reaching him from Bolton at Niagara and Joseph Brant near the Mohawk Valley indicated that two large armies were assembling for some sort of campaign against the Indian country, one Rebel army of more than 2000 under General Clinton gathering in the Mohawk Valley and another, much larger, moving up the Susquehanna River from the deserted Wyoming Valley of Pennsylvania. [KI-p.254]

Sorting through the pile of letters on his writing desk, Haldimand found the petition of Alexander McKee that he had not, as yet, made any determination on. Writing to McKee directly, Haldimand not only granted him back pay in the Indian Department, but appointed McKee "to the post of deputy agent to replace Jehu Hay" at Fort Detroit. Going forward, Alexander McKee would be known as an officer in the Indian Department at Detroit, holding the rank of Captain, who could give orders to the growing list of white men paid by the Department such as the three Girty brothers, Matthew Elliott, McKee's cousin Robert Surphlit, and many others.

"Remained With Us to the Last"

Joseph Brant was worried. The choice for the site of the ambush of the approaching combined Rebel armies of Sullivan and Clinton did not suit him well, nor that of Major John Butler. There was little room to maneuver on the wooded hillside and if anything went wrong when the ambush was sprung, the steep flanks on the left of the ridge that faced the enemy would not allow Brant room to move his men. John Butler commanded his own Rangers, a small detachment of the King's Eighth Regiment, and all the members of the Indian Department that had arrived from Fort Niagara. Together with Brant's own Volunteers and a mixed force of Iroquois and Delaware warriors, Brant and Butler could only count about 600 men to oppose an army of over 5,000 seasoned American troops with artillery approaching up the Chemung River towards the Delaware village called Newtown on the morning of August 29. Of Brant and Butler's force, only 180 were white men, and almost half of Butler's own Rangers were hungry and sick, having had little to eat in the past week and a half, foraging in the woods with little success. Both Brant and Butler wanted to fall back farther into Seneca lands, pick a defensively better position and send out parties to harass the Rebels while they were on the march, after giving their men a chance to recover their strength. [KI-p.259]

However, both Brant and Butler had been overruled by the Delawares and the Seneca under their war chief Sayengaraghta, who deemed it their right to determine where to meet the Americans in battle. The Indian village at Newtown was one the Delawares held dear, and one which they did not want the Americans to destroy. Influencing their decision was the fact that the Seneca did not hold either Joseph Brant or John Butler in high esteem, Sayengaraghta resenting them both. Reluctantly Butler and Brant conceded to the Seneca and Delaware plan, deploying their men along the half-mile ridge overlooking the old Indian trail called the "Forbidden Path" which paralleled the Chemung River, a path the American army would have to use on their march. Some hastily constructed breastworks of logs were camouflaged with fresh cut branches to conceal firing positions as the loyalist and Indian force prepared to wait for the advancing Rebel army to enter the ambush. As they passed the time on the morning of August 29, many of the Indians and Rangers remembered their great success the year previous at the Wyoming Valley when the Rebel militia walked into a similar ambush and were cut to pieces.

General Sullivan, commander of the huge American army, was a capable and cautious soldier who refused to allow himself to be ambushed, and his troops were "not green militiamen, and were not reckless," but "disciplined and experienced Continental soldiers" who knew that the enemy was somewhere ahead in the wilderness of the Indian country, waiting to strike. [KI-p.261] Consequently, Sullivan sent out a screen of riflemen and scouts well ahead of his army on the march, learning from all the mistakes of previous ambushed armies in the wilderness, such as Braddock's 25 years earlier on the Monongahela. An army needed expert intelligence on a hidden enemy a great

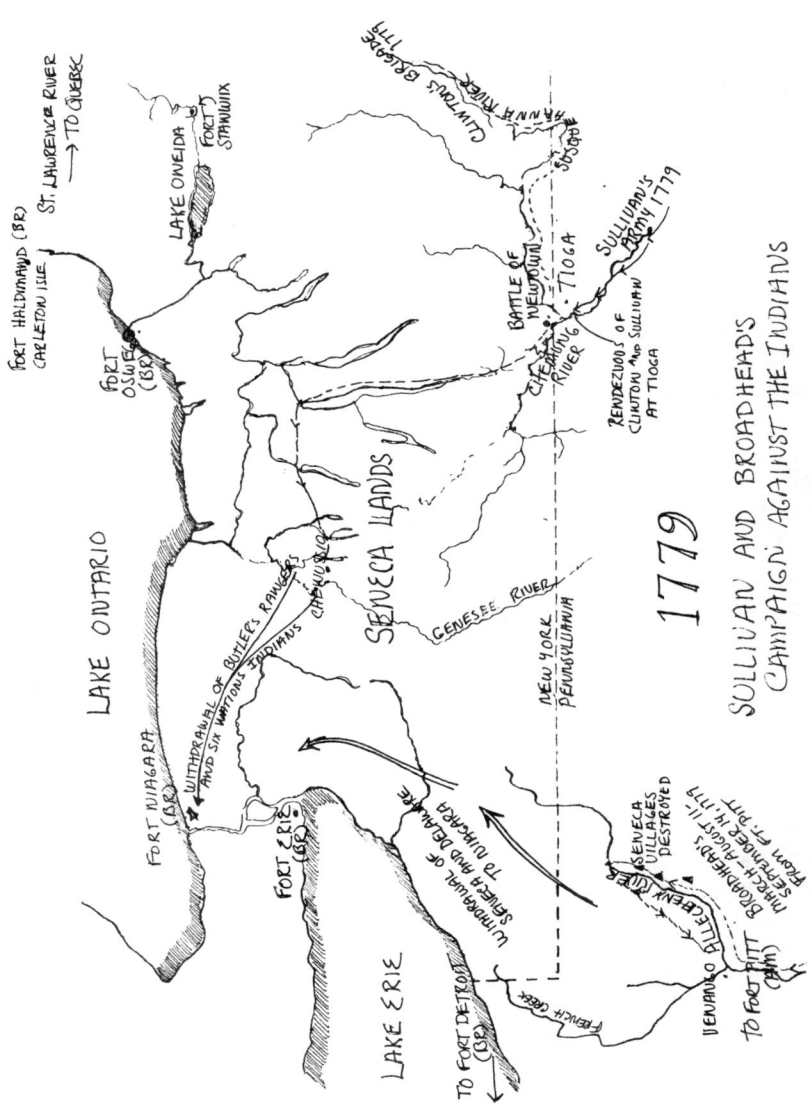

Map of 1779 American campaigns against the British-allied Indians.

distance ahead of the main body to allow the trailing army to deploy and meet any threat. It was the job of the advance party of scouting riflemen and two Oneida Indians to detect any potential ambushes ahead, and that is what happened when "one of the riflemen climbed a tree and glimpsed some brilliantly painted bodies, for it was hot and the warriors were almost naked" in the bushes on the ridge to the right of the trail. [KI-p.261] The patrol stopped and sent a runner immediately back to Sullivan's advancing vanguard under General Hand. At the sound of gunfire, Joseph Brant knew that the ambush had been spotted and the effort of the Indians to ambush the approaching Americans was thwarted.

At the news of an entrenched Indian and loyalist enemy ahead, General Sullivan had the artillery brought up and opened fire with solid shells and grapeshot on the ridge while his forward regiments opened fire from behind trees and the creek banks. Meanwhile, Sullivan sent a well-reinforced flanking force of 1,700 men through the woods on his right to attack the British and Indian left by surprise, while the cannon and Hand's brigade engaged the front of the enemy. On the hillside above the Americans now under a fierce cannonade from below, the bulk of the Indian warriors with Butler panicked and broke and fled the lines, and "ran away at full speed," thinking they were surrounded. [CE-p.72] It was then that it came to the attention of both Butler and Brant that a grave error had been committed by some Senecas and Delaware warriors in their earlier deployment on the left flank. "Some officious fellows among the Indians altered and turned the left wing along the mountain, quite the contrary way from its original situation," Butler wrote later, "which was in great measure the cause of our defeat, as it gave the enemy room to outflank us on that wing without opposition." [CE-p.71]

Joseph Brant was watching the demoralizing effect of the American artillery on the Seneca when a runner came in from the far left of the ridge with the startling report that a strong force of Americans were advancing up the hill on Brant's far flank in an attempt to cut in behind the Indians and Rangers. This was what Butler and Brant had feared. In an instant, Joseph Brant realized that the cannonade of the ridge was a diversion and the badly outnumbered Indians and Rangers were in danger of being cut off and surrounded. With what Indians and Volunteers he could muster, Brant met the advancing Continentals near the hilltop on the flank, but could not stop them with the few numbers and sporadic fire from his own force. Quickly he sent word to Butler that he was falling back and urged the Rangers to do the same before they were overrun. John Butler did not need any convincing to retreat, as the cannonade had now stopped and rows upon rows of Continental troops were advancing up the hill to his front, in an attempt to join with the American force trying to cut off the escape route. Rallying his outnumbered, hungry and exhausted men, Butler's force fell back along the mountain to the rear with the victorious Americans in possession of the ridge.

Late in the evening and far upriver, John Butler counted his casualties: five Rangers dead or missing and three wounded. The Indians had suffered greater losses, though many had fled the field early in the battle. Butler wrote to Bolton the details of the affair, noting that "Joseph Brant's Conduct through the

Whole of this affair does him much honor, he with Kiangarachta and Several Other Chiefs and Indians remained with us to the last." [KI-p.262] However, it was not lost on Butler that with his most able Captain and the best Rangers of the Corps stationed at Detroit, the loss of the field at Newtown now left the road open for the Americans to enter and destroy the Seneca lands, and "the path was open before them all the way to Niagara if they had the ability to take it." Still, John Butler endeavored to rally his men and the dispirited Indians at the Seneca village of Canadasego, but more than "half of Butler's men were sick and absolutely unfit for duty" and the bulk of the Indians not interested in fighting. Butler wrote to Bolton at Niagara on September 8, "I endeavored, but to no purpose to prevail upon the Indians to make a stand at Canadasego." [BW-137] Eventually the whole force fell back further in the face of Sullivan's advance.

"The Nests Are Destroyed, but the Birds Are Still on the Wing"

To the north of Pittsburgh, General Brodhead's force of over 600 Continental troops and militia made slow progress up the Allegheny River on their way to the Iroquois villages nestled on the upper reaches of the watershed southwest of Fort Niagara. Brodhead had supplies "sent by canoe as far as the river was navigable, and then transferred to packhorses" to keep pace with the movement of the army. [WGA-p.90] Well ahead of the main column, the General sent a strong advance party to scout the many trails for hostile Indians, and like Sullivan, detect Indian ambushes before the rest of the army arrived. On the morning of August 25, the scouts led by Samuel Brady and the Seneca half-breed, Thomas Nicholson while more than a mile ahead of the army, spotted a war party of over 40 Senecas, Munceys, and Wyandot warriors coming their way down the trail towards them.

Brady laid an ambush of his own, allowing the Indians to pass by them undetected, then catching them between Brodhead's vanguards, who fired on the war party. Many of the warriors were killed or wounded in the skirmish, but some managed to get away to warn the Seneca and Muncey villages to the north. The scouts suffered nothing more than a few scrapes and minor wounds, and no one seriously injured. The scouting party stripped and scalped the bodies of the more than a dozen dead warriors. Without wasting much time, the scouts then moved quickly ahead again to the nearest Indian village, finding it deserted, as was expected, due to the alarm by the war party. On arriving, Brodhead ordered his men to torch the Indian cabins and huts, and destroy any crops of corn found nearby.

As the days passed and Brodhead's march proceeded north, more and more villages were burned until Brodhead's army reached the upper tributaries of the Allegheny whereupon he turned around and marched the army back to Fort Pitt, satisfied that he could go no farther through the impassible wild country, having destroyed a dozen deserted Iroquois towns with their ripening crops as he had been ordered. Hardly another hostile Indian was seen from the time of the first encounter until the army arrived at Fort Pitt on September 15. While the purpose of Brodhead's mission to destroy the Indian towns on the Allegheny was accomplished without suffering a single casualty, Brodhead had not been able to destroy the Indians who were raiding the frontier settlements from that quarter. Like Sullivan, Brodhead had accomplished his task only if the sense that villages and cornfields were ravaged. Yet as one veteran officer of the Indian campaign recorded, "the nests are destroyed but the birds are still on the wing." [CE-p.75] Only time would tell if the Indians would continue to fight for the British, for as yet, they had not been conquered, only driven and harassed by the Rebel campaigns into their lands.

Washington complimented General Brodhead on his return to Pittsburgh, telling him, "I am exceedingly happy in you success in the expedition up the Allegheny." However the American commander added his orders on any further campaigns of the season to the west. "With respect to an Expedition against Detroit, I cannot at this time direct it to be made, as the state of the force at present with you is not sufficient to authorize the clearest hopes of success." [HW1-p.138] Brodhead would have no choice but to go into winter quarters at Fort Pitt and plan for a renewed campaign against Detroit in the spring.

"To Rouse the Indians to Act with Vigor"

At Fort Niagara, Lt. Col. Mason Bolton had good reason to be upset in early September. There were daily reports coming in from John Butler, detailing the advance of the sizable Rebel army marching through the lands of the Seneca, with every apparent intention attacking at Niagara. If that were not enough to distress him, word arrived from Butler on September 8 that an Indian runner had come into his camp from the Ohio, "informing that the Rebels were coming up the Allegheny, and had penetrated as far as Canawaga" [HW1-p.138] Bolton's guess on Brodhead's real mission had been correct all along, and now Niagara was being approached by two Rebel armies from different directions. "Seriously alarmed for the safety of his post," Bolton issued a series of orders to attempt to alleviate the military situation, first sending to Major Butler reinforcements to support another attempt to confront Sullivan's army. "I have ordered the Light Infantry Company of the King's [8th] Regiment with the few Rangers here to embark in bateau…in order to join the Major as soon as possible, and have also sent the Grasshopper (3 pounder artillery piece) with ammunition and provisions in hopes to rouse the Indians to act with vigor," Bolton wrote on September 7 to Haldimand. [HP-87] He added "when the Light Company of the 34th Regiment…arrive" from Carleton Island at the fort at head of the St. Lawrence River, "I shall send him (Butler) another reinforcement."

Realizing that his own garrison was extremely undermanned, and thus vulnerable to attack from a sizable Rebel army, Bolton judged that "I have the greatest reason to suppose the Rebels have laid aside all thoughts of an Expedition this year against that post (Detroit), their whole force I believe is certainly intended against the Six Nations and possibly Niagara." Consequently, Bolton took the initiative to write to Captain Lernoult, recalling the company of the

King's Eighth Regiment from Detroit, as well as Captain William Caldwell's company of Rangers. Bolton's reasoning was sound. If Niagara fell, Detroit would be completely cut off from reinforcement and supply, and would be lost anyway. All that mattered now was to keep Fort Niagara from being taken by the Rebels, and time was of the essence once again for Bolton. By mid-month, the precious reinforcement of over 100 men was on its way to Niagara by sloop across Lake Erie. Unknown to Bolton, General Sullivan decided on September 15 to turn his army homeward some distance from Niagara, as "his provisions were just barely enough to get back to Tioga" on the Susquehanna River. [KI-p.267]

"This is All I Have to Acquaint You With"

Simon Girty thought it best that he send a report to Captain Lernoult at Detroit informing him of what had transpired since his arrival at St. Duski, and of the information he had gathered from the Indians who met with Girty there. Finding a white trader at the post who could write, Girty dictated the letter to Lernoult, telling the officer of the party of 25 Wyandots led by their war chief Seyatahita, and 10 Mingo warriors commanded by Sandithtas, that Girty met with at St. Duski, who were preparing to go out on raiding parties against the Virginians. Girty wrote to Lernoult that a war party was preparing to set out for the Falls of the Ohio to raid into Kentucky, while another party of Wyandots "brought here their prisoners from Kentucke" who Girty questioned for intelligence. "They say there is nine Forts in and about Kentucke, and 300 men under Pay in that parts." The prisoners told him all they knew, hoping that by doing so that Girty could influence the Indians to spare their lives. However there was little he could do for them, nor that he cared to do, without offending his savage friends. [BC-p.71]

On the question of the Rebels at Fort Laurens, Girty reported "there is no certain accounts of the Rebels leaving Tuscarawas," adding, "I intend to go there directly and shall send you the Token you gave me at Detroit if they are not there, if the Delawares are in possession of the Fort, I intend to turn them out and burn the Fort (if my party are able) as you gave me the liberty to act as I thought best, as they and I are not on the best of terms." Girty thought long and hard for a moment on the missionary Zeisberger and his cohort Heckewelder near Goschachgunk, as well as the Christianized Delawares that were doing the bidding of those Rebel sympathizers. Girty spat on the ground when he thought of them. Eventually, something should and would be done about the two preachers, to either remove them from the Delaware, or dispose of them in another way. With the trader becoming impatient to finish the letter so he could return to his Indian customers awaiting him at the post, Girty closed the letter to Lernout, adding, "Yesterday Sandithtas arrived here with the account of 10 Parties of Shawanese that are gone to War. This is all I have to acquaint you with at present. I am, Simon Girty." Then sealing the letter, Girty gave it to a Huron squaw who was setting out in the morning for Detroit, with a gift for her troubles in exchange for a promise from her to deliver it to Lernoult once she got there. With so much to do, Girty got up from where he sat and returned to his preparations for the morning journey into the Ohio Country. [HP-71]

"Parties of Indians are Gone in Quest of Them"

Captain William Caldwell was like a man possessed since arriving at Niagara in the middle of September. Lt. Col. Bolton immediately ordered Caldwell into the field, "with a Party of Rangers and Indians to follow the Rebel Army and if possible to take a Prisoner." [HP-89] Caldwell set out at once, pushing his force to quickly cover the distance between Niagara and Sullivan's army which was withdrawing from the Indian Country. Reaching the Rebel fort at Tioga on the upper reaches of the Susquehanna River, Caldwell found it had been abandoned and burned, "and there were unquestionable signs that the American army had retreated with great haste." [CE-p.74]

Caldwell drove his men onward towards the Wyoming valley 16 miles further from Tioga in hopes that he could capture a prisoner there and harass the American rearguard. However the Indians in his party balked at accompanying Caldwell any further, caring little to engage the Americans so late in the season. Caldwell knew what was really on their minds, for at Tioga the Indians had come across a considerable number of horses and cattle abandoned by Sullivan's army that were left to wander in the surrounding woods. "Parties of Indians are gone in quest of them," and though irritated with the desertion of the Indians, Caldwell could hardly confront them, knowing the distressed and hungry condition of the dozens of Indians he had passed on the trail headed to Niagara from their devastated homelands. Turning around, Caldwell "returned to Niagara, where he would winter." [WM-p.12]

"We Made Them Pay Prittey Well for That"

In the early morning light of October 4, two Shawnee warriors stealthily moved through the underbrush beneath the thick forest canopy that bordered the north shore of the Ohio River several miles below the mouth of the Little Miami River. Without making a sound, the two hunters closed in on several unsuspecting deer that were grazing close to the water's edge, when one of the Indian hunters noticed that something had caught the attention of a deer closest to the river, causing it to stand motionless with its eyes and ears riveted to the water. Curious, the Shawnee scanned the waters of the main channel that he could see through the forest of tree trunks, looking to see what had caught the deer's attention, when his ears picked up the sound of paddles dipping in the water, and the low murmur of voices coming from the overhanging mist. In a moment, he spied the outline of a boat with white men in it, and two others behind it, working their way up the Ohio River, unaware that they were being watched. After counting heads, the two warriors silently backtracked their way undetected to the trail that would lead to their camp a half mile away to warn the rest of their war party, in the company of Simon Girty, his brother George, and Matthew Elliott, of the approach of a large party of Virginians on the river. [BC-p.82]

At the main camp of the war party, a hasty council was held to decide what to do, in light of the fact that over half of their mixed force of over 100 Mingo, Wyandot, Delaware and Shawnee warriors were still out hunting and unaware that the Enemy were nearby. As there was no time to call in the parties, Simon Girty quickly devised a scheme to lure the Virginians close to the north shore as they neared a bend in the river near the mouth of Licking Creek, where they would be susceptible to an ambush by the 40 or so warriors preparing themselves in camp. In the middle of the discussion, a gunshot was heard in the distance coming from the vicinity of the river, which could only mean that one of the hunting parties had encountered the Enemy boats. Girty sent a runner to the sound of the gunshot to determine what was happening while he advised the warriors to lay to their arms and prepare to go. [HP-90]

Coming up the Ohio River were three boats loaded with supplies destined for the Virginian settlements in Kentucky, commanded by Colonel David Rogers of the Virginia militia with a detachment of nearly 70 men split evenly among the keel-boats to man the oars. Rogers had originally left from Fort Pitt in June 1778 on a mission to purchase supplies for Kentucky from New Orleans. Having to return upriver to St. Louis to obtain the goods, Rogers and his party set out up the Ohio River with their precious cargo in the autumn of 1779, reaching the Falls of the Ohio in mid-September, where he was reinforced by a detachment "of 23 men under Lt. Abraham Chapline, sent by Clark" to help Rogers on the most dangerous leg of his journey upriver. [HW1-p.139]

The trip upriver had been uneventful for Rogers and his men until the morning of October 4. Just as the mid-morning sun was burning off the last of the fog that clung to the water, Colonel Rogers and his party heard a gunshot ring out nearby, and one of the men in the lead boat spotted a small party of Indians disappear into the woods on the north shore. Fearing that he was about to be ambushed, Col. Rogers "ordered the boats to run ashore, on which he landed about 40 of his men", including himself, in order to pursue the party of Indians and sweep the north shore ahead to prevent any Indian ambushes. Rogers' men primed and loaded their weapons and set off in the direction that the Indians had fled, with Rogers in the lead. In a matter of moments, Rogers' party unexpectedly collided with the main camp of the war party. Shots rang out from the Virginians, and a surprised Simon Girty yelled at the warriors to repulse the attackers.

Rogers' men managed to get off the first volley into the Indian camp, felling several warriors as they scurried for safety, before fanning out in an attempt to surround Girty and the rest of the Indians. But the warriors got over their initial surprise and according to Matthew Elliott, "we all flue to our arms like good soldiers, and fired away till we Drived (sic) them out of the bush." [HP-90] The firing was hot and heavy from both sides, however the Girtys, Elliott and the warriors increasingly found their mark, felling more and more of Rogers' men, and forcing them to retreat to the boats, where the Indians followed them closely, shooting down many of the men as they attempted to push off. Rogers

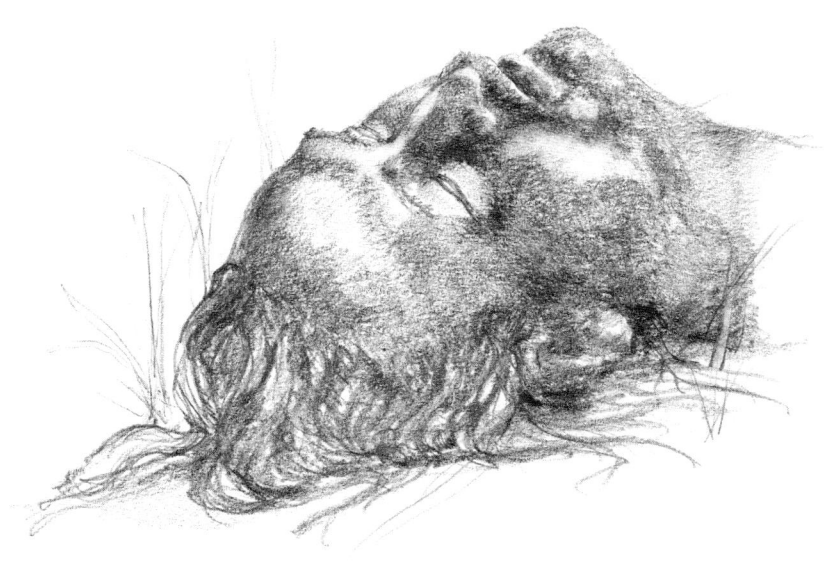

*A militiaman caught in the exchange of gunfire
with the Indians is slain.*

himself was shot, according to Elliott, who wrote that "Simon Girty says that he wounded Rogers in the bush, that he (Rogers) flinged away his gun." [HP-90]

The Indians swarmed over the surviving Virginians on the shoreline and captured the first boat before it could set off, killing, wounding or capturing all of the men in it. Hearing the intense gunfire, more and more warriors who had been in the field hunting quickly returned and joined the battle in progress, cutting down many of the Enemy as they now tried to escape total annihilation. A second of the three boats was "able to get off with about six or eight men in her," but a Sergeant Chapman (Chapline) and "six more men that was prisoners of with him" convinced all of the remaining men alive in the boats to surrender, Describing the fight, Elliott reported that "we got all the Prisoners without any hurt." [HP-90] With that, the short, sharp battle on the Ohio River was over.

The Indians were enraged at the loss of "two of our Indians Kild by their first shote and three Sleytley wounded" in the initial engagement. The warriors scoured the surrounding woods for any wounded Virginian they could find and mercilessly hacked them to death, as well as returning to scalp and mutilate the corpses of those already killed. In a rage the warriors demanded Girty and Elliott turn over the remaining prisoners to them for burning to avenge their dead. As a result, Girty and Elliott could only save five of the captured Virginians from the stake.

It was enough for Elliott to say in his report to Lernoult that when the affair was all said and done, "we made them pay prittey well for that [the Indian casualties]. What was kild on the shore and Drounded in the River was about two or three and 40. Elliott reported "Collonel Camble, Lieut. Chaplin, one French man, and 2 privates as their prisoners. Colonel Rogers, shot by Simon Girty was not one of the survivors. Of Rogers' total command of nearly 70 men, others escaped the Indians, but only 13 were able to eventually make their way to the Kentucky settlements alive. [HW1-p.139] Before destroying the keelboats, Girty, Elliott and the Indians methodically unloaded a treasure trove of goods and supplies stowed inside them, finding to their surprise and great delight a substantial quantity of gunpowder and ammunition destined for the Kentucky settlements. Realizing the necessity of getting the precious gunpowder back to Detroit along with the prisoners for questioning, the entire war party set out for Detroit at once. Elliott sent a runner ahead to Captain Lernoult with his letter reporting of the encounter, along with all the papers of importance that were taken from the bodies of the dead Virginians that might prove to be useful intelligence. In all, the Girtys and Elliott could claim that the whole affair with the Rebels had been a resounding success. [HP-90]

"I Cannot Spare a Soldier Now"

Word of the victory on the Ohio River traveled fast through the wilderness. George Rogers Clark at Vincennes heard of the defeat of his men from a straggler arriving at his post. Clark, with only 40 men left under his command by mid-October, was distressed at the terrible news of the loss of so many men and precious supplies, especially the gunpowder that was so badly needed to defend the settlements. Captain Lernoult arrived at Niagara late in the month from Detroit. He brought with him word of the successful strike against the Virginians on the Ohio from the runner sent by Matthew Elliott. Lernoult reported to Bolton that the destruction of the Rebel force "has raised the spirits of the Indians in that neighborhood," coming on the heels of news from the Mingo scouts that there was solid evidence "the Rebels have left Tuscarawas fort and have given it up entirely." [HP-88]

On November 1, Major DePeyster wrote to General Haldimand from his new posting at Detroit, "I have the pleasure to acquaint you that Lernoult sets off with the accounts of Simon Girty, his brother, and Matthew Elliott having defeated a Colonel Rogers on the Ohio, a stroke which must greatly disconcert the Rebels at Pittsburgh." [HP-249] If there was a bright spot occurring in the Ohio Country for General Haldimand since the capture of Hamilton early in the year, Rogers' defeat was a stunning victory for the British cause, in the wake of a year of Rebel advances on the Wabash, the Tuscarawas, and the upper Allegheny.

While Haldimand at Quebec could take heart in the recent stroke of success in the Ohio Country, he still had many complex and pressing problems with the year coming to a close. For one, just as Captain Lernoult was preparing to embark for Niagara, Lernoult informed Haldimand that he received a new report from the Wabash that the Rebels were preparing once again to move against Detroit. James Girty of the Indian Department, currently visiting Detroit from the Shawnee villages, was the only available person capable to "raise a party to reconnoiter towards the Weas" villages on the Wabash to determine if the rumor was true. Lernoult enlisted Girty's help, telling Bolton that "I cannot spare a soldier now our numbers are reduced." [HP-88] But before Girty could set out, Elliott's runner came in with the news of the victory on the Ohio, and a report from one of the prisoners that Clark had too few men to make any attempt on Detroit. With that, James Girty set off for the Shawnee village of Wapatomika to inform Alexander McKee of the developments, but not before Bolton and Haldimand had been informed of the new alarm against Detroit.

"Little or Nothing May Be Expected to be Done"

Another problem for Haldimand was that from all quarters, he was receiving requests from his officers in the field to send reinforcements, provisions, and ammunition to the western posts, not only to defend the forts, but bolster the Indians still allied to the British. Haldimand wrote to Lord George Germain in England in September when he received word of Sullivan and Brodhead's advancing expeditions aimed at Niagara. A worried Haldimand warned Germain "that if he expected to preserve the Upper Country and fur trade, a body of 1,000-1,500 men with the necessary supply of provisions must be employed for that service alone, as soon as the River became navigable in the spring." [CE-p.75]

Obtaining provisions from England alone was proving to be very difficult. By the time Haldimand learned that Sullivan's army had finally turned back to the east, Haldimand was relieved to discover that his remaining supplies for all of Canada and the western posts had not run out, as "the provision fleet from England having arrived when Haldimand was down to five days' supply" at Quebec. [KI-p.269] The ships had come in the nick of time for more than just Quebec. Along with the garrisons to feed, Haldimand knew he must find food for the more than 2,600 destitute Iroquois refugees alone gathering at Niagara or have them starve during the coming winter and lose the possibility of enlisting them to fight the Rebels in the spring.

DePeyster, too, was feeling the pressure of the Indians gathering late in the season at Detroit. Like Bolton, he wrote to Haldimand, requesting more troops to be sent to support the Indians and thus keep their loyalty. "The demands of the Indians are great. If Captain Caldwell's Light Infantry Company was here, I would comply with their request, but that not being the case; I have it not in my power to assist them with troops." [HP-249] For that matter, neither did Haldimand. When he looked at the Disposition of his troops in the Upper Country, Haldimand could count only a total of 1,543 men under arms from the fort at Carleton Island to the upper post of Michilimackinac—1,500 men to hold a the entire flank of Canada, and spread over almost a 1,000 miles of wilderness. [HP-375] The challenge facing Frederick Haldimand was daunting.

Adding to Haldimand's consternation late in the year, was a letter that reached him at Quebec from Lord Germain in England, giving Haldimand detailed instructions on the manner in which he should conduct the war in the Ohio Country. It was obvious to Haldimand that Germain had not as yet been apprised of the major events that had occurred in the changing wilderness war in the Indian country which made Germain's advisements irrelevant. Writing to Bolton on the 12th of December, Haldimand commented on Germain's latest dispatch, "in the present situation of affairs in the Indian country together with Lieutenant Governor Hamilton's misfortune, little or nothing may be expected to be done in consequence of it." [HP-136]

"A Few to Act in Conjunction with a Good Body of Indians"

Far to the west and deep in the Ohio Country at the upper Shawnee Indian village of Wapatomika, Alexander McKee wrestled with the problems facing him in conducting the affairs of the Indian Department to support the tribes still willing to fight the Virginians. McKee was in a unique position at Wapatomika, for the coming and going of many Indian scouts kept him appraised, more than any other man, of the mood of the various septs of the tribes, as well as their wants, needs, and complaints, which he forwarded to Detroit whenever he could, and "communicated to them, endeavoring to convey to them in the most favorable light" the wishes of the new commander at Detroit, Major DePeyster. [HP-91]

Likewise, McKee was at the center of all the intelligence on the designs and movements of the Enemy brought in by Indian scouts traveling far and wide.

They provided McKee with the "eyes and ears" to accurately determine the intentions of the Rebels from Fort Pitt to the Falls of the Ohio and beyond. One startling piece of important intelligence reached him at Wapatomika in mid-November. A Shawnee warrior confided to McKee the proceedings of a meeting held at Fort Pitt between the Americans and the Delaware chiefs friendly to the Rebel cause. The warrior had been able to find out that the nature of "the determinations of the Cooshawking Delawares to assist the Virginians." The Delaware intended to pledge to help the enemy attack the Shawnee in the coming spring, and McKee wrote that "this discovery undoubtedly points out more and more the necessity of troops to support His Majesty's Interest in this Quarter, and a few to act in conjunction with a good body of Indians in an incursion towards Cooshawking would have a good effect upon the greatest part of the Delawares, notwithstanding their promises to the Rebels." [HP-91]

Nonetheless, as winter set in at the end of the year, one thing was for certain on the minds of Haldimand and McKee alike. They had weathered the storm of Rebel advances and their own setbacks in the wilderness war, and all things being considered, could count the stalemate at the year's closing as a blessing. On the bright side, the British posts at Detroit and Niagara had not fallen, and Canada was safe for the moment. More than anything else, the wilderness of the Ohio Country still remained in the hands of the Indians despite the efforts of the Rebels to drive the Indians out. Both men counted on the Indians to fight for those lands in the coming year, and in turn, drive the Rebels from their lands once and for all. If both men had anything to do with it, the Indians would succeed, and do much more.

Chapter 12

1780: Kentucky Wilderness War

In early November 1779, winter weather descended with a fury on the Ohio Country. It came earlier in the season than it had in many years, forcing Indians and white men alike to seek shelter, as the wilderness lands were plunged into an icy landscape. For weeks at a time, bitter cold temperatures and deep snows kept all but a few men confined in their quarters at the military posts of Niagara, Fort Pitt, and Detroit. From the frontier settlements east of the Ohio River to the dozens of Indian villages scattered throughout the wilderness of the Ohio Country, the early winter forced nearly everyone to huddle close to their fires for warmth and relief from the howling frigid winds. Impassable trails and frozen waterways gripped the land and made hunting, scouting, and wilderness war all but impossible. [KI-p.271]

Yet men ventured out into the icy hinterland of the Ohio Country between snowstorms, driven by the need to firm up allegiances during the respite from fighting, and to make plans for renewed warfare in the spring. In spite of the severe winter weather white men and Indians moved on snowshoes along the snowbound trails from the Shawnee and Mingo villages along the Scioto River and the villages of the Upper Sandusky to council at the Upper Shawnee town called Wakatomika on the Muskingum River. An important Indian council had been called for early January 1780. It was imperative that Alexander McKee of the British Indian Department, Matthew Elliott, and the Girty brothers consult with the Indian chiefs and war captains to decide what to do in light of the Rebel peace overtures recently made to the neutral Goschachgunk Delaware and a delegation of Cherokee visiting from the south.

Wapatomika was a cluster of three to four Shawnee villages nestled on the west side of the Muskingum River, sitting on the north bank of the mouth of the creek called Wakatomika, which emptied into the Muskingum. The main village of Wakatomika where the council would be held rested several miles south of the main Delaware town of Goschachgunk where the confluence of White Woman's Creek and the Tuscarawas River formed the Muskingum. [BR-p.135] McKee, Elliott, and the Girtys made the arduous trip to Wakatomika in the first days of January 1780, wishing not only to meet with several prominent Delaware and Shawnee chiefs allied to the British cause, but also to speak with those Delaware Indians and their Cherokee guests still favoring neutrality in the war.

The Delaware nation as a whole, like their Iroquois brothers to the northeast, was split in allegiance to the white men, some favoring the British, some supporting the Americans, and others choosing neutrality. At the village of Goschachgunk, most of the Delaware tribesmen "had not yet taken up the hatchet against the Americans." [BC-p.87] The Delaware living in the villages to the east, under the leadership of Captain Killbuck and White Eyes, were aligned to the American cause because of the influence of the Moravian preachers Zeisberger and Heckewelder, whereas those villages "westward, up the Walhonding, across to the Scioto, thence to the Mad River" and beyond to the Upper Sandusky were hostile to the Virginians and supportive of the British cause. Delaware chiefs at each village spoke for their own clan people as to their particular alliance. [BR-p.xxi]

"I Open Your Hand Gently"

Word had reached McKee that a deputation of Cherokee from the south, who were visiting the Delaware at Goschachgunk, had been approached by the Moravian Delawares and asked to accept a token of friendship sent by the Rebels from Fort Pitt. Simon Girty was aware that Heckewelder and Brodhead had sent the Delaware envoys. A war hatchet from the Rebels had been presented to the Cherokee war chief named Raven from the Cherokee of Chola. [HP-250] Girty sent word to McKee that, in spite of the weather, something must be done to neutralize the situation before the Cherokee returned to their homeland with the war hatchet.

McKee called for a meeting of his own with the Cherokee. The Shawnee village of Wakatomika was chosen because Girty received word that "the Rebel hatchet must be in the hands of those Cherokee at Wakitamiky," [HP-250] who had since left the Delaware village to the north and were staying with the Shawnee. McKee knew that by meeting with the Cherokee at Wakatomika, he would be able to exclude any Delaware of dubious loyalty who would want to pass on the information of the council to the Rebels through Zeisberger and Heckewelder. It was an opportunity for McKee to meet with the neutral Delaware and gauge their mood as well.

On January 17, 1780, the council began in the central longhouse of the village. Joining McKee were the three Girty brothers acting as interpreters for the Mingoes, Delaware, and Shawnee present. Along with McKee was Lieutenant Caldwell of the King's Eighth Regiment acting in place for Major DePeyster at Detroit, and seated next to McKee were the principal war chiefs of the Hurons, Delaware, Shawnee, Miami, and Six Nations who favored McKee and the British cause. Across from them sat the Cherokee delegation with the Delaware chiefs from Goschachgunk who favored neutrality. No Moravian Delawares were present. The Girtys had seen to it that the Rebel sympathizers were excluded from this important meeting of the Indians. What was at stake at the council was more than the allegiance of the Cherokee. McKee knew that he had a unique opportunity to make an impression on the still uncommitted

Delaware and attempt to influence them to join the British cause, and spurn the Moravians. It was to that end that McKee shrewdly counseled the Delaware war captain "Buck Anguiles" to speak first to the Cherokee, knowing that the prestige of the warrior would carry more weight than McKee's own words. [HP-250]

The principal Delaware warrior, Buck Anguiles, rose to his feet and addressed the silent audience, speaking first to the Cherokee about the Rebel hatchet in their possession, which had been given to them recently at Goschachgunk. "Graced Children of Chola. You see here before you at this Council Fire, all the Chiefs and Warriors of the several nations inhabiting this country and in their presence I open your hand gently, and take out of it a Hatchet delivered to you by a few drunken People of my Nation, in conjunction with the "Big-Knife, our Enemy," the respected Delaware war captain said. A murmur of approval echoed through the lodge from the assembled Indians as they thought about the Delaware's words. "In delivering it up, I hope you will throw up every bad impression you have received from them, to the satisfaction and desire of all Nations present," Buck Anguiles impressed on them. [HP-250]

When he was finished, other Delaware headmen allied with McKee in turn rose and spoke, castigating those Delaware favoring the Rebels, and pledging their warriors to continuing the war against the Big Knives, as the Virginians were called, as soon as the weather would allow war parties to set out to the white frontier. The oratory continued late into the evening and when it was finished, the Cherokee who had remained silent throughout the day, informed the council that they would have an answer in the morning, to Buck Anguile's petition.

Alexander McKee was pleased at the next council when the Cherokee warrior Raven delivered the Rebel war hatchet to the assembly, whereupon it was thrown into the fire, signifying a unity of purpose among all the tribes present. It was then that McKee rose to speak to the Indians for the first time, asking them to take up their own war hatchets against the Virginians as soon as the spring thaws arrived. He promised them that the British at Detroit would supply them with provisions and ammunition if their war parties were sent to attack the frontier. Pointing to the fact that the Enemy had been driven from their fort on the Tuscarawas, McKee repeated his claim that the invasion of the Big Knives was over. It was now up to the warriors to take the initiative and attack the Enemy wherever they could be found.

"They Came Empty-Handed and Almost Naked"

At Fort Niagara, Lt. Col. Mason Bolton of the King's Eighth in command of the British post struggled with the dire situation facing him in January. With Lake Ontario completely frozen, he knew he could expect no help from Canada in the near future. Somehow he must make do with the meager supplies on hand in the garrison's depleted larders to feed the multitude of starving Indians huddled about the fort walls in the hundreds of squalid huts barely visible under the heavy snowdrifts. The refugees from the devastated Iroquois villages of the Seneca, Cayuga, Onondagas and some Oneida had made their way to Niagara to join the Mohawks already there, seeking shelter and sustenance. "They came on foot and on horseback: men, women, and children, the old and the young, the vigorous and the crippled, the healthy and the sick, many with babies on their backs." [KI-p.269]

Adding to the Indians already at Niagara came Tuscaroras, Mahicans, Nanticokes, and Delawares from the destroyed villages on the Susquehanna River and the upper Allegheny, all arriving "bereft of food and shelter and country. They came empty-handed and almost naked." Bolton had the monumental task of feeding and clothing more than 3000 Indians at the fort. He knew that if a large number of the native allies perished in the winter, those that survived would desert the British in the spring. Bolton knew he could rely on Joseph Brant to help him see that all the Indians received fair and equitable treatment. However, that was not the case with Guy Johnson, the head of the Indian Department for the Six Nations at Niagara. Johnson's partiality for a handful of favored sachems and warriors did nothing to alleviate the crowding, discomfort, and suffering of the rest of the Indians with whom Bolton had to concern himself. Because of Johnson's lack of concern for the Indians as a whole, the burden fell on Bolton to ease the misery of the Indians.

"As Soon As I Can, Disclose the Object of Their Mission"

While the winter winds blowing in from Lake Superior howled outside the far-flung British post of Michilimackinac, Lieutenant Governor Captain Patrick Sinclair huddled in the warmth of his quarters, putting the finishing touches on a plan he had devised since receiving an important letter from Lord George Germain late in 1779. Germain had advised the new Lieutenant Governor to send a substantial force of garrison troops which could be spared with a sizable body of allied Indians in the spring to attack the Illinois Country to the southwest, particularly the French, Spanish and Virginian posts on the upper Mississippi Country since Great Britain was at war with all three countries. How Sinclair was to assemble that force and command it was up to him—however, Germain was adamant on one point. Sinclair was to stay at his post at Michilimackinac. Germain would not risk the safety of Sinclair, as Hamilton had done, and become a victim of unforeseen circumstances and unpredictability of a wilderness war. As a newcomer to the wilderness, Sinclair agreed to the directive. [WGA-p.106]

In late February, as McKee, Elliott, the Girty brothers and a following of Indian chiefs were traveling from the upper Shawnee towns to the Sandusky villages to Detroit to meet with DePeyster, Sinclair met in council with the Indians of the upper lakes. He called upon the Ottawa, Sioux, Sauk, Fox, Chippewa, Menominee, and Winnebago Indian chiefs to support his proposed spring campaign against the enemy posts on the Mississippi, promising them a chance to "strike at their traditional enemies, the Indians of the Illinois Country." [WGA-p.106] Satisfied with the results of his meetings, Sinclair wrote to DePeyster,

Bolton, and Haldimand that the wheels had been set in motion for an expedition to the southwest as soon as the weather broke sufficiently in the spring for bateaux to traverse the waterways. Noting to them by letter in early March that in response to "My Lord Germain's Letter, I have sent a War Party from hence to join and act with the Sioux under Wabasha their Chief, Mr. Roque the Interpreter for that nation, if he can go, with a Mr. McKay as English Interpreter and Commissary, will join him; and I hope that they will proceed sufficiently early and in force to be of Service. I shall prepare other small bands and send off as soon as I can, with safety, disclose the objects of their Mission." [HP-381]

"If I Would Send Some Soldiers"

At Detroit, the winter weather of early March was losing its strength, with milder days tempering more and more the snow and ice, hinting at spring to come. Major DePeyster had been busying himself with preparations as well for offensive action against the Rebels in the Ohio Country and the Virginian frontier to the east and south to the Kentucky settlements once the weather allowed sufficient movement of war parties into the field. It was to this end that he welcomed on March 10 "from the Shawanese Country Captain McKee, Mr. Elliott, the Girtys, and about 50 Indians, amongst them the principal chiefs of the Mingoes, Shawanese, and Delawares," who wished to meet with DePeyster for a War Council." [HP-382]

DePeyster shared with them the recent intelligence he had received from Mr. Louis Chevalier, a Frenchman and British agent at the post of St. Joseph's to the northwest of Detroit who had sent a letter to DePeyster acquainting him that he believed that "the Rebels have totally quitted the Illinois Country." In addition, though DePeyster was not at liberty to discuss the details of the mission, he informed the delegation that a force of troops and Indians from the upper posts would soon be setting off for the Illinois Country and the Mississippi to attack the enemy there and clear the entire region of those Indians and Frenchmen providing support to the Virginians under Clark at his posts in the Illinois Country. With Detroit now secure, and the western flank of the Ohio Country soon to be cleared of the Enemy, DePeyster assured the Indian delegation that the time would be ripe with the coming warm weather to strike the Big Knives to the south and east of their villages. Unlike his predecessor Lernoult, DePeyster promised them a firm hand of support if they would send their warriors out.

In return, McKee reported to DePeyster that "the Rebels failed in their attempt to build a fort at Cooshocking" as the fort on the Tuscarawas had been abandoned, and it was reported to him that the Moravian preachers had been unable to convince the Rebels at Fort Pitt to build another closer to their missions. However, intelligence from Indian scouts from south of the Ohio indicated that the Virginians "had now surrounded the Indian Hunting Ground of Kentuck, having erected small Forts at about two days' journey from each other" so as to be able, in McKee's words, to come to the aid of each other with mounted men to intercept war parties raiding the country. Further, McKee stated that the chiefs with him had knowledge that the enemy intended to build a fort in the spring on the north side of the Ohio River at the mouth of the Little Miami. With these renewed threats from the Virginians against the tribes of the Ohio Country, it was evident to DePeyster what the chiefs were preparing to ask of him, if they were to command their warriors in a renewed war against the encroachment of the Virginians. [HP-382]

However, Major DePeyster was surprised when the chiefs of the Ohio Country, in their preparation to speak to him at the Council, produced the wampum belt and strings of beads given to them almost two years previously at Detroit by Lieutenant Governor Hamilton, saying to DePeyster that "to prove their assertion that it was now time to fulfill the promise" which was made to them previously by Hamilton to provide them with the assistance needed "in case the Enemy should approach their villages" as was done the previous summer during the raid against the Shawnee village of Chillicothe. The Indian chiefs asserted to DePeyster that without aid in provisions, ammunition and British soldiers to fight with them "they would soon be under the disagreeable necessity of falling back and thereby becoming a burden to their Father, or else they must retire to the southward." [HP-382]

DePeyster thought on the matter for a moment before responding to the Indians. During the pause, the "Principal chiefs of the Hurons, Pottawattamies, Chippawas, Ottawas, Ouiattonons, Miamis, Weas, Peorias, and Kickapoos (being) present in the Council" requested to speak to DePeyster, "declaring that if I would send some soldiers till a greater body could be spared, they would use and assist their Elder Brothers, and for the future act in conjunction for the good of the King's Service." [HP-382] Unlike Lernoult, DePeyster had experience in dealing with the Indians from his service at Michilimackinac. Instinctively he knew with all the Indian eyes in the Council on him, he must seize the moment and give them what they wanted. Truly, the events of late 1779 had changed the mood of the Indians for the better, offsetting their despondency and fear resulting from the earlier successes of the Rebels. A great deal of that change had to be credited to the tireless efforts of McKee, Elliott and the Girtys who, by living with the savages, had been able to do much. Now it was up to DePeyster to give the Indians what they wanted so that they would fight the Rebels. Not one to shy away from an opportunity to take the offensive, DePeyster was more than eager to provide the assemblage of chiefs before him with the words that he knew they wanted to hear. He must give them promises that he would be able to fulfill, which would motivate the Indians to fight as they had not before. In the balance, he hoped the Rebels could be driven out forever from the Indian Country.

"Brought the Ill Will of the Indians Upon Him"

The chiefs hushed as DePeyster, resplendent in his red officer's coat, began to speak to them through his interpreters. DePeyster promised them that if they would pick up the war hatchet again against the Big Knives and send their warriors against the white frontiers of the Virginians, he would not only provide them with ample ammunition and provisions, but send them many soldiers of his own to accompany the warriors, and cannon to batter down the gates of the enemy forts in Kentucky, as soon as the weather permitted soldiers and provisions to arrive at Detroit by vessels on the lakes. This was the year, DePeyster emphasized to his audience, that the King intended to help his children to drive the Big Knives from the Indian Country, and force them back across the eastern mountains from whence they came. DePeyster's pledge was met with overwhelming approval by the assembled chiefs. Plans were quickly made to supply the Indians at Detroit with what provisions they needed so they could disperse to their respective villages as soon as possible where preparations could be made to send out war parties against the Virginian frontier to scout, harass, and attack the enemy, keeping them on the defensive while DePeyster put together his force at Detroit for the coming spring offensive.

Before setting out for the Ohio Country with the various chiefs, the Girty brothers, McKee, and Elliott met in private with Major DePeyster to work out the details of his plan. DePeyster confided to his Indian Department agents that he had high hopes for the major offensive against the enemy's Kentucky settlements, which were numerous. Besides destroying the Virginians and their posts in Kentucky and demoralizing the population there, DePeyster was convinced that "the raid would divert American attention from Detroit," while encouraging all the Indians of the Ohio Country still uncommitted, such as the Goschachgunk Delaware, to seek or "renew their allegiance to the British cause." [NL-p.113] Keeping the Indians in the field until the objectives of the raid were accomplished would be the challenge for McKee and his men. With concerted effort, and a little luck, a great deal could be achieved, DePeyster believed.

As a final adjunct to the meeting, Major DePeyster called into the room Captain Henry Bird of the King's Eighth who was well known to all present from their past service of the previous year at the Upper Sandusky villages, and the brief siege of the Rebel fort on the Tuscarawas. DePeyster announced that Bird would hold overall command of the expedition, which should be ready to leave by mid-May if all went well. At Bird's disposal would be regular troops from Detroit, some trusted Canadian militia, all of the men of the Indian Department, and any reinforcements yet to arrive from Niagara that could be spared. To ensure the campaign be successfully led once in the field, DePeyster told the officers present that Captain Alexander McKee was to "coordinate the actions of the large contingent of Indians" rather than Bird, remembering the unfortunate incident involving Bird at Sandusky the previous year that had "brought the ill will of the Indians upon him." McKee was to act as a liaison between Bird and the Indians. In the event that Bird became ill or "incapacitated during the raid, his successor was to take no action without first consulting the deputy agent," Captain McKee. As DePeyster saw it, good communication with the Indians was paramount for success. He demanded Captain Bird be on his best behavior, no matter how difficult the Indians became. Captain McKee would have to see to it that the Indians stay focused and did not become disgruntled over trifling matters.

"We Have Heard Nothing At All What the Enemy Are About"

With the coming of warmer weather, the Delaware, Wyandot, Shawnee and Mingo war parties soon set out from their villages with the coming of warmer weather and hit the Virginian frontier. Wyandot warriors attacked across the Ohio River below Fort Pitt in the vicinity of Raccoon Creek, surprising a party of 11 settlers gathering maple sugar. Five of the men were instantly killed and scalped. Three young women and three boys were taken prisoner back across the river to Indian country, to the shock of family and neighbors. [BC-p.86]

Twenty-one miles south of Fort Henry, near the mouth of Captina Creek on the west side of the Ohio River, three boatloads of settlers traveling down the Ohio were attacked by a war party of Delaware Indians, called Munceys, late in March. Two of the boats managed to escape the Indians. The third boat was overtaken by the Muncey warriors, who killed three men and captured 21 men, women and children. Heading with their prisoners and plunder from the boat to the interior of the Ohio Country, the group halted to rest on the Muskingum River where Moravian Delawares sent word to Zeisberger of the attack, who wrote to General Brodhead at Fort Pitt on April 2, informing him of the attack. [BC-p.87] Zeisberger's letter coincided with Heckewelder's report to Brodhead on March 30 in which he relayed to the General the news from friendly Delawares that "five or six companies of warriors have gone out; two parties of Wyandots toward Beaver Creek and the others down this river [Muskingum]." [BC-p.86] With the coming of warm weather, it was apparent to Heckewelder that the Indian raids against the frontier settlements had commenced once again. "We have heard nothing at all this whole winter what the Enemy are about," he wrote Brodhead, until now. Any thoughts of a further respite from wilderness warfare against the settlers living along the frontier borders was dashed.

Soon, the Kentucky settlements came under Indian attack as well. Shawnee war parties raided near Boones Borough and Bryan's Station in early April, ambushing settlers in their isolated cabins. As increasing calls went out to the forts for help, the mounted militiamen coming to the rescue found settlers slaughtered in their burned homes, their horses stolen and their cattle killed. The small but numerous war parties attacked with impunity, as "the increased number of settlers were too scattered to help and only provided defenseless, attractive targets for the warriors." [WGA-p.106] Though apprehensive, the Kentuckians had not as yet faced any large-scale raids like that of previous years.

Far to the west in the Illinois County, Captain Sinclair's mixed force of a handful of British soldiers accompanied by a large body of Canadians and Indians, set out from the posts of Michilimackinac and St. Joseph for the upper Mississippi River. At the village of Prairie du Chien, more Indian warriors from the Fox, Sauk, Menominee, Sioux and Winnebago nations joined the force now led by a British trader named Emanuel Hesse. Sinclair sent enough ammunition with his own troops to enable Hesse to outfit the hundreds of Indians with him, hoping that the expedition could destroy not only the Illinois villages, "but the

Spanish settlements of St. Louis as well; for Spain was now at War also with Britain." [BC-p.88]

In the spring of 1780, George Rogers Clark was at the mouth of the Ohio River overseeing the construction of a Virginian post to be named Fort Jefferson on the east side of the Mississippi River just five miles below the Ohio. A frantic call for help from his men at the Illinois towns of Cahokia and Kaskaskia forced Clark to rush north with as many militiamen as he could muster, arriving at Cahokia on May 26, only one day before Hesse and the Indians attacked. A skirmish resulted, and Hesse diverted his force across the Mississippi to attack the Spanish at St. Louis. After several hours of siege against the well-defended post, the Indians became bored and broke off the attack, favoring instead to burn and pillage the surrounding countryside, seeking easier prey among the scattered settlers.

When the Indians, British and Canadians finally withdrew to the northeast, they could count over 70 killed and many others taken captive. A pursuit force of 350 Virginian, French and Spanish troops "accomplished little beyond burning Indian villages up the Illinois and Rock rivers." [WGA-p.107] While not a great success, Sinclair could take heart in the news arriving at Michilimackinac that a significant blow had been struck against the Illinois Country, which Sinclair hoped would cause Clark to re-think leaving the frontier undefended while he pondered moving against Detroit.

"You Are to Entirely Disregard Every Such Pretended Capitulation"

General Haldimand had spent a great deal of time thinking over the events that transpired at the upper British posts in the latter half of 1779, during the ensuing winter. While pleased that Detroit and Niagara were safe from the Rebels by the end of the year, Haldimand nonetheless realized that his officers at those posts had come within a hair's breadth of losing them to Clark, Sullivan, and Brodhead. Though the assaults by the Rebels had not materialized, Haldimand could not think that the reason was more to chance than by design. He worried that if the Rebels had mounted a serious campaign to take those posts and provided the logistical supplies, the men under arms, and the necessary artillery as they had done in the Sullivan campaign against the Indian country, his British officers in command of the posts in jeopardy would be unable to make critical decisions sufficiently well on their own without the forthcoming orders from headquarters to guide them, which would take too long to reach them. It was clear to Haldimand that the British command structure in the wilderness was too rigid for officers to adapt to a quickly changing military situation while so far removed from Haldimand himself in Quebec.

It was with this in mind that Haldimand directed a Circular "to the Officers Commanding at Niagara, Detroit, and Michilimackinac" on April 1, addressing the issue of communication and command with Quebec. "Sirs, From considering how precarious the Communication between the uppers posts will unavoidably become should an enemy penetrate into any part of that Country, I think it essential for his Majesty's Service in that case to make every Officer responsible for the particular post he commands, and therefore should it happen that your communications are interrupted or any of the posts invested, you have full authority to afford any assistance to the besieged which you judge will best promote the King's Service." Haldimand hoped this directive to Bolton, DePeyster, and Sinclair would make it clear to them that in a time of crisis they should act quickly and decisively on their own, without reluctance or hesitation while waiting for orders from Quebec. In Haldimand's mind, Bolton had already proved himself able to do so in the last year. DePeyster and Sinclair needed to see that the face of wilderness war, so far removed from the battlefields in the east, demanded they make decisions on their own, which their conventional military training had not permitted.

Tempering the need for his officers to command in the field, Haldimand knew he must address the possibility that under duress they find themselves in the disagreeable position of being called upon to surrender a post, when the situation itself did not warrant it. He wrote "You are not upon any account or pretence whatever to make any Capitulation or even to enter into or propose any Terms of Convention for any post except that you have the honor of commanding, and should the Enemy attempt to deceive you by any false Capitulation...you are entirely to disregard every such pretended Capitulation but to defend yourself with that determined bravery which zealous and experienced Officers have always done when they consider that delaying an Enemy for a few days may frequently be the means of persevering a whole Country."

"Lest the Enemy Should Make a Dash Upon Him"

Haldimand left the orders to his officers at that, without explaining to them why he had felt it necessary to do so. It was simple for him to see that the fate of Canada was hanging in the balance of the activities of three men, Bolton, DePeyster, and Sinclair, moreso than anything he, himself, could do as Commander in Chief. To hold Canada, Haldimand reasoned he must prevent an invasion by the Rebels. The greatest threat lay in the vast wilderness to the west, which was an open door. Therefore, to prevent an invasion from that quarter, it was imperative that the upper posts be maintained at all costs. Yet that could only be done by capable, experienced officers who could fight a wilderness style of warfare.

Haldimand reflected that Hamilton had been a fighter, but his conventional thinking had eventually bested him, boxing him in at his post at St. Vincent. He had outwitted himself by thinking that a fixed defensive position in a very fluid wilderness war was impregnable. Hamilton had allowed himself to give up the military initiative. Contrary to officers like Hamilton, Haldimand believed to win in the wilderness one needed to be able to think one's tactical moves in an unconventional manner. An officer needed to command like a partisan leading irregulars who could maneuver, counter, and out-fight the enemy from constantly changing positions. But also, at the same time an officer must be able to use the defensive strengths of the fixed position of a fortification to one's best advantage, in a war where one paradoxically needed all the advantages one could muster to defeat an enemy who was unforgiving of tactical mistakes. This was what Haldimand was trying to communicate to his officers at the upper posts. Haldimand knew more than anyone else that the true test of their understanding of his words to them would come only when they found themselves in a crisis situation and were forced to out-think the enemy, or perish. Such was the nature of the crucible of wilderness war, Haldimand reflected, thinking on his own experience.

Haldimand's thoughts drifted back in time more than 20 years to a different wilderness war when it was he who was faced with the paradox of command in a crisis. It was in early July 1759, during Prideaux's campaign against French Fort Niagara. Haldimand remembered he was a Lieutenant Colonel then, the senior officer left in command of a British force of nearly a 1,000 provincial New York troops and regulars at the former site of Fort Oswego on the south shore of Lake Ontario. While Prideaux and his army had gone on to Niagara, Haldimand's orders were simply to select a new site for a fort, and "fortify Oswego to protect Prideaux's line of communications" between Niagara and New York to the east. [DB-p.35] However, Haldimand remembered it was not as simple as that, for he had good intelligence that the French and their Indian allies might attempt to attack his force in the vulnerable position they were in before the fort construction could be completed. He did not have long to wait before the crisis came.

Sensing that if his exposed camp were attacked by a superior enemy force of French and Indians his men could be overrun out in the open, Haldimand decided to hastily "barricade his camp with pork and flour barrels" to provide some sense of a defensive position "lest the enemy should make a dash upon him." He needed a temporary fort for the tactical advantage. However much the provisional wall afforded his men a sense of security and protection from enemy fire, it was not enough in Haldimand's mind to prevent his own destruction, due to the inability to maneuver his own confined men. If an attack came, Haldimand reasoned that his force would be surrounded, and the only hope for success lay in preparing for offensive action, which an enemy would never expect him to do. That was the paradox, and that was exactly what he did. On the morning of July 5, Haldimand remembered clearly the surprise attack of more than 1,000 French and Indians who had arrived by canoe the previous night and had quietly surrounded his own force in the dark. The fighting began as a party of his woodcutters were attacked by French and Indians. Haldimand immediately sent a force of his own men racing to the sound of the firing with muskets loaded, which Haldimand had prepared in advance for just such an occasion. Haldimand's men crashed into the unsuspecting French and Indians who had surrounded the woodcutters, and dispersed them with several volleys of musket fire. The enemy had not expected such action on the part of the British, and panicked. When the French and their Indian allies returned to take up positions around Haldimand's encampment, his work party and the relief force had safely returned, and the enemy could only fire upon Haldimand's men from some distance till breaking off the fight for the night.

The next morning the French and Indians returned to their firing positions. Haldimand remembered the din of blood-curdling shrieks from the mass of howling Indians and the terror they struck in his own men. Only later did Haldimand learn that the French priest, the Abbe Piquet, had solemnly blessed the savages the day before, and "told them to give the English no quarter". [PF-p.380] Haldimand was undeterred by the Indians for he had a surprise waiting for them. Again, he was not content to let the Enemy take the initiative, but recalled that if he could out-think them by taking the offensive himself and attack them where they were the weakest, he had a chance to beat them. Throughout the night, Haldimand had his men move his three cannon forward and place them opposite the Indian positions of the previous day, thinking to himself that the Indians would likely return to the same spot in the morning. When they did, Haldimand had his cannon open fire upon the Indians, catching them completely by surprise, and scattering them in terror. Haldimand had reasoned correctly that the Indians were the weakest link for the French and their fear of cannon bombardment alone might have the desired effect of stripping them from the French, and forcing the numerically superior enemy to give up the fight. [PF-p.380]

The French and Indians had fled that day, Haldimand recalled, leaving him and his army intact at Oswego with slight losses, when to all appearances, the enemy had thought the English already beaten. Their complacency had allowed them to be out-maneuvered and out-fought as they thought they possessed all the advantages. All Haldimand could do was hope that Bolton, DePeyster, and Sinclair would be able to think on their feet when the time came. Haldimand chuckled to himself. If there was one thing that he wished he could give them, it would be a dash of cunning and daring that the Rebel commander Colonel Clark possessed. However Haldimand doubted that his officers would find that thought as amusing as he did at the moment.

At Detroit, Captain Bird assembled his force for his campaign against the Virginians to the south. Major DePeyster provided Bird with a combined detachment of men from the companies of the King's Eighth Regiment and Aubrey's 47th Regiment of Foot from the Detroit garrison. In addition, all of the men of the Alexander McKee's Indian Department still at Detroit including the three Girty brothers and Matthew Elliott prepared to set out with Bird, along with "nearly 100 Indians from the upper lakes region." This time Bird succeeded in bringing along with him the necessary artillery pieces that he had lacked during the siege of the Rebel Fort Laurens. Two cannon, a six pounder and a three pounder, "both on wheeled carriages" with "a detachment from the Royal Regiment of Artillery to man them" from Detroit were at Bird's disposal. [NL-p.115]

On April 12, his force of nearly 150 whites and over 100 Indians set out by boat from Detroit "moving along the western basin of Lake Erie" for the

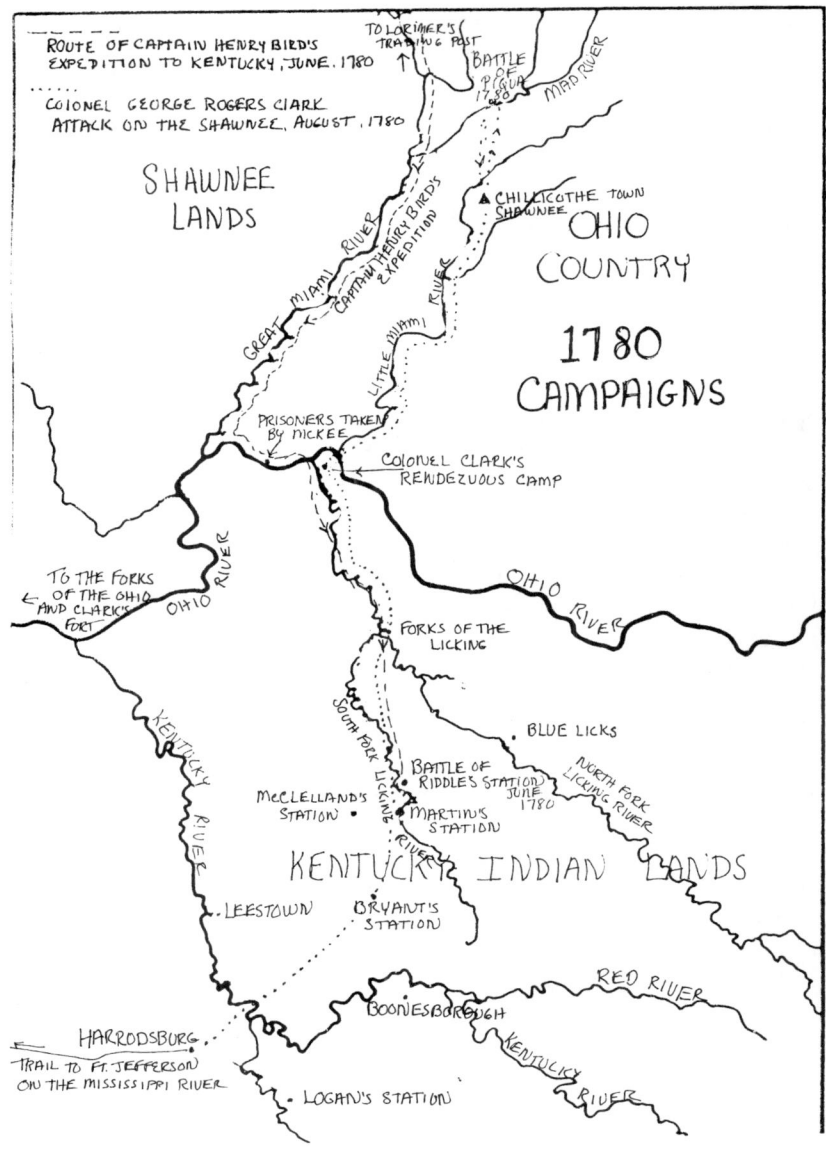

Map of the 1780 Campaigns

mouth of the Maumee River. [NL-p.115] Bird was confident that this time he would succeed in taking the Enemy forts his force encountered. First on his mind was an assault upon Clark's "fort at the Falls of the Ohio." When that fell, Bird and his force would then move across the Ohio River to "attack other forts in Kentucky" as well. [BC-p.88] While Captain Bird knew that the expedition leaving Detroit did not have nearly enough Indian warriors, he expected to meet Alexander McKee with several hundred Shawnee, Mingo, and Delaware gathered along the way, which would bolster the numbers of Indians necessary for the campaign. Despite the fact that Bird personally disliked deploying the savages at all, he realized he had no choice if he expected to accomplish anything without them.

"Which Bring Down the Earth in Great Clods"

On May 15, a private named Hamilton, from the 47th Regiment of Foot who had volunteered to accompany Bird's detachment of soldiers, came into Detroit with a letter from Captain Bird for Major DePeyster, dated May 9. Bird's force had successfully made its way by boat up the Maumee River to its confluence with the Auglaize, and from there had proceeded up that river where "Bird expected to pass the Carrying Place in four or five days." [HP-97] DePeyster studied the letter intently, while occasionally glancing at the hand-sketched map on the desk in his officer's quarters. DePeyster was impressed with the progress Bird had made, considering the inclement weather of the past few weeks, and the length of the waterways his officer had to navigate. Bird's accounting could only mean that his force would soon be able to descend the Big Miami River, once he was able to portage his bateaux and supplies, an enormous task taking considerable time.

Having just finished with the interrogation of the most recent batch of Virginian prisoners brought to Detroit for ransom by returning war parties from Kentucky, DePeyster could only hope that Bird's campaign against the settlements would be successful enough to discourage the further arrival of people to those Indian lands which seemed lately to be a torrent. From the questioning of the captives, DePeyster could see that the settlers were hardly interested in the politics of rebellion, being entirely consumed with acquiring land for themselves. In many cases, it appeared to him that they were "flying from the oppression of Congress, in order to add to the numbers already settled at Kentuck, the finest Country for new settlers in America." [HP-97]

The problem for these settlers, now prisoners of the Indians, was that no one had told them, nor did they understand that the ground they wished to acquire was Indian territory, part of the Ohio Country; land that was already spoken for, already taken, and not to be given up to fulfill their desires for settlement. "Unfortunately for them, it happens to be the Indian's best Hunting Ground, which they will never give up," DePeyster wrote. "In fact, it is in our interest not to let the Virginians, Marylanders, and Pennsylvanians get possession there, lest in a short time they become formidable to this post," and attempt to attack

Detroit, for men like the Rebel Colonel Clark wished to enlist these poor farmers to do.

DePeyster knew that Captain Bird would do all in his power to discourage them, but as cruel as it may sound, DePeyster implicitly understood that whomever Bird was unable to dissuade by both persuasion and force of arms, the Indians would teach with the hatchet and scalping knife. For the moment, DePeyster had more important things on his mind, such as the deplorable condition of the parapets of Fort Lernoult. "The ditches are filling faster than we can stop, owing to severe weather, and springs breaking out in all parts, which bring down the earth in great clods" making it all a muddy mess. In addition, another problem needed his immediate attention. Word had just reached DePeyster that the sloop "Wyandot" was "beached on the east shore of Lake Huron with all her Cargo" still aboard. DePeyster shook his head in disgust. [HP-97]

"Of Distressing the Enemy in That Quarter"

At the same, Lt. Col. Bolton at Niagara had a number of difficulties of his own to deal with. First was the fact that it was May 16, and Bolton had not as yet had a vessel arrive from Detroit, so that he could return it with supplies for DePeyster, as well as important dispatches from Quebec and reinforcements. Not knowing if the vessels "Gage" or "Dunmore" were completed to sail, nor what had happened to the sloop, the "Wyandot," Bolton "found it necessary to send off an express to Major DePeyster and enclose for him extracts of letters with such orders" necessary for his Post, as well as for Sinclair at Michilimackinac. [HP-98]

After the recent arrival of the detachment of the 34th Regiment of Foot from Carleton Island to reinforce the Niagara garrison and be "employed in carrying on such works as are absolutely necessary for the safety of this Post," Bolton consulted with Major John Butler of the Ranger Corps. He decided that a company of Rangers must be sent forward to Detroit at the first possible moment to support DePeyster's campaign against the Rebels in Kentucky, now that they could be spared. [HP-98] Captain Peter Hare's Ranger company had been selected by Butler to go to Detroit, and Hare and his men were put on alert to make the necessary preparations. [CE-p.88] Bolton and Butler both agreed that Captain Caldwell and his men would be much needed at Niagara to support Sir John Johnson's major campaign against the Mohawk Valley, which General Haldimand had ordered in his letter to Bolton on April 16. "I wish to communicate to you my intention of sending a strong detachment composed of Regular Troops, Provincials, and Indians under the Command of Sir John Johnson into the neighborhood of Johnstown in order to furnish a number of Loyalists with an opportunity of Escaping from thence, and at the same time of Distressing the Enemy in that Quarter." [HP-138]

Bolton knew that Johnson's Royal Yorkers, Brant's Volunteers, and the best of the Ranger Corps would be required for the expedition, including the services of Captain William Caldwell. He had little doubt that the Iroquois would need any persuading to accompany the expedition. Bolton's only fear was that in their current mood, no one would be able to stop the Indians from butchering every Rebel man, woman, and child that should be unfortunate enough to fall into their clutches, once they found an opportunity to satisfy their vowed blood vengeance against the Rebels, as a result of Sullivan's campaign the previous year which had devastated their homes and crops.

Still, Bolton had more pressing worries. He did not have enough workable weapons to outfit the entire force, and ordered "all repairable and unserviceable arms to be sent down as soon as possible to Montreal." Bolton calculated he did not have enough provisions for the upcoming campaign that would last weeks, in light the families still arriving from Albany as refugees, as "we find it a difficult matter to supply those already here with Provisions." And though the Indians were intent on seeking revenge against the Rebels, Bolton knew from past experience that he would need to supply them with presents, in addition to provisions and ammunition. Serving them with gifts was a long-held custom of the British that appealed to the vanity of the Indians, flattering them for the necessity of their allegiance. However outrageous it seemed to him at the moment, "without the usual presents to them, we cannot count on for any assistance from our Indian allies," in spite of the great expense they had already cost the Crown at Niagara. While Colonel Guy Johnson, Superintendent of the Indian Department at Niagara boasted to Bolton that he had "near 400 Indians out on different expeditions," Bolton knew otherwise. In his estimation, the Indians were at times more trouble than they were worth, and if he had not conservatively doled out the provisions to the Indians at Niagara during the winter, in spite of Colonel Johnson's wishes to the contrary, "this Garrison must have been put on short allowance three months ago." [HP-98]

Far afield in the wilderness of the Ohio Country, Captain Henry Bird congratulated himself that so far, everything had gone favorably for his expedition. It was the May 21 and his force was now encamped "Six Leagues below the Portage" between the Auglaize and the Big Miami River, at the post of Peter Lorimer, an English trader and friend of the Shawnee. [HP-99] His men and the Indians present were busy making pirogues, or dug-out canoes to add to their flotilla, which Bird hoped would not retard their progress in joining with McKee downriver at the appointed spot. Several developments had occurred since their arrival which was disconcerting to Bird.

First, a runner came in to Bird's camp the first day with news from the upper Shawnee towns concerning "the Hurons of St. Dusky" who "will give the Shawanese no answer about joining" the expedition. Bird could not understand the petty bickering and jealously between the tribes which prevented them from doing anything in a concerted manner, including going to war. In addition, an Indian scout soon after arrived from McKee's Shawnee village with the report that "Colonel Clark is advertised of our coming, though ignorant of our numbers and artillery." Apparently two prisoners taken the previous autumn had managed to escape the Indians and had, as yet, not been recaptured. [HP-99] The revelation of Indian laxness in handling their prisoners disturbed McKee.

Then, a wretched Rebel prisoner taken somewhere near the Falls of the Ohio was brought into Bird's camp by an Indian party. The man revealed that word of Bird's expedition had indeed reached the Rebels on the Ohio, and though Clark had said "he will wait for us, instead of going to the Mississippi, his numbers do not exceed 200," the prisoner told, and "his provisions and ammunition short." [HP-99] With the latest news fresh in his mind, Captain Bird thought it prudent to send a note to McKee at the upper Shawnee village, urging him to send more Indians to help with work on the pirogues to hurry them for the appointed rendevous. If the information on the movements of Clark were to be believed, Bird could only surmise that time was of the essence if his force was to attack the fort at the Falls of the Ohio before Clark could reinforce it.

"He May Have Them Intercepted Should They Take That Way"

Alexander McKee at the upper Shawnee Indian village carefully studied the message that had been placed in his hands by the Indian runner from Captain Bird at Lorimer's. McKee could see the urgency in Bird's words, but did not feel the same compulsion as the Englishman to hurry himself or advise the Shawnee chiefs and warriors to do the same. How could he possibly make Bird understand that the Indians did not move by his or Bird's bidding, but by their own tune and design. "I have endeavored all in my power to expedite them going to you and collecting themselves" McKee wrote to Bird in his reply, "but there is no bringing them out of their usual method of proceeding." [HP-96] McKee thought to himself that if Bird took a Shawnee wife it might enable him to see that his impatience with the Indians was impertinent. The Indians would move when they were ready to. A great deal of counseling among themselves was necessary and the signs must be right. Until then, Bird could harangue them all he wanted but the Indians would not move at the orders of a white man. However, McKee knew that explaining all this again to the captain was a waste of time.

What was important, was for McKee to inform Captain Bird of the unfortunate incident that happened many days ago, that no doubt, would have some bearing on Bird's campaign, and surely affect the Indians, once they became entirely apprised of the situation, and its possible ramifications. McKee believed that it was the fault of the Hurons that the two Virginian prisoners in the village were allowed to escape, and not the fault of the Shawnee. There was no point in keeping the news from Bird any longer, as he was sure to discover the news of what happened himself. Better that the Captain hear it from McKee first, than from the Hurons, who would undoubtedly, due to their animosity towards McKee and the Shawnee, create their own version to suit themselves, and absolve themselves of responsibility.

"An unlucky accident (which they ought to have prevented) has retarded them some days—two white prisoners made their escape from the Hurons upon receiving some intimation of our designs. They lived with one [named] Zeans, who is strongly suspected by the Indians of not only assisting them of, but sending intelligence by them. One of the prisoners is a Lieutenant in the Rebel Service and was taken last fall at the Ohio- as I had received an account, last writes that they might attempt to escape, I spoke to the Indians upon my first arrival, to have them secured, which they neglected. They have sent different courses after them, and I have offered a reward to have them brought in and delivered to me, to be sent to Detroit." [HP-96]

McKee guessed that Simon Girty and his brothers would be enraged when they heard that the two had escaped, remembering that they had a hand in their capture the previous fall in the engagement on the Ohio, when one the two men, a Lieutenant Abraham Chapline, was saved from the wrath of the Indians by Simon Girty himself. The other man McKee did not know, but had heard was named Hendricks, had been captured earlier with the Virginian Boone. [WGA-p.107] As McKee was about to seal the letter to Bird and send it with a runner to the British camp, he was summoned by one of the Shawnee chiefs who informed him that a white prisoner of their own had given them important information on the escape, which McKee should become aware of. "I have just received an account from a prisoner who lived with them [the two prisoners] during the winter, that Zeans had directed them to the Miami River to a Frenchman there, who would assist them in getting clear," McKee added to Bird, in his letter of May 3. "Perhaps by sending Mr. Branbeau he may have them intercepted, should they take that way." [HP-96]

"And By One Ridiculous Day and the Other"

Within the week, Captain Bird's expedition was once again able to set out down the Big Miami River from Lorimer's post in their flotilla of bateaux and pirogues. On May 31, he reached the forks of the Big Miami River, which was "the place appointed by the Indians," for the purpose of rendevous for all the Indians of the Ohio Country who were intent on accompanying the campaign against the Enemy in Kentucky. [HP-43] True to his word, Alexander McKee met Bird and his men there, bringing with him over 300 Shawnee warriors which, along "with those from the Lakes," McKee noted, "makes as near 400 strong," adding that "the Six Nations with a large band of Shawanese upon the way to join us, compacted to 200 more, will make our party about 600 Indians in addition to Captain Bird's detachment. Thus we shall not be able to meet all our force, till after our arrival at the Ohio, which will be tomorrow, where it is thought most expedient to wait for those in our rear, as we shall have there an opportunity to intercept any boats that may be passing down the river," our Enemy. [HP-44]

McKee decided that he would not pass up an opportunity to criticize the conduct of the Hurons to Captain Bird whenever the chance should arise, for his dislike of them was as deep as theirs of him. On June 3, while waiting in the combined camp, McKee informed Bird that "no satisfactory answer has been had from the Hurons, notwithstanding that several messages has been sent to them to expedite their joining us." [HP-44] McKee wanted to be sure to lay blame against the Hurons if anything should go awry in the campaign, which the support of the Hurons could have forestalled if they had participated. "About the time we were on the way out, I am informed that a small party of them (Hurons) was stopped by the Wakitumikee Indians from going to war, which those Indians declare was far from their design, having on the contrary, called upon them there several times since, for their assistance in the present undertaking." This, McKee reluctantly communicated to Bird, knowing that the information would only add to the officer's growing frustration with the Indians.

Bird took McKee's information at face value. The Hurons were the problem, not the Indians at Wakatomika, he believed. McKee informed Bird that the Hurons had repeatedly refused to join him. "The Hurons, glad of the opportunity, returned, but have, though repeatedly invited, refused to join the Confederacy." [HP-106] Whatever the problem was with the Hurons, perhaps due to jealousy or a long-standing enmity with one of the other tribes, Captain Bird could not figure it out, nor did he wish to at this point. It was beyond his comprehension that the Indians continued to squabble amongst themselves, even under the current conditions that they faced with a common enemy threatening them all.

In light of the news reaching the Indians in camp that the two Rebel prisoners of the Hurons had "arrived some time ago at the Falls, with intelligence of our approach," the chiefs of the various septs and tribes decided that a council was needed to discuss what they intended to do. [HP-106] Captain Bird was beside himself with anger. Precious time was being wasted with more talk, when the whole force could easily descend the Miami, "a day's march from the Ohio," [HP-106] and strike downriver for the Rebel post at the Falls without any difficulty. "I went to Captain McKee and told him - I could wish he would attempt to bias the Indians as far as proper to proceed immediately to the Falls," rather than proceeding anywhere else. [HP-43] Bird stated his reasons unequivocally to McKee. First, Captain Clark would "not be able to join the rebels assembling at the Falls before the first of the month- he has certainly 200 soldiers with him." Secondly, "it is possible before Clark's arrival they may raise 800 men, probably may raise 600, certain they can raise 400. It is also possible we may beat 800- probable we can beat 600, certain we can beat 400. Col. Clark's arrival will add considerably to these numbers, and to their confidence; therefore the Rebels should be attacked before his arrival- now it is possible that he may return be the 14th, probable by the 22nd, certain by the 1st of July," Bird counseled.

Now Bird came to the real crux of the matter in his argument to McKee. Rightly, it concerned the Indians. "It's possible for us to get to the Falls by the 10th of this month, certain by the 14th, the Indians will have their full spirits- the ammunition and everything plenty, and in the state we could wish it. After taking the Falls, the country on our return will be submissive, and in a manner subdued; but if we attack the heavier forts first, as we advance, we shall have continual desertion of the Indians- the ammunition wasted or expended, and our people far from fresh, our difficulties will increase as we advance, and Colonel Clark will be at the Falls with all his people collected to fight us at the close," adding to his argument "I have another reason for attacking the Falls-should we succeed, we can ambuscade Mr. Clark as he returns." [HP-43]

Bird's words made a strong unintended impression on McKee, stinging him with the feeling of rebuke concerning the inconsistency of the Indians, whom he was charged with overseeing. However McKee was not one to argue with Bird at this critical juncture in the campaign, and he remained silent for the moment, knowing that the officer had not intended to insult him. Recognizing that there was an element of truth in what Bird had said, McKee finally spoke, agreeing with Bird's reasoning, and promised to extend all his efforts to persuade the Indians in the favor of Bird's plan. "Captain McKee thinks my reasons just-if this plan is not followed, it will be owing to the Indians who may adopts others", Bird responded. [HP-43] What McKee could not tell Bird was that the Indians would have little consideration of Bird's proposal anyway, in light of the word of Clark's advance. All that McKee could do was warn Bird that "the Indians would also consider these new developments and arrive at their own conclusions" irrespective of any white man. He and Bird would just have to wait and see the outcome. [NL-p.115]

The Indian Council went on for two days at the Forks, without results. Bird's initial anger turned to total exasperation with the Indians as the time passed and they could not arrive at a consensus on what they should do. "It is now 16 days since I arrived at the Forks, appointed by the Indians to meet, and by one ridiculous day or the other, they have prolonged or retarded to this day," Bird noted on June 11. Unable to speak with the Indians directly when they came to him with their petty requests and complaints, Bird directed them to McKee for fear that he would lose control with them as he had the previous year at the Upper Sandusky villages, and if that happened, any hope remaining of a campaign against the Rebels would be gone. McKee, who was not bound by the same constraints as Bird, performed admirably in the role given him by Bird. "I confess to you, my patience have received very severe shocks, and would have been very long ago exhausted, had I not had an excellent example before me as the one Captain McKee sets- indeed he manages Indians to a charm," Bird wrote to DePeyster. [HP-102]

On the following morning, the assembled chiefs of all the Indians present, met with Bird to give him their answer. Through McKee and the Girty brothers, Captain Bird was informed that the Indians would not advance down the Ohio to attack the Virginians at the Falls of the Ohio, but instead, had "determined for Licking Creek, and tomorrow by daybreak we move up the stream." [HP-102] Bird was more than disappointed, but could do nothing. McKee quietly explained to the officer their reasons for setting out for the mouth of Licking Creek on the Ohio River that lay a short distance upriver from the mouth of the Big Miami. The Indians "determined to proceed to the nearest forts by way of Licking Creek, giving for their reasons that it could not be prudent to leave their villages naked and defenseless in the neighborhood of those forts." [HP-104] Bird again was enraged.

The Indians' decision was based on the information received by them of Clark's advance. In Bird's mind, it was entirely the fault of the Indians that Clark had forewarning of Bird's expedition, alerted by two escaped prisoners of the Indians. It did not make good tactical sense for the Indians to attack the forts on the Licking that intelligence suggested were far too weak to mount any attack on the Indian villages across the Ohio. "Their attack on the littler forts, their numbers so great, is mean of them" Bird replied, a waste of precious provisions and ammunition when a more strategic target at the Falls was within reach. Captain Bird lashed out at the Indians to McKee, suggesting that their decision was based more on an unreasonable fear of Clark which bordered on cowardice.

Sidestepping Bird's angry conjecture, McKee defended the decision of the Indians, reminding him of the destruction wrought by Bowman's raid of the previous year against the Indians and pointing to their genuine concern for their families who would suffer greatly if another attack were mounted against them while the warriors were so far away. McKee then reminded Bird that the problem of information reaching Clark had nothing to do with the Indians who were with him at the moment. The perfidy was a result of the negligence of the Hurons who should be the object of Bird's anger and chastisement, not the Shawnee. With McKee's remarks, Captain Bird calmed himself and accepted with resignation the decision of the Indians to head to the Licking. It was just that with all that had passed in Bird's frustrating dealings with the Indians since his arrival in the Ohio Country more than a year before, the distinction between Indian differences was completely lost upon him.

"It Is Hoped In a Day or Two"

At Detroit, Major DePeyster had no recent word recently from Captain Bird and his expedition deep in the Ohio Country, nor from the party of Indians he had sent in the direction of Post Vincent to scout the location and strength of the Rebels in case they might be mounting a campaign against Detroit while Bird's force was gone. Waiting and worrying, DePeyster occupied much of his time supervising the troops of the garrison who were improving the works of Fort Lernoult which had suffered from the winter snows and spring rains. With a mound of correspondence waiting for his response, DePeyster wrote to Bolton on June 8, "whenever I have it in my power I will lose no time in sending the detachment to Michilimackinac - the men are with Captain Bird, and until his return we have no more men than are indispensably necessary for the duty and works of the garrison." [HP-99]

DePeyster was presently irritable from the tension of watching and waiting for word of Captain Bird and the enemy. He was unhappy that more reinforcements had not arrived to bolster Bird's own detachment of troops, knowing intuitively that somewhere or somehow the Indians would run afoul of Bird with their unpredictableness which both he and Bird privately despised. Light infantry and Rangers in sufficient numbers would have had a greater chance of success than the bulk of Indians that McKee had summoned to accompany

Bird. Writing again to Bolton, DePeyster remonstrated for the lack of good men, stating, "I wish the Rangers I wrote to you for were arrived, in order to send them to support Captain Bird in case of necessity, and at all events, to relieve his detachment after he has seen the Enemy." [HP-99]

Clearly, Bird and his men were on DePeyster's mind at all times, in despite the spate of vexing problems with the lake vessels. "As the 'Angelica' cannot get upriver (to Detroit) I have for dispatch ordered bateaux to fetch up her cargo, she with the 'Faith' shall sail, wind and weather permitting, by tomorrow evening," DePeyster told Bolton. "The 'Dunmore' and "Gage" are not yet finished, and the latter has just broke her mainmast in three." On the condition of the beached sloop "Wyandot", "the 'Wyandot' has not arrived as you will see by the enclosed letter, and the 'Welcome' has gone to assist her for some days past, to that I have only the 'Adventure' no ways calculated for a Mackinac voyage. It is hoped in a day or two, the 'Felicity' will make her appearance from Michilimackinac, when I shall forward everything to that Post." [HP-99] If DePeyster was in ill-humor in recent days, as was whispered by junior officers at Detroit, he could find good reason for it in the exasperating business of keeping the King's lake vessels under his charge at Detroit afloat and moving in a timely manner.

"The Way This Intelligence Came Was by Two Men"

The entire force comprised of Bird's detachment and the body of Indians numbering well over 700 warriors arrived at the Ohio River the next day, June 12. After stopping for a brief rest, they turned upriver to paddle several miles to the mouth of Licking Creek which flowed into the Ohio from the south. Alexander McKee reached the mouth of the Licking hours before with an advanced party of warriors traveling in canoes and on the river trails scouting for sign of the Enemy ahead of Bird's main body. It was near the Licking the scouts encountered a small party of Virginians in their lone boat, and seized them before they had a chance to fire on the Indians or make their escape. McKee had had a hand in their bloodless capture. He had called out to them in English, telling them that if they surrendered immediately that the Indians would spare their lives. McKee knew what he told them was a lie, but he needed them alive to question them about the Rebel forts ahead. Unfortunately their fate was inconsequential to McKee, for he knew that the Indians would take no prisoners with them while scouting for Enemy. Since they could not be left behind for fear they would alert Clark's militiamen, the Indians would kill them when McKee was done with the questioning. That was the harsh reality of wilderness war, and McKee considered it fortunate that Bird, who did not fully understand these things, was not with them to witness what was about to happen next to the doomed captives.

McKee took the opportunity to talk to the men while the warriors decided among themselves how the white men were to be killed once McKee was finished questioning them. McKee could see fear written all over the faces of the worried men. Without betraying what he knew was going to happen to them, McKee calmly asked the men what they knew of the strengths of the forts on the Licking River. Without hesitation, the captives told him that they had come from the Falls of the Ohio, having left on June 1 and were on their way to Pittsburgh. They knew nothing about the forts on the Licking and none of the men admitted that they were in the Virginia militia. By occupation they were farmers and not Rebels. They told McKee that Colonel Clark and his militia were not at the Falls, nor expected for some time. Most of the inhabitants at Clark's post were settlers like themselves, not soldiers, and had come to seek land to farm, and not to enlist to fight against the British or Indians. By McKee's judgment, he believed from the sincerity of their answers that what they told him was true, and that these men who were about to die, were good people. But with the talking done, McKee stood up and moved aside from them, motioning to the Indians that the time for the execution had come. Seeing this, the captives began to tremble and cry out to McKee, begging him for their lives, which he knew could not be spared.

Alexander McKee turned away from the macabre spectacle that was about to unfold, knowing from the beginning that the warriors would not trouble themselves with the unnecessary nuisance of taking prisoners along with them before they attacked the forts, when the scalps of the dead men could adorn their belts just as well. Though McKee was hardened to the harsh realities of wilderness fighting, he nonetheless could not watch those living men bloodily butchered alive before his eyes by his delighted companions. For a few terrible moments, the shrieks of the men pierced his ears. One by one, the gruesome deed of slaughtering the unfortunate men was completed and their lifeless bodies stripped naked. The warriors disemboweled the corpses as if they were game, and then mutilated beyond recognition what was remaining. Then to the derisive laughter of the warriors involved, the bodies were dumped into the current of the Ohio River where the Virginians downriver on the island at the Falls were sure to discover them in horror.

One of the warriors dropped the blood-spattered packet of letters taken from the hapless men into McKee's hands. He opened them, one by one, and read the contents more out of curiosity than in the hopes of gaining intelligence. One letter was written to family in the east, stating, "Dear Brother, I arrived at this place about 10 days passed and can't help saying that I think nature never before formed a country equal to it, but would never advise any friend or acquaintance of mine to bring their family." [HP-95] Another young man had ironically written to his uncle on May 30, saying, "the Indians have been very successful in killing and scalping the people here," concluding the letter that would now never arrive, "your dutiful nephew, William Elliot." [HP-95] McKee cooled himself from any twinge of sentimentality, as the Indians were eager to move up the Licking now that the smell of blood had heightened their senses. As McKee jammed the packet of letters into his breast pocket, he was sure of one thing that he had gleamed from each man before they had died, which was also reflected in all of the letters. The Rebels had been well alerted on the approach of Bird's force for some time, if McKee could judge by the words "the way this intelligence came was by two men that left the Indian towns about 4 to 5 weeks ago," which kept running through his mind. [HP-95] Hopefully the element of surprise was not completely compromised.

"The Carelessness of Some Indians Upon Our Left"

Alexander McKee and the advance party of Indians paddled up the Licking "as far up as the forks, where we found it unpractical to get farther by water on account of its lowness." [HP-104] Here McKee set up camp to wait for Bird and the main body, while sending warriors to reconnoiter the fort ahead and scouts to watch the trails used by the Virginians. He hoped that a prisoner could be taken alive who could provide them with intelligence on the strength of the posts that were to be attacked. Within a day, Bird's vanguard arrived at the forks of the Licking, and Bird, McKee, the Girty brothers and the Indian war captains and chiefs conferred. It was decided that McKee would accompany a party of about 200 warriors who would lead the way to the first enemy fort called Ruddel's station several miles distant by a shorter overland route that had been already scouted. Bird and his detachment, with the main body of Indians and the two artillery pieces would take the longer route following the trail that followed the Licking. On the June 26, McKee prepared to leave. The Indians stripped to their breechcloths, each man carrying only his hatchet, scalping knife, a pound of powder and ball for his musket, and a couple of handfuls of corn to eat along the way. After painting themselves for war in vermillion and black, the warriors with McKee slipped out from camp towards the first enemy post that the Virginians called Fort Liberty. [HP-104]

In the fading light of dusk, McKee and his force of warriors arrived undetected in the woods surrounding the fort without encountering enemy settlers, militia, or their scouts on the trails leading to the post. Through the night, McKee carefully deployed the warriors "and surrounded the enemy's first fort, before day, this done before they were in the least apprised of us." McKee gave strict orders to the chiefs with him to tell their warriors to remain hidden at all costs, and rest through the remainder of the night. Under no circumstances were the warriors to fire on anyone coming to or leaving the fort "and by no means to alarm the fort, if it could be avoided, until the arrival of the main body with the cannon," in the morning. McKee again hoped that the Indians would be fortunate enough to quietly capture a prisoner leaving the fort without the knowledge of those still inside, "in order to gain intelligence of the enemy's force and situation," for neither McKee, Bird, or the Indians had a true evaluation of the fort's defenses as yet. [HP-104]

The light of dawn slowly filtered through the dense forest canopy of the woods surrounding Ruddel's fort alerting the more than 200 Indians who lay hidden in the woods just beyond the picketed walls. By the sounds of the settlers and their children beginning to go about their daily chores, and the melodic bellowing of the hungry cattle within the fort's interior stockade, it became apparent to McKee and the Indians that the inhabitants were indeed unsuspecting of the presence of the force concealed around the fort in readiness to attack them. In spite of a growing edginess that McKee could sense among the hidden warriors, McKee and the chiefs would not allow any move on any warrior's part that would compromise their position. Then almost an hour after sunrise, the gates of the fort opened, and a small party of Virginians came out of the fort with sickles in hand to cut hay. As the men sauntered towards a patch of tall grass growing near a cluster of dense thickets "the carelessness of some Indians upon our left fired upon the small party" dropping several of the Enemy in their tracks. As warriors emerged from the woods to scalp the dead and dying, the survivors raced to the safety of the fort, hollering to those inside that Indians were attacking. Once the men were inside, the gates were shut, and "this commenced a firing, both from the fort, and our Indians, which lasted till about 12 o'clock," with shots being traded with the fort defenders with little effect. [HP-104]

This was exactly what Captain Bird had feared would happen, and what he warned McKee and his Indian officers to avoid at all costs. "Persuade them not to engage with the fort until the guns were up, (for) if any were killed, it might exasperate the Indians and make them commit cruelties upon the Rebels surrendered." [HP-103] Bird's pleas had been in vain once the shooting began, as the Indians had given away any element of surprise, and now the outcome of the battle rested upon Bird's arrival with his detachment, the artillery, and the larger body of Indians with him. However, while on the trail to Ruddel's fort, Bird's Indians received word by runner that the attack had begun, and they immediately took off at a run, outdistancing Bird and his men, fearing they would miss out in the killing, scalping and distribution of plunder.

"That They Would All Be Killed"

By noon, Bird and his force arrived at Ruddel's, and the Captain appraised the situation, while his men moved the three-pounder cannon to within striking distance of the fort gate. Already McKee's advance party had taken casualties. "Poor McCarty," the white trader and interpreter from the Upper Sandusky villages, "in every respect an extreme, attentive, serviceable fellow perished by disobeying this order" issued by Bird to wait until he arrived, rather than risk oneself in the fire from the Enemy. "An Indian was shot through the arm" Bird noticed, but so far, none had been killed in the fusillade. Bird had his men "raise a battery of earth within 80 yards of the fort, taking some advantage of a very violent storm of rain, which prevented them being seen clearly. [HP-103] The artillerymen loaded the three-pounder and fired the little gun twice with little effect; one shot "only cut down a spar," and the other shot "stuck in the side of a house" to the cheers of the fort defenders. However their mood of defiance changed when they saw a much larger cannon, the six-pounder, rolled across the field from the woods and into position next to the smaller piece, which many Virginians had "thought the three pounder a swivel gun the Indians and their Department had got with them." [HP-103] As the artillery crew prepared to fire the larger gun against the fort gates, the defenders struck their colors, signaling Bird and the Indians that they had had enough, and were "determined to surrender the place." [HP-104]

Captain Bird called to McKee to have his Indian officers pass the word to the warriors in the woods surrounding the fort to stop shooting at the fort. It took several minutes for the musket fire from the Indians to trail off and end, creating an eerie silence that descended upon the battlefield. Smoke from the gunfire drifted low to the ground, mixing with the rising mist from the morning's rainstorm. With the firing halted, Bird hastily convened a meeting of his officers and the Indian Department to determine what to do next. Simon Girty suggested that he approach the fort alone under a flag of truce and call on the defenders to surrender immediately. Bird agreed to Girty's request, but not without urging him to warn the Rebels as he neared their guns that if anyone of them fired upon Girty while he was parleying with them, Captain Bird would give the order for his gun-crew at the six-pounder to fire upon the gates till they battered them down, whereupon he would no longer be able to restrain the Indians from entering.

Simon Girty emerged from the woods and made his way across the field to the fort, waving a scrap of cloth tied to the end of his musket as a signal to hold their fire, as he was approaching to parley. He could hear the intermingled sounds of crying babies, wailing women, bellowing cattle and the moans of the wounded echoing from behind the picket walls as he got closer. On the edge of the woods on all sides of the fort, Girty could see the hundreds of painted warriors emerging from cover to watch what was unfolding. Quickly covering the distance to the stockade walls, Girty called to the defenders whom he could see on the parapet with their weapons trained on him that he wanted to talk to the officer in command of the fort. In the same breath, Girty warned them that they had better not fire upon him while he was under the flag of truce, conveying Bird's warning of what would happen if he should be shot down. Girty again asked to speak to whoever was in command, and for a few tense moments, he waited under the guns of the enemy for a response, not sure of what would happen next. Then slowly the gates were opened wide enough for a man to enter, and Girty was motioned to proceed inside, "while many rifles were pointed at him as he entered the stockade." [BC-p.89]

Once in the fort, Simon Girty quickly scanned the interior, noticing the large number of women and children who were crowded inside the walls next to the animals. Obviously, their large numbers meant Ruddel's fort was civilian and not military. To Girty, the men and their families looked liked farmers and not Rebel militia. He could see by the distraught looks upon their faces as his gaze met theirs, that they were gripped with terror at the spectacle of the Indians surrounding them, and the fate that was in store for them if they should fall into the hands of the savages. Girty was met by Isaac Ruddel, the commander of the Fort and his comrades who gathered around Girty to hear what he had to say. Keeping cool, Simon Girty informed Ruddel and all "those inside the pickets that, unless they surrendered" and did so immediately, "they would all be killed," owing to the six-pounder which had been brought up to "batter down the frail stockade," and the large number of Indians whom the British would not be able to restrain from massacring the women and children once they gained entry. [BC-p.89]

However, Girty was surprised to find Ruddel not easily intimidated, despite the hopeless situation in which he and the people inside the fort found themselves, facing cannon and an overwhelming number of attackers outside the fort. Isaac Ruddel refused Girty's demand to surrender and open the gates. He was adamant the he would only consent to surrendering the fort after speaking with the British officer, Captain Bird. Ruddel explained that he wished to personally discuss with Bird the terms of capitulation, telling Girty that "he could not consent to open the gates but on certain conditions, one of which was that the prisoners should be under the protection of the British and not suffered to be held by the Indians." [BC-p.89]

"That the Savages Would Adopt Some of Their Children"

Realizing that he had done all that he could under the circumstances to convince the stubborn Ruddel to surrender unconditionally, Girty reluctantly agreed to return to Bird with Ruddel's request for a formal meeting. As Girty walked back across the field to speak with Bird, he could sense the palpable restlessness and growing frustration of the Indians who watched him. Girty was sure that he knew what the Indians were thinking; what Alexander McKee was already aware of, and what Captain Bird remained totally ignorant of. The warriors had not come all this way to the Kentucky lands to watch white men talk of peace and then go home empty-handed, without scalps, plunder and prisoners. The Indians were thinking that the white men might talk, but the fight was far from over for the warriors as yet.

Shortly, Captain Bird, with Alexander McKee, Simon Girty and an armed guard of soldiers trudged across the field to talk to Isaac Ruddel about the terms of capitulation. However before leaving, Bird had spoken in a brief council to the Indian chiefs through the interpreters, laying out to them the terms of the surrender and what he expected of them. On the advice of McKee, Bird promised the Indians all of the plunder within the fort, in equal distribution "amongst their several nations to prevent jealousies or dissatisfaction" [HP-104]. In return, however, the Indians must promise that the cattle within the fort be given "for food for our people," and the prisoners must all be given up to Bird and his men unharmed. In addition, Bird told the Indians that they "were not to enter (the fort) until the next day" after the prisoners had been secured and removed. [HP-103] After talking among themselves, "the Indian chiefs agreed to the proposals as well as for the preservation of the prisoners" assuring Bird that they would talk to their warriors and not break their promise to him. With the agreement of the Indians in place, Captain Bird with his officers and guard proceeded to the fort, "to settle the terms of capitulation with Captain Ruddel." [BC-p.89]

Bird met with Ruddel inside one of the cabins. To Ruddel's conditions of surrender that he had requested Girty convey, Captain Bird consented to honor the terms with certain provisions. Bird informed Ruddel that though "the conditions granted that their lives should be saved" it would mean that they would be "taken to Detroit" as prisoners and all their property confiscated by the Indians. What could not be taken would be destroyed and the fort and their homes burned. McKee then spoke up, telling Ruddel that under the circumstances, sparing their lives would be a very difficult thing for the Indians to agree to. Ruddel and his people were occupying the hunting grounds of the Indians and that violation demanded that the Indians seek revenge against the intruders. McKee warned Ruddel that to appease the Indians, it was unfortunately necessary that he should expect "that the savages would adopt some of their children" as a condition to saving everyone's lives. [HP-103]

Knowing the large number of children within the walls, Isaac Ruddel swallowed hard at this chilling demand. Ruddel appealed directly to Bird as a fellow Christian, asking the officer how could he possibly tell his family, friends and neighbors that they must give up some of their children to the savages in order to spare everyone's lives, when their children were all that they had in this world that was worth living for? Before Bird could answer, the piercing sound of a chorus of war whoops, shrieks and hideous screams instantly erupted outside the cabin, riveting everyone's attention for one brief horrifying moment. Pandemonium had broken out within the fort's walls, as a horde of terrifying, painted Indians had rushed inside the gate with tomahawks and scalping knives in hand, driven into a frenzy by blood-lust, and possessed with an insatiable, murderous rage.

"The Poor Children Had Been Torn From Their Breasts"

Bird and his officers rushed out the door of the cabin but it was already too late. Charging Indians had seized a half-dozen of Ruddel's unarmed men and cut them down with tomahawks where they stood. As those dying men were scalped on the spot, more and more Indians continued to pour into the fort, stepping over the bloody bodies to join in the slaughter. Bird and McKee immediately entered the melee in an attempt to intervene, and stop the killing. By now, a savage struggle for survival was occurring as unarmed settlers hopelessly fought off the savages to protect their wives and children until they themselves were killed and their family seized. The Indians were grabbing any child they could and dragging them from inside the fort to the gate. Mothers who fought with the warriors to prevent the abduction of their screaming children were either clubbed or tomahawked by the maddened warriors, or themselves dragged by the hair to the gates, kicking and screaming along with their children, until they either gave up their fight or were killed and scalped in front of the children as a result of their attempt to save them.

Captain Bird, Alexander McKee, and Simon Girty were momentarily stunned by the spectacle of horror that greeted them. Bird screamed at the top of lungs at the Indians, barking orders to them with no effect, as McKee and Girty waded into the struggling mass of warriors, pulling them away from their victims in an attempt to stop the killing. The Shawnee, Wyandot, and Mingo warriors were among the attackers who more readily listened to McKee and Girty's demand that they stop, knowing and respecting the two Indian agents who lived among them. But the large number of Indians from the area of Fort Detroit, composed of Ottawa, Chippewa, and Pottawattamie Indians who had accompanied Bird on the first leg of his expedition ignored the pleas of the two Indian officers, as well as the orders of Bird himself. "The Lake Indians, in seizing the prisoners contrary to agreement, threw everything into confusion." [HP-104] While struggling with the most prominent of the warriors, Bird called upon the handful of men from the King's Eighth guard still standing to one side of the fort to prime, load, and present their weapons on the Indians, for if he could not stop the Indians by orders alone, though outnumbered, he must shoot down the worst offenders to attempt to restore order, for "neither Bird nor McKee could stop the slaughter." [NL-p.116]

As this was happening, a reinforcement of red-coated soldiers led by a quick-thinking subordinate officer burst into the fort with Matthew Elliott, George and James Girty, and French Canadians of the Indian Department who immediately forced themselves between the Indians and the remaining settlers to dissuade them from further killing. Gradually a semblance of order was restored, but not before the Indians had "killed a number of the defenders." An American survivor of the massacre later recalled, "The pickets were cut down like cornstalks, and 20 persons were tomahawked in cold blood." [NL-p.116]

The scene before Bird was beyond his description. Bloody, scalpless bodies of butchered settlers lay on the ground intermingled with the wounded and those still living. Dazed sobbing children clung to the bodies of slain fathers and grieving mothers wailed uncontrollably for their lost babies, calling out the names of "the poor children that had been tore from their breasts" during the confusion, when several hundred of the warriors inside the fort not directly involved in the killing had used the chaos as an opportunity to carry off dozens of children from inside the fort for adoption into their own tribes. Still, the frightful affair was not over yet.

"I Talked Hardly to Them of Their Breach of Promise"

The Ottawa and Pottawattamie warriors stood their ground before an angry Captain Bird, glaring at him with wild, hateful stares for the unwelcome interruption. In spite of the fresh scalps that hung from their belts and the blood that covered their bodies, their lust for killing was still not satiated. Knowing that Bird would not let them kill any more prisoners, the warriors turned to the 20 head of cattle that nervously stood penned in a corner of the fort, and unleashed their fury upon the poor beasts, wildly tomahawking the bellowing animals and cutting their throats to bathe and drink from the flow of blood before Bird could stop them. The Indians did not halt until "they killed every one of the cattle,

*Once inside Ruddel's fort, warriors lusting for blood
and scalps begin to massacre defenseless captives.*

leaving the whole to stink" as the carcasses quickly began to rot in the hot afternoon sun, attracting swarms of blowflies laying their eggs in the spoiled meat. Before Bird's eyes, the cattle which he had counted on for providing food for the expedition was gone. "We had brought no pork with us, and were now reduced to great distress, and the poor prisoners in danger of being starved." [HP-103]

The fitful night of June 26 passed. In the morning, a large body of Shawnee, Wyandot and Mingo warriors approached Captain Bird with heads hung in shame and turned their prisoners over to him and his men whom they had taken from the fort the previous day, seeking to mollify the Captain who was obviously disgusted with them. "The other Nations next morning returned all they had taken back into Captain Bird's charge," which McKee, with the help of Elliott and the Girtys through no small effort had managed to convince the Indians to do so through the night. [HP-104] However, the recalcitrant Lake Indians refused to do likewise with their prisoners, deciding among themselves during the night that they had come the greatest distance from their villages and had suffered the most during their arduous trip to Kentucky. They were not about to return home without captives for their troubles. Over 100 white prisoners of all ages remained in their hands, and Bird knew he was helpless to do anything more about the situation, as the Indians in question would not speak to him further on the matter of returning the prisoners, and threatened to leave him if he persisted. For his part, as Bird prepared his force to leave for the next Rebel fort named Martin's Station with nearly 300 hungry, frightened prisoners in tow, he could only glare in disproval at the Lake Indians to whom "I talked hardly to them of their breach of promise" [HP-103], and of the "wanton destruction of the cattle" by their hands. [BC-p.89]

"As I Had Then Fasted Some Time"

On the morning of June 27, Bird turned to the task ahead and had McKee dispatch "some spies towards the enemy's second fort" to learn what they could about the strength of the Rebels. The Indians were successful and "returned in the afternoon with a prisoner, having intercepted two men going express to alarm the other forts of our approach, killing one and capturing the other. The intelligence received from this prisoner determined us to set out immediately for the second fort, and we reached it the next morning about 10 o'clock, being the 28th." McKee advised Bird that he had reason to believe from the man that Martin's Station could be easily forced to surrender without a fight, and had the Indians bring the prisoner forward. The frightened man was advised that his own life would be spared if he would convince the fort to surrender without a fight, guaranteeing the man that if he was not successful, that he would be put to death by the Indians in a gruesome manner once the fort fell to Bird's cannon. Before the picket walls of Martin's post, "the prisoner taken the day before was sent in to inform them of the situation - they agreed to surrender" [HP-104] to Captain Bird's satisfaction, "without firing a gun." [HP-103]

While on the march to Martin's Station, Captain Bird had "demanded that the Indian headmen restrain their warriors and promise that any prisoners they took would be placed directly under Bird's personal protection" [NL-p.116] to avoid at all costs repeating the debacle that occurred at Ruddel's. "The Indians agreed, but when the station surrendered" and the defenders lay down their guns to place themselves under Captain Bird's guard, "the same promises were made and broke in the same manner [HP-103]" as a body of Indians rushed into the fort seeking prisoners, plunder, and scalps. "Once again, the Indians killed some prisoners and slaughtered the livestock [NL-p.116] and when Captain Bird finally managed to restrain the Indians and restore order, he found "not one pound of meat" fit to eat, with his own men and "near 300 prisoners" under his control to feed. [HP-103]

With the fall of Martin's Station, the Indians began to squabble among themselves and Captain Bird. The Lake Indians were content to leave for home at the first possible moment as they were loaded with so much plunder and prisoners without food, they worried their captives would die before they could reach their villages far to the north. The Shawnee, on the other hand, were determined to continue on, if only to obtain possessions of their own, and "several parties set out towards the adjacent forts to plunder for horses. [HP-104] Leaving Bird and his force behind at Martin's Station, the Indians set out farther up the Licking Creek where "the Rebels ran from the next fort, and the Indians burnt it" [HP-104] after stripping it of anything of value.

Meanwhile, back at Martin's Station, Bird decided that he had no other choice than to head back to the Ohio River, as "the prisoners now becoming numerous, amounting to between 300 and 400, with a scarcity of provision, added to many other insurmountable difficulties [MK-104]" for Bird. If the Shawnee did not want to go back "I must have insisted on, as I had then fasted sometime, and the prisoners were in danger of starving." [BD-103] Captain Bird turned his force around in the morning and "by the next day, we were back at the first fort [HP-103]," resting next to the ruins of Ruddel's, when a war party of Shawnee arrived in the camp. "Here we were overtaken by one of the small parties with a prisoner, who had left the Falls of the Ohio eight days before, he says that Col. Clark was daily expected there, and was to command an army against the Indians who were to leave that place on the 10th of July." [HP-104] It did not take long for the news of Clark to spread among the Indians, some of whom decided to set out immediately with or without Bird's approval for the Ohio River.

"Many of Them Laid Up With Agues and Fluxes"

Back at Fort Detroit, Major DePeyster had not heard any word more on the progress of Captain Bird's campaign against the Kentucky settlements since receiving the bundle of captured Rebel letters sent by Alexander McKee taken from prisoners near the mouth of Licking Creek on the Ohio. Studying the letters, DePeyster was astonished by the determination of the Virginians to possess the

Indian lands of Kentucky at all costs. Writing to Lt. Col. Bolton at Niagara on June 27, DePeyster noted, "you see it will become absolutely necessary to support the Indians with troops" as the efforts of the Indians alone, "whose success however great may be expected, will not be sufficient to deter those people from settling that country." DePeyster reflected upon Bird's current efforts, judging that however successful Bird might be in destroying the Rebel forts, "still it will only be temporary. Their letters plainly show that they will use all means to repair any loss they may receive from so small a detachment." [HP-101]

In the interim since Bird's departure from Detroit, the company of Rangers under Captain Peter Hare had arrived from Niagara to support the garrison. DePeyster was more concerned for the welfare of Bird's expedition than his own. Within days of the arrival of the Rangers, DePeyster ordered Hare to board the sloop "Wyandot" and set out for Sandusky and Kentucky to join with Bird's detachment. The "Wyandot" had only recently returned from Lake Huron where it had laid beached by a severe storm for several weeks. "Captain Barnett and the people with him had great fatigues in getting the 'Wyandot' afloat—their working mostly in the water have reasoned many of them to be laid up with agues and fluxes." [HP-100] When Captain Alexander Grant arrived at Detroit from Fort Erie a few days later, he informed DePeyster "of my meeting the 'Wyandot' on her way to Sandusky with the Company of Rangers." [HP-100] DePeyster had wisely decided to send extra provisions for Bird and his men with the Rangers, knowing that the extra weight would slow their progress but be of infinite help if Bird's force had found provisions along their trail too scarce to support the men and Indians.

"A Very Smart Fellow Escaped From Me"

At the moment, the welfare of the Indians was the furthest thing from Captain Bird's mind as he struggled from the Forks of Licking Creek to reach the Ohio River and Lorimer's post on the Big Miami before he, his men, and all the prisoners died from starvation. Bird's opinion of Alexander McKee had changed considerably for the worse at the Forks. There, McKee had informed Bird that he was leaving with the Shawnee who were intent on returning to their villages, in spite of Bird's exhortation for help. His appeal to McKee did no good, as the Indian officer attempted to reason with Bird that "the scarcity of provisions oblige the Indians to disperse. I engaged a few of the chiefs to stay with Captain Bird, more would be useless and troublesome" and in McKee's mind, "there could be no apprehension of danger immediately from the Enemy." [HP-104] Bird was not so sure. "It was with difficulty I procured a guide through the woods - I marched the poor women and children 20 miles in one day over very high mountains, frightening them with frequent alarms to push them forward," Bird wrote. "We came 90 miles in 4 days, with all our cannon and ammunition, we have no meal and must subsist on flour, if there is nothing at Lorimer's, I am out of hope of getting any Indians to hunt or accompany us, however George Girty I detain to assist me. Mud and rains have rotted our people's feet, and the Indians almost all left us within a day's march of the Enemy." [HP-103]

On the first of July, Bird and his exhausted, hungry force reached the mouth of Licking Creek on the Ohio River, where they rested a day. Bird took the opportunity to write a letter to Major DePeyster, sending it by express with a runner to Detroit, detailing the dire condition facing him, and lamenting his failure to achieve the original objectives of his expedition. "I could, Sir, by all accounts have gone through the whole country without an opposition, had the Indians preserved the cattle. Everything is safe so far, but we are not yet out of reach of pursuit, as a very smart fellow escaped from me within 26 miles of the Enemy." Bird worried that the escaped prisoner would be able to lead Clark's relief force right to him with little trouble, in an attempt to free the prisoners he held. [HP-103]

"I Have Left the Bombardiers Robson, Crow, and Galloughy"

Bird was able to move more swiftly once his force began their ascent up the Big Miami River during the first week of July. At nearly the same time, Alexander McKee with Simon Girty, his brother James, and Matthew Elliott reached the Shawnee villages on the Scioto with the returning warriors. On July 8, McKee thought it wise to write to Major DePeyster at Detroit, recounting to the officer the details of the raid into Kentucky, and explain to him why it was necessary to leave Captain Bird's returning expedition. Concerned for Bird's welfare, McKee wrote, "I have engaged the chiefs of the lower villages since my arrival to send a party down upon the Ohio in his (Bird's) rear, and to send spies towards the Falls." Appraising DePeyster of the latest intelligence received from war parties still in the field, McKee noted, "The Enemy abandoned two other Forts, which has been set on fire by the Indians. These are the most material circumstances relative to this expedition carried on by the Indians in conjunction with the King's troops." [HP-104] As for the behavior of the Indians at Ruddel's fort, McKee thought it best not to include any account.

On the morning of July 4, a runner reached Detroit and delivered Bird's letter to an expectant Major DePeyster. The news was better than DePeyster had anticipated. He learned that several enemy forts had been destroyed, and a large number of prisoners taken. As a sloop destined for Niagara had just left its mooring not more than a half hour before the letter arrived, DePeyster hastily penned a note to Lt. Col. Bolton, and sent it post-haste to reach the sloop while it was still in the Detroit River, to give the letter to Bolton. "Sir, this instant I received the enclosed from Captain Bird, which I send to overtake the sloop. You see that my little expedition will have missed of doing great things, from the want of resolution in the Indians, who are not fond of going in search of Rebel troops." However, DePeyster thought it wise, also, to content Bolton with the positive effects of Bird's campaign. "A prisoner woman just brought in from the Falls declares that two-thirds of the people there wished for Captain Bird's arrival in order to join him, being sick of oppression." [HP-102] If there was truth in what she said, both he and Bolton could be assured that an invasion of the Ohio Country by Clark was out of the question.

By July 15, Captain Bird and his expedition reached Lorimer's post on the Big Miami River, running into a scout of Rangers along the way, who were sent by Captain Hare to search for Bird and his people, and help bring them in. Arriving at Lorimer's, Bird was overjoyed to find "the provisions he had were of infinite service. Three days after we arrived at the Standing Stone our provisions were out—his stock will serve us." Bird had been delayed along the way with the burden of the artillery which was difficult to transport by pirogue, due to the low water of the river. Captain Hare assisted. The artillery "we have got to Mr. Lorimer's by going and returning with the few horses Captain Hare brought us. The waters are so low they will not furnish sufficient depth for a bark canoe within 50 miles of Mr. Lorimer's. I have left the rake until the waters are sufficient for their transportation." [HP-107] Leaving Captain Hare and his company of Rangers in his rear for protection against any pursuit by Clark, Bird proceeded on to the portage of the Auglaize River, sending ahead a letter to Major DePeyster written on July 24 informing him of his painfully slow progress, as well as "much news from the private conversations with the prisoners, and other means, respecting the situation of the Country." Confiding to DePeyster on the character of the prisoners, "I don't believe we have more than two families really Rebels" out of the dozens under Bird's guard, whom Bird judged, "are composed of good farmers with extreme industrious families who are desirous of being settled in Detroit with some land. They say they fled from persecution and declare if government will assist them to get them on foot as farmers they will, as militia, faithfully defend the country that affords them protection." [HP-107]

"Bow to the Urging of Kentucky Leaders"

Upon learning from a scout arriving downriver from the Falls of the Ohio that a British and Indian force was intent on attacking the Kentucky settlements from Fort Detroit, Col. George Rogers Clark set out at once for Kentucky "making all haste with what men he could spare" [BC-p.90] from Fort Jefferson on the Mississippi River. To save precious time that would be wasted ascending the current of the Ohio River, Clark took an overland route along the trail leading east to the settlement of Harrodsburg. There, Clark found to his dismay that he had arrived too late to avert the disaster that befell the forts on the Licking Creek. Rather than facing the enemy, Clark had to endure bitter recriminations from Kentuckians who had earlier in the year warned Clark that he needed to concentrate his military efforts against the Indian villages of the Ohio Country, rather than drain men away to garrison his posts in the Illinois lands, as well as the new forts at the Falls of the Ohio and on the Mississippi. Clark's critics needed only to point to the charred remains of Ruddel's and Martin's stations as proof for their contention. Embarrassed and embittered by the setback, Clark was forced to admit that he had inadvertently stripped the Kentucky frontier of protection afforded by the presence of the militia.

Clark faced the fury of his friends and neighbors who challenged his notion that attacking the Indian towns "would only dissipate his strength and squander his resources." With the forts on Licking Creek destroyed and the people carried off by the Indians and British, Clark had "no choice but to bow to the urging of Kentucky leaders" that he take the war to the Indians to end their depredations once and for all. [WGA-pp.106-7] Reluctantly Clark agreed that he would lead an attack against the Shawnee Indian villages in the Ohio Country in an attempt to prevent further raids against Kentucky settlements. In the last weeks of July, Clark set about raising and provisioning a large force of mounted militiamen to cross the Ohio River by the end of the month and attack the nearest Shawnee towns.

"Take A Calculated Risk"

Through early August 1780, General Haldimand at Quebec finalized his plans for the second expeditionary invasion of the year into the Rebel-held Mohawk Valley. Sir John Johnson, at the head of a force of over 600 provincial troops, regulars, and Mohawk Indians had surprised the inhabitants of the valley in early May when his force swept down from Lake Champlain to attack his former home area of Johnstown. Johnson had with him over 300 men from his own provincial regiment, the King's Royal Regiment of New York, and regular troops from the 53rd, 29th, and 34th Regiment of Foot. [FM-p.93] On May 21, Sir John Johnson's force attacked Johnstown, "destroying all before us as we marched along.... The Indians and Rangers burning and laying Waste everything before them." [FM-p.94]

Johnson's force had caught the valley by surprise, and before a serious reinforcement of Continental and militia troops could be assembled to oppose him, Johnson's expedition completed their foray and left by the way they came, but not before burning 120 houses, barns and mills, taking Rebel prisoners with them back to Canada along with 143 loyalist men, women, and children who were rescued from the Rebels. As to the devastation his army of Indians and provincials wrought, in addition to the buildings burned, "vast quantities of flour, bread, Indian corn and other provisions were seized or burnt in the houses and mills," with cattle slaughtered and horses appropriated. Sir John Johnson's raid had been a stunning success, in General Haldimand's estimation. Now with word reaching Haldimand from spies in the valley, that the summer crop had been good, "and the Rebels were not in a position to send a large reinforcement after any expedition that might enter the country," Haldimand decided the time was ripe to "take a calculated risk" and send a second expedition through the Mohawk Valley to destroy everything that had been missed in the first raid. Only this time, Haldimand intended to bolster Johnson's force of his own provincial troops and regulars with over 250 Rangers of Butler's Corps, two artillery pieces, and all the Indians who could be mustered, including Joseph Brant and his

Volunteers, to complete the work that Haldimand and Johnson envisioned. [FM-p.100] "If the people on the frontier had hoped that Sullivan's expedition might bring peace or at least reduce the number of Indian raids" [KI-p.288] the Americans were about to find out how wrong they were, and how vengeful the loyalists and Indians could be in the autumn raid to come.

"Simon Girty and Alexander McKee Had One Each"

On the morning of August 4, Captain Bird and his expeditionary force finally reached Detroit, to the relief of Major DePeyster. "Captain Bird arrived here this morning with about 150 prisoners, mostly Germans who speak English." DePeyster knew from Bird's count that of all the prisoners taken in Kentucky, "the whole will amount to about 350" but the balance of captives missing were those that the Lake Indians had personally seized at Ruddel's and Martin's forts and taken with them directly to their own villages, avoiding Detroit and Major DePeyster's disapproval entirely. Many of the women and children would be adopted into the tribes. Of the men taken by the Ottawas and Pottawattamies, some would be later exchanged to the British for goods, and a few were stripped and painted with lampblack, signifying that they were destined for the torture post and the cooking spit.

Of the prisoners taken to Detroit by Captain Bird, almost all of them were "greatly fatigued with traveling so far, some sick and some wounded. Thirteen of the men had already decided to "enter into the Rangers" under Captain Hare still in the field near Lorimer's post. Upon questioning, many expressed a desire to DePeyster "to remain and settle at this place." Impressed by their willingness to support the British cause, DePeyster decided to "defer sending them down (to Montreal) least it be attended with bad consequences, the remainder to save provisions." Writing to Bolton at Niagara, DePeyster reported that the bulk of the prisoners "I shall distribute in different farm houses to help in the harvest" [HP-108] until Bolton or General Haldimand decided otherwise.

A sticky issue concerning a few of the prisoners needed resolved by DePeyster once the problem came to light. It seemed that a number of Negro slaves taken prisoner at Ruddel's fort had been placed in the custody of Alexander McKee, Matthew Elliott, and the Girty brothers for safekeeping by them. When Bird reached Detroit, Mrs. Agnes La Force petitioned DePeyster for the return of her 13 Negro slaves. The task proved simple in proving that La Force owned the slaves, however, the problem was that they could not be found for La Force to rightfully reclaim. "DePeyster had to inform Haldimand," who had been made aware of the claim, that "though the owners were known the slaves could not be produced," owing to the fact that "the slaves had been divided among the members of the Indian Department and the Indians. Simon Girty and Alexander McKee had one each, and Elliott had two. The rest had been divided among the other Indian officers and the Indians" to the chagrin of Major DePeyster, who thought it best not to "risk alienating the Indian officers by ordering the restoration of the slaves." [HR-p.30]

"Upon the Holy Evangelists of Almighty God"

However, on the heels of Bird's arrival at Detroit came unsettling word from the Ohio Country that was cause for alarm. As Major DePeyster was congratulating Captain Bird and his men on their successful strike against the Rebel forts, a deserter from the Rebels named John Clairy made his way in to Detroit with Captain Bird's rearguard. He brought disturbing news from the area of Logan's Fort in Kentucky, which he had left only 12 days prior. Clairy claimed to have defected from "a detachment of the Enemy consisting of 250 men upon their march towards Licking Creek, under the command of a Colonel Logan." Clairy told DePeyster that on the same morning of his defection, he witnessed that "an express arrived from Colonel Clark who commands at the Falls (of the Ohio) desiring the said Colonel Logan to meet him at the mouth of Licking Creek with all the force he could raise, by the last day of July, from whence they would march across the Country by land to the Shawanese towns." [HP-109]

DePeyster immediately sent express runners with word of the intelligence to Alexander McKee at the upper Shawnee villages at Wakatomika on the Muskingum River, and to Captain Hare who was either at Lorimer's or on his way with the Rangers to join with McKee. If Clairy were telling the truth, DePeyster reasoned that both the lower Shawnee villages and Detroit as well could be in possible jeopardy from Rebel attack. DePeyster would not have put any weight to Clairy's words, rationalizing to himself that the Rebels were still reeling from the devastation of Bird's recent campaign, if it were not for the amount of detail that Clairy was able to convey, causing him to take the threat more seriously. Clairy knew that "several stations had not yet joined Col. Logan, viz. Bryans, Todds, Lexington, Strouds, and Boones, which collected would make Col. Logan's party about 400 men, and when added to those coming from the Falls with Clark, will make the whole force coming out against the Indians amount to about 800 men" or more.

If that were not enough, Clairy stated that the same morning, "a letter was received from General Brodhead that it was out of his power to afford them any assistance from Fort Pitt that they therefore must depend upon themselves." Finally, when DePeyster asked Clairy what cannon, if any, the Rebels could bring with them, Clairy said that "it was reported among some men" he had overheard talking, "who had served under Colonel Clark, that he would bring with him one brass six-pounder, and two iron four- pounder" cannons. [HP-109] John Clairy had signed the affidavit with his mark, swearing to DePeyster "upon the Holy Evangelists of Almighty God" that everything he had said was the truth. That was what troubled DePeyster the most, for he believed that Clairy was telling the truth about the enemy. That could only mean that Colonel Clark was advancing at that very moment into the Ohio Country with a mounted, mobile force four to five times the size of the Detroit garrison, and armed with artillery at a time when the Indians had just dispersed to their villages throughout the wilderness, and were ill-disposed to fight again anytime soon.

With the possibility of renewed trouble from the Rebels, DePeyster thought it best to inform Lt. Col. Bolton at Niagara at once, in the hope that reinforcements could be sent in time to Detroit. Sending Clairy's intelligence to Bolton, DePeyster added, "The Indians are much alarmed at it, especially as all their chiefs with some of their principal warriors are now on the way here. This afternoon or tomorrow morning, the Indians here will assemble in Council, as there are some Mingoes, Delawares, and Shawnee already arrived, I am convinced they will call upon me for assistance." DePeyster sized up the grim situation facing him at Detroit and the Ohio Country if the Rebels should attack in great numbers. "The troops just arrived are much fatigued, and you know this garrison is very weak. The company of Rangers will be trifling without a detachment of soldiers, DePeyster wrote. "The Canadians, Captain Bird declares, are not worth sending still something must be done, if the Indians insist upon it. In this situation I will not send a detachment to Michilimackinac till I receive your further orders, which I hope will be accompanied with a reinforcement." What Detroit and the Indians needed to decisively turn the tables on the Rebels, DePeyster estimated, was not a company of troops that he was doubtful that Bolton could currently spare at the moment, but an entire regiment of soldiers from England, and then some.

"An Opportunity of Making Their Way Through Him"

Colonel George Rogers Clark was very pleased with the army of nearly 1,000 seasoned militiamen who prepared themselves to leave their encampment at the mouth of the Licking River. It was the largest force of mounted militia that Clark had ever brought together for an expedition against the Indians. Without wasting further time, on the morning of August 1, Clark gave orders for his force to cross the Ohio River and move up the trail on the east bank of the Little Miami River north to the nearest Shawnee Indian towns many miles away. With Clark were the principal veteran officers from the interior posts, stations, and settlements of Kentucky who were of the same mind as Clark and the men they led, that the time had come to punish the Indians severely once and for all, for their past raids and terrible depredations committed against them, their friends and relatives. Vengeance was on all of their minds as their horses splashed across the shallows of the Ohio that morning. "As taste of their own medicine was in store for some soon-to-be surprised Shawnee" was everyone's thinking. [HW1-p.146]

Clark knew the success of his campaign depended upon moving his army swiftly enough to catch the Indians off-guard and unaware of its approach. Consequently, Clark had the able scout, Simon Kenton, guide the army directly by the trail that led to the Shawnee village of Chillicothe, while moving the artillery and stores up the Miami River by boat for a distance. However, Clark's attempt to surprise attack the unsuspecting Indians at Chillicothe did not materialize. Though Clairy's information on Clark's intentions did not reach Detroit in time for DePeyster to warn the Shawnee, the Indians, at Alexander

McKee's urging, had not been entirely idle. A small Indian scouting party sent by McKee to cover Bird's return to Detroit had spied the Virginians massing on the Kentucky side of the Ohio River and warned the village of Chillicothe once the direction of Clark's attack was known. In addition, a deserter from Clark's army, "a Tory sympathizer, sneaked off into the night and gave the Shawnee notice of Clark's approaching army." [HW1-p.146] To Clark's dismay, the village of Chillicothe was abandoned and burned by the departing Shawnee, "so that when Clark arrived, there was nothing but smoking ruins." [HW1-p.146]

Clark gave orders for his army halt for a day or two at the Indian village to methodically destroy the surrounding acres of ripening cornfields, which he had his men burn to deny the Indians their source of food for the winter, all the while being watched by Shawnee spies. "The Enemy, finding no opposition there (Chillicothe), halted two days to cut down the corn fields, after which time they advanced to Pekawee" intent on destroying the Indians and the village there on the branch of the Mad River which flowed into the Big Miami, some miles distant from Chillicothe. However, at the Shawnee village of Piqua, the Indians were waiting. Shawnee spies had been seen by Clark's advanced scouts moving ahead of the main body, "obviously drawing them to a fighting ground of the Indian's choice." [WGA-p.109] By midday on August 8, Clark's force at last came into sight of the Indian village, which they immediately prepared to assault.

Clark deployed his men in a broad front facing the Indian skirmishers who began firing from the cornfields between him and the Indian town. From what Clark observed, the Shawnee Indians had been forewarned of his arrival for there was no sight of women and children, whom he presumed had fled. However, by all other appearances, the Shawnee were attempting to make a stand to defend the town which pleased him, as Clark hoped finally to be able to encircle and destroy a large number of warriors once and for all. Clark had the cannon brought up to the front of his column that was deploying in a line, and had the cannon primed and loaded. Meanwhile, out of sight of the skirmishers, Clark gave orders for two mounted flanking columns of 200 men each under the command of Colonel Logan to move off from the fields and attempt a wide encircling movement around the village from each side, while Clark and the main body kept occupied the attention of the Indians in the fields before the town. If all went according to plan, Clark's flanking movements would catch the Indians unaware from the rear of the village and cut off all escape, whereupon they could all be slaughtered.

Clark's plan was a bold maneuver, but due to his hasty arrival at Piqua town, he was unable to scout the surrounding terrain, nor take into account the swampy ground to the east. Immediately Logan's flanking column on the right became bogged down in soft ground soon after leaving the main body and was effectively neutralized as a fighting force for some time. Unaware of this, Clark's "main body advanced through a plain adjoining to the south end of Pekawee" [HP-304] and "savage fighting broke out at once in the fields around the village." [WGA-p.109]

According to McKee, who arrived too late to the Shawnee village to take part in the affair, the Enemy "entered the edge of the town at the same time a party of Indians who had been sent to spy on them was making their report. In this surprise, many of the Indians who had been collected there to make a stand broke off and did not come into the engagement, however the few, about 70, who stood, make a resolute resistance, and defended their village the greatest part of a day against 900 of the Enemy." [HP-304] With the Indians who remained to fight were George and James Girty. The two men realized that their small force was greatly outnumbered and could not defeat Clark's army. Nonetheless, the two directed the warriors in delivering a volume of musket fire upon the Virginians to inflict as many casualties as possible while not exposing themselves to direct fire from the cover of the fields. Gradually the Girtys and the Indians were pushed back through town, fighting as they withdrew till word coming from scouts reached George Girty near dusk that the enemy was appearing to either side, Clark's flanking forces having finally found and fought their way through the swampy woods that had encumbered them most of the day. Seeing a concentration of warriors around the central longhouse, Clark had the six-pounder cannon fire upon it until it was destroyed, scattering the Indians there. However, with no sign of Logan's columns to be found, Clark realized that this inadvertent tactical error had allowed "the Indians an opportunity of making their way through him." [HP-304] With darkness falling, the strength and exact whereabouts of the attackers unknown, and a number of wounded men among his ranks needing immediate attention, Clark called off the attack and organized a guard around camp for the night.

"The Road is Besprinkled With Blood"

George Girty questioned the Virginian prisoner brought in by the Indians to their position in the heavy woods just north of the Pekawee town. The shaken militiaman declared the Enemy "to be 970 men, amongst whom were a great many French from Post Vincent and the Illinois, that out of the above number, 40 were left at the Ohio to guard their provisions, boats and two 4-pounders, that they had but three days provisions, and depended for subsistence entirely upon the Indian fields" [HP-304] George Girty listened intently, realizing that Clark's force must be at the end of their food, and consequently, at the farthest point of their advance into the Indian Country. However he lamented the fact that the bulk of the warriors had earlier chosen to retreat from the fight in the face of Clark's six-pounder when overwhelming numbers could now have made a decisive difference in the battle. The warriors still with Girty and his brother were "too few in number to advance into the plain and take possession of it." [HP-304] With the fighting spirit of those warriors still high, in Girty's estimation, if more warriors had joined in at this point as Clark's army halted, "300 would have given them a total rout." [HP-304] Unfortunately that was not to be.

At first light, Clark ordered a large reinforced detachment of men to secure the deserted Indian town and put all the buildings, including the ruins of the palisade long house to the torch, while other parties of men set about destroying what corn in the fields could be easily cut and burned, regardless of the constant sniping from the Indians. As this was being done, Clark began moving his sizable number of wounded with the artillery piece back by the way his army had come, leaving 14 men who had been killed the previous day to be hastily buried. With as much of the destruction of Piqua completed as was possible, Clark pulled the rest of his militiamen out from the burning Indian town and headed for the Ohio River, satisfied that a great deal of the material support for the Indians had been eliminated at the town.

However, Col. Clark left with a certain amount of disappointment too. Few Indians had been actually killed in the battle. While Clark had set his mind on proceeding further north to attack more Indian villages, if not Detroit itself on this campaign, his officers did not agree with him. Pointing to the few number of Indians killed, they advised Clark that more fighting could be expected and if the Indians were reinforced, as was likely to happen, the odds would no longer favor the Kentuckians, especially if the Indians were supported by British Rangers. Then, too, almost all the provisions brought with the men had been eaten, except for the small amount of Indian corn that could be gathered from the fields. Clark's officers reasoned with him that the dire condition of the seriously wounded men dictated he break the campaign off at Piqua, or risk destruction himself. Reluctantly, Clark gave the order to withdraw, as the Indian campaign was over.

Alexander McKee arrived within two days of the battle with more than 200 Shawnee, Mingo, and Wyandot warriors from the upper Shawnee villages. The warriors still at Pekawee brought in their casualties to the ruined town, amounting to "six killed and three wounded, but that of their own will be a very distressing one to their families" as the grieving for the dead commenced. At the same time, scouts and small war parties set out to dog Clark's army as it headed back to Chillicothe and the trail to the Ohio River. Soon a constant stream of information flowed back to McKee on the condition of the enemy. "Upon the road they went, some small pieces burnt of the carriage of their cannon" were discovered, "which gives some reason to suspect they have left it behind as no trace is to be seen farther than that. I shall have diligent search made, as far as the Indians have pursued them in their retreat they say the road is besprinkled with blood and several places where litters were made which they conclude they must have had a great many wounded men to carry off." [HP-304]

"They Build Much on the Promises of Their Father"

Alexander McKee assessed the damage done by Clark's attack on the Shawnee. Though Indian casualties were relatively light, considering the duration of the fighting at Pekawee and the numbers involved, two villages were entirely destroyed and more importantly, a major portion of the corn crops at both villages lost completely, which was the Indians main source of food for the upcoming winter season. With their homes and crops destroyed, McKee could see that the initial anger of the Shawnee was quickly turning to demoralization. "They have already devoured almost all the fields of corn in their neighborhood, what remains the others are unwilling to part with unless they receive payment."

McKee hastily scrawled a note to Captain Peter Hare of the Rangers still at Wapatomika to send what men he could to Pekawee as quickly as possible with what provisions could be spared, and with as many warriors who would accompany him. McKee needed Hare's Rangers to "restore the spirits" of the Pekawee Indians "who were inclined to abandon their country." [CE-p.88] More importantly, if Clark had re-provisioned his men and should decide to make another attempt to attack into the Indian Country, McKee and the Indians would have a force in place in the area to repel the Virginians decisively, as McKee knew the character of Hare and his men, all seasoned veterans of wilderness fighting, who were more than willing and able to give Clark's men a good drubbing if the opportunity should present itself.

To DePeyster at Detroit, McKee sent a note by Indian runner on the 22nd of August requesting immediate assistance for the Indians in the form of provisions, ammunition, and reinforcements if possible. "I find it will be impossible to avoid making some expenses on their account, as they build much on the promises of their Father, in case of necessity, and they now really stand in need of his support or without it must perish. I have told them whilst they hold steadfastly to their engagements with him they will find he will always assist them." [HP-304] If McKee was to properly execute the duties of his position as Captain of the Indian Department, then the time had come for DePeyster to unequivocally send help to the Indians. In McKee's mind, the welfare of the Indians and their ability to continue this war for the Ohio Country could not suffer any more excuses from Detroit.

"Spades, Shovels, and Pickaxes are Much Wanting"

Unfortunately for McKee and the Indians, little help could be forthcoming from Major DePeyster at Detroit, because fewer provisions earmarked for the upper posts had been brought up from Niagara, so little was planned to be allocated to the Indians by Bolton on Haldimand's general orders to conserve resources. Major DePeyster, entrusted with the safety and preservation of his command at Detroit, chafed under the weight of legitimate requests made to him from the various tribes of the Ohio Country, the least of all Alexander McKee's plea for aid. However he had no practical way of fulfilling McKee's request beyond sending some meager supplies. General Haldimand had been unable to send reinforcements of any kind to him, and the news of the war in the east, along with whispers of an acquiescing sentiment in England against continuing the war in general with the Americans were not encouraging to him. Finally, DePeyster decided by September 1 that the needs of the Indians of the Ohio Country were too great and pressing to delay acting any longer and therefore resorted to taking matters into his own hands. Without orders to do so, DePeyster commandeered the provisions destined for the post of Michilimackinac that arrived at Detroit on the sloop, the "Wellcome."

Openly acknowledging to Lt. Col. Bolton on September 3 his actions, DePeyster listed the needs of the Indians from every corner of the Ohio Country following Clark's foray. 'The "Wellcome' was loaded with provisions for Michilimackinac but to satisfy the demands of our Indian allies, have been obliged to send her to the Miamis," for unloading and distribution up the Miami River and on to the Indian villages. Aware that reinforcements were unlikely, DePeyster wrote requesting at least materials necessary to improve the works at Detroit. "I cannot think the Enemy mean an attempt on up this post but to guard against the worse, least they should endeavor to winter in the settlement as reported by some of the prisoners, I am taking every precaution necessary." DePeyster specifically requested "Spades, shovels, and pick axes are much wanting, as well as proper ordinance for the new fort, although the cannon we have in general being too light, and much of it has already been returned as unfit for real service."[HP-111]

"If It Is To Be Done, There Is No Time To Lose"

Major DePeyster was unaware of the major offensive General Haldimand planned against the Rebel settlements in the Mohawk Valley in September which had diverted most of the ammunition, provisions, and troops to the fort at Carleton Island for the upcoming attack. Haldimand and Sir John Johnson had insisted on a shroud of secrecy to cover the campaign so that maximum destruction could be wrought against the Rebels without leaks from spies and deserters. Sir John Johnson's raid against the Rebel valley in May had been a stunning success, yet much of the valley had not suffered from his incursion; many homes, barns, mills and granaries remaining untouched due to Johnson's limited field of operations. Now General Haldimand decided that another, more thorough and encompassing campaign be initiated against "both banks of the Mohawk and even Schoharie" valleys with "the main object to destroy as much of the enemy's grain crop as possible before it could be sent to Washington or before the rebel farmers themselves could get much good out of it." [KI-p.295]

Preparations were made in secret, with instructions being sent from Haldimand directly to Sir John Johnson at Carleton Island on August 24. Sir John was to proceed by boat to Oswego with the bulk of his 1st Battalion of green-coated loyalist Royal Yorkers, many of whom had participated in the first raid of the year. Likewise, Lt. Col. Bolton and Major John Butler, along with Joseph Brant were likewise alerted with instructions to send "two light infantry companies of Regulars, 200 of Butler's Rangers, and a large body of Indians" to join Johnson at Oswego on the appointed date of October 1. The exact force that finally assembled at Oswego in the first days of October were 150 Regulars of the 8th and 34th Regiment from Niagara, 165 of Butler's Rangers and Colonel Guy Johnson's Indian Department also from Niagara with 10 men from the Royal Artillery, 265 Six Nations warriors with Brant's Volunteers from the same, and

312 troops from Sir John Johnson's provincial 1st Battalion Kings Royal Yorkers, Leake's Independent Company of Loyalists, and German Hesse Hanau Jager Riflemen. The total men under arms of all ranks under the command of Johnson numbered 893. [WG2-p.164]

By October 3, Johnson's expedition to the Mohawk Valley was underway, setting out "by the old trade route up the Oswego River, some troops by land and some by water; but instead of turning east for Fort Stanwix and the Mohawk, they went farther south to Onondaga Lake and then to the eastward, deep into Oneida country." [KI-p.296] Johnson's goal was to traverse the deserted Oneida lands and attack the unsuspecting Enemy at the southern end of the Schoharie Valley by marching some 250 miles from Oswego. Moving north through the Schoharie Valley would enable Johnson's force to not only devastate the homes and farmland there, but also reach the Mohawk Valley to the north which he had not been able to attack in his earlier raid. Haldimand now wished to put the Mohawk Valley to the torch, reiterating to Johnson in the planning stages of the campaign that "if it is to be done, there is no time to lose as the Corn will be hurried away the moment it is fit to Transport." [WG2-p.157]

"I Know That It Is In Vain to Hope For A Reinforcement"

On the morning of September 15, Captain Peter Hare brought in his weary detachment of Rangers back to the Shawnee village of Wapatomika and was greeted by McKee and the Indians. Hare was immediately concerned for the whereabouts of Lieutenant Caleb Reynolds, who had not returned as yet with his a handful of Rangers accompanied by a sizable party of warriors that had gone directly south across the Ohio River to scout "some time ago after being informed that there was an army of the Rebels at the River Kanawha," [HP-38] McKee assured Hare that "the return of the party is hourly expected, by whom it is probable we shall receive some material accounts," of the activities of the Rebels. [HP-112] Captain Hare had brought with him the six-pounder cannon from Lorimer's post as safekeeping, sending it "off to the Rapids by Mr. Clench who goes with some of the Rangers and some Indians and some Canadians, as that is one of my greatest cares least it should fall into the hands of the Enemy, as I shall always keep it in my rear." [HP-38]

Captain Hare's men were glad to rest at Wapatomika. Besides the arduous trip transporting the six-pounder over the rough, narrow Indian trails to the Muskingum, a part of their time had been occupied with building a blockhouse on the Miami River, and the rest was spent continuously on extended scouts south of Piqua to the Ohio River in search of sign of the approach of the Enemy. As none had been found, "the danger of an invasion had passed," [CE-p.88] however the constant movement in the field had taken its toll on the weapons, clothing, shoes and stamina of the Rangers, prompting Captain Hare to write DePeyster on September 15 that among other things, "the Rangers are almost naked for want of clothing." [HP-38] Constant exposure to the elements combined with daily exertion had caused their issued coats, trousers, and shoes to rot away, forcing the men to wear whatever could be found from Indian and civilian clothing, including breechcloths, leggings, and moccasins.

Alexander McKee liked Hare, and found the Captain easy to work with, as well as being compatible with the Shawnee. McKee wrote to Colonel Guy Johnson that "Captain Peter Hare is here with his company of Rangers, which gives those Indians some spirits, as he is already much respected by them, it is a pity more could not be spared to support and encourage them being willing to oppose the Enemy as far as in their power." Soon after Hare arrived, he and McKee received information from scouts that the Rebels at Fort Pitt may be preparing for a campaign again against the Upper Sandusky villages. Both men took the necessary action to find out more information on the reports. "I am sending other parties (of Indians) with white men towards Fort Pitt so that a few days will put us in certainty of their (Rebels) designs."[HP-112]

For his part, Hare decided to wait at Wapatomika and see what developed. His own men were too worn out to move until they rested. "I have thought it proper to send Mr. Elliott to the Wyandot towns to see what the Indians are about there" Hare reported, before he would move his exhausted Rangers into the field again. [HP-38] When the intelligence sent by McKee and Hare reached Detroit, detailing the possibility of an attack against the Indians and Detroit from Fort Pitt, Major DePeyster could not restrain himself from writing to Bolton at Niagara on September 22, again requesting that Bolton send troops to bolster Detroit and the Indians. "I assembled the Indians present, and am sending them off to join at Wapatomika. I know it is in vain to hope for reinforcements, till the fleet arrives with troops" DePeyster declared," but it is my firm opinion that a regiment should be quartered at Detroit." [HP-112] What Major DePeyster did not know was that Bolton had already received instructions from General Haldimand concerning the matter of reinforcements for the western posts. Haldimand wrote that "another company or two of Rangers would have a good effect...against the Encroachments on the Ohio," but until more troops arrived from England, "every available man was needed at Oswego" for Sir John Johnson's campaign. DePeyster and the Indian Department at Detroit would have to just make do.

"Forced to Withdraw the Garrison From Fort Henry"

Events had gone from bad to worse by September for General Brodhead at Fort Pitt. His planned offensive against the hostile Indians of the Upper Sandusky villages in the Ohio Country had stalled in May due to a lack of artillery, provisions, ammunition and packhorses. Fuming at the postponement of his campaign until June, as the days wound down, Brodhead found he was unable to procure the supplies he needed from eastern Pennsylvania, and was forced to reschedule his attack. General Washington wrote to Brodhead in July, informing him that no Regular troops could be spared in the east to take part in an offensive into the Ohio Country. As for the militia, Washington warned Brodhead "against placing any faith" in them. Still, Brodhead was not easily discouraged, and planned for a "rapid mounted attack" with what forces he could muster in August. By then, however, "the low water in the rivers prevented mills from grinding corn so provisions became even more scanty." Adding to his frustration was the constant desertion of men from the Pennsylvania militias, who either slipped away to return home or fled down the Ohio River to join Clark's force at the Falls of the Ohio. [WGA-p.110]

In September, Brodhead sent orders to the surrounding counties of Pennsylvania to have their militiamen ready to march to Fort Pitt in an October campaign against the Indians at Upper Sandusky. Brodhead struggled to assemble the necessary ammunition and supplies but found increasing objections to the campaign arising from militia officers. By the first week of October the consensus of opinion among Brodhead's officers at Fort Pitt was that it was too late in the season to mount an extended campaign against the Indian Country. Not only was the weather threatening to turn worse, but a spate of Indian raids by the Mingo, Wyandot, Munsee, and Shawnee war parties had hit the length of the Virginia and Pennsylvania frontier on the east side of the Ohio, preventing the local militias from sending men to Fort Pitt, as Brodhead had directed. The war parties "continued to kill, burn, and capture," forcing the "people of Westmorland County to fort-up" and protect their own families and friends from immediate attack. A thoroughly frustrated Brodhead was forced to "withdraw the garrison from Fort Henry at Wheeling and give up his plans" entirely for the year. [WGA-p.110]

"Everything Except the Soil is Destroyed"

By the morning of October 18, Sir John Johnson's force of British raiders had effectively managed to destroy every house, mill, and barn on both sides of the Schoharie River without any opposition from the scant Rebel militia in the valley, who wisely remained holed-up in their forts rather than risk annihilation by the Indians, Rangers, and Regular Light troops. Joseph Brant and Lieutenant Thompson of the Rangers were the last to cross the Mohawk River from the south side with their detachment of Rangers, Volunteers, and Mohawks. Johnson had sent them on a mission to destroy the outlying Fort Hunter settlement which they did with great relish, setting ablaze all the homes and barns in the area, causing great plumes of black smoke visible for miles to rise in the air. Brant and Thompson were able to rejoin the main British column on the north side of the Mohawk with their force intact, and reported to Johnson the success of their efforts that had been unopposed by the Rebels.

However, the smoke from Fort Hunter had alerted the American militia marching with artillery from Schenectady under the command of General Van Rensselaer whose army reached Fort Hunter at midnight. Once there, Van Rensselaer sent word across the river to Colonel John Brown, the Continental officer of the Massachusetts State Levies garrisoned at Fort Paris in Stone Arabia, the next target of Johnson's raiders, informing Brown that he intended to bring his troops across the Mohawk at daybreak and engage the British. [WG2-p.205]

On the morning of the October 19, Colonel Brown decided to take the entire garrison of Fort Paris and the surrounding posts and attack Sir John Johnson's column which was moving westward up the Mohawk, burning the homes and barns on both sides of the river. Colonel Brown marched out with "about 300 Massachusetts men with perhaps 80 militia and rangers" to attempt to pin down Johnson's Crown forces until Van Rensselaer's army could arrive and engage the enemy. Brown's advance guard collided with 50 men of Joseph Brant's Volunteers who were acting as an advance screen for Johnson's vanguard. At the first musket fire from Brown's men, "the Volunteers quickly drove these men back upon Brown's main body" who had deployed behind a stone fence in the wooded heights above Johnson's main force.

Sir John Johnson was with the vanguard composed of MacDonnell's company of Butler's Rangers, and the light companies of the 34th and 8th. Assessing the situation, Johnson could see Joseph Brant lead his mixed force of Volunteers and Indians as a screen to "work around the Rebel's right flank." He ordered Captain MacDonnell to take his Rangers and turn the Rebel left flank, while leading the light companies of the 8th and 34th up the hill to attack the Rebel center, deploying "about 160 men against 170 of Brown's leading units— a very even match." As Johnson closed his men on Brown's defensive position, "a brisk skirmish commenced in which Colonel Brown, who was prominent atop his black horse, was killed." At the same moment, Brant and his force of Volunteers and Indians were able to turn the Rebel right flank, while MacDonnell of the Rangers had likewise done on the left of the Rebels, threatening to encircle and annihilate the entire Massachusetts force. [WG2-p.207]

With Colonel Brown dead, Brown's force fell back in disorder, "the routed Rebels either fled towards the Stone Arabia forts or took to the woods heading south towards the Mohawk River, "while being pursued and cut down by the Indian "bloodhounds" of Johnson's force. When the battle was over, more than 40 of Brown's Levies, militia and Oneida Indian scouts had been slain, with dozens of wounded littering the battlefield. As for Sir John Johnson's losses, Joseph Brant had received a minor flesh wound in his foot, "and a private of the 8th and three Indians were killed and three Rangers were wounded." Johnson commended Brant and MacDonnell for "their leadership in this action", knowing that "it was not numbers that won, it was nerve, skill, and decisive leadership." Throughout the minor engagement, the main body of Johnson's force had continued their business of burning the homes, barns, and mills to the west unopposed.

When Johnson's exhausted troops reached the safety of Oswego on October 26, Sir John sent a letter to General Haldimand reporting on the success of the raid in which "we destroyed every grain before us for nearly 50 Miles, their loss at the most moderate computation, cannot Amount to less than 600,000 Bushels of different kinds." [KI-p.298] The Rebels could hardly disagree with the devastation wrought by the British and Indians. "Governor Clinton" of New York State "estimated the property loss as at least 200 dwellings and 150,000 bushels of wheat" alone. A witness from the arriving Continental army attested that "everything except the soil is destroyed from Fort Hunter to Stone Arabia" with all the hamlets of the Schoharie Valley burned to the ground. [KI-p.298]

"She Nearly Escaped Being Lost"

With the onset of winter and colder weather, the Shawnee, Wyandot, Mingo and Delaware war parties organized by Alexander McKee in October to raid the settlements along the Pennsylvania and Virginia frontier made their way back to villages deep in the Ohio Country, loaded with scalps, prisoners, and plunder. Snow storms of late November discouraged new war parties from setting out, so the Indian raids tapered off. Alexander McKee, Matthew Elliott, and the three Girty brothers resolved to spend the winter months with the Indians in their respective villages. Captain Hare and his company of Rangers were recalled to Detroit the same month by Major DePeyster, with a detachment sent "to take post with at the Miamis Town, to act in concert with that nation," which now is fairly entered" to the British cause. [HP-230]

With the coming snows, Major DePeyster could breathe a sigh of relief that the possibility of a Rebel campaign against Detroit from either quarter of Kentucky or Fort Pitt had ended. The reinforcements which he had sorely requested from Bolton and Quebec had never materialized. DePeyster could count no more than 393 effective fighting men in the garrison, "50 of Major Butler's Rangers, 125 men of the 47th Regiment, Three companies of the King's Eighth Regiment amounting to 168 men, and 50 men, part of the King's Regiment to be sent in the Spring to Michilimackinac" which DePeyster delayed releasing, because of the threatening reports received at Detroit of a Rebel advance against that post. [HP-376] When DePeyster finally decided to send the troops to Sinclair, he found "the season too far advanced," and the men returned to Detroit. "The sloop which sailed from hence on the 7th of October with troops on board for Michilimackinac, returned here on the Instant (Nov. 13th) having met with much rough weather, in which she nearly escaped being lost. Till I can send an Express through the woods, Lieutenant Governor Sinclair will of course think I have still neglected sending the Detachment which was not in my power to send before." While the men of the 47th Regiment considered themselves lucky to be alive, others on Lake Ontario were not so fortunate. [HP-114]

Disaster struck the British sloop "Ontario" as it sailed across Lake Ontario to Carleton Island, leaving Niagara on October 31. Lieutenant Colonel Bolton was on board the sloop, glad to be returning to Quebec where he would not have to face another Niagara winter that was a contributing cause of his declining health. "On the night after Bolton sailed, a terrible storm roared across the lake, swamping the sloop which broke up in the pounding wind and waves. The next day, a scout of Royal Yorkers at Oswego spotted the wreckage washed up on the shore, "but no sign of a human being anywhere." [KI-p.300] Bolton, "along with 32 soldiers and 40 seamen" were drowned. Word spread quickly to the upper posts and Quebec of the grievous loss to the King's Service.

"The unfortunate Fate of Lieutenant Colonel Bolton from all circumstances appears conclusive in the loss of the "Ontario," Captain Potts of the 34th Regiment wrote to Brigadier General Henry Watson Powell at Niagara. [HP-113] When word reached General Haldimand at Quebec on November 14, Haldimand lamented the loss of such a good officer and gentleman under his command. "I yesterday was greatly affected by receiving the news of the unfortunate fate of Colonel Bolton, and together with the loss of the "Ontario." [HP-138] While dealing with the great loss, Haldimand ordered that Powell, already at Niagara, take official command of that post with DePeyster at Detroit and Sinclair at Michilimackinac reporting to Powell as overall officer in charge of the upper posts.

When Captain Hare and his company of Rangers finally arrived at Detroit from many months of service in the wilderness of the Ohio Country, Major DePeyster and the garrison were stunned by their appearance. Hare's men were barely recognizable as Rangers. Their uniforms were reduced to tattered rags covered by filthy Indian blankets. Major DePeyster was aware from Captain Hare's reports that his men needed a rest and refitting at Detroit. Yet it was not too long after their arrival that the Ranger Captain had his men engage in physical work improving the works of the fort. Hare's service had been commendable, Powell reported to Butler. Likewise, Major DePeyster mentioned "Captain Hare to have exerted himself upon every occasion." [HP-133] Captain Thompson, with Lieutenants Clinch and Pawling, were sent by Major Butler to Detroit on the last sloop to sail to that post before the lake froze to assist Captain Hare. [HP-346]

While at the Shawnee village of Wakatomika on the Muskingum late in December, a Shawnee warrior returning from the Delawares at Goschachgunk brought news to McKee of General Brodhead that caused McKee to laugh. The Ohio Delaware had recently been sent a letter from Brodhead at Fort Pitt, warning them that it would be in their best interest to "make war on the British" since "McKee and others in the Indian Department were doing "great harm to your Grand Children by the Lies they tell them." Brodhead was offering a reward to the Delawares of "60 Bucks" if they would capture McKee and bring him to Fort Pitt, and "20 Bucks" for each of the three Girty brothers. [NL-p.117]

The idea that Brodhead would offer a reward to the Delaware for McKee's capture amused McKee. The Shawnee warriors, who saw great humor in the fact that Brodhead thought the Shawnee to be the children of the Delaware, when the relationship, in their minds, was quite the opposite, howled with laughter. But what McKee found the most amusing was not the amount of "60 bucks" placed upon his head by Brodhead but the thought that the Rebel general was now resorting to paying the Indians to do what his own army of regulars, militia, and scouts were unable to do. Brodhead had not be able to stop McKee. It gave McKee great satisfaction to know that he was the cause of Brodhead's desperateness. However, what was more fulfilling to McKee was the knowledge that another season of wilderness war had passed and the Indians of the Ohio

Country were still firmly in control of their lands, in spite of the best efforts of Brodhead and the Rebels.

Chapter 13

1781: Bloody Struggle on the Ohio

By December 1780, the onset of winter in the Ohio Country promised a brief respite from the wilderness war of the previous months. With the coming of winter snows, the Indian war parties still in the field returned to their villages from raiding the border settlements. Cold weather forced the Virginia militia from Kentucky to Fort Pitt to seek security behind picketed walls. The end of hostilities brought another year of war for control of the Indian Lands in Kentucky and the Ohio Country to a close, while the American war for independence continued unabated into its sixth year to determine if Great Britain would re-establish sovereignty over its rebellious colonies. Neither east of the Alleghenies nor in the western wilderness had the outcome to the warfare been determined decisively.

December 1780 gave way to January 1781 without severe winter weather manifesting itself in the Ohio Country. With the mild weather, an uneasiness spread through the people of the wilderness as both Indian and settler alike realized that without heavy snows, frozen waterways, and frigid temperatures to impede the movement of troops or warriors, attacks against the frontier settlements by the Indians and offensive action against the Indian villages by the Virginians were a real possibility, forestalling any hope of a respite. Rather than enjoying a cessation of hostilities that the winter months should have promised, the thoughts on everyone's minds from Detroit to Kentucky, was when and where the next blows would fall in the continuing battle, if winter did not bring a pause.

Several men in the western wilderness used the mild weather to their own advantage to prepare for continued war. Colonel George Rogers Clark of the Virginian militia left Kentucky in December 1780 for a journey east over the mountains to the Virginian capitol with a plan in mind which he believed would successfully end the war in the west in Virginia's favor. Clark intended to meet with Governor Thomas Jefferson and gain the support necessary to strike a decisive blow against the British and their Indian allies. While he was away, Clark left his trusted militia officers to command the posts from the new fort at the Falls of the Ohio, to Vincennes and the Illinois Country, where Clark still held on tenuously with small numbers of loyal men. Traveling for days on horseback with a group of aides and friends, Clark headed first to Williamsburg, and then to Richmond, where the government of Virginia had moved during the previous summer.

Clark met with Governor Thomas Jefferson near the end of December and presented to him his ambitious plan to end the western war by a decisive campaign against British-held Detroit, which was the source of British support for the continuing Indian raids against Kentucky and the Virginian settlements east of the Ohio River. Capturing British-held Detroit by military assault, Clark argued, would permanently secure the western lands, thus eliminating the route by which the British supplied the Indians of the Ohio Country. Without ammunition, provisions, and logistical support from the British, the Indians would be forced to end their attacks on the settlements. However, Clark proposed to Jefferson that there was much more to be gained for Virginia by an attack than just an end to the Indian wilderness war.

For if Clark could take Detroit from the British, not only could the Indians of the Ohio Country be compelled to end their alliance with the British and sue for peace, but the wilderness lands which they called their own from Kentucky to Lake Erie and west through the Illinois Country to the Mississippi could be relinquished by the Indians to become part of the state of Virginia. Virginia stood to acquire thousands of square miles of virgin wilderness with its wealth in timber and potential farmland as part of its own territory. Clark presented a compelling argument to Jefferson for a campaign against Detroit that fueled both men's ambitions beyond ending the war in the west. [WGA-p.110]

On Christmas Day 1780, Jefferson agreed to Clark's plan and issued orders for a spring campaign in the west against Detroit by means of an expedition led by Clark himself at the head of a force to number 2000 men raised from the state of Virginia. He would be joined by 1,000 men to be gathered from the Kentucky and Illinois Country, making the expedition "almost wholly a Virginia enterprise." [WGA-p.111] Clark and Jefferson poured over maps of the Ohio Country, determining elaborate plans for Clark's campaign that accounted for a secure supply line from Virginia to support Clark's army, the garrisoning of the existing forts in Kentucky during the expedition, and the logistics of moving the large army up the Wabash River from the rendevous point at the mouth of the Wabash on the Ohio River, to the post at Vincennes and on to Detroit by movement on the rivers.

Clark's idea was to use the Wabash River as a means of travel "as soon as the ice was out of the stream in the spring but before the ice cleared from Lake Erie, ensured that the British would get no help" from the fleet of sloops on the Lakes. Clark was convinced that if he could get to Detroit before reinforcements could be sent from Niagara and Michilimackinac that the fort there would easily fall. His own French spies at Detroit reported that the outer works of Fort Lernoult were insufficiently defended and a negligible number of British troops manned the garrison with little hope for reinforcement from Canada. In Clark's mind, the success of the expedition would rest on a direct attack upon the Fort Lernoult at Detroit. Clark believed he could brush aside the Indian allies of the British, whose style of wilderness warfare would be negated by the overwhelming size of his own army, the presence of artillery, and his refusal to meet the Indians in battle in the wilderness where his advantages were negated. He preferred instead to crush them before the gates of Detroit itself. As proof for his contention, Clark recounted how Hamilton and his British troops capitulated at Vincennes once the Indians proved themselves unreliable allies by deserting into the forest rather than face cannon and massed riflemen. If Clark could get to Detroit quickly, he assured the Governor that the fort would fall by conventional means.

The plan for Clark's expedition against Detroit received General Washington's overwhelming approval, who wrote to General Brodhead at Fort Pitt in early January, "directing him to begin assembling the necessary supplies, and to give Clark every assistance in his power, as well as provide him with the largest possible detachment of regulars from Pitt that Brodhead could spare." [HW1-p.147] For his part, Clark immediately dispatched several officers with orders for the militia in Kentucky to begin preparing for the spring campaign, and for his men at the fort at the Falls of the Ohio to begin at once to send out parties of hunters to bring in deer and buffalo meat for curing, to be used as provisions for Clark's army.

However, just as Governor Jefferson was issuing orders for the raising of recruits for Clark's militia army, the British navy unexpectedly sailed unopposed up the James River and disembarked a British army outside of Richmond. The 1200 man force composed of "loyalist troops from Canada, New York, and Pennsylvania," was led by the American traitor Benedict Arnold, now a newly-commissioned Brigadier General in the British army. Arnold and his force marched on Richmond at once, and though George Rogers Clark was pressed into service with Von Steuben's outnumbered Regulars in the defense of Richmond, the American army failed to prevent Richmond from falling to Arnold's army, who plundered and burned the captured city. Jefferson and the Virginian government were forced to flee inland, eventually to Charlottesville.

By mid-January, Clark was able to detach himself from Von Steuben's command to prepare for his western expedition; however circumstances had greatly changed in a few short weeks. With Arnold and his army occupying Portsmouth on the coast, and a British army under General Cornwallis on the move north through the Carolinas to join Arnold, Virginia was in disarray. Jefferson was unable to find the men and provisions to supply Clark as he had earlier promised because all possible resources were committed to the desperate defense of Virginia against the British invasion. Before leaving Virginia for Fort Pitt and the western frontier, George Rogers Clark requested a commission in the regular Continental army from Congress, but was denied. Clark, who held the rank of a Virginia militia colonel, turned to Jefferson for help, who granted Clark an appointment as "a brigadier general for the campaign" for the western expedition, giving Clark senior authority over General Brodhead at Fort Pitt which he desired. Near the end of January, Clark was headed back west over the mountains. In spite of the best of intentions of Jefferson and the Virginia legislature, Clark was returning empty-handed as no militia troops could be spared. Left to his own devices, Clark decided to attempt to raise the men he desperately needed along the way, by recruiting volunteers from the Virginia settlements bordering the Monongahela River. [WGA-p.111]

"Colonel Clark is gone Down to Williamsburg"

However, Clark was not the only commander actively preparing for renewed hostilities in the Ohio Country during the mild winter month of January 1781. In early January, Major DePeyster at Detroit met with Simon Girty and Matthew Elliott, who at Alexander McKee's urging, had traveled to Detroit to obtain ammunition and provisions for the Indians. McKee had taken up residence at the upper Shawnee town named Wapatomika on the Mad River, north of the destroyed village of Piqua and east of Peter Lorimer's trading post on the upper Miami River. McKee wanted to be closer to the Shawnee who were attempting to rebuild their village at Piqua and Chillicothe. At DePeyster's urging, Simon Girty agreed to take "up his residence at Upper Sandusky, among the Wyandots, sent thither from the Mingoes because his services would be greatly enhanced by the change." [BC-p.93] While Girty could speak their language, he was not as fluent among the Wyandot as he was with the Ohio Seneca, the Mingoes, who considered him an adopted blood brother. However, DePeyster wanted Girty to help bring the Upper Sandusky Wyandots more closely into the British fold, for their warriors were more numerous than the Mingo of the Ohio Country. DePeyster gave Girty official instructions to live with the Wyandots, "interpret for them, and go to war with them when occasions offered." [BC-p.93] Though not adopted into the Wyandot tribe as one of their own people, Girty's relationship with them was to be "the beginning of a long intimacy with those Indians." [BC-p.93]

Matthew Elliott, on the other hand, was instructed by DePeyster to prepare the necessary provisions to take back to the Shawnee villages, in order to supply major war parties to set out at the first possible moment, with Elliott in command, to attack the Kentucky settlements if the weather still permitted. DePeyster's plan was two-fold. On the one hand, he hoped that Elliott and the Indians would be able to keep the Virginians off-balance by a series of hit-and-run attacks that would force the militia to remain bottled up, not knowing where and when Elliott and the Indians would strike next. In addition, vital intelligence could be obtained from captured prisoners that would reveal to McKee the intentions of the Rebels. McKee could then relay that information to DePeyster, so that the Major could send what troops he had to counter an enemy attack, to avert a strike against the Indian villages and Detroit. With no promise of reinforcements to be sent from Niagara, DePeyster gambled that a screen of Indian attacks against the wilderness border settlements would buy him time to shift the forces available at his disposal to where they would be needed most. As yet, Haldimand had not agreed to commit troops to the western posts in any great number. Elliott agreed to confer with McKee as soon as he returned to the villages, so as to coordinate his efforts in the field. By late January, he was on his way into the Ohio Country leading a string of loaded packhorses destined for the Shawnee war parties. [HR-p.30]

The main reason that Major DePeyster sent Girty and Elliott into the wilderness of the Ohio Country to organize the Indians for winter campaigning against the Virginians was the troubling intelligence that he had received at Detroit from three prisoners brought in by Lieutenant Du Quidre in early January. During Du Quidre's pursuit of the party of 16 men from Cahokia who raided the post of St. Joseph, the party of the enemy were overtaken, surrounded, and attacked by the Indians with Du Quidre. Seven men were captured and the remaining men killed, wounded or escaped. Three of the captives were brought to Major DePeyster at Detroit for questioning. One of the prisoners named Brady admitted that he was a Virginian, and held the rank of Superintendent of Indian Affairs for the Illinois Country under Clark. Major DePeyster took note of what Brady had to say concerning the whereabouts of Clark. "Brady informs me that Colonel Clark was gone down to Williamsburg to solicit a detachment to join with a Spanish colonel in an expedition against this place." [HP-115] When the other two men were interrogated, they revealed the same information concerning Colonel Clark's intentions, confirming Brady's account, and verifying to Major DePeyster that the threat of an attack by Clark was undoubtedly true. Without confirmation from other sources, Major DePeyster was not about to sound the alarm so early in the year, but he found the information troubling enough to pass it on in a letter written on January 8 to General Haldimand at Quebec. Summing up his reaction to the possibility of an full-scale attack on Detroit by Clark, DePeyster remarked, "when the heavy cannon and ammunition arrives, which I have returned wanting, I shall be ready to give them a warm reception, should they be rash enough to attempt it," although noting on a more sober note on the deplorable condition of Fort Lernoult, "Our works are however yet in a shattered state." [HP-115]

Meanwhile, at the Shawnee village of Wapatomika deep in the wilderness of the Ohio Country, Alexander McKee had not been idle. The mild weather allowed him to meet with the Shawnee war captains and chiefs and relay to them the string of messages that McKee had received from Major DePeyster at Detroit, as well as from Simon Girty at the Upper Sandusky Wyandot villages. McKee met with Captain Thompson of the Rangers, who arrived from Detroit to replace Captain Hare in the field at the Ranger blockhouse on the upper Miami River near Lorimer's trading post. Thompson relayed to McKee the news that both Wea and Miami Indian war parties had already crossed the Ohio River to raid the settlements to the south of them in Kentucky. [HP-35] Then at the end of the month, McKee received word by runner that Simon Girty was leading a Wyandot war party to the Falls of the Ohio and would reach McKee at Wapatomika in a few days to request the help of the Shawnee. In addition, McKee learned that Matthew Elliott, who had set out from Detroit to meet with McKee, would soon arrive to raise as many warriors who would assist Elliott to attack the Virginians in Kentucky. All in all, it was encouraging news to McKee who hoped that the concerted efforts of the Indians against the Enemy would have the desired effect of buoying their lagging spirits due to "the constant alarms amongst the Indians that made it necessary for me to assist and encourage them being in great perplexity and undermined since the destruction of their villages." [HP-141]

The mild winter weather allowed Captain Thompson of Butler's Rangers to employ his men at the blockhouse on the Miami River with improving the modest fortification. Having arrived from Detroit with his detachment of Rangers near the end of December to prevent the incursion of parties of Virginians and Frenchmen from the vicinity of Vincennes and the Illinois Country, Captain Thompson brought enough provisions with him to winter over. DePeyster had urged Thompson to complete the blockhouse in his letter written on February 7, delivered to Thompson by a Pottawattamie Chief by mid-February. While keeping a work party close at hand, Thompson found time to send small scouting parties along the Indian trails to bring to him intelligence on the movements of the enemy in the vicinity of the Falls of the Ohio. The troublesome lack of sufficient horses for his men forced Thompson to send "people out every day looking for the horses" that had been lost in the preceding month. "Am afraid most of them are dead. They were so poor last fall. The six that McClinch took to Detroit is dead, and two that Serj't. Whitewells is also." [HP-35]

Late in the month, a war party of Miami Indians paid Thompson a visit, bringing with them a captive. "The prisoner Huntington was taken from Col. Clark at the Falls of the Ohio by a party of Indians from La Riviere d'languille, and delivered up to me in February." Thompson interrogated the Virginian, who in regards to the military intentions of the enemy knew only that Colonel Clark had gone east over the mountains to Virginia to seek support for a campaign against the Indian Country and Detroit to be conducted in the spring. Thompson turned the prisoner back over to the Indians and sent the information on to Major DePeyster with one of the men returning to Detroit with a list of provisions requested by the Rangers. "I would be much obliged to you as the men are in want of a number of necessaries. You would permit John Wilson who was formerly a Serjeant in the Rangers to come out and supply them. 'Tis a request of the men to me. I can safely recommend him as a good man when in this Corps." [HP-35] Captain Thompson made sure that Wilson carried with him the speeches of all the Weas and Miami Indians who had brought intelligence to him in the past month, which Thompson had the Frenchman, Beaubien translate for him. "The Indian speeches I was obliged to ask Mr. Beaubien to write in French as I do not understand but a third of what he says." Of one thing Thompson could be sure of, in regards to the Miami who came to see him. "I never seen people in higher spirits. They have been talking to me several times to write to you for assistance to go and destroy Post St. Vincent," Thompson reported to Major DePeyster. [HP-35] Whether or not the Rangers could be spared for such a campaign remained in doubt, in Thompson's mind. He knew that the Miami would have to fend themselves if the Rangers were called upon to assist the Shawnee in the Ohio Country, if they were attacked again in the spring. [HP-149]

"Their Intention is to clear the Indian Country"

On the Ohio River several miles upstream from the Virginian post on the island above the Falls of the Ohio, the two parties of hunters slowly rowed their bateaux against the current to the north shore of the river, making for the mouth of the small stream flowing into the Ohio just below the buffalo ford at the shallows. Lieutenant Hinton of the Virginia militia scanned the shoreline for the wooly animals, intent on carrying out the orders given to him by Colonel Clark in Virginia, for Hinton to hurry to Kentucky and the fort at the Falls. Considering the amount of work that needed done by the hunting parties in early February to lay in a quantity of buffalo meat for salting, in preparation to feed Clark's sizable expedition, Lieutenant Hinton had to make sure that enough of the animals were killed, butchered and salted each day to meet Colonel Clark's high expectations. With that goal in mind, and little time to waste, Hinton ordered the 16 men to paddle up the stream entering the Ohio River, so that he could get a better look in the low brush for buffalo cows and their yearlings that often rested once crossing the Ohio at their fording spot.

Just as the men in the two boats had rowed a couple of hundred feet upstream, one of the men pointed to Hinton a buffalo in a thicket. At the very instant that the men looked to the spot in the woods, a volley of musketry erupted from the shoreline, as 30 or more Wyandot and Shawnee warriors fired at once on the hapless Virginians caught out in the open, killing several of the men instantly and wounding most of the others in the close fusillade. The horde of warriors instantly dropped their muskets and plunged into the knee deep water with knife and tomahawk in hand, reaching the stunned militiamen in a flash, before any of them were able to get off a shot. Simon Girty, who accompanied the warriors, signaled to the Indians that those men unharmed must be taken prisoner; however of the five men unscathed in the two boats, two were cut down with tomahawks before Girty could intervene. Motioning to the warriors that the three remaining men were his prisoners for interrogation, Girty was able to save them for the moment, while the warriors went about their business of dispatching the wounded, scalping and gutting the dead, and plundering the valuables of the two bateaux which included weapons, ammunition, personal packs, and provisions. All in all, the attack had produced a very successful haul for the Indians, who were elated at their newly acquired scalps and presents. In a short while, the bloodied water and mutilated corpses had floated down the stream to the Ohio, as the Indian war party, with Simon Girty and the three trussed prisoners in tow, made their way up the buffalo path to the Indian trail leading to the Miami River and northeast to Wapatomika. [HP-141]

Alexander McKee questioned the three men brought in by Simon Girty and the Indians at length, one at a time. He encouraged them to tell the truth by reminding them that he had already received a great deal of information taken from other prisoners to which McKee would compare their own stories. If he found them lying in what they were about to tell him, McKee motioned to the warriors gleefully watching, implying that he would not be able to prevent the savages from cruelly burning them over a slow fire for entertainment. On the other hand, if they told the truth, McKee would see to it that they were taken to Detroit to be exchanged at the first opportunity. McKee's bluff had the desired effect on two of the terrified men, who were quick to tell McKee all that they knew. The third prisoner, named Lieutenant Hinton, was not so easily frightened, however McKee discovered that the reason for his reticence was due to the amount of information that Hinton knew concerning Clark, that he was not readily willing to give up. Nonetheless, the constant threat of torture by the Indians finally unnerved the officer, who revealed to McKee the plans of Colonel Clark's campaign.

McKee listened intently, taking some notes during the questioning, and comparing it to what he already knew from the other two prisoners. "The most material part of their information is, that the Enemy, have been laying in Buffalo Beef during the winter for an expedition into the Indian Country as early as possible in the Spring, and that Colonel Clark is gone into the Settlements to procure an army of 2,000 men to join almost 1,000 men already in Kentucky—the whole to assemble at the Falls of the Ohio and to consist of 3,000 men." McKee thought it best to send the information immediately to Major DePeyster at Detroit, considering the imposing number of men that Clark was quoted by the prisoners to be raising for the expedition. Writing to DePeyster on the day of the interrogations, February 27, McKee added, "Clark is to return by Fort Pitt and to bring a quantity of flour down the Ohio in March." [HP-141]

The prisoner Hinton was subdued by his unfortunate capture by the Indians and the loss of the bulk of the men under his command. While impressing upon McKee Clark's planned expedition into the Ohio Country in the spring, Hinton openly worried that "it will be their last effort, should they be unsuccessful, their settlements on the south side of the Ohio must undoubtedly fall." Still, he was, at the same time, able to alarm McKee, by telling him that he believed that the Virginians would not fail. "Their intention is to clear the Indian Country and penetrate as far as Detroit." With the questioning completed, McKee conferred with the Hurons and Shawnee headmen who had captured the three men and now owned them, advising Simon Girty to assist him to bargain for Hinton to send to Detroit in exchange for trade goods. When the deal was completed, McKee motioned to the warriors that he was finished with the two other men, who were separated from Hinton and led off by the Indians who stripped the prisoners and painted their faces black in preparation for burning at the stake. "The most intelligent person amongst these prisoners will be delivered with this to you by a party of Hurons from a village near this place, whose services upon several occasions deserve some notice as, they say, they are not in the way of receiving any part of the arms or ammunition delivered to their Nation." [HP-141]

"I Have Desired of Him to Send for Some of the Rangers"

At Detroit, Major DePeyster perused the letter just delivered to him by the Huron runner who arrived at the post from Wapatomika on March 4. The news conveyed by McKee alarmed DePeyster, for the intelligence gleamed from the prisoners taken near the Falls of the Ohio substantiated what DePeyster had learned from the Virginian prisoners Brady and Huntington concerning the intentions of the Rebels. It appeared more than ever to DePeyster, that Colonel Clark had every intention to invade the Ohio Country to attack the Indians and Detroit in the spring and with the backing of the Rebel government in the east, Clark would now have the means to do so.

A day after McKee's letter arrived, a runner arrived from the Upper Sandusky Indian villages with a disturbing dispatch from the resident trader and British Indian agent, Abraham Coon, written on March 1, concerning a man just brought in by Moravian Indians from Fort Pitt who claimed to be a deserter. "A few days ago, Mr. Graverot arrived here from Fort Pitt in company with four Moravians who conducted him here from Coochocking. I not knowing his intentions of coming, took him under my call with much difficulty, as the Indians wanted to Barbecue him, with orders from you to take care of anyone coming from there. I send him in haste to you as he seems to have a great deal to say to you, so as you may take your measures accordingly in the spring." As to Graverot's intentions for deserting, Coone warned, "as to pretend to give my opinion whether he ran away from them or was sent, I can't say, but in my opinion he should be taken care of till you are fully persuaded of his good will towards government." [AC-140]

Within the week, the British trader William Arendel with a party of Indians from Upper Sandusky brought the Rebel deserter Albert Graverad to Detroit as a prisoner for Major DePeyster to interrogate. DePeyster was skeptical of Graverad's assertion that he was a deserter from Fort Pitt. DePeyster distrusted everything the man said because "he was formerly a deserter from this post," and in DePeyster's mind, a Rebel spy sent to gain information on the strength of Detroit. Major DePeyster questioned Graverad at length, learning from him "that Colonel Brodhead commands 150 men in garrison at Fort Pitt and Beaver Creek, and that they receive one ration and a half of flour but no meat, are very ill-clothed, and that many of the settlement would come off if a road was opened for them, and that they knew how they would be received here." While that news was heartening, but quite possibly a lie, DePeyster judged what Graverad had to say about George Rogers Clark to be true, for it was what DePeyster had already learned from other prisoners. "He reports that Colonel Clark has obtained a draught of 3000 men to enter the Indian Country at the Miami River and penetrate if he can into Detroit." [HP-144] Though it was old news to DePeyster, nonetheless Graverad inadvertently verified without a doubt that Clark would attempt an invasion of the Ohio Country and an attack upon Detroit itself.

The repeated news of an expedition by the Rebels against the Indians and Detroit made Major DePeyster uneasy about his own situation at Detroit.

From every quarter, the Indians were making demands upon him for provisions and ammunition. However, with his stocks at the garrison severely depleted, very little could be spared for the Indians, whom DePeyster now needed to assist him in repelling Clark more than ever. Writing to General Powell on March 17 concerning the deplorable situation, DePeyster noted, "You may depend that I shall take every method to secure the provisions at this place. I am however sorry to say from the scarcity of crop the year before, and the severity of the winter before, which killed most of the hogs and numbers of the cattle together with the last fall crop turning out worse than was expected- I do not believe I shall be able to purchase above 100,000 lbs. of flour, 2000 bushels of Indian corn, and about 80 head of cattle, being very poor, and the grain, as yet, in the sheaves," DePeyster complained to Powell. "The provision return will show that the flour we have and what can be purchased will not serve this garrison long, rating it at one thousand strong, including Indians, and I expect soon to have all the Shawanese families to feed," [HP-144] whom DePeyster knew would soon arrive at Detroit for the Indian Council planned for the first week of April.

What DePeyster needed now to avert the looming disaster was a reinforcement of troops and an ample supply of provisions be sent to Detroit. If provisions were not sent, DePeyster feared that, being unable to feed or arm the Indians sufficiently they would desert him before Clark reached Detroit. His garrison of several hundred regulars at Fort Lernoult would be no match for 3000 Rebel troops, no matter how hard his men fought. Consequently, while requisitioning General Powell for the necessary provisions to be sent, DePeyster ordered that all prisoners be shipped to Niagara as soon as he was done with them to avoid having to feed them from his meager stores. Writing to General Powell, DePeyster stated that in the event reinforcements could not be sent to Detroit in the near future, he would request more Rangers be sent from Niagara, but not until the last possible moment. "I have desired him to send for some of the Rangers from hence, in order to be employed at Sanduski or wherever they may be most wanted, but as the state of our provisions will not admit of their being long in camp, it would be wrong to send for them until they are really wanted." [HP-150]

"No Artificer to Give the Least Assistance"

In the meantime, DePeyster turned his attention to his plan to outfit schooners upon Lake Erie to support the defense of Detroit, as well as protect the Maumee River from its mouth on the Lake up to its juncture with the Auglaize and to prevent Clark from using the river to transport his troops by water, it they should come. DePeyster wrote a formal request to Captain Alexander Grant, the British senior Naval Department officer in charge at Detroit with "commanding His majesty's Armed Vessels on the Lakes Erie, Huron, and Michigan." [HP-146] Grant complied with DePeyster's order, but informed

General Powell at Niagara on March 18 that the task given to him by DePeyster was not without its problems.

"Major DePeyster informed me that he had accounts of the enemy intending or advancing this post, and directs two of the armed vessel that could be best spared from the transportation to be well armed so that they might be stationed in the river Miamis (Maumee) or where most necessary. I have accordingly fitted out the schooner 'Faith' and the sloop 'Adventure' for that purpose," Grant wrote. "The Major says he cannot spare troops to be put on board these vessels, in that case its out of my power to man them properly for defense being as much as I can do with the numbers of men we have in the Department to man the vessels for the transportation. This will prevent our having it in our power to give any assistance in the transportation between Little Niagara and Fort Erie as two vessels usually allotted for that business were 'Faith' and the 'Adventure'" Adding to growing list of problems at Detroit, Grant continued, "by the express the day before yesterday from Michilimackinac, the senior officer of the Department there informed me that he thinks the 'Welcome' is not repairable, and that they cannot ascertain the damage done the 'Angelica' till the ice breaks up." [HP-145]

Captain Grant fretted that while the lack of manpower and resources to refit the vessels was his most pressing problem, it did not help that the violent storms upon the Lakes were tearing apart the King's ships as fast as he could get them afloat, and leaving them stranded far from Detroit where it was nearly impossible to work on them. "He further tells me there is neither white oak nor pine on that island or near at hand, so as to have good planks sawn for the repair of them, and also no artificer to give the least assistance." [HP-145] Aware of Grant's complaints, Major DePeyster remained undeterred. He wrote to Captain Grant on March 31 with additional orders requesting Grant to conduct "a Survey upon His Majesty's Armed Schooner 'Hope.'" Grant ordered Mr. Joseph Williams, the Master Builder at Detroit, along with his shipwrights to "hold a survey upon His Majesty's armed schooner 'Hope,' as she is represented to me unfit for Service, and you will order the said schooner 'Hope' to be condemned or repaired for the ensuing season." [HP-146]

At Fort Niagara, all was not well with the Mohawk war captain Joseph Brant. Unlike past winters when he ventured out to attack the Rebel settlements, Brant brooded much of January behind the confines of the overcrowded fort walls. On the one hand, he chaffed under the yoke of inaction brought about the heavy winter snows coming off the Great Lakes early in the month which hindered war parties from heading southeast to the Rebel frontier. More than ever, Brant wished to attack the contemptible Oneida Indians for their insolence in deserting the Iroquois Confederacy to side with the Rebels. On the other hand, Brant was despondent that there appeared no end in sight to the war which kept him and his sister Molly from returning to their former home at the Mohawk village Canajoharie on the Mohawk River after six long years. Finally wishing to do something of consequence, Brant accompanied a party of 30 Rangers under the command of Lieutenant Andrew Bradt, with 150 Indians "intending to cut off supplies moving toward Fort Stanwix." [KI-p.306]

Returning to Niagara on March 17 with Bradt's party, after achieving only limited success, a discontented Joseph Brant paid a visit to General Powell, telling the commander that he wanted to resign his commission as captain of the Volunteers and wished for some sort of change. Powell was taken aback by Brant's sudden request and "asked him to wait and consider" before resigning his company. On April 6, 1781, Joseph Brant, "the most sober and quiet and good natured Indian I ever was acquainted with," as his good friend Daniel Claus in the Indian Department liked to call him, got involved in a drunken brawl with one of Guy Johnson's men from the Indian Department, setting off an investigation into the incident by General Powell at the insistence of Molly Brant, Joseph's influential sister. With gossip abounding at the post, Guy Johnson, with General Powell's approval, thought it best to send Joseph Brant away to Detroit, giving Brant the change that he desired. On April 8, Brant set out with "17 young warriors, probably the greater part of the small Indian party who had stood by him since Oriskany. Though he told Powell he hoped for some military action in the west, his white Volunteers seem to have been left behind." [KI-p.308] Ahead, Joseph Brant hoped to encourage the western tribes to defend the Ohio Country from any invasion from the enemy in the spring.

"I Hope They Get What They Deserve"

Meanwhile at Fort Pitt, Colonel Brodhead in command of the post was not amused when he received the deeply disappointing news that Colonel Clark had been promoted to General in order to lead an expedition of several thousand men into the Ohio Country as soon as the coming of spring. Brodhead had wanted to lead a similar force against Detroit and the Indians of the Upper Sandusky villages by way of Fort Pitt. "Informed by both Washington and Jefferson of Clark's mission, Brodhead fumed. The glory would go to Clark while Brodhead was consigned to a defensive role." [WGA-p.111] The situation only grew worse for Brodhead when he received a request by Jefferson for Colonel Gibson and his regiment at Fort Pitt to be consigned to Clark's mission, along with Washington stripping Fort Pitt of an artillery company destined for Clark, and orders from Washington for the number of Regular soldiers at the American posts on the upper Ohio River to be reduced, and the surplus men sent east to support Washington's desperate campaign against the British. The actions appeared to Brodhead to be purposely slanted against him, and it was more than Brodhead could bear.

At Fort Pitt in early March, Colonel Brodhead wrote to the president of Congress, Samuel Huntington, listing his complaints, and then to Washington, protesting the order to give up Gibson's regiment to Clark. Brodhead's letters had no effect but to embitter him more deeply. However, new developments with the Delaware Indians residing at the villages surrounding Goschachgunk on the Muskingum River late in February promised to give Brodhead the diversion he needed from his troubles, and at the same time, provide him with an opportunity to draw off some of the military support destined for Clark that could only undermine the good intentions of Brodhead's rival.

Brodhead was informed on February 26 by a letter from the preacher John Heckewelder residing at one of the Moravian Delaware villages on the Tuscarawas that the formerly neutral Delaware Indians of the region were about to meet in council to pledge their allegiance to the British at Detroit. "The people of Coshocton have been very busy in trying to deceive you this long time," Heckewelder wrote. "I indeed believe that the greater part of them will be upon you in a few days, as they have arranged themselves in three parties, ... And if I am right, one party is gone already; but I hope they will get what they deserve." [BC-p.92] Brodhead considered the information from the Moravian preacher, and decided to move against Indians at the first possible moment, which he now considered hostile. In raising men for the campaign to attack the Delawares, Colonel Gibson "pointed out that men so engaged would not be willing to serve again" thus depriving General Clark of the volunteers from the region that he was desperately seeking for his own expedition. [WGA-p.112] Many men would rather accompany Brodhead's brief campaign to avoid enlistment with Clark, whose expedition deep into Indian country promised to be a lengthy time far away from their homes and families.

"That Bind Us Together and Make Us One Flesh and Blood"

A major Indian Council of a confederacy of tribes from the Ohio Country was planned at Detroit on April 5 by Major DePeyster. A few days prior to the important meeting, Alexander McKee arrived at Detroit accompanied by an entourage of Indians from the Ohio wilderness. DePeyster met briefly with the chiefs before the Council to hear their complaints and demands they wished resolved by the end of the meeting. "Alexander McKee arrived here with some principal chiefs of the Mingoes, Delawares, Wyandotts and Shawanese who declare they have every reason to believe that Mr. Clark is to enter their country this summer with three thousand men and some cannon," DePeyster wrote. "They therefore have brought the Belt of Alliance with them to claim the assistance heretofore promised upon the like occasions, declaring that, if not affected, must fall back and be maintained here, or make the best peace for themselves they can." [HP-149]

Writing to Powell on the details of the information gleamed from McKee and the Indians, DePeyster noted "thence accounts from all quarters that this Expedition is intended against the Indian Country and even to this part if they can find passage- I wish it was in my powers to assist the Indians with a body of troops to give a decisive stroke to Mr. Clark's incursion into the Indian Country." Quoting from McKee's information taken from prisoners, DePeyster added, "being informed by some of the prisoners that should he (Clark) fail in this attempt, the settlers upon Kentuck will leave that country together." Yet DePeyster wished Powell to know that the Rebels were not idly waiting for Clark, but "the people of Kentuck are night and day employed in removing their families and effects to a large settlement called Bryant's Station, where they hope to remain in security during Clark's expedition, and that they are gathering magazines in different quarters, one of which some of our Indians under Mr. Elliott (who I sent from here) have burnt. I now send down one of the Deputy Commissaries by the name Hinton, who confirms the same." As to what the outcome of the Council with the Indians would be, DePeyster noted that Alexander McKee "will be able to give the result of a council held at this place as soon as the Indians can be assembled." [HP-149]

On the morning of April 5, Major DePeyster with Major Gamble of the 47th Regiment, and a dozen junior officers of the King's Eighth, the 47th, and the Royal Artillery, including Captain Henry Bird, sat down on the blankets laid out in the Indian Council Lodge before the host of nearly 100 Indian headmen, chiefs and war captains from the major tribes of the Ohio Country. The members of Guy Johnson's Indian Department at Detroit took up their positions between the Indian chieftains and the red-coated British officers so as to act as liaisons between the two groups and sworn interpreters for the proceedings. Alexander McKee, as senior officer of the Department and Johnson's deputy agent, was flanked on the left by Isidore Chesne and Duperon Baby, both Frenchmen from Detroit. On McKee's right sat the brothers Simon and James Girty. Once the solemn introductions were completed, the Shawnee delegation signaled to McKee that they wished one of their most esteemed chiefs named "Wry Neck" to speak to Major DePeyster on the important matter that had brought them all to Detroit.

A hush fell over the throng of Indians as the respected chief of the Shawnee rose from his place and prepared to speak. McKee motioned to James Girty to translate the Indian's words as DePeyster listened intently, his eyes never leaving those of the Shawnee chief. "Father," the chief began, directing his comments to DePeyster, "we return the Great Spirit thanks for permitting us to meet you this day in our Council House, but am sorry that several nations of Your Children are absent. The Ottawas, the Chippewas, and the Pottawattamies," the Chief named the tribes of the Lake Indians conspicuously absent from the council, are "equally concerned, but we suppose the season has prevented them, and shall therefore proceed to inform you of My Errand." [HP-253]

Wry Neck cleared his throat and continued. "Father, I am now to acquaint you that after the destruction of our Villages by the Enemy last fall, our Chiefs have been in constant Councils, and early this spring whilst they were engaged in one, Simon Girty...." the Chief paused and pointed to Girty seated before him, "Simon Girty with a party of Hurons and some of our own Nation, delivered us a Prisoner they had taken from the Enemy who confirms their designs against us as early as possible this year. He was brought for the purpose of giving us and you Intelligence, therefore we now deliver him to you." The Chief motioned with his arm to the warriors stationed at the door and they brought forward the Virginian prisoner named Hinton to the side of Wry Neck, who nodded to the captive to sit. It was a formality for DePeyster who had already spoken to the prisoner, and gleaned all that was to be learned in advance of the Council from Girty, McKee and Hinton himself. Wry Neck pointed to the prisoner, adding, "I hope that what he will tell you will convince you of the danger with which we are threatened by the Enemy." [HP-253]

Coming to the point of his lengthy dialogue, the Shawnee chief stated to DePeyster, "Father, notwithstanding the misfortunes that have happened to your Children of our Confederacy, we can assure you they are not cast down, but that they still hold up their heads and are determined to revenge themselves upon the Enemy." Reaching for the three beaded belts of wampum given to the tribes by former Governor Hamilton, and formally kept in possession of the Shawnee, Wry Neck solemnly draped the belts over his outstretched arms for DePeyster and the other officers to see as he continued to speak. "Therefore I am come to speak to you in their behalf on business of importance to you and us both. For Father, this is the Council Fire at which you and the different Nations of your Children were united, those are the Belts that bind us together and make us one Flesh and Blood, and you must remember the Promises of assistance whenever they are presented before you, as on this occasion." [HP-253]

The Shawnee Chief closed his speech to Major DePeyster with what amounted to a formal request from the confederacy of the tribes present to provide them with the necessary arms, ammunition, provisions, artillery, and troops to aid them in repelling Clark's army, if it should come into their Indian lands. A veteran of dealing with the Indians at Michilimackinac, DePeyster was not at a loss of words in his reply to the chief and the Indian assemblage, knowing that he must promise to support them in every manner they requested, while remaining hazy on the details, and keep from them the true unfortunate state of affairs at Detroit concerning the dire lack of everything that the Indians wished for. Assuring them of the King's love for them, and thanking them for their presence, DePeyster made sure that precious food, ammunition and gifts were liberally distributed among the chiefs, while pointing to the next Council to be held late in the month of April as the appointed time that he would determine what was to be done, once the ice on the lakes permitted supply ships to reach Detroit from the east along with orders from General Powell at Haldimand's direction.

In the meantime, with the Indian Council over and the chiefs temporarily satisfied with the response to their requests, Major DePeyster thought it wise to send word through Simon Girty to the Delaware Indians at the village of Goschachgunk on the Muskingum, inviting them into the alliance of the Indian Confederacy of the Ohio Country with the British, in response to their appeal to DePeyster. DePeyster conferred with Girty, who then prepared a speech to the Delaware on April 12, which Girty would deliver to the Delaware through Half King and Captain Pipe, once Girty reached the Upper Sandusky villages. "Indians of Goschachgunk! I have received your speech sent me by the Half King of Sandusky. It contains three strings, one of them white, and the other two checkered. You say that you want traders to be sent to your village and that you are resolved no more to listen to the Virginians, who have deceived you. It would give me pleasure to receive you again as brothers, both for your own good and for the friendship I bear to the Indians in general." [BC-p.93] What neither Girty nor DePeyster could know was that on the morning of April 10, General Brodhead at the head of a small army of about 300 mounted men, had crossed the Ohio River at the settlement of Wheeling below Pittsburgh, and headed west up Indian Wheeling creek intent on attacking the unsuspecting Delawares at Goschachgunk to destroy the rebellious Indians before they could attack the settlements on the east side of the Ohio River. [BC-p.94]

"Likewise Send the Indians That Are About You to Assist Us"

Brodhead's force was composed of 150 regular troops from Fort Pitt who were joined at Fort Henry in Wheeling by 134 militiamen who had been raised for the expedition from the surrounding settlements by Colonel David Shepherd whom Brodhead had sent word ahead. [HW1-p.148] On April 19, the Moravian preachers at Salem were alerted that Brodhead's force "was seen at White Eye's Town (ten miles from here) and was marching right to Goschachking. This put us in a great predicament because of the Brothers and Sisters we believed to be in the village. Before evening we had some refugees here, who had been captured by the army but immediately set free." [BR-p.198] Brodhead had with him a friendly Delaware chief named Pekillon, who not only helped guide the expedition, but also pointed out to Brodhead those Delawares whom he knew to be openly hostile to the Americans.

Early on April 20, by means of a rapid march, Brodhead's army succeeded in surprising the Delawares at Goschachgunk. Dividing his army into three wings and approaching the village from all sides he surrounded the Indians and took them captive "without firing a single shot." [HW1-p.149] Deliberations were now held by the militia officers to determine what was to be done with the captive 35 Delaware men, women and children. It was decided on the advice of Pekillon that the 15 male prisoners whom he knew to be "active in raids against the frontier settlements" and should be put to death on the spot, thereupon they "were bound and taken a little distance below the town, and dispatched with tomahawks and spears, and then scalped" by the Virginian militiamen from Wheeling. The rest of the Delaware prisoners, mainly women and children, "were taken back to Fort Pitt as hostages, although they were soon released." [HW1-p.149] Unable to continue his campaign any further against remaining hostile Delawares in the area due to the fact that the militia, now loaded with scalps and plunder, voted to return home, a disappointed Brodhead ordered the Delaware village burned to the ground before leaving.

Simon Girty was still at the Upper Sandusky Indian villages when word reached him of Brodhead's attack on the Delaware village on the Muskingum. "We sent 20 of our men to Goschachgunk some time ago, and this day they have returned with the following news. On the 20th of April" Girty wrote to Major DePeyster, "Colonel Brodhead, with 500 men, burned the town and killed 15 men. He left six houses on this [west] side of the creek that he did not see. He

likewise took the women and children prisoners, and afterward let them go."
Girty continued to dictate all the information that he had learned of Brodhead's
activities. "He let four men (Delawares) go that were prisoners who showed
him a paper that they had from Congress. Brodhead told them that it was none
of his fault that their people (the Delawares slain) were killed, but the fault of
the militia that would not be under his command. He likewise told them that in
seven months he would beat all the Indians out of this country. In six days from
this date, he is to set off for this place (Upper Sandusky) with 1,000 men; and
Colonel Clark is gone down the Ohio River with 1,000 men." [BC-p.95]

The Delaware and Wyandots with Girty were furious at news of the
killings and vowed immediate revenge upon the Virginians, but did nothing.
"There were 120 Wyandots ready to start off with men, until this news came,"
Girty reported. He knew that pursuit of Brodhead's force was out of the question
because the Americans had, by this time, already safely returned to Fort Henry
and Pittsburgh even after a reported stop at Heckewelder's mission.
Consequently, Brodhead's force, particularly the militia, could not be attacked
directly behind the walls of Fort Henry. The anger of the Indians was tempered
too by the fact that they desperately needed supplies and assistance for any
extended war party across the Ohio. "I have 160 Indians at this place. Their
provisions are all gone; and they beg that you will send them some," Girty
informed DePeyster. "Your children (the Wyandots) will be very glad if you
will send those people you promised to send their assistance; likewise send the
Indians that are about you, to assist us. The Christian (Moravian) Indians have
applied to us to move them off before the Rebels come to their town. I will be
much obliged to you, sir, if you send me a little provision for myself as I was
compelled to give mine to the Indians." [BC-p.95] Writing to DePeyster for
help was all that Simon Girty could do at the moment for the Wyandots had no
provisions to set out on an extended raid into enemy territory. Unfortunately
for the Delawares, in one surprise blow, the Rebels had entered the Ohio Country
and destroyed their village of Goschachgunk with impunity and there was
nothing the Indians could do. Revenge would have to wait.

"The Rangers Are Obliged to Sell Their Necessaries"

At Fort Niagara, Brigadier General Watson Powell mulled over the stack
of letters on his writing desk recently received from his officers in command of
the upper posts who reported to him. He rose from his desk to pace the floor of
his officer's quarters, trying to formulate an assessment of the reports which he
must send to General Haldimand in Quebec. Powell considered for a moment
the enormity of the problem facing the British if they were to hold the Ohio
Country in their possession during the coming year. From every quarter under
his command, requests for provisions, ammunition and reinforcements had been
forwarded to him, but Powell had no way of providing the necessary supplies
and troops until they were sent from Canada upon arriving from England. Powell
judged DePeyster's situation at Detroit the most pressing for when the Major

made a closer estimation of the provisions that could possibly be purchased by him from the French inhabitants at Detroit, he found that amount "precarious, at this time" on April 3, and since the current shortage of food compelled DePeyster to count every mouth under his command, "the prospect of getting up little provisions this summer and the Rebels threatening a visit, obliges me to send down prisoners" to Quebec, rather than having to feed them. [HP-148]

Finishing his report to General Haldimand on April 10, detailing his evaluation of the needs of the upper posts, Powell outlined to Haldimand the necessity of sending provisions at once to Detroit if the General expected the garrison to be able to defend itself from the Enemy's expected incursion. "The enclosed letter will lay before Your Excellency such further information as has been received, relative to the intentions of the Rebels. Should Major DePeyster find that their movements are intended against Detroit, I have desired him to send for some of the Rangers and Indians from hence, in order to be employed at Sanduski or wherever they may be most wanted" Powell wrote. Yet, he stated for the General the inherent problem with that course of action, since no food was available to feed the additional troops. "But as the state of our provisions will not admit of their being long in camp, it would be wrong to send them until they were really wanted." Because of a shortage of food at both posts, "as fast as prisoners arrive here they shall be forwarded." [HP-150]

Many of Major Butler's Rangers had pressing debts that needed settled, which General Powell could not authorize without Haldimand's consent. Commenting on the Ranger Corps, "on the 31st of March, I saw the Rangers mustered, they were all clothed and made a very good appearance," Powell stated to Haldimand. Yet when it came to the essential needs of the Rangers when out on campaign, they had felt the sting of a lack of adequate supplies that forced Powell to submit an account to Haldimand, to address the inequities. Since the Rangers were the only experienced and capable troops in the field that Powell could rely upon to counter the Rebels in the western war, it was imperative, in his mind, that they be adequately supplied and paid. "As the Rangers, when they are out on scouts, are frequently obliged to sell their necessaries to supply themselves with provisions, which is seldom reimbursed, I send the account of expenses incurred by some of the men of Lt. Tierney's last party. Your Excellency will please to observe that the things mentioned in it were sold to supply the whole party, and as they received no provisions from Government at that time, I beg leave to submit it to your consideration, whether it would not be right, upon that and such occasions, either to reimburse them the money laid out for provisions, or to make their provisions up to them for the time they received none from the garrison." [HP-149]

"To Intercept Mr. Clark on His Passage Down"

Deep in the wilderness of the Ohio Country, Matthew Elliott was stunned by the news that he had just been told by the three prisoners standing before him. Elliott had recently returned to the Shawnee villages on the Scioto with the

Shawnee war party from raiding the Virginian settlements deep in the Kentucky lands south of the Ohio. Elliott, with the party of Shawnee warriors he accompanied, had managed to stay in the field for more than a month. The war party lived off the land as they moved between the Kentucky stations, attacking outlying settler cabins, and making off before the local militias could be summoned to pursue them. Coming close to the stronghold called Bryan's Station, Elliott observed the heightened activity of the Rebels in mid-March, and learned from a captive that many of the militia were bringing their families to Bryan's Station for safety during the expected campaign by Colonel Clark as soon as he could muster his forces in the upcoming month. Elliott had wisely counseled the warriors to avoid attacking the fortified Rebels whom he knew had more than enough men and horses to give chase once the alarm was sounded.

Crossing the Ohio River late in March, Elliott and the Shawnee made their way up the Scioto with their load of plunder, scalps, and horses in tow. It was several days later, on March 8 that another war party returned, sounding the war whoop that they had captives. Matthew Elliott took notice. "Three Prisoners were brought in the Shawanese villages by a party of that Nation taken upon the Ohio." After the two adult men and the youth had been thoroughly beaten with sticks by the villagers, Elliott asked their Indian captors if he could speak to the men to question them, before the Indians decided to burn the prisoners. Without reservation, the warriors brought the three bloody, frightened white men to stand before Elliott for his examination.

Elliott asked the men who they were and where they were from. "They say they were deserters from Wheeling, a Rebel post upon the Ohio below Fort Pitt." Questioning them on the strength of the Rebel army in that part of the country, one of the men stated to Elliott "that the whole regular force of that country does not exceed 200 men, divided in the following manner, 110 men at Fort Pitt, 30 at Beaver Creek, 30 at Wheeling, the place they deserted from, and about 30 more dispersed through the country at farm houses." Elliott's eyebrows raised when he heard the scant numbers, and thought if he had only 100 Rangers and as many Indians, that he was sure the frontier could be rid of the Enemy, if the information was correct. [HP-151]

Elliott asked the captives what they knew of the whereabouts of Colonel Clark, whom Elliott had heard was on his way to Kentucky with an army. The younger of the two men nervously told Elliott that "Colonel Clark who commanded upon the Kentucky is appointed a General, and his command now included Fort Pitt and all the Enemy's forts upon the Ohio." [HP-151] General Brodhead at Fort Pitt had gone to Philadelphia, the man stated, having been recalled. [WGA-p.112] Colonel Clark "had applied some time in the winter to the convention of Virginia for two regiments, to join those that could be raised upon the Kentucky to make a campaign in the spring, in order to subdue the Indians and penetrate to Detroit." [HP-151] However that was not to be, the prisoner remarked to Elliott, which caused the Indian Department officer to come to his feet before the man, and ask him what he meant by that.

The prisoner mumbled to Elliott that Clark "was referred from thence to Congress who refused that number and gave him an order for only two companies, which made about 100 men. At present he is building boats upon the Redstone above Fort Pitt to transport him with eight families to the Falls that his intention is to leave there some time in the beginning of May." Matthew Elliott was stunned at this latest news, and questioned the three again until he was finally convinced that the intelligence was truthful, although the older of the two men had said little to corroborate the other man's testimony, and the boy was too frightened to be coherent. Nonetheless, Elliott was sure now that George Rogers Clark was not a the head of an army of several thousand men making their way to Kentucky, but rather, far upriver in the mountains, with only two meager companies of troops.

A council with the Shawnee was quickly held to determine what to do next, in light of the latest news on Clark. "This information determined the Indians to send Elliott to this place (Detroit) to request a few men with a cannon to join them as quick as possible at the Ohio to enable them to intercept Mr. Clark on his passage down, being fully of the opinion that if they are successful against him, they will have nothing to fear again from the Enemy this season." [HP-151] Matthew Elliott prepared to set out at once for Detroit, but parleyed with the Indians on the delicate matter of the prisoners. Elliott wanted to take the talkative captive with him to meet with Major DePeyster. He offered to buy the man outright from his own funds, or seek restitution for the Shawnee owners from the Major upon reaching his destination. The warriors agreed, but on the question of the other two, they dismissed the notion that they were deserters, and decided to burn the elder man in the evening, while adopting the boy into one of the families that had lost a son. On that matter, knowing he could do nothing to change the warriors' minds, Elliott acquiesced, and in a matter of hours, the elder of the two adult men was reduced to a pile of smoldering, blackened bones in the coals of the village fire.

"Wishes That Some Rangers from Niagara Were Sent"

Just as Major DePeyster at Detroit received the disturbing news from Simon Girty at the Upper Sandusky villages that the Goschachgunk Delawares had been attacked by the Rebels from Fort Pitt and their village destroyed, word reached DePeyster from James Cochran at the Indian village of Roche de Bout on the lower Maumee River. Cochran was the British trader who had been planning to set out for the Delaware on the Muskingum to supply them with trade goods, now that they had embraced the Crown's cause and requested support. Writing to DePeyster on April 22, Cochran reported, "Sir, just arrived Indians with the news that Rebels is at Cooschuckunk and has took the vilige and all the Indins that was in- it only ten escaped and they say that by this time they are at Upper Sandusky. Likewis they say ther is a Nother Partey of Coos Coming up Ston Creek by way of Mr. Lorimies. How true it is I cannot tell as it is Indin News." [HP-151] Cochran's intelligence from the Indians confirmed

Girty's report of the magnitude of the Rebel attack against the Delaware. While DePeyster found it discouraging that the Rebels had successfully struck a blow against the formerly neutral Delaware on the Muskingum before DePeyster could support them militarily, he knew now that the attack was limited to the Indian village and not the Upper Sandusky villages themselves. In the long run, he felt that the attack would serve to harden Indian sentiment against the Virginians all the more, rather than persuading them to seek peace with their enemy. It was a sign to DePeyster that the time had passed for any of the tribes to remain neutral in the fight for the Ohio Country any longer.

On April 26, an Indian Grand Council was held at Detroit, with all of the tribes of the Ohio Country and the Great Lakes present. Attending the Council was Joseph Brant and his contingent of Iroquois warriors who had arrived the previous week by sailing vessel from Niagara. It was Brant's first Indian Council at Detroit and he would play a role as ambassador of the Six Nations tribes of the Iroquois Confederacy, along with the notable Seneca war chief of the Mingoes, Kayashuta, "who had also come with encouraging messages from Guy Johnson and the Six Nations" at Niagara. [KI-p.309] Presiding over the British officers at the council was Major DePeyster, commanding at Detroit, with Alexander McKee as officer in charge of Johnson's Indian Department at Detroit. As Simon Girty and his brothers, along with Matthew Elliott, were busy accompanying Indian war parties to the Ohio River and Kentucky, McKee had Indian Department officers currently at Detroit serve each of the tribes as sworn interpreters during the Council, "Duperon Baby for the Shawanese, Isidore Chesne for the Ottawas, Pierre Druilliard for the Hurons, and William Tucker for the Chippoweys." [HP-254] Representing the Confederacy of the tribes of the Ohio Country were no less than "six Huron chiefs, including the famed Andesherry, nine Ottawa chiefs," [HP-254] "two Pottawattamies, eight Chippewas, and one Miami," [KI-p.309] along with many Shawnee chiefs, and "a large number of warriors of various nations," [KI-p.309] who had come to witness the important proceedings. The Grand Council began by noon on April 26, with a deputation of Shawnee speakers "describing George Rogers Clark's latest movements and threats" against the Ohio Country.

One by one the Shawnee chiefs outlined their great need for Major DePeyster and the British to support all the tribes of the Ohio Country with arms, ammunition, food, and troops to counter the threat from the Virginians. When they were finished, it was time for Joseph Brant and Kayashuta to speak to the assembly, and they delivered to the Indian Confederacy of the Ohio Country the pledge of support from the Six Nations of the Iroquois to help the western Indians defeat their common enemy, with the help of the British and Guy Johnson, the Superintendent of the Indian Department. On the surface, the western tribes embraced the message of Brant and the Six Nations which extolled the spirit of friendship and cooperation between the Six Nations and the western tribes, "as though they were all the greatest friends in the world." But privately, Joseph Brant "was not exactly welcomed with open arms." [KI-p.311]

The Hurons, Delawares, and Shawnee all knew who Brant was and the Mohawks who he represented, and their impression was negative. Brant had acquired a reputation for being too forward in presenting himself to other Indians, a trait that was not liked by the western Indians. In addition, Brant represented the Iroquois Confederacy whom the western Indians had "long memories of old grievances which went back many years." Ill feelings had persisted for years since the signing of the Treaty of Fort Stanwix of 1768 by which the Iroquois had surreptitiously sold the Delaware lands east of the Ohio River to William Johnson and the British government for colonial expansion without consulting the Delawares who considered themselves the rightful owners. [KI-p.311] Old resentments among the Indians against the Six Nations could not be forgotten easily, even in spite of the common war both Indian Confederacies fought to win against the Americans. Brant was soon to find that a mixed welcome awaited him by the Indians of the western tribes wherever he went in the Ohio Country. "There was something about Joseph Brant as an individual and his people en masse which raised the hackles of the western brethren," that was greater than the petty jealousies and squabbles that occurred between the tribes. [KI-p.311]

DePeyster ended the Grand Council much in the same way as he had the last, urging the Indians to embrace the common cause of defeating the American enemy which threatened them all, and promising to send them the necessary aid and support as soon as it was forthcoming, without being specific on what he would do. DePeyster allayed their fears by pointing to the latest intelligence on Clark's movements gleaned from Matthew Elliott's prisoner which revealed that Clark did not have an army of 2000 men with him, but rather two companies totaling only 200. DePeyster was confident the Indians could easily defeat this force. "Mr. Clark has failed in his application for procuring a sufficient body of troops to enable him to penetrate this far," DePeyster noted. However the Indians wanted some evident show of support from DePeyster, and as "it is nevertheless thought he will enter the Indian Country with about 1,000 men," DePeyster was forced to provide those tribes with some assistance, telling Powell, "you will see the steps I proposed to take and which will be necessary for me to pursue in order to please the Indians who still persist in having the assistance of their Brethren from Detroit." [HP-152]

After much discussion, DePeyster urged the chiefs to rendevous their warriors at the Upper Sandusky villages in the coming month, whereby he would send the necessary supplies and ammunition, along with a small contingent of men to help the Indians to set out against Clark at the first possible moment, to intercept him and his troops on their way to Kentucky. Joseph Brant and his Mohawk warriors agreed to accompany the war party for the Upper Sandusky; however, on the day after the Council adjourned, Brant met with DePeyster to discuss the subject of the conduct of the war from the Upper Sandusky. DePeyster confided that "the Indians are extremely troublesome in order to procure troops to be sent with them to St. Dusky," believing that the Ohio tribes could conduct the war against Clark by themselves if the Indian Department officers could exert the right amount of influence upon them. Being a Mohawk and an outsider to the Ohio tribes, Joseph Brant was not so sure the Indians would cooperate sufficiently if DePeyster were unable to send troops. "Joseph being convinced it is not in my power wishes that some Rangers as could be spared from Niagara were sent." [HP-152] Already Joseph Brant was feeling some degree of uneasiness and if not suspicion towards the Ohio tribes who had remained standoffish towards him during the Council.

"It Won't Be Long Before We Shall Meet the Enemy"

Joseph Brant and his party set off for the Upper Sandusky loaded with provisions. On the way there, he met Matthew Elliott returning to Detroit from the Scioto, whereupon the two men conferred; Elliott informed Brant on almost all of the happenings in the wilderness war in the Ohio Country of the past year, thereby bringing Brant up to date on the latest intelligence. Brant then continued his journey up the trail that followed the Sandusky River to the cluster of villages near the head of the Sandusky River adjoining the Carrying Place or portage with the upper reaches of the Scioto River. Arriving there by the second week of May, Brant met with Simon Girty in the company of a large band of Wyandot Indians, who were awaiting supplies before setting out for the Ohio River. On the night of the May 16, two Moravian Delaware Indians came into Girty's camp while he was meeting with Brant, reporting "that there are 2000 Rebels coming to this place, in four parties, each of them 500, they intend to meet themselves about two days journey from this place." [HP-301]

Joseph Brant was alarmed at the news. Simon Girty cautioned the Mohawk to wait until confirmation from Girty's own people when they came in before reacting too quickly, as the Christian Delawares were not to be trusted because they were known to spread unfounded rumors. Brant, writing to Matthew Elliott and Isidore Chesne at Detroit on May 19, repeated the news he had heard, but added Girty's warning, "I think you better remain still where you are till you hear from us again, because the news are not certain till our own spies return to us." [HP-301] On that same day, George Girty came into the Sandusky village returning from the Shawnee, unaware of the latest news. "George Girty and one Indian just arrived from the Shawanese town brought a string of wampum beads, message from those different nations that they would be glad if they could get them ammunition as soon as possible which the Major DePeyster promised them and also would be happy if the Major would send some of his men to assist them because they are now sure the Rebels will soon get into their country. They think if he does not send men immediately, it will be too late to assist them as it happened the last summer. They have sent four different parties as spies, but not yet returned." [HP-301] The flurry of rumors and the activity of the local Indians stirred Brant to excitement, in anticipation of a good fight with the Rebels. "It won't be long before we shall meet the Enemy" Brant wrote to Elliott, encouraging him to get horses and ammunition to the Upper Sandusky as soon as he could, as well as "encourage the Indians that came from

Detroit who are not yet tired of staying there," to join him at the Upper Sandusky. [HP-301]

Far up the Monongahela River, above the site of Braddock's disastrous defeat 26 years previously, General George Rogers Clark privately despaired in the middle of May of ever raising an army to go to Kentucky. For weeks he had tirelessly harangued the militiamen in the isolated Pennsylvania settlements of Westmoreland County in an attempt to recruit sufficient men to accompany him for his campaign from Kentucky against the Indians, but to little avail. At the settlement of Redstone on the Monongahela, Clark labored to build dugouts and bateaux to transport those men he had been able to procure, but desertions were rampant and potential recruits indifferent to Clark's plea for support. To add to his misery, word reached Clark from Captain George at the far-flung Fort Jefferson at the mouth of the Ohio River on the Mississippi that the meager provisions were spoiled and the post had no means to induce the local Indians to hunt game for the garrison. Clark wrote to Jefferson on the deplorable failure of his campaign, which by mid-May was stalled. "My situation is truly disagreeable," Clark stated. "There is an indignity in it that often hurt me." [WGA-p.113] Brodhead had despaired when he had been ordered to turn over his command at Fort Pitt to Colonel Gibson, in order to return to Philadelphia on May 6, to face charges of mismanaging public funds earmarked for the garrison of Fort Pitt. Now it was Clark's turn, for by the end of May, he was "was tasting failure" of his own. How much more bitter would his setback have been if Clark had only known that the British and Indians were fully aware of his intentions as a result of their ability to intercept and capture Clark's envoys on the Ohio River and interrogate them for vital information on the movement of his men. While he remained in the dark, his enemy, the Indians and the men of the British Indian Department were "receiving fairly accurate intelligence concerning Clark's intentions." [NL-p.118]

"It Is Said That Governor Hamilton Was On His Parole"

At Quebec, General Haldimand studied the recently received letters from the western posts which Captain Matthews had placed before him, concerning the latest intelligence on the movements of the Rebels along with status reports on the strength of the garrisons and requisitions from the commanding officers. Something troubled Haldimand more than the reports that George Rogers Clark intended to lead an expedition against the Indian Country to strike at Detroit. What was disconcerting to him was the inadequate provisions and lack of reinforcements sent by ship from England destined for the defense of Canada and the western posts, and for the conduct of the war in the western wilderness. There was not enough of either, in Haldimand's mind, to do more than to barely hold on. Ordinance, provisions, and reinforcements were in short supply.

Haldimand kept Brigadier General Powell at Niagara in the center of the tempest of re-supplying the western posts. Powell dutifully kept his Commander-in-Chief apprised of the situation of the western posts, and the complexity of the problems regarding vital supplies. All of the latest news from Powell revolved around requests for supplies and troops. From Governor Sinclair at Michilimackinac, Powell wrote on May 28, "it is not in my power to comply with Sinclair's requisition, in respect to ordinance you will of course give orders to send it from Canada as there is none to spare here." [HP-155] As to the problem of outfitting and supplying Indian war parties to take to the field in light of the scarcity of provisions, Powell was unsure as to what to do. "If you have formed any particular plan, I wish to be informed that I may try to keep them in such a situation as will be most likely to cooperate with." [HP-155] And in regards to Powell's need for troops to sufficiently garrison Niagara, Powell added "Though this post is very weak, as soon as any reinforcement is sent to Oswego, I hope Your Excellency will be pleased to order the detachment of the King's Regiment and as many of the Rangers to be sent back as can be spared." [HP-155] Unfortunately, Haldimand would have to inform Powell that he had none to spare as none had arrived from England by early June.

Detroit added to the dilemma facing Powell. From DePeyster, Powell sent to Haldimand requests for provisions and reinforcements for Detroit, as Powell had no provisions to send from Niagara and could not spare a man. Though DePeyster had not asked Powell for any more Rangers from Niagara to be added to Thompson's company already deployed in the Ohio Country, Powell anticipated that DePeyster would "make an acquisition of some Rangers and Indians to be sent to Sandusky." Asking for direction on the matter from Haldimand, "When I receive your dispatches I shall probably be able to judge how the Rangers are to be employed this summer, and if any of them can be sent to Sanduski." [HP-153] On June 7 Powell wrote again with bad news. "Major DePeyster informed me that the large powder magazine at Detroit fell in on the 23rd of May. I understand it has long been in ruins." [HP-156]

Powell received news written by DePeyster on June 27 concerning developments with the Enemy which Powell immediately passed on to Haldimand. "By a prisoner just brought in taken ten miles from the other side of Fort Pitt, we are informed that Brondhurd (Brodhead) after having struck the Cooshocking's went down to Philadelphia- we can give no account of Clark- the Indians and other prisoners still keep up the news of Clark's coming into this Country." [HP-157] However, what Haldimand found of equal interest was news that reached Detroit on the whereabouts of Lt. Governor Hamilton, who was a prisoner with the Rebels. "By a prisoner brought in from Pittsburgh, we are informed that a messenger from Lieut. Gov. Hamilton for this place was taken, and sent with the dispatches to Fort Pitt. It is said that Governor Hamilton was on his parole at Chesterfield Court House, in Virginia." [HP-157] Haldimand shook his head at this word on his former officer, and sincerely hoped for the sake of Henry Hamilton that the news was not true, and Hamilton's clandestine activities not exposed to the wrath of the Rebels, whom he was sure, would have little mercy on him for what they would see as treachery.

"Clark Has Not Yet Joined From Fort Pitt"

Since leaving Detroit in early May to return to the upper Shawnee Indian village of Wapatomika, Alexander McKee had not been idle. From what his friend Matthew Elliott had learned from captives as to Clark's whereabouts and plans, McKee had formulated a scheme to help the Indians defeat Clark, which depended upon sending a large enough body of Indians and white men to the Ohio River as soon as possible. McKee reasoned that since Clark intended to rendevous soon with his troops in Kentucky, that Clark must travel down the Ohio by boat with his men and provisions to reach the Falls of the Ohio where McKee believed Clark would mass his troops before entering the Indian lands. Hearing that Clark would pass down the Ohio with at most several hundred men and not several thousand, the possibility of attacking and defeating Clark while he was most vulnerable in boats, without room to maneuver on the water, was a tempting possibility that convinced McKee that it could be done by the Indians, with the help of the Indian Department and the Rangers that Captain Thompson had available.

Nonetheless, McKee faced the daunting task of collecting as many warriors of the Ohio tribes from all parts of the Indian Country and "then trying to hold them together once collected," as McKee knew that as he assembled them to intercept Clark, "some of the young warriors insisted on leaving for the hunt, some would go out horse-stealing, and others {would lose} the new clothing and ammunition sent them from Detroit." [KI-p.312] McKee turned to the men of the Indian Department, the three Girty brothers, Matthew Elliott, Isidore Chesne, Robert Surphlit, his cousin, to assist him in the task of preparing the Indians for the coming campaign to destroy Clark once and for all. At the same time, McKee sent small scouting parties to the Ohio and Kentucky to keep him informed on any movements of the Enemy up or down the river, reporting to him if word of Clark's force was sighted. By the end of June, while McKee was still working at raising sufficient Indians to accompany him, Joseph Brant arrived at Wapatomika with his party of Mohawk warriors, waiting there to join the expedition once it got underway. However, upon learning that a war party of Ottawas from Detroit had set out a few days earlier for Kentucky to raid the settlements there, Brant became impatient. With McKee's reluctant approval, Joseph Brant decided to set out for the Ohio River, taking with him George Girty and nearly 90 Indians and white men, itching for action. [KI-p.312] Accompanying Brant and Girty on June 26 for the trip down the Miami River was a small war party of Shawnee "headed by the Principal Warrior of Chillicothey" who bade goodbye to Brant's force when they reached the Ohio. There, the Shawnee crossed the river to "endeavor to discover the Enemy posted upon Kentucky." [HP-14]

The Chillicothe Shawnee war captain counted 10 days since his party had left the Ohio River heading for the Kentucky River to watch the trails from the Enemy forts to the south. The wide trail of militia footprints that he had discovered on this day was alarming. The tracks told the warrior that the enemy from Kentucky was on the move. Instinctively he realized that he must get word to the chiefs of the upper Shawnee villages, as well as Alexander McKee and the British at Detroit that the enemy appeared to be moving towards their villages. Carefully he had the two Shawnee runners recite the intelligence he had just given them to make sure they had left nothing out. First, they had come "upon a large road leading towards the Ohio, in following, which found that a large body of the Enemy had passed before them marching in several columns. And as they pursued, saw several encampments till they arrived at a large breastwork which had been lately built, and found this to be the place the enemy had made Canoes and also that three parties of them had joined at this place by different roads and were but just gone from hence down the Kentucky towards the Ohio." [HP-14]

The Shawnee war captain counted for McKee the number of the enemy "joined together here to be about 1,200 and he counted in their way 30 places were large canoes had been put into the water, but as they did not take the time to scout, there must have been many more they did not see." The Shawnee told the runners to go as quickly as possible with the news by the most direct route to Wapatomika, crossing the Ohio near the Big Bone Lick, and he and the rest of their party would follow as quickly as possible. He concluded that "it would not be prudent for them to follow the route of the enemy longer, as they must reach the Ohio before them, being fully convinced that the Enemy was now upon their way against their villages." [HP-14] Without further word, the runners set off for the north to inform everyone at Wapatomika.

Several days later, as the Chillicothe war captain and his warriors were crossing the Ohio River near Big Bone Lick, they "heard a great deal of firing below them" which he took to mean that the enemy was coming up the river towards them. They did not know until later when they met up with the party of Ottawas on the trail leading to Wapatomika that the Ottawas had an unlucky run in with the enemy as they were going down the Ohio, and "discovered the Enemy at an island below the Big Bone Lick and with difficulty escaped from them." They had managed to get away with only two warriors slightly wounded by musket balls. When everyone was reunited at Wapatomika, the Shawnee war captain confirmed the intelligence to McKee that the enemy was moving against them. It was his opinion from tracking the Virginians that, "Clark has not yet joined them from Fort Pitt nor had those who are to cross the country to them with forces and that this is their main body from Kentucky with provisions for who they expect to meet at the mouth of the Rocky river or Licking Creek." [HP-14] If that was the case, McKee reasoned that Clark and his men would soon be coming down the Ohio River. It was paramount that he send word to Brant and George Girty to make ready, as well as a request to Captain Thompson to join him as soon as possible with his Rangers, and summons to the Detroit for more help.

On the very next day, July 15, McKee sent a dispatch to Major DePeyster at Detroit in the care of Robert Surphlit, whom he trusted to take the information in haste to that post. "I received the enclosed intelligence last night and the Indians seem so desirous to have it forwarded immediately to you." As McKee had seen off several war parties that morning that left to meet the enemy, "I shall take the opportunity of sending to you every account we receive of their approach." Requesting DePeyster send supplies for the Indians, McKee noted, "it is indeed true they are scarce of provisions and obliged to hunt for their families. But at this critical juncture, it is necessary to watch the enemy as it is certainly drawing near the season for them to make their push into Indian Country." Food would be in short supply until the corn ripened, "unless we receive a supply from you. I endeavored to get all that was left at Sandusky to this place.... Captain Thompson writes that he is also in want so that we shall have to divide with him," once the Rangers joined McKee on the Scioto River, before he and the remaining Indians and Rangers set out for the Ohio River to join Brant and Girty. [HP-19] In McKee's mind, they would have to make do with the scant provisions at hand, as it was doubtful, at this point, that DePeyster would be able to supply them with anything at all.

"To Gain Strength Enough to Penetrate to Detroit "

Far up the Ohio River at Pittsburgh, George Rogers Clark made his final preparations during the last week of June to depart Pittsburgh for the Kentucky settlements and Fort Nelson at the Falls of the Ohio. Despite numerous setbacks that put his campaign against Detroit more than three months behind, Clark had made some modest progress in the latter part of June, finally amassing enough boats, provisions, ammunition, and artillery to outfit his expedition. While falling far short of the 2000 men he envisioned to lead from Virginia, Clark had nearly 400 men ready to set out with him, with nearly 100 more militia volunteers promised to join him under the command of the able Colonel Archibald Lochry of Pennsylvania's Westmoreland County. Where Clark had been unable to convince many Pennsylvanians to enlist with him, Lochry, "who had constantly tried to cooperate with the Continental and Virginian contingents in the upper Ohio region," had promised to join Clark as soon as he could get the militia ready to leave. Fearing further desertions if he lingered longer at Pittsburgh, Clark "moved his force of 400 down-river to Wheeling" and Fort Henry where he planned to wait for Lochry to unite with him. After several frustrating days of idleness during which a handful of militiamen managed to desert during the night, an "angry and upset" George Rogers Clark decided he could wait no longer for Lochry and his reinforcements, sending word to "his second in command, to follow immediately with his troops." [NL-p.118] On the morning of the August 7, Clark ordered his men to set off down the Ohio River for the Falls. Little did Clark know that dozens of Indian war parties were keeping watch on the river below Wheeling, on the lookout for his boats.

From every quarter where the Indian war parties were dispersed, a steady stream of reports traveled back by runner to Alexander McKee at Wapatomika, keeping him informed on the movement of the Rebels, as he patiently waited for more provisions, Indians, and Rangers to arrive. A prisoner named William Tyler, "taken by a party of Hurons on the 11th of July going between the Forts upon Kentucky and the Falls of the Ohio" gave the information that "the militia of that country are now completed to 1,500 men." Tyler added what he had heard that "a boat had arrived with letter from him (Clark) at the Falls about a week ago," intimating that Lochry was to leave Fort Pitt about the middle of July. Another Shawnee war party came in "from the Enemy's forts upon Kentucky with one scalp and several papers detailing the expedition against the Indian Country. The Shawnee reported "all the tracks upon the roads lead towards the Falls, from which they conclude the Enemy to be assembling there." On July 27 a party of Delawares lurking on the east side of the Ohio River below Fort Pitt, took a prisoner named James Boggs "upon Buffalo Creek in Ohio County" who stated, upon questioning, that "it was the common report in the country that General Clark would be able to collect a sufficient number of men from the different counties upon this side of the mountains to accompany him down the Ohio and that he is to be joined by a body of men at the mouth of the Miamis River, and that the reason for his delay has been to gain strength enough to penetrate to Detroit." [HP-21] As McKee reviewed the intelligence and passed it on to Detroit, he was sure of one thing – that the plethora of reports from prisoners was sufficiently truthful and accurate, for they did not contradict one another. Soon, George Rogers Clark would be on his way down the Ohio, and soon, a decisive victory for the Indians might be within their reach.

"We Will Proceed After You As Quickly As Possible"

Upon reaching Fort Henry at the settlement of Wheeling by the afternoon of August 8, Colonel Archibald Lochry was disgusted to find that he had missed George Rogers Clark by only a day, in spite of doing everything possible to meet the General at Wheeling. To make matters worse, after seeking quarters for his men inside the walls of the fort, he was disappointed to find that Clark had taken all of the provisions for Lochry's men with him, leaving nothing for his men to eat. Writing a note to Clark which he would send immediately with a scout downriver to find the General, Lochry wrote, "I arrived at this post this moment. I find there are neither boats, provisions, nor ammunition left. I have sent a small canoe after you to know what is to be done. If you send back these articles mentioned and with direction where I will overtake you, I will follow. We are upwards of 100 strong including Light Horse." [HP-24] Sealing the note and giving it to the scouts, Lochry watched them cast off their canoe from the wharf below the bluffs of Fort Henry, and paddle their way into the main current of the Ohio River flowing to the southwest. With that business done, Lochry paused to re-read the letter he had received just the day before leaving Fort Pitt from his old friend, scout, and Indian fighter, Samuel Brady. "You may be assured that nothing gives me greater pleasure than to find that you and a number more good men are going with General Clark. ...I am in hopes the country will turn out to go against Sandusky. ...I wish you a very successful campaign and a safe return, and am with every sentiment of esteem, Your very humble Servant, S. Brady." [HP-20] The warm words from his close friend helped Archibald Lochry to cast aside his frustration of the moment, and quell his private fears for the future.

Lochry's scouts in their canoe had no way of knowing how close they had come to discovery by the war party of Wyandot Indians who arrived at their well-used vantage point on the bluff overlooking the Ohio River. Only moments before, the militiamen's canoe had disappeared from view around the bend in the river. Several hours later, Lochry's scouts reached the islands that lay in close proximity midstream in the Ohio, below the mouth of the Kanawha River, known as Three Islands to the Virginians. Uneventfully arriving at General Clark's camp on Middle Island on August 8, they delivered to Clark Lochry's letter late in the day. The next morning, as Clark made preparations for his army to set off once more, he wrote a dispatch to Lochry, which he intended to leave with Captain Wallace and eight men on the lower of the three islands, who were to wait to rendevous with Lochry. "Sir, I this moment received yours of the 8th Instant, I am heartily sorry that after waiting so long for you, I should set out but a day before your arrival. I also learn that you were so kind as to send an express but he did not arrive, and I of course supposed that you shared my fate in meeting with every disappointment from the populace," Clark wrote. Clark was frustrated with his current situation, and added to Lochry, "I am exceedingly unhappy in our not joining at Wheeling, but don't know that either of us is to blame. The militias with us continue to desert and consequently I cannot remain long in one place, otherwise should be happy in forming a juncture here. The following plan is proposed, I have augmented the command of Mr. Wallace to eight alert men, furnished with 15 days provisions for the whole of your troops, and there will be left at the lower point of the third island below Middle Island, for your exception one large horse boat and a sufficient of small ditto with what you will be able to collect on your passage. I shall move on slowly for the reasons before stated and you will use the greatest industry, as you cannot possibly pass us without our knowledge. I have suffered much lately but you again encouraged me." [HP-13]

General Clark left explicit orders with Major Cracraft and militia Quarter Master Richard Wallace on the morning of August 10. "Sir, you will take charge of the large horse boat and eight small dittos together with a command of six choice men for the use of Colonel Lochry's troops, and wait at this place for his arrival which will probably happen in about six days from this day. Should Colonel Lochry fail to arrive in eight days, you are hereby directed to proceed with your command and stores down the river until you overtake me." As an afterthought, Clark added, "you will follow in one small boat the stores in case you are not overtaken, observing to leave the towlines safely secured." Clark hated to leave anything to chance when it came to preserving the precious provisions, which could not be replaced if they were lost by the negligence of his own men. [HP-18]

As Clark and his army set off down the Ohio, Major Cracraft made sure all precautions were taken concerning the boats before he allowed the men to relax under the trees. Once Clark and his flotilla were out of sight, several of

Cracraft's men began playing cards, while another fished by the water's edge. Not having seen an Indian during the entire trip, none of the men thought it important to post a scout on either end of the island after the first day of uneventful waiting for Lochry. Unfortunately for Cracraft and his men, their lack of vigilance would soon be their undoing, for they had no knowledge that an unseen enemy was quickly closing in on them, with the intent of discovering the location of the Virginians.

As dusk began to fall on Cracraft's little camp at the end of the lower island on the evening of August 14, their boredom was broken by the sounds of someone or something approaching their position through the woods and brush of the island, that caused the men to reach for their muskets in alarm, and begin to prime and load them, not knowing if the noise was an Indian or an animal. As Cracraft's men stood in apprehension peering into the darkness of the trees with their silhouettes outlined by the light from the campfire, they failed to notice in the river the approach of two canoes, one to each side of them that had silently drifted with the current towards them, both boats filled with men pointing muskets in their direction. In an instant, Cracraft and his little detachment realized that they were surrounded, and lowered their weapons as one of the men in the canoes yelled a warning. To Cracraft's surprise and chagrin, the men in the canoes were Pennsylvanian scouts, an advanced party of Lochry's force, who had spied the campfire from the middle island, and decided to cautiously investigate, intending to surprise a probable party of foolhardy Indians and lift their scalps. One of the scouts signaled upriver, and within minutes, Lochry's flotilla of boats appeared out of the deepening darkness and beached on the shore, everyone glad to find themselves in the company of friendly faces.

Early on the morning of August 15, Lochry gave Major Cracraft the brief note to General Clark that he had penned the previous night, after reading Clark's letter delivered to him by Captain Wallace. Lochry intended to catch up with Clark at the first possible moment, but realized that Cracraft and his party could travel faster by single small boat than Lochry could, as he was slowed by the large horse boat and various bateaux which were much more difficult for his men to maneuver in the water. Sending Cracraft ahead with the news of his pending arrival, Lochry wrote, "My Dear General. This evening we arrived at camp Three Islands. We are every man in great spirits and determined to go where ordered. There is no desertion in our troops. We had the pleasure to apprehend an officer and 15 deserters on our march which I hope we will safely deliver to their duty. We will proceed after you as quick as possible." [HP-17] Within minutes, Major Cracraft and his party of seven men paddled their boat into the main current of the Ohio and disappeared from view as they headed downriver to find General Clark.

"We Suppose the Enemy to be Clark's Army"

On the night of August 18, Joseph Brant with George Girty and the large war party of over 90 Indians camped on the wide sandbar at the mouth of the Big

Miami River after the day's travel down the Ohio towards the Falls. Knowing that the enemy might be nearby, Brant took the precaution of posting scouts upriver and near their camp, as well advising everyone to extinguish their small cooking fires that had been lit before dusk. Close to midnight, one of the Mohawk scouts posted a nearly a mile upriver swiftly came into camp and alerted Brant and the warriors that a large undetermined number of white men in boats were coming down river in the middle of the current. Brant deployed the wakening warriors and told them to prepare to fire on the boats, but no to do so until he could determine their numbers, and give the signal. As the minutes ticked by in silence with no sound from the river to be heard, all eyes and ears of the Indians strained to detect the approach of what must surely be the enemy. Then, ever so softly at first, Brant and the Indians heard the sounds of paddling, accompanied by the muffled voices of many men, which grew louder and louder with each passing minute. It was then that Brant spied the lead boat, which was piloted by several men holding lanterns to illuminate the main channel.

By the light of the stars, Brant could see an unending line of larger boats following the first, each carrying dozens of men, and some with horses. The flotilla of the enemy coming out of the dark was much larger than he had imagined. It stunned him for a moment; for he had not anticipated that the enemy would attempt a nighttime maneuver. Quickly, Brant surmised to himself that the Americans must have had some forewarning of the approach of his own party, and were determined to avoid an attack or ambush on the water by cleverly using the cover of darkness to pass by his force. Undeterred by the tactic which had already allowed several boats to pass by the hidden Indians, Brant decided to have his force fire a volley upon the slower moving boats which he could see were still up ahead, realizing that those which had passed were filled with troops, while the larger ones yet to come were laden with supplies and horses, which the troops would have great difficulty in turning about to support, once the attack was sprung.

Just as Joseph Brant was about to give the signal to fire, the unexpected happened. For some inexplicable reason, just as the largest of the flatboats reached the mouth of the Miami where Brant and the warriors lay hidden, "when they got past the mouth, (the Enemy) fired a cannon." The cracking sound from the fire of the swivel-gun mounted on the side of the boat took Brant and the Indians completely by surprise. It spewed a shower of fire and sparks towards the shoreline, but in a direction that suggested to Brant that the enemy was firing blindly, if not by complete chance, for they could not know that his force was present before them. Regardless, in that instant, the cannon struck terror in Brant's compatriots. The Indians lay in shock, and none of them would have returned fire on the boat even if Brant had given the order to do so, for fear of giving away their positions to a cannonade. As a consequence, Brant did not give the signal, much to the relief of the rattled warriors. In a matter of minutes, the entire flotilla was passed, and Joseph Brant could only shake his head in disbelief. "When they got past the mouth, fired cannon, we were going to attack but we could not." To his growing anger and embarrassment, Brant realized he had been foiled by the enemy, a clever enemy. "We suppose," Brant wrote after some discussion, "the Enemy to be Clark's Army." [HP-01]

"We Determine to Attack the Enemy As Well As We Can"

Three days later, Brant with Girty and the party of 90 Indians had moved 10 miles below the mouth of the Big Miami River, after stopping the day before at Big Bone Lick "to see whether he (Clark) was there. I could not see no signs of it" as the Indians looked for evidence of an enemy camp. While they continued downriver, an Indian scout following the rear of Brant's party hurriedly caught up with the main force to report that a large canoe or boat was approaching from upriver with eight white men in it, and would soon be upon them. Quickly Brant scanned the shoreline ahead and picked a spot where the river widened, and the main channel was shallow. Deploying the Indians to the woods, he suggested to George Girty to call to the white men from the riverbank when he could see them approaching in an attempt to lure them ashore, and Girty agreed. The trap was set.

As Major Cracraft and the seven men paddled the small bateau around the bend in the river, the monotony of the uneventful day of travel was broken by the sight of a white man ahead on the north bank of the river, who was waving frantically to them and calling out to come ashore to pick him up. Cracraft had the men maneuver the cumbersome boat from the main current to the shallows near the shoreline, as he replied to the stranded stranger, asking him if he was another deserter from General Clark's militia. Girty answered to the officer that he was, but was in need of help, for his food had run out, and he wished to return to the army. As Cracraft had one of his men step into the knee deep water to pull the boat to shore, it was then, to his astonishment that dozens of garishly painted Indian savages stepped into view from the shadows, with muskets trained on the eight unfortunate militiamen and tomahawks held in readiness if Cracraft should attempt to escape. Once the terrified captives were roughly stripped of most of their clothing, their papers confiscated, and their arms tied uncomfortably behind their backs, Brant and Girty had the men brought one at a time for interrogation, telling them he would turn them over to the warriors for unspeakable torture if they did not tell him all that they knew. While the questioning proceeded, the Indians argued over their newly found plunder in the boats.

Soon Brant knew everything from the prisoners that was important concerning the movements of their forces. "We took the boat with seven men, one Major amongst them, Militia named Cracraft, who was following Clark as he is gone down sure enough and has about 350 men with him, they deserting from him very fast. The prisoners does not know how far Clark is gone down the River, they suppose to be at the Falls. Likewise the prisoners says there is hundred and about fifty men more coming down the river with ten small boats, one large, and one still larger horse boat, number of them it is which is expected to be here next day after tomorrow the longest. They was at the three Islands five nights." Brant began to formulate a plan in his mind. He told Girty and the chiefs that he intended to intercept the enemy force that would soon come downriver and take them all by ambush, capitalizing on the ruse that Girty had accomplished so easily. Turning to the trussed prisoners, Brant told them that they were in luck, for he wished to keep them alive for the moment. They would serve as the bait to lure their comrades ashore, into the trap. If they refused to do so, or alerted the enemy to the ambush, Brant would see to it that they died a very slow agonizing death by roasting. To a man, the prisoners nodded to Brant that they would do whatever he asked.

With much yet to do, Brant decided it best to send a runner up the Miami River trail to Wapatomika with a message for McKee or Thompson, whoever could be found first at or near "Chilikathity" asking them to come at once with all the Rangers and Indians who could be found to support him. "We are about 90 strong at present with different tribes. These Indians and chiefs particular desires you and the Indians that is with you to come on as fast as possible you can to join this party. Whilst the Enemy are scattered we can easy manage them and further desires express should be sent to different villages for every man of them should come immediately to this place for there is no signs any other party can go against the Indians except Clark, as the prisoners says there is no other can be sent. No more at present, please to excuse my writing, I wrote in a hurry. P.S. Please let all the Indians know if they don't come to assist us, we determine to attack the Enemy as well as we can." [HP-01] This time Brant intended to fight, for his pride was not about to let another party of the enemy float by without a shot being fired.

"Your Patriotism, Valor, Conduct, and Fidelity"

Late in the morning of August 24, Colonel Archibald Lochry and his men in the 12 boats had traveled more than ten miles on the Ohio River below the mouth of Big Miami River where they had beached their boats and spent an uneventful night in camp on the sandbar. Although Lochry and his men had not seen a soul neither white nor Indian since leaving Three Islands, the discovery of the worn out Indian–style moccasin and many fresh footprints on the sandbar did not sit easy with Lochry, though he had no reason to believe that there were Indians in the area. He attributed the footprints to Clark or Cracraft's party who had traveled the same route or deserters from Clark's expedition who would be following the river. Still, the moccasin find bothered Lochry. If the owner had been an Indian and the footprints those of his comrades, then it was likely that a large party of savages were somewhere in the vicinity, within reach of his detachment. Luckily, the water lay to their advantage, for while they were in the boats and not on land, there was little way that the Indians would be able to stop them or do them harm.

As Lochry's men had been unable to find sufficient forage for the horses near the sandbar at the mouth of the Big Miami River, Lochry ordered his men in the lead boat to keep an eye out for a suitable place to put in and cut grass, a place usually found on the lowlands adjacent to the mouth of a creek flowing into the Ohio. After questioning the prisoners on the habits of Lochry's expedition, Brant picked a spot for the ambush, at the mouth of a creek flowing into the Ohio from the north shore, some 11 miles below the Big Miami. A tall hill lay to the west side of the mouth of the creek, "a tall cane break grew on the other side of the river." [KI-p.313] Brant believed the grasses would help entice Lochry's force to come to rest at that precise spot, on the flat land bordering the east side of the creek, where Brant intended to lure Lochry's force ashore with sufficient bait to succeed.

Passing a bend in the river, the men in the lead boat called out to Colonel Lochry that they could see several white men up ahead, standing in the river shallows on the north bank of the Ohio on the edge of a low grassland. Lochry immediately gave orders for the men in the string of boats to come to the alert, as he scanned the riverbank up ahead to the right of them, looking for the men in question. Seeing that they had been noticed, the eight men on the shore began waving to the men in boats, and calling out to them to come ashore. Lochry strained his eyes to identify who the strangers were, but upon hearing his own name called out from one of them, realized to his relief, that it was Major Cracraft and his detachment. As he could see now that their empty boat was listing to one side in the water, having sustained some sort of damage, Lochry ordered his detachment to row to the shoreline to rendevous with Cracraft and pick up the stranded men. As his boats glided towards the shadows, Lochry noticed the particular odd looks on the faces of the eight men, who appeared awkwardly silent under the circumstances.

Just then, from the thick grass on the shore came a shrieked war whoop and then the deafening crash of a volley of muskets from the hidden ambush positions of the Indians with Brant, who directed their fire upon the helpless militiamen in Lochry's boats who were in the process of rising from the vessels. Dozens of the militiamen were hit and fell into the water by the initial shots of the Indians. Many of Lochry's men slumped dead or wounded into their boats, as a horde of painted savages splashed into the river shallows with tomahawks and scalping knives in hand, intent on dispatching the militiamen before they had a chance to prime and load their weapons laying in the bottom of their boats. With weeks of pent up frustration, anger, and strain against an unseen enemy now released, the warriors with all the viciousness and savagery they could muster, waded into the floundering militiamen at the water's edge and struck them down with hatchet blows to the head and face. Skulls of their victims were crushed under repeated blows while scalps were ripped from heads and flesh was butchered with Indian knives. The slaughter of the militia about the boats was horrific. Amid the shrieks, screams, cries and groans of the dying, the dwindling survivors surrounding Colonel Lochry pleaded to surrender and be spared.

Joseph Brant with George Girty at his side, waded into the bloodied water and barked a series of commands to the warriors while pointing to the surviving enemy, signaling that those not already wounded were to be spared the hatchet

After ambush and capture by the Indians,
Lochry and his men await their fate.

for the moment, as he wished to take prisoners. Those militiamen who were unscathed were hustled ashore by the warriors and stripped of most of their clothes and bound. With few exceptions, the men that had been wounded were seized by the warriors, who buried their hatchets deep in the men's skulls time and time again, in spite of the pitiful attempts on the part of those men to parry the inevitable blows in an attempt to live. In a matter of minutes, the entire affair was over. Brant beamed with pride as he looked over the shocked, dejected, and terrified prisoners huddled together on the riverbank. To his credit, his ambush had worked, and not one of the enemy had been allowed to escape, nor had any of the warriors in his company suffered as much as a scratch. [KI-p.513]

In the boats floating in the shallows before Brant and the Indians lay a virtual treasure in horses, provisions, ammunition, weapons, and prisoners resulting from their short work, not including the 37 bloody trophy scalps of the enemy hanging from warrior's belts. As the hefty plunder was distributed among the Indians, and the mutilated naked corpses of the dead militiamen floated out into the current of the Ohio to send to Clark's army downriver at the Falls of the Ohio, one of the young warriors who was angry that he had no scalp of the enemy to take home with him, wandered among the prisoners, intent on obtaining one. He approached Colonel Lochry, and for a long moment stared malevolently at the bound officer. Finally, the warrior removed the tomahawk from his belt and swung it over Lochry's head, burying the blade up to the shaft in Lochry's skull, which killed him instantly. Lochry's comrades were spattered with blood, as the warrior deftly removed the officer's scalp and placed it carefully in the belt tied about his waist, his wish for a trophy fulfilled.

Joseph Brant looked through the pile of blood-soaked papers taken from the dead and living that was destined for Detroit. He perused its contents for pertinent intelligence, stopping once to read the commission of a militiaman. "In the Name and by the Authority of the Freemen of the Commonwealth of Pennsylvania, Who Espousing Especial Trust and Confidence in your Patriotism, Valor, Conduct, and Fidelity, do by these Presents Constitute and Appoint you to be Ensign in the Company in the Third Battalion of Militia, in the County of Westmoreland. You are therefore carefully and diligently to discharge the Duty." [HP-07] Brant had read enough. A smirk crossed his face when he thought about the Rebel Ensign's duty, which he had just been discharged from by the hand of Joseph Brant, the great war captain.

"Being Four Days without Provisions"

After loading all the plunder on the available horses and the rest on the backs of the Rebel prisoners, Brant, with George Girty and the Indians set out for the Great Miami River, to retrace their steps to the upper Shawnee villages. On August 27, his party met up with Alexander McKee and Captain Thompson of the Rangers who were heading towards the Ohio River with a force of two companies of Rangers, several French volunteers from Detroit, and over 400 Indian warriors from the Ohio tribes. With McKee was Simon Girty, George's elder brother, who had recently joined McKee at Wapatomika with his large party of Wyandots who had arrived from Sandusky only days before. At their juncture on the trail, Brant related to McKee, Thompson, and the Indian chiefs the details of his defeat of the Rebel detachment, whereupon "the rejoicing of the savages over Lochry's defeat was great." [BC-p.97]

McKee and Brant agreed that all the prisoners, provisions, and plunder should be left in the care of "a sergeant and 18 men" so that Brant and his force could turn around and accompany McKee on his expedition against Clark. On August 29, the British and Indian expedition reached the banks of the Ohio River, determined to pursue Clark and attack him at the Falls of the Ohio and destroy him.

Moving downriver, McKee's mixed force of whites and Indians reached the mouth of the Kentucky River by September 5. With no sign of Clark's army in sight, the Indians requested that McKee call a council to determine what to do, as a great difference of opinion among the tribes had developed since the force reached the Ohio days before. McKee attempted to hold them all together. "The Indians seemed to think that their success two days before against the second division of Clark's army would assure them peace for some time in their villages. I endeavored to convince them that as there was so large a body of them then collected that it would be prudent to watch his (Clark's) motions some time longer and to send scouts towards the Falls and endeavor to gain some certain accounts of his future intentions, McKee wrote to DePeyster. "In consequence of this we fell down the river some miles when I found again that it would be difficult to keep them together long, therefore advised keeping out scouts continually before us, and that if the Enemy did not advance, that we should attempt drawing them into action in the neighborhood of the Falls where their main body lay, and by a further success totally destroy their designs of carrying an expedition into the Indian Country." [HP-52] Captain Thompson of the Rangers, Captain Brant of the Indians and the Girty brothers and the Frenchmen were in agreement with McKee as to proceeding. However, many of the Indians remained unconvinced, desiring to break up into smaller parts to hunt, steal horses, raid the border settlements in Kentucky or return to their villages as no enemy on the river could be found. McKee was persuasive, but the Indians demanded another meeting to talk about it.

The hastily convened Indian council was held on the morning of September 5, with all the chiefs and principal war captains of the various tribes taking their positions on the ground surrounding the main campfire. Pipes of tobacco were passed around the assemblage, as each of the headmen had their say as to what to do. Captain Thompson of the Rangers was present, along with McKee and the Girtys, and all the Frenchmen of the Indian Department from Detroit. Of the consensus of the Indians, Thompson noted that "the major part of them were all of the opinion that a stroke should be made at Boon's Fort." Following them, McKee, Simon Girty and Captain Thompson each spoke and "dissuaded them from that notion by convincing them they had nothing to fear from that Quarter, and that we ought to keep in a Body and move down the River if we did not meet Clark we should strike at the Falls and by those means disable the Enemy from making any further attempts upon the Indian Country this fall." [HP-256] The chiefs considered what McKee and the other white men said, speaking mostly among themselves before "they agreed to send a scout" to the Falls to gain further intelligence, before they would move as a whole. [HP-256]

Idle now at their camp at the mouth of the Kentucky River, "we waited the return of our scouts who joined us the next day with two officer's scalps taken the day before at the Falls. As nothing material was learned by this, of the Enemies' intentions, we prevailed upon them still to keep on towards this place, and to keep out other scouts who could meet us upon our way." [HP-52] Consequently, the Indians agreed to break camp on the morning of September 7 and "we proceeded and arrived within 30 miles of the Falls on the 9th, where the Indians, after holding a council, sent off another scout who arrived with two prisoners soon after." [HP-256] Finding themselves amid a horde of painted, armed Indians, the two unlucky captives did not need much coaxing to tell the interpreters all that they knew for the questioning Indians. Their account was that recently "Clark had called a general council of the field officers of the several counties, that the result thereof was not then made public, but that it was the general opinion of the country that they could not assist him in carrying on an expedition this season." [HP-52]

Upon hearing this heartening news, the Indians openly rejoiced "who when they heard what the prisoners said, got entirely out of the notion of going any further" and many of them began to make plans to break up into small parties, "some going home, others going after Horses, which they had done all along," [HP-256] and a yet a number of them how still expressed an interest to continue on to the Falls with McKee, which "determined me to follow them as far as there was a probability of getting them to do anything." [HP-52] The bulk of the Shawnee decided to leave for home, and as they "had the directions on how we were to proceed, gave it (directions) over. We got Captain Brant and the Mingoes to take their place," however within the matter of an hour, the numbers of Indians still present were "reduced to a small number, not able to attack the Falls." [HP-256] Captain Thompson thought the matter over carefully, as his men were wore out and had no food to speak of with them. "Being four days without provisions induced me to return, during which we had nothing to subsist on but two Bears that luckily fell in our way." Thompson and his men headed for the Shawnee village of Chillicothe where he would arrive on September 26.

"It Would Be Good Policy to Watch Him"

McKee and the Indians with him broke camp at once and headed downriver, intent on approaching the Rebels at the Falls of the Ohio to see if some sort of attack could be executed against them. "The same evening we arrived within 15 miles of the Falls and not finding ourselves in numbers sufficient to put in execution our first plan, it was here agreed to cross the country and attack some of their small forts or invest the roads." [HP-52] At this juncture,

Joseph Brant, with George Girty, the Mohawks, and a small party of Mingoes decided to advance a little further downriver, rather than cross the Ohio into Kentucky and accompany McKee. They did so but with no result, after encountering neither enemy patrols to ambush, nor acquiring any Indians who would follow Brant further. In a few days, Brant's party returned upriver to the Great Miami, for the trip northward.

Crossing the Ohio, McKee accompanied a mixed party of Huron, Shawnee, Mingo, and some Delaware warriors numbering close to 200 fighters. On September 9, the war party met up with a war party of Miami Indians returning northward "on a wagon road leading from the Falls to the Upper Forts." The Miamis explained that they had just given battle "a few hours before upon this road" when they had fallen in ambush upon "a party of the Enemy's light horse escorting a number of families, who were flying from the upper forts upon being apprised of our being out. They (Miami) killed a number and dispersed the rest." [HP-52] McKee held a quick council with the Indian war captains and proposed to them a plan to ambush the enemy who would surely return to recover and bury their dead. "This intelligence induced us to take possession of the ground they had driven the Enemy from, and to wait their coming." The next morning, a scout reported to McKee that a detachment of enemy mounted militiamen was nearing them, and McKee deployed the Indians into the woods and brush to wait in ambush.

Mounted Virginians led by a Captain Cloyd rode into the trap set by McKee and would have been cut down to a man, if it had not been for some of "the Indians who were not posted to receive them, owing to their being bound in collecting plunder found upon the field. The greatest part of them were killed and taken, with some officers of rank," including Cloyd who was killed. "We lost three Hurons among who was their principal warrior, one of the best Indians with us, and a great loss to our party." The slain Huron would prove to be the undoing of any further campaigning against the enemy. "After we returned to our baggage in order to consult what could be further done, the Lake Indians would listen to no proposals, thinking they had prisoners and scalps sufficient, did not even halt upon this ground here," but picked up their gear and deserted McKee and the remaining Hurons and Miamis. McKee attempted to persuade the warriors in "taking Boon's Fort in one way and endeavor to draw them out, destroy their cattle, and otherwise distress them as much as was in our power," but they would not listen to McKee, as they were distraught by the loss of the well-liked warrior. "The Hurons, discouraged by the loss of their chief and likewise being left by their younger Brethren, desired that the whole might return home which was agreed to by the other nations." [HP-52]

McKee, too, was discouraged by the sudden turn of events after coming so far. "We were never able to ascertain our numbers, being constantly left by small parties whose view was only to plunder." With the war party in agreement to return to the Ohio, McKee had no choice but to acquiesce to their decision, as there was no fight left in them. While traveling back north, he could take some satisfaction that "upon the whole since our first setting out, from the best computation I am able to make, there has been near to 200 of the Enemy killed and taken, amongst whom are near 30 officers, some of considerable rank." What impact that loss would have upon the Enemy, McKee was uncertain. "How far it may effect their future operations it is hard to say, however should they still attempt anything, we are certain their numbers will not be so great." As to the intentions of Clark, McKee thought "it would good policy to watch him till the season is farther advanced, if the Indians could be possibly prevailed upon." [HP-52]

Upon McKee's return to the Ohio River, his party caught up with Brant's force, as well as Simon Girty and all the small parties of Indians who were slowly making their way up the Ohio to the Big Miami River and the major trail leading to Chillicothe and the upper Indian villages. At one of the evening camps, a keg of rum was opened and the Indians began to drink freely with the white men of the Indian Department. It did not take long for Joseph Brant to become drunk and begin boasting to everyone "of the great victory which he had won and of the numbers of the enemy that he had captured single-handedly" [KI-p.314] and the men he had killed. Simon Girty, who was drunk as well, took issue with Brant by calling him a liar. "In the heated exchange that followed, the enraged Mohawk drew his sword and brought it down across Girty's forehead," [NL-p.121] knocking him senseless and cutting him severely. Thinking he had killed the desperately wounded Girty, Brant fled for his life, running into McKee on the trail not far from camp, "who calmed him down and urged the Mohawk to return" [NL-p.121] whereupon they found that Girty was alive. A deeply remorseful and sober Brant made "offers of money and services" to Girty "if he would make up with him." [NL-p.121] However Simon Girty was incapable of dealing with Brant due to the severe wound. The Wyandots carried him by litter "back to Sandusky where he spent months recovering from the wound" which left a deep, long scar across his forehead as lasting evidence of his encounter with the great Joseph Brant. McKee, who could see that no good could come for either man if Major DePeyster and Colonel Johnson were made aware of the brawl, made sure that "no recognition of this ever got into the official British reports." [KI-p.314]

"Two Powerful and Mighty Gods Are Standing"

On September 25, Alexander McKee finally reached the Shawnee village of Chillicothe from the campaign to Kentucky. There, he found that Captain Thompson and his Rangers had just left for Detroit, while Matthew Elliott had just arrived the same day from the Muskingum River valley in the Ohio Country, after completing Major DePeyster's mission to expel the Moravian missionaries from the Indian lands and see to it that they were escorted under guard to the Upper Sandusky Indian villages. Elliott recounted to McKee all that had transpired since the two men had left the Upper Sandusky in early August, each in a different direction. Elliott had orders to remove the troublesome missionaries, who were suspected "as early as July of 1779" by McKee of passing intelligence on the activities of the Indians to the American authorities at Fort Pitt. [NL-p.121]

Elliott set out in early August for the Christian Delaware Indian villages where the Moravian priests resided in three missions. He was accompanied by a large war party numbering over 250 Wyandots, Delawares, and a smattering of the Lakes tribes under the leadership of the "Wyandot half king (Pomoacan or Sweet House) and Captain Pipe (Hopocan), a Delaware war captain, who were antagonistic to the Moravians Heckewelder and Zeisberger, having "complained to British officials about the Moravian's aid to the Americans" for some time. Ever vigilant, Zeisberger got word from the Christian Delawares of Elliott's advance. "Somewhere about August 13, we heard that a strong party of warriors was on the march for our towns." [BR-p.199] DePeyster, Elliott and McKee had good reason to suspect the preachers of duplicity. As soon as Zeisberger received word of the approach of the hostile Indians, he wrote a dispatch to the commander of Fort Pitt and "warned him that of party of some 250 Indians led by Matthew Elliott would probably advance on Wheeling, Fort McIntosh, and Fort Pitt." [HR-p.31] Colonel Brodhead, back in command at Fort Pitt, immediately sent a letter to Captan John Boggs, in command of Fort Henry at Wheeling on the August 24. "I have this moment received certain intelligence that the Enemy is coming in great force against us, and particularly against Wheeling."

At Heckewelder's mission called Salem, Elliott dined with the missionary and his family, where "he went out of his way to be pleasant to Heckewelder" though he had another plan in mind yet to revealed, for what he had in store for the Rebel sympathizer. The next day, Elliott and the force of Indians moved to the main village up the river at Gnadenhutten, where they set up camp at the west end of the Indian town. Here, the preacher Zeisberger resided, who entertained Elliott, and agreed with Heckewelder that Elliott "likewise behaved in a friendly way toward us, but had secret guile and we could trust him not in the least. [BR-p.199] On the morning of August 20, "the first move was taken to effect the business at hand" as the Wyandot Half-King called all the Christian Delaware Indians together to speak to them and the missionaries, [HR-p.32] telling them that "I see you live in a dangerous place. Two powerful and mighty spirits or gods are standing and opening wide their jaws toward each other to swallow both. And between them, are you placed. You are in danger, from one or from the other, or even from both. Therefore I take you by the hand, raise you up, and settle you where I dwell," [BR-p.200] demanding that they should come and settle at Sandusky. The Moravian Indians promised to have an answer by the next day.

"Appears to be a Jesuitical Old Man"

The morning of August 21, the Moravian Indians, on the advice of Heckewelder and Zeisberger, told Half King that they "would give a definite answer sometime before the next spring." [HR-p.32] Elliott recognized that the preachers were trying to buy themselves time so to be able to secure protection from the Americans at Fort Pitt. Elliott recommended Half King express his dissatisfaction with their vague response and press the matter again before the Indians. On August 25, Half King demanded once again that they leave; however, the Christian Delawares resisted the pressure, telling him and Elliott that "they had to have time to harvest their crops otherwise their women and children would perish."

As some of Half King's Wyandot warriors were satisfied with the answer from the Moravians, Elliott decided that it was time to show firmness. Elliott's patience was running out at the game being played by the missionaries, who had caused him to be "detained there a long time and amused by the Moravians." [HP-52] Elliott spoke in private to the Wyandots, telling them, "if you go home without these ministers, expect no favor from your English Father; if you fail to seize them, I will leave this place and report your faithlessness. Then you will not have a father, but a powerful enemy at Detroit; and the English and the Americans both against you, what awaits your tribes but destruction?"

Elliott's speech had the desired effect upon the Wyandots. On September 1, the Half King and his warriors ordered the missionaries and all the Christian Indians from Salem and Schonbrunn to come to the village at Gnadenhutten. Zeisberger, up to that point, had "reason to believe that the Half King and the captains had already as good as given up their purpose to use force against us" could now plainly see that "the English, who were with them, left nothing undone to excite the captains and warriors, and to spur them to drive us out by force." [BR-p.201] Seeing all the missionaries now gathered together under guard at one spot, the Indians proceeded to shoot the cattle and pigs at the mission, leaving the dead carcasses to rot about the village. On the morning of th September 3, Half King sent his warriors to seize the terrified missionaries, who were stripped of their clothing, and had all their possessions plundered by the Indians, while the Indians sang their war song, the "fearful Death Hallow," [HR-p.33] implying to Zeisberger and Heckewelder that they were about to be slain.

Matthew Elliott had no intention of letting the missionaries be killed, as Major DePeyster wished to interrogate them. Elliott called for the preachers to be brought to his tent, telling them that though he wanted to treat them compassionately, he had "express orders from the commandant in Detroit to bring them away by force if they resisted," and Elliott was going to see to it that those orders were carried out, one way or another. "In fear of their lives, the Moravians agreed to move" and on September 11, the white missionaries and close to 400 Moravian Christian Delaware Indians were forced to leave Gnadenhutten and their surrounding homes, in the company of the Wyandots, directed by Elliott himself. [HR-p.34] Joining them were a number of warriors returning from pillaging the abandoned village of Schonbrunn, which they set on fire when done. [BW-175] On September 14, the entire force reached the destroyed village of Goschachgunk, and moved up Walhonding or White Woman's Creek to the headwaters of the Sandusky, arriving at the Upper Sandusky villages late in the month.

At nearly the same time that the Moravians were forced to leave, a large war party of Wyandot and Delaware warriors detached themselves from the main body and headed directly east along the creek trails to the Ohio River, intent on attacking Wheeling. There the warriors crossed over to the large island in the river opposite Fort Henry and the settlement of Wheeling, and attempted to take the fort by surprise, but without success, as the fort defenders had been forewarned by dispatch from Fort Pitt. With no means of laying siege to the fort, nor any desire to do so, the Indians quickly split up into several smaller parties to raid the surrounding neighborhood in search of plunder, horses, scalps and prisoners, after looting and plundering the settler's cabins around the fort, killing the cattle and hogs, and setting fire "to all the buildings within reach." [BR-p.173] In a few days, the war parties had re-crossed the Ohio with prisoners in tow, and rejoined their comrades along the trail to the Upper Sandusky.

Matthew Elliott rejoined Alexander McKee at the Shawnee village of Chillicothe where the two set out for the Shawnee village of Wapatomika. Informed by Elliott of the successful removal of the Moravian preachers and their Christian Delaware Indians to the Upper Sandusky, McKee disagreed that "the Hurons are disposed I understand to place them at Upper Sandusky where they will still be too convenient to correspond with the Enemy, and though they may not be even concerned for the future, yet from this situation they will be blamed for it." [HP-52] Sensing the potential threat that Heckewelder and Zeisberger still posed, McKee advised Major DePeyster that "there is six of their teachers taken with them. The principal appears to be a Jesuitical old man and if I am not mistaken, employed by the Enemy though he denies it. If the whole of these white people can be removed from the Indians it will be so much the better, for it is not likely they will be our friends whilst they have such teachers." [HP-52]

"Poor Brant is Very Ill"

Major DePeyster agreed. In early October, DePeyster "sent word to McKee that he wanted the Moravian missionaries to be brought to Detroit" for questioning. [HR-p.35] As there were not enough provisions at Detroit to feed the Christian Delawares, DePeyster advised McKee that the Moravian Indians would have to remain with the Wyandots at the Upper Sandusky. On October 4, McKee asked Captain Pipe and a Delaware shaman named Wingenund to go to the Upper Sandusky to deliver McKee's message to the Wyandots and Delawares, "congratulating the two nations for the firmness they had shown in their earlier actions against the Moravians," [NL-p.122] and inviting them to go to the village of Roche de Bout on the Maumee River to receive their share of provisions and presents. "Captain Pipe and Wingenund have undertaken to carry in the Moravian Teachers immediately. They are both sensible men and their activity upon the whole of this business merits some notice," McKee thought. [MK-15]

At the same time, McKee observed "several small Parties of Indians are come in since our return from Kentucky and a prisoner they have brought confirms the account of the Enemies not being able to carry on an expedition into the Indian Country this Season." The prisoner stated further "that their Intention is to take post at the mouth of the Kentucky and Salt Creek where it empties into said River, the design of this is to cover their small Forts advanced from the inroads of the Indians as they otherwise would remove into the Settlements." [HP-257] McKee was satisfied, knowing that this latest movement of the Rebels was due to the ambush that he and the Indians had successfully laid for Captain Cloyd and his men.

McKee thought it wise to inform Major DePeyster of "a meeting held here yesterday by the Chiefs of the several nations at which they returned thanks to the Six Nation Deputies for the amicable speeches delivered by them in the name of the English and the Six Nations, giving the strongest assurances of their always continuing to adhere to their advice.' [MK-257] At McKee's urging, the Shawnee chiefs asked the Iroquois representatives if they would "turn their attention towards Fort Pitt, as the Source of all the Enemy's capability to distress their Country, and that whilst the Enemy are in possession of this door into it, they can never live in either Ease or Safety." [HP-257] The Iroquois assured the chiefs of the western tribes that they would present that request to Colonel Guy Johnson of the Six Nations Indian Department and their own chiefs upon returning to Niagara the next month. McKee reminded the Shawnee chiefs from Chillicothy "the necessity of watching the Enemy till the season was so far advanced that they would not be able to come." The Shawnee agreed that they would do so.

McKee sent all this latest news to Major DePeyster in a packet of letters entrusted to a young white man whom Matthew Elliott identified to McKee as one of the three captives taken the previous spring from the Rebels at Wheeling. "The Bearer of this, Brice Reagen, is one of the Young Men taken up by the Shawanese last spring upon the Ohio having deserted from the Enemy at Weeling. He is adopted into a principal Family of the Shawanese, who do not now lay much restraint upon him, having served as a Volunteer with us during the summer against the Enemy, and behaved as becometh him." McKee recalled the ambush on the road in Kentucky. Reagen had been there, fired his gun upon the Rebels. "I take the liberty of recommending him to you for a few Cloaths," McKee added as an afterthought, for the youth with striking blue eyes was nearly naked in the cold morning air of October 18, save for the breechcloth he wore with the scrap of a blanket draped over his shoulders. [HP-15]

Word reached McKee late in the month from Elliott that Wingenund and Pipe reached the Wyandot village where the preachers were held on October 14, and "escorted the missionaries" to Detroit, arriving there on the October 25, whereupon Major DePeyster questioned the six preachers at length, before allowing them to return to their ministry to the Christian Indians living at the cluster of huts at the Upper Sandusky called Captive's Town, under the watchful eye of the Wyandot chief Half King who assured DePeyster that the Rebel collaborators would not have an opportunity to pass information to Fort Pitt. [NL-p.122] When Joseph Brant and his party of Mohawks arrived at Detroit early in the month, DePeyster presented Brant with the orders from General Powell and Colonel Johnson at Niagara, requesting him to return on the next vessel leaving down lake. Brant spoke to Powell before leaving in the spring for Detroit, "informing me when he went away, that he wished to meet the Enemy before he returned." [HP-162] While Powell had previously wrote to General Haldimand on September 18, telling him that although "Captain Brant had received directions to return to this Post," Powell was informed by DePeyster that Brant had gone to the Ohio, and "it was probable he will now remain above to see the issue of Mr. Clark's intended enterprise." [HP-164] However, once at Detroit, Brant was in no condition to travel anywhere but to a bed.

Somewhere during Joseph Brant's excursion to the Ohio, he had received a leg wound that had become infected. Brant would not reveal to anyone how the wounding had occurred, saying only that he had "accidentally cut himself with his own sword" which could have happened either on the campaign trail or during a bout of drunkenness. [KI-p.315] Rumors abounded at Detroit that Simon Girty had been the cause of the cut due to their previous altercation. By the time Brant arrived, the news of his fight with Girty had already reached the post from the Upper Sandusky, where Girty lay recovering. DePeyster had the post surgeon investigate the festering open wound. The doctor said that there was little he could do to treat it, "but bathe them (the wound) in rum" to disinfect the infection, and hope for healing, or resort to removing the limb if it began to rot, before the infection spread to the rest of the body, which would result in death. DePeyster notified Powell at Niagara, that "Poor Brant is very ill" and that he "would have to remain in Detroit for the winter" if he were to recover.

"He Is Now Out of Danger"

More bad news began to filter in to Niagara. Captain Thompson and his company of Rangers had returned to Detroit at the same time that Brant arrived. The men were on the brink of starvation, their uniforms and gear in tatters, and many had inoperable weapons with broken springs and no flints due to their extended stay on the march in the Ohio Country since leaving Fort Niagara almost a year before. Captain Thompson requested to Major DePeyster that he leave for Fort Niagara, "to come down to this Place to settle the amounts of his Detachment with Lieut. Col. Butler" to which DePeyster agreed without question, because of the officer's outstanding service at Detroit. On October 15, Thompson boarded the sloop that was scheduled to leave for Niagara. Hoping for a good headwind to take them across the lake the next morning, the captain of the vessel floated down the Detroit River and anchored at its mouth on the lake to await the morning's rising breeze. During the evening, the officers and men aboard opened a small keg of rum and began drinking. Sometime during the night, a wobbly Captain Thompson, who was unaccustomed to consuming any quantity of liquor after his long stay in the wilderness, climbed the steps from the quarters below to the top deck to relieve himself. At the railing, Thompson slipped and fell overboard into the waters of the lake. In a matter of seconds, the heavy wool coat he was wearing became saturated, and he sunk beneath the surface. "He had unfortunately fallen overboard and was drowned."

When Thompson's Rangers, and the garrison of Detroit learned of the Captain's death, everyone was saddened as Thompson had been well-liked by all that knew him, including the Indians. DePeyster informed Powell and Butler at Niagara. Butler recommended to Powell on October 20 that Thompson's men be recalled to Niagara while he found a successor to fill the vacancy due to Thompson's death. "Colonel Butler has represented to me that the Company of his Corps now at Detroit, having been promised to be relieved during the course of the summer, he was afraid they would be much dissatisfied if it did not take place. In consideration of which, and the constant hard duty they have been upon, I have permitted him to send up Captain Caldwell with 25 men which were all they had fit for that Service, to relieve part, or all of that Detachment if they could be spared, and I shall take some other opportunity to complete Captain Caldwell's company." [HP-167] Upon receiving Powell's order, DePeyster informed the 45 Rangers of Thompson's company at Detroit to prepare to depart on the next ship for Niagara. [HP-145] With the returning Rangers came word from Detroit on Brant's condition. "A mortification was at first apprehended, but he is now out of danger." [HP-167]

"You Must Be Sensible, Sir"

Further difficulties with Butler's Rangers surfaced near the end of October. While Haldimand noted that Butler recently completed the 10th Company of Rangers, who were mustered before General Powell at Niagara on September 18, Butler had sent only 150 Rangers on September 29 to accompany Major Ross' expedition to the attack the Rebels in the Mohawk Valley. [HP-363] General Haldimand wished to know why there were so few Rangers mustered to join the 33 men of the King's Eighth and 200 Indians from Niagara. As the rest of Ross' complement were several hundred 34th regular troops and loyalist King's Royal Yorkers from Carleton Island, Haldimand naturally felt that more Rangers would ensure the success of the October campaign. Haldimand demanded an answer from Powell, and so Lt. Col. Butler was summoned to provide an explanation.

Major Butler, stung by Haldimand's veiled allegation of impropriety, prepared to respond directly to General Haldimand with an accounting. John Butler was already under considerable strain by November 1, as "we have yet had no accounts from the detachment on the expedition to the Mohawk River," in which his eldest son, Captain Walter Butler, was employed, commanding all the Rangers. Before John Butler could write to Haldimand, word reached Butler and Powell "from the troops returned here yesterday" at Niagara on November 13, concerning the tragedy that had befallen two officers accompanying Ross' expedition. On October 19, after marching from Otsego Lake to the Mohawk

River, Lieutenant Dockstader, of the Indian Department, "who had distinguished himself on so many occasions, died very suddenly," for reasons unknown to Ross. [CE-p.99]

Then on the return trip, after devastating the valley to within 12 miles of Schenectady, Ross withdrew his detachment westward by way of West Canada Creek. An advanced guard of Colonel Willett's American troops pursued Ross, who called upon the Rangers to form a rearguard. Walter Butler and "a few of the Rangers halted to engage the pursuers," and slow them down. On the west bank of the creek, four of the Rangers were felled by a volley of Willett's men. One of them was Captain Walter Butler who was shot through the head and died instantly. The rest of the Ranger rearguard retreated, leaving the bodies of Butler and the three others for the Americans to recover. By the time the news of Butler's death reached Niagara, the entire New York frontier was celebrating the death of the "scourge of the frontier" and the man blamed for allowing the Indians to slaughter the innocents at Cherry Valley in 1779. Walter Butler was dead, and it was said that he had been scalped by an Oneida Indian who had been with Willett's men. [CE-p.102] Powell reported the loss to General Haldimand saying, "Captain Butler, who behaved very gallantly, was unfortunately killed at the Passage of Canada Creek," on the New York frontier. [PO-168]

John Butler was in seclusion grieving for the loss of his son, and in no condition to defend himself. Instead, he turned to General Powell to write to Haldimand for him. "Your Excellency has remarked in one of your letters that only 150 Rangers were sent upon the Expedition, tho' Lt. Col. Butler returned 10 Companies complete, and the nine here consist of 450 men," Powell wrote. "This was certainly a mistake of his, and he must have meant that the 10th Company was complete, for I suppose the others might want 40 of their complement, to which if 110 sick and convalescents, with 50 recruits, who were upon duty in this Garrison are added, it appears only 100 remained for cutting timber and firewood, servants, guards, etc. When the detachment went off, I think Lt. Col. Butler informed me he had only eight men left fit for that kind of service, and some time after, it was with difficulty 25 men could be mustered to send to Detroit." [HP-170]

Powell spoke plainly to Haldimand, knowing that Butler was under tremendous strain. "You must be sensible, Sir," General Powell testily wrote to General Haldimand, "that a Regiment when called upon is never able to furnish the number of men returned in the column Fit For Duty, and allowances should always be made for Servants, Convalescents, etc. I think it is right to observe that whenever demands are made upon this Post for Troops to be employed in the Enemy's Country, very large allowances must be made, as there are very few of the King's Regiment, equal to the fatigue they must necessarily undergo upon that Service, and in the summer there are frequently 100 of the Rangers upon the Sick List, owing to the ague which generally rages here at that Season, which with cutting timber and firewood, providing hay, guards, servants, etc., will prevent their furnishing that number of men for Active Service, which, from their Returns, might be expected." [HP-170]

"My Chain Appears to Have Run Out"

By early November, colder weather marking the onset of winter began to make itself known across the Ohio Country. Major DePeyster at Detroit, on October 21, had sat in "a conference held with the Hurons from Sandusky" that included their chiefs "Orotondy, the Snipe, and Sindaton" with Duperon Baby, Isidore Chesne, and a recovering Simon Girty interpreters for the Indians. Sindaton spoke to DePeyster on the situation with the remaining Moravian Delaware Indians in the Ohio Country. "Father! Listen to what I am going to say before you and the Six Nations present. I speak in behalf of the Half King, who says he was formerly a Six Nation Chief and therefore wishes they may know his Sentiments. Our Half King says he is sorry to find that there yet remain a few Delawares nigh and about Fort Pitt who are too headstrong to listen to his advice, he therefore looks upon them as Rebels and recommends to you to treat them as such." [HP-258] DePeyster listened to the allegation, and nodded his head in agreement, though his patience was wearing thinner than ever with the Indians and their constant conflicts with each other over and who was not listening to whom.

Burdened on November 2 with the accounting of the Indian Department, Alexander McKee assured DePeyster that "I have received the Invoice of Goods sent out for the use of the Indians and agreeable to it have made divisions suitable to the numbers of the Several Tribes and Nations which I have forwarded to Mr. Elliott with directions to deliver them in bulk as soon as the people to be appointed, go for them." To keep the Tribes from their incessant squabbling over who should get what provisions and presents, "I have advised the Indians to send a few people from each Nation for their shares and divide them here in their villages to prevent too many of them going to that place who not being satisfied with the part they get will still be troublesome at Detroit." [HP-259] McKee did not envy Matthew Elliott's upcoming duties at the village of Roche de Bout, where he would mediate between the quarreling Indians. The only good that could come of it for Elliott would be the share of the provisions that Elliott would cut for himself, as payment for his troubles. That, McKee knew, the savvy trader and friend of his would do.

With Elliott handling the distribution of goods for the Indians now that Major DePeyster had seen to it the Indians were amply supplied for the coming winter and rewarded for their efforts in successfully thwarting the Rebel advance into the Ohio Country, McKee was content that he could relax his grip upon the Indians and allow the superb network of war parties and scouts in the field return to their villages with the onset of cold weather. One of the last parties of Shawnee to return from the area of the Falls of the Ohio brought with them a prisoner captured near Clark's post. The man claimed to be an Englishmen deserted from the Rebels. Upon questioning him about the strength of the Rebels on November 2, McKee found that "the man reports them to be only about 130 strong, these Continentals, and that they have given up all thoughts of coming against the Indians this year. All the proposals made by Clark for this purpose to the

Inhabitants of Kentucky were rejected, their numbers being greatly diminished since last year, and most of their Regular Troops returned into the Country, as the Enlistments expired." [HP-259] McKee wondered if the information from the prisoner was entirely accurate. The man said "that Clark's Aide-de-Camp is gone into Virginia to make application for two thousand men next year to support the settlement," and McKee pondered whether Clark would make another attempt in the coming year against the Indian Country.

McKee had no way of knowing if the information gained from interrogating the prisoner was totally correct. A weary, disheartened, and discouraged George Rogers Clark decided in November to let the militia officers decide what to do, after additional desertions of men had weakened what was left of Clark's troops, rendering them incapable of making an assault upon the Indians so late in the season. While the General could at least take heart in the fact that while the Kentucky stations and posts had been spared a major assault by the British and Indians during the summer, as they had experienced the previous year along the Licking River, the campaign Clark dreamed of against Detroit had never materialized, and all the efforts on his part to prepare for that campaign had been negated by a series of setbacks.

First, recruiting able men from Kentucky had been negligible due to "many people moving away to escape military service." Clark complained about the lack of troops to the Governor of Virginia on October 6, from his post at the Falls. "We should have made a much better figure this campaign had it not been for an act passed empowering your Excellency to stop the expedition. It seems it alarmed the country. The Greenbrier militia returned the drafts in this country dispersed; great numbers returned to Virginia that were for the enterprise. It had equally as bad an impression on the Monongahela country; as the report happened about the time of the rendezvous, and proved an excuse for numbers that otherwise would have joined the camp." If that insult for Clark were not enough, due to the ineptness of his men, the large quantities of meat stored for the campaign at great expense and effort, had been improperly prepared in kegs, resulting in all of the precious provisions spoiling.

Then word came from returning scouts of the disaster that had befallen Colonel Lochry and his command. General Irvine, who had taken command of Fort Pitt from Colonel Brodhead, informed William Moore, the president of the Supreme Council of Pennsylvania on December 3, the news just reaching the Pennsylvania frontier that Clark had recently been made aware. "I am sorry to inform your Excellency that this country has got a severe stroke by the loss of Colonel Lochry and about 100 (tis' said) of the best men of Westmoreland county, including Captain Stokely and his company of rangers." [WIC-229] Clark's personal friend and second in command had lost his life, and all his men killed or captured. Clark was deeply saddened by the great loss. In addition, men were constantly being killed or taken prisoner by small war parties of the Indians from nearly every part of the country bordering the Ohio River and Clark was powerless to stop it.

Word reached Clark that the fort at the mouth of the Ohio River on the Mississippi had to be abandoned by early fall, due to the constant harassment of parties of Indians who prevented the small garrison from hunting for food. Clark decided to remain at his fort at the Falls, now called Fort Jefferson, but could only spare "an Officer and 15 men to Post Vincent," [HP-259] which Clark hoped to hold at least until the coming spring, knowing that of all the Indians he had once held in alliance with Virginia after his defeat of Hamilton, only a few Wabash now remained loyal. Though word reached Clark late in the year of a great victory for the Americans over the British in Virginia, Clark "gloomily concluded he would never be able to take control of the Ohio Country he so desired, saying, "I have lost the object that was one of the principal inducements to my fatigues and transactions for several years past- my chain appears to have run out." [WGA-p.118]

"I Cannot Help Expressing My Surprise"

At Detroit, Major DePeyster ended the year on a sour note. One matter bothered him to no end and that was the problem caused by the Indians, their constant meddling in his affairs, their bickering, indecisiveness, and pettiness plagued him daily. There never seemed to be a moment when there were not Indians at his door with demands or complaints. Most irksome to DePeyster, which tried his patience beyond its limits, were the Indians incessant requests to him, combined with their rudeness, lack of respect, and haughtiness when he was unable to give them something they asked for. Perhaps that was why when he read the letter from General Haldimand that had lain on his desk since arriving in mid-October, that he could not bring himself to reply to the General. DePeyster could feel the anger welling up inside himself at Haldimand's total lack of appreciation for what it took for him to deal with the Indians at Detroit. And then to heap such praise upon Joseph Brant, while condemning himself for not meeting Haldimand's financial budget was almost more than DePeyster could bear.

Reading from the General's letter again, DePeyster slowly shook his head in disbelief. "Joseph's persevering and spirited Conduct will furnish the Indians in that Country with an example worthy their Imitation, and you," DePeyster winced, "with an Opportunity representing to them the facility of defending their country against any incursion." DePeyster could hardly contain himself. If Haldimand could only know how the drunken Joseph Brant had nearly killed Simon Girty, a man much endeared by both the Mingoes and Wyandots. If it had not been for the intervention of Alexander McKee, the Ohio Indians would have likely killed the Mohawk on the spot, as he was generally not well liked, and was a boastful Iroquois who constantly claimed his self-appointed status was inherited from Sir William Johnson. However, that was not the crux of Haldimand's comments that disturbed DePeyster the most.

It was the scolding DePeyster received from Haldimand concerning the Indians that he found humiliating. "The Bills for L35,225 agreeable to your

Letter of Advice, have appeared, and I have accepted them, but I cannot help expressing my Surprise, not only at the astonishing Amount of those Bills, so soon following the last, but as so great expense being incurred at all, after you were made acquainted with my Intentions, and were given to expect an immediate supply of Indian presents from hence." DePeyster chaffed at the implication of the General's comments, arguing with himself that while Haldimand wanted him to support the Indians with provisions, gifts, and ammunition, at the same time the General demanded that he reduce the amount of goods flowing to the Indians to keep within an intended allotment. How could DePeyster dole out to one party of Indians and not to another, when they would not keep quiet among themselves, and eventually were all clamoring to DePeyster for more and more, and yet always threatening to abandon the British at the least provocation, or when he tried to reduce the amount of goods to try to adhere to Haldimand's request. Where was he to draw the line when the Indians constantly demanded more and more? [HP-219]

"I Shall Attend to What You Have To Say"

The winter winds whipped over the settlement of Detroit on the morning of December 10 bringing the first heavy snows of the season to the western post, isolating it and the people there from the rest of Canada until spring. With the thought in mind that no more provisions would be forthcoming from Niagara, Major DePeyster prepared to counsel with the Indians who requested to speak to him. Sitting before DePeyster and the junior officers present from the King's Regiment, Lieutenants Bennett and Saumarez, and Ensigns Sheehan, Pollard, McDougal and Frey, were the principal chiefs and war captains of the Delaware, along with a smattering of Shawnee, Wyandot and Mingo Indians from the Upper Sandusky villages who demanded to speak to him on what they termed "matters of importance." Duperon Baby had already briefed DePeyster on what the Indians wanted which amounted to more provisions for they had already eaten their allotment that was to last them until spring. As George Girty had accompanied them from the villages, he told DePeyster that feeding the Moravian Indians settled at the Captive's Town was taking more food than previously expected for there were many hungry mouths to feed.

However, Mr. Baby privately informed the Major that the Indians were out of food because they had traded some of their precious provisions for rum from an unscrupulous trader in the Delaware village. The Indians were going to claim that the Moravian Delawares had eaten up their own supplies, when in fact, those Indians were at the point of starving, subsisting on green corn, and having been given no share of any of the food destined for them. If all this were true, Major DePeyster could see no point in holding a council with the savages under such pretentious conditions that only pandered to their duplicity, except for the fact that he was bound to his duty to do so, as the commandant of the post. Rising up before the throng of chiefs seated before him who were smoking their pipes, DePeyster signaled to his interpreters, Duperon Baby, William Tucker,

Pierre Druilliard, and George Girty, that he was about to begin the council meeting. DePeyster looked over to Captain William Caldwell of the Rangers. Caldwell, with Lieutenants Andrew Butler, younger son of Lt. Col. John Butler, and Clinch, had just arrived at Detroit a few days before by boat from Niagara, bringing with them a half company of Rangers for duty at the western post. Captain Caldwell, a welcome friendly face whom Major DePeyster had become acquainted with during the officer's previous duty at Detroit, gave the Major a nod. [HP-260]

George Girty quickly approached DePeyster before he had a chance to speak. Girty whispered in the Major's ear, informing him that the Indians had not yet eaten a morning meal, and were hopeful that DePeyster would supply them with food and drink before the council began, so they would not suffer from empty stomachs before counseling with him. DePeyster looked over Girty's shoulder and noticed the "Delaware chiefs Captain Pipe and Buckagihelas" watching him and Girty. DePeyster nodded to the chiefs, saying to them, "it gives me pleasure to see my Children at all times, especially such as have executed my orders. I'm persuaded you would not have taken this journey had you not something very interesting to communicate but as you are fatigued, I shall order you wherewith to refresh yourselves and as soon as you are ready I shall attend to what you may have to say." Then motioning to Ensigns McDougal and Frey to see to it that the Indians were fed, DePeyster and the other officers adjourned the council.

"Unless Dispatches Were Found Upon Them"

By late December, winter had descended upon Quebec with a fury, locking the city in its icy grip, and isolating the British headquarters in Canada from New York City and the rest of North America. In the cold, drafty officer's quarters of the old Citadel on the bluff overlooking the St. Lawrence River, General Frederick Haldimand sat motionless in his chair, staring at the letter of secret intelligence that Captain Matthews had placed on his desk. The dispatch had just arrived from General Henry Clinton commanding at New York City. The letter had come by land and not by sea, having made its perilous way up the Hudson River valley sewn into the clothes of one of Sir John Johnson's undercover scouts from Captain Crawford's company, the spy company of the 2nd Battalion of the King's Royal Regiment of New York, the men of the 2nd Battalion recently incorporated into Johnson's regiment from Captain Leake's Independent Company of Volunteers. Not all of the important mail destined for Haldimand in Quebec had reached him by this clandestine method. Some of it fell into the hands of the Rebels when the scouts carrying it were discovered and arrested as spies.

Only two months before, two of Johnson's couriers were apprehended by the Rebels near Johnstown in the Mohawk Valley, when they strayed too close to their former homes for a chance opportunity to see their wives. Johnson notified Haldimand on September 17. "Two men of Captain Leake's Corps, who were to go to Hudson's River, but were unfortunately taken and gave information of the destination of the three first mentioned, which occasioned so strict a search for them that our "friend" at Albany and Schenectady was deterred from sending some dispatches which they say were received from New York for Your Excellency, to go by way of Saratoga." [HP-383]

The two men, Peter Fitzpatrick and Dennis McGraw, were recognized by one of their former neighbors and identified as Tories. Upon arrest, the men were found to have British documents in their possession. Being in civilian and not military clothes, the two were arrested and taken to Albany in chains to be tried as spies for the British. The important information in the documents had unfortunately not reached Haldimand. Rather, from the papers, the Rebels were informed of the intelligence from the British in New York City. An angry Haldimand was prompted to write to John Johnson. "I am favored with your letter of the 17th communicating the return of three men you sent to Johnstown for Intelligence and the Capture of Two Men of Captain Leake's Corps who accompanied them, whose Infidelity has prevented my receiving Sir Henry Clinton's Dispatch, and might have proved fatal to your three men. It has no doubt been hurtful to the object of their Mission, as it is probable they have been intimidated by the Threats of the Rebels." [HP-384]

Haldimand advised Johnson to counsel his scouts and couriers immediately. "You would do well to represent in the Strongest Terms to all Scouts the Dangerous Consequences of yielding to those Inquisitions, and how unnecessary it is to their Personal Safety, for whatever the Enemy may threaten, they will not venture to take their Lives, unless Dispatches are found upon them, which is always to be avoided by Precaution." [HP-384] John Johnson knew exactly what the nature of the problem was. Because the bulk of his scouts were drawn from men of the Mohawk Valley like Fitzpatrick and McGraw, they were tempted while on a mission to slip into the valley, regardless of the risk, because their families were still there, and they had not seen nor heard word from them in many, many months. The agony was too great for many men to resist.

John Johnson spoke to Captain Crawford of the scout company, telling him to instruct his men that in the future while on a scout, they were to avoid altogether the trails leading to the Mohawk Valley, as the information they carried was far too valuable to risk losing. Every man was told that the Rebels would have no mercy on them if they were captured and found to have documents on them. They would be arrested on the spot and taken to Albany where the Rebels would hang them in the public square adjacent the Old Stone jail. This had already happened, so the best course was not to stray off the mission given to them, and keep from being recognized and captured.

While attempting to correct the situation and prevent another future disruption to his line of communication with Clinton, Haldimand realized that with the loss of the dispatches, he had no way of knowing the latest developments in the war in the Colonies. The riskier land route for carrying dispatches was far quicker than the longer sea route from New York up the St. Lawrence, which often became impassable by January when the river froze, preventing the movements of ships. At this critical juncture in the war, Haldimand needed to know more than ever what was going on to the south of him. The secret dispatch on his desk had just been brought in from the Colonies to Montreal by courier, and swiftly sent to Haldimand without delay, its contents undisclosed until General Haldimand had opened it, and read it. That was why he now was motionless in the chair, stunned by the news that had just reached him which plunged him deep in thought. For Haldimand realized, by implication from what he read, that the safety of Canada itself which was entrusted to him along with the welfare of the men in the King's Service at the string of posts to the west keeping watch over the Indians and the vast wilderness lands of the Ohio Country, were now in jeopardy as never before. Something unexpected and terrible had happened.

The dispatch that General Haldimand had just read contained secret intelligence from Sir Henry Clinton at New York City. It informed Haldimand that a military disaster had befallen Lord Cornwallis's Expeditionary Army in Virginia, the past October. Cornwallis had been forced to surrender his entire army of over 6000 men on the October 19, 1781 to a combined army of American and French troops besieging them. Terms of the capitulation were unknown. To Frederick Haldimand it could mean only one thing. Great Britain's war to put down the Rebellion in its former colonies was all but finished.

Chapter 14

1782: Bloody Battle for the Ohio Country

The winter of January 1782 was not what anyone expected in the Ohio Country. The icy weather and deep snows were more harsh than the previous winter, yet not as severe as the early months of 1780 which had brought on such hardship to settlers, soldiers and Indians alike from Fort Pitt to Detroit. Nonetheless, the first weeks of 1782 in the Ohio Country were daunting for the Indians scattered throughout the wilderness. With so many hungry mouths to feed and so little food to go around at Wapatomika, Upper Sandusky, Roche de Bout, and Detroit, the perils of the previous summer's war had brought major changes to the Indian way of life. Few Delaware remained at their villages on the Muskingum River which had once teemed with people. The Shawnee had been forced to abandon their lower towns at Chillicothy and Piqua, once the center of Shawnee culture, which the Kentuckians burned. Everywhere, the Indian preoccupation with making war had left them little time to plant and tend to crops, and without their normal source of food for the winter, more and more Indians were moving northward to be closer to the source of the meager provisions doled out by the British at their western post of Detroit.

At the Upper Sandusky Indian villages, the lack of food was most severe because of the influx of the Christian Delawares from the Moravian settlements who had arrived with nothing to eat and in need of everything. The Wyandot Half King, in whose charge the Delawares were placed, did the best he could to see that they did not starve, but food even for his own people was scarce. Heckewelder, who resided with the Indians, was helpless to alleviate their suffering. "Towards the end of January, the cold during the nights became almost insupportable; the more so, on account of the smallness of our huts, not permitting the convenience of our having large fires made within them, and even wood being scarce where we were. Our houses having no flooring, whenever a thaw came on, the water, forcing passages through the earth, entered in such quantities that we scarcely could keep our feet dry." [BC-p.101]

The situation with the Moravians went from bad to worse by the end of January when their food began to run out. "The cattle finding no pasture in these dreary regions, and we being able to procure any for them, now began to perish by hunger, and, as provision for so many people could not be had even for money, famine took place, and the calamity became general; many had now no other alternative but to live on the carcasses of starved cattle, and in a few instances suckling babes perished for want of nourishment from the mothers' impoverished breasts." [BC-p.101] However, the Wyandot chief, Half King, had become more calloused to their plight, as he lost his sympathy for them. Two of his sons had been killed by the Americans the previous fall, during an Indian raid against settlers on the east side of the Ohio River when they were unexpectedly pursued by the militia and attacked. Half King was not done grieving for his loss, and vowed vengeance against the whites who had killed his sons, and anyone who sympathized with the Americans. Naturally, he turned his hatred towards the Moravian preachers, whom he knew to have supported the Americans in the past, to vent his enmity. [BC-p.102]

"I Suffer Myself to Be Flattered"

At Detroit, Major DePeyster had his hands full trying to feed everyone at the settlement and the Indians too from the scant stores in the garrison. To add to his woes, another letter from Haldimand in Quebec had arrived late in the season just before the Lakes froze, in which the General demanded an explanation from DePeyster why he had neglected to send Thompson and his company of Rangers in time to help Joseph Brant intercept Clark and his detachment on the Ohio. DePeyster realized that Brant, still at Detroit, must have sent a dispatch of his own to Colonel Johnson at Niagara, and then on to Haldimand, complaining of the lack of sufficient support made available during his campaign to the Ohio the previous summer. Despite the fact that the lakes were frozen, which prevented dispatches being sent by water, DePeyster decided he must write to Haldimand directly on both the issues laid before him, that of Brant's allegation, and Haldimand's previous complaint of poor management of goods to the Indians. On January 25 and 26, DePeyster finally wrote to Haldimand.

DePeyster addressed the issue of the Indians first, attempting to describe to Haldimand the nature of the problem he faced dealing with them, which he was privately sure the General did not fully comprehend. In regards to Haldimand's claim that DePeyster was superfluous when it came to giving the Indians what they wanted, DePeyster explained, "They say they are all provided with horses (canoes not being used by the Shawnee, Mingoes, Delawares, Pottawattamies, etc.) and having been accustomed to saddles, they cannot do without them. The Enemy uses rifles, they therefore must have rifles to be on a footing with them. It would be tiresome to repeat all their impertinences but I must give Your Excellency some insight into the temper of those people." [HP-231] DePeyster described a recent incident hoping it might illustrate to Haldimand the true nature of the Indians that made it nearly impossible to deal with them. "About a week ago, Mr. Alexander McKee Deputy Agent sent in an Indian named Morgan, who had not been in here for two years past, recommending him in the strongest terms. I ordered Mr. Baby to equip him handsomely, to give him some articles for his family, and send him to me to receive a present of silver works, with which I decorated him as fine as a Miami." DePeyster now related the conversation that he had with the Indian named Morgan. Morgan, are you content?' 'Yes, father, but won't you give me a rifle, it will be well bestowed. I know how to use one.' I gave him a rifle. 'Father, you have only given milk at one Breast! I would willingly have a Keg (rum) to speak to the young men when I get home, in order to rouse their Spirits to Martial Deeds.' I gave him the keg. 'Father! My saddle was stolen last night, you surely will give me a saddle!" [HP-231]

DePeyster continued with the account. "In consideration of his great services, and what he still might be of, I gave him a conditional order on Mr. Baby, which he protested, not having any in the store. Now my Intentions were to have give him my own saddle and housing, rather than he should be discontented. But the first accounts that I heard of him were that of being refused at the store, he threw down his load in the street, and rode off to his village." Summing up this example of what was typically an everyday encounter with the Indians, and the inherent difficulty in attempting to transact anything with them, DePeyster concluded to Haldimand, "these are the circumstances which will frequently happen. I shall not in the future trouble Your Excellency with a detail of them, nor would I suffer them lamely had I a Regiment in this Garrison, in which case, I would dictate to My Children as they are pleased to call themselves."

Unfortunately, DePeyster was unaware that other factors contributed heavily to the difficulty of dealing with the Indians. In the case he had just cited to General Haldimand, the Major did not know that Mr. Duperon Baby, DePeyster's "Captain and Indian Agent at Detroit" [HP-379] in charge in overseeing the other Frenchmen in the Indian Department at the post as well as supervising the major trading post attached to the garrison, had spoken to Morgan in words only the two men shared. Baby did not like the haughty Miami Indian to begin with, and did not think the Indian worthy of DePeyster's special treatment. Furthermore, Baby was part Shawnee by birth like McKee, having an Indian mother, but while Baby had served the British at Detroit for years, McKee was a relative newcomer whom Baby believed had risen to his position as Department Deputy Agent at Baby's expense. The remarks he made to Morgan in private were more than a slight to the Indian whom he felt did not deserve a saddle, and was not even a Shawnee. The words of insult to Morgan were indirectly pointed at McKee, who had sent the man to DePeyster in the beginning. The Indians were not the only problem for the Major, though he was not aware of the animosity in the Indian Department that ran high among the Frenchmen.

Next in his letter DePeyster turned his attention to addressing the question of the Rangers' late arrival to the Indian Country. Citing previous reports sent to General Powell at Niagara detailing the specifics of the campaign, DePeyster outlined for Haldimand the reasons why the Rangers were unable to make the juncture with Brant. DePeyster wanted to present the facts to Haldimand which contradicted the General's conclusions that a unique opportunity to destroy Clark on the Ohio River did not occur due to reasons other than to the negligence Haldimand was intimating. "The chief reason which prevented the Rangers joining Brant before Clark passed was owing to want of provisions which neither proceeded from neglect in me or those employed by you. Captain Chesne an active officer had the transporting of the provisions, and was detained by a series of the heaviest rains known in this country, which rendered the roads impassible. The Rangers, some Volunteers and Indians, however, pursued Clark to within a few miles of the Falls." [HP-232] DePeyster remembered the conversation he had with Captain Thompson when the officer returned from the field. Thompson recalled how the Indians sat in two councils on the Ohio, without any urgency to move towards the Enemy, eating up the last of the provisions as they smoked their pipes and discussed what to do, and when they did send out scouts with explicit orders to bring in prisoners for interrogation, the warriors returned with the scalps of prisoners as they were unable to resist their urge to kill prisoners to obtain trophies for their belts. In the time that was wasted, Thompson believed, the initiative to attack and destroy Clark was lost, and if blame must be laid, it was at the feet of the Indians. Unfortunately, Thompson was now dead, and unable to support DePeyster's claim, if further explanation were needed.

Major DePeyster continued his defense to Haldimand. "With regard to the Indians in general, they are not under better discipline. I have wrought hard to endeavor to bring them to it, but find it impossible altogether to change their natures. I assemble them, get promises, and send them out, but when once out of sight the turning of a screw might divert them from the original plan. If too severe with them, upon such occasions, they tell us we are well off that there are no Virginians in this quarter, but such as they bring here against their inclinations," DePeyster related. Continuing, DePeyster wrote, "the treasure given to them is immense, I cannot however think it altogether thrown away the last Campaign. The Indians in this country must be looked upon as a large body of irregulars, fed, and clothed, to prevent the inroads of the Virginians into this country, and, who must be delicately managed to prevent their favoring those Rebels."

DePeyster felt that he had made his point to Haldimand, and defended himself against accusations of impropriety by demonstrating to the General the difficulties faced by long distances of communication and re-supply in the wilderness, combined with the unpredictableness of the weather that could make travel at times next to impossible, when using a native ally who was prone to as many vagaries as could be imagined of a savage in the wilderness. All in all, Major DePeyster believed in his own heart that he had done the best he could in managing the Indians under the circumstances and though not saying it to Haldimand, implicitly challenged the Commander-in-Chief to find one who had done better. Summing up his defense to Haldimand, DePeyster stated that his dealing with the Indians "in the execution of which during seven years application, I suffer myself to be flattered with having used some degree of judgment." [HP-232] It would have been too bold for Major DePeyster to remind General Haldimand that a man of lesser experience in dealing with the Indians, such Captain Lernoult, DePeyster's predecessor at Detroit, had not been able to accomplish as much as DePeyster had in holding the Indians together as native allies for the Crown.

"Never Serve Under Ross Again"

General Haldimand in Quebec had spent a great deal of time during the early weeks of 1782 formulating a plan for the defense of Canada in lieu of specific orders from England and in light of the military developments to the south of him. Haldimand reasoned that once the Americans consolidated their gains after Cornwallis's defeat, if England showed no signs of continuing the military offensive in the Colonies, the Americans would undoubtedly turn their attention to Canada, and attempt to seize it by invasion, as they had attempted to do in 1775 and 1776. Further, the key to holding the western posts from becoming severed from Canada was to maintain the string of forts along the St. Lawrence and Lake Ontario that protected the sailing vessels plying the Great Lakes with provisions and reinforcements for the British garrisons and the Indians of the Ohio Country and beyond. Tantamount to the success of such a defense, in Haldimand's mind, was the occupation of Oswego on the southeast shore of Lake Ontario.

"From the turn affairs have taken to the Southward admitting the late reports concerning Lord Cornwallis to be authentic, it is highly probable that the Enemy will resume their Intention to reduce the Province upon their original plan, which has been already communicated to you in which event our having possession of Oswego becomes more than ever necessary," Haldimand wrote to General Powell at Niagara on February 18. Haldimand found it most ironic that Oswego, the site of his victory over the French and Indian War battle with the French force sent there to sever the western British army from the east, would once again play such a vital pivotal role in linking the west with the east. "I have therefore determined to take post there as early in the spring as the lake will permit, and for that purpose have directed Major Ross to make such preparations during the remainder of the winter as will facilitate the measure, and by some degree alone for the want resources an undertaking of this kind demands, but which, the uncertainty of what may happen in the lower parts of the Province absolutely forbids. I have nevertheless no doubt of success, persuaded that every effort in your power will be exerted to further it" [HP-139] Haldimand detailed to Powell the transfer of troops under Ross from Carleton Island, and the men that would be needed from Niagara to assist him, but cautioned his commander on the need for secrecy at his post, lest the venture be compromised by forewarned knowledge reaching the Americans, which would result in their possession of Oswego before Ross could get there.

"As the Rebels have no doubt many friendly Indians who resort there for the purpose of communicating with them it would therefore be risking too much to mention the Affair to a Second Person not even to Colonel Butler, and when the past preparation are making which indicate a movement, it would not be amiss to give out that it is intended for Detroit until the troops embark, and then declare it for Carleton Island. No bad consequence can follow those hints from a band of Indians as the few that happen to be at Niagara with those that accompany the troops from Carleton Island will be sufficient to keep Major Ross quiet until his Work's put him out of danger." [HP-139] Noting to Powell that "I could wish it were possible to recall Joseph Brant, he would be very useful on this occasion," Haldimand ordered Powell to "send off an Express immediately to him that you have something of importance to communicate and desiring he will return to Niagara with all possible expedition." Haldimand was looking ahead to Ross's upcoming mission to rebuild and fortify Oswego. Indian scouting parties to ascertain the movements of the Rebels would urgently be needed once Ross landed at the mouth of the river there. And there was something else that Brant could do of merit, in Haldimand's estimation. Ross had blamed the Indians for the debacle that had befallen their expedition the previous fall. While his assessment of their performance was correct, the Indians who accompanied his force were "admittedly a poor selection, being recruited at Niagara on less than a week's notice." On hearing this, the Six Nations as a whole had "swore they would never serve under Ross again." [KI-p.323] Haldimand knew that Brant could assuage the Iroquois to mend fences with Major Ross for the sake of everyone involved.

"1,600 Indians Needing Rations"

By the end of February, General Haldimand now had before him an accurate accounting of the troops spread out across the western posts of Michilimackinac, Detroit, and Niagara, sent to him from the Monthly Return calculated from General Powell on February 1. It was vital that he know the disposition of the troops, so that he could plan for Ross's mission to Oswego, drawing men from where he could, to support those earmarked to leave Carleton Island. At the far upper post of Michilimackinac, only 107 men were on active duty with seven sick in their quarters, a total of 114 men under Lt. Governor Sinclair's command. At Detroit, Major DePeyster had 367 men on duty drawn from the King's Eighth Regiment, the 47th, and the Ranger Corps. 242 of these men were from the King's Regiment, and now at Detroit were a total of 56 Rangers of Caldwell's Company with two Lieutenants, Thomas Butler and Ralfe Clench, on hand with Caldwell. Niagara could boast a garrison of 642 men under arms, but the total troops, excluding the Indians, at the three posts spread over the enormous distance across the Great Lakes amounted to no more than 1,100 men. Of the 2,300 persons "Drawing Provisions out of the King's Stores" at Niagara alone, slightly more than 650 were soldiers. The rest Powell attributed to Brant's Volunteers, the Indian Department, a hodge-podge of Loyalists, and over 1,600 Indians needing rations. [HP-356]

"The Half King Is To Help Me"

By the middle of February, Simon Girty had decided, with Alexander McKee's approval, to push the Wyandot chief Half King to have the Moravian missionaries removed from the Upper Sandusky village and taken to live permanently at Detroit. Girty had many reasons to persuade the Half King, whose hatred towards the preachers had been increasing. While Girty himself harbored hostility for the two preachers, he too had reason to believe that their clandestine operations had not entirely ceased with their removal from the Muskingum. Girty suspected that Heckewelder and Zeisberger were still communicating by letter with Fort Pitt, and though without proof, he had a letter written for the Half King sent to Major DePeyster at Detroit, requesting the commandant "to take them away as soon as possible" saying that if he refused, "he himself would know what to do." [BC-p.102] Major DePeyster had been preoccupied with an Indian council held at Detroit on February 25. On that date he met for the first time with the deputation of the Lakes tribes known by the French as the "Masoutins and the Qui, quabous Nations" where "Major DePeyster addressed himself to the Chiefs and warriors" of the two tribes, with the officers of the King's Eighth and the Ranger Corps present. "Duperon Baby, Isidore Chesne, and Charles Beaubin" served as sworn interpreters. "Children! Since it is your desire that I should call you my Children, it is this day I call you so, as it gives you pleasure to hear it so." [HP-261] It was DePeyster's duty to forge the alliance of these tribes to the King's Service, regardless of the fact that it would cost the post provisions and gifts to cement the questionable relationship. At the end of the council, DePeyster had word sent to the Half King and Simon Girty to have the Moravians brought to him at the first opportunity.

On March 1, Heckewelder and Zeisberger received a message from the Half King and Girty, ordering all six of the Moravian preachers "to appear before them tomorrow morning at the house of McCormick, there to hear a letter read written by the commandant at Detroit to the Half King and Captain Girty respecting us." [BC-p.102] When only Heckewelder and Zeisberger made the arduous eight mile trip through the snow the next morning to Half King's lodge, "the latter, seeing but two of us arrive impudently insulted us, for having disobeyed their orders," whereupon Girty addressed the two men, telling them "you have brought upon ourselves what you have so long deserved, by means of your attachment to the Rebels! Your deeds are no more hidden!" Girty threatened the two Moravians if they refused to go, saying that while he was personally appointed to bring them in to Detroit, if he "should be otherwise engaged, or should need any assistance, the Half King is to help me," implying that the Wyandot could take care of the preachers permanently in any manner that suited his savage nature. [BC-p.103] On the morning of March 13, the six Moravian preachers with their families were at last escorted from the Upper Sandusky villages for the trip to Detroit, leaving behind several hundred Christian Delaware converts. Simon Girty was unable to make the trip with them, for he had left already with a war party of Wyandots headed for the Ohio River to the east. In his stead, he had a Frenchman named Le Villiers conduct the missionaries to the village at the Lower Sandusky to await transport by boat to Detroit.

"That They Intend For Sandusky"

When the severe winter weather of January turned milder in the Ohio Country by mid-February, several dozen Indian war parties set out from the cluster of villages of the Upper Sandusky intent on raiding the white settlements on the east side of the Ohio River. War parties struck the frontier with a vengeance from below Fort Pitt to deep into Washington County to the south. The Indians killed and scalped settlers, and took what prisoners and plunder from cabins that they could, before setting them on fire and disappearing across the Ohio River. One man named Carpenter was taken prisoner by the Indians, "but by great daring, managed to escape, bringing back word that his abductors had been Moravians." [HW1-p.177] A settler named Wallace returned to his home to find it ransacked, his livestock slain, and his wife and three children taken captive by the Indians. Everywhere, word reached Fort Pitt, Fort McIntosh and Fort Henry that hostile Indians were marauding throughout the settlements. An alarm was raised in the counties to call out the militia to protect against further incursions, and to pursue the war parties and attempt to recover several dozen prisoners who were already taken by the Indians into the wilderness of the Ohio Country.

Likewise, Simon Girty set out from the Upper Sandusky on March 17 with orders from DePeyster to meet with loyalists on the Virginian side of the river near Wheeling. "I left in company with the Half King's son and eight others, but as to the place I intended to go, I found it impracticable, for the Virginians was too thick a scouting in that Quarter, which rendered my design abortive, and the paper that you gave me, I had no opportunity of seeing them that I wanted to see." [HP-30] Girty with Scotosh and the eight warriors joined with another war party of Wyandots led by the war chief Abraham Kuhn. [BC-p.104] Reaching the Ohio River below Fort McIntosh, the combined party of 30 warriors divided, and Girty accompanied the Wyandots that crossed at Mingo Bottom with Scotosh, while Abraham Kuhn took the others to raid near Fort McIntosh in "hopes of ambuscading some of the soldiers at that post." [BC-p.104] Upon crossing the river, Girty and Scotosh divided into two groups who raided above Wheeling and Fort Henry, taking several prisoners on April 1. "I was obliged to go another way to make a stroke and push off as fast as possible. We killed one soldier and took one man prisoner and arrived at Upper Sandusky April 8," with a captive named John Stevenson who was in the Virginia militia. [BC-p.104]

"Mr. Simon Girty arrived at the upper town from war three days ago, and brought a prisoner and a scalp. They were taken at the other side of the Big River (Ohio) about nine miles below Beaver Creek." An intensive interrogation of Stevenson was begun to gain intelligence on the intentions of the Americans at Fort Pitt, Major DePeyster related. "Girty asked the prisoner where the rest of his people were. He answered that they were gone to Fort Pitt to Council. He asked them what Council they were going upon," DePeyster wrote. [HP-171] "The said prisoner informs me that General Irvine had returned from the Congress to Fort Pitt. That he had been down for two battalions of troops, but whether he had obtained them or not, he could not tell. He further says, that on his arrival at Fort Pitt, he had called all the militia officers together, and likewise the regular Captains to a Council of War, and that it was determined to start in a few days on a small campaign. Their numbers to consist of about 500 foot and 300 horse- that they intended for Sandusky and are to march from Fort McIntosh," Depeyster concluded in his letter to Haldimand. To Girty, all this information was confirmation that the Virginians were up to something, and he gave his opinion freely to DePeyster. It appeared to him that the threat to the Indian Country was coming from Fort Pitt and the settlements in the east, and not from Clark in Kentucky.

"They Came Upon a Grisly Discovery"

At nearly the same time that the Moravian preachers had been summoned to hear the message of the Half King ordering their removal to Detroit, the Moravian Delaware Indians under the charge of the missionaries at the Upper Sandusky had reached a crisis trying to survive through the winter. Beginning in January, several of the Christian Indians who were reaching the point of starvation had pleaded with the Half King to allow them to return to their abandoned homes on the Tuscarawas River to gather up what little of the crops that had been left standing the previous fall when they were forced by Elliott and the Half King to leave their homes for the Upper Sandusky. Half King relented, letting some of the Indians leave unescorted to search for food for he knew that he could no longer feed the Delawares, nor cared to, as his attitude had grown more hostile towards them. By late February, when the weather had turned milder, "permission was granted for about 150 of the starving Christians to return to the Tuscarawas" [HW1-p.176] to join those who "had started, some on the 16th and others on the 19th of January, 1782, neither of the missionaries nor any other white persons accompanying them." [BC-p.115] However, "it was a bad time to return, because at almost the same time that they were searching the fields on hands and knees, picking up each kernel found in frozen fields" war parties of Indians from the Upper Sandusky were crossing the Ohio River and striking the frontier settlements. [HW1-p.176] The inevitable reaction was about to happen.

By early March, the alarm was spread along the length of the eastern frontier south of Fort Pitt and bordering the east side of the Ohio River. "James Marshel, lieutenant of Washington County, Pennsylvania, ordered out, according to law, some of the militia to march across the Ohio and attack them." [BC-p.116] Militiamen from the surrounding countryside were quickly assembled to pursue the Indian war parties that were known to be still in the area and carrying white prisoners. The main force of over 100 mounted men, some drawn from the Wheeling area, was commanded by Colonel David Williamson. They collected at Fort Henry at Wheeling around March 1 and on the morning of the 4, crossed the Ohio River into the Indian Country, following a trail that had been found by scouts. The fresh tracks were apparently made by one of those war parties of Indians returning home in the direction of the of the Moravian Indian villages on the Tuscarawas, where Williamson and his men believed the Indians had set out from.

Williamson's reasoning came from the discovery of "the signs of a large Indian encampment which had been in existence over an extended period of time" at the deserted village of Gnadenhutten the previous early fall. Then, Williamson with a detachment of mounted militia, had been pursuing a party of Indians who had raided isolated settler cabins on the east side of the Ohio River in September, after a brief attempt to surprise the inhabitants at Fort Henry and lure them into an ambush, which failed. The tracks of the war party led Williamson to Gnadenhutten, however they found no warriors there, except for a few stray Christian Indians who Williamson took as prisoners for Fort Pitt, having difficulty restraining his men from killing them on the spot. For on the outskirts of the village were found the remains of a large deserted Indian camp, proof to all the men that the "so-called Christian Indians had been the staging ground from the assaults on the frontier settlements". [HW1-p.176] Williamson did not know that the Indian camp had actually been that of Elliott, Half King, and several hundred of his warriors from the Upper Sandusky who had stayed at the village to remove the Moravian preachers and their Indians.

Williamson and his men were no more than eight miles up the trail headed west from the Ohio River when they "soon came upon a grisly discovery," the mutilated remains of Mrs. Wallace and her infant daughter who had been captured only days before by one of the Indian war parties. The spectacle was horrific. "The Indians, safe from pursuit, had stopped to have a little sport with their victim. When they had finished they cut off a sapling about two feet above the ground, and sharpened the point. Two or three of them then lifted up the screaming woman and forced her down on the sharpened point, leaving her there to suffer a drawn-out, agonizing death, knowing that she was sure to be found, impaled on the stake, by the next traveler who happened by. There would be no rescue of Mrs. Wallace, or her infant daughter. Nearby, the militia found its bloody and scalped corpse. It, too, had been impaled on a stake." [HW1-p.177] After hastily burying the corpses as best as could be done in the frozen ground, Williamson's detachment headed towards the Moravian Indian villages, intent on attacking and killing the savage murderers of Mrs. Wallace and their neighbors with a newfound vengeance motivated by the terrible sight they had just witnessed.

"Two Boys Succeeded in Eluding the Militia"

On the evening of March 6, Williamson's party reached the abandoned village of Gnadenhutten undetected, and found the Indian village was not deserted, but occupied by a large group of Indians living there. Early on the next morning of March 7, Williamson ordered his men to approach the village from several directions, and round up the Indians who were headed to the fields. While a few of the Indians who were first encountered had been killed outright by Williamson's men, the bulk of them had not witnessed these killings and the militiamen were able to approach the Indians in a friendly manner, identifying them as Moravian Christian Delawares and not the warriors they were in search of. Telling the Moravians "in a sincere manner...that their intention was to take them to Pittsburgh, where they would be fed and housed until the war was over," [HW1-p.178] Williamson and his men were able to round up the entire population of the Moravian Indians at Gnadenhutten and the nearby village of Schonbrunn, who were unarmed and unsuspecting of the danger posed by the militia. Those Delawares at the village of Salem had managed to escape, due to a runner who warned them of the approach of the militia who had killed several Indians they encountered in the fields outside of Gnadenhutten.

Williamson's men herded the Indians together into the village of Gnadenhutten and locked up the men and boys in one of the houses, and the women, children and babies in another while a search of the village was begun. Horses were found at the village that militiamen identified as some of the "animals which belonged to white families." [HW1-p,178] And inside one of the houses, the "torn and blood-stained dress of Mrs. Wallace" [HW1-p.178] was discovered, along with other "garments and other articles" [BC-p.117] that were known to have been taken from settlers' cabins. On closer inspection of the Indians, it was "discovered that some of the Indians were wearing their friends' clothes who had been killed and scalped; and they also saw various kinds of plunder that had been taken in war." [BC-p.117] Upon questioning where these things had come from, some Moravians responded that they had been given to them as presents by a party of Indians that had passed through the village some days before, but as some of the Indian men observed their hair plucked and painted in the manner of a warrior and not a peaceful Indian, it could only mean there were both hostile warriors among the Moravians, as well as Moravians who had gone to war against the settlements, both living with those Indians who had returned to the village with the sole intent of finding food. The distinction between the guilty and innocent Indians could not be determined, nor did it really matter to Williamson's men who had just recently seen the horribly tortured and mutilated corpses of Mrs. Wallace and her baby on the trail. There was more than enough proof for the militiamen to conclude that the Moravian Indians had "just been raiding into the settlements, and that it was their trail which had been followed by the militia; which belief, as to about 30 of those Indians, there can be no doubt was well founded." [BC-p.116]

A hasty council was convened among Williamson's men to decide the fate of the Moravians in light of the discovery of the settler's property in possession of the captives, and the overwhelming conviction that the Indians were guilty of raiding the frontier. After a brief discussion, during which some of the militiamen advised that the Indians should be taken back to Pittsburgh for General Irvine to decide their fate, a vote was called by those men in favor of executing the guilty Indians, whereupon the fate of the Moravians was sealed, although 18 of the militiamen refused to vote to execute the Indians.

Those few men in opposition to the whole declared they would not take part in the "ghastly retaliation" which would put to death 96 men, women, children, and babies, most of whom could not have possibly taken part in any raiding parties across the river due to their sex and age, saying "that it would be murdering a people whose innocence was beyond question." [NL-p.124] Nonetheless, the majority of the votes from the men decided that none of the Moravians should be spared. Those men who considered themselves God-fearing Christians and stood in opposition to the killings "wrung their hands, and calling God to witness that they were innocent of the blood of these harmless Christian Indians, they withdrew from distance from the scene of slaughter," riding to a spot outside of town where they would not see or hear the act of vengeful murder, which in their minds, was no less terrible as that perpetrated against Mrs. Wallace.

On the morning of March 8, the slaughter of the Moravians began. It was decided that a large cooper's mallet found in one of the houses would be used to knock the victims on the head to dispatch each one of them. Each one of the Indians submitted without a struggle to the executioners, who were forced to take turns swinging the mallet, as the work quickly became tiresome, crushing the skulls of the prisoners, and then scalping them in turn, inside the buildings. The horrible work took a great deal of time, during which the dwindling Indians still alive awaiting their turn were forced to hear the terrible shrieks and the hammering of human skulls as the executions proceeded. When the killings were finished, the militiamen gathered up all the plunder they could carry, and then put to the torch all of buildings in the village of Gnadenhutten and nearby Salem, including the churches as well as the two buildings filled with the corpses of the slain Indians, determined that the villages would never again be used by Indians "as their jumping-off point for attacks on the pioneers." [HW1-p.187] With their work done, Williamson and the militia gathered up nearly 100 horses taken from the Indians, and headed back east along the trail leading to the Ohio River and Wheeling, with more than 90 Indian scalps taken as trophies of their recent handiwork. The only survivors of the mass execution of the Moravian Indians were "two boys who succeeded in eluding the militia," [BC-p.116] who ran to the Upper Sandusky with the news of the massacre.

"Were Surrounded by 15,000 of the Enemy and Taken"

Once the two boys reached the Upper Sandusky with their shocking tale, news of the mass murder of the Moravian Delawares spread like wildfire throughout the Indian villages of the Ohio Country, inciting among all the tribes an outrage against the Americans that called for revenge. Simon Girty, who had just returned to the Lower Sandusky Indian village with the war party of Wyandots who had been raiding the settlements across the Ohio at the same time the Moravians were slain, was informed of the news that just reached the village on April 12. "The Moravians that went from Upper Sandusky this spring to fetch their corn from their towns where they lived last summer are all killed by the Virginia militia. The number of dead amounts to 96 men, women and children. There is a Delaware man arrived that has been sometime confined at

Fort Pitt has made his escape, and he informs that all the Delawares that lived there as friends of the Americans, are all killed by the Virginians." [HP-30]

Though Girty had always expected the Virginians to respond in kind against the Indians, he was shocked by the number of Indians killed, of whom almost half were women and children. Girty knew this would incite the Delawares and Wyandots to retaliate against the frontier settlements and commit untold atrocities against the settlers which Girty would be powerless to stop, even if he were ordered to do so. If that should happen, he expected that no more white prisoners would be brought in by the Indians for questioning, for the Indians would undoubtedly kill them all. Already, Girty was having a difficult time convincing the Indians at Sandusky to turn over a white prisoner to him for questioning. Rather, the Indians wished to burn him over their fires in revenge for the massacre of the Moravian Delawares. Noting that a war party just returning from the frontier, "have brought in 14 men's scalps, and four male prisoners, so that there have neither women or child suffered this time." [HP-30] Simon Girty knew as he left for the Upper Sandusky, that the policy of the Indians which spared captive women and children would soon change. With the merciless killing of the Moravian women and children at the hands of the Enemy, no white woman or child would be exempt from the hatchet, scalping knife, or the fire again.

Alexander McKee had a great deal of important news to send to Major DePeyster on April 10 which had come to him at the upper Shawnee town from various Indian runners arriving from different directions. Several Delaware warriors whom Williamson had taken as prisoners to Fort Pitt the previous fall, upon release, had reached McKee's village with the startling news about the massacred Moravians which McKee felt was sure to "fuel retaliatory raids of unprecedented brutality" [NL-p.124] once the Indians reacted fully. "Some of the Moravian Indians who were taken last fall at their Corn Fields by the Enemy, having returned with messages to inform their friends that they would not be molested in their returning to save their corn, most of them went thither upon this business and upon their arrival there, took the first opportunity of informing their Brethren the Virginians thereof, who upon hearing it, assembled and came there to the number of between 400 and 500 and massacred all that fell into their Hands which has been 80 persons, who made no resistance, relying upon the promise of safety, and holding up the speech wampum which they had received from the Virginians to encourage their going there who now paid no regard to it, but Slaughtered and Scalped without distinction it is said," McKee wrote to DePeyster. "They have not taken a single prisoner, which appears as if those of their people who are now and may hereafter fall into the Hands of the Indians are held in no great estimation by them." [HP-262]

The news worried McKee. Now that all the Indians knew what had happened, war parties were preparing to hit the frontier with a vengeance previously unheard of. The Delaware warriors especially were vowing to kill every white man, woman and child that they could find, and to burn any prisoner unfortunate enough to fall into their hands. McKee's source of intelligence on the enemy, gleaned from captives taken by the Indians was now in jeopardy, for he could see soon none would be brought in alive, but killed for their scalps. Even the party of 11 men brought in "a few days ago by the Delaware, whom they took upon the Ohio with two boat loads of flour going to the Mississippi" were not all going to be sent up to Detroit. "The chief of the party takes with him five of the above prisoners to deliver up, the rest are in the hands of the chiefs." [HP-49] McKee could see the fires being kindled around the unfortunate prisoner who stood bound to the post naked and painted black. Soon his shrieks of pain would fill the air, as the first of the six men would be slowly burned alive by the Delawares avenging their dead cousins.

Major DePeyster at Detroit sat stunned at his desk. He could hardly believe the news that he just read, on April 18 from the dispatch reaching him that morning. Apparently the rumors told to him were true. "The Army under the Command of Lord Cornwallis, which consisted of Five Thousand British troops and Two Thousand Loyalists, were surrounded by 15,000 of the Enemy and taken at York Town in Virginia, at the same time the Harbor was Blocked up by the French fleet, however that he had made the best Terms he could was himself returned to England upon Parole." [HP-262] Equally shocking in importance to the loss of the British army which undoubtedly spelled the end of the British effort to put down the rebellion by force, was that the news had not come to DePeyster from Haldimand at Headquarters in Quebec, but sent to him by Alexander McKee in the Ohio Country, taken from independent confirmations from separate prisoners brought in from the frontiers. No word had as yet arrived from Quebec, the British command was strangely quiet. DePeyster did not know what to think. He wondered what would happen if the Rebels attempted another expedition against Detroit from the direction of Fort Pitt, as the dispatches from both Simon Girty and Alexander McKee predicted would occur, from intelligence taken from captured Virginian soldiers in the past month. Would DePeyster receive the necessary provisions, ammunition and reinforcements he requested if Detroit was to be held?

"I Now Send Joseph Down"

General Powell at Niagara opened the packet of orders labeled "Private" just received from General Haldimand written on April 21. Powell had already been privy to Cornwallis' surrender and Haldimand's decision to refortifying Oswego, but he had followed his explicit orders and had not informed either DePeyster at Detroit or Sinclair at the post of Michilimackinac of the latest developments, awaiting further word. "I have lately received a dispatch from Sir Henry Clinton dated the 2nd of February, an extract I send you, another dated the 10th of March says that notwithstanding his former Intelligence, he has more reason to think that New York is the object of the Enemy's design, and not Canada. If an attempt against Detroit was really in agitation, I conceive it must have been upon the original Co-operating Plan, and if that is laid aside for New York, it must have reached the knowledge of Major DePeyster and of course have been communicated to you. My not having yet heard from you confirms me in the opinion that every thing is quiet in that quarter," Haldimand wrote to his officer. "You will nevertheless communicate the enclosed to Major DePeyster, giving him orders to take every precaution possible for the safety of his Post, as will in regard to securing all the provisions he can from the settlement should the Enemy advance. Should you therefore find it absolutely necessary to reinforce Detroit, there is no alternative but withdrawing one or two companies of the Rangers from Oswego," which Haldimand did wish to do (at all costs). That would weaken Oswego just as it was in the process of being turned into a stronghold by Major Ross and the troops under his command, now underway. Becoming philosophical about attempting to do so much with so little in the face of an apparent hopeless situation, Haldimand commented, "We are governed by Contingencies and not Contingencies by us, we must therefore act for the Best." [HP-176]

Major DePeyster said farewell to Joseph Brant as he boarded the sloop for Niagara, as his leg now well enough for him to travel. "I now send Joseph down agreeable to your desire, he takes his band of Senecas." Returning with Brant was Lieutenant Thomas Butler of the Rangers along with "19 recruits for Colonel Butler's Corps" drawn from professed Loyalists at Detroit. "I hope soon to see an Officer to replace him as the Rangers will soon move for the Indian Country. When the Sick and the Lame are taken off, the Rangers are so few, that Captain Caldwell hopes, and I am sure I have reason to hope, it will not be insisted upon that he sends the remainder of Captain Thompson's detachment, and that the remainder of Captain Caldwell's Company will join him by the first opportunity." [HP-174] General Powell was not so sure. "As to the Rangers, it was impossible to comply with his demand, for when 200 men are detached from this Garrison, it will be with difficulty we shall be able to carry on the works. If an attack should be made upon it, a strong reinforcement will be required to defend it properly," Powell responded. As to DePeyster's request for an eight-inch howitzer for Fort Lernoult, "it is now, as it was then," last fall, "impossible to send one, but I have sent everything we had to spare" for DePeyster to bolster the fortifications of Detroit by mid-April. [HP-173]

"Lend The Fort's Surgeon, Dr. Knight"

By early May 1782, it became apparent to General William Irvine, in command of Fort Pitt, that Colonel Williamson's militia expedition to the Tuscarawas in pursuit of Indian raiding parties, and his subsequent execution of the Christian Delaware Indians, had stirred up a hornet's nest of hostile Indian activity against the Pennsylvanian and Virginian frontier on the east bank of the Ohio River. Report after report was brought to him detailing accounts of atrocities committed against isolated settlers' cabins by small war parties of Indians slipping across the river unnoticed and striking before anyone could stop them or give chase. Frontier scouts reported to Irvine that the tracks of the Indians led in the direction of the Upper Sandusky Indian villages where it was known that the British-supplied Indians were coming from. With the inhabitants of the surrounding counties clamoring for something to be done to stop the Indian attacks, General Irvine, having been granted by Congress the power to call out the militia in the defense of the countryside, weighed all the possibilities before calling on the militia captains to discuss a proposed strike against the hostile Upper Sandusky Indian villages. The garrison at Detroit, the bastion of British authority in the west, was well beyond the reach of the Americans at Fort Pitt, [HW1-p.181] and would not be the ultimate target.

The militia had considered a plan to attack Detroit from Fort Pitt, but after reviewing the abortive attempt by General McIntosh years before, and taking into consideration Clark's inability to march from the Falls of the Ohio against Detroit, "it was finally determined, with the consent of General Irvine having first been obtained, to organize a volunteer force and assail these savages in their homes," [BC-p.120] at the Upper Sandusky villages. The Indians attacking the frontiers of the militia were leaving from those villages, and not from Detroit. It was to utterly destroy once and for all the Indians, "for their aggressions had become wholly intolerable to the border men" [BC-p.120] and that was of primary importance. As a result of the meetings, General Irvine gave the orders in the first week of May for recruiting to begin at once in "Westmoreland and Washington counties of Pennsylvania, and of Ohio County, Virginia," [BC-p.120] for the undertaking planned for the end of the month.

There was no problem finding volunteers for the expedition once word circulated through the settlements that the object of the campaign was to destroy the Indians attacking the frontier. General Irvine had let it be known as general knowledge to all the men recruited, that due to the lack of ample material support from the meager stores at Fort Pitt, each man would "have to supply his own weapons and ammunition, provisions for the entire trip, and a horse." [HW1-p.181] If they were to be successful, Irvine envisioned that the army would need to be mounted and travel as fast as possible to reach the Indian villages, take them by surprise, and catch the Indians before they had a chance to disperse and elude the attackers. Furthermore, Irvine reluctantly declared that he was unable to provide any regular troops stationed at Fort Pitt for the expedition, having been ordered by General Washington to strictly keep the regulars defending the vital fort which was the key to holding the frontier from British attack. What Irvine would agree to do was to lend "his own personal aide-de-camp, Major Rose, and the fort's surgeon, Dr. John Knight," [HW1-p.181] for any assistance they could provide the militia force.

"Children! This Belt is Shown to You to Sharpen Your War Hatchets"

Major Ross read the letter with disgust. The note written on May 4 by General Haldimand at his headquarters in Montreal had just reached Ross at the new post of Oswego a week later. An impatient man, Ross was in the midst of the heavy construction on the fortifications of the post at the mouth of the

Oswego River. Every one of the 809 men employed at the post were engaged in the long tiring task of either cutting timbers upriver, transporting wood to the site of the fort, or laboriously digging the entrenchments. [HP-354] Now, at the height of the work when every man was desperately needed if Major Ross were to complete the work ordered by Haldimand, he was going to have to give up men. "I am sorry to acquaint you that there is a probability of your losing a Company or two of the Rangers, should a Report from Detroit prove well-founded, as it says that an Expedition against that Place and the Indian Country under Mr. Clark, with a considerable Force in forwardness. Major DePeyster has already applied for a Reinforcement, and should Clark advance, it will be absolutely necessary to send one." [HP-321] Ross wondered how the General expected him to complete the fortifications on time if the enemy should decide to intervene.

General Powell at Niagara was sure he was doing the right thing on May 10 by sending reinforcements immediately to Detroit without consulting Haldimand. In light of the information just reaching him from DePeyster from intelligence gathered from Rebel prisoners captured by the Indians on the Virginian frontier, it appeared that a Rebel expedition from the area of Fort Pitt was soon to leave for the Ohio Country and the Upper Sandusky. There was no time to request Rangers be sent to Detroit from Major Ross at Niagara. Although it weakened Powell's position at the fort, it was imperative that he send reinforcements as quickly as he could. "I sent off Lieutenant Turney with 24 Rangers, which were intended to relieve an equal number of the late Captain Thompson's Company, but I have now desired Major DePeyster to keep the whole if he finds it absolutely necessary, and propose to complete them to the number mentioned, should I receive advice of the Enemy's advancing in Force." [HP-175] Major DePeyster at Detroit was more certain than ever that the Rebels intended to attack Detroit from the direction of Fort Pitt in light of the information that Alexander McKee had brought with him to Detroit. The recent prisoners taken by the Indians now arrived for interrogation and their stories proved that a major Rebel expedition was soon to leave Fort Pitt. It was more important than ever that DePeyster address the Indian chiefs and warriors from the Ottawas, Wyandots, Chippewas, and Pottawattamies on the morning of May 10. They had come to the Council from their villages surrounding Detroit, and he felt he must prepare them to accompany the Rangers to meet the new threat. With "Mrs. Baby, Chesne, and Druilliard interpreting," Major DePeyster asked that Alexander McKee and Captain Caldwell speak to the Indians after he was finished, with the aim of convincing the tribes to send as many warriors as possible to support Caldwell who was readying his men to leave by boat for Sandusky.

Raising the wampum belt signifying the alliance between the western Indians of the Ohio Country and the English King, DePeyster spoke. "Children! This belt has been already shown to you for to sharpen your War hatchets as it was sent here by the Six Nations for that purpose. I shall not show you again the Belts on which Our Alliance is founded nor repeat to you that the King of England

and his Indian Children are but one. I shall only present this War Belt that you may all again sharpen your hatchets as it is necessary you should do so, and I hope you will not leave any of them dull. It is a good thing to have this belt by us to keep our hatchets always in order, and it enables us always to succeed." [HP-264] Major DePeyster raised the belt again high over his head, shaking it for emphasis to add to his words. The warriors and chiefs immediately howled their war cries in support, and waved their hatchets in unison, high above their heads. Alexander McKee and Captain Caldwell could see that the Major had done a good job in convincing the Indians to go to war. The two men hoped that they would be as successful in the field in defeating the Rebel army, if it should come, a far more difficult task than stirring the blood of the Indians to fight.

"Take Up Lieutenant Turney on Their Way"

On the morning of May 16, Captain Caldwell inspected the "68 Rangers" [HP-354] of his own Company and those men of Thompson's still at Detroit. With a nod of approval at the smartly dressed green-coated Rangers who carried the heavy packs loaded with provisions, gunpowder and shot for the trip to Sandusky and the upper Indian villages, Caldwell ordered his detachment to form up in column and board the "Faith" docked at the Detroit wharf. Major DePeyster had given Caldwell his orders after the Indian Council. DePeyster had written to General Powell, relaying his orders to Caldwell, and he hoped that the General would understand. "I see by the Intelligence that it confirms the attack now intended upon Sandusky. I hope, Sir, that this necessary movement will apologize for my not sending back the remainder of late Captain Thompson's Detachment, which will be most assuredly wanted with Captain Caldwell." Thinking of how the Indians would react if "the offering to delay, or lessen the small assistance promised to them would throw a damp upon the minds of the Indians, I shall therefore let the troops under orders proceed."

With the Rangers loaded, Captain Caldwell arranged for their horses to be sent by the long route overland to Sandusky, accompanied by parties of the Wyandots and Ottawas. The warriors of the Lake Indian tribes promised to leave in a few days to join Caldwell as soon as they were adequately supplied. As the sloop "Faith" with the Rangers aboard was preparing to cast off from its moorings and edge into the waters of the Detroit River, the sloop "Hope" came into view from the mouth of the river with dispatches for DePeyster from Powell at Niagara. Powell's dispatch confirmed that the two officers were thinking alike. Powell had ordered Caldwell and his Company of Rangers were to advance to Sandusky, and to either "take up Lieutenant Turney and his men on their way, or should they miss of him, he can be sent after Them," [HP-176] to Sandusky. This would reinforce Caldwell's detachment with an additional 15 men, bringing the total number of Rangers to 84 officers and men under arms to throw against the Rebels. Caldwell would not need to wait for long for them. On board the "Hope" gliding into the wharf, Caldwell could see on deck Lieutenant Turney and his men.

.

"Six Days of Incessant Rain"

With the Rangers and Indians underway at last for Sandusky, Major DePeyster prepared a letter to General Powell on May 16 reporting the details to the commander, the latest intelligence brought in from an express received from Sandusky, "informing that two of the scouting parties fell in with the Enemy on this side of the Ohio opposite to Wheeling, on the road to Sandusky. Some of the Indians were wounded and escaped with difficulty, not having been able to estimate the number of the enemy. A deserter from them arrived at Sandusky, who reports that their number amount to one thousand from the neighborhood of Wheeling, designed against the villages of Sandusky. The chiefs have sent for assistance promised upon them the like occasions, which I cannot refuse them without running the risk of losing the confidence of the Indians." [HP-27] Reporting on the movement of the Rangers, "I send off Captain Caldwell with the Rangers and some Canadian Volunteers, and the Lake Indians, with a proportion of ammunition which I hope will give spirits to the Wyandots."

DePeyster had two additional reports to make. One concerned the prisoners, Major Cracraft, and Captains Orr and Irwin, taken "on the river by Joseph Brant" during the campaign of the previous summer. "By this opportunity I send down one Major and two Captains, with some women and children, desirous to follow their fortunes, and some other prisoners as per enclosed." [HP-27] Thirty-one of them were loaded on the "Angelica" for Niagara and eventually Quebec, and Major DePeyster was glad to see them go. Providing housing and food for the prisoners and their children had put a strain on the men of the garrison. They were forced to give up their quarters to Margaret Reynolds and Margaret Link and their 12 children taken prisoner by Captain Bird and the Delawares during the campaign to Kentucky during April and June of 1780. [HP-365] In the meantime, DePeyster now had to concern himself with an old reoccurring problem at Fort Lernoult. Powell was informed by DePeyster that "I am returned from reviewing a disagreeable situation which is no less than the destruction of a great part of our works occasioned by six days of incessant rain." [HP-27]

"Their Future Existence As A People Depending Upon It"

Alexander McKee had a loose end to tie up before leaving with the Shawnee to the upper villages to raise the alarm of the Rebel expedition and rally as many warriors as possible to meet Caldwell's force and the Wyandots whom Simon Girty was preparing to accompany. This would be McKee's last chance to write to Haldimand to request compensation for his losses and expenses before he left. Why Major DePeyster at Detroit, and General Powell and Colonel Johnson at Niagara could not simply help McKee with this important matter was beyond him. Sitting down at last on May 15, McKee wrote, "I beg to inform Your Excellency that since my residence in this country, I have done myself the honor to write to Your Excellency several letters." That none of them had elicited a response from Haldimand, vexed McKee at the moment. Listing once again to Haldimand his long service in the Indian Department and the debts he had accumulated in living with the Indians, McKee noted that "to my disappointment I find they still remain unpaid which is disadvantageous to me having interest to pay for a considerable amount and though I had authority to make expenses, yet it was difficult for me to preserve papers in the dangerous situation I was in," McKee wrote. "I came here but a few days ago from the Southward where I have been several months past upon Service, and as Intelligence is received of some designs of the Enemy to invade the Indian Country, am about returning again. That Your Excellency will be pleased to give directions for the payment of my accounts which I flatter myself will appear just and reasonable." [HP-265] With that done, McKee sealed the letter and gave it to Major DePeyster to send with the packets destined for Niagara and Quebec, McKee now set his sights for the Ohio Country and the Shawnee whom he must rally for war.

In the past month General Haldimand moved to Montreal to be closer to the western posts including Oswego. He busied himself with the reports reaching him from those posts, including Detroit. In picking up the correspondence from DePeyster, he read the officer's lengthy rebuttal of Haldimand's request for an explanation of the inconsistencies in DePeyster's accounting of the post in relation to supplying the Indians. The General realized that DePeyster had taken the matter as a personal affront, which was not intended. Perhaps Haldimand considered that his tone might have been construed by Major DePeyster to be pointed and direct, but Haldimand had not intended to offend. Yet with so much at stake in the western wilderness, Haldimand could not allow himself the luxury of apologizing to a man whose Dutch sensibilities had been jarred by Haldimand's Swiss forthrightness. Haldimand had a war to conduct and a country entrusted to him to hold. Consequently, as a matter of duty, he did not need to explain himself to his officers. "I depend upon your exerting your utmost efforts and abilities as well to convince the Indians of the indispensable necessity there is for their resisting this shock with Unanimity and Firmness, their future Existence as a people depending on it, as in taking every possible Precaution for the security of Your Post in which I persuade myself I shall not be disappointed." [HP-11] Firmness would be needed at Detroit now more than ever, Haldimand told himself, with all indications pointing to an enemy on the move towards that post and the Indian Country.

"Would Simply Stop Where They Were"

Colonel William Crawford, at age 50, was a veteran of many wilderness war campaigns against the Indians, having served in the French and Indian War, Pontiac's Rebellion and Lord Dunmore's War. Having just be elected by the militia on May 24 to command the expedition to attack the Indians of the Upper Sandusky, Colonel Crawford advised the scouts leaving ahead of the 480 man force assembled at "Mingo Bottom on the Virginia shore about 20 miles above Fort Henry," [HW1-p.181] to keep a sharp lookout for Indian scouting parties on the trail across the river from their camp, leading to the Muskingum River and Sandusky beyond. Colonel David Williamson, who led the militia in the Gnadenhutten campaign, was elected by the men to serve as Crawford's second in command. As the mounted troops crossed the shallows of the Ohio on the morning of May 25 to begin the expedition, Williamson urged Crawford to set a swifter pace, knowing that the "the usual lack of discipline among the militia" [HW1-p.182] was the cause of their slow going, once they had crossed the river and began ascending the trail to the interior of the Ohio Country. Williamson worried that their force would not be able to reach the Upper Sandusky in time to take the Indians by surprise, as he had done with the Moravians at Gnadenhutten.

Colonel Crawford, a survivor of Braddock's defeat at the hands of the Indians years ago was not so sure that a quick pace was entirely warranted. He did not want his force to ride into an enemy ambush without the handful of scouts deployed ahead having time to adequately scour the trail for hidden Indians. Crawford worried that with so many men crammed together on the narrow path through the woods, in the event of an unforeseen Indian attack, the men would become easily targets on their mounts, being unable to turn the horses to escape an enfilade, if it should occur. They would be cut down, as Braddock's troops were felled by Indians firing from cover on either side of the trail. Besides, Crawford had taken a serious look at the condition of some of the horses that the militiamen were riding. He estimated that better than half of those horses were draft animals, adequate for farm work, but not suited for a forced march of any distance, and in danger of giving out if pushed too hard.

Williamson's advice to Crawford to take the Indians of the Upper Sandusky by surprise was not without merit, however the expedition was much greater in size than Williamson's smaller force, which meant that it took more time to move almost 500 men on a single trail. Also, the distance was much farther to the Upper Sandusky region than to Gnadenhutten, and the number of Indians opposing them was more sizable and formidable than, by and large, the peaceful Moravian Delawares. In reality, the Indians at Upper Sandusky had been on alert ever since the skirmish between a handful of militiamen and a returning Indian war party, which occurred more than a week before as the Indians were crossing the Ohio. The Indians at Upper Sandusky sent out scouts to the Ohio to watch for any sign of the Virginian expedition if they indeed should come as prisoners had informed them. Thus, when the militiamen began assembling on the Virginia side of the river at the designated spot for a camp, unseen Indian eyes were watching from the west side of the river, counting horses and heads, and reporting those numbers by runner to the Upper Sandusky villages, where preparations were underway to meet the Enemy. In fact, at every leg of the journey, the militiamen were watched by the Indians who were advised not to give away their positions, but to keep the villages informed on the movement of the column.

By May 29, four days after leaving the Ohio River, Colonel Crawford had to admit to himself that the expedition was proceeding far slower than he would have liked it to, having just reached the banks of the Tuscarawas River, with several days yet to go to reach their objective. Their lack of progress was due to the great difficulty in keeping the militia moving as one body, as men were "often wandering away from the army, in little groups of two or three, to hunt. Quite often they would simply stop where they were to debate what course of action they should next follow," [HW1-p.182] until either Crawford, Williamson, or McClelland would demand the men keep moving. The indiscriminate shooting by some of the men irked Crawford to no end. No only was it a waste of precious ammunition that might be needed later, but it served to attract unnecessary attention, giving away their position to any Indians in the area, alerting them to their presence. The scouts John Slover and Jonathan Zane were ordered to apprehend any Indians they should come upon on the trail ahead to prevent them from escaping to the Upper Sandusky villages to inform the Indians there on the approach of the militia. As yet, the two men reported no sign whatsoever of Indians.

While Crawford was glad that no Indians had as yet been encountered, it bothered him too. Common sense told him that as the expedition drew closer to the enemy, his scouts should have come across someone accidentally on the trail, yet not an Indian man, woman, or child had been spotted. Williamson and the other officers did not give any credence to Crawford's misgivings when voiced to them, dismissing the lack of Indians as a sign of their own good fortune, and proof that their expedition would take the Indians by surprise. While not disconcerting to Crawford, he did recall that Braddock's scouts had not spotted Indians until they were on top of them. Crawford acknowledged to himself that while having not seen an Indian since leaving the Ohio River could mean that his army might surprise them a the Upper Sandusky, common sense also told him that possibly their expedition was already known to the Indians, who were preparing to attack his army somewhere up ahead on the trail. With many pressing matters to worry about, the veteran officer decided to put his apprehension to the back of his mind, knowing that if he started drawing any similarities between his expedition and Braddock's, he would end up talking himself and his men out of proceeding any further.

"To Direct the Movements of the Indians"

At the cluster of Indian villages at the Upper Sandusky, the Delaware, Wyandot and Mingo warriors and the men of the British Indian Department hurried their preparations on June 1 to meet the approaching enemy. A steady stream of runners came in with the latest word of the advance of the Virginians, now known to have crossed the Muskingum River, heading in the direction of Half King's Wyandot town. Simon Girty and his brother George were everywhere, urging the Chiefs of the Delawares, Wyandots and Mingoes to call in their absent warriors who off hunting or visiting at the Lower Sandusky village. "Girty was with the Half King when the account reached the Wyandots of the actual marching of Crawford." [BC-p.121] Girty had word sent immediately to the Delawares at Wingenund's village, and at Captain Pipe's town near

Wingenund's, and to all the villages southward as far as the upper Shawnee towns at Wapatomika and on the Scioto River to bring their warriors in haste to Half King's town, where the Virginian army was apparently headed to attack.

Girty saw to it that ammunition and provisions were divided up among the arriving warriors, who busied themselves with cleaning their guns, sharpening their knives, plucking their hair, and painting themselves for war. Preparations were made to move all the women and children of the village to a hidden location in a deep, wooded ravine some distance to the north of Half King's town, near the juncture of Tymochtee Creek and the Sandusky River, where they would be safe from the enemy, if the enemy should reach the Wyandot village. A runner from the north brought word to Girty informing him that Captain Caldwell and his Rangers reached the Lower Sandusky, but were waiting the arrival of their horses before setting out for the Upper Villages. Girty learned that Matthew Elliott was at Lower Sandusky, preparing the Lake Indians from Detroit to set out in the morning or the next to join with him at the Half King's town. No word had reached Girty or Half King on the progress of Alexander McKee and the Shawnee chief Black Snake who were expected to arrive from their villages to the south on the Mad River with a large body of warriors. Simon Girty could only hope that once the battle commenced, that McKee and the Shawnee would reach them with a large enough force of warriors to defeat the Virginians.

On the morning of June 3, Crawford and his army left the wooded rolling hills west of the Tuscarawas River valley, and entered the flat, open grasslands called the Sandusky Plains by the scouts, which extended all the way to the upper reaches of the Sandusky River and the Indian villages. Moving in column, the militiamen could see in the distance isolated groves of trees dotting the wide, expansive plains covered with thick, high grasses which made an army traveling on horseback highly visible to any Indians who might be scouting. Gradually, the boisterousness of Crawford's men began to change to apprehension as each man realized that they were getting closer to their intended target and the high grasses might conceal Indians who might try to ambush them. Still, the three men scouting ahead of the column had not spotted a single Indian. Unfortunately, this did nothing to ease the growing fears of many of the men, who now were clearly apprehensive. Reaching a shaded spring along the trail, Crawford ordered a halt. It was late afternoon, and Crawford thought it best that the men and horses refresh themselves, and camp there for the evening. Jonathan Zane, who had been to the Upper Sandusky previously as a captive of the Indians, remarked to the officers that they were only seven miles from the first of the Indian villages, called Half King's old town.

At nearly the same time, Matthew Elliott and his large party of warriors painted for battle settled into their own camp along the banks of the Sandusky River halfway between the lower and upper villages, preparing to set out at first light on the trail leading to the south. They kept their weapons and packs close at hand, ready to move immediately at daybreak. Upon arriving at Sandusky, Captain Caldwell in command of the Rangers, had met with Elliott at the lower village, telling him that in the event of hostilities, Major DePeyster had ordered Elliott "to direct the movements of the Indians" [BC-p.122] in conjunction with McKee, if he should arrive with the Shawnee, and to support the Wyandots under the Half King with Simon and George Girty assisting. Elliott agreed with the leadership role, and immediately informed all the Indians of the various tribes present. In the dim light of their campfires, warriors of the Chippewa, Ottawa, Pottawattamie, Wyandot, and Mingo tribes sang their war songs into the night as they prepared themselves to meet the enemy at last. [HR-p.37]

"Dance The War Song, Whooping and Stamping"

Just before dawn on June 4, Colonel Crawford had his officers rouse the militiamen to break camp for an early start on the final leg of their journey to attack the Indians, knowing that a confrontation with them was highly likely, especially if they were to catch any of them by surprise in their villages ahead. Crawford's scouts were already in the field moving far ahead of the army, searching for the Indians, and alert for any ambush by them, if it should come. The militiamen moved slowly on the advance, for it was now evident to Crawford and his officers, that many of the farm horses were in no shape to move any quicker, not being suited to the rigors of extended riding, and were thus exhausted and played out by the morning of June 4, some being unable to move at all. However, Crawford had no choice but to keep the army moving ahead. With provisions for the men running low, he knew they could not tarry to allow the horses several days to rest at the spring. Within a couple of hours of dawn, a rider was spotted returning from the scouts to the north. He reported that while they had seen some Indians in the distance, upon reaching the first village on the east bank of the Sandusky River, the village known to be the Wyandot town of Half King's where the Moravians held been settled during the previous winter called Captive's Town, it was found to be completely deserted.

Soon the scout John Slover arrived to confer with Colonel Crawford and his officers. He told them that he was "of the opinion that the Indians of the upper town had moved to the lower one," and if the army crossed the river and moved in the direction of the trail which headed north along the river, "settlements, he thought would soon be reached," [BC2-p.202] recalling the whereabouts of the lower villages from the times he had been there years before. Agreeing with his scout, Crawford gave the order for the army to move out to cross the Sandusky River to the west side, "just below the site of the old town, at a point half a mile from the deserted Moravian huts." [BC2-p.202] At a point about three miles north of the river ford, the army reached a springs along the trail, where several men stopped to water their horses, and complain to their officers that as their provisions were low, and their horses spent, they thought it wise to turn around, "for the first time expressing a desire to return home." Hearing the argument, Colonel Crawford ordered a halt to his division of men at one o'clock in the afternoon of June 4, and called his officers to a council of war, inviting both Dr. Knight, and Major Rose, Irvine's aide-de-camp, to determine their next move, now that Jonathan Zane had just returned from scouting the enemy downriver. More than anything else, the men wanted to hear what Zane had discovered and what he thought was going to happen. [BC2-p.203]

Unknown to the militia, several miles to the north of them, a force of nearly 200 Indians and a handful of white men were preparing to leave Half King's village to cross the Sandusky River and lay an ambush for them. The Delaware war chief, Captain Pipe, with Wingenund and the Delaware warriors made up nearly half of the force. The Wyandot chief Half King with Simon and George Girty accompanying him had nearly as many Wyandot warriors at the rendevous, and at noon on June 4, Matthew Elliott resplendent in a British officer's red coat of the King's Eighth, arrived with the Indians collected from the lower Sandusky village, with news that Captain Caldwell and nearly 90 Rangers and Canadians were on their way from Sandusky to meet them. After stripping off their excess clothing and carefully painting their bodies and faces in the garish colors and symbols of war, each of the warriors began to sing and dance the war song, "whooping and stamping" in wide circles around the central blackened post erected in the camp for that purpose. Many warriors struck the post with their hatchets, signifying their hatred of the Americans, and their intent to strike a death blow against them in battle, if they should meet. The Frenchman Le Villiers and a few other men from Detroit, along with Simon and George Girty, painted themselves as well in the custom of the warriors about to meet the enemy in the field of battle. Then when all was ready, Elliott, Half King, and the Girtys signaled with war whoops to begin crossing the river at the ford, and the wild assemblage of warriors with a resounding chorus of whoops and yells, waded through the shallows, to set out south towards the Americans, their muskets in hand, and scalping knives and war hatchets in their belts.

Captain William Caldwell and the Rangers had spent the night of June 3 at the trader's post at Lower Sandusky. There he had his men open the sealed kegs of gunpowder and by candlelight and oil lamp, rolled pre-measured amounts of powder and ball into cartridges from the scraps of paper that William Arundel and Abraham Coon were able to provide him. With no horses to spare, Caldwell realized that he had little way of transporting the small carriage-less artillery pieces that had been off-loaded with him and his men from the crew of the "Faith." However, Caldwell was sure from the information brought in by runners that the Rebel army had no artillery either, and were not about to fortify themselves in any position where that artillery could be used. As the enemy was mounted, and with few provisions, Caldwell reasoned that they would be constantly on the move. Consequently, artillery of his own would be more a nuisance for him to bring up to the upper villages, and would not only slow him down, but if he were able to bring the pieces into position, he would have to detach some of his men to fire the cannon, which he did not want to spare. Having heard from Captain Bird at Detroit that these Virginian militia were not of the same caliber and quality as the men of the Mohawk Valley, Caldwell determined that volley fire from his companies of men would be far move effective against the enemy than a cannon, which in the open field, would cause to Indians to hesitate. At the first light of dawn on the morning of June 4, Caldwell had his Rangers check their equipment one last time, then saddle up and set out up the trail to the upper villages at a good pace. Accompanying him were a handful of French volunteers and the last Indians left at Lower Sandusky.

"In a Moment, The First Shots Were Fired"

The Virginia militia watered their mounts and checked their weapons and gear at the resting spot near the springs at first light. Colonel Crawford asked Jonathan Zane for his opinion of what he thought was the situation facing the militia force so that the officers present in the council of war could come to some decision as to what to do. The scout spoke up so all the men could hear, "advising an immediate return" of the army to the Ohio, for he feared that at this point in their advance, the Indians not only were aware of their presence, but also because "none of the Indians had, as yet, been discovered in the Plains was a sure evidence, in his judgment, that they were concentrating at some point nor far away for a determined resistance." After listening to Zane, Colonel Crawford told the officers that he was in agreement with Zane, and although "a further march into their country…would only be giving more time to the enemy to gather reinforcements." [BC2-p.203] A heated argument ensued between some of the men, who argued they had come a long way at great personal expense to themselves and their men, and as the purpose of the expedition was to destroy the Indians preying upon the homes and families of their neighbors and friends, which they had not as yet even attempted to do, and if they returned home now without killing even one Indian, they would be called cowards by everyone on the frontier for not attempting to fight. After much debate, "it was finally determined by the council that the army should continue its march that afternoon, but no longer." [BC2-p.203]

With Indian scouts returning by the minute with news that the enemy force, which had halted for an hour at the springs on the west side of the Sandusky River about three miles below Half King's old village, was again on the move northward, Matthew Elliott conferred with Half King and the Girtys. He outlined a simple plan by which their force would spread out on a wide front across the grassland as they moved southward, so that they would be able to either lay an ambush for the approaching Americans and catch them in a wide Vee-shaped trap with the trail forming the center of the ambuscade, or force the Americans to the steep banks of the river and outflank them across the open plain, cutting off their avenue of retreat. While Half King and his chiefs agreed in theory with Elliott's plan, putting it into execution was a problem, for less than a mile since leaving Half King's town, the large body of warriors had already broken into several smaller parties, and keeping some semblance of order was going to be difficult with the warriors now strung out. Ahead, Half King pointed to the grove of trees that stood out in the distance on the higher point of ground more than a half mile away, and indicated to Elliott that he was going to take some of his warriors there to "secure the grove before the arrival of the Americans" which would give the Indians a decided advantage. Looking at Simon Girty who shrugged his shoulders, Elliott disagreed with the Wyandot chief who commanded so many warriors. Breaking their force in two was not a good thing when the enemy had a decided advantage in numbers. Nonetheless, Elliott acquiesced.

It was nearing two o'clock in the afternoon when Captain Caldwell and his mounted Rangers reached Half King's village, and stopped briefly to water their mounts and fill their canteens. An Indian runner sent by Matthew Elliott to find Caldwell and urge him to hurry to join the Indians reported that their scouts had seen the enemy force no more than a few miles ahead of the main body of Indians and a battle was sure to take place on the grassy plains bordering the trail to the south within the hour. As the Rangers mounted up and headed south, Captain Caldwell called Lieutenants Clench and Turney to his side, telling them that, depending on the disposition of the Rebels and whether they remained mounted or not, Caldwell decided his force should engage the enemy to their center, and by keeping up a constant fire and pressing them hard, that would allow the Indians time to flank the enemy force and attack their rear. Once the pressure from the Indians became too great, Caldwell hoped the militia would break and run, allowing them the opportunity to overrun their front and destroy them all. Caldwell wanted the Rangers divided roughly into three companies of two ranks of men. While the front rank was loading, the rear would fire over them, and then re-load while the front rank fired again, which would allow for a constant front of fire to be exerted against the Rebels at all times. Lieutenant Clench would command the left company, Lieutenant Turney would take the right, and Captain Caldwell himself would direct the center. Standing high in his stirrups, Caldwell could make out a copse of trees far in the distance to which it appeared the Indians were heading for. In a moment, the first shots were fired.

"A Quick Forward Movement With Brisk Firing"

While the officer's council was being held at the springs, Colonel Crawford sent ahead a small number of mounted men that he "previously formed into a company of light horse to act as scouts in advance of the army," [BC2-p.204] now that the trail through the woods had given way to the vast openness of the grassy plains. The mounted scouts "followed along the Indian trail, and were now reconnoitering the open country northeast of the spot where the council of war was deliberating," when "to the left of the trace they saw a beautiful island, or grove, which seemed to beckon them from the fierce heat of the sun. They drew up for a moment to enjoy the cool shade of its clustering oaks." [BC2-p.204] Halting under the trees for a moment, the scouts looked out over the high grassy plain "to the north and west spread out before them."

Finally deciding to move once again northwardly into the grasses bordering the Indian trail, the light horse scouts had gone a short distance when they suddenly and unexpectedly came into "full view of the enemy." Ahead of them the scouts could see a large body of warriors running towards them, having spotted the scouts on their horses before being seen themselves. Startled, "the scouts immediately drew together, and dispatched one of their number, riding their fleetest horse as an express, to inform Crawford of the discovery of the savages; and then wheeling about, retired slowly as the foe advanced." [BC2-p.204] The approaching warriors began to fire their muskets and rifles at the mounted men, thus indicating to the rest of their force the enemy's location, and that the battle was now engaged. Not only did Matthew Elliott and the Girty brothers take notice of the gunfire, and stop to prime and load their muskets, but William Caldwell's keen ears picked up the sound of gunfire in the distance, coming from the direction of the grove of trees. The battle was on.

The officer's council had just broken up and the militiamen as a whole were mounting up when the sound of gunfire was heard in the distance, and soon one of the scouts "from the north came riding up a full speed, announcing the discovery and advance of the savages." [BC2-p.206] While each man was filled with trepidation at the sounds he heard and the word swiftly passed that some of their men were engaged with the Indians, there was no longer any talk of heading back now that some of their own men were attacking the enemy ahead, and would need their support. Once every man had primed and loaded their weapons, orders were shouted by the officers for an advance of the troop by a column of four. Moving towards the sound of gunfire, Crawford's battalion met with the retiring light horsemen who were falling back along the trail, having been driven out of the copse of woods ahead and to Crawford's left, as the Indians, whom they reported were "just ahead and in considerable force, evidently prepared to offer them battle," [BC2-p.206] having taken possession of the grove of trees. Seeing the advantage the grove of trees on the higher spot of ground would give the Indians over his own men on the plains, Crawford immediately ordered the vanguard of the militiamen to dismount, and by means of a "quick, forward movement, with brisk firing," attempt to drive the Indians out of the trees and force them into the open prairie to the north, where the rest of his force could cut them down during the retreat. Crawford's plan worked in part when his men poured fire into the trees and then rushed the Indians, driving them from the island of woods into the prairie in panic. What he did not see until it was too late was that those Indians were only a part of the force opposing him. It was just at the moment when Crawford's men were rejoicing at their success that Matthew Elliott with the rest of the Delaware and Wyandot warriors entered the battle to reinforce the Indians retreating from the woods.

Elliott with the Delaware warrior Captain Pipe quickly appraised the situation and decided that Pipe would take the warriors with him and flank to the right of the militiamen in the woods working their way around the enemy and attacking them in the rear, thus sealing off their escape route. Elliott would urge some of the Indians to flank on the enemy's left while the Girtys with Half King would hold the center and pour a hot fire on the men in the woods, knowing that they could do nothing more than keep them pinned down on the higher ground to the front of them. As the volume of firing increased along the breadth of the tree line of the woods, Elliott could hear in the distance, firing from the other side of the woods that could only mean that the Indians under Pipe were attacking the militiamen in their rear. Knowing that their numbers were less than evenly matched with the enemy with the decided advantage over the warriors, Elliott worried that the Rebels might attempt to charge through the thin lines of the Indians and turn his own flank, and by doing so, envelop his own force and pin them against the woods. Thus, to Elliott's great relief, the mounted column just discovered by some alarmed Indians to be moving in the direction of Elliott's own force was not that of the enemy but of a friend. In the distance, Matthew Elliott could make out Captain Caldwell and his Rangers coming to reinforce him.

"If I Had Not Been So Unlucky"

Caldwell brought the Rangers up to the rear of Elliott's position and had his men dismount. Immediately the Rangers were deployed in a broad front covering almost 200 yards, in three companies, each comprising two ranks. As Matthew Elliott heartily greeted Caldwell and brought the officer up to date on the position of the enemy, Lieutenants Turney and Clinch gave the order for the front rank to advance under the cover of the high grass and then fire in volley on the Rebels in the trees. The thunderous roar of their muskets and the cloud of smoke caught the attention of those militiamen firing from the edge of the woods, who paused to see who had just fired upon them in regular order. It was at that moment that the second rank of the advancing Rangers fired into the woods, dropping several of the militiamen who had momentarily left the protection of the trees. To their utter surprise and horror, the militiamen who had not fallen quickly passed the word to the other men, that a troop of white men in green coats had suddenly appeared on the battlefield to support the Indians and were engaging them directly to the north of the woods. Crawford and his officers reacted with shock at the new development. No one, not even General Irvine at Fort Pitt had calculated that the savages would be able, in any event, to obtain aid from Detroit." [BC2-p.217] Crawford realized that there was little doubt the white men opposing them were experienced British Rangers. He could count on the fact that any advantage his men had in numbers over the Indians had been suddenly neutralized by the Rangers, and it struck some degree of uncertainty and fear in his men to know that they were no longer fighting just Indians, but white men as well, who were intent on killing them.

Elliott asked Caldwell for instructions now that the Rangers were putting pressure on the front of the Rebels, thus freeing up a number of the warriors who had engaged the enemy. As a runner from Pipe had just arrived with news that the Delawares had successfully attacked the enemy in their rear, and drove them and their horses into the woods for protection, Caldwell wanted to be sure that the militiamen did not remount and attempt a foray against the thinly held lines of the Indians commanded by Pipe. He urged Elliott to take some of the warriors to help Pipe while keeping a small party between the Rangers and the

*Captain Caldwell has his Rangers take up positions
against the militiamen in the woods.*

rear of the woods for good measure. Caldwell remounted his horse to get a better look at the Indians on the left of his Rangers who were unsuccessfully working their way to a small grove of woods to the northeast of the grove, which the Rebels were clearing. Elliott warned Caldwell that as the enemy had men with rifles stationed in the woods, he should take care not to make himself an inviting target on his horse. It was no more than a minute later, when Caldwell turned his horse to get a better glimpse of what was happening in the little grove, that he was shot in the buttocks by a Rebel rifleman, the ball knocking him off his horse, and sprawling him to the ground to the rear of the Rangers.

Elliott yelled to Turney that Caldwell had been hit, and the two men rushed to the aid of the fallen officer. Captain Caldwell writhed on the ground in excruciating pain, having been shot through the buttocks with the ball passing through the flesh on the right side and lodging in the left. Examining the wound, Turney could see "Caldwell wounded in both legs, the ball lodges in one," [HP-178] and would need to be cut out. As the wound was bleeding profusely and the officer in great pain, Turney was concerned that the wound was mortal, perhaps having broken the captain's leg bones, or severed an artery. However, when the little old Ottawa chief named Linderwattone who had accompanied Caldwell from Detroit was brought up, the chief cut away Caldwell's trousers and after examining the wound and asking two of the Rangers to lift Caldwell momentarily to his feet to see if he could walk, to determine if any bones were broken, the Indian pronounced that the wound was not fatal, but that Caldwell would not be able to fight any longer. Caldwell, in great pain but entirely in possession of his senses, uttered a string of curses, saying to Turney that "if I had not been so unlucky" he would remain in command of his men, but as the loss of blood, which the Linderwattone was attempting to stem, was having the effect of weakening Caldwell beyond his ability to stay lucid, Caldwell called Lieutenant's Turney and Clench to his side, gave command of the Rangers to Turney and instructions to both men before the "ball through both my legs obliges me to leave the field." [HP-177] Then with the help of two Indians, Linderwattone had a crude travois constructed to haul the Ranger captain, as he was incapable of sitting or riding a horse, for the trip back to the lower village of Sandusky where Mr. Coon and Mr. Arundel would be able to help treat the wound.

"One Ranger Killed and Two Wounded"

The fighting went on, with both sides exchanging heated shots around the perimeter of the woods until darkness began to descend on the battlefield, with both sides having sustained men killed and wounded in the close fighting. "Our loss is very inconsiderable" Lieutenant Turney noted in his report made on the results of the day's fighting. "We attacked them about 2 o'clock. The Enemy immediately retreated to a copse of wood at a little distance where they made a stand, and had every advantage of us, as to situation of Ground people could possibly wish for," referring to the slight rise in elevation the woods afforded the defending militiamen. "As there was but a small neck of woods that we could get possession of, which when we once gained, the action became general and was dubious for some time, till we obliged them to retreat about 50 yards, after which we were able to cover most of our men, the battle was very hot till night, which put a stop to the firing, both parties kept their ground all night." [HP-23] Still, in spite of the tall grass which afforded the Rangers a great deal of cover, in Lieutenant's Clench's attempt to drive the enemy from the adjacent small neck of woods, several Rebel shots had found their mark, and Turney could count "one Ranger killed and two wounded," along with "LeValliers, the French interpreter killed" while he was carrying a message to Elliott from the Rangers. Turney had no idea how many of the Indians had been killed or wounded, nor numbers of the enemy, only guessing that the militiamen near the edge of the woods had taken some casualties due to the enormous amount of firing the Rangers poured into the grove in the early shooting. Giving orders to his men to keep to their positions and lay on the weapons for the evening, Turney saw to it that several of the men returned to the horses to bring up provisions and water for the men, as they were thoroughly exhausted by the day's fighting and exposure to the hot sun.

    With the fall of darkness, Matthew Elliott and Lieuts. Turney and Clench met with Pipe, Wingenund, Half King and the other chiefs for the first time since the battle had begun. It appeared to him Indian casualties had been relatively light, with less than a half dozen killed and a handful wounded, but none serious. As the chiefs smoked their pipes around the campfire, and warriors lay down for the evening, after posting sentinels around the perimeter of the copse of woods, a Shawnee runner arrived from the trail to the southwest with encouraging news that Captain Snake, with Alexander McKee and about 150 Shawnee warriors were on their way to join them, and were camped no more than 12 miles away at that very moment. The chiefs asked Elliott for his advice on what they should do, and Elliott in turn asked them if they knew if there were a spring in the woods where the enemy could get water for their men, their wounded, and their horses. The Indians replied that there was not. Elliott advised them to keep up their fire on the Virginians in the morning, and make sure that the warriors on the southern end of the woods had ample ammunition and warriors in case the enemy should attempt to sally out.

    With no water to be found in the woods, and with the Rebel force surrounded, the Rangers and Indians need only keep the pressure on the enemy until Snake and the Shawnee arrived. It would only be a matter of time until the men trapped inside the woods would attempt to break out due to thirst, and no hope of reinforcements arriving. Elliott calculated it would happen tomorrow afternoon, if not sooner, depending upon how soon the water ran out inside the woods. The longer they waited, the weaker the enemy would become and their horses would begin to die. The Rangers and Indians would be waiting for that moment, and would strike them down when they attempted to break out. Everything would have to be held in readiness until then.

"A General Attack the Next Night"

While the fall of darkness brought relief from the battle for Crawford's militiamen inside the grove of trees, the moans of the wounded men and the lack of sufficient water was disconcerting. "No spring was near, nor running stream" found in the woods, and with the river over a mile from the woods and that avenue cut-off by the Indians, the men had to content themselves with sharing what little was left in their canteens. None could be spared for the thirsty horses. In addition to the five men killed during the day's fighting, 19 militiamen were wounded, some of them severely. All were in need of water to ease their suffering and there was none to be had, until a militiaman named John Sherrard, whose weapon had fouled beyond firing, searched the grove of trees, and found a pool of stagnant water laying in the cavity created by an overturned tree. Sherrard brought water in his hat and canteen to some of the men until others could follow. While the water was foul, it nonetheless aided tremendously in slaking the thirst of many of the militiamen and the wounded who were without water at all. Colonel Crawford met with Williamson and his officers to discuss their situation, now that it was evident that their force in the woods were surrounded by the Indians. Though the morale of the men was generally good, the lack of water and the large number of wounded who could not ride made Crawford apprehensive that a blow would needed to be struck very soon against the Indians, and the white men fighting with them, before the militiamen became incapable of fighting their way out of the woods, and the predicament turned into a disaster. [BC2-p.213]

On the morning of June 5, the Indians commenced firing upon the militiamen in the woods, who in turn, returned a steady fire on the Indians. Matthew Elliott had seen to it that sufficient water and ammunition had been brought up during the night and distributed to the Delaware warriors under Pipe covering the south, and to all the other Indians in their positions surrounding the woods. The warriors, as instructed, did not attempt to advance on the enemy in the trees, rather favoring to keep up a constant but spaced firing on the militiamen from a safer distance of "200 or 300 yards." This caused some of the Americans to take heart in believing that the skirmishing and long-shots by the Indians indicated that "the slackness of their fire" was due to the drubbing that they were believed to have taken during the previous afternoon, causing them to keep a healthy distance. Little did they know that Elliott and the chiefs were in fact waiting for McKee with Black Snake to arrive with the Shawnee warriors, while allowing for the heat of the day to do its work on the enemy, who Elliott surmised, must be suffering from a lack of water. Turney and Clench had the Rangers keep the pressure on their side of the enemy to keep them pinned to their positions. "On the 5th at daybreak we again commenced firing, which we kept up pretty briskly, till we found the Enemy did not wish to engage us again, however we kept firing at them whenever they dared show themselves. They made two attempts to sally, but were repulsed with loss." [HP-178]

Throughout the morning, Crawford discussed with his officers the possibility of sending a mounted force to sally out of the woods in an attempt to roll up the enemy to the south to re-open the trail to their rear. However, the success of such an attack depended upon the vigor of the horses to be ridden at a gallop. Many of the officers pointed out that the horses had no water since their drink at the springs. Because they were incapable of moving at a trot, the mounted men would make easy targets for the Indians to hit with their muskets. In addition, it was brought to Crawford and Williamson's attention that an increasing number of men were incapacitated in the woods and in need of immediate aid. "Some of the men were sick from the fatigues of the march, some from the extreme heat of the weather, and others from the bad water they had been compelled to drink since leaving the river," which by mid-morning was having an ill-effect upon them, causing them to be violently ill. Consequently, with so many of the men tending to the sick and wounded, it left the proposed attacking force with too few numbers. By late morning, it was decided by the officers, with Colonel Crawford's approval, that they would prepare "for a general attack the next night, "making every effort to be fully prepared to strike a decisive blow" that evening. [BC2-p.215] Subsequently, while the desultory firing continued to noon, Crawford began discussing plans "for the attack in force" that would take place at dusk. However, all of Crawford's plans were about to change.

"I Find Him Very Useful and of Great Service to Me"

Sometime shortly after noon on June 5, one of Crawford's scouts serving as a sentinel on the edge of the woods to the west, spotted a huge party of Indians, "apparently 200 strong" which he identified as Shawnee, advancing in the distance from the south towards the wooded grove. As the Indians drew closer, several white men could been seen with the Chiefs at the head of the warriors, and soon a chorus of war whoops resounded from the body of Indian reinforcements that was answered in kind by the Indians and Rangers surrounding the militiamen. The Shawnee war chief, Captain Black Snake, with Alexander McKee and James Girty at each side, had arrived from the Shawnee country with more than 150 painted, armed warriors, who took up positions to the west of the Delawares, and reinforced Pipe's men to the south with added warriors. At "about 12 o'clock we were joined by 140 Shawanese, and had got the Enemy surrounded," noted Turney. [HP-178] Soon Alexander McKee, with the Snake, and James Girty reached Matthew Elliott, Lt. Turney, Pipe, and Half King where the officers and chiefs greeted one another, rejoicing that the added force of warriors had sealed the fate of the hated enemy, and allowing for many scalps for the warriors and much plunder and horses to be had for all. All through the rest of the afternoon, as the firing continued, more and more parties of warriors kept arriving to the battlefield, as bands of Indians that had set out many days before from the Mingo and Munsee Delaware villages to the east and the Miami to the west finally reached their destination, to take part in the fighting. As the added reinforcements tipped the scales in favor of the Indians and Rangers who now greatly outnumbered the enemy, Matthew Elliott was confident that in the coming morning the Virginians could be dislodged from the grove of trees and finally destroyed in the open, as they gave way in retreat.

By late afternoon, Captain Caldwell was brought into the lower Indian village at Sandusky on Lake Erie, in the care of the old Indian chief Linderwattone. The wizened old man had Caldwell taken by litter to the home of Abraham Coon, the British trader, where the Indian prepared to remove the ball still in Caldwell's upper buttocks. Carefully cutting away the bloody remains of Caldwell's trousers, the Indian skillfully used a small skinning knife to probe into the coagulated wound, while Coon poured a stream of his finest liquor over Caldwell's flesh. The officer grunted in severe pain while the operation was done, and in a matter of a few minutes, Linderwattone held in his hand the 50-caliber lead ball of a Rebel militiaman's rifle that had pierced Caldwell's flesh. Under Linderwattone's direction, Coon again disinfected Caldwell's wounds liberally with the liquor, allowing the officer a drink now and then to ease his sufferings. Coon then dressed the wounds with linen, after applying a poultice that Linderwattone carried in his pouch just for that purpose. Barely conscious from the intense pain and the loss of blood, Caldwell thanked the two men for saving his life, noting later to Major DePeyster that, "Linderwattone, your friend the little old chief remains with me. I find him very useful and of great service to me." Of the man who had expertly dressed his wounds and kept them from becoming infected, Caldwell remarked to the Major, "I must beg leave to recommend Abraham Coon, whom I found very useful." [HP-177]

"Prudence Therefore Dictated a Retreat"

John Rose, General Irvine's aide, had watched the arrival of the large body of Shawnee warriors and the movement of more Indians throughout the afternoon to reinforce their positions, reporting to Colonel Crawford and the other officers that "they kept pouring in hourly from all quarters." [BC2-p.217] With confirmation of the added Indian reinforcements, and growing awareness that the white British Rangers were seasoned and experienced soldiers who had not budged an inch during the afternoon fighting, Crawford called together a council of his officers to the center of the woods to discuss the changed situation which no longer appeared to them as favorable. The officers reported that the apprehension among the men was turning to fear as the volume of gunfire from the total force arrayed around them had intensified by late afternoon. After discussing the alternatives that could be taken, the officers resolved unanimously to call off any attempt at attacking the enemy. "It was evident" to all of them that "there was no other course to be pursued," [BC2-p.217] but to "gather their forces and make a sudden concerted break out of the woods and back along the trail upon which they had arrived." Crawford agreed that any further thought of attacking the enemy had to be given up in favor of breaking out, as "it was now fairly to be presumed that the enemy would continue to be reinforced." [BC2-p.217] Rose supported the decision, pointing out that with the last of the water gone, and ammunition running low, "prudence therefore dictated a retreat." [BC2-p.217]

"A Loss We All Regretted"

A plan was devised by the officers for a breakout from the grove "to commence at nine o'clock. By sundown, the arrangements were all complete," [BC2-p.218] and the militiamen informed of the plans. Occasional firing from the Indians could still be heard by their sentinels posted around the copse of woods, to let their warriors know that the position was secure. Just an hour before the appointed time for the militia to mount up and move, one of the posted scouts on the edge of the trees was brought forward to Crawford and Williamson with important news. He reported that he had observed as the Indians regularly fired from the edge of their camps, that there was a spot to the southward direction where no firing was coming from, indicating the probability that there were few, if any, Indians posted there, or he would have heard most certainly from their sentinel. He thought the Colonel should know that it was a likely weak point in the Indian lines, and one that the army could chance to breach during the break out. Crawford thanked the scout for his keen observation, and incorporated that knowledge into the plan.

Just before the appointed time to set the army in motion, Colonel Crawford gave his final orders to the men. He ordered them to remember to stay together at all times, in one body for added protection and to keep this discipline to preserve the safety of the wounded and sick men who would be riding in the center of the formation of four divisions, once it left the woods. Those men too seriously wounded to ride a horse would be carried on a litter strung between two horses. Their successful extrication depended upon the army staying together at all times. As darkness began to descend, Crawford had the sentries light many small fires around the perimeter of the woods to give the impression to the Indians that they were settling into their camp for the night. Crawford ordered those men killed during the two days of fighting to be "now buried, and fires burned over their graves to prevent discovery" [BC2-p.218] by the Indians who would undoubtedly dig up the corpses and scalp them. "It was no sooner dark, than the officers went on the outposts and brought in the men as expeditiously and quietly as possible. The whole body was then formed to begin the march with Crawford at the head," [BC2-p.219] the nervous and fearful militiamen waiting only for the order to be given. At close to nine o'clock, Crawford ordered the withdrawal from the woods to begin, with the army to head in the southeastward direction by which they had come. The men were divided into four loose groups commanded by many of the same officers as they had come with. Each group left the woods at nearly the same time for the dark open plain ahead of them. Without any light to direct themselves but that from the stars, the divisions of men quickly lost their coherence, as some men inadvertently splitting off from the main body, and others who were grouped together with their companions decided that the best course of action to take was to set off on their own, judging that the Indians would undoubtedly pursue the main body. In a matter of a few minutes, with fear and expectation of Indian attack driving the militiamen on in the darkness, the body of troops that had been an army disintegrated in many smaller parties, each taking a route of their own determined by those men in the front who judging as best they could the general direction away from the grove and toward the darkened horizon ahead where they presumed there were no Indians due to the lack of fires.

Suddenly, firing erupted in a long outburst, as some of the Delaware scouts were alerted by the sounds of the militia horses neighing, and by the conversations of men in the column closest to the trail (who rode closest to the warriors stationed in the darkness to guard against a breakout.) Sparks flew from muskets as warriors shouted their war whoops to alert their comrades that the enemy was near. The startled militiamen closest to the Indians whipped their mounts in panic. The frightened horses reared up and screamed in terror at the sight of the shower of sparks from the gunfire lighting the darkness close to them, and the loud report of the weapons discharging suddenly in the quiet of the night.

Pandemonium reigned everywhere. Some of the men were dropped from their panicked horses, others were shot and wounded while in the saddle, but the overall effect of the Indian gunfire was to cause the militia force to dissolve completely into a mob of groups of men heading in all directions to escape the Indians. In the resulting terror, most of the seriously wounded men who were in the center of the original formation were abandoned, left to fend for themselves. At the same, many officers became separated from their own men in the darkness and confusion, not knowing where anyone was, nor what had happened to them. Such was how Colonel Crawford became separated in the dark from the division he led when it broke up in the melee and everyone ran in all directions for their lives. Somewhere during the night, the men riding with Colonel Williamson informed him that Colonel Crawford was missing, but with so many men "consequently separated," Williamson could do little more under the circumstances than agree that the loss of Colonel Crawford was a "loss we all regretted." [BC2-p.374]

"They Never Alarmed Our Camp Till Daybreak"

While the gunfire had alerted many of the Indians closest to the scene of the enemy breakout, many of the Indians farther away from the action did not come to any assistance owing to the lateness of the night and the fact that they could still see the light of the campfires of the enemy in the grove of woods. This assured them that the gunfire was the result of a local action with some small part of the enemy. Elliott was awakened by the noise, and peering into the night, wondered if the enemy were indeed taking the initiative. He decided it best to send off runners to the sound of the noise and find Pipe's men to ascertain what was going on. Sending a man to the Ranger camp to wake Lieutenant Turney, Elliott decided he would remain awake till a response was forthcoming. The officer did not consider the sound of isolated gunfire strong enough to rouse himself and his exhausted men, rationalizing to himself that whatever the problem, at morning's light he would give assistance once he could clearly see what was going on. No good would come from wakening his men and sending them out into the darkness to accidentally get shot by Indians mistaking the Rangers for the enemy. Glancing toward the grove of trees, he could see the light of the enemy's campfires, and with the knowledge that they were still in the present positions, Turney laid down on his bedroll and returned to his much-needed sleep.

However, well after midnight, a runner from Pipe's camp, followed by a warrior from the Snake, confirmed to Elliott that it appeared that the enemy had left the woods in considerable force southward on their horses. Elliott roused the warriors in his makeshift camp, and at the first streak of faint light in the eastern sky, several warriors of an advance party led by Elliott carefully approached the edge of the woods, and finding no sentries on guard entered the grove to find the enemy gone. A general alert was sent to all the parties of Indians to the east, west and north, informing them that the enemy was making their retreat, and that everyone must come as quickly as possible to pursue them. Lieutenant Turney was awakened by Lieutenant Clench who informed him of the startling news of the enemy's retreat. Astonished, Turney asked Clench how their army had been able to get away, and Clench told him that it appeared that "through some mistake of the Indians, there was one pass left unguarded, through which they made their escape about 12 at night, though some of the Indians pursued them." Turney cursed the Indians as "they never alarmed our camp till daybreak" [HP-178] discounting the fact that he had been awakened at the sound of the first gunfire, but which he had dismissed it as inconsequential.

"The Enemy Was Mostly on Horseback"

Now Turney roused his men to action with the disconcerting news of the escape of the enemy. With the sky brightening from the approaching sunrise, Lieutenant Turney had his Rangers quickly saddle up and as a body they set out at once for the trail leading southward. "As soon as I heard of it, I pursued them with the Rangers." [HP-178] Soon they could see evidence of the rout of the militia during the night, as many of the escaping men had discarded their unnecessary gear which they feared would slow down their flight. As other mounted Indians joined the Rangers in the pursuit of the enemy, from the grove of trees isolated shots and war whoops could be heard as warriors scouring the woods came across a few stragglers hiding in the tangles, which they dispatched and scalped on the spot. On the horizon to the west of the Rangers, Turney could see several groups of Indians moving in the same direction as he, while others were returning from the manhunt loaded with plunder, scalps, and horses. Turney and his men passed the mutilated remains of several militiamen who had been overtaken by the Indians while they lay wounded on their litters, abandoned by their comrades to their own fate. Pounding down the trail with all the strength their horses could muster, Turney and the Rangers headed south across the open plain towards the sound of firing that told him the enemy could not be far ahead. Soon the Rangers caught up to the mounted Indians in hot pursuit of the retreating Rebels. Turney and his men were able to catch sight of the Rebel rearguard, which appeared to be nothing more than handfuls of militiamen who had been outdistanced by their own companions. Due to the exhaustion of their own mounts, some of which had collapsed on the trail, these Rebels were now firing on the Indians coming up on them. Many of the Indians broke off to hunt down the scattered smaller parties of men, those who were straggling on horseback or on foot, while Turney and the Rangers headed on with a large body of mounted warriors intent on attacking the bulk of the enemy who were still ahead on the plains, and now visible to the pursuers. "The Enemy was mostly on horseback, some of the Indians who had horses followed and overtook them, killed a number, and it was owing to nothing but the country's being very clear, that any of them escaped," [HP-178] remarked Turney later. However the real reason some of the retreating Rebels would escape was due to Turney's own hesitation in flanking the militiamen once he caught up with them, cutting off their escape route when he was still in a position to do so.

"It Was Evidently Their Design to Retard Our March"

By dawn of the morning of the June 6, those militiamen who were able to rally themselves together on the trail leading to the south did so, and collected themselves "into a sizable force of about 300" men. [HW1-p.184] With many officers and men missing, including Colonel Crawford and others, "Colonel Williamson assumed command and headed the men" in the southeast direction following the trail they had come by. All hope of holding the remains of the army to wait for small parties of men and stragglers who were separated during the night was lost. Williamson correctly deduced that with daylight, the Indians would soon be on their trail, and their survival depended upon putting as much distance as possible between themselves and their pursuers, who were sure to follow. It did not take long for that to happen, for by early afternoon, the Indians caught up with the rearguard of the main body near Olentangy Creek, "close to the eastern verge of the prairie not very far ahead." [BC2-p.228] With the Rangers closing in behind, the Indians attacked Williamson's body of men, and a hot brisk battle ensued, with the mounted Indians and Rangers beginning to flank Williamson's force. The Indians pressed hard, firing into the militiamen, who in turn, fired back upon the Indians, forcing them to pull up. "It was evidently their design, to retard our march, until they could possess themselves of some advantageous ground in our front, and so cut off our retreat, or oblige us to fight them at a disadvantage. Though it was our business studiously to avoid engaging in the Plains, on account of the enemy's superiority in light cavalry, yet they pressed our rear so hard, that we concluded on a general and vigorous attack, whilst our light-horse secured the entrance of the woods," commented Rose, General Irvine's aide-de-camp. [BC2-p.228] Williamson ordered a large party of the men to dismount and take up a firing line, while others primed and loaded their weapons while still on their mounts to prepare to repel the charging Indians. At the first assault of the Indians, the militiamen successfully drove them off with several hot volleys of concentrated fire, which played in their favor.

"Whereupon the Indians Gave Up the Pursuit"

Once Turney and the Rangers arrived, a second attack on the American positions was attempted while flanking parties tried to cut off the rear of the enemy, but Williamson and Rose shuffled men from side to side of their position to deliver fire upon them, while the mounted troops on the best horses left, sallied out to drive away any Indians who were closing in on the American rear near the woods. Turney had the Rangers deploy across a broad front facing the enemy, and deliver several volleys of fire at the Rebels. Turney did not order them to press the enemy closer, but took up more of a defensive stance, waiting to see what the Indians would accomplish, and fearing that his men might be caught in a mounted charge by the militiamen to their front. After almost a hour of exchanging shots with little effect upon the Americans, the Indians began to slacken their efforts, primarily due to the fact that they were getting little help from Lieutenant Turney, who unlike Captain Caldwell was not aggressively taking the initiative and pressing the enemy with everything he had. Though Lieutenant Clench suggested to Turney that he could take a detachment of Rangers to the enemy rear, and deliver a volley of fire into their dismounted ranks while Turney advanced his men from the front, Turney was indecisive and not sure that he should divide the Rangers when the exact numbers of the enemy were not known, and what their intentions were. In a matter of an hour, the shooting died off as the Indians broke off the battle.

Though several men had been killed and wounded in the latest foray, Colonel Williamson realized that the stand of his men had had the desired effect to push the pursuing Indians and Rangers back on their heels, if only momentarily. Seizing the opportunity created by the pause in that attacks, Williamson had the men with him mount what horses were available as quickly as possible, and with the wounded in tow, resumed their march from the plains of the Upper Sandusky following the trail now through the woods hills leading to the Muskingum River many miles distant. Knowing they would likely be attacked again, and a potential disaster could result if those men in the rear of the column panicked, and "began pressing forward, breaking up the line of march," [HW1-p.184] Williamson devised a tactic of a fighting withdrawal by which the men in the rear company would turn to face any Indians in their rear, and after firing upon them, move to the front of the moving column, while the next group of militiamen who had the weapons readied, took up the position of the rearguard to face and fire upon whoever might be attempting to attack the rear of the column. By this method, the retreating militiamen, with their wounded, were able to stave off several more Indian attacks with concentrated volley fire by the rotating rear guards, "whereupon the Indians gave up the pursuit." [HW1-p.185]

Retreating and fighting as they went, "on the evening of June 13, the survivors of the expedition" [HW1-p.185] reached the banks of the Ohio River, and crossed over to their former camp in relative safety, the returning men very glad to be alive with so many others, killed, wounded or missing.

"We Have, With Your People, Defeated the Enemy"

Calling off the attack on the enemy when it was clear that they were entering the woods, Lieutenant Turney had his Rangers mount up to return to their camp by late afternoon of June 6. Along the way, they encountered parties of warriors setting off into the grasslands of the plains following the trails of straggling militiamen. Other Indians were returning to their camps of the previous night loaded with scalps, plunder, and horses taken from any of the enemy soldiers whom they had managed to run down after the men had become separated during the night's retreat, and were discovered in the light of the morning. As the Rangers headed north to retrieve their gear still at their previous camp, Turney could spot an occasional enemy prisoner who had been captured by the Indians and was being led, stripped and bound, towards the Upper Sandusky villages. He also came across many grisly mutilated corpses of the militiamen that lay not only upon the trail by which they had attempted to escape, but also in the surrounding fields, naked and scalped.

Turney reached Elliott's camp and met with the Indian Department officer who had just finished interrogating a Virginian prisoner. Turney was informed by Elliott that "the loss of the Enemy is 100 killed and 50 wounded, as we are informed by the prisoners, the number killed we are certain of." It appeared to Turney that the engagement was a stunning success in spite of those militiamen who had been able to escape. Just to be sure that the services of the Rangers would not be needed further, and owing to the fact that his men desired to rest and eat after three days of exertions, Turney decided, "I intend to march to Lower Sandusky likewise in a day or two, where I shall wait for orders, unless something should turn up before." [HP-178]

With no news on the whereabouts of the enemy, nor any chance that their army would return soon, Turney moved the Rangers on June 7 to Half King's town on the Sandusky River where they could relax and refresh themselves. McKee, Elliott, the Girtys, Black Snake, Pipe and Half King soon arrived with word of many enemy soldiers killed in the battle of the day before, and prisoners taken by the Indians who would soon be brought to the villages, including the commander of the Virginian army, Colonel William Crawford. In spite of that, McKee lamented the fact that so many of the militiamen had been able to make their escape, after having been "surrounded by near an equal number of the Rangers and Indians." As they compared notes on the last day's events, Elliott found out for the first time from McKee that "our unlucky maneuver of the Indians ordering the sentinels posts round them to fire, showed the Enemy their weakest part" of the Indian lines where few warriors were posted, "through which, they escaped under cover of a dark night." [MK-57] While Pipe and Black Snake responded saying that "as the Indians are still bringing in prisoners and scalps, and numbers are still after them, whose intentions are to follow them to the Ohio," by their own reckoning, the enemy, "many by the prisoner accounts, must perish in the woods, having left their clothes and baggage." [MK-57] While admitting that the battle against the enemy was not a total victory, it nonetheless, a great victory, the Shawnee war chief Black Snake boasted to McKee, Elliott, and the Girtys, for "we have with your people defeated the Enemy." [HP-179]

"They Never Alarmed Our Camp Until Daybreak"

Each of the leaders at the Upper Sandusky village of the Half King dictated a letter to Major DePeyster at Detroit, informing him of the victory. "Sir, I am happy on having the pleasure of acquainting you with our success on the 4th and 5th," wrote Turney. [HP-178] McKee added his own summation, beginning with, "Sir, you have already an account of the repulse of the 500 of the enemy who advanced near to this place," [HP-57] and Captain Caldwell would add his own report to those being prepared to forward to Detroit. "I now have the pleasure of transmitting to you as true an account as possible, which is killed and wounded 250, the Enemy's loss, amongst the prisoners, Colonel Crawford and some of the officers." Assailed by the Indians with requests for provisions and ammunition, each officer forwarded the demands to DePeyster. "I am desired by the Wyandots to return you thanks for your assistance you have sent them just in time of need, and they hope their Father will send some clothing as they say they are quite naked and beg in possible a few more men and the Half King a little rum to drink," [HP-58] reported Turney. "They beg you to send them what further assistance you can, with a further supply of ammunition and stores suitable for warriors, as that on the way they think will not be sufficient and having already expended all they had," McKee noted. Caldwell sent his request from Lower Sandusky. "The chief with One Eye and Dewantate with their bands are going to Detroit, as it is their custom after striking a blow to return to see their families. The Indian demands are great, and I have not a simple thing to suffice them with. Provision is mostly their cry, which I hope you will send us a fresh supply of. Ammunition, tobacco, and such other things as are necessary for warriors, are requisite if you please to send them." [HP-177]

On the morning of June 9, at Abraham Coon's cabin at the lower Sandusky village, Captain William Caldwell was so furious with Lieutenant Turney that the Rangers in their camp nearby could hear Caldwell lambaste his officer inside the cabin. Still unable to do more than lay on his stomach due to the excruciating pain from the healing wounds, Caldwell insisted that Coon and Linderwattone help him to his feet so he could face Lieutenant Turney when he accused him of dereliction of his duty. Reiterating to Turney that his last orders to pursue the Rebels and prevent their escape, "if I had not been so unlucky, to receive a ball though both my legs, I am induced to think from the influence I have with the Indians, the Enemy would not have left the place we surrounded them in." [HP-177] Lieutenant Turney asked to speak in his own defense of Caldwell's charge.

Placing the blame for his inability to contain the enemy in the grove of trees first on the fact that the enemy chose to break out from the grove on the far side from his camp. Naturally, this prevented Turney from taking any immediate position to stop them during their escape. Turney commended both Lt. Clench and Captain Elliott for their tireless efforts in motivating the Rangers and Indians on the first day to keep the enemy contained. "Captain Elliott and Lieutenant Clench, in particular, who signalized themselves," [HP-178] Turney reported, adding that the real fault in allowing the enemy to escape lay with the Indians guarding the perimeters of the enemy camp who "never alarmed our camp till daybreak." [HP-178] Caldwell remained unconvinced by Turney's explanation. Several warriors sent from Pipe had already confided to Caldwell that while it was true that some of the Indians sentinels were to blame for allowing the enemy to break out of the woods, it was due to Turney's lack of aggressive action that the enemy had been allowed to escape when the Indians and the Rangers caught up with the retreating enemy and engaged them later the following day. In the fight that ensued, Turney had allowed the remnants of the enemy to slip away.

"Slapped Them in Their Faces With The Reeking Scalps"

Enemy prisoners were brought in from the surrounding countryside for several days after the initial battle, numbering more than a dozen men. Though many more militiamen were initially captured, the Indians killed a number of them on the spot, in personal acts of revenge on the part of the warrior who had captured the man. Men like Colonel Crawford and Dr. Knight were taken prisoner as they wandered alone on the plains in search of their comrades whom they had become separated from during the breakout of the previous night. On the morning of June 6, they were chased down by roving bands of Indians as they attempted on foot to elude any pursuers. Crawford and Knight, who had met up with four other men, were surprised by a war party of Delawares, and captured on the spot. When the four men broke and ran from the Delawares, they were chased by some of the warriors who soon returned to the main party of Indians holding Crawford and Knight with the scalps of two of the four men hanging from their belts. [HW1-p.186] By the evening of June 7, Crawford and Knight were brought into the Delaware camp of Wingenund, where they joined nine other prisoners, and soon two more, who were all closely guarded by the Indians.

On the morning of June 10, the 13 prisoners of the Delaware were "led out of Wingenund's camp along the trail west towards Half King's town on the Sandusky River, with a party of Pipe's Delaware warriors. Along the way, Colonel Crawford learned from his captors that Simon Girty, his old acquaintance from the days at Fort Pitt prior to the Revolution, was currently at the Half King's village. Crawford determined to ask his Delaware captors if he could be taken there to speak to Girty, to ask him to see what could be done to obtain his release from the Indians. "This was agreed to, especially as, in so doing, two horses that had been left by Crawford's party while retreating on the same route, were to be hunted for." Separated from the other prisoners who were to be escorted to the old town of the Half King, Crawford was taken to the Half King's village and arrived sometime during the night. Colonel Crawford was given an opportunity to speak to Simon Girty in private. During that conversation, Crawford learned that William Harrison, his son-in-law, and William Crawford, his nephew, both of whom had come out with the army, and had been missing since the night of the retreat from the battlefield, had in fact been captured by the Shawnee." [BC-p.129] As to their fate, Girty already knew that the two men had been horribly tortured and burned alive that day by the Shawnee, but he told Crawford only that the Shawnee had decided to spare the lives of the two men.

Crawford asked Girty what was to be done with him and the prisoners. Girty replied that he did not know, though it was likely that the Delawares would call for the deaths of some of the men. Girty "assured Crawford that he would do all he could for him," and talk with his captors, the Delaware, about sparing Crawford's life. Crawford offered Girty a deal, declaring "he would communicate something of importance if his life could be saved, but that nothing else would induce him to do it- intimating that some great blows would be struck against the country." [HP-31] Girty told Crawford he would pass the offer along, but could not say what might become of it. The next morning on the 11th, Colonel Crawford, was taken to the Old Town under guard to join Dr. Knight and the other prisoners already there, where Crawford found that their faces had been painted black by Pipe, signifying that the men were marked for death. Now the Delaware chiefs Pipe and Wingenund "came forward and greeted Crawford for he was personally known to both," from their acquaintances made years previous at Fort Pitt. While telling Crawford that he was to be adopted by the Delawares once he made the journey to the Half King's town, Pipe painted Colonel Crawford's face. [BC-p.132]

The party of Delawares, with their prisoners under guard, now began their march from the Old Town on the trail leading to Half King's village eight miles to the north. Immediately, Crawford and Dr. Knight were held back by their guards, while the rest of the prisoners were ordered forward with some of the Delawares. Pipe and Wingenund accompanied Crawford and Dr. Knight on the trail. Passing the same springs that Crawford's army had stopped at on the morning of June 4, they had not gone much further when Pipe's party encountered the fresh corpses of four militiamen laying near the trail. Shocked, Crawford identified them as four of their own comrades who had been sent ahead of them on the trail no less than an hour before. Each of the men had been tomahawked, scalped and horribly mutilated. Their naked bodies were left where they had been slain to rot in the sun.

Soon, the party of Delawares with Crawford and Knight in tow reached the juncture of a trail branching off to the northwest well past the grove of trees visible to the left where the army had fought for two days before their disastrous retreat. At the fork, Pipe ordered the warriors escorting the two prisoners to take the left trail that would lead to Pipe's own village several miles distant on the Tymochtee Creek. Reaching the Little Tymochtee creek in less than an hour, Pipe's party, now within a mile of the Delaware village, caught up with the other

Indians and the five prisoners "who yet remained alive." [BC-p.133] Here they were briefly reunited for the last time, while a large body of Indians, including women and boys, held a council with Pipe and Wingenund.

After a few moments, the warriors approached the prisoners and separated Colonel Crawford and Dr. Knight from the other five men, who were forced to remain sitting on the ground. Knight was given a Shawnee guard who was responsible for taking him to the Shawnee village of Wapatomika in a day or two, while Crawford was told only that he would be taken to Pipe's town very soon. Then without warning, the crowd of squaws and boys with knives and hatchets in their hands, approached the five other captives who were in sight of Crawford and Knight, and began to beat them mercilessly. Then, one at a time the five were stripped, tomahawked, and scalped. Methodically, the mob of Indians mutilated the prisoner's remains beyond recognition with hatchets and knives before Crawford and Knights' eyes. Then the Indian youths brought their bloody trophies over to the two captives, and "slapped them in their faces with the reeking scalps." [BC-p.133] With the killing of the prisoners completed, the march of Crawford and Knight to Pipe's town was resumed, the two men much distressed at what they had just been forced to observe, and fearful of what might lay ahead for themselves.

"Girty Answered Yes"

They had not gone too far before the party was approached by Simon Girty and a party of Indians with him on horseback, who caught up with Pipe and his two prisoners from the cut-off trail to Half King's town almost eight miles away. Girty already knew what lay in store for the two men. He had been told on June 9 that Colonel Crawford had been taken prisoner of the Delaware and given to Pipe and Wingenund to decide his fate, which was to be burned alive. Girty saw to it that Matthew Elliott still at Half King's town and Captain Caldwell at lower Sandusky were informed of the news. "Amongst the prisoners, is Colonel Crawford and some of the officers" [CW-51] Caldwell informed Detroit on the morning of June 11, as word had just reached him the previous afternoon from Upper Sandusky. It was then that Matthew Elliott, whom Caldwell had appointed to command the Indians on the morning of June 4, and who was called by the warriors "Captain Elliott" in light of their high esteem for him, had attempted to convince Pipe and Wingenund that Crawford would be more valuable alive than dead to Major DePeyster at Detroit for the amount of military intelligence that he possessed. Elliott pledged that he would see to it that the two chiefs were handsomely compensated for giving up Crawford to him alive, but the two Delawares would hear none of it.

When Elliott asked Simon Girty for his advice on the matter, Girty cautioned Elliott that he knew the temper of Pipe and Wingenund, and there was nothing anyone could do to save Crawford at this point. Girty remarked that the Indians believed that even if Crawford had nothing to do with the Moravian massacre, he nonetheless had no business being with the enemy army coming to the Upper Sandusky in the first place. In Girty's opinion, Crawford was doomed, and not even Major DePeyster in Detroit could save Crawford, for Crawford had sealed his own fate by leading this army against the Indians. Girty pointed out to Elliott that Pipe was correct in his presumption that Crawford's army would have massacred the women and children of the Upper Sandusky villages if they had been given the opportunity. To Pipe and Wingenund, Crawford was guilty and that was all that mattered. Regardless, Elliott tried to speak with Pipe on the matter of sparing Crawford, but the Delaware chief refused to discuss the matter with Elliott. Elliott's "attempt to intercede on Crawford's behalf was to no avail." [HR-p.39] As a result, he made his way to Pipe's town to observe Crawford's execution. Having been appointed by Caldwell and DePeyster to command the Indians during the defense of the Upper Sandusky, Elliott knew that he must be present at Crawford's execution, out of respect for the Delaware chiefs, or they would have taken offense at the slight, if he were not there. Accompanying Elliott to the burning were George and James Girty.

Simon Girty, on the other hand, had decided to make the trip to Pipe's town from the Half King's because "he wanted to be present at his (Crawford's) torture, and had started out on the trail to meet the Delawares with their prisoners." When Girty caught up with the two men, he did not speak directly to Crawford or Knight but followed them on his horse. At a point on the trail, the two captives were separated by the Indians and beaten severely with sticks and clubs by a mob of Indians from Pipe's town who had come out to meet the two men on their final leg of their journey. After the beating, Simon Girty rode up to the bloodied Dr. Knight and told him that he "was to go to the Shawanese towns" the next day, where lived about 30 Delawares, and there he was to be tortured and burned. Then leaving Knight, Girty rode ahead to the spot designated by the Delawares for Crawford's torture, which was about three quarters of a mile from Pipe's village on the banks of Tymochtee Creek.

At the execution site, a fire had already been kindled in preparation for Crawford, and a post nearly 12 feet high sunk in the ground by the villagers awaiting Crawford's arrival. When the two men were brought in, each were stripped naked by the Indians and forced to sit down in front of the fire, where they were beaten again by the Delaware with "clubs, sticks, and thorn-covered blackberry canes, until the blood poured freely from the wounds." [HW1-p.188] With that done, several warriors took Knight some distance away from the fire to a spot where he would be forced to witness the spectacle that was about to unfold. The warriors now grabbed Crawford and tied his hands behind his back, passing a woven leather thong of 12 to 15 feet in length through his bound hands and tied to the top of the post which allowed him to "set down or walk around the post once or twice and return by the same way." [BC-p.134] Upon seeing these preparations, Colonel Crawford called out to Simon Girty sitting nearby, asking him if the Indians intended to burn him. Girty answered "yes," to the horror-stricken Crawford. [BC-p.134]

"Until Death Put An End to His Frightful Suffering"

With the preparations for the torture completed, "Captain Pipe made a speech to the Indians," who numbered about 30 or 40 men and up to 70 women and boys. "When the speech was finished, they all yelled a hideous and hearty assent to what had been said" by the Pipe, and began loading their guns with large amounts of gunpowder wadded with no ball. At Pipe's command, the Indians fired their weapons from the distance of a few feet away "into Crawford's body, the genitals being the preferred target," with the effect of "the stinging, burning particles of coarse black powder penetrating the skin" of Crawford, causing excruciating pain. In a few moments, "every inch of Crawford's skin was charred, burned and smoking" from more than 70 rounds fired at him. [HW1-p.188] With that done, several of the warriors approached Crawford, and while they held him immobile, his ears and his genitals were sliced off, causing blood to pour down Crawford's face and legs. [HW1-p.188]

Next, the warriors reached for the hickory poles that had been placed over the fire that was burning about 20 feet from the stake. Each of the poles was about six-feet in length, and their ends were alit. Each warrior took a pole and touched the burning end to Crawford's body, causing him to run around the post to avoid the burning sticks, but as three or four of the warriors participated at a time, in turn, they made a sport of making his escape impossible from the blazing sticks, so that Crawford was gradually burned on all parts of his body, leaving no place untouched and immune from the painful sizzle of the red-hot ember of the hickory stick put to his flesh. "In the meantime several squaws, not to be outdone" by the warriors in the playful torture of the prisoner, "scooped up some of the burning coals onto slabs of bark, and began throwing them on Crawford's naked body, so that in a few minutes the unfortunate man had nothing to walk on but red-hot coals. [HW1-p.189]

Having been tortured for nearly two hours by various means of burning, the hideously burned Crawford sank to his belly on the hot coals, insensible any longer to pain. One of the warriors approached him and expertly cut the skin above his eyes in a circle around his skull, yanking off his scalp, and then took it to Dr. Knight where he slapped the prisoner's face several times with the bloody trophy. Then one of the squaws gathered up a heap of hot coals from the fire and dumped them over Crawford's bare skull, the new pain causing Crawford to raise himself up. "Incredibly, the charred remains of what had once been a human being gave a low groan, and as all watched in amazement, slowly regained its feet and once more commenced its slow shuffle around the stake" [HW1-p.189] to the delight of the Indians, who howled with pleasure. Quickly they jabbed him once again with burning poles, but this time Crawford barely reacted. As two Indians raised Dr. Knight to his feet to take him away to be bound for the evening, Crawford was "roasted by a slow fire until death put an end to his frightful suffering." [BC-p.136] What was left of the corpse of the officer was thrown upon a pile of heaped-up burning wood and coals, and "around his charred remains danced the delighted savages for many hours." [BC-p.136]

"They Came Out On a Party of Pleasure"

With the torture of Colonel Crawford over, Simon Girty came to his feet and prepared to leave. He had always been morbidly attracted to the deeply lurid sight of a prisoner slowly being burned alive with the sounds of their pitiful shrieks and screams piercing the air. Since his capture by the Indians at the age of 15, and adoption into the fierce Seneca tribe, Girty had attended many tortures and burnings of prisoners brought to the village by war parties for that purpose, beginning with the burning of his step-father John Turner by the Delaware at Kittanning, when they were captured in 1756. The burning of prisoners by the Indians was routine for them, and routine for Girty to observe. While he could tell himself that it was unfortunate that Crawford had got himself caught by the Indians, Girty knew that Crawford had no business coming to attack the Indians in the first place. If anything, Girty told himself, Crawford was getting what he deserved for coming against the Indians and their villages, even if Crawford had befriended Girty in the past. The Delaware had made him pay for it. Rising from his spot in the grass near the post, Girty felt nothing and said nothing as he left the scene of the torture. Crawford's death mattered not in the least to him, at the moment. For Simon Girty was tired, and wished for some much-needed sleep after the long day.

In the morning, Simon Girty and Matthew Elliott headed for Half King's town to join Alexander McKee, who had remained there with the Shawnee after the battle. They passed by the spot of Crawford's burning and observed Dr. Knight being brought to the place of execution by his Shawnee armed guard to view the grisly charred remains of Crawford that still smoldered on the last of the hot coals. Arriving at the Half King's town, Girty and Elliott found a large temporary encampment erected on the outskirts of the village to accommodate several hundred warriors from the tribes who had come to the Upper Sandusky to help fight the Virginians. Dozens of warriors lounged around campfires, engaged in cooking food, cleaning their weapons, showing off trophy scalps taken from the enemy in battle, and recounting the events of the previous fighting that they personally took part, swapping stories about their own particular deeds of bravery to the point of argument.

In other spots of the camp set aside for treating the wounded and dying, Indian women worked to clean and dress those men wounded in the battle, while others ministered to the handful of mortally wounded warriors who were dying. A steady stream of warriors continued to come in and go out to the battlefield in search of plunder, for the retreating army of the Virginians had discarded a huge amount of weapons, ammunition pouches and powder horns along with packs containing all sorts of personal items that the warriors found valuable. Once at the encampment with their newfound goods, warriors bartered with each other for what they did not already possess, from spare flints and gun springs to cooking pots, combs, and items of clothing. The liveliest trading was reserved for those warriors purchasing one of the scores of horses taken from the enemy that had fallen into the hands of the Indians, and now changed owners as the warriors bid with their newfound plunder for the choice mounts they desired from the growing herd tethered at the edge of the village. With a treasure trove of plunder for the victorious Indians and relatively few casualties, Girty and Elliott could see that the Indians had profited greatly from the battle, and would likely fight again if the opportunity arose.

By the evening of the following day, June 13, Simon Girty reached the lower village at Sandusky, after leaving Elliott and McKee. There he found Captain Caldwell recovering from his wounds at Abraham Coon's home. "Simon Girty arrived last night from the Upper Village who informs me that the Delaware had burnt Colonel Crawford and two captains at Pipes town, after torturing them a long time," Caldwell wrote to Major DePeyster. "Crawford died like a hero, never changed his countenance, though they scalped him alive and then laid hot ashes upon his head, after which they roasted him by a slow-fire. He told Girty if his life could be spared, he would communicate something of consequence, but nothing else could induce him to do it. He said some great blows would be struck against this Country. Crawford and four captains belonged to the Continental Forces. He said 14 Captains were killed. The Rebel Doctor and General Irvine's Aide-de-Camp are taken by the Shawanese. They came out on a party of pleasure," Caldwell sarcastically noted in his report to Major DePeyster, and the Indians had made that party quite hot. [BC2-p.31]

"The Lake Indians Are Very Tardy"

By the middle of the month, Indian war parties and scouts were once again heading out from the villages of the Upper Sandusky for the frontier settlements in the east, and Kentucky to the south with renewed vigor to attack the Virginians and Pennsylvanians wherever they could be found. James Girty left with Matthew Elliott and Alexander McKee to join the Shawnee at Wapatomika to participate in a council of war. James Girty wanted to go to observe the burning of the two remaining prisoners from Crawford's campaign who had been taken there, Dr. Knight and the scout John Slover, but was disappointed upon arrival to find that Dr. Knight had escaped his Delaware guard on the trail, thus eluding torture and death at the stake. George Girty accompanied a large party of Delaware to their village on the Mad River adjacent to the Shawnee village, these Delaware not being a part of Pipe and Wingenund's band. Simon Girty elected to stay with Caldwell a few days more, until he set out for the nearby Wyandot village called Solomon's town, there deciding to accompany a large party of warriors to Wapatomika, [BC-p.142] where Captain McKee was calling his Indian Department officers to join him in advising the Indians chiefs at the council of their decision as to what they should do.

The Indian Council had been called primarily by the Shawnee chiefs, whose lands and villages were the most exposed to the Virginians from Kentucky. The Shawnee believed a strike would be made against them first, in retaliation for the defeat of Crawford's army. However, chiefs and warriors from many tribes decided to attend the major council, and Captain Snake, one of the Shawnee chiefs requested Captain Caldwell and his Rangers to come from Sandusky to Wapatomika at the first possible moment to join him, sending Caldwell "three strings of black wampum" to pass on to Major DePeyster with his request. "There is another army coming against us from Kentuck, that we are certain of, not only from prisoners, but from our young men who are watching for them. "Father," Pipe implored Caldwell to write to DePeyster, "we hope you will again grant our requests, and let the Rangers remain at Lower Sandusky about ten days, and then march to our villages." [HP-179]

As Captain Caldwell was feeling better, though not well enough to ride a horse, he did not need to wait for permission from Major DePeyster to decide to join the Indians headed to the south to Wapatomika. Caldwell sent word to them that he would gather up his resupplied Rangers and set out with them at the first possible moment that he was able to travel. Caldwell sent in his stead several Rangers immediately to Wapatomika to keep him apprised of the intentions of the Indians which would be determined at their council. Accompanying them on the trip was a large contingent of the Lake Indian tribes, including Ottawas, Chippewas, some Wyandots from Detroit, and Pottawattamies, who had arrived too late at Sandusky to participate in the battle at the upper villages. "The Lake Indians are very tardy. We had but 44 of them in the action. I should be glad they would hasten as I expect we will have occasion for them…for Clark, I believe, will soon be on his way for the Shawanese country," Caldwell informed Major DePeyster at Detroit.

"Rheumatism, My Constant Companion"

At Detroit, Major DePeyster had received the news on June 15 [HP-235] from Caldwell, Turney and McKee detailing to him the great victory over the Rebels at the battle of the Upper Sandusky. He was relieved to learn that the casualties suffered by the Rangers and Indians had not been large. DePeyster took satisfaction in the knowledge that the Rebels had suffered greatly, and that finally a decisive blow had been struck against the enemy which might deter them from attempting again to invade the Ohio Country with the aim of possessing the Indian Lands and Detroit. However, on the heels of those dispatches, word quickly arrived from Sandusky informing DePeyster of the burning of the Rebel captives by the Indians, including Colonel Crawford. DePeyster was aghast at the thought of the Indian barbarity, but quick to come to the conclusion that the Rebels had brought it upon themselves. "Your Excellency will see by the enclosed, that the late acts of cruelty perpetrated by the Enemy at Muskingum, at the times the Indians were almost weaned from it, have awakened their old custom of putting prisoners to most severe tortures. By what I can learn the unhappy victims were themselves at the Massacre of the Moravian Indians. Nearly the same body of troops certainly were present and had similar intentions upon Sandusky," [HP-277] DePeyster dutifully informed General Haldimand.

General Haldimand had something of far more importance pressing upon his mind at the moment than the outrageous conduct of the Indians in the Ohio Country. For what lay upon his writing desk at headquarters in Quebec was a dispatch from England which had reached him by the middle of June, the orders contained within it, what Haldimand had dreaded would be issued since first hearing of Cornwallis's defeat the past winter. While he had delayed informing his staff in Canada and the officers of the upper posts in the wilderness, the time had come for Haldimand, as Commander in Chief, to order those officers to cease all offensive operations of the troops under their commands against the Rebel frontiers. A cease fire was ordered by the Crown, the Foreign Ministry, and the new commander of British forces in North America, as truce talks with the Americans had been proposed for the purposes of ending the war, and granting the former colonies their independence. While Haldimand had "known for some time that Lord North had fallen, " he did not know that Lord George Germain "had resigned his office," nor that General Sir Henry Clinton in command of British forces in America had been replaced with Sir Guy Carleton at New York. The Americans were being told by Carleton that "he was stopping all offensive operations" and Haldimand must do so as well to comply with Carleton and the new orders by the end of the month.

Now, on July 11, Haldimand picked up his quill to respond directly to Major DePeyster on the subject of the Indian cruelties at the Upper Sandusky. "I have received your letters communicating the Defeat of the Rebels at St. Duskey by the Rangers and Indians under Captain Caldwell. While I very much applaud the conduct and bravery of the officers and men who have so much distinguished themselves, it is unfortunate the Affair was tarnished by the cruelties committed on Col. Crawford and the two Captains, and the consequences may be very prejudicial should an accommodation be in agitation," referring to the proposed peace talks to be held. "I have not a doubt that every possible argument was used to prevent that unhappy event, and that it alone proceeded from the Massacre of the Moravian Indians, a circumstance that will not extenuate the guilt in the eyes of the Congress. When you see a fit occasion, express in the proper terms the concern I feel at their having followed so base an example, and the abhorrence I have had throughout the War, of Acts of Cruelty, which, until this instance, they have so humanely avoided." Adding a note to DePeyster on the proposed orders to call off all offensive actions against the Rebels Haldimand got personal. "Circumstances, as would have informed you Affairs are, I Regret the Necessity of the Rencontre." [HP-289]

At Niagara, Lt. Col. John Butler in command of the Ranger Corps was ill. He had been suffering from ague since learning the news of his son's death at the onset of the last winter. Overseeing the progress of the settlers attempting to farm the land adjacent to the Ranger barracks across the river from Fort Niagara, Butler had worked with Powell at fulfilling Haldimand's orders that the land be cleared and crops grown to help the post at Niagara become more self-sufficient. With orders reaching Butler and Powell concerning the cessation of offensive operations against New York and the western wilderness, Butler's thoughts turned to that of his men, who's future remained clouded, if talk of the end of the war became an actuality and the Corps were disbanded. A settlement across the Niagara River might prove to be a good opportunity for them. "Seven or eight Rangers got their families from the frontier last fall. These, with some others that have been here for some time, are desirous of being discharged and leave to settle on lands near the place."

Privately, John Butler brooded. His bout of ill-health continued into June, often keeping him from his duties, with a host of complaints. "I would wish much to have an agreeable gentleman appointed Major to the Corps. If I am to take care of the Indian Department, it will be necessary for me to stay on the other side of the Niagara River, for crossing the river twice a day does not agree with the Rheumatism, my constant companion." [HP-32] Always, his thoughts turned to his son Walter, his eldest child named after his own father. John Butler agonized when word reached him from returning Rangers that his dying son had been scalped by an Oneida Indian allied with the Rebels, and left where it lay unburied, for the wolves to devour. Rumors abounded at Niagara that Lt. Col. Butler had "offered a large sum" of money to the Rebels to have his son's "remains delivered in Canada, but it was not done." [SH-p.245] An unconfirmed report reached Niagara that loyalists still in the Mohawk Valley had discovered Walter Butler's body and took it "secretly to St. George's Church in Schenectady, and that he was buried there," [SH-p.243] though John Butler had been unable to verify it.

In any case, the death of Butler's eldest son had "evidently stricken him by the loss," and affected his health for a long time. "Butler recovers slowly. He is the only man here equal in any degree to the management of the Indians," wrote Colonel Allan MacLean at Niagara. [SH-p.244] Once Butler's health improved, he resumed his duties as commander of the Ranger Corps and officer in the Indian Department. Daily, Butler would be rowed by whaleboat across the Niagara River from his quarters in the Ranger barracks on the west side of the river to the post headquarters in the old stone castle within Fort Niagara's walls. Yet to those officers in the British army who knew Butler, he appeared to be a changed man, much more quiet and withdrawn. With his eldest son dead, his former home of Butlersbury overlooking the Mohawk River confiscated by the Rebels, and his name reviled by everyone along the eastern frontier for his use of Indians to fight alongside the Rangers in a wilderness war against the settlements, John Butler had come to realize that because of the war, he would never be the same again, regardless of the outcome. Butler's thoughts often turned to his own questionable future once the general armistice took effect and the war effectively ended, for he would never be able to return to his former home. Yet far to the west, in the wilderness of the Ohio Country, his Rangers, Butler's Rangers, prepared for a new round of wilderness war.

Chapter 15

Bloody Battle for the Ohio Country: Blue Licks and Fort Henry

"The Virginians at Wheeling Must Be Destroyed"

At the Shawnee village of Wapatomika deep in the wilderness of the Ohio Country, the Indian Council of the tribes of the Western Confederacy got underway by the third week of June, with the Shawnee, as host, overseeing days of speeches by the chiefs and head warriors of the tribes. Each emissary wanted to speak before the assemblage to give their opinion on what course of action should be taken in their war with the Long Knives. Alexander McKee and Matthew Elliott "attended their most important councils, and gave advice to the savages." [BC-P.142] Elliott was now held in high esteem for his personal bravery in the battle at the Upper Sandusky and how he "handled his Indians for most of the battle." For the escape of some of the Virginians, "no blame was placed on Elliott for the Indian mistake in allowing the Americans to break out of their position." [HR-p.38] After more than a week of deliberations by the Indians, it was decided that Captain Caldwell's Rangers should be called for, and with their support for the Indians, a major attack should be made to the east against the settlement called Wheeling, from where many of the men responsible for the Moravian massacre had set out, and where Colonel Clark staged his advance down the Ohio River the previous summer.

The Shawnee were discontented that a decision to attack both the Virginian settlements in Kentucky and Clark's post at the Falls of the Ohio was not made. While they stood to bear the brunt of any expedition of the enemy from Kentucky because their villages lay closer to the Kentuckians than any other tribe, the Delaware and Wyandots held sway over the council. Pipe and Wingenund appealed to the chiefs and warriors to help them avenge their own people, the Delaware of the Muskingum, whose blood was spilled by the Virginians at Gnadenhutten, and whose deaths, especially those of the women and children, had not been avenged against the men, women and children of the Virginian settlement of Wheeling. That enemy, led by Williamson and Crawford, had killed, scalped and burned 96 Delawares, which must be avenged.

The Delaware chiefs call for revenge was strong. Those Indians in the delegations from the other tribes implicitly understood that vengeance must be exacted before all else. Many now echoed Pipe's sentiment that the Virginians at Wheeling must be attacked and destroyed. A unanimous decision was reached to do so, and the council ended with the chiefs and warriors prepared to set out to their own villages to gather their warriors. With deliberations over, Alexander McKee and Simon Girty set out on the trail late in June for the Upper Sandusky villages with a large force of Indians to rendevous with Captain Caldwell and his Rangers. [BC-p.143] On his way there, a runner reached him from the northeast with a message from Colonel Guy Johnson and Lt. Col. Butler at Niagara, informing him that "King Guyashutta," the western Seneca war chief, "is gone to a place called Wheeling near Fort Pitt, with 250 men" who would somewhere meet with McKee and Caldwell. [HP-32]

"Represent to Mr. Bradt the Impropriety of His Conduct"

At Niagara, Brig. Gen. Powell was worried. Since July 1, reports were arriving daily from the Ohio Country and Detroit with word that, in spite of the defeat of Colonel Crawford's expedition, the Rebels were planning to make another attack against the Indians and Detroit from both Fort Pitt and Kentucky with two separate armies, demonstrating that they had every intention of taking control of the Indian lands before the peace negotiations began. Powell mulled over Haldimand's last order to begin to cease offensive operations. Regardless, he decided that he must act to protect Detroit and his men already in the field. Powell ordered Col. Butler to have a company of Rangers assembled as soon as possible from the garrison to send at once by sloop to Sandusky. "Corroborating reports of the intentions of the Enemy have determined me to send a company of the Rangers immediately to Sandusky from hence, and I shall write to Captain Caldwell, that if it should happen that he has no occasion to employ them, he will send them to Detroit, where their assistance will be of very great use in repairing the works, which I am informed the late heavy rains has quite leveled." [HP-180] Powell was hedging his bets, for if Caldwell would not need the added Rangers in the defense against the Rebels thought to be coming from Fort Pitt, then DePeyster at Detroit could put them to good use in defending that post from the threat posed by Clark to the south in Kentucky. Either way, in Powell's mind, the Ohio Country must be reinforced. By the middle of the month he would know more, for Powell intended on leaving for Detroit as soon as possible to inspect the post. "I shall intending setting off about the 10th, and I shall wait there to see the event of Mr. Clark's expedition, should it appear to be intended against that Post." [HP-180]

Lt. Col. John Butler summoned his nephew, Captain Andrew Bradt, commanding the recently-raised 10th Company of Rangers to his quarters in the Ranger Barracks on the west side of the Niagara River on July 2. Informing him of Powell's orders to send another Ranger company to the defense of the Ohio Country, Butler told the zealous officer that he was to report to Captain Caldwell once he got to Sandusky with his men, and reinforce the Rangers who were already there. Butler reminded Bradt of the allegations made by Joseph Brant during their joint expedition to Fort Stanwix in February 1781, when Brant accused Bradt of being arrogant with the Indians, and in particular, of ignoring Brant's captaincy during the campaign. While a lieutenant at the time of the incident, Bradt disputed Brant's accusation, inferring that the Mohawk disliked him because of his relationship to Butler, whom Brant had never seen eye-to-eye from the time the two men left the Mohawk Valley at the beginning of the war.

Yet controversy continued to dog Bradt. He aroused the ire of both Powell and Haldimand when he struck a Sergeant Smith of a rival loyalist corps called the Loyal Rangers commanded by Captain John Walden Meyers. Both Smith and Bradt claimed the recruits for themselves. Bradt had Smith arrested at Niagara, calling him a Rebel spy, but General Powell overruled him and "had Smith released, and the eight recruits turned over to Meyers." [FM2-p.154] Bradt protested to Powell, but to no avail. "I therefore expect said guilt will be punished for so falsely exhibiting charges against me," Bradt wrote to Haldimand in defense against Captain Meyer's charges. All charges and counter charges were dropped against Smith and Bradt; however the affair had embarrassed Lt. Col. Butler. Haldimand sent a letter to Powell, informing him to "please such orders as will prevent anything of the kind in future, and let Col. Butler represent to Mr. Bradt the impropriety of his conduct." [JWM-153] Consequently, Lt. Col. Butler ordered his overly-aggressive nephew with a reputation at Niagara for being quick to anger and difficult to work with, to be sure to restrain himself in the field from acting rashly with the Indians or his fellow Rangers. Butler pointed out to Bradt that the success of his mission would hang on his ability to work closely with those that he found himself with. Captain Bradt assured his uncle that he understood what he needed to do, and left at once to begin preparations for the departure of his company.

"We Set Off For Wheeling To Strike"

As General Powell made his own preparations to sail on the next vessel headed for Detroit, he received a dispatch from Major DePeyster on July 10, several days after Captain Bradt and his Rangers had sailed from Fort Erie to Sandusky. Powell was informed that Captain Caldwell at Sandusky had sent word to DePeyster on June 27 that "all the Lake Indians had joined him, and were ready to proceed towards Wheeling, as soon as McKee and the Indians arrived with a large force of warriors from Wapatomika. However, Caldwell had received no word from scouts to the east or south that the Rebels were advancing with an army either from Fort Pitt, or by way of the Big Miami River from Kentucky. "As Captain Caldwell makes no mention of an Enemy coming from Fort Pitt, it convinces me that the Shawanese chiefs' reports must have been false." [HP-34] Realizing too, that Captain Caldwell intended to leave Sandusky with his men as soon as McKee reached the Upper Sandusky villages by the first week of July, "the company of Rangers which were sent from hence would be too late to join Captain Caldwell, Major DePeyster will employ them upon the works at Ft. Detroit. He has now 125 of that Corps acting under his orders," [HP-34] which meant there were more Rangers now than ever before deployed in the Ohio Country.

On the afternoon of July 11, Alexander McKee and his party of warriors numbering several hundred men arrived at the Half King's town of the Upper Sandusky villages. The next day, July 12, Captain William Caldwell at the head of his Corps of Rangers, reached Half King's town from lower Sandusky accompanied by over a 100 Lake Indians and Sandusky Wyandot warriors who came to join their brothers from Detroit already in the Ohio Country. McKee, Elliott and the Girtys heartily greeted Caldwell. They were glad to see the Ranger Captain up and walking, though he did so with obvious discomfort. He had healed enough to ride a horse and was ready to campaign against the enemy. However, relations between the Indian tribes were strained again. The Shawnee were late in arriving, which irritated the Lake tribes who wanted to set out at the appointed time. "Consequently, the Indians at Sandusky were not feeling extremely cooperative." [WM-p.24] "When Matthew Elliott delivered wampum to them from the Shawnee, Caldwell held a council and acquainted the Wyandots and Lake Indians with a request from the Shawnees, Mingoes, and Delawares that the Sandusky Indians remain stationary a few days so as to be nearby for assistance in the event of attack." The Wyandot and Lake Indians, having "waited with a great deal of patience," refused the offer telling the Shawnee that they could go "to the Shawnee towns or the Miami" for help. [WM-p.24]

With the various tribes squabbling with each other again, McKee knew that he must get the Indians moving to keep a sense of unity and cohesion among them lest internal bickering split them apart before they had been able to strike at the enemy. With more and more Indians pouring into Half King's town and with the warriors there increasingly disgruntled with waiting, McKee had the provisions and ammunition doled out to them, and on July 15, "after a few days consultation with the Indians collected there, we set off from thence towards Wheeling to strike the nearest settlements of the Enemy." [HP-47]

"Captain Caldwell Will Be Here Tomorrow With the Lake Indians"

Advancing along the same trail to the southeast which Crawford's army had traveled on its way to attack the Upper Sandusky villages, McKee, Caldwell, Elliott and the Girtys accompanied a force of hundreds of warriors in addition to Caldwell's 80 Rangers. Moving across the open plains, the force entered the trail through the woods which would take them to the Muskingum River valley and then Wheeling on the Ohio River directly to the east. "We had advanced as far as the Whetstone branch of the Scioto between that place and Kooshawking when we were overtaken by a message from the Shawanese." [HP-47] A Shawnee runner brought important news on the movements of the enemy. "I expected to have struck at Wheeling as I was on my march to that place but was overtaken by a messenger with the Shawanese who informed me the Enemy was on their march for their (Shawnee) country, which obliged me to turn their way." [HP-45] A council was immediately held. McKee and Elliott learned from the runner "that their scouts were returned with a prisoner and scalps from the Falls, who reported the enemy are assembled to come this way, and in a few days would be upon their march to the Shawanese towns." [HP-47] The runners gave information that "General Clark was approaching with a train of artillery and a large body of troops." [BC-p.143] The startling news threw the Indians into a quandary as to what to do. The Shawnee refused to go further eastward away from their own villages which were in danger of attack again by Clark, whom they believed would show them no mercy for their role in defeating Crawford's army. The Shawnee worried that their women and children left behind undefended in their villages would soon perish at the hands of Clark's men.

McKee and Elliott, who had Shawnee wives and families of their own, expressed sympathy for the Shawnee. The Wyandots, Lake tribes, Mingoes, and Delawares, on the other hand, were undeterred, and wanted to go on to attack the Virginians at Wheeling. But with their families in danger, the Shawnee decided to leave at once for the upper towns, and nothing could change their minds. Acquiescing to the abrupt change of plans, Captain Caldwell agreed to accompany the Shawnee with his Rangers, as their need was great. He and McKee implored the warriors of the other tribes to join them. "After some difficulty, the Lake Indians were prevailed upon to turn their course this way, and we are now upon their march hither." McKee and Elliott decided to leave immediately in an advance party ahead of Caldwell with the Rangers and Lake Indians, to ascertain quickly from the scouts, the exact location and size of the enemy's force and the direction in which they were moving. On the night of July 22, McKee and Elliott reached the upper Shawnee village of Wapatomika, but only after agreeing to send "40 warriors with two Frenchmen to watch the frontiers to the eastward, and give intelligence of any expedition in progress." [BC-p.143]

By early afternoon on the following day, July 22, while McKee and Elliott were still resting, "a runner came in from the lower villages with an account that another scout which had been sent out after the arrival of the one mentioned, was (sic) returned and had discovered the Enemy in their march below the Big Bone Lick, and that they had dispatched three of their party to apprise their villages of their approach, the rest remaining to watch their motions." [HP-47] McKee was not entirely sure that the intelligence was completely accurate. However, as the runner had come directly from the lower Shawnee village of Standing Stone he produced "belts and strings of wampum in so earnest a manner, that could not but gain credit with us." [MK-28] Soon, another Indian runner arrived with news that scouts had discovered evidence near the mouth of the Big Miami River of "a body of the enemy who they suppose to be an advanced party that had either fallen in upon their tracks, or were (sic) come to take post till the arrival of their main army." [HP-47] McKee learned that the chiefs of the lower villages had "sent messengers to the Wabash Indians and all those in the neighborhood of the Miami to desire (sic) their assistance as soon as possible," saying that "they are now about 250 men there," in the area of Piqua and Chillocothe, and they "are determined to meet the Enemy before they arrive in their neighborhood, and therefore desire to be joined with all speed by the rest of their brethren." [HP-47]

McKee wisely decided to wait an extra day or two before setting out, rationalizing that "Captain Caldwell will be here early tomorrow with the Lake Indians." [HP-47] McKee wanted more intelligence on the size of the Rebel force that was assembling on the Ohio. "There is (sic) several parties gone to endeavor to discover their force and number. I hourly expect a prisoner and some further intelligence and hope it will arrive in time to go by this opportunity." Another Indian runner arrived in the morning with "an account that they viewed the Enemy from the top of a hill near the mouth of the Miami three days ago, and that the Enemy had two large boats in their front from which two cannon were fired every evening upon coming to their encamping ground and that they saw a number of Indians with them. They say they are the most formidable army that has yet come into their country and from their appearance must intend more than attacking their villages." [HP-47]

"I Had 1,100 Indians On The Ground"

Alexander McKee was plainly worried at the startling reports coming from the Indian scouts on the Ohio. It appeared to him that Clark was planning an expedition of considerable size, and McKee could not see how the Rangers and Indians would be able to stop Clark's army, if it possessed cannon in addition to an army of mounted troops, as it had when Clark attacked the village of Piqua two years before. By the following afternoon, Captain Caldwell and the Rangers had arrived with the Lake Indians, and McKee informed him of the latest intelligence on the movements of the enemy. "July 23rd, Captain Caldwell is (sic) just come up with the Lake Indians but is apprehensive that the reinforcement with Captain Bradt will not arrive in time." [HP-47] Judging from everything that Caldwell had been told about the strength of the enemy, he feared that his force of Rangers and Indians would be too small to confront the Virginians, whom the Indian scouts reported had artillery with them. After conferring with all the chiefs present in the camp, a decision was made to advance their combined force to join the Shawnee, Miami, and Wabash warriors already massing at the village of Piqua, while sending scouts out far and wide to the Ohio Country villages urging those warriors to come in haste to Piqua as the enemy was near. "Whatever force we are able to collect we shall endeavor to be between them and Detroit which must undoubtedly be the object by all accounts." [HP-47] In the meantime, on the way to the Shawnee village of Piqua, Captain Caldwell asked his Indian scouts who were familiar with the lay of the land between Piqua and the Ohio River, to describe to him possible ambush sites along the route that Clark's army likely would take, where the enemy could be lured into a trap, or where their advantage in numbers could in the least be neutralized and their artillery incapacitated. In Caldwell's mind, there was no question that the enemy had to be attacked. However, he knew the coming encounter would be far more difficult than the previous battle with Crawford's army, due to the size of Clark's army and the quality of its veteran mounted troops.

Arriving at Piqua, which lay almost 40 miles south from Wapatomika, Caldwell assessed the area "which Clark had driven the Shawnee from two years before, and after extensive talks with George Girty, who had been in that battle, and with the Shawnee chiefs and war captains, came to the conclusion that it would be best "to meet and fight the enemy near the town" [BC-p.144] where the ground offered the Rangers a sweeping field of fire, as well as the possibility for the Indians to outflank the enemy as they advanced in column along the narrow trail leading to the partially rebuilt town. Here Caldwell, McKee, Elliott, the Girtys, and the principal chiefs met in council and decided that it would be best to wait for more Indian reinforcements who were known to be on the way. Caldwell sent out a new wave of Indian scouts with Rangers to re-assess the strength of the enemy force, and determine the direction of their advance while possibly bringing back prisoners for interrogation and intelligence. While waiting, Caldwell, "having the general marshalling and oversight of all the savages," could count on the number of warriors from the tribes of the "Shawnee, Delaware, Wyandot, Mingo, Muncey, Ottawa, and Chippewa" [BC-p.144] to steadily increase, as more and more warriors arrived at Piqua by the hour to join in the coming fight.

By August 1, McKee could take heart in the swelling army of warriors, "the greatest body of Indians collected to an advantageous piece of ground near the Piccawe village that have been assembled in this quarter since the commencement of the war, and perhaps may never be in higher spirits to engage the Enemy." [HP-28] Though they consumed precious provisions in great quantities as they busied themselves with preparations for war, Captain Caldwell was much more confident that the increased size of their force was now on more equal footing with the Rebel army, as from all accounts, "I had 1,100 Indians on the ground and 300 within a day's march of me." [HP-45] Caldwell was pleased with the martial spirit of the Indians and Rangers, which led him to believe that in the coming battle, he would see to it that the enemy was not allowed an opportunity to get away. His luck, he hoped, would be better than at battle of the Upper Sandusky, where a near-fatal wound forced him to relinquish command, and the enemy escaped his grasp, a thought which still irked him.

All that was left to do was to wait until the scouts returned from the field with their reports from the Ohio River. Part of that waiting involved witnessing the unfortunate deaths of three prisoners brought in by a Shawnee war party from the Falls of the Ohio. The frightened men had little information to offer McKee on the movements of Clark's army. Swiftly, the Indians re-took possession of the men, and in full view of the camp, the Shawnee stripped the prisoners naked and ran them through several gauntlets of warriors who beat the men mercilessly with great enjoyment. Finally, the bloodied prisoners were bound and slowly tortured with fire one at a time into the evening, before perishing by burning to the satisfaction of the large crowd of singing, dancing warriors. Only the Ottawas did not take part in the festivities, as they sulked in silence before their own fire, angry that their attempt to obtain one of the prisoners from the Shawnee in trade to burn for themselves had been rebuffed. In the morning, several of the angry Ottawas broke camp and left for Detroit.

"Do All In Your Power to Instill Human Principles in the Indians"

At Detroit, Brig. Gen. Powell arrived on July 31 for his inspection of the Post as ordered by General Haldimand. "I found the works here in a very ruinous state from the depredations occasioned by the continual heavy rains, but from the indefatigable zeal with which the garrison continues to repair them, I do not doubt but they will be in a very defensible state before the Enemy can appear before them, as Captain Caldwell is now supposed to have two thousand Indians with him, which with the two armed vessels that will be stationed at the mouth of the Miami River (Maumee) must retard their progress very much, if not totally defeat them." [HP-184] Powell ordered the sloops "Adventure" and the "Faith" under the command of Captain Grant to set sail by August 3 for the mouth of the Maumee River to protect against a Rebel advance by water if that should occur. "Immediately after my arrival at Detroit, Captain Grant went off to the Miami," [HP-185] Powell informed Haldimand by dispatch.

While evaluating the defenses of Fort Lernoult at Detroit, Powell took time to discuss with Major DePeyster what should be done with the Indians in respect to their torture and burning of prisoners. "During my stay at Detroit, Major DePeyster received some very disagreeable reposts of shocking cruelties lately committed by the Indians, upon which a Belt was immediately sent to them, representing the impropriety of their conduct, that I very much disapproved of it and that if they continued to treat the people with cruelty who fell into their hands, I was confident they would be deprived of every assistance and protection, the Troops used to give them; which I hope will have a proper effect, as the Belt which was sent was one to which they had promised to pay the strictest attention, whenever it should be sent." [HP-185]

Major DePeyster was privately skeptical at Powell's naivete in dealing with the Indian style of conducting war in the wilderness. While obeying Powell's order to send a letter at once to Captain McKee of the Indian Department admonishing him to exert his greatest efforts to stop the Indians from burning their prisoners, DePeyster knew that the effort would fall on deaf ears deep in the wilderness. Nonetheless, he dutifully wrote McKee on August 6 to satisfy Powell. "It having been represented to me that the Shawnee and Delawares push their retaliation to great lengths by putting all their prisoners to death, whereby if they are not prevented they will throw an Odium upon their friends the English as well as prevent their Father from receiving the necessary Intelligence of the Enemy's motions so essential to carry on the service for their mutual interest. I must therefore reiterate my Injunctions to you of representing to the Chiefs that such a mode of War will by no means by countenanced by their English Father, who is ever ready to assist them against their common Enemy provided they avoid Cruelties, tell them I shall be under the necessity of recalling the Troops, who much be tired of such scenes of Cruelty, should they persist. Assure them that the Lake Indians complain much of their late treatment of the three prisoners taken near the Falls." [HP-182]

DePeyster knew that Powell was a career British officer with little field experience with the Indians in the wilderness and that Colonel Johnson of the Indian Department took care of those duties at Niagara. Powell would have no way of knowing Captain McKee's reaction to Powell's directive, as DePeyster could only imagine. "I am confident, Sir, that you and the officers do all in your power to instill Human Principles into the Indians. It is a duty however incumbent on me to beg of you once more to speak to the Chiefs. I assure them that Brigadier General Powell was greatly shook at hearing the reports, and strongly recommends that it may be stopped. ...I request to hear from you and Captain Caldwell as soon as you receive this letter. Please to show this letter to Captain Caldwell to whom I shall write by the next opportunity." [HP-182] DePeyster harbored no great love for the Indians as he knew McKee did. With no hope of more troops reinforcing Detroit from Niagara, on Powell's orders it seemed ludicrous to DePeyster to chastise the Indians on such a point of contention, when their services were needed most. Powell's directive could be taken by them as an insult, and cause the Indians to withdraw their support. DePeyster was glad when the disagreeable dispatch was finished and sent on its way, so that he could get on with the wilderness war that showed no signs of abating anytime soon. With that in mind, he prepared to send the last of the Rangers recently arrived from Sandusky on board a sloop to the Indian Country to reinforce Captain Caldwell in what appeared to be a final stroke to destroy the Rebel army and Clark. Captain Andrew Bradt began assembling his company of 50 men for the trip. [HP-04]

"We Advanced Towards the Ohio with 300 Hurons"

Captain Caldwell tried to maintain his composure with the Indians when the Ranger scouts who just returned to his camp reported their findings to him on the morning of August 3. When they were done, Caldwell angrily dismissed the men. He was disgusted at what had just been told to him. Several scouting parties had returned at the same time to the large encampment at Piqua with the same disappointing news. Apparently, all the previous reports from Shawnee scouts on the movement of the enemy were false. Clark was not advancing towards them with an army of the enemy. In fact, Clark and the Virginians had not been seen at all upon the Ohio River. Rather, to Caldwell's chagrin, what he surmised had happened was "that it was owing to two Goudals," or large, flat-bottomed gunboats that had been seen by the previous scouts, "coming up to the mouth of Licking Creek, and landing some men upon the south side of the Ohio, which when the Indians saw, supposed it must be Clark." [HP-45] Caldwell could hardly contain his anger with the Shawnee for their intransigence which he realized had not only cost him the bulk of the provisions brought to Piqua, but prevented what would have been a successful attack upon Wheeling, where he had intended to go in the first place. While Caldwell fumed at the news, the Lake Indians gloated over the Shawnee, taunting them with disrespectful jibes at the apparent loss of face. Angered at what had transpired, some of the Shawnee warriors began to pack their possessions to prepare to leave camp, as "many of them had left their towns no way equipped for war, as they expected as well as myself to fight in a few days," Caldwell noted. [HP-45]

Alexander McKee was disheartened at the bungling of the Shawnee who presumed that the sighting of a party of the enemy on the river was construed as evidence of George Rogers Clark and his army. The disheartening news immediately caused a great commotion throughout the Indian camp as the various tribes began to argue among each other as to who was to blame and what should be done. In no time, their previous spirit of unity was broken. McKee tried his best to mediate between them in an attempt to quell the deep discontent he knew would lead to dire consequences. "When the return of the scouts from the Ohio informed us that the accounts we had received were false, this disappointment notwithstanding, all our endeavors to keep them together occasioned them to disperse in disgust with each other." [HP-28] That was not the worst of it. Since the Shawnee had been the ones who had called upon the Rangers and Indians on their march to Wheeling to divert to protect their own villages from the supposed advance of the enemy into their country, their Chiefs suffered humiliation in the eyes of the other Indians. Rather than endure the blow to their pride and redouble their efforts against the enemy, or redeem themselves by striking a blow elsewhere, "the inhabitants of this country who were the most immediately interested in keeping in a body were the first that broke off." [HP-28]

Matthew Elliott was torn between accompanying the departing Shawnee or staying with McKee and Caldwell. After some deliberations, he decided to stay with McKee and try to keep the few remaining Shawnee from leaving. James Girty set off with the bulk of the Shawnee to Wapatomika where they planned to disperse to their respective villages. Both Simon and George Girty elected to remain with McKee and the Rangers, as Captain Caldwell was intent on advancing at once to the Ohio with whatever force he could, to seek out the enemy and attack them. "I was determined to pay the Enemy a visit with as many Indians as would follow me," [HP-45] as long as food and ammunition would hold out. A decision was made by Caldwell, now in charge of the military operation, to move the greatly-reduced force of Rangers and Indians south along the path following the Big Miami River to its mouth on the Ohio, going by "the same route taken by Captain Henry Bird two years earlier." [HP-28] McKee readily agreed, as did Matthew Elliott and George and Simon Girty, for McKee, Elliott, and Simon Girty had been with Bird on that expedition, and could "advise Caldwell from their experiences." [HP-28] At first light, they set off on the morning of August 9. "We advanced towards the Ohio with upwards of 300

Hurons and Lake Indians. A few of the Delaware, Shawanese and Mingoes followed us." [HP-45] Caldwell had still with him 69 Rangers [HP-358] comprised of parts of his own company and parts of Thompson's and Turney's. To his displeasure, he still had no word on the whereabouts of promised reinforcement of Captain Bradt and his Rangers.

"The Indians Were In Too Great a Hurry"

On the morning of the August 11, Caldwell and McKee's force reached the banks of the Ohio. Runners who had been scouting the river in both directions for several miles returned with no word on the whereabouts of the enemy. A quick council was held to discuss what to do. "On our arrival at the Ohio we remained still in uncertainty with respect to the Enemy's motions, and it was thought best from hence to send scouts to the Falls." [HP-28] Accordingly, Elliott immediately sent several parties of Indians along the trail downriver to ascertain if Clark and any sizable force were at his post at the Falls of the Ohio. Caldwell hand-picked 30 of his most able, veteran Rangers [HP-10] from the 68 men available to accompany him to Kentucky while ordering Lieutenants Turney and Clinch to take the remaining Rangers, numbering 36 men, to stay on the Ohio River in case word arrived that the enemy was moving up the Ohio from the Falls, whereupon they were to engage them with whatever Indians they could muster. Meanwhile, it was decided "that the main body should advance in the Enemy's country, and endeavor to lead out a party from some of their forts by which we might be able to gain some certain intelligence." [HP-28] The Virginian post called Bryant's Station was chosen because it was relatively close and could be reached by the trail that led from Ruddel's destroyed fort on the Licking River. As the settlements of Harrodsburg and Boones Borough lay farther south near the Kentucky River, if the enemy chose to send reinforcements to Bryant's fort, they would have to come from the south, and not from the rear of the Rangers and Indians, thus providing a secure avenue by which to withdraw to the Ohio River, if the Rangers and Indians were pursued.

Caldwell, Elliott, and McKee with the body of Rangers and Indians crossed the Ohio and ascended the trail following Licking Creek, "with 300 Indians and Rangers, and marched for Bryant's Station on Kentuck." [HP-45] Arriving at the forks of the Licking, about 100 of the warriors decided to leave the bulk of their personal gear there rather than carry their packs any farther, despite the warning by McKee and Elliott that if something unexpected should occur while they were in enemy territory, there was no assurance that they would be able to return by the same route, and thus be forced to abandon their possessions. The warriors wouldn't listen, and stowed their packs in trees off the creek trail, rather than carry them further, taking only minimal necessities and weapons. After a short rest, Caldwell got the tired force of Rangers and Indians moving again. Provisions were running low with only a few days supply of food remaining to feed everyone, so Caldwell dared not let his force waste time on the trail to Bryant's fort, knowing that they might not be able to find food once they got there.

With several scouting parties well ahead of the main body, Caldwell's force passed the ruins of Ruddel's fort and Martin's beyond it by mid-afternoon, before approaching the vicinity of Bryant's Station at dusk, having left the south fork of Licking River at Martin's station, and taking the trail to Harrodsburg that would lead them first to Bryant's fort. Unfortunately, the scouts had encountered no one whom they could have captured to provide them with critical intelligence on the strength of the well-fortified post. Reconnoitering the fort from cover, Caldwell surmised that his force had arrived undetected by those inside the fort. Consequently, he held out hope that the fort could still be taken by surprise in the morning, if a plan could be executed to draw out the defenders into an unsuspecting ambush. Caldwell ordered the fort surrounded by the Indians and Rangers once darkness had fallen, and told everyone to lie on their weapons and get some rest, while he with McKee and Elliott discussed well into the night a plan for a morning ambush. Caldwell reasoned if they showed to the fort a small party of Indians attempting to raid for horses, that perhaps the enemy would send a substantial force out of the fort in pursuit of the Indians, who would withdraw along the trail leading to the north. Caldwell would have in place his 30 Rangers in an ambush along the higher ground opposite the Elkhorn creek trail that led to the Licking. With everyone moved into position by midnight, Caldwell thought about his plan for the ambush. He reasoned that it would work only if the small Indian party showing themselves to the fort were convincing enough to draw out the defenders. Caldwell was not entirely sure that the enemy would come out of the fort to pursue them. Something about the appearance of the fort did not seem right to him. While Caldwell was sure that the defenders had no knowledge of his hidden force, the fact that so few horses were tethered outside the walls made him think that the people of Bryan's post could possibly be aware of his presence in the area.

Soon after first light on the morning of August 16, as the people within the fort walls could be heard going about their routine morning chores, Caldwell gave the order from his place of concealment for the party of warriors to make their way from the trail to within sight of the fort walls and the nearby cabins. Within minutes, the popping of Indian guns could be heard as the 14 warriors fired upon the fort from the edge of the field while two of their comrades attempted to steal the tied horses nearby. All eyes and ears of the hidden, painted warriors surrounding Bryan's Station were glued to the party of warriors and the fort, to see if the ruse would work. From within the fort came a great commotion in reaction to the Indian attack, as the fort bell was rung in alarm, and men quickly appeared at the fort walls with the weapons readied. However, 10 minutes after the alarm had sounded, no one had opened the fort gate to indicate that the enemy militia was about to give chase. Watching from the dense brush near the edge of the woods, Caldwell cursed his bad luck under his breath. Whatever had happened behind the walls of the fort to prevent the enemy from coming out, it was apparent to Caldwell that they were not about to take the bait.

What Captain Caldwell did not know was that the 44 men inside Bryant's fort "were not surprised; they were under arms, intending to march to the aid of a neighboring settlement that had been threatened," [BC-p.145] only a day before Caldwell's arrival, had they "learned that Hoy's Station, south of them, was under attack, and they were busy inside the stockade with preparations to ride to the aid of Hoy's." [GJ-p.36]

Still, Caldwell wanted to give his decoy war party a little more time to lure the defenders, who had begun firing their rifles and muskets at the Indians from the walls of the fort while the Indians whooped and hollered from a distance. Noticing some movement inside the cabins outside the fort walls, Caldwell sent an Indian to join the war party with the suggestion that they attempt to enter the cabin farthest from the fort to capture a prisoner, to see if the fort defenders could be induced to come out. We "tried to draw them out by sending up a small party to try to take a prisoner and show themselves." [HP-45] It was to no avail. As three warriors worked their way to the cabin, the riflemen on the fort walls fired a barrage of shots that wounded one of the Indians, and drove them all off. Caldwell concluded that his strategy of the decoy war party was not going to bring the Rebels out of the fort, so he patiently called for McKee and Elliott to discuss what to do. But as they pondered the possibilities, which included waiting until dark, shooting suddenly erupted from the woods on all sides of the fort as the bulk of the warriors who had remained hidden from view grew impatient with the apparent stalemate, and opened fire on the fort from all sides which prematurely exposed Caldwell's entire force of Indians to the fort defenders. "The Indians were in too great a hurry and the whole showed themselves too soon," Caldwell noted in disgust.

"Pulled Up and Destroyed Their Potatoes"

McKee and Elliott attempted to make the best of the situation, now that their ruse was exposed and a general assault by the Indians underway. Unfortunately, at the first shots, two riders were able to gallop away from a rear sally port of the fort, successfully getting through the thin cordon of the Indians. "Two couriers from the garrison managed to make their way through Caldwell's lines unobserved, and hastened to Lexington with the news of the presence of the Enemy," [BC-p.145] so that the nearest forts at Lexington, only six miles to the south, and Boones Borough, Harrod's Burg, and Logan's fort could send reinforcements. Caldwell was undeterred by the setback, and ordered an all-out assault. "I then saw it was in vain to wait any longer and so drew nigh to the fort." [HP-45] Caldwell brought the Rangers quickly up from their former position in ambush and directed them to concentrate their musket fire on the fort walls nearest the buildings to support the Indians as they assaulted the fort from that side. They were attempting to set the cabins on fire, hoping that the flames would ignite the close fort picket walls. Under McKee's advice, "the Lake Indians rushed up to the fort and set several out houses on fire." [HP-28]

The Indians were successful in firing the three buildings close to the fort wall; however the unfavorable wind did not blow the flames, smoke, and sparks toward the fort pickets as expected. McKee could see that while "several out houses were on fire," they were "but at too great a distance to touch the fort, the wind blowing the contrary way." [WM-p.28] Caldwell urged the Indians on with the added support of the Rangers, however they were able to "burn three houses, which was part of the fort, but the wind being contrary prevented it from having the desired effect." [HP-45] With the flames from the destroyed cabins dying down, and no means by which the walls or gate could be breached under the accurate rifle-fire from the defenders, the attackers settled into trading gunfire with the fort defenders. Caldwell spoke briefly with McKee and Elliott in command of the Indians, telling them to keep up a steady fire on the fort while he pulled the Rangers out of the line for special duty. If there was no practical way of taking the enemy fort without artillery, then he would have his men concentrate on methodically destroying the livestock and crops of the enemy which were outside the fort, as well as burning any other cabins yet standing. By early afternoon, the Rangers began their task of slaughtering the cattle, sheep and hogs that were grazing in pens outside the fort, in full view of the fort defenders who were helpless to intercede unless they sallied out.

Early in the afternoon, intense gunfire suddenly erupted from the woods adjacent to one of the overgrown fields outside the fort that had been left lightly guarded by the Indians. A reinforcement of nearly 30 militiamen had arrived unexpectedly and "attempted to throw themselves into the fort; a number on horseback succeeded," [BC-p.145] as they rode straight through the surprised Indians and reached the rear sally port of the fort where they were let in. Captain Caldwell was informed of the reinforcement of enemy troops and hastily formed up a small detachment of the nearest Rangers to support the Indians in repelling the enemy, some of whom were on foot, and still attempting to reach the fort. The firefight was over before the Rangers were able to join the Indians. "A party of about 20 of the Enemy approached a part (of the fort) which happened not to be guarded, and about one half of them reached it, the best being driven back by few Indians who were near the place." [WM-p.28] The rest of the militiamen who could not make it to the fort fell back immediately rather than risk being overwhelmed. "Those on foot were driven back with the loss of one killed and three wounded." [BC-p.145] The Indians killed the wounded militiamen who were unable to escape and scalped them in view of the fort defenders. Soon, the warriors paraded their bloody trophies and parts of the mutilated bodies of the militiamen before the fort walls, but out of rifle range, as their comrades surrounding the fort whooped and hollered in triumphal delight.

Due to the surprise attack of the enemy reinforcement, Caldwell ordered a party of Indian scouts to cover the trail leading to the south for several miles. He was sure that the small detachment of militiamen had been local. However, more men were sure to come, and with his force of Rangers and Indians spread out around the perimeter of the fort fields, a large party of the enemy might be able to roll up the Indians, if allowed to approach without warning. In the meantime, Caldwell ordered the Rangers back to their work of killing the livestock, which had to be done by hand, as their was not enough powder and shot that could be wasted on the animals. By early evening, the Rangers finally completed their task, "killing upwards of 300 hogs, 157 head of cattle, and a number of sheep." [HP-45] Caldwell was determined that if the enemy was to be left in possession of the fort, that they would have it, but everything else of value outside the walls would be destroyed by the time the battle was over. Two more out-cabins were set on fire, and all the horses that could be found outside the fort were gathered up to be taken by the Rangers and Indians on their withdrawal. In addition, Caldwell had his men methodically destroy the nearby crops of the enemy, whereby the Rangers "pulled up and destroyed their potatoes, cut down a great deal of their corn, burnt their hemp and did other considerable damage." [HP-45] By nightfall, there was nothing left standing outside the fort walls of value to the Virginians.

"Nigh 100 Indians Left Me"

A council was called after dark by Caldwell at the urging of the Indians. McKee, Elliott, and Simon and George Girty attended, to listen to the chiefs of the Lake Indians, and the few warriors of the Wyandots, Shawnee, and Delaware. The Indians explained to Caldwell through the interpreters that they had enough of attacking the fort, and wanted to break off the battle in the morning, as there was no way they could envision assaulting the fort without taking more losses. They needed only to point that five warriors had been killed and two wounded, which the Indians blamed on Caldwell not having cannon with him, as Bird did during the successful attack on Ruddel's post two years before. Caldwell responded to their complaint by pointing out to them that the casualties were due to "the Indians exposing themselves too much" to the accurate fire of the enemy riflemen. Yet he could see no practical way of taking the enemy fort, and so agreed with the Indians to call off the fight in the morning and withdraw their force in the direction of the Ohio River after a night's rest.

At dawn on the morning of August 17, Caldwell had the Rangers prepare the horses to carry the meager food gathered the previous day from the settler cabins and the green corn and potatoes in the fields that could be eaten. The small, unripe vegetables would be needed to supplement their own provisions of cornmeal and flour which were almost gone. By mid-morning, the Indians vacated their posts around the fort, "finding it to no purpose to keep up a fire longer upon the fort as we were getting men killed, and had already several men wounded which were to be carried" [WM-p.28] back to the Ohio Country if possible. Then after a few parting shots, "the force under Captain Caldwell began their return march in a leisurely manner," [BC-p.147] heading northwards on the trail that they had come by to the south fork of the Licking River. "We retreated and came as far as Riddle's (sic) former station," [HP-45] when the Indians called to him to rest and council. Caldwell had no choice but to agree, and decided to camp for the night in the ruins of the enemy post. Unfortunately, some of the

Indians had other ideas. Not wanting to stay at Ruddel's, a large body of the warriors who had left their personal belongings at the forks of the Licking during the advance to Bryan's now decided to leave Caldwell and McKee, in spite of his warning that they should keep together in the safety of one large body in the event the enemy might attempt to pursue them. The bulk of the Indians were Shawnee, Delaware and Wyandot warriors who expressed great determination to keep moving by that trail to gather their things and rejoin their comrades at Wapatomika. Caldwell could not keep them from leaving as he had wished. "Nigh 100 Indians left me, as they went after their things they left at the forks of Licking." [HP-45] Though perturbed at the loss, Caldwell could still count nearly 200 warriors of the Lake tribes who chose to stay with him, in the hopes that they could find an enemy outpost to ambush or attack. Caldwell remained optimistic that an enemy force might attempt to follow his own, providing him an opportunity for an Indian-style ambush. His 30 Rangers would be ready, if called upon, to do so.

"The Enemy Was Within a Half Mile of Us"

Caldwell did not have long to wait. On the morning of August 17 just as his force had gotten underway, word reached him by a mounted Indian scout that a large force of mounted enemy militiamen had arrived at Bryant's fort soon after dawn. Captain Caldwell took interest, and questioned Matthew Elliott, who knew a great deal about the lay of the land between Ruddel's and the Ohio River, as to the best spot for an ambush, or at least the whereabouts of higher ground than that of the Licking bottomland which the trail from the forks ran through. Elliott informed Caldwell about a path ahead which led cross-country to the salt licks and a natural ford across the north fork of the Licking River. Elliott remembered that the hills on the north side of the ford gave a commanding view of the approach from the south, and were cut with wooded ravines which could provide an excellent opportunity along the buffalo trace for an ambush of Caldwell's choosing. Caldwell sent his scouts forward to secure the ford and "took the road by the Blue Licks as it was higher, and the ground more advantageous in case the Enemy should pursue us." McKee saw to it that a rearguard of mounted scouts posted themselves out of sight along the trail from Ruddel's at predetermined spots where they could view the trail in the distance without being seen by the enemy, and inform him and Caldwell if the enemy were in pursuit. Then Caldwell and McKee moved on with the body of Rangers and Indians, where they "got to the Licks on the 17th and encamped" [HP-45] for the evening, "near an advantageous hill, and expecting the Enemy would pursue, determined here to wait for them, keeping spies at the Lick." [WM-p.28] In an attempt to provide himself with accurate intelligence, after reaching the heights of the hills overlooking the Licking, Caldwell sent one of his best Rangers on horseback to scout the trail south of the Licking by the way they had just come. There, Caldwell's scout could keep a lookout on the trail from

Ruddel's, and have ample time to warn Caldwell if any of the militiamen came in pursuit.

Unknown to Caldwell and McKee, there were, indeed, mounted militiamen from the surrounding forts and stations in Kentucky who responded to the alarm and "soon gathered in considerable force at Bryan's Station and determined to pursue the retreating army" [BC-p.147] of British Rangers and Indians, "having little idea of its numerical strength." Caldwell had with him at the Licks "30 picked Rangers and about 200 Lake Indians," [HP-10] where at first light, he prepared an ambush, "on a hilltop, a half-mile beyond a ford over the Licking River." [GJ-p.38] When the Kentuckians left Bryan's Station on August 18 to pursue the Indians, they could count "182 men...under the command of Colonel John Todd." [BC-p.147] Responding to the call for the militia were Colonel Stephen Trigg and Major Hugh McGary both of Harrodsburg, with Colonel Daniel Boone from Boones Borough, who each brought their own men comprised of their neighbors, friends, and family respectively, to join Todd's force from Lexington. [GJ-p.37] Word reached the combined militia force at Bryant's Station that Colonel Benjamin Logan was on his way to join them with over 400 men from Logan's fort, but Todd dismissed the idea of waiting for the added reinforcement, arguing with the militia officers on August 18, that they needed to "set out at once, lest the Indian raiders escape." [GJ-p.38] After some argument, the officers decided to leave Bryan's in pursuit, and the entire force of 182 men set off at once to overtake the Indians.

Early of the morning of August 19, Caldwell's scout came riding hard into camp with an alarming report for Caldwell and McKee that a large mounted force of the enemy had been spotted heading towards the river ford. "One of my party that was watching the road came in and told me the Enemy was within a mile of us." [HP-45] The Ranger brought Caldwell the first good news that he had heard since he set out on the expedition to Kentucky. It meant that the Rebels were riding in hot pursuit of the Indians, which presented Caldwell with the possibility of ambushing them if they were reckless enough to fall into the trap he planned to set. There was no time to waste to make ready. Morning cooking fires were quickly doused, the horses were taken to a ravine and secured, and Caldwell had McKee make sure that the tracks of the horses and the footprints of the Indians at the other side of the ford were plainly visible in the soft riverbank soil to convince the approaching militiamen that the trail of the Indians led across the Licking River and up the slope of the wide ravine that made its way to the crest of the hills where Caldwell's ambush had been positioned.

"The Indians Were Trying to Conceal Their Numbers"

With little time remaining, Captain Caldwell remembered the successful ambush of the militia when they advanced from Forty Fort in the Wyoming Valley to pursue the Indians who had led the militia to believe that they were withdrawing by burning several settler cabins. The militia had then come in hot pursuit, looking for the rearguard of the Indian war party. Caldwell had been there when Colonel

Butler had used an old ruse learned from the fight with the French and their Indians 20 years prior. To ensure that the militia would rush headlong into the awaiting ambush, Butler had made sure that the enemy vanguard found what appeared to be the rear of the Indian war party. Butler had purposely instructed a handful of warriors to tarry on the trail and allow the Rebel vanguard to catch sight of them, creating for the militiamen the mistaken belief that they had, by their hot pursuit, caught up with the Indians they had been chasing, and all that remained to do was to run the Indians down. As the militiamen threw all caution to the wind in their rush to attack the Indians, they were ambushed by Butler's hidden force of Rangers and Indians and slain almost to a man.

Caldwell asked McKee to place two warriors on the forward slope of the hillside in plain view from the ford of the river. These two Indians were to act as decoys, and McKee instructed them to act as if they were straggling behind the main body of the retreating Indian war party, and allow the enemy to see them as they approached the ford from the trail to the south. Caldwell hoped the militiamen would presume the rest of the Indians they were pursuing were just over the crest of the hill, and this belief that they had finally caught up with the Indians would spur them on to cross the river and enter the ambush. Caldwell put his Rangers in a firing line slightly beyond the crest of the hill where they could not be seen. Then, he had all the Rangers and Indians load their weapons, and lay on them in their hidden positions and wait.

If everything went as planned, the militiamen would be sorely tempted to cross the river and fall into the ambush that was waiting for them. If this enemy militia were no different than any other that Caldwell had encountered, he hoped that due to their grueling ride to catch up with the Indians, they would throw all caution to the wind, and defying good sense, allow themselves to be deceived by the situation and be ambushed. It was a clever plan that could work if given the chance, Caldwell thought to himself. Making sure that everyone was well hidden, Caldwell settled down to his own position to wait.

At 7 a.m. on the morning of August 19, the mounted Kentucky militia came into view across the Licking River as they thundered down to the ford on their horses, and stopped there to decide what course of action to take. Caldwell could see from his hidden position that the officers were dismounting to discuss the matter. Colonel Boone was alarmed that the tracks of the Indians were too plainly visible, as if the Indians wanted them to follow the trail they left. To Boone that could only mean danger in the form of an ambush lay ahead across the river shallows, warning "the rest of the group that they were being lured into a trap," [GJ-p.38] that judging from his years of experience as a woodsman and Indian fighter no retreating war party would commit such an error unless they wanted their pursuers to follow them. Too, he pointed out that some of the footprints indicated to him that the Indians were "trying to conceal their numbers by walking in each other's footprints," a sign that could only mean that there was a dangerously large force of Indians ahead, which might outnumber their own force. Boone advised that the prudent course of action was to wait on the south side of the Licking until Colonel Logan came up with reinforcements the next day.

"We Rushed in Upon Them When They Broke Immediately"

However, Boone's advice was quickly dismissed by the other officers, particularly Major McGary who called Boone's courage into question for his apparent timidity. He pointed out they had come to far too let the Indians escape, especially when two warriors were spotted on the hillside opposite their own position across the ford of the Licking. The two Indians could be clearly seen headed up the hill, loaded with some sort of plunder from the cabins looted outside Bryan's fort, and by the way they picked up their pace upon seeing the militiamen in the distance, it could only mean that those Indians were stragglers lagging behind the main Indian war party which could not be too far ahead. McGary was adamant that they attack before the Indians had a chance to get away. While Todd agreed with Boone that they should not take the chance of crossing the ford to pursue what appeared to be Indian stragglers until they were supported by Logan's reinforcement and were positive no Indians lay hidden in ambush, the two experienced officers were overruled by the other men who were more determined than ever to attack the Indians at once. Todd and Boone had no alternative but to throw their lot in with the other men. Quickly, the militiamen divided into three columns, headed by Colonels Todd, Trigg, and Boone. Major McGary would lead a vanguard of 20 mounted men ahead, while the three columns of attackers dismounted after crossing the shallows of the Licking and prepared to move up the low, rising hill, roughly straddling the animal trace in the three separated units of militiamen.

Captain Caldwell could see everything that was happening from his hidden position on the heights overlooking the ford some distance away. Caldwell was pleased with the way the two warriors were taking their time moving up the hill on foot, which he hoped would be enough to do the trick to lure the militia to chase them. He was delighted when he saw the enemy divide themselves up, and "they advanced in good order." [HP-45] The ruse provided by the two apparent stragglers had worked. "They had spied some of us and it was the very place they expected to overtake us," [HP-45] for by understanding that the pursuing militia had wanted to find Indians, Caldwell had obliged them, and presented the militia with what appeared to be the rear of the Indian war party the militia were pursuing. All was going according to Caldwell's plan.

The three columns of dismounted militia advanced up the separating gullies with the vanguard of mounted men ahead in the center, working their way up the trace to the top of the hills. Caldwell ordered the Rangers and Indians to allow the vanguard to reach the crest and fire on the decoys in the distance which would spur on the unsuspecting columns to fully enter the ambush, while more of the warriors could work their way around the advancing militiamen to be able to seal off the escape route, once the fighting began. As McGary and his men reached the hilltop, one of the straggling Indians ahead fired a lone shot at the vanguard which caused them to spur their mounts on in haste to catch up with the Indians, firing wildly at the small party ahead from their saddles. "We had but fired one gun till they gave us a volley and stood to," Caldwell remarked. It was the last thing they were able to do while still alive, he observed, for "the Kentuckians indeed thought they were pursuing a retreating force" [WM-p.28] when in fact, they had unknowingly played into Caldwell's hand. "Caldwell had used the same strategy as in New York a year earlier; he would feign retreat, draw the enemy in, and attack from favorable positions." [WM-p.28]

From the bushes and low scrub bordering the buffalo trace, Caldwell's Rangers rose up and fired a solid volley of buck-shot and lead ball into McGary's men, killing and wounding all but three, who dropped from their saddles and were pounced upon by Indian warriors who dispatched them with a fury of slashing knives and tomahawks. From all sides of the gullies below the hill, the Indians responded to the firing with volleys of musket fire of their own from their hidden positions, dropping dozens of the surprised militiamen in their tracks. Captain Caldwell called to the Rangers to move forward, which they did, to confront Todd and Trigg's troops who had momentarily halted to face the Indian onslaught. The Rangers skillfully reloaded their Brown Bess short-barreled smoothbore muskets on the run by simply pouring some black powder down the muzzle of the weapon and then putting buck shot and lead ball down the barrel the same way, and then securing the load by tamping the butt of the musket on the ground. Priming the pan with a little powder and cocking back the hammer holding the flint was all that was needed to fire again, unlike the militiamen who had to load their rifles by a laborious method that involved tamping the powder, greased lead ball, and wadding with a ramrod, which took much more time to complete than a musket. While rifles were more accurate than muskets, the Rangers knew that in close-quarter fighting, all that mattered was dropping as many of the enemy as quickly as possible. For every one shot that an enemy rifleman could get off in slightly more than a minute, a Ranger could re-load and fire up to five shots in the same amount of time, and with the use of buckshot that discharged from their weapons in a wide spread of lead, the Rangers could hit most of the militiamen at least once at close range before they could reload their rifles.

Caldwell moved the Rangers quickly from their ambush position slightly over the crest of the hill back down the reverse side to confront the center column of Colonel Todd and the men on the right under Colonel Trigg. Unaccustomed to the sight of uniformed soldiers opposing them, the militiamen hesitated for a moment while preparing to fire a volley up hill. Seeing the militiamen present their weapons at them, the Rangers had enough time to fall to the ground just as the militiamen of Todd's column fired their weapons. As the bullets whizzed harmlessly over the heads of the experienced Rangers, their own front rank quickly came to the kneeling position and presented their muskets at the enemy. Colonel Todd looked on in horror and disbelief at the leveled muskets that spewed out a concentrated volley of lead into the ranks of his stunned men, every ball finding a mark and dropping dozens of the Kentuckians where they stood. It was the last thing that Todd saw before a musket ball hit him squarely in the head, killing him. Immediately the second rank of Rangers kneeling slightly behind the first who had just fired, stood up and fired another deadly volley into the enemy, just as the first rank was finished loading and were priming their muskets to fire again. The militiamen had no chance to respond at all to the precision firing that withered their ranks. With the Indians pressing in from the sides and the Rangers firing at the exposed men from the higher ground, the militia columns began to disintegrate, as dozens upon dozens of fallen militiamen writhed on the ground and screamed in pain from their wounds, as their comrades turned and ran in terror, many dropping their weapons to the ground.

Caldwell could see the warriors below the hill moving in on the flanks of the retreating militiamen in an attempt to cut them off from their horses. Quickly he ordered the Rangers to fix their bayonets, and signaled to McKee that the time had come to turn the rout of the enemy into total defeat. Giving the order to attack and annihilate the enemy, "we rushed in upon them when they broke immediately." [HP-45] Pandemonium resulted, as dozens of Rangers and Indians caught up and engaged the retreating militiamen in hand-to-hand combat. After the initial volleys, the bodies of the enemy were savagely thrust with bayonets, clubbed with rifle butts or crushed with war clubs and bloodied hatchets. Some of the Kentuckians threw down their weapons and attempted to surrender. Those men who were fortunate enough to be taken prisoner by a Ranger were spared. However, the Lake Indians who waded into the retreating enemy with hatchets and knives flashing lost all self-control when they smelled the blood of those men already killed and sensed the panicked flight of their prey. The warriors slaughtered whoever fell into their hands as quick as they were able to reach them, whether the militiamen tried to surrender or not. The warriors fought with a fury fueled not only by blood lust but a pent-up thirst for vengeance. Soon their near-naked painted bodies were streaked with the blood of their victims and their hands bathed red from the butchery at hand.

"We Killed and Took 146"

Colonel Boone could see from his position with his besieged column that the militia had blundered into a hopeless ambush and must now fight their way out by whatever means to reach the horses and safety by crossing the river. Rallying what men he could, Boone had them retreat by means of a fighting withdrawal, to protect from being overwhelmed. As he turned to see if anyone was left of Trigg's and Todd's columns, his son, Israel, at his side, was shot through the neck and fell to the ground, blood pouring profusely from the young man's mouth. There was nothing Boone could do to save him, and seeing that he was in danger of being killed himself, had to leave Israel in his death throes on the hillside gully. It was almost more than Boone could bear. Still, knowing there was nothing more he could do for his son, and with so many of his men in dire need of help in escaping the Indian onslaught, Boone forced himself to turn away from Israel, and he rallied what straggling men he could and escorted them "into dense woods to the left, with orders to cross the Licking downstream, beyond range of the warriors' muskets," after which Boone himself "cautiously made his way back to the river," [GJ-p.39] rejoining what men who had escaped the Indians and were remounting their horses on the far shore. Conspicuously absent were Colonels Todd and Trigg, and the bulk of their men. Only McGary and another man of the vanguard were alive. Quickly the remains of the militia force took off back down the trail they had come by, for they could surmise that the Indians and Rangers were intending to pursue them soon.

Captain Caldwell gave orders for the Rangers to bring up their horses and begin the pursuit of the remaining militia whom he had observed on the opposite side of the Licking riding away. Few Indians would agree to accompany the Rangers, for with so many dead, wounded, and captured enemy on the battlefield, the warriors were too preoccupied to want to leave their gruesome work on the battlefield which they delighted in. The bulk of Caldwell's Rangers rode down the hill and crossed the river ford. "We pursued for about two miles, and as the Enemy was mostly on horseback, it was in vain to follow further." [HP-45] On the battlefield itself, Caldwell and McKee began to take count of the enemy casualties, and the sizable number of prisoners whom Caldwell questioned at length. "We killed and took 146, amongst them is Colonel Todd, the commander, Colonel Boone, Lieutenant Colonel Trigg, Major Harlin who commanded the infantry and a number more of their officers." [HP-45] Caldwell was misinformed about Colonel Boone, as Daniel Boone had, indeed, managed to escape. McKee assessed the losses of the militia, which were staggering. "We were not much superior to them in numbers, they being about 200 picked men from the settlements of Kentucky, commanded by Colonels Todd, Trigg, and Boone, with Majors Harlin and McGeary, most of who fell in the actions. From the best inquiry I could make upon the spot, there was upwards of 140 killed and taken with near 100 rifles- several being thrown into the deep river that were not recovered." [HP-28]

"He Died Like a Warrior, Fighting Arm to Arm"

With the battle now over and no more shots fired, the warriors emerged from the woods and brushy gullies adjoining the area where the militia columns had marched and began their grim work. Methodically, each one the scores of wounded militiamen who still lay upon the field of battle thrashing in pain and moaning for help were approached by the warriors and knelt over one at a time, to be disposed of by the Indians. Each wounded man was stripped of his clothes and then while still alive, was butchered, hacked, brained, and scalped by the warriors in bloody triumph. For more than a half hour, their pitiful screams for mercy were pierced by the shrill screams of men being dismembered alive, combined with the monotonous thudding and chopping sounds of hatchets hacking into human flesh. Caldwell wanted to save the prisoners who were not wounded who he could to take with him back to the Ohio Country. In sparing them, he saw no point in rebuking the Indians for massacring those militiamen who were already wounded, as he knew that the wounded were already doomed, and could not be saved. From years of experience in wilderness fighting, Caldwell knew that the warriors believed that it was their right to slay the hated enemy they had fought for so long, many of whom were responsible for the killing of their brethren in previous campaigns. For Caldwell, it was a simple tradeoff, to save those prisoners who were able to physically make the trip to the Ohio Country. Intuitively Caldwell knew that if the Indians already had many scalps of the enemy hanging from their belts that he would have greater bargaining power with them when they came to him demanding the prisoners to burn in their fires, which he would refuse. There was little Caldwell could do to help those men who were taken prisoner by the Ottawas and Chippewas, who would not give them up. Because he would not risk insulting the Indians and have them desert him at such a great distance from Detroit, he did not order them to turn over to him their property taken in battle, for that would provoke a confrontation he could not win. If the Indians wanted to burn those prisoners, he would have to let them do so.

As soon as the wounded were all slain, the warriors turned to the task of scalping the dead, and mutilating and dismembering the corpses until they were unrecognizable, hacking off genitals, heads, and arms, while disemboweling the torsos, and in some cases, cutting out the hearts of the corpses. Gradually the work turned to the search for valuables, plunder and food. Many warriors concentrated on rounding up the scores of horses left by the dead militiamen that were still wandering about the area. The Rangers returned to the battlefield from their pursuit, and joined the Indians in plundering the dead, however for different reasons. The Rangers searched the dead militiamen for food, clothing, and ammunition, for they knew beyond a shadow of a doubt that, with no reinforcements coming from Detroit, they would have to make do with whatever means of re-supply that was at their disposal, and at the moment, the dead Kentuckians were providing a rich source. Many of Caldwell's men tried on the shoes and moccasins of the militiamen to see if they would fit, for their own footgear were rotting off in shreds or non-existent due to the length of time the men had been out in the field exposed to the elements since leaving Niagara. Since what was left of their wool uniforms was in tatters, the Rangers hunted for shirts and trousers that would fit them, and any leather pouches or cartridge boxes that were usable. At a premium as they searched the packs of the fallen Rebels were spare flints, gun springs, powder, ball, and of course provisions which both the Rangers and Indians were sorely lacking, having almost exhausted their own food by the time of the battle.

Caldwell, McKee and Elliott walked over the battlefield strewn with corpses. Thankfully, their own casualties had been surprisingly light. McKee counted 10 Indians killed by the enemy, with an additional 14 wounded, [HP-28] to Caldwell's partial count of "six Indians killed and ten wounded." [HP-45] None of the 30 Rangers with Caldwell had been slain, nor wounded in the engagement, however one white man had died, and McKee took Caldwell and Elliott to the body of La Butte, the French interpreter from the Indian Department,

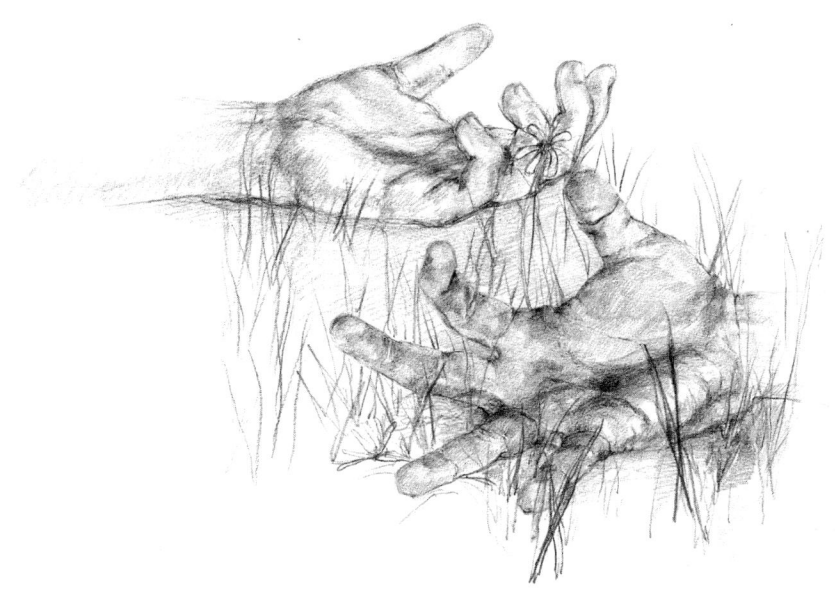

*The corpses of fallen Kentucky militiamen litter
the field after the battle of Blue Licks.*

who laid on the field partially covering the corpse of one of the Rebels. McKee had witnessed La Butte's death, which occurred when La Butte agreed to save a young militiaman who was pleading for mercy to surrender. As La Butte lowered his musket, one of the young man's comrades had shot La Butte in the chest at point-blank range, killing him instantly, and triggering the Indians nearby to kill both of the militiamen as a result. It was an unfortunate circumstance, as La Butte was a personal friend of McKee and Elliott from Detroit. "Mr. La Butte of the Indian Department, who by sparing the life of one of the Enemy and endeavoring to take him prisoner, lost his own," noted McKee. "Our loss is Monsieur La Butte killed," noted Caldwell. "He died like a warrior, fighting arm to arm." [HP-45]

"We Waited Upon the Ground For Him This Day"

A council of the Indians was called by Caldwell to decide what to do. Naturally, the Indians wanted to leave immediately for the Ohio River and home to their villages in the Ohio Country and Detroit with what scalps, horses, and prisoners they had. Caldwell was not in favor of leaving so soon, and argued that everyone needed a rest, and as most of the Indians and Rangers had not eaten much in days, he pointed out that the meat from the freshly slain horses could provide them with a much-needed cooked meal. What was on Caldwell's mind was that he had learned from interrogating the prisoners that another body of the Rebels might be on their way to the Licks, now that nearly 50 of the enemy who escaped the Indians would soon inform their friends of what happened, and how many men Caldwell had with his force. "It is said by the prisoners that a Colonel Logan was expected to join them with 100 men or more," [HP-28] McKee was able to find out from some of the captured men that in regards to Clark's army at the Falls of the Ohio "there is no talk of any expedition from that quarter, nor indeed are they able without assistance from the colonies, and that the militia of the country have been employed during the summer in building the fort at the Falls." [HP-28]

Some of the prisoners who had recently returned from there, described to McKee and Caldwell "what they call a Row Galley which has made one trip up the river to the mouth of the Big Miami River, and occasioned that alarm which created us so much trouble. She carries one six-pounder, six four-pounders, and two two-pounders and rows 80 oars." [HP-28] Upon hearing this, Caldwell roared with laughter at the thought of the Shawnee scouts who spotted the big boat on the Ohio and heard the enemy fire one of the cannons, scampered in terror all the way back to Wapatomika, convinced that Clark and his entire army was aboard. McKee added that the prisoners told him the boat at one time carried "at the Big Bone Lick 100 men, but being chiefly draughts from the militia, many of them left her on different parts of the river." [HP-28]

Caldwell advised McKee, Elliott, the Girtys, and the Indians that they should wait until the next day before leaving as there was a chance that the enemy under Colonel Logan might ride to the Licks to come to the aid of their comrades, or to bury them, in which case, Caldwell wanted an opportunity to ambush them too. The dead bodies of the militiamen were bloating in the sun and would provide the ample bait if the Rebels should be unlucky enough to attempt to cross the river again. However, Caldwell advised that they move their camp to a spot over the hill some distance from the bodies which were creating a horrible stench as they began to decay in the stifling heat. An agreement was reached to wait a day to see if Logan would arrive. "We waited upon the ground for him this day." [HP-28] At the same time, Caldwell sent out several hand-picked scouts to patrol the trail to the south across the river in the direction of Bryan's station to keep a look-out for signs of the enemy's approach, while sending a party of men north along the buffalo trace towards the Ohio to look for signs of the enemy along the route Caldwell intended to march the next day if no signs of Logan were forthcoming.

"Captain Bradt Is Setting Out For the Neighborhood of Wheeling"

By mid-morning of the next day, August 20, Caldwell called in his scouts on the trail to the south. They reported there was no sign of Colonel Logan's militia force. "Seeing there was not much probability of his coming, we set off and crossed the Ohio the second day after the action," [MK-28] learning there, from Indian scouts from Wapatomika, that Turney with the balance of the Rangers and Indians had moved downriver in search of the enemy but found no one. They were forced to return to the Shawnee village of Wapatomika for want of food. Caldwell and McKee turned their force of Rangers, Indians, and prisoners for that village as well, arriving there on August 26. On the brink of starvation, they discovered "to our disappointment we find no provisions brought forward to this place, or likelihood of any for some time, and we have entirely subsisted since we left this, on what we got in the woods and took from the Enemy." [HP-28] The strength and health of the Rangers, in particular, were fading fast, as Captain Caldwell, like many of his men upon reaching Wapatomika, was stricken with sickness.

Several important messages were waiting for Caldwell and McKee at Wapatomika. First, a dispatch written by Major DePeyster had been addressed to each of the two men, which they opened immediately. To their utter surprise, Caldwell and McKee found a formal directive from DePeyster sent by Powell and Haldimand "ordering them not to make any incursions into the Enemy's country, but to act on the defensive only." [HP-33] The war with the Americans was coming to a close as peace negotiations were in progress, and an armistice had been called in the eastern former colonies. DePeyster had sent a message to Captain Bradt of the Rangers too, who had reached Wapatomika only days before from Sandusky, but left immediately with James Girty and a large body of Indians for the settlement of Wheeling on the Ohio River. Bradt was reacting to a dispatch informing him that the Rebels were massing there in preparation for another expedition into the Indian Country. "I am informed by a deserter the Enemy are determined to march, from one thousand to 1,500 strong. When the deserter left them in the beginning of this month, they were assembling in the neighborhood of Wheeling and Fort McIntosh, under the command of the blood thirsty Colonel Williamson who so much distinguished himself in the massacre of the Christian Indians, at the settlement of Muskingum, which cruel proceedings have been the cause of the later retaliation of the Delawares and Shawanese on the person of Colonel Crawford." [HP-33]

"We have since our arrival heard something of this matter and that the particulars have been forwarded to you," McKee wrote to DePeyster. "A detachment of Rangers with a large party of Delawares and Shawanese are gone that way, who will be able to discover the truth of this matter." [HP-28] However DePeyster was worried. "I hope the courier will be in time to stop Captain Bradt who is on the point of setting out for the neighborhood of Wheeling" [HP-33] which would run contrary to the orders given him to prevent any more attacks on the enemy. In regards to Bradt and Caldwell, DePeyster clearly needed them to bring their men in. "My endeavors, however shall be to turn their attention towards Sandusky" [HP-33] where it appeared enemy intended on attacking, and the Rangers must defend. Antoine Chesne of the Indian Department thought it wise to inform DePeyster on August 18 at Sandusky of renewed word of the enemy's intentions from a party of Delaware warriors arriving from a scout on the Ohio. A day later, Chesne's information was confirmed by a party of Pottawattamie warriors who "came in here, they have been at Cross Creek but could not take a prisoner, and on their return home on this side of the Big River they found a Negro they think he was horse hunting." [HP-291]

"Hanna's Town Was Burnt"

Chesne and Arundel interrogated the prisoner. He told them that he was not out horse hunting as the Indians had reported, but that "his master's name was Epharain Hart from whom he deserted," [HP-291] and that he was more than willing to tell Chesne and Arundel everything that he knew about the plans of the Americans, of which he was well informed. From the Negro, the two British agents learned that "General Irwin is mustering men at Fort Pitt to come against Sandusky and they are to come 1,500 in number. This is what he heard at his Master's house, where all the meetings of the country are kept and where several hundreds of that place had already given in their names to join General Irwin." Because the Negro had been in attendance at those meetings of the militia, he was able to tell Chesne and Arundel that in "the beginning of September they are to set off for this place, they are not to have cannon as the expedition is to be carried on with all the secrecy possible, and they intend it shall be as expeditious as possible, as their intention is to kill and burn all before them. As soon as this matter was mentioned, there was 400 rose and said they would go to revenge the Death of Colonel Crawford." [HP-291] While on the one hand it seemed incredulous to Chesne that the slave would know so much about the movements of the Rebels against Sandusky, on the other hand, Chesne realized that he could not take a chance that the prisoner was in fact telling the truth and Sandusky was again to be threatened from Fort Pitt.

Chesne sent a message to DePeyster with this intelligence: "The Enemy is assembling at this side of the Big River, of which Captain Bradt at the Shawnee towns is informed, so there's no time to lose to send the assistance to this place. The Indians from here are going off on a scout to see the Enemy, and begged I would let you know, hoping you'll be so good as to give them all the assistance you can this time, as you were pleased to do before, and they are in good hopes they'll meet with the same success." [HP-387] The Negro had one more important thing to tell Chesne and Arundel, which he thought they might find of interest, concerning the fate of a small settlement in Pennsylvania about 35 miles east of Fort Pitt, named Hanna's Town. It seemed that sometime in July, a large war party of Indians had attacked the settlement. "Hanna's Town was burnt by some white people and about 200 Indians," the Negro had heard. "They killed seven and took nine prisoners. They killed all the cattle there." [HP-291] Chesne could only guess that the raiding party was that of King Guyashutta with his Seneca warriors accompanied by rangers from the Indian Department from Fort Niagara which Chesne knew had set out from Fort Niagara in early July for Wheeling before diverting eastward into the Pennsylvania highlands.

"Being Notoriously Known For a Disaffected Person"

There was another matter awaiting Alexander McKee when he arrived at Wapatomika, which he found offensive. Major DePeyster had written a separate letter to him, dated August 6, concerning the recent conduct of the Indians, which in essence, laid blame for the cruel acts of the Indians at McKee's feet. Major DePeyster's letter, directed by Powell and Haldimand, was clearly a reprimand. McKee was angry at the tone of the letter and the duplicity on the parts of his superior officers in their policy regarding the use of Indians. The commanders wanted him to urge Indians to attack the Rebels and expel them from their lands since the British officers had no troops to do so, other than the handful of Rangers. Yet Haldimand wanted the Indians to fight like white men, which they were not. They fought in battle in a manner suited to the wilderness that was a part of their ancient customs. That style of warfare included the disposing of their prisoners by methods that white men found savage and barbaric. To McKee it was simple. If you employed the Indians to fight in the wilderness, they would do so in the only manner they knew how. Vengeance drove the Indians to fight the enemy and vengeance drove them to burn their prisoners, like Crawford, for Indian blood that had been spilled.

Further, McKee thought it was hypocritical for DePeyster to criticize the Indians for cruelty towards prisoners when the enemy on the frontier did not adhere to the same civilized standards of warfare that Haldimand was espousing. When it came to the Indians, the Virginians were equally brutal and barbaric, as was demonstrated with the massacre of the Moravian Delaware men, women, and children who were clubbed, scalped, and burnt. In McKee's mind, the wilderness war between the Indians and the Americans was a fight to the death. Both sides were determined to exterminate the other. The Indians were fighting for their very survival. How could Haldimand and DePeyster chastise them for burning a handful of enemy prisoners, when the Indians had done so much for the British to oust the Rebels from their lands? McKee did not believe the criticism of the conduct of the Indians was justified, nor the attack upon himself.

As Indian Agent and officer in the field responsible for the Indians, McKee fought back his own anger and frustration at DePeyster's admonishment. Part of the problem had been caused by an old adversary, Isaac Zeans, who informed DePeyster of the burning of the prisoners to attempt to stir up trouble for McKee. McKee decided to respond to DePeyster's allegation by discrediting the source of the reports. "I am this day favoured with yours of the 6th of August containing the report of Isaac Zeans concerning the cruelty of the Indians. It is true they have made sacrifices to their revenge after the massacre of their women and children, some being known to them to be perpetrators of it, but is was done in my absence or before I could reach any of the places to interfere and I can assure you Sir, that there is not a white person here wanting in their duty to represent to the Indians in the strongest terms the highest abhorrence of such conduct, as well as the bad consequences that may attend to it to both them and us, being contrary to the rule of carrying on war by civilized nations." [HP-28] McKee paused for a moment, wishing that Haldimand and DePeyster could see this war through his eyes for one day, fought in the wilderness between two adversaries, each bent on exterminating the other with disregard for any rules of civility. Continuing on, "However, it is probable that Zeans may have exaggerated matters greatly being notoriously known for a disaffected person, and concerned in sending prisoners away with intelligence to the Enemy, at the time Captain Bird came out as we were then informed." [HP-28] Satisfied that he had said all he could in writing to DePeyster under the circumstances, he added a note to the officer that Matthew Elliott "is to be the bearer of this who will be able to give you any further information necessary respecting matters here." [HP-28] At least McKee knew that his friend, who was preparing to leave for Detroit, was of the same mind as his own.

"Captain Caldwell Is Conformable To My Orders"

Just prior to dawn on the morning of September 11, Captain Andrew Bradt and his company of nearly 50 Rangers and over 230 Wyandot, Mingo, Delaware and Shawnee warriors got underway on the trail leading east from the Muskingum River Valley to the crest of the hills that separated the watershed of the Muskingum from that of Indian Wheeling Creek. Captain Bradt and the Rangers [HP-358] "having arrived at Sandusky too late to overtake Caldwell" [CE-p.109] on his march into Kentucky, made his way with his men to the Shawnee village of Wapatomika, where he met James Girty by August 15 with a large party of Shawnee warriors returning from the village of Piqua having left Caldwell, McKee and Elliott on their expedition to the Ohio River and beyond. Bradt had explicit orders from DePeyster and Powell to find Caldwell and place his company of Rangers under the senior officer's command. However James Girty quickly acquainted Bradt with what had transpired at Piqua, telling Bradt that while Caldwell wondered where Bradt and his reinforcement might be, Caldwell had given Girty no orders for Bradt if he should encounter him on the trail from the Upper Sandusky villages to Wapatomika. At nearly the same time, word reached Girty and Bradt at Wapatomika from Indian runners to the east and from Chesne at Sandusky that it appeared that the Rebels intended to march on the Upper Sandusky villages from the area of Fort Pitt, where they were assembling troops. In council with the Delaware, Wyandot, Shawnee and Mingo warriors at Wapatomika, Captain Bradt discovered that Captain Caldwell had originally intended to march against the settlement of Wheeling in July before he was diverted to the south. Consequently Bradt decided to gather "all the Indians that could be mustered- 238 in number, to march at once against Wheeling," [BC-p.149] having received no orders at Wapatomika from DePeyster or Caldwell to do otherwise, and not having heard as yet DePeyster's directive to him, to take only defensive action in the Ohio Country.

By early afternoon on September 11, Bradt, on his march to Wheeling with the Rangers and Indians, inadvertently learned from the Indians that his force was no more than a couple of miles away from crossing the ridge of hills that would take them down the trail to the Ohio River and the settlement of Wheeling. Bradt was disturbed to find that the Indians had no scouts out ahead of the main body. He felt that it was most critical that they do so, if they intended on taking the enemy at Wheeling's Fort Henry by surprise. Bradt called to James Girty to inform the chiefs and headmen that he wished to halt their column and council with them concerning the necessity of posting forward scouts before the Rangers would proceed any further. Girty reluctantly did so, knowing that the head warriors would not react well to this latest suggestion of the young arrogant Ranger captain, who had been grating on their nerves ever since leaving Wapatomika. While Girty knew enough about Bradt to understand that the officer meant well, nonetheless, his constant counseling to the Indians had already annoyed the warriors to the point that they privately informed Girty that they did not like the Ranger Captain at all and would abandon him if he took to giving them orders. James Girty found himself in the awkward and unpleasant situation of having to mediate between Bradt and the Indians to ensure that the attack against Wheeling did not disintegrate before the Rangers and Indians had an opportunity to get there. Girty could see that Bradt had no rapport with the Indians. Bradt masked his inexperience in working with Indians and his fear of them with aloofness and distain. The warriors, on the other hand, reacted to the young officer's haughtiness, mistaking his inexperience with Indians for hostility directed towards them. All that Girty could do, under the circumstances was to try to temper both parties' icy responses to one another through the words Girty chose in translating, in hopes of keeping peace. Bradt's latest suggestions to the Indians was trying Girty's patience to the limit, for when it came to asking the Indians to do something, Bradt was no Captain Caldwell.

Captain Bradt could not bring himself to sit before the Indians in a formal council setting just to talk to them. Rather, he paced before the handful of chiefs, as he attempted to explain to them the importance of sending out scouts ahead on the trail at this critical point in their march. Since they were nearing the vicinity of the enemy, if they hoped to take the small settlement and fort by surprise and catch the inhabitants outside the fort walls, it was imperative that they send out scouts and flankers to intercept any enemy scouts that might he encounter up ahead, who if allowed to escape, would be able to bring word to the settlement of an of an impending attack. Girty dutifully translated the officer's words to the Indians. While he knew that Bradt's words made perfect sense, he worried that the Indians would take the officer's suggestion as a personal slight, for Girty could see that the Indians did not need an interpreter to understand the officer's cold manner with them. No reaction was forthcoming from the Indians in response to Bradt's directive. The Ranger officer asked Girty what the Indians were saying. Unfazed, the Indians whispered to each other, ignoring Bradt altogether. Girty could not bring himself to tell the Captain the truth that Indians wished that they had a real Ranger captain with them like Thompson or Caldwell whom they found more agreeable than this one strutting before them. Rather, Girty made the mistake of telling Bradt that the Indians did not understand him.

Hearing this, and wishing to make himself more clear, Captain Bradt felt that further explanation was needed. He told the Indians that before he was appointed a captain of the Rangers by his uncle, Lt. Col. John Butler, as a lieutenant he had accompanied several Indian war parties into the Mohawk Valley where the Iroquois had employed the use of advanced scouts and flanking troops with much success. When Captain Bradt described how he and Joseph Brant had ambushed the enemy supply train approaching Fort Stanwix by using scouts and flanking units to intercept the enemy column's own vanguard, the chiefs seated before Bradt suddenly took notice of the Ranger captain, and fixed their eyes upon him. The Indians had not understood a word that Bradt uttered but one, and that was the name of the Mohawk Thayendanegea. It had a catalytic effect upon them, causing the chiefs to bristle with hostility at the mention of that arrogant, boastful Iroquois who had attempted the year before to command them in the field as if they were his children, and he a great war chief over the Shawnee and Delaware.

At the mention of the name Thayendanegea, the chiefs sitting before Bradt came to a unanimous conclusion about him. If this Ranger Captain strutting before them was a friend of that despised Mohawk, then it would be much easier to desert him when the time came, though some of the Indians argued that they should abandon Bradt now and go on alone. However, calmer heads prevailed among the chiefs, and while Bradt waited, the headmen finally agreed that they should continue on the trail to Wheeling in one body with the Rangers. They would send scouts ahead as the Ranger Captain desired. For the moment, it was important that they keep it in their minds that they had come to strike a blow against the enemy at Wheeling who had taken part in the slaying of their relatives at the Muskingum villages. Until that was done, they would not break up into smaller parties and leave this arrogant white man to his own devices.

By September 1, Captain Caldwell, with all of the Rangers and many of the Lake Indians, arrived at the Upper Sandusky villages to await orders from Detroit after being summoned by Major DePeyster to go there because of the threat of Enemy incursion from Fort Pitt. Caldwell sent a dispatch immediately to DePeyster, who on September 4, informed Haldimand that "Captain Caldwell conformable to my orders is at present encamped with the Rangers and local Indians at Upper Sandusky, there to wait for a body of the Enemy which I am informed are to make another attempt upon that place." [HP-292] Caldwell had not wanted to make the trip. Many of his men, including himself, had been stricken with a sickness that spread among the Rangers and debilitated them with bouts of fever and intestinal flux that made them unfit for duty of any kind. Hardly able to ride a horse himself, Captain Caldwell nonetheless had seen to it that the Rangers followed DePeyster's orders and move from Wapatomika to Pipe's Town. McKee, who was not sick, agreed to stay with the Shawnee at Wapatomika until he could determine for sure what the intentions of the enemy were. To do that, McKee sent scouting parties south to the Ohio River in hopes of gaining intelligence on the whereabouts of Clark, and if he intended an expedition against the Indians and Detroit in retaliation for the Indian and Ranger victory at the Licks in Kentucky.

"I Have Received Information That Mr. Grenville Was Sent To Paris"

General Haldimand at Quebec decided that it was imperative that he act now to avert serious trouble with the Indians. Report after report was reaching him from the upper posts concerning growing discontent among the tribes, as more and more troubling news reached them in their villages across the Ohio Country and beyond. The Indians were becoming aware that the war in the east between the British and the Americans was over, and there was talk of negotiations with the enemy to bring about peace. They had heard of Haldimand's orders for the British to remain on the defensive and to not to attack the American frontier any more, which they could not understand. Further, the Indians learned of the General's displeasure with them for torturing and burning of Enemy prisoners, which they had done with impunity in the past. No one had interfered with them previously. However, now everything was changing and those changes were causing discord among the tribes, of which Haldimand had been kept informed. With Brigadier General Powell leaving Fort Niagara for England, Haldimand thought it was time he inform his new commander of the upper posts at Niagara, Lieutenant Colonel Alexander Dundas, what could be done to keep the Indians in the Ohio Country in check.

On September 9, Haldimand wrote a private communiqué to Dundas on the matter of the Indians. "If the Enemy should hear of the Indians' discontent, they will not fail to attempt their corruption, and there is no saying what lengths the influence and disappointment may drive them to. I would there recommend to you, without discovering the least distrust, narrowly to watch over their conduct, and by the strictest vigilance and attention at all your posts, to prevent a possibility of surprise." [HP-191] To Haldimand, that surprise could take many forms, from disaffection of the Indians to the point where they would sue for a separate peace with the enemy, to their unwillingness to fight as allies if the British posts were attacked by the Americans even at this late date. "From Colonel Butler's influence and zealous attention, you will always be furnished with the best intelligence from the Indian Country, and have timely notice of any event of Consequence. I have no apprehensions on this account but precautions are so easily taken, that it were unpardonable to risk anything by neglecting them," Haldimand noted. With all the rumors reaching him of threats of enemy attacks coming against the Indians, Haldimand did not want to chance losing any part of Canada due to the intransigence on the part of the Indians before the peace was settled. On that particular issue, Haldimand added to Dundas the chilling news that "I have received certain information that Mr. Grenville was sent to Paris, about the middle of June, on a conference to bring about a Peace, the result of which must ere long be communicated to us." [HA-191] The future of the Indians and their lands of the Ohio Country remained much in doubt in Haldimand's mind.

"The Siege of Fort Henry Was About to Begin"

What was unknown to Captain Bradt and the Indians on their march along the trail leading to the Ohio River and the settlement at Wheeling was that Colonel Ebenezer Zane, the veteran Indian fighter from Virginia who had founded the settlement at Wheeling and made his home there, had been considering the possibility of an Indian attack upon Wheeling for some time. Zane had given a great deal of thought to his vulnerable situation since he received word from General Irvine at Fort Pitt of the possibility of a major Indian raid against the settlement in mid-August. With no aid forthcoming from Fort Pitt after a detachment of regular troops briefly stationed at Fort Henry were withdrawn to Fort Pitt late in August, Zane knew that the few families remaining at Wheeling were on their own to defend themselves if the Indians should attack. Zane had about 20 able men to defend Fort Henry in that event. Most of the settlers did not realize the dire situation they faced if they were caught by surprise by Indians while they were outside the walls of Fort Henry tending to their crops, their livestock, or in their cabins. But Zane realized that, with so few men and women available to handle a rifle or musket in defense, a surprise attack by the Indians on the settlement would likely result in the wholesale slaughter of everyone.

Zane knew the consequences of being caught outside the walls of the fort by the Indians. He was a survivor of the Indian attack of 1777 against the settlement in which two companies of militia were lured outside by a small party of Indians into an ambush just east of the fort, in which many of the those unfortunate men paid for the blunder with their lives. Zane remembered warning the impetuous militiamen to remain in the fort in case the war party was a ploy to lure them into an ambush. Unfortunately, his advice was ignored by the younger men who viewed Zane's cautiousness as timidity. The fort defenders had been able to hold on in spite of losing almost two dozen militiamen in the ambush. They successfully defended the fort because of plenty of hands still inside who could handle a weapon. But the situation was different now in early September 1782. Only 20 men remained at the settlement to defend their homes, their wives, and children in the event of Indian attack. That was far too few, Zane believed, to take any chance of letting the settlement by taken by surprise.

Alarm after alarm of eminent Indian attack had been raised through July and into August along the breadth of the Virginia frontier below Fort Pitt. Word reached Zane at Wheeling from scouts that small Indian war parties were crossing the Ohio to raid isolated settler cabins. While Zane had no hard evidence of a concerted Indian attack against Wheeling, in mid-July Major Samuel McColloch and his brother John were ambushed by a large party of Wyandots several miles east of the Ohio River and almost 12 miles upriver from Wheeling. Samuel McColloch had served as the eyes and ears of Fort Henry ever since escaping from Indian pursuers during the siege of Fort Henry in September 1777, when he had spurred his mount to leap off a cliff near the crest of the hill overlooking Wheeling to avoid certain capture and a horrible death. McColloch and his brother had kept constant scouts out along the trails crisscrossing the hills between Wheeling and Van Metre's fort on Short Creek. It had been a blow to everyone at Wheeling, especially to Ebenezer Zane, when the sad news reached them from Van Metre's that Major Sam McColloch had been killed by the Indians when he and his brother John "were riding leisurely along" the trail to Van Metre's from the river and were ambushed by Indians firing from cover "a deadly discharge of rifles, killing Major McColloch instantly," [HW2-p.42] on July 30, 1782.

The next day, "a party of men from Van Metre's went out and gathered up the mutilated remains of Major McColloch." [HW2-p.42] John McColloch led them to the spot of the ambush which he himself had barely escaped. They found want was left of Sam, his corpse disemboweled and his heart cut out by the Indians who recognized the famed militiaman and remembered him as the white man who had escaped capture by bravely leaping over the cliff at Wheeling. With Sam McColloch gone, Ebenezer Zane worried that he had no one to rely upon who knew the trails as well as Sam, and who would be able to give Zane the advance warning that he needed to sound the alarm and warn the settlers of impending attack while they were outside the fort. Having requested gunpowder from General Irvine on July 22 just before McColloch's untimely death, Zane had fatefully stated the conditions of Wheeling to the General, telling him "five militia are all the strength we have at present, excepting the inhabitants of the place. A few Indians have been viewing our garrison yesterday and have returned on their backtrack, in consequence of which, we may shortly expect an attack. If any aid can be afforded, it will be very acceptable; if it cannot, we mean to support the place or perish in the attempt." With such long odds in his disfavor,

Zane reasoned that, in spite of being a God-fearing man, he must do something more to even the odds to avert a disaster at Wheeling than just put their fate in the hands of the Lord.

Ebenezer Zane thought long and hard about the precarious situation at Wheeling in the early days of September 1782. With his request for gunpowder forthcoming from Fort Pitt, Zane realized his thinking ran opposite to Captain John Boggs who had actual command of Fort Henry. Boggs believed that with ample warning, the settlement of Wheeling could easily be reinforced by militiamen from the surrounding posts at Van Metre's to the north and Catfish Camp (Washington, Pennsylvania) to the east, by sending riders post-haste at the first sign of trouble. Zane, a veteran of many clashes with the Indians, could not agree with Bogg's thinking, having known the Indians time and again to cross the Ohio unseen by anyone until it was too late. While he agreed with Boggs that reinforcements could be summoned by a rider to defend Wheeling, Zane worried that without ample warning, the effort would be in vain if the Indians managed to attack Wheeling by surprise, ruse, or ambush as they had been able to do in 1777. Zane had never allowed himself to forget the bloodied, scalped, and mangled corpses of his friends and neighbors who had lost their lives to the cunning of the Indians in the ambush of Ogle and Meason's militia companies, and Captain Foreman's massacred men several miles south of Wheeling during the fall of 1777. Without more militiamen or regulars from Fort Pitt, what Zane reasoned Wheeling needed most, if the people were to survive an Indian attack, was time to get inside the fort if the Indians suddenly attacked. Time was needed to sound the alarm of an impending Indian attack. Enough time to get everyone into the safety of the fort would decide whether the settlement at Wheeling survived, including his own family. With that in mind, the experienced Indian fighter hatched a plan to buy the time that he knew was what Wheeling needed most.

Perched high in the crotch of a large tree overlooking a part of the trail leading from the headwaters of Stillwater Creek, a tributary of the Muskingum, the veteran scout John Linn shifted his cramped legs once more on the morning of September 11. Linn scanned that part of the path that he could see in the distance, almost a quarter of a mile away from where he sat. He had left Wheeling only a few days before on Ebenezer Zane's urging, with instructions to take a few days water and provisions with him, and to find a spot on the crest of the ridge some 14 miles west of the Ohio river, where the headwaters of Indian Wheeling creek met those of the Stillwater.

Zane knew it was a tremendous gamble to send Linn out on the trail that followed the creek westward and leave so many other trails unwatched. But having no one else available for the job that needed many scouts to cover all of the trails leading from the interior of the Ohio Country to the frontier at Wheeling, Zane decided to hedge his bets and gamble. If the Indians did come in force, Zane figured they would come by way of the most direct trail to Wheeling, using the same path that many scouts and mounted militiamen used on earlier forays into the Ohio Country. Zane had already been forewarned by scout John Slover, who had recently escaped from the Indians during Crawford's ill-fated campaign that the Delaware desired to attack Wheeling. Slover told Zane that, while in captivity, he overheard the Delawares under Captain Pipe swear a blood oath to avenge the deaths of their cousins against the settlers at Wheeling whom the Indians believed were responsible for the massacre. Consequently he sent Linn to scout that trail in the hopes that Linn would be lucky enough to spot an Indian war party if one were on its way, and buy the settlers at Wheeling the time they would need to get inside the fort with their families, if Linn could sound the alarm. All hinged on Linn. If the Indians did come by that trail and Linn spotted them before they saw him, he might have a chance to make it back to Wheeling in time. If not, it wouldn't matter, for Linn and Zane would both be dead, along with everyone else.

John Linn instinctively knew that vigilance was everything in fulfilling the task that Zane had given him. The problem for him at the moment was how to keep himself from falling asleep in his perch due to the monotony of sitting in one place. Linn picked his lookout spot carefully, choosing a tree that gave him a commanding view of the ground to west and a glimpse of the trail descending from the ridge top where he sat, to the creek waters of the Stillwater in the distance. With his horse hobbled nearby to graze as it pleased on the undergrowth, Linn shifted and re-shifted his cramping legs, as he focused his eyes on that spot of the trail that he could clearly observe. It was past noon and unusually warm on the afternoon of August 11. As Linn adjusted his aching legs again, being careful where he put his numbed feet, something caught the attention of his horse, causing it to raise its head from grazing, instantly alerting Linn to possible danger, and riveting his attention to that bare patch of ground through the wooded horizon to the west of him, where he was at once able to see the movement of men. A quick glimpse told him beyond the shadow of a doubt that there were Indians moving rapidly in his direction, and instantly Linn sprang from the crotch of the tree to the ground below. He knew from the stories told about scouts who had failed to come back alive, that his own life was now measured by minutes, for if the Indians had seen him in the tree, he could be sure that pursuers would soon arrive to cut off his escape. Leaving his pack and provisions where they lay next to the tree trunk, Linn sprinted to his horse. Quickly untying the leather thong securing its front legs, John Linn mounted his horse to begin the ride of his life.

Several hundred yards behind Linn on the trail just below the ridge crest, one of the advancing Delaware scouts trotting on foot up the slight grade of the trail, heard the slight whinny of a horse. Immediately the warrior whistled a signal to the flanking parties traveling parallel at some distance on either side of the trail. Those warriors were supposed to move through the woods ahead of the main body to cut off any enemy spies who might be watching from the vantage point of high ground like the ridge crest ahead. The flankers were to advance beyond the high point and then double back on the trail and capture any enemy scouts before they had a chance to escape. However, the Delaware scout at the head of the vanguard determined from the reply from his fellow warriors in the woods almost even with him, that the flankers had not been able to advance far enough to pass the ridge top due to the heavy underbrush that impeded them. Quickly, the warrior called to several mounted Delaware warriors several dozen yards behind him. He motioned to them that an enemy scout was somewhere up ahead. Without further delay, three warriors thundered ahead on their horses, intent on catching whomever might be on the trail.

John Linn had barely enough time to mount his horse and turn down the trail leading to the Ohio River when he could hear the sound of horses pounding on the trail behind him. The chase was on, and Linn could only hope that his head start was enough to give him the advantage to reach he Ohio River before the Indians could catch him. On a particularly straight stretch of the path leading to the Ohio, the Indians caught sight of Linn up ahead, and one of the warriors fired a shot from his musket at the Virginian scout, which missed. Far back on the trail, just east of the crest of the ridgeline, Captain Bradt halted momentarily to examine the contents of the abandoned haversack. When the report of the musket shot in the distance reached his ears, Bradt deduced that one of the enemy had been sighted by the Indian scouts who were giving pursuit. Bradt ordered those Rangers and Indians who were mounted to make haste at once down the trail with him, figuring that even if the enemy scout reached the fort and warned the settlers of the pending attack, they might have little time to prepare. Bradt judged that possibly the Rangers and warriors on horseback could still mount an attack on the settlers before they had a chance to reach the stockade. However, as tired as their mounts were, there was no time to spare for his Rangers and Indians in the vanguard to close the distance and get to Wheeling.

With only a few more miles to go, John Linn was elated that he had been able to outdistance the mounted Indians pursuing him. He attributed it to the fact that his own horse was well-fed and rested before the race to the Ohio River had begun, while the mounts of the Indians far behind him must have been tired and worn before they had given chase. Still, Linn checked himself from becoming overconfident by thinking that he had gained a tremendous lead on the Indians to a point where he could slow his pace. Linn was all too aware that his own horse might begin to give out at some point, allowing the Indians a chance to close the gap. With the one thought in mind that he must reach the Ohio River to give Zane the warning of the approach of the Indians in order to save everyone there, Linn keep putting his heels to the flanks of his horse and whipped the mount from side to side with the loose end of the leather reins. He continued along the trail to the river with all the speed his horse could muster. When he reached the last mile of the trail to the river, where the path ran relatively straight along the north side of the creek lowlands, Linn could feel his horse begin to falter, as it had run the entire distance without a pause, and was now in danger of collapsing.

Arriving at the bank of the west channel of the Ohio that separated the trailhead from the island in the river across from Wheeling, Linn leaped into the water as his staggering horse collapsed from exhaustion. After swimming the short distance to the island, Linn raced to the Wheeling side where he alternatively splashed through the shallows and swam across the deeper current to reach the east bluffs of the riverbank below Fort Henry. Screaming at the top of his lungs, Linn caught the attention of a sentry on the fort walls who summoned Silas and Ebenezer Zane. Reaching the fort, Linn blurted out to the apprehensive group of militiamen that a large war party of Indians were on their way to the settlement, their advanced scouts no more than a couple of minutes behind Linn on the trail directly west from the Muskingum. Quickly, Captain Boggs was informed of Linn's news of the approach of the Indians. Boggs ordered the swivel gun on the wall of Fort Henry fired to alert everyone outside the fort walls to grab their family and guns and get inside the stockade. Within minutes, Captain Boggs mounted his horse and raced off down the trail leading east along Wheeling Creek to bring reinforcements raised from the militia surrounding Catfish camp in western Pennsylvania.

In the meantime, Ebenezer Zane prepared to defend his fortified blockhouse home which sat 40 yards outside the fort walls to the southeast. Ebenezer decided that with Captain Boggs going for help, his brother Silas should command the fort rather than join Ebenezer and his family in the blockhouse. With little time to waste, the settlers bustled about, "the women carrying what food and blankets they could lay their hands on in a few minutes, and dragging the children behind them, the men rounded up the horses and herded them into the fort." [HW1-p.216] Once inside, all of the 40 men and women set about loading every musket and rifle that could be found, in the event the fort was attacked. Powder horns were filled with gunpowder from the limited stores inside the fort and bullets were passed out to each of the men and women, as they climbed to the shooting platforms around the three walls of the fort facing away from the river to see if an Indian attack would actually come.

The defenders did not have long to wait. Within 15 minutes of the initial firing of the signal gun, a large war party of Indians was spotted on the large island in the river directly across from the fort. Within minutes, several hundred painted warriors emerged in force from the woods and crossed the main channel of the river, quickly surrounding the fort and outlying cabins while screaming their war whoops and firing their guns at the men and women on the fort walls. One of the fort defenders fired the swivel gun of the fort for a second time in the direction of the advancing Indians, alerting Captain Boggs, no more than a mile from the fort that it was now under attack. By late afternoon on September 11, the siege of Fort Henry was about to begin.

"They Rushed Hard On the Pickets In Order To Storm"

Captain Bradt was angry with the Indians for not having intercepted and captured or killed the lone Rebel scout who had spotted their approach on the trail from the Muskingum. In managing to get away, the scout had been able to warn the inhabitants of Wheeling of the pending attack, before Bradt was able to lay an ambush for the settlers and take the fort by surprise. It irked him that the Indians had not followed his orders completely, for with the sound of the wall gun at the fort being fired as an alarm, Bradt realized the element of surprise was lost as the fort defenders had been warned of his approach. If that were not all, he felt the Indians still had an opportunity to show only a small party of warriors as a decoy before the fort in an attempt to draw the settlers out before resorting to an all out assault; however Girty told Bradt that the Indians were impatient, and did not believe that the ruse would work again since it had been so successfully executed in the September 1777 attack on Wheeling.

Captain Bradt was uncertain what to do next, given the fact that Captain Caldwell and Lt. Col. Butler had told him many times that if Rebel militia were properly coaxed with a ruse, they would predictably react in the same manner again and again and throw caution to the wind by leaving the safety of their fort to chase a small Indian war party. The officers recounted to Bradt the ambush of the militia in the Wyoming Valley in 1778 and how well it had worked. But now at Wheeling, with the Indians intent on showing their entire numbers before the walls of Fort Henry, Captain Bradt could see that it was useless to discuss the matter of a ruse with them, for they seemed to have a mind of their own and were not interested in telling him their thoughts. Disgustedly, Bradt led his Rangers across the river to the abandoned settlers' cabins to the north and east of the fort, and deployed them in a skirmish line as the Indians completed their encirclement of the fort to ensure that no one could get in or out of the fort. With that done, Bradt had James Girty signal the Indians that he wished them to cease firing on the fort, as he wanted to parley with the Enemy, to try to convince them to surrender.

In Bradt's mind, there still was a chance that the fort could be taken without a fight if he could convince the defenders to open the fort gates and lay down their arms in return for his assurance that they and their families would not be harmed by the Indians. He hoped that the fort defenders, in realizing that they were vastly outnumbered by the Indians, could be coaxed to surrender out of fear. However, without artillery, Bradt knew that he had no means of battering down the gates of the fort. He had everything to gain by the bluff; nothing to lose by attempting the simple ploy. If the defenders were naïve enough to chance opening the gates of the fort, Bradt knew that there would be no way that he could prevent the Indians from pouring inside and slaughtering all the men, women and children as they were laying down their weapons while under the protection of his word as a British officer. He knew the Indians would not listen to him even if he were on better speaking terms with them, as they had one thing on their minds since the beginning of the campaign, and that was to quench their thirst for vengeance with the blood of the whites at Wheeling. Until that was done, Bradt realized that nothing else mattered to the savages.

Bradt gave the signal for the Rangers and Indians to stop firing on the fort. He ordered one of his men to attach a scrap of white cloth to a pole and wave it at the fort to indicate that he wished them to stop shooting so he could approach the fort to parley with them under a flag of truce. Hopefully, this would prevent the defenders from firing upon him at close range. Quickly the firing from both sides ceased, and Bradt, with James Girty and a squad of Rangers at his side, slowly made his way towards the fort walls, calling out to the enemy not to fire upon them, as he wished to approach and talk with whomever was in command of the fort to discuss the terms of capitulation.

A fort defender signaled to Bradt and Girty to come forward to a point within earshot of the walls. He shouted to them that those inside the fort were willing to hear what he had to say. With the British flag now unfurled, the squad of Rangers marched with their muskets at the ready behind Bradt and Girty as the little party advanced under the protection of the white flag of truce. Captain Bradt called out to a man on the walls to identify himself if he were in command, but there was no reply. Nervously, Bradt called out again to the fort, telling them who he was, and that as the representative of the King of England, that he demanded the fort's garrison to surrender, for which he would grant them protection from the depredations of the Indians. In an instant, Bradt received his answer. Silas Zane rejected Bradt's call to surrender by ordering one of the men inside the fort to fire the swivel gun in the direction of Bradt and the colors, which was done. "Without uttering a word," Zane had given Bradt "as much of an answer as he cared to give." [HW1-p.214] Realizing the futility of continuing with the ploy, Bradt and the Rangers scampered quickly out of range of the fort shooters, for fear that they would be fired upon. Once safely out of danger, the battle resumed with the Indians beginning a general assault on the fort to test the strength of the defenders. Stymied, Bradt ordered the Rangers to support the Indians with musket fire.

"Their Cannon Burst; its Slivers Flew In Every Direction"

Bradt watched as the Indians pressed their attack from the north and east. Immediately they were met with a fusillade of gunfire from the fort and the detached blockhouse which drove them back to a safe distance. In a matter of moments, Bradt could see the Indians advance again, this time under the protection of what little cover they could find, exposing themselves a lot less to the fort defenders, but again, they were quickly forced back by the accurate rifle fire coming from the two-story blockhouse which held a commanding view of the positions of the Indians once they showed themselves in the open ground surrounding the fort walls. As the Indian fire slacked off into sporadic shooting at the fort, a stalemate developed. The Indians informed Bradt through Girty that they would not attempt another assault on the fort during daylight due to the intense rifle fire coming from the blockhouse which prevented them from getting close. Bradt, who had viewed the failed attempts by the Indians to attack the fort, could see that it was futile to continue, as there was no practical way to approach the fort without being seen. There was only one possibility left that he could imagine working, and that would have to wait for darkness, for "if only the wall could be set afire the Indians stood a good chance of breaking through." The only problem with that was the fact that the riflemen in the enemy blockhouse would be able to shoot down anyone attempting to fire the walls. Captain Bradt reasoned the "necessity of first reducing that abode to ashes" [HW1-p.214] once darkness had fallen which would give some protection to those trying to set it on fire. Quickly Bradt had Girty communicate his suggestions to the Indians, to which they agreed.

Soon after dark on the evening of September 11, a lone warrior crawled to the foundation of the blockhouse "carrying a smoldering firebrand under him." [HW1-p.214] While attempting to rekindle the ember into flame, one of the blockhouse defenders spotted the Indian and fired upon him with success. At around midnight, the Indians tried again. In attacking the fort, the Indians "rushed hard on the pickets in order to storm but were repulsed" [BC2-p.277] noted Ebenezer Zane in the blockhouse. Twice again during the night, more attempts were made by warriors determined to rush the walls with piles of combustibles in their arms to set the old pickets on fire. Again and again, the fort defenders beat them off in the darkness with rifle fire from the walls and Zane's blockhouse. Slowly the shooting tapered off until dawn as the Indians, exhausted by the exertions of the evening, slept or rested in their positions around Fort Henry. With the return of daylight, several warriors began sporadically shooting at the fort, letting the inhabitants know that they were still there and had not given up their siege. Faced with another day of an impasse, Captain Bradt resolved to have his men begin destroying the outlying cabins, livestock, and crops of corn in the fields while the Indians pressed their renewed attempt to attack the fort.

Soon after first light, Captain Bradt considered the possibility of another parley with the fort on the chance that the fort defenders, after the previous day and night of fighting, might be more amenable to persuasion, and could be convinced to give up and surrender. But Bradt feared that a second attempt on his part would likely get him killed due to the gunfire that the British flag had attracted. Instead, Bradt had the Negro brought forward to him from the rear of their camp where he was watching the horses. The former prisoner had been captured by the Indians and taken to Sandusky from somewhere upriver. Once at Sandusky, the Negro was released and accompanied Bradt to Wapatomika. Bradt instructed the former Rebel slave in what to say when he reached the fort. The frightened man advanced slowly to the walls, waving the flag of truce in his hands. Told by Zane in the blockhouse to halt, the terrified messenger "informed us that their force consisted of a British Captain and 40 regular soldiers and 260 Indians," [BC2-p.277] though he was too fearful to demand those inside the blockhouse and fort surrender, with all the rifles pointing at him. With the parley abruptly over, the Negro quickly retreated to the safety of the woods once Zane motioned him to go.

By mid-afternoon, the Indians were frustrated that they had been unable to find a way to reduce the fort. Bradt knew that it was all but impossible to do so without artillery. Consequently, several Indians decided to construct a cannon from the trunk of a hollow tree, when a boatload of cannonballs was discovered at the wharf below Fort Henry, apparently destined for Clark and his army downriver at the Falls of the Ohio. [HW1-p.357] Well into the morning of September 12, the Indians and some Rangers worked with tools to enlarge the bore of the tree trunk so that it would be the right size to fit a cannonball with a load of gunpowder into the muzzle. To strengthen the barrel of the crude wooden artillery piece, the Indians wrapped it with a piece of chain found in one of the settler cabins. When it was finally completed late in the morning, several warriors came to Captain Bradt and requested that he order the Rangers to fire the improvised gun, arguing that white men were more adept in the ways of handling cannon. Bradt refused the Indians. After an inspection of the wooden gun, Bradt informed them that it would be impossible for the crude gun to work, and it would likely explode in their faces. Bradt's critical attitude and lack of cooperation enraged the Indians who constructed the gun, forcing them to handle their makeshift weapon alone without Bradt's help. The loaded cannon was carried by the Indians to a spot where it could be pointed at the fort walls without those igniting it coming under enemy rifle fire. Unfortunately, when the powder charge was ignited by an Indian, "their cannon burst; its slivers flew in every direction; and instead of being the cause of ruin to the fort, was the source of injury only to themselves," as those Indians close to the makeshift gun felt the effect of the blast, "several were killed, many wounded, and all dismayed by the event." [HW1-p.358]

"At About Ten O'clock At Night They Made a Fourth Attempt"

An assault on the fort by the Indians was resumed again, but only half-heartedly. Meanwhile, Bradt directed his Rangers to kill all of the cattle, hogs, and sheep that could be found in the surrounding woods and set fire to the isolated settler cabins some distance from the fort. Bradt knew that there was always the remote chance that someone in the fort would attempt to sally out to save their homes, and if not, at least he could have the satisfaction of depriving the enemy of shelter and sustenance once the battle were over. Soon, plumes of dark smoke rose into the air from the burning homes, as the Rangers labored to pull up the ripening corn in the nearby fields and pile them onto the flames. Bradt could see many of the fort defenders watching the methodical destruction but no one opened the gates to try and stop him. Unknown to Bradt, a crisis had been developing inside the fort that overshadowed all else for the fort defenders. "The supply of powder, deemed ample at the time, by reason of the long continuance of the savages, and the repeated endeavors by them to storm the fort, was now almost entirely exhausted, a few loads only, remaining." [HW1-p.358]

Upon that dire discovery, Silas Zane quickly called a meeting of those inside the fort to decide who would risk their life to run to his brother's blockhouse over 100 feet from the southeast corner of the fort, to bring back a supply of gunpowder before the Indians attacked again. During the ensuing debate, a young woman named Elizabeth Zane, the younger sister of Silas and Ebenezer, [HW2-p.74] volunteered to make the run, arguing that the fort could not spare one man, however, "a woman will not be missed in the defense of the fort" [HW2-p.359] if the runner should be felled by gunfire. After some debate, it was finally agreed to let the young Zane woman attempt the run, and "a little after noon the sally port gate on the south wall suddenly opened and a young woman ran out; quickly she covered the distance between the fort and the blockhouse, and disappeared inside." [HW1-p.215] Some distance away, Captain Bradt heard the Indians yell "Squaw, Squaw" and catching sight of a woman running from the fort to the blockhouse, realized that something was amiss in the fort. [HW2-p.p.75]

Calling out to James Girty to alert the rest of the Indians of what had just happened, Captain Bradt motioned to the Rangers north of the fort to come as quickly as possible in the event that the enemy was about to sally forth and attack. Instead, as Bradt watched, the "door of the blockhouse was flung open, and the same woman appeared, racing back up the slight incline toward the fort, but this time carrying a large, bulky bundle with her." [HW1-p.215] Bradt instantly realized that she must be carrying something of great value to the fort that would cause her to risk her life outside the fort walls. He correctly deduced that the fort must be out of gunpowder and the woman was making a run back to the fort with a load of powder in her apron. Bradt realized if she could be stopped, the fort would be forced to surrender or fall, if the Indians attacked it again. Here was the break that Bradt had been looking for since the start of the siege.

Bradt screamed at the top of his lungs to the Indians nearest to the running woman to shoot her. As he watched, the woman closed the distance up the slight incline from the blockhouse to the fort gate, the Indians began to fire at her, but all their shots missed. By the time any of the warriors had reloaded, the woman was safely inside the fort, enraging Captain Bradt to no end. The Indians had missed an ideal opportunity to finish off the fort, without themselves realizing what had just transpired by the young woman's run. Beside himself with anger, Bradt could barely keep himself from insulting the Indians, for he had had his fill of their incompetence. For the rest of the afternoon, through the desultory long-range firing on the fort that the Indians amused themselves with, Bradt refused to speak to any of them through Girty. With maximum damage inflicted to the settler's cabins, livestock, and crops, Bradt prepared his men to leave in the morning for either Wapatomika or the Upper Sandusky villages. By nightfall, the Indians were equally discontented with Bradt, and called a council of their headmen to decide what to do, but excluded the Ranger captain from sitting in.

One last assault on the fort was agreed upon by the warriors to try to set the walls on fire. When that attack failed, as had all the rest, the Indians resigned themselves to giving up the siege in the morning. "At about ten o'clock at night they made a fourth attempt to storm to no better purpose than the former," [BC2-p.277] noted Zane in his blockhouse. Sensing the desperation of the Indians, Zane felt if the defenders were able to hold out one more day, he was sure that the enemy would finally relent. When dawn broke on the morning of September 13, the Indians again began firing on the fort as the day before, though Zane was sure he had spotted the Rangers saddling their horses far north of the fort from the spy port in the loft of the blockhouse. Within an hour, Indian scouts to the east of the fort along the trail which led to Catfish Camp, came riding into the Indian camp with news that a large party of mounted enemy reinforcements were on their way to relieve the fort. With no one eager to set an ambush, the

Indians decided to break off the attack and divide into smaller parties to "engage in their usual raids against smaller stations and individual cabins." [HW2-p.217]

"Our Strength Will Be Greatly Diminished and Divided"

With no casualties to burden them, Captain Bradt and the Rangers re-crossed the Ohio River to the head of the trail on the west bank leading to the interior of the Ohio Country. James Girty refused Bradt's invitation to join him on the return trip, telling Bradt that he was going to accompany a party of about 70 warriors and a few Frenchmen who intended to raid a small enemy station called Rice's fort more than a dozen miles to the northeast. With additional war parties heading up the Ohio River to attack the vicinity of Beaver Creek, only a few Delawares were willing to go with Bradt and the Rangers to Wapatomika where Bradt hoped to join with Caldwell and his men. Bradt was relieved that more Indians had not chosen to come along, as he had little food to spare, outside of a few ears of corn his men had been able to stuff in their haversacks at Wheeling. Taking the trail to the Muskingum and across to Wapatomika, on September 21, Bradt and his men reached the Shawnee village finding Alexander McKee there who informed them of Caldwell's subsequent illness and forced march to Sandusky. Noting "Captain Bradt is arrived here with the Rangers and a few Delawares," [HP-46] McKee was surprised to learn James Girty had not accompanied Bradt and the Rangers, but rather, continued on with the Indian war parties. It did not take him long to understand there had been a problem at Wheeling. The handful of Delawares returning with Bradt filled in McKee with the details of the raid on Wheeling, and the estrangement between Captain Bradt and the Delawares.

Later the same day, a Delaware came into McKee's camp with news from the James Girty and the Indians still on the frontier. "A runner from a party of Indians who after the unsuccessful attempt on Wheeling, made another upon a small fort between that and Beaver Creek, in which they also failed, having two Indians killed, but took a man passing from Beaver Creek to that place" [HP-26] as a prisoner. The Indian said he had come alone as "his companions who were two Delawares gave out upon the way," [HP-192] and told McKee no Indians were returning to the Upper Sandusky to join the Rangers there. Rather, he had been told to go directly to Wapatomika by the war party "of 70 men," [HP-192] to inform McKee of the important intelligence on the movements of the Enemy at Fort Pitt which was learned from the prisoner who had been taken near there.

Girty and a Canadian had questioned the white prisoner, "who upon examination informed them that he belonged to an army of 1,200 men assembled at that place with an intention of cutting off the Huron villages, and that they were to set out in two or three days, and this Indian being three days upon his way, suppose the Enemy to be now on their march." [HP-191] The Frenchman with Girty and the Indians decided to head directly for Niagara with the alarming news, leaving "Wheeling about the 16th of September when there was a great stir in that quarter by troops arriving which he supposed were on their march to join Irvine's army" [HP-08] at Fort Pitt. Without orders for Bradt from Caldwell, McKee decided it best to advise the Ranger Captain to join Caldwell at Sandusky, since it appeared from the intelligence the enemy was intending to march again upon the Upper villages.

With Bradt, McKee sent a note to Caldwell, informing him of the recent word of the movement of an enemy army on the Ohio River aimed toward Caldwell's direction. "I shall assemble all the Indians that can be found in this quarter to oppose them. I wish the Hurons now to watch towards Kooshawking and inform us of their discoveries from time to time. Perhaps Upper Sandusky is their object. This only can be known by the way they take from Kooshawking or Tuscarawas. I wish you would forward this intelligence to Detroit and Roche de Bout. The Ottawas there may come at least in time to Sandusky." [HP-194] McKee promised Bradt that he would not be far behind him, as he hoped to head for Upper Sandusky as soon as he could raise enough warriors from the Shawnee villages to accompany him to repulse the Rebel army. McKee sent a separate dispatch to Major DePeyster at Detroit, telling the officer that he worried what effect the continuing reports of George Rogers Clark's gathering army on the Ohio River below at Kentucky might have on his own attempts to raise Indians for the Upper Sandusky in this growing crisis. "From the number of parties still out from the lower villages and the report of the Enemy's coming the other way, our strength will be greatly diminished and divided. Perhaps the neighboring Indians of Detroit and Roche De Bout may be prevailed upon to join there as they will still be in time, if they are expeditious. I have dispatched an express to Captain Chesne to invite the Miamis to assist us." [HP-191]

"I Have But Few Rangers to Face Them"

By September 26, it was clear to McKee that a crisis was at hand in the Ohio Country as word from every quarter indicated that two separate enemy armies were massing to begin expeditions against the Indians and Detroit from two opposing directions. Clearly, there were too few Indians to defend their lands against both. On September 24, two Delawares who had been held in confinement at Fort Pitt arrived at Wapatomika with further information concerning the Enemy force at Fort Pitt. McKee wrote, "They made their escape from that place 12 days ago, and says that General Irvine who commands the army this way, was arrived with 500 troops from below joined to those collected on this side of the mountains, will make the army 1,500 strong. They were to leave Beaver Creek September 18 or 20, and after passing the Huron villages to meet Clark at the Shawanese villages who they say have orders to move this way before this time. They are of the opinion that the Enemy are five or six days now upon their march, and are to bring two field pieces with them which was sent to Beaver Creek from Fort Pitt before the above Indians left it." [HP-25]

The news appeared grimmer than ever to McKee. Sending the two Indians on to Sandusky with their account, Shawnee scouting parties arriving from the

Ohio River and Kentucky reported more and more militiamen assembling near the Falls of the Ohio for what looked like an intended strike into the Indian lands. Warriors who had been preparing to depart with McKee to the Upper Sandusky changed their minds and refused to go with him, worried that their women and children would be left unprotected if Clark should march against their villages. McKee could hardly argue with them, reflecting, "we shall find difficulty to collect Indians sufficient in this Country now to oppose this army." [MK-25] Everything would rest with Caldwell and the Rangers to throw the enemy back, McKee reasoned. Though outnumbered, there was no other force of substantial size, strength, and determination to make a stand against the Enemy about to invade the Ohio Country.

On the morning of September 24 far to the north of McKee at the lower village of Sandusky, Captain Caldwell had two of his men raise him up from the cot upon which he had been laying prostrate with fever since arriving from the Indian Country with his men. Though dizzy and weak from the unrelenting illness that had sapped his strength, Caldwell insisted that the two Delaware Indians just arrived from the vicinity of Fort Pitt be brought to him with their important news on the movements of the enemy in that quarter. With a shaky hand at times, Caldwell scrawled a note to Major DePeyster, recording everything that the Indians had to say. "Two Delawares informed us there were 1,200 Rebels gathered in that country to come against this place, part of them, they says when he saw them were already crossed the Ohio, which makes me think they will be shortly with us. I send you a letter I this moment received from Captain McKee." [HP-192] Having sent the Indians on their way, as weak as Caldwell was, he demanded that he be taken to the huts housing the Rangers for an inspection of his men. Inside the dimly lit squalid shelters, lay row upon row of men stricken with the same illness, and incapable of standing on their own feet due to the severity of the flux infecting them. A handful of Sandusky Wyandot women, at the behest of Mr. Arundel and Abraham Coon were busy ministering to the sick men in an attempt to ease their sufferings until recovery was possible. It was a bleak picture for Caldwell to face, and one he knew he must communicate to DePeyster, for out of the force of 68 Rangers under his command, less than half were fit for duty. [HP-360] "I am sorry to be obliged to tell you that I will have but few Rangers to face them with as there is 38 of them sick. I could wish you to send all assistance you possibly can and as quick as possible." [WM-p.-22] The only saving grace Caldwell could count on, as he was taken back to his quarters, was that word had reached him Captain Bradt and his company were no more than a day's march from him, and that should add at least 40 more men to the Rangers able to fight. With the dispatch to DePeyster on its way to Detroit, Caldwell collapsed on his litter from exhaustion and fever.

"That Their Intentions Are to Exterminate the Savages"

Major DePeyster watched from the window of his quarters as the sloop "Faith"bearing Captain Caldwell's sick Rangers slipped into its moorings on the morning of September 30. One by one, the litters carrying the ill men were brought into the special barracks set aside for them, in the hopes that the Rangers could be brought back to health at Detroit, rather than the fever-stricken lowlands at the village of Sandusky. Not only was Caldwell "very ill with an intermitting fever" but so too were "40 of his men in the same situation" as well as the entire "crew of the "Faith" and most of the Indians in the lower town of Sandusky." [HP-192] Luckily, Captain Bradt and the Rangers of his company, having arrived late at Sandusky, had not become stricken by the flux and ague. Captain Bradt and his Rangers arrived in Sandusky from Wapatomika unscathed by the rampant illness, and there they received orders from DePeyster to return with Caldwell's men to Detroit.

Now the entire complement of 120 Rangers [HP-360] who were crowded aboard the vessel began to disembark at Detroit just as Major DePeyster walked down to the barracks with the officers of the King's Eighth. He was aghast at what he saw. The Rangers for the most part, were unrecognizable as such, their uniforms and clothes but tattered torn remnants held together with rags and pieces of leather. Many men were without shoes, hats, coats, or trousers, and had replaced those missing and worn-out pieces of clothing with Indian moccasins and breach cloths, or articles taken from the enemy dead. Their long term of duty in the wilderness of the Ohio Country had left them so thin, haggard, unkempt and gaunt that the commander of Detroit whispered to his officers the Rangers appeared as "walking specters." [CE-p.109]

Major DePeyster ordered Captain Grant "to relieve the "Faith's" crew and to take off the provisions and ammunition" [HP-192] that had been sent from Niagara. Unfortunately, the horde of Indians at the landing had been able to examine the vessel's cargo, and having seen that there were no gifts for them among the load of provisions and garrison supplies, made their way as a mob to DePeyster's office to protest the intransigence of the King in fulfilling his promise of supplying them with presents. To DePeyster, the Indians made open threats to abandon Detroit to Colonel Clark if and when he should attack. DePeyster handled the situation as best he could, distributing what little tobacco that he had from his own commissary, but it did little to alleviate the troubling situation. "Lt. Col. Hope and Sir John have been eye witnesses to the straight I have been put to with respect to the Indian presents not arriving in time. I have made every shift in my power, and if we are not supplied soon, I shall not know what to do. The Indians are really becoming troublesome, a disagreeable prelude to what must soon happen," [HP-237] DePeyster wrote to General Haldimand on September 29.

But something else was on Major DePeyster's mind that he needed to communicate to Haldimand concerning the situation facing him at Detroit which was "a very difficult card to play at this Post and its dependencies, which differ widely from the situation of affairs at Michilimackinac, Niagara and others in the upper district of Canada." [HP-237] With the war lost in the eastern colonies and peace soon at hand, two armies of the enemy were still intent on campaigning into the Ohio Country where this wilderness war continued with no end in sight. Yet, as the enemy prepared to invade the Indian lands, DePeyster received orders to keep the Indians on the defensive at all times. However, he knew the Indians could not possibly defend their homes when the enemy was on their doorstep. Rather, their best defense was to meet the enemy on the frontier, take offensive action. "It is evident that the back settlers will continue to make war upon the Shawanese, Delawares, and Wyandots even after a truce shall be agreed to, betwixt Great Britain and her revolted colonies, in which case, while we continue to support the Indians with troops (which they are calling aloud for) or only with arms, ammunition and necessaries, we shall incur the odium of encouraging incursions into the back settlements, for it is as evident that when the Indians are on foot occasioned by the constant alarms, they receive from the Enemy entering their country, they will occasionally enter the settlements and bring off prisoners and scalps. So that while in alliance with a people we are bound to support a defensive war- it will, in spite of humane prudence, almost always terminate in an offensive one." [HP-237]

Major DePeyster got to the point of his letter to Haldimand, the subject of which was causing him great turmoil as always. "These matters considered, I hope Your Excellency will urge the necessity of the back settlers holding out the olive branch instead of setting foot, one expedition after another, declaring in their setting out, that their intentions are to exterminate the whole savage tribe. I wait with impatience to hear from Your Excellency, and in the mean time I shall continue to discourage small parties as much as possible, and endeavor in every respect to act for the honor of the British Nation." [HP-237] Major DePeyster was concerned that he had said too much to Haldimand. As a career officer and a gentleman, it was his duty to follow orders, whatever they may be. Yet, as much as he despised the duty of dealing with the Indians, he could not help but feel that the shrinking supplies for them coupled with the demand that they stay on the defensive in the face of a determined hostile enemy entering their own lands, could only mean that the Crown was in some measure, preparing to ignore the Indians in an effort to find a suitable peace.

"I Shall Be Very Ill Off For Want of Officers"

As the month of October opened, there still was no report from Indian scouts that either of the two enemy armies had been spotted on the move towards the Indian lands of the Ohio Country from Fort Pitt and Kentucky. In the meantime, Brigadier General Powell at Niagara had been granted leave to return to Quebec. In his stead, Lt. Col. Dundas had been placed in command of the upper posts from his headquarters at Niagara. On October 11, Dundas wrote to DePeyster ordering him to send Captain Bradt and his company of Rangers back to Niagara, as no alarm in the Ohio Country had as yet been sounded on an enemy incursion. DePeyster was hesitant to do so without further reports from scouts, but followed orders on October 23 by sending Bradt and his detachment aboard the sloop "Dunmore" to Niagara. The ship anchored at the mouth of the Detroit River for the night within sight of the "Wyandot" to await the morning breeze coming from the west.

During the night, Major DePeyster was awakened by Edward Hazel of the Indian Department, "one of my interpreters and runner who came express in three days from Pipe's Town at which place he had spoken with two decent men, one an old country Englishman, deserters from Fort Pitt who offered to take their oaths or be burnt at the stake." [HP-07] The two men, "William Bruce, a native of North Britain and lately an inhabitant of Pennsylvania...on the 5th of October left Whitely Creek on the Monongahela, in order to make his escape from the Rebels in company with a Robert Hinds, and arrived about the 20th same month at Upper Sandusky." [HP-293] The two men had related important intelligence to Hazel, who came directly to DePeyster as quickly as he could with the news.

Bruce told Hazel that "an expedition against the Indians at Sandusky under command of General Irvine was proposed and in agitation, to consist of 1,200 or 1,300 men, and that provisions for the purpose were collected, and that they were to set out from Fort McIntosh on the waters of Beaver Creek the 29th of September, but was prevented by an express from below Fort Pitt, ordering them to wait until the 6th of October for 300 Continentals, and 100 militia which were to join them at that time." [HP-293] By the time that Bruce and Hinds had "set off, the 5th of October, that said reinforcement was not arrived, but that he learned it was on the way by a person who accompanied it a days journey." [HP-293] Furthermore, Bruce knew that "an expedition under General Clark from the Falls of the Ohio to consist of about 1300 men, was to set out and join General Irvine at the plains of Sandusky, and that they expected to return home about Christmas if possible." [HP-293] Both Clark and Irvine would have artillery with them, and would advance to take Detroit once the Indians were dispersed.

Major DePeyster was alarmed at the disturbing news brought from the Ohio Country by Hazel. Having no time to waste, "I immediately dispatched a boat to stop the vessels at the mouth of the river and I now send orders to Captain Bradt to shift his detachment on board of the "Wyandot" and return to Detroit. The "Dunmore" is to proceed to Fort Erie." With Caldwell and the Rangers at Detroit ill, DePeyster worried that he might have to send some of his own men and officers to help the Indians at Sandusky "in order to keep up the spirit of the Indians," in which case, he realized "I shall be very ill off for want of officers." [HP-07] Discussing what strategy to take in light of the latest news, DePeyster confided with his officers "I propose to get everything ready but not to make any movement until I have certain intelligence of the Enemy being in motion." [HP-07] Regarding the latest information, DePeyster reasoned he would not have long to wait to know if the enemy was, in fact, on the move towards Detroit.

"Hearing the Welcome News That Peace Preliminaries Had Been Signed"

Alexander McKee found the Delaware village of Pipe's Town abuzz with activity when he reached it in the early evening of October 24, 1782. War preparations were being made by the Delaware, Wyandot, and Mingo warriors already there to attack the enemy army believed to be headed to the Upper Sandusky along the same route as Crawford's expedition. McKee had come in a hurry with warriors "from the Shawanese towns in consequence of a message delivered there from the Hurons and Delawares informing us that they had received certain intelligence of the Enemy's intention to strike those villages and requesting the assistance of the Shawanese and Mingoes who by this time are chiefly on their way thither." [HP-194] McKee was disappointed to find that Caldwell and the Rangers had gone on to Detroit as well as Captain Bradt and his men. No Rangers were available to help stop the Americans if and when they should come, and without the Rangers, McKee privately began to despair that all would be lost.

The months of unrelenting wilderness warfare and constant alarms on the movements of the enemy were taking their toll not only on the Rangers and the Indians, but on Alexander McKee, who was beginning to show the strain. Few Indians were heeding McKee's call to meet at Pipe's Town in great numbers. Some warriors, like the Shawnee, feared leaving their own villages to the south undefended. Other Indians, like the Ottawas near Lorimer's, "are mostly gone a hunting, though I had sent to them not to disperse." [HP-194] The situation looked grim to McKee. It was apparent that if the enemy should "make a push this way not withstanding the season is so far advanced, that if they find the Indians an easy conquest, their design is to reach Detroit." [HP-194] McKee penned a note to DePeyster on October 25 from his camp at Pipe's Town, detailing for the Major the critical situation the Indians found themselves in, with only a few hundred warriors at best, and wanting for every necessity to fight. McKee also had to worry about the Shawnee at Piqua and Chillicothe who were left behind to guard against Clark. "There is a general complaint for want of ammunition among the Indians of the Lower Villages. I was in hopes to find some at Lower Sandusky, but am informed it has been delivered to the Hurons and Delawares of this place." [HP-194]

There was some good news awaiting McKee at Pipe's Town. William Arundel delivered a letter to McKee which he had had in his possession since its arrival from Detroit soon after McKee left the Upper Sandusky villages for the Ohio River and Kentucky in August. McKee noted that the letter was directed to him from Haldimand's secretary in Quebec, Captain Matthews, dated July 8. "Sir, I am directed by His Excellency the Commander in Chief to acquaint you that he has received your letter of the 25th of May requesting permission to leave Your Duty for some time to settle your Private Affairs, and representing that your Accounts settled through the channel of the Superintendent, remain unpaid to your Great Loss and disappointment. In answer to which I am commanded to acquaint you that you have his Excellency's Permission to come to this Place as soon as Major DePeyster shall think your attendance on the Service can be dispensed with. In regard to Your Accounts, I am to acquaint you that His Excellency Honored a Bill for the amount five months ago, payable to Mr. Taylor and Forsyth, and upon His Excellency's inquiring into the reason of your not having received the money, the enclosed extract of a letter from Col. Johnson was laid before Him, from which it appears that by Virtue of Taylor and Forsyth's note of Hand, you have only to draw upon them at sight for the amount." [HP-288] McKee was stunned at the news. In an instant, his troublesome financial problems going back to his escape from the Rebels in 1778 had been resolved once and for all.

McKee worried about the invasion of the Ohio Country by General Irvine with an army of 1,200 to 1,500 men, including regular troops and cannon, bound for the Upper Sandusky villages. However, by the first week of November it was becoming apparent to him that the attack was not materializing, and for some reason, Irvine was not coming. McKee was holding the Indians at the Upper Sandusky in readiness, while word was sent to DePeyster to send what Rangers he could to Sandusky once the scouts returned from the east with word that the enemy army was in motion. However, the scouts reported no sign of the enemy to the east. McKee could only wait and wonder why. Finally, by the first week of November, Indian runners returned from scouting on the east side of the Ohio near Fort Pitt to report they had obtained word from several prisoners that General Irvine was not coming with an army at all. Apparently, his part in the campaign against the Ohio Country had been earlier "canceled by orders from Congress and the Board of War," [WGA-p.126] which had ordered an end to the expedition upon "hearing the welcome news that peace preliminaries had been signed" in Europe. [WGA-p.126] Wisely, General Irvine had not let his own officers know the change of plans. Irvine's own intelligence had told him that the Indians were assembling at the Upper Sandusky to meet him and Irvine wished to keep them there waiting for him for the longest possible moment to keep them from reinforcing their Shawnee brothers to the south who were soon to be the target of George Rogers Clark, who at that very moment, was coming against them.

"The Road I Am Afraid Will Be Open to Detroit"

The blow from Clark was unexpected by the Indians. Irvine's ruse had effectively worked to keep McKee and those Indians at the Upper Sandusky preoccupied with preparations to meet him, thus allowing Clark the opportunity to move quickly against the Shawnee before they had a chance to be reinforced. Clark had been able to assemble over a 1,000 mounted militiamen by late October, and "he crossed the Ohio at the mouth of the Great Miami on the 5th of November," [HW1-p.217] headed north to the Shawnee villages, intent on attacking the Indians in retaliation for the battle at the Blue Licks. Clark's army moved quickly up the trail following the Big Miami River to attack the village of Chillocothe. Surprisingly, the Shawnee had "only scant minutes after the alarm had been given, but it was all the time the inhabitants needed to gain the safety of the surrounding woods." [HW1-p.218]

Clark sent Colonel Logan ahead into the village with 150 picked mounted men as an advanced guard. Few warriors opposed them, and of those that did, "the advance guard killed a few and took some prisoners." [WGA-p.126] With Chillicothe in smoldering ruins in a matter of a few minutes, Clark sent detachments which were able to "destroy five towns, along with their crops," as no warriors opposed them. The re-built village of Piqua was burnt again, and Clark sent a force under Logan as far north as Lorimer's trading post at the portage between the Big Miami and Auglaize Rivers where the detachment plundered the trader's goods and horses before burning his home to the ground in retaliation for supplying the Indians with British goods. Nowhere was Clark able to draw the Shawnee out into a fight with his troops. After four days in the Ohio Country, Clark finally gave the orders for his army to withdraw, "as bad weather was approaching, and the Indians could not be forced into an engagement." [HW1-p.218] Leaving a force of mounted men as a rearguard, Clark and the main body returned southward to the Ohio, content that he had devastated five Shawnee Indian towns before plundering them, "killed ten warriors and taken another seven prisoner" while being able to repatriate three white captives of the Indians and suffering only one man killed and one wounded. [HW1-p.218] All in all, it had been a profitable operation.

McKee was aghast at the shocking news of Clark's advance against the Shawnee lower towns which reached him unexpectedly by a messenger from Wapatomika on the night of November 11. "I received an account 12 o'clock at night that the Standing Stone Village was surrounded by a body of the Enemy." [HP-294] McKee hurriedly left with what few warriors he could muster the next morning to reinforce the Shawnee under attack. "The next morning I set off from hence to their relief with all the Indians I could collect, which did not exceed 70." [HP-294] Arriving too late to intercept Clark's army which had already withdrawn to the Ohio, McKee and the warriors with him attempted to attack Clark's rearguard still in the vicinity. "We were met near that place by a body of their horse which proved too powerful for us and obliged us to retreat. We had several Indians killed, and learned from some who joined us that day that the village is entirely cut off, being surprised, and most of their men dispersed." [HP-294] McKee and the warriors with him fell back to Wapatomika to regroup on November 15. News from scouts to the south told McKee that the enemy rearguard was showing no intentions "to leave the country soon. As soon as they have made themselves strong there, we expect them this way which will be in a day or two at the farthest." [HP-294]

McKee despaired again that all was lost. Writing to DePeyster for help, he reported the situation at Wapatomika. "I am endeavoring to assemble the Indians, but find I shall not be able to collect a number sufficient to oppose them (Enemy). The chiefs are now met here upon that business who desire me to inform you of their situation requesting you will communicate it by the enclosed strings to their Brethren the Lake Indians, and without speedy assistance that they must be drove off from their Country, the Enemy being too powerful for them. We have no certain account of the number of the Enemy, but the Indians are of the opinion they must be 1,200-1,500, and have two pieces of cannon which they know from their firing them upon different occasions." [HP-294] With no Rangers to help, few provisions to feed themselves, and scant ammunition at hand to defend against the Kentuckians, McKee did not know what more to say. In his mind, he could not shake the feeling that the Shawnee were purposely being abandoned by the British at Detroit, Quebec, and England.

Still, it was important for McKee as the Crown's agent for the Indian Department to let DePeyster know that he had done all that he could, and the consequences of Clark's advance and Irvine's own expedition soon to come would undoubtedly be disastrous, if British policy was to abandon the Indians in the Ohio Country. In the eyes of the Shawnee at Wapatomika, McKee could see their defiance against the Big Knives at its lowest ebb. Enemy alarm after enemy alarm had finally taken its toll on them. Their constant vigilance against the advance of Clark was sapping their morale. "The Indians here are really tired out watching," McKee reported to DePeyster. Where once the tribes of the Western Confederacy had flocked to each other's aid, now, only indifference remained among the Indians. "We have sent to the neighboring Indians but here they are gone to their wintering grounds, and are not to be expected." [HP-294] All in all, with Piqua, Standing Stone, Chillicothe and Lorimer's in ashes, it was a bitter pill for McKee to swallow. As to Irvine and Clark's next move, "whatever their intention may be, the road I am afraid, will be open for them to Detroit," McKee lamented to DePeyster. Late in the day a Delaware Indian arrived at McKee's cabin at Wapatomika with unexpected news. "We were informed from a messenger from Fort Pitt, a Delaware Indian, that the army designed to come from that quarter was dispersed by orders that arrived there two days before the time they were to set off." [HP-294] McKee could take heart that Irvine was not coming after all. The Indians would not be crushed between two enemy armies as they feared, after all.

"I Must Beg to Repeat What I Have Formerly Said"

Major DePeyster at Detroit opened with trepidation the official document from General Haldimand, written on October 21, that had just been delivered to his quarters from the sloop which arrived from Niagara that morning. DePeyster guessed the letter contained Haldimand's response to the Major's previous letter sent weeks ago to Quebec. He could only nervously wonder what Haldimand's response would be to his protest over the question of the Indians. "Sir, although extreme hurry prevents my writing fully at present, I wish to acknowledge the receipt of your letter by Lieutenant Colonel Hope. The Defensive Measures you have taken will, I hope, prevent the Enemy from prosecuting their Incursions into the Indian Country, at least this season, or should they persist, render their attempt abortive." [HP-300] Haldimand now got down to the crux of the matter that DePeyster had addressed. "Your observations upon the consequences attending the unavoidable Hostilities between the Indians and the Americans upon the frontiers as long as the latter continue their present system of Invasion are very just, and I shall attend to them in their place." [HP-300] DePeyster breathed a sign of relief that Haldimand had not chastised him for bringing the matter up.

DePeyster read the General's orders on the matter of the Indians. "In the meantime, I have to recommend to your serious attention a steady adherence to the instructions you have received concerning a strict observance of Defensive Measures as far as the safety of your Post will permit. Before any operations can be undertaken by the Enemy's next campaign, I hope to be able to send you such Orders as will, in all events, be decisive," Haldimand wrote, adding for the present, your Attention must be employed to restrain the Indians from every act, of Hostility, except in their immediate defense, and to that Economy of the Public money, I have so repeatedly and so earnestly recommended." [HP-300] While Haldimand had addressed DePeyster's concerns, the Major was not entirely satisfied with the General's response, which left many questions on policy towards the Indians unanswered.

However, there was one thing that Major DePeyster was sure of, and that was General Haldimand's displeasure with him over finances, particularly the expenses of the Indian Department. Where Haldimand had previously found fault with the amount of money spent supplying the Indians with presents, now the General was displeased with the amount of the payroll of the Indian Department at Detroit under DePeyster's charge. "Your list of Indian officers and the amount of their Pay are enormous and greatly increased in the Course of Your Command," Haldimand wrote unhappily. "Which ought not to have happened without my particular Approbation and Consent, and I now desire that you will make as great a reduction in that Expense as the Absolute, indispensable necessities of the Service will admit of, for which the late adopted system of Defense affords a very favorable opportunity, and I expect you will improve it to the Greatest Advantage, reporting to me thereon, and specifying the Particular Services those Continued are Employed in." [HP-300]

DePeyster felt the sting of Haldimand's criticism. He wondered how the General intended for him to restrain the Indians in their villages deep in the Ohio Country from sending out war parties against the Rebel frontier, if there were no men of the Indian Department willing to live with the Indians and advise them correctly, as the General advocated cutting the roll of the officers thus employed, and reducing their pay for such services. Nonetheless, DePeyster felt that a new policy ordered from England must be at the heart of what was driving Haldimand to emphatically reduce expenditures at the western posts. As an officer not privy to that information, DePeyster realized that he had no choice but to comply or risk the charge of insubordination, for Haldimand had made himself clear. Responding to the General on November 21, DePeyster yielded. "I must beg to repeat what I have formerly said, that I have and ever shall pay the strictest attention to a proper economy of the public money.... The list of people employed in the Indian Department I reduced upon the breaking up of the campaign and I shall in future attend to Your Excellency's Instructions thereon." [HP-9] DePeyster's personal rebellion over the paradox of Indian policy had been effectively quelled by other contingencies.

"You Will However Recollect That We Have Injuries to Revenge"

To DePeyster and his officers of the Indian Department living with the Indians, it was apparent that the wilderness war in the Ohio Country was winding down with the onset of another winter. However the coming snows brought with them more discontent among the Indian tribes of the Western Confederacy than ever before, as each nation attempted to ascertain the intentions of the British at Niagara, Detroit, and Michilimackinac now that word had reached them that a general peace between the British and the Americans was being negotiated in the east. The Indians in general were unable to stifle their growing feeling they were being betrayed by the King and his officers, for less aid and fewer provisions were reaching them from the east. Many Indian tribes had sent "deputies to Montreal to talk with Sir John Johnson, and then on to Quebec, if possible, to talk with General Haldimand. They were getting anxious about their prospects; being withheld from war disturbed them." [KI-p.329] Never before had they been asked to restrain from attacking the enemy frontier, while the Virginians continued to pour westward across the mountains and make more and more incursions into their lands. It was disconcerting that the British now wished them to not defend themselves by making war on the settlers, as had always been done. This alone was enough to cause their disgruntlement, and General Haldimand was flooded with alarming reports from the posts on the vacillation of the Indians.

Haldimand requested Sir John Johnson of the King's Royal Regiment of New York to call for a Grand Council of the Iroquois and the tribes of the Western Confederacy to come to Niagara so he could speak to them in place of Guy Johnson, Superintendent of the Indian Department, who had left for England. Haldimand had instructed Sir John to emphatically assure the Indians that "they could confidently rely on the King's favor and protection in all situations, no less in peace than in war." [KI-p.334] Sir John met with a partial delegation of the Indians by mid-November "at the village at the landing- now formally christened the Loyal Confederate Village," [KI-p.333] where he soothed the Indians, telling them that contrary to the rumors they had heard, there was no firm peace with the enemy, but that "the King, had only stopped the bloodshed for a time so that his rebellious children could have an opportunity to reflect on their folly and return to their senses." [KI-p.333] After the meeting, Johnson reported to a worried Haldimand that the Indians seemed pacified for the moment.

However, Haldimand himself was in a quandary. In spite of Johnson's Council, he remained unsure of what the Indians might do, remembering "Pontiac's conspiracy and the terrible scenes after the last peace, and he meant to guard against sieges and ambushes and all unpleasant surprises." [KI-p.334]

Considering all that DePeyster had detailed to him in regards to the handling of the western tribes of the Ohio Country, Haldimand wrote to the Commander-in-Chief of British forces in America, Sir Guy Carleton at New York, discussing with him the unsettling situation with the Indians. "I think it necessary as a Commissioner to inform you that my having Restrained them from Hostilities has occasioned a general discontent among them. They are alarmed at the appearance of an accommodation so far short of what our Language, from the beginning, has taught them to expect, deprived of their lands and driven out of their Country." [KI-p.334] Coming to the crux of his argument that the Indians needed to be included in any negotiation with the Americans, Haldimand stated, "I persuade myself they will be amply considered by Your Excellency either in a Representation to the King's Ministers or by such arrangement as shall be agreed upon in this Country." Adding to his request, Haldimand noted that not only should the Six Nations be represented, but that "many of the Western Indian Nations in the neighborhood have suffered equally by shameful encroachments of the Virginians upon their most valuable Hunting Grounds, and have been equally attached and serviceable to the Royal Cause." [KI-p.334] Still, without privy to the delicate peace negotiations being conducted with the Americans, Haldimand had no way of knowing whether his remarks and suggestions to Carleton would carry any weight for future policy being decided.

Still, Haldimand worried that Carleton would not understand the true situation in Canada, being so far removed in New York City from the current desperate conditions he faced in holding Canada with a vacillating Indian population. Haldimand took a bold step and wrote directly to the new Secretary of State, Thomas Townsend, in the Ministry in London, explaining to the Secretary his own views on the Indian situation. "From an apprehension, Sir, that the Disposition of the Indians, and the indispensable necessity of preserving their affections may not be Sufficiently understood at Home, I think it my duty to assure you that an unremitting attention to a very nice management of that People is inseparable from the safety of this Province, which has been indisputably preserved in a great measure by their Attachment." [KI-p.335] In no small part, Haldimand felt himself echoing the sentiments of Major DePeyster, though he was not about to inform his officer at Detroit of the impact his past arguments on the issue of the Indians, had had upon himself. Whatever the outcome of the negotiations might be, Haldimand knew that both he and DePeyster had to attend to their duty, even if they found it personally disagreeable.

On December 1, a "band of Senecas from the Shawanese Country" (otherwise known as Mingoes) requested a council with Major DePeyster at Detroit. They were angry at his call for all the western tribes to refrain from attacking the frontiers, and wished to speak with him on the subject. Present with DePeyster at the Council was "Captain Potts of the King's Regiment, and Captain Caldwell of the Rangers," now satisfactorily recovered from hs illness. "Duperon Baby and William Tucker acted as interpreters" as Simon Girty, once close with the Mingoes, was at Half King's town in the Ohio Country with the

Wyandots. Ay-on-ini-amsh, Mingo chief, stood up before DePeyster with three strings of wampum in his hands. "Father, I must remind you of your promises, at the time you first engaged us to espouse the King's cause, you told us that not only the wants of the warriors but those of our families should be supplied in great profusion." The Chief delivered the wampum to DePeyster as to demonstrate the veracity of his words. Then picking up another six strings, he continued. "Father, we have received a message last summer through you, from the commander in Chief, forbidding us to treat our Prisoners with cruelty, assuring us that it was contrary to the laws of God and custom of Nations, which speech I have accepted and shall preserve." But now with his voice rising, the Chief voiced his complaint. "You will however recollect that we have injuries to revenge and although you protect the Enemy from the Stake, you shall not leave our people defenseless in the face of the Enemy who continues their incursions into our lands and shows our women and children no mercy." [HP-296] DePeyster could not argue with the Mingo, for he knew that the Indian's complaint was justified. At the moment, there was no truthful answer that DePeyster could give him that would not be construed by the Indian as a lie.

"Brothers! You Are Still Strong"

Reports of the attack by George Rogers Clark and his army against the Shawnee in the Ohio Country reached Niagara by early December. The Six Nations tribes at that post were angered by the news and felt betrayed by the words spoken to them only weeks before by Sir John Johnson. They demanded to see the new General in command of Niagara and the western posts, Brigadier General Allan Maclean. On December 11, "the Principal Chiefs and Warriors of the Six Nations Indians assembled in Council at Niagara." [HP-195] Before Maclean and the British officers of the post, including Lieut. Col. John Butler, the Iroquois orator Tioquanda arose to speak to voice his angry complaint with Maclean. Referring to Clark's attack on the Shawnee, which occurred "at a time when they, the Rebels, and we were forbid to go to war, and directed to cease hostilities by the great General of Our Brother the King of England, and upon our agreeing to obey the Orders of the General, the perfidious Rebels have taken the advantage of our inactivity, and have come like thieves in the night, when the Shawanese warriors were out at their hunting grounds, surrounded one of their towns and murdered all the women and children. We therefore think it proper to acquaint you that you may let the Great General know that we shall remain no longer idle and see our Brethren and people destroyed."

Continuing with the angry speech that brought many murmurs of approval from the assemblage of Indians in Council as he spoke, Tioquanda reiterated to Maclean, "we are persuaded there is no reliance to be had on the faith or promise of the Rebels, whose unparalleled cruelty lately destroyed the poor, innocent Moravian Indians.... Under the cloak of friendship they murdered them in cold blood, and reduced their bones to ashes that the murder might not be discovered.... We are therefore resolved that in future we will act upon our own principle, and show them no mercy...and though we have hitherto, in general, refrained from retaliating their cruelties except in the instance of Colonel Crawford, the principal agent in the murder of the Moravians, and he was burned with justice and according to our Custom, yet we make no doubt the Rebels will imagine that our not going to war proceeds from fear.... We shall in future follow the example set us by themselves, seeing it is their intention to destroy the Indians and possess themselves of our Country." [HP-195] Maclean found Tioquanda's argument eloquent and compelling; however he knew it would be contrary to Haldimand's orders if he were to allow the attitude of this Indian to remain unchecked on the issue of attacking the American frontier. Maclean had the evening to think about the response he would give to the delegation in the morning in which he had to attempt to both mollify and restrain them at the same time, without disputing their valid claims. It would be a delicate balancing act, Maclean was sure as he pondered the vagaries of what he must say.

On the morning of December 12, Brigadier General Maclean confidently rose before the Indians from the various tribes in the Great Council, reaching out to them with the words that he knew he must say to ease their minds, even if they were not entirely true. "Brothers! I thank the Great Spirit for giving us this opportunity of meeting together this morning at this Great Council Fire.... Brothers! You acquainted me yesterday with your great uneasiness on the account of the misfortunes of your younger Brothers the Shawanese. ...Your being desired to cease from going war by your Brother the General was for very good reasons. But he repeatedly requested that you should send out frequent scouts, to be upon your guard, and not allow yourselves to be surprised. ...Had the Shawanese kept out scouts as they were advised to do, they could not have been surprised; and now I recommend it to your particular care, that you will keep out scouts to watch the motions of the Enemy. There will then be no danger of your being in the same situation with your younger brothers, the Shawanese. And should the Rebels attempt to come into your Country, in that case, I have orders to sharpen your ax, and not permit it to be dull." [HP-196]

Maclean knew that he was stretching the truth. Haldimand wanted no more Indian raids upon the American frontier while negotiations with the Americans were ongoing. He had instructed Maclean to "discourage any ideas the Indians might have of revenge for Clark's attack on the Shawnees." [KI-p.337] Haldimand knew how difficult it would be to dispute what the Indians believed to be their natural inclination and who "found their rights, and Even their Existence upon the Principle of Retaliation, and Who consider themselves and in fact are a free People." [KI-p.337] Yet every possible argument had to be used on the Indians to keep them from attacking the border settlements, even if it meant blaming them indirectly to coerce them to remain in place. Without knowing the nature of the negotiations which must include the future of Canada and the Ohio Country, Haldimand ordered his officers to make sure that the Americans were not given any pretext to lay claim to the Indian lands under the excuse that they needed to protect themselves from continuing Indian raids, and by virtue of their need to expel the Indians in order to guarantee security along their frontier. It was Maclean's duty to convince the Indians to remain on the defensive for entirely different reasons.

"Brothers! You are still strong, and I have orders to tell you that you shall be well supported provided you don't allow yourselves to be surprised. The Enemy cannot come into any of your villages easily without being discovered. They live at a great distance from you.... It is not in their power to proceed two days march with a body of troops without your discovering them, and in that case, I doubt not, but with our mutual strength, we shall be able to make them pay dear for the attempt." [HP-196] Maclean knew he could not say more on the subject to them. In reality, he and Haldimand could only wish that the Americans made no further incursions into the Indian Lands, Indian vigilance or not mattering little. For Haldimand had no intention of making the enemy pay dearly for any such attempt, nor had the means to do so. Maclean hoped that the Indians were satisfied with his directive to them and would not see through the thinly-veiled disguise that hid the real truth which Haldimand feared the Indians would discover soon enough: no more British troops would be sent to support them. Direct British military involvement in the wilderness war of the Ohio Country had come to an end.

"I Wish I Was In the Interior of Tartary"

Maclean reported to Haldimand on December 24 on the success of his Council, stating in regards to the Indians, "its surprising in what good humor he had sent them away, after he had acquainted them with his being short of several articles of clothing for them this year." [HP-197] All and all, General Maclean told Haldimand "he thought that the Indians were behaving well." [KI-p.338] Yet Haldimand had his misgivings about the welfare of the Indians, fearing that the government in England would be tempted to abandon them in negotiations with the Americans for the sake of expediency. Writing again to Thomas Townsend, the Secretary of State in London, Haldimand warned "Policy, as well as gratitude, demands of us an attention to the Sufferings, and future Situation of these Unhappy People involved, on our account, in the miseries of War with an Implacable Enemy." [KI-p.338] Haldimand prayed that the highest British authorities in both Britain and America, in their quest for peace, would take the welfare of the Indians of the Ohio Country into account.

Deep in the wilderness of the Ohio Country, Simon Girty relaxed with Pipe, Wingenund and the Half King around the cook fires in their lodges and cabins at the Upper Sandusky villages, now blanketed with winter snows. Another year of campaigning was over, and there were many scalps to show for their efforts, and dozens of stories to tell and retell of the battle of the Upper Sandusky Plains and the fight at the Blue Licks in Kentucky. In spite of all their troubles, and the loss of some of their friends to the enemy, it had been a good year, Girty reminded the Indians, one in which they had defeated the Big Knives at almost every turn. Simon and his brother George roared with laughter when they were told from arriving scouts on the frontier that the Virginians were offering "1,500 pounds, being one half of Colonel Crawford's estate, as a reward for Simon Girty, dead or alive, for having been present when Crawford was put to death by Pipe." [HP-07] Simon was sure that their brother James, who was living with the Shawnee at Wapatomika, would laugh as loud as the two of them, and probably tell his comrades that he might claim the reward on his brother for himself, as Simon was becoming too important.

At Wapatomika, Alexander McKee bade farewell at the end of the year to his dear friend Matthew Elliott, sending his best wishes to Elliott's Shawnee wife at their home in the little village on the Scioto, where Elliott was now headed. McKee would stay put at his own cabin in the village for the weeks to come, spending time with his wife and children whom he had sorely missed during the long campaign of the summer and fall which had kept him constantly on the move. One thought continued to trouble McKee as he settled into his winter quarters with the Shawnee. While their victory over Crawford and the Kentuckians led him and all the Indians to believe that they were winning the war for control of the Ohio Country in spite of Clark's late incursion into Shawnee lands, the fact that the expected enemy attack from Fort Pitt had not materialized, after so long in the making, was puzzling.

McKee did not deceive himself, as he saw many of the Indians do, into believing that the enemy had called off their campaign against the Upper Sandusky villages due to their cowardice and fear of the Indians. McKee knew the Americans too well to accept that. Something else made them retire, McKee concluded, and it was this "something else" that he could smell in the wind that troubled him as the year was about to end. McKee could not deny the cold truth that the Americans were stronger than ever on the other side of the Ohio from Fort Pitt to the Falls. In spite of the best efforts of the Rangers and the Indians, the Kentuckians under Clark had not been dislodged, nor the Americans forced to abandon Fort Pitt. On the contrary, hundreds of settlers were streaming across the mountains as never before in search of good land, Indian land, to clear and cultivate in spite of the wilderness war.

While McKee knew that the Indians had been able to provide him with the best intelligence on the movements of the enemy from prisoners taken in the field, he also recognized that news arriving from east of the mountains on the conduct of the war for independence always reached the enemy frontier first, before Niagara and Detroit were informed from Quebec. The frontier settlers had known of Cornwallis' defeat before anyone in Canada. Rumors of an armistice and negotiations for settling a peace between Britain and her former rebellious colonies were circulating as far west as Kentucky, while the British at Detroit were telling the Indians that the war was not over and denying the possibility of talks. In the end, McKee could see that all of these rumors and denials "flying on the wing" over the Indian lands, carried from runner to runner, did not bode well for the Ohio Country.

McKee stirred the coals of the fire as he sat in the darkened cabin, deep in thought. What was it that was bothering him? Were the Americans restraining their armies, such as the one gathered by Irvine at Fort Pitt, because they did not want to chance another debacle as befell Crawford's army, or was it something else more sinister? Did the Americans not attack because they already had knowledge of the terms of the peace which McKee and the Indians were ignorant of? Did they restrain themselves from invading the Ohio Country, not because they were afraid to seek revenge against the Indians or provoke them to attack the frontier so that they could say that Indians had violated the terms of the peace, but rather, because they already knew something about those very terms that favored them, and that would alleviate their need to attack the Indians and fight them?

Would not the Americans, the implacable enemy that they were, have not continued the wilderness war against the Indians from their undeniable point of strength if the terms of a peace were disagreeable to them? Was this the foreboding that McKee felt? What possible peace with the enemy would make them refrain from continuing their war, just when the Indians believed it to be true that they had won it? McKee peered into the darkness, as if waiting for an answer that would never come. The twinge of dread that lurked in the depths of his mind and knotted itself in his stomach, finally made itself palpable, and gave form to words that McKee had not considered thinking before: had the Americans called off their attack because Britain and the King had ceded the lands of the Indians, the Ohio Country, to the Americans as the prize for settling the peace? Those thoughts, like the shafts of arrows piercing the duck in flight or the deer on the run, shook McKee's very being, impaling him with the revelation of a great betrayal that was about to unfold.

Lying restlessly on the bed of straw in the Ranger barracks at Detroit on the cold February day of 1783, Captain William Caldwell tried to find relief under the wool blanket which covered him, his body again wracked with intermittent spells of fever from the sickness which had not entirely purged itself of him. While recovering, Caldwell had plenty of time to ponder his future and that of his men, now that an end to the war was almost a certainty, and their own fates as Rangers more cloudy than ever. Caldwell remembered the Memorial that Lieutenant Colonel Butler sent to General Powell and Haldimand over a year ago, on October 1, 1781, on behalf of Butler and "the Officers of his Corps." [HP-329] Butler had stated clearly the dilemma of any Ranger captured by the Rebels while in uniform. The commission that each officer carried on his person had been the cause of "the ill treatment they are subject to should any of them be captured by the Rebels" due to certain words of their Commission, viz. "to serve with the Indians"- The Idea the world in general conceive of the Indians, and what has not been in a small degree blackened by false representations to the world by the Rebel Congress and their adherents, in order to blacken the characters of those who are sent on service with the Indians, to give them a pretence to treat such unfortunate persons, serving aforesaid, who may fall into their hands in the most inhuman manner with impunity, Your Memorialists to be considered as possessing the same if not worse principles than is thought to be the innate ones of the Indians." [HP-329]

Caldwell paused to recall what he had heard over the years of stories circulating at Niagara and Detroit, concerning the fate of Rangers captured by the Rebels and identified as the men who fought alongside the Indians. There was the unceremonious hanging of Ranger scouts Hare and Newberry in the Mohawk Valley before the military tribunal, and stories of the few men taken prisoner on the battlefield during Johnson's and Ross' raids into the valley during 1780 and 1781. Those Rangers had endured severe beatings and ill-treatment at the hands of their Rebel captors, once they were identified as men of Butler's Corps who were serving with the savages, against the American frontier. Butler's request to change the wording of each man's commission had come too late in the war, considering that by 1781, the Rebels on the frontier from the Hampshires to Kentucky knew only too well who the men were who were fighting with the Indians. "Your Memorialists therefore humbly request you will be graciously pleased to lay this Memorial before the Commander in Chief, praying his Excellency will ease their minds in this particular, and renew their Commission, without those words, viz. to serve with the Indians, and Your Memorialists, as in duty bound will ever pray, John Butler." [HP-329]

It mattered little to William Caldwell now. What Butler had tried to do for the Rangers, in the face of mounting hatred by the Americans against Butler's men who were known to have fought at the side of the Indians in the wilderness war waged against the frontiers of New York and Pennsylvania had been in vain. With the war winding down, every man in the Ranger Corps knew that the Americans were not about to forgive and forget the men who had served under Lt. Col. Butler. Their fate was now sealed. Brigadier General Maclean at Niagara was one of the few men who understood the fate of the Rangers, for in spite of the cessation of hostilities, the Americans were intent on seeking retribution against Rangers, if they were able to get their hands on them. Mclean aptly described the situation facing Butler's men, when he spoke in council to the principal warriors of the Six Nations assembled at Niagara, only a couple of months before. He responded to the complaints of the Iroquois that, by their support of the King, they had forfeited their ancestral lands to the Americans when Sullivan and Clinton expelled them from their villages during the campaign into the Indian lands in 1779. The Indians wanted, more than anything else, to be able to return to their homes, but without British support forthcoming, they had no way to drive out the American settlers who were streaming into those lands. They were angry with Maclean that he and the King did not seem to be interested in addressing their losses.

Maclean put their complaints in perspective for them. "In respect to your situation being worse," Maclean described to the Iroquois the fate of the Rangers, which he deemed more anguished. Caldwell was told of Maclean's speech to the Indians from men arriving at Detroit from Niagara. "There are now men upon this ground, whose situation is exactly similar to yours, with respect to the Rebels and in some degree, worse. Many of their friends have been put to death, and, they have been obliged to take banishment, forsake their country, and leave all their property behind them." [HP-196] Caldwell knew why Lt. Col. Butler was opening land on the west side of the Niagara River for his men to settle and farm. He knew why Major DePeyster had suggested to Caldwell, Bird, Elliott, McKee, and other men that they take up lots of land for themselves close to Detroit, on land proposed to be given to them as grants by the Hurons. The die had been cast for the Rangers as a result of their service with the Indians against the Americans. None of the Rangers or the men of the Indian Department could ever return to their former homes in New York and Pennsylvania now that peace with the Rebels was being made, leaving the Rebels in control of the former colonies. William Caldwell knew he could never go back to Philadelphia because he was a Captain in Lt. Col. Butler's Ranger Corps, and if recognized by the Americans for his former service to the King, he would likely be shot or hanged. [WM-p.3] What he and the Rangers had done in the course of their duty to the King, fighting alongside the Indians at Wyoming Valley, Cherry Valley, Ohio Valley, and elsewhere, had marked each man for life as a traitor, a scoundrel, a savage, and a fiend by the Americans. Caldwell and the Rangers had traversed the wilderness beyond the borders of the frontier with their savage allies to wage an Indian-style of warfare against the Rebel settlements from the Hudson River to Kentucky lands over the course of the years. They had forsaken their former friends and left their homes to support the King. Now they found themselves to be more than simply men without a country, for the Americans judged that they were men whose duty had left them with blood on their hands, the blood of innocents slaughtered by the Indians without mercy.

Too many men, women, and children had perished under the hatchet and scalping knife of the brutal, heartless savages accompanying the Rangers for anyone now to forget what had happened, nor forgive those white men, like Caldwell, for their part in the wilderness war that had brought immeasurable suffering and grief to so many people. In doing their duty which they had unfalteringly carried out in the wilderness war, the Rangers learned from word arriving from the American frontier in the early months of 1783, that the white men who had fought with the Indians were to be held accountable for their actions. William Caldwell knew beyond the shadow of a doubt that he was one of those men.

Several months later, far to the north at Quebec, General Frederick Haldimand sat alone at the writing desk in his damp, cold living quarters in the stone Citadel, as the harsh wind howled outside. Finally finding the words to express the feeling that overwhelmed him, Haldimand picked up the quill and dipped it into the ink well to write to his old friend of long standing, General Riedesel. "My soul is completely bowed down with grief," Haldimand wrote, "at seeing that we, with no absolute necessity, have humbled ourselves so much as to accept such humiliating boundaries. I am heartily ashamed, and wish I was in the interior of Tartary." [KI-p.339]

On his desk lay the open letter from General Carleton at New York that had come by express to Haldimand on the night of April 25, 1783. The contents of the letter detailed a proclamation by King George ordering an end to the war in America and a cessation of arms. A preliminary peace treaty had been signed on November 30, 1782, by the commissioners meeting in Paris. The rebellious American colonies had been granted their independence. Both sides had agreed that the boundaries between the two countries, Britain's Canada, and the new United States, was to run through the middle of the Great Lakes. With the stroke of a pen, all that Haldimand had worked to protect and hold during the long years of war had been given away. No provision had been made to secure the lands of the Ohio Country for the Indians living therein, and by not doing so, the Indians of the Ohio Country, and the white men living with them, could call no place their home in the future, and no land they lived upon their own.

Chapter 16

Epilogue – The Aftermath

The Last Battle of the American Revolution

We know now from American military archives and the Haldimand Papers that the Battle of Fort Henry, fought on September 11, 12, and 13, 1782, was the last battle of the American Revolution in which British troops engaged American forces. While many Kentuckians historically consider the Battle of Blue Licks fought in late August 1782 to be the last battle, the Siege of Fort Henry postdates the engagement at Blue Licks by several weeks. In both battles, British provincial rangers attacked American militiamen. At Blue Licks, Caldwell's Company of Butler's Rangers engaged Kentucky militia forces and at Fort Henry, Bradt's Company of Butler's Rangers laid siege to the militia fort. Yet despite the plethora of information from the Haldimand Papers that has brought to light the British conduct of the wilderness war from 1778 to 1783, controversy and questions surround the British and Indians at the siege f Fort Henry, due to lack of a first-person account from the British side. While Captain William Caldwell wrote a report after the Battle of Blue Licks, no evidence exists to substantiate the fact that Captain Andrew Bradt did likewise after the siege of Fort Henry.

A personal report written by Bradt has never been found and most likely was never written. An exhaustive search conducted on May 6, 1996 by Caroline Forcier Holloway, Reference Archivist at the National Archives of Canada in Ottawa, Ontario, Canada, failed to turn up an after-battle report written by Captain Andrew Bradt from either the Sir Frederick Haldimand Papers index (MG 21, Add Mss 21661-21892) or the British War Office 28 Papers, MG 13, W.O. 28 Great Britain War Office Headquarters Records, Finding Aid 90 relating to the provincial loyalist military unit know as Butler's Rangers in Canada, 1777-1783. Subsequent searches by the author at Archives Canada have likewise proved fruitless. Consequently, from the research, it can be presumed that Captain Bradt did not file a report after the Battle of Fort Henry ended on September 13, 1782.

Why is this so? The answer could be as simple as the officer had no writing materials with him to compose a letter to either Major DePeyster at Detroit, or Captain Caldwell at Sandusky. We do know that Captain Bradt could read and write because he wrote two letters in 1781, defending his actions in a dispute over recruitment. However several possibilities exist that might explain why he did not write, which can be inferred from what we do know about Bradt and his mission. First, there exists the possibility that Bradt disobeyed orders to join Caldwell's force once he reached Wapatomika from Sandusky. If he were to join Caldwell, Bradt would have relinquished command of his company to the senior Ranger officer. By marching his men in the opposite direction towards Fort Henry raises the question whether Caldwell would have approved of Bradt's actions, when Bradt was clearly ordered by DePeyster to join Caldwell. Because Bradt was Lt. Col. John Butler's nephew, Bradt may have been tempted to disregard previous orders and take it upon himself to lead an independent expedition to attack Fort Henry once he met James Girty at Wapatomika, who informed him that Caldwell had intended to attack Wheeling but was diverted instead to Kentucky. Unfortunately, Bradt had established a reputation the previous year as an impetuous and impertinent officer when he took matters into his own hands in the New York wilderness, after confronting another loyalist recruiter. At that time Bradt struck the man, had him arrested and escorted to Fort Niagara whereupon Bradt was chastised for his brash actions, and only by the grace of his uncle was he able to keep from military arrest himself.

Another possibility as to why Bradt did not write an after-battle report is that he did not want to reveal to his superior officers the unflattering details of his conduct while on the campaign. It is clear from the historical record that after the siege of Fort Henry was broken off by the Rangers and Indians, the Indians, almost to a man, abandoned Bradt and his men, and decided on their own to break up into smaller raiding parties to attack isolated settlements, like Rice's Fort in western Pennsylvania. This suggests that the Indians had developed some degree of animosity towards Bradt during the course of their expedition to Wheeling and during the subsequent attack, causing them to leave Bradt once all hope of destroying Fort Henry was gone, and the necessity of joint cooperation lifted.

If Captain Bradt had antagonized the Indians to point that they would desert him when the opportunity arose, then Bradt would not want to record this fact, and conceal it by laying blame upon the Indians for the failed siege, knowing in either case, that Caldwell, McKee, DePeyster and Butler would see through the lie, and know that Bradt had been at least partly responsible for botching the attack on Fort Henry. If Bradt alienated the Indians with him, we can guess that it was due to his lack of experience in cooperating militarily with Indian allies and his divisive character.

Bradt had recently been promoted to the position of captain from that of lieutenant. There is some reason to believe that Bradt did not earn his promotion through merit, but rather due to the influence of his uncle, Lt. Col. John Butler. Bradt's scandalous conduct the previous year drew a reprimand from General Haldimand who wrote, "Let Col. Butler represent to Mr. Bradt the impropriety of his Conduct." [FM-p.157] Butler was clearly embarrassed by the affair, yet still he chose to promote his nephew over other candidates in the Ranger Corps, when normally a reprimand from Haldimand, the Commander in Chief, would have disqualified another man from a promotion, and possibly ended in his career with dismissal from the Rangers.

Becoming a captain put Bradt in the position to command a company of Rangers in the field. With little actual experience, he could have easily made the mistake of believing that he should exert command over the Indians accompanying his Rangers on the expedition to Wheeling. As the Indians with Bradt were from the tribes of the Ohio Country, Bradt had had no previous exposure to them prior to his arrival at Sandusky. If Bradt resorted to giving them orders, he would have antagonized the warriors, rather than have gained their trust and support. When Lieutenant Bradt led 30 Rangers and a party of about 150 Indians on a winter expedition against Fort Stanwix in New York in early February 1781, Bradt had with him Joseph Brant to advise him and to command the Six Nations warriors himself. At Fort Henry, Bradt was alone with only James Girty to advise him on Indian relations. Apparently Captain Bradt irritated, angered, and/or insulted the Indians who lost all respect and confidence in him.

Are there any clues from the historical record that we can draw upon that would lend credence to this possibility, besides the knowledge that the Indians did not accompany Bradt on the return trip? We can compare Bradt's raid on Fort Henry with Caldwell's attack on Bryan's Station in August 1782, and Bird's assault on Ruddel's Fort in 1780. On each of these separate raids, we know that neither Caldwell nor Bird themselves approached the enemy fort and called for a parley. Both officers remained with their troops and studied the fort defenses while other men went forward with the risky business of calling to the defenders to hold their fire under a flag of truce to speak.

We know from the American historical record, that the defenders at Fort Henry did not know that the white men they witnessed fighting alongside the Indians were in fact a company of British provincials called Butler's Rangers from Fort Niagara. However, they were able to identify the white officer who approached the fort under a flag of truce as a "Captain Pratt," the one and the same man as Captain Bradt. That Bradt took on the task of parleying with the fort himself, rather than asking a subordinate to do so, supports the notion that Bradt was accustomed to taking risks. Combined with the incident of the previous year, there is evidence to suggest that Bradt's behavior was brash and arrogant for a Ranger officer. Bradt could have manifested this character trait with the Indians by becoming impatient and openly critical with them once upon the trail to Wheeling where he was in command and had no one to answer to, and therefore would have no need to restrain himself from becoming overly critical and self important. Continually imposing himself as the appointed leader of the expedition, Bradt would have quickly grated upon his native allies and turning them against him.

A more cautious officer with some command experience could have turned to a junior officer for advice, but Bradt did not, although he had such a man with him. A 1783 Company Return lists Bradt as 28 years old in 1783, thus

27 at the time of the attack on Fort Henry, and Lieutenant Ferris of Bradt's Company, the subordinate officer, aged 35 at the time of the attack, considerably older, and ostensibly, a man with more experience, to whom Bradt could have turned for advice. However it is Bradt ("Pratt",) who approaches Fort Henry and who speaks with the defenders, not Ferris. [DW-pp.263, 265]

Without Bradt's own words to clarify for us what happened, we can only surmise what he was thinking and doing during the siege of the fort. Aside from the fact that Bradt successfully destroyed the homes, crops, and livestock surrounding the fort, lacking the ability to take the fort by surprise and with no artillery to batter down the gates as was done at Ruddel's fort in 1780, the attack on Fort Henry was unsuccessful. Bradt must have considered the attempt a failure, especially since he personally called upon the fort to surrender at the beginning of the siege and in the end, could not take the fort. From the account of Colonel Ebenezer Zane, in command of Zane's blockhouse outside the fort walls, we hear of the attempts of the Indians to breach the fort walls over a period of three days. Yet nowhere in Zane's account do we hear of the actions of the Rangers under Bradt. Apparently Bradt did not lend the support of his men in close quarter fighting, which the Indians were sure to relate to McKee and Caldwell, once they returned. When the battle was over and Bradt and his company arrived at Sandusky without the large body of Indians he was known to have left Wapatomika with, Bradt would have had enough explaining to do without committing any of it to a written report.

Without that report, we do not know for sure why Fort Henry was given ample warning of the impending attack, other than the brief report from American Colonel James Marshel, at Catfish Camp (present-day Washington, Pennsylvania) who wrote a letter to General Irvine at Fort Pitt on Thursday September 12, 1782, after news of the attack on Fort Henry was brought into camp by Captain John Boggs. "Dear Sir, by an express this moment arrived from Wheeling, I have received the following intelligence, namely, that a large trail, by supposition about 200 Indians, was discovered yesterday about three o'clock near to that place." [HW3-p.4] Mr. Bill Hinzten clarifies in his article "Rice's Fort Attacked" that "no doubt a number of scouts (American) were out; Linn may have been first to reach the fort (Henry) with information concerning the actual numbers of the approaching war party." [HW3-p.4] In Allan Eckert's "Dark and Bloody River" Eckert surmises that John Linn "encountered a huge party of war-painted Indians that he estimated to number upward of 400," and that Linn "had been seen, fired at and hotly pursued, but had managed to escape." [EA2-p.418]

While we have no hard evidence to support how Linn was able to do so, there is no reason to dispute that he did. However once Linn spotted the Indian war party, he was able to escape capture or death and warn the settlers at Wheeling. Knowing something more about the makeup and likely actions of such a large party of Rangers and Indians can help us make a more accurate educated guess. First, we know that Bradt and the Indians numbered at least 238 warriors, claimed by a deserter, and a company of Rangers that had a maximum of 49 men [HP-

337] of whom at least 35-40 were with Captain Bradt. This force of close to 300 men were several days on the trail to Wheeling, and because all their provisions were carried in their packs, it was of the utmost necessity that they waste no time getting to Wheeling and attack the fort before the food would run out, acknowledging the possibility that little or no food might be found once they got there. By DePeyster's own description of the Rangers as "walking specters" [BR-p.109] when they returned to Detroit late in 1782 after the attack on Blue Licks and Fort Henry, it is apparent that provisions were scarce during the campaigns, and thus the necessity of moving quickly to their objectives, once they left their base of operations, from which no re-provisioning would be forthcoming.

Moving nearly 300 men along a narrow wooded trail as quickly as possible presented some difficulties for Bradt and the Indian war captains. The need for stealth and caution to avoid an ambush would be negated by their own numbers and the noise created by horses and men. We do know that Ranger and Indian joint military expeditions in New York dictated that an advanced guard of flankers move parallel to the trail the main party was traveling, once the expedition reached a point within a day's march of their objective, so as to anticipate and apprehend any enemy scouts ahead watching the trail for Indian war parties. There exist many accounts from New York historical records detailing the deaths of American scouts sent to watch the trails for sign of approaching Indians who were intercepted by flanking parties of Indians sent ahead for that purpose. We know that Bird sent ahead an advanced party of Indians before attacking Ruddel's fort, and after the successful attack on that fort, an advanced party of Indians headed towards nearby Martin's fort, capturing a scout while on the trail.

It is safe to presume that Captain Bradt and the Indian war captains, their provisions dwindling, knew that they must attack Fort Henry directly and as quickly as possible, hoping that their one chance of taking the fort by surprise would be successful, as long as no American scouts were able to give the settlers at Wheeling ample warning of the pending attack. Since John Linn managed to see the huge war party, and was able to evade apprehension by flanking parties who must have been out, we can guess that he picked a spot where he would be able to remain stationary and view any oncoming Indians from some distance so that he might have enough time to get away before they spotted him and killed him. If he had stumbled upon their tracks after they passed, the Indians would have been between him and Fort Henry, cutting off any chance of warning the fort. If he were advancing on the trail and stumbled into the advance guard of the Indians, it would be highly unlikely that he would have survived an initial volley, turned his horse around, and outraced the Indians coming at him back to Wheeling, judging the necessary time needed to make those maneuvers on a narrow trail with Indian warriors rapidly closing the distance.

Consequently, it is likely that John Linn picked a spot overlooking the rising trail following a creek flowing into the Muskingum River watershed, where it met the Indian Wheeling creek tributary and made its way to the Ohio

River. That spot could have been a rise of ground or a particular tree that could serve as a lookout which gave Linn the necessary line of sight vision to spot the Indians before they spotted him. In all likelihood, Linn's observation post was somewhere near the rising ground at present-day Flushing, Ohio.

The End of the War

With the lifting of the siege of Fort Henry at Wheeling, Virginia on September 13, 1782 by Bradt's company of Butler's Rangers and the Indians, the last battle of the American War for Independence came to an end, although small Indian war parties still in the field continued to skirmish with American settlers and militiamen on the western frontier. When Captain Bradt and his men returned to the Upper Sandusky Indian villages, they found a dispatch waiting them from Major DePeyster at Detroit, ordering them to cease all offensive operations against the Enemy and remain on the defensive until further orders arrived. All Indian war parties not yet returned from the frontier were called in, as both the Indians and the white men fighting with them in the Ohio Country were surprised by the news that the western wilderness war seemed to be coming to an end. An armistice between the British and Americans had been officially declared, and while negotiators worked out the details for ending the war which lasted eight long years, British and American officials at the highest levels called an end to hostilities between combatants. Nervously, the Indians, British regulars, provincial Rangers and the white men of the Indian Department strung across the western posts of the Great Lakes and the Ohio Country waited apprehensively to see what would happen next. As the autumn of 1782 turned to winter, no orders to resume the wilderness war were forthcoming from General Haldimand in Quebec.

The stunning defeat and surrender of Lord Cornwallis' British army at Yorktown almost a year before had far-reaching effects on the British conduct of the war, which only a year later was making itself known to the British and Indian forces in the western wilderness. After Cornwallis' surrender to the American and French army, British military operations effectively ceased in Virginia and the Carolinas as Sir Henry Clinon awaited a response from England as to what to do after the substantial British loss of men and material at Yorktown. When word of Cornwallis' defeat and surrender reached London on November 25, 1782, the shock to both Parliament and the Crown was great. According to Lord George Germain, who brought the news to Lord North, North reacted, "as if he would have taken a ball in his breast, crying out wildly as he paced to and from, 'Oh, God, it is all over!'" Though equally distressed, King George stubbornly refused to believe the war had come to an end, saying, "When men are a little recovered of the shock, they will then find the necessity of Carrying on the War." [MB-p.186]

King George's wishful thinking was not to be. The English public was war-weary, and no longer in the mood to support the King in what was increasingly seen as an unwarranted personal vendetta against the colonials. In the ensuing months, Lord North's government fell due to the lack of public support for continuance of the war in America. By early 1782, as Crawford's army was preparing to leave from the Virginia frontier to attack the Upper Sandusky Indian villages, in England, Parliament was voting to "authorize King George to seek peace." Commissioners were appointed by both sides by the end of summer to meet in Paris, France. By November 30, 1782, not only was an armistice agreed upon by both sides, but provisional articles for a formal peace treaty between Britain and the United States were signed. Word of the agreement was officially sent to Sir Guy Carleton in New York City who had taken command of British forces in North America from Sir Henry Clinton.

By the close of winter in early 1783, rumors began circulating among the Indian tribes of the Ohio Country that the Americans at Fort Pitt and in Kentucky were preparing to resume their attacks upon the Indians once the weather improved. Concerned that the rumors were true and that the Americans would use the armistice as an opportunity to grab Indian land for access to the lucrative fur trade before any peace was agreed upon, [JB-399] General Haldimand in Quebec ordered his officers at the western posts to keep Indian scouts constantly in the field on the lookout for movements by the Rebels. When Haldimand's orders reached Major DePeyster at Detroit, he turned to the Indian Department to see they were carried out. Through the early months of 1783 Simon Girty, in particular, kept constantly on the move in the Ohio Country, bringing reliable word to Major DePeyster at Detroit from Indian scouts returning from the Rebel frontier to the Upper Sandusky villages. [BC-p.150] Nowhere along the frontier did the rumors of Rebel armies moving into the Indian lands prove to be true.

In fact, when word of the armistice reached George Rogers Clark at his fort at the Falls of the Ohio River, Clark shelved his plans to invade the Ohio Country in the spring of 1783. After the disastrous defeat of the Kentuckians at Blue Licks the previous August, Clark had been rebuked by many prominent Kentuckians, including Daniel Boone, who criticized Clark for lavishing his attention on his own fort at the Falls at the expense of defending the Kentucky settlements. [WGA-p.124] Further, the new Governor of Virginia, Benjamin Harrison, added his own criticism of Clark by questioning the General as to why he had failed to construct the additional forts in Kentucky which he had requested. With recriminations flying between Kentucky and Virginia over Clark's conduct, George Rogers Clark remained idle during the winter at Fort Louisville at the Falls of the Ohio, reluctant to take any action against the Indians or the British at Detroit.

In early April 1783, a British ship arrived at New York City with official word for Sir Guy Carleton from England that preliminary articles of peace had been signed on November 24, 1782, in negotiations by commissioners for both the Americans and the British meeting secretly in Paris, France. [KI-p.339] Carleton was ordered to inform all his commanding officers throughout the colonies and Canada of the pending peace treaty and end of the war. On the same day, Carleton sent a letter to General Haldimand in Quebec with the news, and on April 9, Carleton wrote a letter to General Washington in command of the American forces, disclosing to Washington his actions, and the need for the General's approval. "Sir, I have written to General Haldimand, acquainting him that the preliminaries of a General Peace have been signed and ratified, and have given my dispatches into the care of Captain Richard Tonge and Lieut. William Robertson of the Naval Department in Canada, with directions to proceed over land to Canada without any delay, but to this end it may be necessary they should be furnished with passports from your Excellency, which I cannot doubt will be immediately given." [CL-208]

As channels for communication between General Carleton and General Washington were opened, in regards to the pending peace, Washington took the opportunity to write to Brigadier General Maclean at Fort Niagara on April 14, 1783, detailing to the British officer what had transpired between him and Carleton. "I have the honor to inform you that on the 3rd of April I received from Sir Guy Carleton the enclosed Extract of a letter from General Haldimand, No. 1. On the 8th, a proclamation from the King of Great Britain was sent me by Sir Guy, No. 2. And on the 10th, a letter of which No. 3 is a copy, was received requesting passports for two Gentlemen bearing dispatches from the British Commander in Chief to General Haldimand announcing the ratification of the preliminary Articles of a general Peace, and a Cessation of Hostilities. A passport was immediately granted and the Gentlemen are on their way to Canada." [HP-207]

Washington now got to the point of his correspondence to Maclean, which concerned the possibility of continuing attacks by the Indians of the Ohio Country against the western settlements. "The distance to General Haldimand being great, this situation is wide from your Post, that great time must elapse before you can receive his dispatches. I have taken the liberty to make this communication to you by the most direct route in my power, in confident hope, that although you may not deem this information official, yet that your benevolence will cause it to be regarded with such attention that, if it does not produce a total cessation of hostilities within your command, yet, it may at least prevent any unnecessary and wanton acts of cruelty which may have been meditated by the Indians on the frontier, and which, in their consequences, may prove disagreeable to them as distressing to the inhabitants of the United States." [HP-207]

On April 25, Carleton's two emissaries reached General Haldimand at Quebec with the important dispatch from Haldimand's Commander-in-Chief. Haldimand read Carleton's letter with shock and dismay, realizing that the war against the Rebels was lost, and worst still, no provisions had been made in the preliminary articles of the peace treaty which Carleton included, for the future of the Indians or their lands in the Ohio Country. Implicit in the omission of the Indians, was the undeniable fact that if they were not included in the treaty, then by their exclusion, their lands were omitted as well. Haldimand realized that the proposed boundary line between Canada and the United States, following the middle of the Great Lakes, without stating it, had in fact, ceded the Indian lands of the Ohio Country to the Americans as a price paid for a lasting peace.

Haldimand decided "not to make public the details of the treaty as long as he could avoid it." [KI-p.339] Knowing that sooner or later word of the treaty's inequity would reach the Indians, Haldimand "hoped he would hear something from England which would mitigate the blow." [KI-p.339]

By the end of April, Haldimand sent word to each of his commanders at the upper posts to keep a close eye on the conduct of the Indians, to both prevent them from attacking the American frontier, and to look for signs that they might react in a hostile manner against the posts once word got out to them concerning the peace terms. To General Allan Maclean in command at Niagara, Haldimand wrote on the matter of the Indians, "I cannot learn that any mention has been made in the Provisional Articles. They will soon, of course, become acquainted with this unpleasant information, and the effect it will have upon them may be easily conceived. It will therefore be highly necessary that you narrowly watch the conduct of the Indians, and without seeming to suspect them, take every precaution to prevent their surprising any small posts or detachments you may have abroad, for there is no saying what their resentment may tempt them to do. Their conduct at the close of the last War was an example of this. Use also your best endeavors to console them and continue your attention to them in every respect." [HP-390]]

In addition to Major Ross building the fortifications at Oswego, Haldimand wrote on April 26, "Having last night received from New York His Majesty's Proclamation for a Cessation of Arms with all the Powers with whom we are at War, in consequence of Preliminary Articles having been signed at Paris on the 30th November last, for treating of Peace, I have to desire that you will, upon Receipt of this, totally cease from carrying on the fortification and all public works whatever at the Post you command, until you receive further orders." [HP-310] No sooner had Ross received Haldimand's letter, than the Indians encamped at Oswego became aware of the pending peace treaty, and Ross noted, "in wonderment, that the news just burst out all over," [KI-p.339] as it spread like wildfire, by word of mouth, between traders, Indians, and regular soldiers.

At nearly the same time, copies of the extract of an alarming American newspaper article taken from the "New Jersey Journal" and re-printed on April 17 in two American newspapers, the "New York City Packet" and the "Fishkill American Advertiser," found their way to Niagara, Detroit and Quebec where provincial troops, particularly Butler's Rangers, found the news disturbing. In reaction to the proposals for peace presented by Commissioners meeting in Paris, "the request of a number of the most respectable inhabitants of this state (New York)" to have the New Jersey newspaper extract reprinted, concerning an article of the peace talks having to do with "giving the Renegades or Tories a temporary residence among us." The published commentary found immediate sentiment and support among New York citizens who agreed wholeheartedly with the argument put forth that "The return of those abominable Wretches, those Robbers, Murderers, and Incendiaries, even to come near us; no method is left us to prevent this great Calamity, but by general associations to render their situation by every means in our power so unhappy, that they will prefer a voluntary Banishment, to the proposed return. Let it be a crime abhorred by Nature to have any communication with them. Like Cain of old, they will carry their mark in their foreheads. Let them be avoided as persons contaminated with the most deadly contagion, and remain as their just demerits, vagabonds on the face of the Earth." [HP-309]

The provincial troops in Canada, including Butler's Rangers, who had fought to regain their families, homes, and property were demoralized when the New York newspaper was circulated through the posts. None held out any hope that reconciliation allowing them to return to their former homes and property in the United States was possible. In fact, the situation for the loyalists enlisted in provincial regiments in Canada went from bad to worse. While the rumors were true that the commissioners in Paris had included an article in the preliminary peace terms allowing for "Congress to recommend to the various state legislatures restitution of confiscated estates of persons who had not borne arms against the United States," and for those men who had served in the provincial regiments, they were to be allowed to "go to the States and remain for a year while trying to get back their property," [KI-p.373] it soon became evident to the men garrisoning the posts in Canada, that the individual states had no intention of carrying out any of the provisions favoring the "hated Tories." Because Congress did not have the means to "force the state governments to abide by the terms," [KI-p.373] the state legislatures were "not repealing their laws against the Loyalists—they were stiffening them, if anything," [KI-p.347] as spring turned to summer in 1783. A handful of Butler's Rangers who had deserted from Niagara and "rashly ventured to their former homes" when the winter weather broke in April, were "savagely beaten" and a few "executed without form of law" by their former neighbors in New York. The remainder were warned to leave the country by June 10, or face arrest and punishment "with the severity due to their crimes and nefarious defection" as Tories. [CE-p.112]

On May 5, 1783, Congress instructed three commissioners to travel from Fort Pitt through Indian country to Fort Detroit, where they were to carry the news of the end of hostilities and peace to the Indians, officially informing all the tribes of the Ohio Country that the British had ceded all the lands from the Ohio River to the Mississippi to the United States. Ephraim Douglass, a former trader at Fort Pitt, led the commission which left Fort Pitt on June 7, but was thwarted by Major DePeyster and the Indian Department, on instructions from General Haldimand, from meeting privately with the Indians at Sandusky, Detroit, or Fort Niagara. Haldimand did not want the Americans driving a wedge between Britain and its allies by disclosing to them the terms of the treaty before the Crown had an opportunity for diplomacy with the Indians.'

In early July, Matthew Elliott of the Indian Department traveled to Fort Pitt to deliver a letter to General Irvine from Major DePeyster, now a Lieutenant Colonel, at Detroit. "I have been honored with your letter of the 6th of July by Mr. Elliott. Report says that the definitive Treaty is arrived at New York, the

While pondering what the future may hold,
a Butler's Ranger awaits orders at Detroit.

enclosed newspapers (which I send for your amusement) contains all I can say of it, as I have not any Official Communication on that subject. Probably, however, is in favor of it being true." [HP-318]

In fact, what General Irvine knew of the proposed Treaty from the newspapers reaching him at Fort Pitt was accurate. The Treaty of Paris was ratified on September 3, 1783 by Great Britain and the United States. Few changes had been made since the original articles were proposed and agreed upon almost a year before. The boundary line between the two countries was fixed at what had been originally proposed- in the middle of the Great Lakes, thus formally giving all the Indian lands previously included as part of Canada west of the Ohio River, from Kentucky to the Mississippi River, to the United States. The Indians were not mentioned in the treaty at all, and once the treaty was implemented, the British were to evacuate all their posts on American soil, including Fort Oswego, Fort Niagara, Sandusky, and Detroit.

News of the treaty ratification reached America by early October, and spread like wildfire to all points of the country, including Canada and the western British posts. Sir Guy Carleton at New York City made plans for an orderly evacuation of all British citizens, soldiers, and loyalists in November, so that the city could be turned over to the Americans. Close to 35,000 loyalist soldiers and civilians, now refugees were believed gathered there to be transported to Canada, for resettlement to be divided between the Maritime Provinces and the valley of the lower St. Lawrence River. [KI-p.307] On November 25, 1783, the last British troops marched from their garrison to waiting ships in the harbor, for transport to England. A woman recalled that the soldiers were "equipped for show, with their scarlet uniforms," as they boarded boats, never to return. [MB-p.192] The war had truly come to an end.

The Indians

As winter turned to spring in 1783, the Indians of the Ohio Country were unaware that a preliminary peace had been signed between Great Britain and the new United States, nor did they know that the King's ministers had not seen fit to include the Indians in that peace, but rather, they had agreed, as a term of the peace, to cede the Indian lands of the Ohio Country to the Americans. While rumors were rampant among the garrison troops and traders circulating the western posts of Oswego, Niagara, Sandusky, and Detroit, that the truce was a prelude to peace with the Americans, the Indians in their villages spread throughout the Ohio Country were more concerned with the threat posed by the Virginians from Kentucky under Clark, and whether Clark intended to attack their villages again, as had happened the previous November with his surprise incursion into Shawnee country.

Major DePeyster at Detroit and General Maclean at Niagara were under strict orders from their commander, General Haldimand at Quebec, to keep word of the peace negotiations secret from the Indians until orders from England arrived with instructions on policy. While DePeyster and Maclean were able to do so, they were not able to keep quiet the rumors spread by traders, civilians, and soldiers arriving at the western posts from the East. Major DePeyster at Detroit was more concerned that the Indians would be demoralized if Clark led another expedition into the Indian lands in the spring, and DePeyster was unable to help them defend their lands. Writing to Maclean on January 7, DePeyster requested that reinforcements for Detroit were needed, "if it were only to keep up the drooping spirits of the Indians, who begin to fear that they are dupes of the War." [HP-198]

On January 13, a council with the Indians was held at Detroit, requested by a visiting delegation of Six Nations Indians arriving from Niagara, who wished to speak to Major DePeyster, his officers, and the Shawnee and Delaware in regards to Clark's incursion into Shawnee lands. DePeyster and Caldwell, with Druilliard, Baby, and Simon Girty interpreting for the Indians, met with the visiting Iroquois, who addressed the war Captains, Black Snake of the Shawnee, and Captain Champion of the Delaware. "Brethren, We the Six Nations are much alarmed to hear that the Enemy has cut off two of your villages." [HP-297] The Iroquois emissaries pledged to the Shawnee and Delaware their support in the spring to repel any further attempts by the Virginians, if they should attack again. In addition, the Shawnee and Delaware listened to the Iroquois request that they accompany them on a mission to Quebec to investigate the question of peace with the Americans. DePeyster strongly advised them against it.

Haldimand wrote to DePeyster on March 12 on the subject of the Indians. "I am willing to hope that the Enemy's retiring from that quarter and being dispersed at Fort Pitt will discourage the Indians from seeking the revenge they seem bent upon. In all events, I depend upon your exertions to prevent it." As to discouraging the Indians at Detroit to meet with Haldimand, the General noted to DePeyster, "You did perfectly right to prevent any of the Chiefs from coming down here, as it would have been attended with much expense, and answered no good purpose. You will receive my answer to the Six Nations upon the same subject. Make such use of it with your Indians as you see fit." [HA-221] Finally, Haldimand noted with approval his previous request to DePeyster that the Indian Department be trimmed in numbers of men and amount of pay, which DePeyster was sure, would send a signal to the Indians that a major change in policy towards them was eminent. "I am glad to find you have made a reduction in the list of persons employed in the Indian Department at Detroit. Transmit to me a return, with the stations and services performed by those officers remaining." [HA-221]

While Haldimand awaited further instructions from England as to what orders should be given to his post commanders concerning the Indians, Major DePeyster at Detroit was joined by Alexander McKee in early March, who just returned from the Shawnee country, and reported "leaving all things quiet" on the frontier with Kentucky. To quell the mood of uneasiness among the Indians at Detroit, DePeyster assured them that troops would soon arrive from Niagara to support them. Writing to Maclean, DePeyster noted, "the prospect of reinforcement gives great confidence to the Indians, but how necessary it will be for them (reinforcements) to come on, I cannot determine, until my scouts return from the neighborhood of Fort Pitt." [DE-199] Unfortunately, the prospects of further aid for the Indians were diminishing daily, and by mid-April, with no word from Haldimand concerning continued British support for the Indians, each of the tribes of the Ohio Country began to suspect the worst.

A Grand Council of the Wyandots was held at the village of Lower Sandusky on April 19, 1783, and with all the chiefs and war captains present, a letter was drafted to petition "their Father at Detroit," Major DePeyster, declaring their concern. "Father, you in the name of our Great Father, the King, requested our assistance against your and our Enemies. You gave us a hatchet, which we have to your knowledge made the best use of we could, in giving you all the help in our power against them. Lately you were pleased to advise us to sit still, which we have, and do hearken to, it being always our intentions. Now, Father, we do not know how to act till we hear from you, and as we have gone on hand in hand together, we hope to continue so, and that you will not allow your poor children to be crushed under the weight of their Enemies. Should a Treaty of Peace be going on we hope your children will be remembered in the Treaty." [IND-316] DePeyster had no choice but to ignore the impassioned plea of the Wyandots, for he was in no position to disclose to them the articles of the proposed peace of which he had privately been made aware. DePeyster had been ordered not to do so, however he knew the Indians would find out soon enough the disagreeable terms by which the British had forfeited the Indian lands of the Ohio Country for the sake of peace with the Americans.

On April 25, Haldimand received the King's proclamation "for a cessation of arms and a copy of the preliminary peace treaty which had been signed at Paris nearly five months before," which Carleton had seen fit to send to Quebec overland by courier from New York. [KI-p.339] Try as he may to keep the news quiet, in succeeding weeks word of the treaty leaked out and spread quickly to the western posts, and to the Six Nations Indians and the tribes of the Western Confederacy. Everywhere, shocked and despondent Indians railed against the perfidy of the English, but nowhere did they "make the slightest attempt to surprise any post or hurt any Englishman," for the Indians "had grown more civilized, and were far more dependent on trade and gifts than before, and were heartily sick of the war" as well. [KI-p.340] The chiefs and war captains of the many tribes complained that the British had no right to give up their lands to the Americans by making the land boundaries between the two countries to run through the middle of the Great Lakes. Only Joseph Brant at Niagara angrily rebuked the British and the King, saying, "England had sold the Indians to Congress." [KI-p.340]

When the Indians had an opportunity to digest the terms of the Treaty as told to them in mid-May 1783, six principal chiefs called for a council with General Maclean at Fort Niagara to voice their dismay and disgust to him, telling Maclean that they "found it impossible to believe that the boundaries actually were run, as reported, and that Britain had not secured to them their own country." [KI-p.340] Clearly worried at what might happen, Maclean wrote to Haldimand his concern for the Indians. "I would by no means answer for what they may do, when they see us evacuate these Posts," adding, "I do from my soul pity these People, and should they commit outrages at giving up these Posts, it would by no means surprise me." [KI-p.341] When Haldimand received Maclean's letter, he quickly sent it on to the ministry in London in hopes that they might consider the consequences of their inactions towards the Indians.

On May 21, 1783, Joseph Brant arrived at Quebec to deliver an important speech to General Haldimand. He demanded to know "the real truth about whether or not the Indians shared in the peace" between Britain and America. Speaking before Haldimand, he reminded the General that the Indians had "joined you from time to time against Your Enemies, Sacrificing Numbers of our People," in the fight to conquer Canada from the French, and the war against the Rebels. "I am now sent in behalf of all the King's Indian allies to receive a decisive Answer from You, and to know, whether they are included in this Treaty with the Americans as faithful Allies should be, or not? And whether those Lands which the Great Being above has pointed out for our ancestors and their descendents, and placed them there from the beginning, and where the bones of our forefathers are laid, is secured to them, or whether the blood of their grandchildren is to be mingled with their bones, through the means of our allies for whom we have often so freely bled?" [KI-p.342]

With no instructions from England to guide him, General Haldimand did not know what to say in reply to Brant's eloquent and reasonable request. At heart, Haldimand was deeply embarrassed, for he knew that the Indians had not been mentioned whatsoever in the treaty signed by the commissioners, "as though they did not exist," in spite of their great service to the King's cause throughout the years of wilderness war. [KI-p.348] To appease Brant and the Six Nations, and convince them that they had not been forgotten by the King, Haldimand asked Brant to accompany the surveyor of the province to the north side of Lake Ontario near the old French post of Cataraqui to look for suitable land for the Six Nations to settle upon in Canada.

From July 18 to 31, a council with the Six Nations was held at Niagara where Sir John Johnson spoke to the Indians on the behalf of General Haldimand and attempted to ease their minds concerning the boundary line of the new treaty, telling them that "regardless of the outcome of the war, their lands," on the American side "still belonged to them, and the King still considered them his faithful allies." [KI-p.344] Hoping that the Indians of the Ohio Country could be likewise convinced, a Grand Council of the Indians of the Ohio Country was called for all the western tribes to meet at lower Sandusky by the end of August. A large delegation from the Six Nations at Niagara left with Joseph Brant to propose to the Indians of the Ohio Country the formation of a union of all the Indians with the Six Nations as the head.

Indians began arriving for the momentous meeting on August 26. On August 27, the vessel "Faith" put into the bay, and on August 28, the crew was "employed in unloading the Indian presents on board." [HP-209] On September 1, the Wyandot chief Half King "and about 300 Indians arrived from the Upper

Town" and on Wednesday September 3 the Shawnee arrived with their delegation, including Alexander McKee and Matthew Elliott. By the morning of September 7, more than a dozen tribes were represented, including Cherokees and Creeks who came from the South. On the morning of the 6, Alexander McKee lit the council fire, and with Simon Girty and Isidore Chesne acting as interpreters, McKee began his speech to the Indians assembled before him, as Deputy Agent for the British Indian Department, preparing them for the business to be transacted by Brant and the Six Nations delegates.

"Children, after saluting the several Nations now assembled at this Council Fire, I am to acquaint you that in consequence of Instructions sent to me by Brigadier General Sir John Johnson Superintendent of all Indian affairs in Canada, I am come here to meet you having found it expedient to call you together at this place in order to avoid delay in apprising of the Councils lately held by him with the Six Nations at Niagara." Given the task by Johnson of explaining to the Indians the nature of the treaty with the Americans in an attempt to ease their minds, McKee told them, "The King, your Father, has found it necessary for the happiness of his more domestic subjects, to conclude a long, bloody, expensive and unnatural war by a peace which seems to give you great uneasiness on account of the boundary line. You are not to believe, or even think that by the line which has been described, it was meant to deprive you of an extent of country of which the right of soil belongs to you," McKee reiterated, as was described by the Treaty of Stanwix in 1768.

"The King still considers you his faithful allies as his Children, and will continue to promote your happiness by his protection," McKee reaffirmed as Sir John Johnson had requested he do. McKee then recommended to the Indians to "bear your losses with manly fortitude, forgiving and forgetting what is past, looking forward in full hopes and expectation that on the return of the blessings of peace and cool and just reflection, all animosity and enmity will cease, and as a proof of your inclination, collect and give up all prisoners that may be among you. As an inducement to comply with what I recommend, I have brought up a large apportionment of everything to supply your wants. Having finished what I had to say, I desire your attention to the deputies of the Six Nations, who will lay before you the late councils held at Niagara." [HP-210] Having done his duty, McKee stepped down to allow Joseph Brant to speak next.

On September 8, 1783, with the business of the Indian council at Sandusky completed, McKee wrote to Major DePeyster at Detroit, detailing to him that "the business which called me to this place is finished and has ended to the general satisfaction of the Indians on this side of the Lakes having fulfilled on our parts the promised made them to their utmost expectation." [HP-319] Yet McKee was not happy himself with what had transpired, knowing full well that the temper of the Indians had been only momentarily appeased with promises and presents, while yet the real problems facing them in regards to their lands in the Ohio Country had not been dealt with directly. "The Indians are not without apprehensions of the designs of the Americans upon their country which by their own accounts they have just reason, for as parties are constantly on this side of the Ohio (River) marking the country." [HP-319] McKee knew that not only were some Americans already crossing the Ohio River into Indian lands to stake claims for settlement, but dozens upon dozens of boatloads of settlers were currently making their way downriver from Fort Pitt to Kentucky [HP-209] with stated designs to "encroach on the Indian Country." [HP-209] McKee could see that with the Indians bound from going to war by the new peace, there was no way to stop the flood of settlers from claiming land on the north side of the Ohio River for their own, now that the agreed-upon boundary line ceded the Indian lands to the United States.

For a while, there was a brief respite in the Indian wars on the frontier with the Americans. Because the United States claimed the Indian lands of the Ohio Country by right of the treaty signed with Great Britain in which the British forfeited the Ohio Country, those lands previously barred from any white settlement by the 1768 Treaty of Fort Stanwix were now property of the United States, and consequently, open to expansion north of the Ohio River. The Treaty of Fort McIntosh of 1785 clarified the position of the United States when the Delawares, Wyandots, and some Ottawas signed away their rights to lands controlled by the tribes in the Ohio Country. The Treaty of Fort Finney of 1786 was a similar agreement between some Shawnee and the Americans that ceded tribal lands north of the Ohio River to the United States. [NL-p.152]

Widespread Indian opposition to the treaties resulted in open warfare against the border settlements by late 1786, and Kentuckians mounted punitive expeditions against the Shawnee villages in the Ohio Country, resulting in destruction of several Indian towns including Wapatomika. Reacting to increasing Indian violence, the United States ordered forts built on the north side of the Ohio River in 1787 and 1788. By 1790, Congress ordered punitive expeditions against the remaining hostile Indians residing in the northwest part of the Ohio Country to eliminate them once and for all. General Harmar's expedition of 1790 up the Miami River Valley resulted in defeat and retreat at the hands of the Indians. A similar advance in 1791 by General Arthur St. Clair was disastrous for the Americans who were nearly annihilated in a battle with the combined tribes of the Indians, however, a third expeditionary force led by General Anthony Wayne met the Indians in battle in August of 1794 at Fallen Timbers in which the Indian nations still fighting the Americans were crushed. The Treaty of Greenville and Jay's Treaty signed in November 1794 effectively ended the attempt by the tribes of the Western Confederacy to oppose the American occupation of their lands. Peace finally came to the Ohio Country as the remaining Indians were expelled westward to the Illinois Country or north to Canada, never to return again. [NL-p.178]

Alexander McKee

Alexander McKee remained active in the British Indian Department at Detroit after the Treaty of Paris brought an end to the war in the Ohio Country in 1783. McKee received a promotion to rank of colonel in the Indian Department, in recognition of his service during the war. As colonel, McKee's responsibilities were increased by Sir John Johnson, the Superintendent General of the Indian Department of Canada, to encompass full management of the Indians of the region. Soon after the end of the war, McKee acquired land for himself "on the Canadian side of the Detroit River, south of Detroit," in conjunction with Matthew Elliott, Captain Henry Bird, and Captain William Caldwell, all of who wished to reside in the Detroit area as they were unable to return to their former homes in the United States. A survey was completed in March 1785 and McKee built a modest home on the land he acquired there, purchased by the Indian Department.

To replace the losses he suffered in Pittsburgh as a result of his flight from arrest by Patriot officials in early 1778, McKee petitioned the British Government in a Memorial dated August 7, 1783, detailing once again those losses of land and property. In December 1788, McKee was granted an award of "three thousand pounds as compensation for his losses," a sizable settlement for the land and property McKee claimed was confiscated by the Americans in Pennsylvania. With the money, McKee invested in real estate in the Detroit area, increasing his land holdings in the region. [HP-333]

By 1790, with the Indians of the confederacy of tribes of the Ohio Country threatening all out war against the frontiers of the United States along the Ohio River, McKee worked with the factions of Indians to obtain supplies and ammunition from the British, by establishing a post at the foot of the rapids on the Maumee River where he could personally distribute to the Indians the goods clandestinely supplied from Fort Detroit. While Great Britain had an official policy of non-intervention in Indian affairs that could damage relations with United States, McKee, as agent to the Indians, was unofficially advised to aid the Indians in any way that he could to oppose any advance by the Americans against the Indians in the western lands.

Consequently, McKee played an active role in meeting with and supplying the various tribes of the western confederacy in their efforts to oppose the coming American military campaigns. In November 1791, an American army under General Arthur St. Clair was soundly defeated by a "large force of native warriors, organized in part by the Indian Department, and aided by arms and intelligence." [NL-p.161] McKee had a direct hand in that victory on the Wabash River in west-central Ohio, but when McKee assembled nearly 1,300 Indian warriors to oppose General Anthony Wayne's American expeditionary force in August 1794 near the rapids of the Maumee River, the Indians did not have a similar success, and when routed by the American army at the Battle of Fallen Timbers, McKee's home and post on the Maumee were burned to the ground by the Americans, and McKee was forced to flee with the retreating Indians, shattering his hope that the Indians would ever recover their lost lands in the Ohio Country, and destroying once and for all the western confederation of the Ohio Country tribes. For all that had happened to the Indians since the close of the American Revolution, McKee, in his capacity as British agent to them, had been unable to convince British officials to commit troops to aid their former Indian allies.

In December 1795, at age 59, Alexander McKee received a promotion to the position of Deputy Superintendent General for Indian affairs for both Upper and Lower Canada, second only to Sir John Johnson. He spent the next few years reorganizing the administration of the Indian Department in Canada, now that an end to the Indian wars had brought relative peace with British Canada and the United States.

By 1797, McKee had semi-retired to his new home on the Thames River following a spate of ill-health that curtailed his daily duties with the Indian Department administration. A "Rheumatic or Bilious fever, attended with great swellings in his feet, hands, and joints" debilitated McKee, and in 1798 he injured his leg just before another severe attack of fever "that left him bedridden and lame." [NL-p.185] On January 10, 1799, Alexander McKee wrote to a close friend, complaining of a "fever and pain in my breast." Within the week, he died in bed at the age of 63, and was buried nearby at the home of his son Thomas, a few miles north of Fort Malden on the Canadian side of the Detroit River. A few months after McKee's death, several hundred Indians arrived at McKee's grave, and with the help of Thomas McKee, they conducted a "slow, measured, and dignified dance that celebrated the memory of their departed friend," a ritual, Simon Girty claimed, was reserved by the Indians "only for men of distinction among them." [NL-p.187]

Matthew Elliott

With the end of the war in 1783, Matthew Elliott had to contend with rebuilding his life far from his former home in Pennsylvania like his close friend McKee. Unlike McKee, Elliott had managed to acquire some assets during the war years that left him far from destitute. During several raids into Kentucky, Elliott was able to capture several Negro slaves which he took with him back to Detroit, and in addition to his many duties serving with the Indian Department during the war, Elliott managed to pursue his private business venture trading goods to the various Indian tribes in the Ohio Country during his coming and going to their villages. Consequently, when the war came to a close, Elliott not only possessed a lot of land near the mouth of the Detroit River adjacent to the lots set aside for many of the officers of the Indian Department and the Rangers, but he was able to build a comfortable estate and settle it with horses, cows, and goods for his slaves to tend.

In subsequent years, Elliott successfully made several land acquisitions through purchases and grants which made him one of the prominent landowners in the Detroit area. Instrumental in acquiring the land was Elliott's establishment of a trading company at Detroit which he formed with his old friend William Caldwell after the war, once Elliott was able to get permission from Governor General Haldimand to conduct a trading business at the western post. For years after the war, Elliott and Caldwell ran their business trading goods for furs with the Indian tribes in the Great Lakes area until the late 1780's.

All the while, Elliott maintained his long, close association with his friends the Shawnee, and frequently visited their villages in the Ohio Country, listening to their complaints against the Americans who were increasingly settling on former Shawnee lands north of the Ohio River and forcing the Shawnee to move their villages further and further towards the Maumee River Valley. Elliott counseled with the Shawnee and was instrumental in encouraging them to renounce the former American treaty they had agreed to and eventually take up the war hatchet against the Americans by resuming raids against the American frontier.

Because of increasing friction between the Indians and Americans over the issue of land in the former Ohio Country which the Americans claimed as their own and called the "Northwest Territory," British officials, who still occupied the post of Detroit and had not turned it over to the Americans, saw the need for closer cooperation with the Indians, and an expansion of the Indian Department there. In 1790, Elliott, through the graces of his good friend McKee, regained official position as Assistant Agent of Indian affairs at Detroit where he was to serve under McKee. With the Americans intent upon putting troops into the field to quell the increasing Indian uprising against the frontier, Elliott was ordered by McKee to rejoin the Indians in the Ohio Country and serve as McKee's liaison and his eyes and ears. Consequently, in the battle between the Indians and General Harmar's invading army in July 1790, and St. Clair's ill-fated campaign of 1791, Elliott was present with the Indians, supplying them with provisions and ammunition, and reported to McKee the extent of the devastating losses suffered by both American armies during the battles and subsequent rout by the Indians. [HR-p.69]

When word reached Detroit in the spring of 1794 of a new invading American army under General Anthony Wayne, Elliott engaged in preparing the Indians of various tribes for Wayne's advance, organizing over 1,500 warriors and arming and supplying them with British goods from Detroit. However, the British refused to commit troops to help the Indians fight the Americans, and at the Battle of Fallen Timbers, both McKee and Elliott, under strict orders from the Indian Department to take no part in the actual fighting, observed the battle and defeat of the Indians by the Americans from across the Maumee River. Everything that McKee and Elliott had worked for to revive the western confederacy of the Indians was destroyed by their defeat, and one by one the tribes made peace with the Americans as McKee and Elliott were forced to return to Detroit. [HR-p.105]

Elliott continued his service in the Indian Department and arranged a large purchase of 3,450 acres of land from Mississauga Indians as McKee's agent for the Crown. In the spring of 1797, Elliott was accused of corruption in the handling of government goods destined for the Indians and was forced to resign from his position in the Indian Department or face prosecution. After Elliott's downfall from office, he spent the next few years attempting to clear his name by petitioning the government in Montreal and Quebec without success. In the summer of 1804, Elliott traveled to England with a petition to appeal the charges against him and clear his name, but "no one was prepared to re-open the case." [HR-p.153] Without recourse, Elliott returned to Canada late in the season.

Back at home, Elliott sent his eldest of two mixed-blood sons, Alexander, to Montreal to receive an education as a lawyer, while his younger son, Matthew Jr. continuing living with his father. Elliott returned to farming and local politics, and in 1806, at the age of 70, he prepared to retire after achieving local prestige and prosperity in spite of his dismissal from the Indian Department. However, with tensions rising between Britain and the United States, Elliott was unofficially called upon by British officials at Amherstburg, across the river from Detroit, to council with the Indians to seek their support. Elliott agreed to do so, and began a series of trips into American territory to meet with the various tribes living on the Auglaize and Maumee Rivers.

Successfully firming up the allegiances of many of the tribes in June of 1808, Elliott was reappointed Superintendent of the Indians at Amherstburg, and in July he arranged a meeting with over a thousand Indian warriors, including Tecumseh, to hear a speech by the Lieutenant Governor of Canada, Simcoe, urging them to join the British and ignore the promises of the Americans. Because of the positive Indian reaction, Elliott believed by the spring of 1809 that with the help of the Indians, the British could regain possession of American Detroit and much of the Ohio Country if war resulted between the two countries.

In the meantime, Elliott, at age 74, married a young woman named Sarah Donovan at Amherstburg in 1810, and within two years she bore him two male children for a total of four sons, and two daughters from his earlier marriage to a Shawnee woman. In 1811, Matthew Jr. attained with the help of his father an appointment as interpreter in the Indian Department, and in early 1812, Alexander was admitted to the bar as a lawyer. On June 18, 1812, the United States declared war on Britain, and by August, Matthew Elliott was involved in leading the Indians in battles around the Detroit area. On August 15, he commanded a force of over 600 warriors in an action that led to the surrender of the Americans at Detroit and the capture of the former British post. But on November 22, 1812, Elliott's eldest son Alexander was killed during a skirmish with the Americans on the Maumee River, and grief-stricken Elliott accompanied his son's corpse back to Amherstburg to bury him at his home.

In September 1813, a strong American force invaded Canada across the Detroit River and forced the British and Indians to retreat up the Thames River. Elliott and his wife and family were forced to flee and his home and estate fell into the hands of the Americans who destroyed all of Elliott's property in revenge for his past service to the Crown. On October 5, Elliott was present when Tecumseh was killed and the British and Indians routed and crushed by the advancing American army when they tried to make a desperate stand. After briefly campaigning with British forces on the Niagara frontier against the Americans, Elliott returned to his family who were residing at Joseph Brant's old home at the village of Burlington at the head of Lake Ontario.

Once there, Elliott was plagued by a persistent sickness through March of 1814, and as the sickness deepened by early April, he decided to dictate his last will and testament on April 22. Lingering until May 7, Matthew Elliott died at the age of 75, his "nature is so much worn out as to be unable to bear the struggle both of mind and body." At his burial at Burlington, a representative from the nearby Moravian mission arrived to pay his last respects. Elliott, who had once persecuted the Moravian priests in the Ohio Country in 1781 and aided in their expulsion from the Ohio Country to exile at the Detroit area, had much later in life "sought to help the local Moravian mission whenever he could." [HR-185]

Simon, George, and James Girty

At the end of the war in 1783, there no longer was a need for the services of the Girty brothers as interpreters for the British Indian Department so the three brothers by-and-large went their separate ways. George, aged 38 and the youngest of the three brothers, returned to live with the Delaware Indians at "Buckungehelas town" which was located "upon the upper waters of the Great Miami River" in the Ohio Country, where he "gave himself up to savage life" living with the Indians, [BC-p.217] and "apparently wanted no other society" than that of the Delaware, by whom he had been adopted many years before as a youth. [BC-p.191]

After the end of hostilities, James Girty moved to the headwaters of the St. Mary's River near the portage where Peter Loramier had built his trading post. With his Shawnee wife, James built a home and established a trading post, where he enjoyed an exclusive monopoly for several years trading with the local Indians. While James dressed much like his Shawnee clansmen, he was nonetheless not as completely immersed in Indian life as his younger brother George, and would frequently travel to and from Detroit to obtain goods to sell.

In July 1783, Simon Girty, the eldest of the three brothers, decided to move to the Detroit area after living continuously with the Mingo and Wyandot Indians for five years in the Ohio Country during the war. Simon, unlike his younger brothers, was not enamored with Indian life, nor had he taken an Indian woman for a wife, like George and James. Simon arrived at Detroit in August, and there met with Alexander McKee, who offered to continue Simon's employment in the Indian Department as an interpreter to the Indians.

A year later, Simon married a young white woman at Detroit named Catherine Mallot, who had been a former American captive taken by the Indians on the Ohio River in 1780, and brought to Detroit. Simon was able to obtain land on the Canadian side of the Detroit River along with McKee, Bird, Elliott and Caldwell, and it was there that he built and home for himself and his new wife to raise a family. [BC-p.160]

The next few years Simon Girty devoted to improving his newly acquired property, raising a family, and trading with the Indians in the Detroit area. In addition, Girty attended to the affairs of the Indian Department when McKee occasionally needed him to travel to the Ohio Country and counsel with the

Indians as McKee's emissary. By 1790, with war between the Indians and the Americans looming over ownership of the Indian lands in the Ohio Country, McKee called upon Girty to meet with the Indians in a grand council on the Maumee River to hear their complaints and advise them to seek an alliance with the British once again.

With an agreement by some of the tribes to renew hostilities against the American frontier and word that the Americans were intent on sending an army against the Indians to quell their uprising, Simon Girty left his wife and a young son and daughter in Canada, and with his brother George, joined a sizable Indian war party of over 300 warriors who intended to attack the American outposts near the mouth of the Great Miami River in early January 1791. Simon led the attack against the Americans at Dunlap's Station and besieged it unsuccessfully for a day and a night during which time an American prisoner of the Indians was horribly tortured to death before the fort walls with both of the Girty brothers approving. [BC-pp.187, 188]

Much later in the year, Simon Girty accompanied a large body of Indian warriors against St. Clair's invading American army and he took part in the battle against the Americans and their subsequent disastrous defeat on November 4, 1791. Simon was said to have fought bravely at the battle and as a leader of the Wyandot warriors, he greatly increased his reputation with the Indians. [BC-p.196] Nearly three years later, Simon accompanied McKee and Elliott in their failed attempt to rally the Indians against General Wayne's American army at the Battle of Fallen Timbers on the Maumee River in 1794. James Girty did not take part in the battle for he had earlier left his trading post on the St. Mary River for Canada for fear that he and his family would fall into the hands of the invading Americans.

After the conclusion of the battle, the Indians sued for peace with the Americans and Simon Girty returned from the Ohio Country to his home near Amherstburg on the Canadian side of the Detroit River to devote himself to his family and farm. James returned to the Ohio Country and built a new trading post on the Maumee River, closer to Detroit, but left his family in Canada near his brother Simon. Sometime before 1810, George Girty, now a habitual drunkard, left his Indian wife and children with the Delawares and went to live with his brother James on the Maumee until his death at the age of nearly 65 just before the outbreak of war in 1812.

James Girty retired from the trading business on the Maumee and returned home permanently to his wife and two children in Canada after the death of his brother George. James's Indian wife Betsy died about this time, and during the War of 1812, James was too old to take part in the campaigns, and suffered from rheumatism, though unlike his brother George, James was thrifty in his investments and temperate by nature. Finally, on April 15, 1817, James succumbed to illness and died at his home in Canada at the age of 74.

When General Wayne sent troops to take possession of Fort Detroit in May 1796, Simon Girty remained long enough to watch the Americans approach before swimming across the Detroit River to safety at the age of 55. In October

1797, Simon's last child was born to him and his wife, for a total of two sons and two daughters, though a few months after the child's birth, Simon and his wife separated due to his increased drinking which resulted in drunken rages against her. In 1800, Girty severely broke his ankle which caused permanent lameness and his eyesight began to fail him, leading him to drink even more.

With the outbreak of war between Great Britain and the United States in 1812, Simon was too blind and infirm to take part in the early battles on the American side of the Detroit River, and when the Americans crossed the river in 1813, Simon was forced to flee eastward to the Mohawk lands, leaving his wife at the home of one of his married daughters. Largely incapacitated, Simon returned to his former home in 1816. He was in ill health and totally blind when in mid-February 1818, he "was taken suddenly ill on the afternoon of February 15, and was taken care of by his wife who had reconciled with him when he gave up liquor the previous year." On February 18, at the age of 76, Simon Girty died at his home, and was buried on his farm two days later. The British at nearby Fort Malden sent a detachment of troops to the funeral, and he was "laid to rest with military honors" for his lifetime of service to the British Crown. [BC-239]

Captain William Caldwell

At the end of the war, Captain William Caldwell decided to leave Butler's Rangers and military life altogether when the unit was disbanded, and by 1784, Caldwell looked for land in the Detroit area where he planned to settle. Caldwell took a new wife named Suzanne Baby who was the daughter of the Frenchman Duperon Baby, the Deputy agent of the Indian Department at Detroit. By 1784, Caldwell was able to secure a land grant on the east side of the Detroit River near its mouth on Lake Erie, along with other former military officers Bird, McKee, Elliott and Simon Girty, and six men of the Indian Department. In addition, Caldwell volunteered to help a group of disbanded Butler's Rangers and other military men staying on in the Detroit area after the war, to secure land grants for themselves as well as acquire tools and equipment necessary for building homes for themselves and to begin cultivating the land once acquired. [WM-p.45]

While working to develop his own land, Caldwell requested permission from General Haldimand, still at Quebec, to secure trading rights at Detroit, and once obtaining those rights, he entered into a partnership with Matthew Elliott to begin a trading company to exchange goods for furs with the Indians in the Detroit area and elsewhere. In the ensuing years, Caldwell and Elliott met with some success, but as American traders from Pennsylvania and Virginia made inroads into the newly acquired American lands of the Ohio Country, they lured the trade away from Detroit and Caldwell and Elliott's enterprise began to fail. By October 1787, Caldwell was forced to dissolve the business and seek protection from creditors, both British and American, with bankruptcy.

With his land grant secure, Caldwell turned to other means to support himself and his growing family which had increased to five sons and three daughters. In 1789 Caldwell invited his mixed-blood son named Billy from a previous marriage to a Seneca woman at Niagara to come live with his new family at Detroit. Though Billy consented, he was a thorn in his father's side in subsequent years due to his unrestrained, unruly behavior which often got him in trouble with the local authorities to the embarrassment of his father.

The elder Caldwell did not take part in the Indian wars against invading American armies under Harmar and St. Clair in the early 1790s. Instead, Caldwell got involved in local politics on the Canadian side of the Detroit River, and in 1791 he became a local justice of the peace for the growing communities across from Detroit. But when American General Anthony Wayne threatened a new and more ominous invasion of the Northwest Territory, Caldwell assumed control of the local Canadian militia by appointment as Colonel of the South Battalion of the Essex County Militia. Throughout the spring and early summer of 1794, he worked to prepare the militia for the new American invasion. [WM-p.64]

At the Battle of Fallen Timbers on August 20, 1794, Caldwell joined in the battle with his company of 53 militiamen, many of whom were former Butler's Rangers, and fought a "stubborn rearguard action" with the Americans, allowing the Indians time to escape the advancing American troops and preventing annihilation of the Indian forces. [WM-p.75] Caldwell did so without approval from the British at nearby Fort Miami, who had strict orders not to engage the Americans with British troops. As such, his company won the undying admiration of the hard-pressed Indians, though Caldwell lost six men in the hot fight.

After the treaty with the Americans in 1795, Caldwell returned to a more sedate life as civic leader, landowner, and farmer on the Canadian side of the Detroit River. With the outbreak of war with the Americans in 1812, an elderly Caldwell returned to military life to support the British cause against the Americans and protect his home, family, and property. Caldwell was called upon to raise a Corps of Rangers of "between four and eight companies from the Western District," using the old "Butler's Rangers as the standard rather than regular troops." [WM-p.94] Caldwell took command of the fledgling ranger corps which numbered only one company of men. When the Americans crossed the Detroit River in 1813, Caldwell and his Rangers accompanied the retreating British and Indian forces which resulted in the plundering and destruction of his home by the Americans. Caldwell and his company fought with the Wyandots at the Battle of the Thames where the Shawnee Tecumseh was slain and the British and Indians routed.

By 1815, with the war over, Caldwell was able to return to the remains of his home, but was devastated to learn that his wife Suzanne had died of illness in his absence. Caldwell once again began to pick up the pieces of his life, and submitted a claim to the Military Board in Canada for the losses he had suffered at the hands of the Americans. However, failing health prevented him from aggressively rebuilding his former estate, and in January 1818, Caldwell drew up his will to divide his properties among his children. Lingering 4 years, William

Caldwell finally succumbed in late February 1822 in his early seventies, at his home in Canada. [WM-p.119]

Lt. Col. John Butler

With the end of the war, Butler's Rangers were disbanded as a military unit in June 1783 although the men of the Ranger Corps had "little hope of being restored to their former homes in the United States due to their previous service with the Indians against the American frontier. [CE-p.112] Lt. Col. John Butler applied for and received permission for his men to obtain grants of land on the west or Canadian side of the Niagara River, upon which many former Rangers began to settle, build homes and cultivate the soil. By the end of July, "258 officers and men had agreed to settle, making, with their families, a body of 620 persons" taking up residence in Canada as permanent exiles. [CE-p.113]

Lt. Col. John Butler retained his office in the Indian Department as Deputy Superintendent of Indian Affairs, though his bouts of ill-health interfered often with his ability to fulfill his duties. At the same time, Butler acquired for himself a substantial holding of land across the Niagara River from the Americans below the escarpment which was the source of the great falls. Butler called his land Butlersbury in memory of his old home on the Mohawk River and around him several former Rangers settled, forming the present town of Niagara-on-the-Lake, Canada. [FM-p.338]

Butler, at the age of 66 in 1791, took an appointment as judge of the Nassau District Court for the local settlement of Newark (Niagara-on-the-Lake,) in addition to raising and organizing three battalions of local militia drawn from former Rangers and their families, totaling "835 rank and file" to defend their homes as tensions rose with the Americans across the Niagara River.

While preparing to attend an important council with the Indian tribes of the Ohio Country to be held in early June 1793 to discuss an American proposal to partition the former Indian lands of the Ohio Country along a new boundary line, Butler's wife Catherine died and he was forced to delay his trip to attend to her burial on May 31. Still grieving over the loss of his wife, Butler cut short his trip to Detroit and returned soon to Niagara, saying afterward that "he could not get along with Alexander McKee, and he differed with him in opinion, for he thought it was the most favorable opportunity the Indians would ever have for making an advantageous peace and saving the greatest part of their country" from the Americans. [KI-p.495]

At heart, and in health, Butler was despondent. He had never been able to reconcile himself with the early loss of his beloved home in the Mohawk Valley which had been confiscated and sold by the Rebels during the Revolution, nor the tragic loss of his eldest son Walter in 1782. Thomas Butler, another son, had attempted to carry on his elder brother's name. "That spring, an infant of Thomas Butler's, named Walter Butler, died and was buried, and again the next year, another infant of that name," died in infancy too, reminding the elder Butler again and again of his heartfelt loss. [SH-p.285]

With much on his mind, by the fall of 1795, Butler was ready to cede his role in the Indian Department once and for all. Returning to his home on the west side of the Niagara River, Butler became "too feeble to carry on his full range of duties" due to his failing health. [KI-p.537] By January 1796, Butler gradually lost the use of his legs due to the onset of paralysis, and while bedridden, he "worried about his old accounts" that needed settled. On May 13, 1796, John Butler died. "The man who had been ailing so long but who had always done whatever he could to help his Indian charges" was gone. [KI-p.568] Joseph Brant conducted an Indian ceremony over Butler's grave in the burial ground on Butler's property, covering it with "a great belt of black wampum" so that Butler might rest forever in peace, declaring of Butler, "his memory will ever be dear to us." [KI-p.568]

As if a postscript to the man who had led his Rangers on devastating raids against the American frontier settlements during the Revolutionary War, during the War of 1812, the Americans crossed the Niagara River in 1813, and during their battle with British and Canadian militia at the town of Newark, (Niagara-on-the-Lake,) John Butler's home and property were pillaged by the Americans. [FM-p.338]

Joseph Brant

After the end of the war with the Americans in 1783, Joseph Brant continued his attempts to petition the Crown to secure land grants in Canada for the Six Nations Indians at Niagara who were homeless and unable to return to their confiscated ancestral lands in New York State. After years of effort, Brant succeeded in obtaining for the Six Nations a substantial grant of land from the government that extended along the Grand River in Upper Canada, and soon became the next home for many exiled Iroquois. A village called Brant's Town was built in the center of those Indian lands, and Brant resided there with his family.

Finally, by mid-summer of 1798, Brant decided that while "he must still look out for his people, for they were helpless without him, he could not live with them any longer," and he successfully obtained a 3,450 tract of land at the head of Lake Ontario from the Mississauga Indians where he moved with his family and began building a grand house. By early March 1803, the house was completed near the beach at Burlington Bay and Brant focused his efforts on cultivating the land. More and more, the elderly Brant suffered from debilitating bouts of illness that were interspersed with periods of heavy drinking, which some who knew him said was the cause of his illness. [KI-p.733] On November 24, 1807, after weeks of severe illness that left him bedridden, Joseph Brant died at his home, at the age of 64.

His last words spoken to trusted friends and family at his bedside revealed his lifelong concern for the welfare of his people. "Have pity on the poor Indians," Brant was said to have uttered. [KI-p.652] In New York and Pennsylvania, the passing of "The Monster Brant" as he had been called by Americans, was little noticed, and only by those old enough to recall the name of the man who was remembered as the Indian war captain responsible for devastating the frontiers of New York and Pennsylvania during the War for Independence.

Sir Frederick Haldimand

At the end of the war in 1783, General Haldimand stayed in Canada to continue his military and administrative service in governing Great Britain's remaining American province. In 1784, Haldimand applied for leave to return to England, and on November 16, 1784, he "left Canada never to return," though he officially remained "the governor until 1786, when a successor was chosen." [FM-p.327] In England, Haldimand was knighted for his services rendered for the Crown in America, including his valiant defense of Oswego in 1759 against an overwhelming force of nearly 4000 French and Indians during the French and Indian or Seven Years War. Retiring from military service, Haldimand, a lifelong career soldier in the employ of the British Crown returned to his native Switzerland, where he died at Yverdun on June 5, 1791, at the age of 73. Many years later, Haldimand's heirs donated his extensive official military correspondence to the British War Museum in England, and copies of his valuable papers were placed in the National Archives of Canada at Ottawa, as historical reference of loyalists serving in provincial regiments during the War of Independence. [Encyclopedia Americana,-Vol.13, p.632]

Patrick "Peter" Fitzpatrick

Patrick Fitzpatrick, often called Peter, was born in Ireland in 1752, and came to America in 1766, at the age of 14. Little is known of his life in Ireland, for there are no records of his life there, nor do we know the port of departure from the British Isles and the ship he traveled on. Peter Fitzpatrick came to America indentured to an Irishman living in the Mohawk Valley, Guy Johnson, the nephew of Sir William Johnson. As an indentured servant, Peter was considered the property of the man he was indebted to and would serve. It was a common practice not to list indentures on the ship's manifest by name, but rather as property, like sheep and cattle. His voyage to America was most likely from an English port aboard a ship that had recently arrived from the West Indies or America laden with raw materials from the colonies.

Most likely Peter was Irish Catholic and poor. It is known that he was illiterate for he was never able to write his own name. Whom he came with from Ireland to America and why he was indentured is not known, as no records have been found to reveal why he left Ireland and who he traveled with. It is generally known that an indenture term of seven years of servitude was a common way for poor Irish to escape a lifetime of crushing poverty in Ireland. Whether he left Ireland with his family and they died during the trip, or whether they disembarked at another port cannot be determined. That Peter Fitzpatrick made his way to the Mohawk Valley at the age of 14 is known for sure, saying in his own words, that he "is a native of Ireland, came to America in 1766." [PEF-01]

In his sworn testimony given for a memorial or petition to the Crown after the end of Revolutionary War for compensation for the losses he had suffered, he made no mention of a family, nor did anyone emerge later that could be determined to be his kin. All that is known for sure about his early years was revealed by Peter in 1784, after the war, at the age of 32.

Patrick "Peter" Fitzpatrick spent seven indentured years, from 1766 to 1773, at Guy Park Manor, the home of Guy Johnson, on the north shore of the Mohawk River several miles west of the settlement at Schenectady and just east of Sir William Johnson's old home called Fort Johnson. Soon after Peter's indenture term was fulfilled, he married a maidservant of Guy Johnson's named Katherine Warren, and the couple received a lease from Guy Johnson for 50 acres of river bottom land which was designated Lot #3 of Johnson's Kayaderroseras Land Patent purchase. However, Guy Johnson did not give the land lease directly to Peter, but to his wife Catherine. "Had 50 acres given to his Wife by Col. Guy Johnson. She had been a servant of his." [PEF-01] The land lay a short distance to the west of Guy Park Manor and abutted the King's Road on its southern edge.

Peter began clearing the land for farming, and built a modest house and a barn, describing his property as "14 acres of land under Good Improvements with a small house and orchard there on, with two cows, one horse, four large swine." Peter owned on his land "one plough and harrow and other implements of husbandry," and had "wheat harvested and put into the Barn in Good Order from six bushels of sowing." A crop of Indian corn stood on four acres of ground," in the late spring of 1775, and his home was furnished with "a bed, bedding, and other household furniture, including three firelocks, and clothing for my wife and children." [PEF-2]

Soon after the outbreak of war at Lexington, Massachusetts in April 1775, Guy Johnson received word from Albany that a warrant for his arrest had been issued by the Rebel authorities there and the Rebels would soon arrive in force at Guy Park Manor to arrest Johnson. Johnson immediately called all his tenants in from their lands surrounding him and had them bring their "firelocks" or muskets to fortify Guy Park Manor in reaction to the alarm. Peter was there, for "14 days at Guy Park attending the alarm" in defense of Guy Johnson. But when Johnson decided to flee the Mohawk Valley or Oswego and Canada, Peter Fitzpatrick left his family at home and accompanied Johnson and the Butlers to Canada. There, it was eventually decided that Peter would return to the Mohawk Valley in the spring of 1776 as a spy for the British.

Arriving home soon after the weather broke, Peter gave his oath of allegiance to the Rebel authorities and was enlisted in the Tryon County Militia, Frederick Vissher's Third Battalion, Emmanuel DeGraeff's Company under the watchful eye of the local members of the Committees for Safety who knew that Peter was formerly acquainted with Guy Johnson and the Indian Department. [NYR-p.180], [NYI-p.372]

On June 7, 1777, Peter and Katherine took their newborn daughter Eleanor to the only local church in the valley still open, the Dutch Reformed

Church at Caughnawaga, where the baby was baptized, having been recorded as born on the 27 of April, allowing for the fact that Peter, the father, had returned to the Mohawk Valley and his wife by August 1776. Soon after the christening, the alarm was given that the British, Tories and Indians under St. Leger were headed from Oswego to the Mohawk Valley and all the men of the Tryon County Militia were required for military service to meet the British threat.

Whether Peter was with the Third Battalion during its rout at the Battle of Oriskany and was able to avoid death at the hands of the Seneca and Mohawk warriors, or whether he remained posted at garrison duties in the valley is not known. If he was there, he may have been spared by warriors who recognized him or by some sign from Molly Brant that he wore which afforded him protection. He is not on the list of men who served at Oriskany, but that list is incomplete and the identities of many men may never be known for sure, although it is evident that he survived when most of his friends from the Mohawk Valley did not. Whether Peter, as an undercover spy for the British, provided intelligence to St. Leger's scouts on the movements of Herkimer's militia force up river can never be known. If he had done so, then the blood of hundreds of men killed and wounded in the ambush of the Tryon County militia at Oriskany stained his hands forever.

Almost a year later, on the July 24, 1778, a warrant for Peter's arrest was issued in Albany, New York, by the Commissioners for Detecting Conspiracies, who acted on a complaint by William Harper, a Patriot official of the Mohawk Valley, who entered a complaint against "Peter Fitzpatrick and John Waters as Persons whose going at large may prove dangerous Consequence to the Safety of the State." Peter was apprehended and arrested soon after. Denying the charges against him, he was permitted to remain on parole in the Albany – Schenectady area, but "not to depart the Limits of this City and appear when called upon by us." [PEF-4] The noose was tightening about Peter's neck, as his spying activities were close to becoming exposed.

Also in the Albany – Schenectady area at the same time were two ardent loyalists who were involved in passing military intelligence on Rebel activities to Sir John Johnson in Canada. One was the former Anglican pastor of Sir John Johnson's church, the Rev. John Stuart on parole for loyalist activities, and the other man was Lt. Peter Drummond, former officer of MacAlpine's provincial loyalist corps who was captured during the surrender of Burgoyne's British forces at Sartoga in 1777. [PEF-3] Peter Fitzpatrick was acquainted with both men. When Sir John Johnson raided the Mohawk Valley in October 1780, Peter Drummond escaped from the Rebels and returned with Johnson's force to Canada. Realizing that he was about to be arrested again, with more severe consequences, Peter and five other men, some former tenants of Guy Johnson like himself, fled the Mohawk Valley for Canada.

At his headquarters of the King's Royal Yorkers outside of Montreal, Canada, Sir John Johnson was surprised in mid-November when Patrick "Peter" Fitzpatrick and five men came into his camp from their arduous trip over the Adirondacks. Johnson wrote to Haldimand of "a list of men lately come in from

Tryon County and desirous of joining the King's Royal Regiment of New York. Of those men, Johnson listed "Patrick Fitzpatrick" at the top of the list, along with "…Magra," [PEF-26] Peter's close friend from the valley, Dennis MCGraw, and four other men. Peter and Dennis were sent to the refugee camp and nearby Vercheres, Quebec to draw rations on Dec. 1, as men of Captain Peter Drummond's newly formed "Company of Royalists." [PEF-10]

On February 28, 1781, Sir John Johnson personally endosed the enlistment of Peter Fitzpatrick and Dennis MaGraw into the 2nd Battalion, Crawford Company, KRRNY. Crawford's Company was known as the spy and scout company and soon Peter was employed to carry communications from Sir John Johnson to loyalists still in the Hudson and Mohawk Valleys as well as transport documents through Rebel lines to the British in New York. It was dangerous work for if a man were caught out of uniform with documents on his person, for he would be tried as a spy and executed by Rebel authorities.

In early September 1781, Peter and Dennis were caught by the Rebels when they strayed too close to the Mohawk Valley and were recognized and captured as spies. By Peter's own account he stated "he was taken prisoner by the Enemy in September 1781, having been sent from St. John's (Quebec) by Order of General Haldimand for Intelligence." [PEF-2] Sir John Johnson soon became aware of the capture of his two scouts and wrote to Haldimand on September 17, 1781. "Two men who were to go to Hudson's River were unfortunately taken, and gave information of the destination of the three men first mentioned. Our friends at Albany and Schenectady were deterred from sending some dispatches from New York," as a result. [PEF-20/HP-383]

Haldimand's reply to Johnson on September 20 concerning the arrest of Johnson's men was terse. "The capture of two men, whose infidelity has prevented my receiving Sir Henry Clinton's Dispatch (from British-held New York City) has no doubt been hurtful. You would do well to represent in the strongest terms to all Scouts the dangerous consequences of yielding to those Inquisitions (of the Rebels). The Enemy will not venture to take their Lives unless Dispatches are found upon them, which is always to be avoided by Precaution." [PEF 21/HP-384]

Peter languished in the squalid conditions of the basement prison of the Albany jail, waiting to be hung after a trial by Patriot authorities found him guilty of treason for spying and sentenced him to death. "Peter Fitzpatrick maketh oath and saith that … he was kept in Close Prison two years in the Common Prison in Albany." [PEF-2] While confined there, and awaiting his sentence to be carried out, Peter witnessed many prisoners die, either by execution or by disease. Dennis MaGraw was one of them. No records exist that show that Peter's closest friend survived the war either in Canada or the United States. The circumstances surrounding Peter's stay of execution are not known. Perhaps his wife's family was able to petition the state of New York to lift the death sentence which ultimately led to his release, and his subsequent exile to Canada once the war was over.

By March 25, 1784, Peter had made his way to Canada, and was residing with his family outside of Montreal, [PEF-2] where he was finally mustered out of the King's Royal Regiment, and had the opportunity to send a memorial to England petitioning the Crown for compensation for his losses in New York due to his years of military service. Peter's memorial resulted in a grant of land near Cornwall, Lower Canada, now eastern Ontario. The date and place of his death is unknown. He was known to be alive in 1806, and was believed to have died in York (Toronto), soon after the beginning of the War of 1812, at around age 60.

However, all was not well with Peter when he was released from prison and re-united with his family in Canada. The war had changed him in some way that can never be fully known. Peter did not make improvements upon his grant of land in Cornwall, but rather, chose to wander. Was it the two years that Peter spent in the Rebel jail in Albany that broke his health or the death of his best friend, Dennis MaGraw that troubled him? Perhaps it was the loss of all that he had owned in the Mohawk Valley coupled with the death of a young son in a refugee camp in Quebec that affected him so deeply. Maybe, upon viewing the poor rocky soil on the north side of the St. Lawrence River above Cornwall Peter fondly rued for the rich deep fertile earth along the Mohawk River that he had grown to love. And too, the memory of so many friends of his youth lost in the bloody carnage at Oriskany battlefield might have made him wonder whether he had made a mistake in serving the Crown.

What is known for sure is that Peter Fitzpatrick was angry and bitter. At a tumultuous town meeting of ex-loyalist soldiers held at Cornwall in January 1787 to protest the possibility that "Gentlemen officers enjoying half-pay from the Crown" were conspiring to "transform themselves into seigneurs," serious questions about "favoritism to officers in the original distribution of land" were raised and many ex-soldiers spoke out. "No officers, no officers" some of the men shouted. "They have rode long enough and now it's our turn. Turn out all those half-pay Gentry," man men called, to which Peter Fitzpatrick shouted, "By the eternal God, they should all be murdered." At this point, the officers present at the meeting quickly adjourned and prudently left. [BW-p.142]

With his passing, Patrick "Peter" Fitzpatrick left a legacy of several children. William, the eldest, was born in the Mohawk Valley in 1778. Elizabeth, Peter Jr., and Eleanor survived the journey to Canada with their mother, Katherine, who was described on January 24, 1784, as "sickly and distressed" when she was counted as a loyalist refugee in a camp near Montreal, drawing rations for herself and her children while she waited for the return of her husband. One male child under the age of six, unnamed, survived the arduous trip from the Mohawk Valley died soon after reaching Canada. [PEF-15] Other children, Hugh, Richard and Francis, were subsequently born in Canada after the war.

Several of Peter's sons, two born in the Mohawk Valley and one born in Canada, went on to serve in the Stormont County militia during the War of 1812 in defense of Canada against the American invasion. William survived the war and took to farming the land granted to his father. Hugh was wounded in the right thigh and died after from the wound that never healed properly. Peter Jr. was not heard of again; presumably killed at the battle of Chrysler's Farm fought on November 11, 1813 or dying of disease.

Their Story is Told

The story of the men of the British Indian Department and Butler's Rangers who fought for the King and the Native-American Indians for control of the Ohio Country during the American Revolution has now been told after 220 years. The quote from William Shakespeare in his play "Julius Caesar" that could aptly apply to them, applies no more.

"Friends, Romans, countrymen, lend me your ears; I come to bury Caesar, not to praise him. The evil that men do lives after them; the good is oft interred with the bones." [SH-JC]

So it can be said of these men who fought with the Indians in that savage wilderness war. Vilified by the victors and banished from their former homes to a new land, I have found them to be ordinary men who were committed to doing their duty, and not "monsters" as some post-war historians recorded. May they rest in peace, and the hatred attributed to them while living, live on no more.

Dedication

Jack Alan Fitzpatrick

My father, Jack Alan Fitzpatrick, was born in 1919 in the little town of Southey, Saskatchewan, Canada, near the family home at Earl Grey. His father and grandfather had come to Saskatchewan in 1903, leaving the rest of the family behind in Cornwall, Ontario, on the farm that their ancestor Patrick Peter Fitzpatrick, had originally been granted in 1788, and homesteaded by his son, William Fitzpatrick. They had come west to the bleak, treeless plains of Saskatchewan along with hundreds of other men intent on obtaining free land from the government for anyone willing to plow the prairie grass under and start a farm.

By February 1914, father and son had made enough improvements on their claims to get the titles to two adjoining sections of land. However, by December 1914, the bank at Earl Grey foreclosed on the property that had been put up as collateral on the loan for lumber and farming tools. By the time of Jack's birth, the family had given up on farming and worked as tenant farmers, moving about the local prairie towns working as sharecroppers. The advent of the Great Depression of the 1930's, coupled with the dust bowl conditions on the northern plains drove Jack's family to move to Regina, Saskatchewan so Jack's father could seek work to support his wife and four young children.

Growing up in Regina, Jack remembered that the family moved around quite a bit because they couldn't make ends meet, because of grinding poverty. "At that stage of my life I never asked why or what was going on. Being the youngest I just went along, of course, and maybe the other kids knew of our life style and economic situation, but I didn't. And I never discussed it with my parents after I had grown up." [FJA-p.6] Great Britain declared war on Germany on Labor Day 1939, and Canada, a Commonwealth country of Great Britain, immediately followed suit. Jack joined the Royal Canadian Corps of Signalers, and on January 23, 1942, he was transferred to the Royal Canadian Air Force. After training and ground crew duty on the West Coast of Canada, Jack was sent overseas to England for duty with the Royal Air Force.

Arriving at Liverpool, England, "after a couple of weeks I was posted to a bomber squadron at Linton-on-Ouse in Yorkshire in northern England. Linton-on-Ouse was an airforce base flying Lancaster bombers." Referring to his war years of service with the RAF, Jack said, "During my time there, I was ground crew in the administration end of it. Didn't have to shoot at anyone." [FJA-p.12]

With the end of the war in Europe on May 9, 1945, Jack returned to Canada and was discharged from the military on November 14, 1945.

Unable to enroll in college because of the long waiting list, Jack took a job as an accountant with Massey Harris, a Canadian farm machinery company on January 4, 1946, and remained with Massey Ferguson for 36 years until he retired on July 2, 1982 in Des Moines, Iowa, at the age of 62. Along the way, he and his wife, Lenore Donison, moved from Regina, Saskatchewan, to Calgary, Alberta; Toronto, Ontario; Des Moines, Iowa; Stow, Ohio; and back to Des Moines, raising three children while he was employed by Massey Ferguson.

Reluctant to give up his Canadian citizenship while living in the United States, when Jack retired from Massey Ferguson, he and Lenore decided to return to Canada. In August 1982, they moved to Kelowna, British Columbia. While retired, Jack became interested in researching his own family's genealogy. All that he knew for certain was that his father and grandfather had come to Saskatchewan by train in 1903 from their home in Cornwall, Ontario, Canada. His father had once told him that he believed that the Fitzpatrick family had come from Ireland to Canada during the Great Irish Potato Famine of 1851. As my father researched first in the genealogical records of the Church of Latter Day Saints and then in the Province of Ontario Archives, he discovered that his father had been wrong. My father learned for the first time that an unbroken chain of Fitzpatrick ancestors dated back to Patrick Peter Fitzpatrick's arrival in America in 1766.

Consequently, on a 1996 trip to the National Archives of Canada in Ottawa, Ontario, to document in detail the loyalist connection of Patrick Peter Fitzpatrick for my father, I inadvertently came across the 1777-1783 letters of loyalist officers serving in the Ohio Country. Sharing these letters with my father, he suggested I bring to light the untold story of these forgotten men, just as he had shed light on our own forgotten loyalist ancestor. I promised him I would do so, but unfortunately he did not live long enough to see this book come to fruition.

In 1995, my mother Lenore, died in Kelowna from congestive heart failure. A year later, my father sold his home and moved to the city of Nanaimo on Vancouver Island in British Columbia to be close to his only daughter, Lana. After overcoming prostate cancer at age 75, he died in Nanaimo at age 81 of lung cancer related-causes.

To my father, Jack Alan Fitzpatrick, this book is dedicated.

Bibliography

Primary Sources – Archival

British Library and National Archives of Canada

Haldimand Papers and British War Office Records

AddMss21756, Correspondence with officers commanding at Niagara, 1777-1783.
AddMss21759, Letters relating to Detroit and Niagara, 1778-1782.
AddMss21760-21763, Letters from officers commanding at Niagara 1777-1784.
AddMss21764, Letters from Haldimand to officers commanding at Niagara, 1779-1783.
AddMss21765, Letters from Haldimand to John Butler, commanding the Corps of Rangers at Niagara, 1777-1784.
AddMss21781, Correspondence between Sir Guy Carleton and Haldimand and the officers commanding at Detroit, 1776-1783.
AddMiss21782-21783, Letters from Haldimand to officers commanding at Detroit, 1779-1784.
AddMss21821, Letters from Officers of Loyalists, 1778-1784.AddMss21841-21842, Papers of secret intelligence of the affairs of the United States, and relating to American prisoners, 1775-1782.

Haldimand Papers and War Office References
(All classified under the designation [HP])

[HP-01] Brant to McKee, 08-21-1781
[HP-02] Butler to Powell, 06-07-1781
[HP-03] DePeyster to Powell, 06-23-1782
[HP-04] DePeyster to Haldimand, 08-18-1782

[HP-05] Powell to Haldimand, 09-18-1781
[HP-06] Brant to Chesne, 05-01-1781
[HP-07] DePeyster to Dundas, 10-23-1782
[HP-08] Powell to Haldimand, 10-06-1782
[HP-09] DePeyster to Haldimand, 11-21-1782
[HP-10] DePeyster to Haldimand, 09-04-1782
[HP-11] Haldimand to DePeyster, 05-31-1782
[HP-12] Butler to Haldimand, 03-26-1779
[HP-13] Intelligence to Haldimand, 06-09-1782
[HP-14] Intelligence to Haldimand, 07-14-1781
[HP-15] McKee to DePeyster, 10-10-1781
[HP-16] Clark to Wallace, 08-09-1781
[HP-17] Lochry to Clark, 08-14-1781
[HP-18] Clark to unknown, 08-10-1781
[HP-19] McKee to DePeyster, 07-15-1781
[HP-20] Brady to Lochry, 08-07-1781
[HP-21] Intelligence to Haldimand, 07-22-1781
[HP-22] Caldwell to DePeyster, 09-24-1782
[HP-23] Turney to DePeyster, 06-07-1782
[HP-24] Lochry to Clark, 08-08-1781
[HP-25] McKee to DePeyster, 09-26-1782
[HP-26] McKee to DePeyster, 09-22-1782
[HP-27] DePeyster to Powell, 05-15-1782
[HP-28] McKee to DePeyster, 08-28-1782
[HP-29] Bradt to Powell, 09-29-1781
[HP-30] Girty to DePeyster, 05-12-1782
[HP-31] Caldwell to DePeyster, 06-13-1782
[HP-32] Butler to Lernoult, 06-27-1782
[HP-33] DePeyster to Powell, 08-27-1782
[HP-34] Powell to Haldimand, 07-10-1782
[HP-35] Thompson to DePeyster, 03-14-1781
[HP-36] Girty to Lernoult, 09-06-1779
[HP-37] Bolton to Haldimand, 10-03-1778
[HP-38] Hare to DePeyster, 09-15-1780
[HP-39] Bolton to Haldimand, 01-26-1779
[HP-40] McKee to Haldimand, 10-25-1778
[HP-41] Grant to Bolton, 06-25-1780
[HP-42] Ferris to Bolton, 07-01-1780
[HP-43] Bird to DePeyster, 06-03-1780
[HP-44] McKee to DePeyster, 06-04-1780

[HP-45] Caldwell to DePeyster, 08-26-1782
[HP-46] McKee to Caldwell, 09-21-1782
[HP-47] McKee to DePeyster, 07-22-1782
[HP-48] Chesne to DePeyster, 08-19-1782
[HP-49] McKee to DePeyster, 05-10-1782
[HP-50] Unknown to DePeyster, 04-08-1781
[HP-51] Caldwell to DePeyster, 06-11-1782
[HP-52] McKee to DePeyster, 09-26-1781
[HP-53] Butler to Lernoult, 11-01-1781
[HP-54] Powell to Haldimand, 08-17-1782
[HP-55] Dundas to Haldimand, 11-02-1782
[HP-56] DePeyster to Powell, 06-12-1782
[HP-57] Intelligence to DePeyster, 06-07-1782
[HP-58] Turney to DePeyster, 06-07-1782
[HP-59] McKee to Lernoult, 10-25-1778
[HP-60] Bolton to Brehm, 04-08-1779
[HP-61] Bolton to Brehm, 04-08-1779
[HP-62] Brehm to Bolton, 05-05-1779
[HP-63] Brehm to Haldimand, 05-08-1779
[HP-64] Brehm to Haldimand, 05-28-1779
[HP-65] Brehm to Haldimand, 07-05-1779
[HP-66] Brehm to Haldimand, 08-02-1779
[HP-67] Bolton to LeMaistre, 04-08-1778
[HP-68] Bolton to Carleton, 05-21-1778
[HP-69] Butler to Bolton, 07-08-1778
[HP-70] Bolton to LeMaistre, 07-14-1778
[HP-71] Girty to Lernoult, 09-06-1779
[HP-72] Bolton to Haldimand, 11-13-1778
[HP-73] Butler to Bolton, 11-17-1778
[HP-74] Bolton to Haldimand, 02-12-1779
[HP-75] Bolton to Haldimand, 03-24-1779
[HP-76] Lernoult to Bolton, 04-02-1779
[HP-77] Bolton to Haldimand, 05-02-1779
[HP-78] Bird to Bolton, 06-09-1779
[HP-79] Bolton to Haldimand, 06-27-1779
[HP-80] Lernoult to Bolton, 06-23-1779
[HP-81] Bolton to Haldimand, 07-15-1779
[HP-82] Bolton to Haldimand, 08-01-1779
[HP-83] DePeyster to Bolton, 07-06-1779
[HP-84] Bolton to Haldimand, 08-10-1779

[HP-85] Bolton to Haldimand, 08-11-1779
[HP-86] Lernoult to Bolton, 08-08-1779
[HP-87] Bolton to Haldimand, 10-24-1779
[HP-88] Lernoult to Bolton, 09-25-1779
[HP-89] Bolton to Haldimand, 11-10-1779
[HP-90] Elliott to Lernoult, 10-11-1779
[HP-91] McKee to DePeyster, 11-16-1779
[HP-92] Burnett to Bolton, 01-05-1780
[HP-93] Mariweather to Clark, 03-10-1780
[HP-94] Randolph to Clark, 05-30-1780
[HP-95] W. Elliott to Holmes, 05-30-1780
[HP-96] McKee to Bird, 05-03-1780
[HP-97] DePeyster to Bolton, 05-16-1780
[HP-98] Bolton to Haldimand, 05-16-1780
[HP-99] Bird to DePeyster, 05-21-1780
[HP-100] Grant to Bolton, 06-25-1780
[HP-101] Grant to Bolton, 06-27-1780
[HP-102] Bird to DePeyster, 07-11-1780
[HP-103] Bird to DePeyster, 07-01-1780
[HP-104] McKee to DePeyster, 07-08-1780
[HP-105] Bolton to Haldimand, 07-01-1780
[HP-106] Bird to DePeyster, 06-03-1780
[HP-107] Bird to DePeyster, 07-24-1780
[HP-108] DePeyster to Bolton, 08-04-1780
[HP-109] Account from a Rebel deserter, 08-05-1780
[HP-110] DePeyster to Bolton, 08-06-1780
[HP-111] DePeyster to Bolton, 09-03-1780
[HP-112] McKee to Johnson, 09-15-1780
[HP-113] Potts to Powell, 11-20-1780
[HP-114] DePeyster to Powell, 11-15-1780
[HP-115] DePeyster to Powell, 01-08-1781
[HP-116] Powell to Haldimand, 02-19-1781
[HP-117] DePeyster to Haldimand, 05-02-1779
[HP-118] DePeyster to Haldimand, 10-05-1779
[HP-119] Haldimand to DePeyster, 06-17-1779
[HP-120] Haldimand to DePeyster, 10-28-1779
[HP-121] Haldimand to DePeyster, 08-30-1779
[HP-122] Butler to Haldimand, 09-24-1778
[HP-123] Butler to Haldimand, 10-04-1778
[HP-124] Butler to Haldimand, 05-02-1779

[HP-125] Butler to Haldimand, 09-01-1781
[HP-126] Bolton to Carleton, 12-14-1777
[HP-127] Bolton to Haldimand, 05-08-1778
[HP-128] Bolton to Haldimand, 02-12-1779
[HP-129] Bolton to Haldimand, 03-24-1779
[HP-130] Lernoult to Bolton, 05-08-1779
[HP-131] Lernoult to Bolton, 11-10-1779
[HP-132] Bolton to Haldimand, 07-24-1780
[HP-133] Powell to Haldimand, 11-10-1780
[HP-134] Powell to Haldimand, 03-23-1782
[HP-135] Haldimand to Bolton, 12-21-1778
[HP-136] Haldimand to Bolton, 12-10-1779
[HP-137] Haldimand to Bolton, 05-01-1780
[HP-138] Haldimand to Powell, 11-16-1780
[HP-139] Haldimand to Powell, 02-18-1782
[HP-140] Coon to DePeyster, 03-01-1781
[HP-141] McKee to DePeyster, 02-27-1781
[HP-142] Bradt to DePeyster, 03-08-1781
[HP-143] Thompson to DePeyster, 03-14-1781
[HP-144] DePeyster to Powell, 03-17-1781
[HP-145] Grant to Powell, 03-18-1781
[HP-146] Grant to Powell, 03-31-1781
[HP-147] Causeland to Powell, 04-02-1781
[HP-148] DePeyster to Powell, 04-04-1781
[HP-149] Powell to Haldimand, 04-07-1781
[HP-150] Powell to Haldimand, 04-10-1781
[HP-151] Elliott to DePeyster, 04-07-1781
[HP-152] DePeyster to Powell, 04-25-1781
[HP-153] Powell to Haldimand, 05-08-1781
[HP-154] Powell to Haldimand, 05-15-1781
[HP-155] Powell to Haldimand, 05-28-1781
[HP-156] Powell to Haldimand, 06-07-1781
[HP-157] DePeyster to Powell, 06-27-1781
[HP-158] Powell to Haldimand, 07-02-1781
[HP-159] DePeyster to Powell, 07-12-1781
[HP-160] Powell to Haldimand, 07-19-1781
[HP-161] Butler to Powell, 07-21-1781
[HP-162] Powell to Haldimand, 08-16-1781
[HP-163] Powell to Haldimand, 08-25-1781
[HP-164] Powell to Haldimand, 09-18-1781

[HP-165] McKee to DePeyster, 09-26-1781
[HP-166] Powell to Haldimand, 10-10-1781
[HP-167] Powell to Haldimand, 10-20-1781
[HP-168] Powell to Haldimand, 11-13-1781
[HP-169] Powell to Haldimand, 11-15-1781
[HP-170] Powell to Haldimand, 12-06-1781
[HP-171] DePeyster to Powell, 04-08-1782
[HP-172] McKee to DePeyster, 04-10-1782
[HP-173] Powell to Haldimand, 04-14-1782
[HP-174] DePeyster to Powell, 04-21-1782
[HP-175] Powell to Haldimand, 05-11-1782
[HP-176] DePeyster to Powell, 05-16-1782
[HP-177] Caldwell to DePeyster, 06-11-1782
[HP-178] Turney to DePeyster, 06-07-1782
[HP-179] Snake to DePeyster, 06-08-1782
[HP-180] Powell to Haldimand, 07-01-1782
[HP-181] Powell to Haldimand, 07-10-1782
[HP-182] DePeyster to Powell, 08-06-1782
[HP-183] Powell to Haldimand, 08-07-1782
[HP-184] Powell to Haldimand, 08-17-1782
[HP-185] Powell to Haldimand, 08-17-1782
[HP-186] DePeyster to Powell, 08-17-1782
[HP-187] Butler to Powell, 08-27-1782
[HP-188] Powell to Haldimand, 08-29-1782
[HP-189] Dundas to Haldimand, 09-12-1782
[HP-190] Dundas to Haldimand, 09-19-1782
[HP-191] McKee to DePeyster, 09-22-1782
[HP-192] Dundas to Haldimand, 10-06-1782
[HP-193] Dundas to Haldimand, 10-23-1782
[HP-194] McKee to DePeyster, 10-25-1782
[HP-195] Indians to Maclean, 12-11-1782
[HP-196] Maclean to Indians, 12-12-1782
[HP-197] Maclean to Haldimand, 12-24-1782
[HP-198] DePeyster to Maclean, 01-07-1783
[HP-199] DePeyster to Maclean, 03-05-1783
[HP-200] Haldimand to Powell, 07-08-1782
[HP-201] Haldimand to Powell, 07-09-1782
[HP-202] Haldimand to Maclean, 10-31-1782
[HP-203] Butler to Haldimand, 09-24-1778
[HP-204] Butler to Haldimand, 10-04-1778

[HP-205] Butler to Haldimand, 10-26-1778
[HP-206] Butler to Powell, 02-12-1779
[HP-207] Washington to Maclean, 04-14-1783
[HP-208] Carleton to Washington, 04-09-1783
[HP-209] Indians, 08-26-1783
[HP-210] McKee to Indians, 09-07-1783
[HP-211] Carleton to Hamilton, 05-21-1777
[HP-212] Carleton to Hamilton, 03-14-1778
[HP-213] Haldimand to Hamilton, 08-06-1778
[HP-214] Haldimand to Hamilton, 08-10-1778
[HP-215] Haldimand to Hamilton, 08-27-1778
[HP-216] Haldimand to Lernoult, 04-08-1779
[HP-217] Haldimand to Lernoult, 04-08-1779
[HP-218] Haldimand to DePeyster, 05-08-1780
[HP-219] Haldimand to DePeyster, 10-06-1781
[HP-220] Haldimand to DePeyster, 05-31-1782
[HP-221] Haldimand to DePeyster, 03-12-1783
[HP-222] Hamilton to Carleton, 02-01-1778
[HP-223] Hamilton to Carleton, 05-25-1778
[HP-224] Hamilton to Haldimand, 05-20-1778
[HP-225] Hamilton to Haldimand, 07-01-1778
[HP-226] Hamilton to Haldimand, 05-26-1778
[HP-227] Hamilton to Haldimand, 12-04-1778
[HP-228] Hamilton to Haldimand, 08-17-1778
[HP-229] Hamilton to Haldimand, 12-18-1778
[HP-230] DePeyster to Haldimand, 11-16-1780
[HP-231] DePeyster to Haldimand, 11-02-1781
[HP-232] DePeyster to Haldimand, 01-26-1782
[HP-233] DePeyster to Haldimand, 06-12-1782
[HP-234] DePeyster to Haldimand, 05-14-1782
[HP-235] DePeyster to Haldimand, 06-15-1782
[HP-236] DePeyster to Haldimand, 09-04-1782
[HP-237] DePeyster to Haldimand, 09-29-1782
[HP-238] Indian Council, 06-14-1778
[HP-239] Indian Council, 06-15-1778
[HP-240] Hamilton to Haldimand, 06-17-1778
[HP-241] Haldimand to Lernoult, 05-08-1779
[HP-242] Bird to Lernoult, 05-17-1779
[HP-243] Bird to Lernoult, 06-09 1779
[HP-244] Doge to Boyles, 07-13-1779

[HP-245] McKee to Haldimand, 07-16-1779
[HP-246] Iago to Lernoult, 07-20-1779
[HP-247] Arundel to Lernoult, 07-31-1779
[HP-248] Haldimand to Lernoult, 08-29-1779
[HP-249] DePeyster to Haldimand, 11-01-1779
[HP-250] Indian Council, 01-17-1780
[HP-251] Indian Council, 01-07-1779
[HP-252] DePeyster to Haldimand, 01-08-1781
[HP-253] Indian Council, 04-05-1781
[HP-254] Indian Council, 04-26-1781
[HP-255] Jefferson, 10-01-1781
[HP-256] Thompson to DePeyster, 09-26-1781
[HP-257] McKee to DePeyster, 10-18-1781
[HP-258] Indian Council, 10-21-1781
[HP-259] McKee to DePeyster, 11-02-1781
[HP-260] Indians to Council, 12-10-1781
[HP-261] Indian Council, 02-25-1782
[HP-262] McKee to DePeyster, -04-10-1782
[HP-263] DePeyster to Haldimand, -05-14-1782
[HP-264] Indian Council, 05-18-1782
[HP-265] McKee to DePeyster, 05-31-1782
[HP-266] DePeyster to Haldimand, 06-12-1782
[HP-277] DePeyster to Haldimand, 06-23-1782
[HP-288] Haldimand to McKee, 07-08-1782
[HP-289] Haldimand to DePeyster, 07-11-1782
[HP-290] Bird to Powell, 08-13-1782
[HP-291] Chesne to DePeyster, 08-16-1782
[HP-292] DePeyster to Haldimand, 09-04-1782
[HP-293] Bruce to Macomb, 10-29-1782
[HP-294] McKee to DePeyster, 11-15-1782
[HP-295] DePeyster to Haldimand, 11-21-1782
[HP-296] Indian Council, 12-01-1782
[HP-297] Indian Council, 01-13-1783
[HP-298] Myers to Haldimand, 08-29-1781
[HP-299] McKee to DePeyster, 09-15-1780
[HP-300] DePeyster to Powell, 06-15-1782
[HP-301] Brant to DePeyster, 05-19-1781
[HP-302] Bradt to Powell, 09-29-1781
[HP-303] Powell to Haldimand, 02-19-1781
[HP-304] McKee to DePeyster, 08-22-1780

[HP-305] Butler to McLean, 03-31-1783
[HP-306] Coleman to Floyd, 09-08-1782
[HP-307] Turney to Lernoult, 01-20-1783
[HP-308] DePeyster to Powell, 09-03-1782
[HP-309] Intelligence, 05-17-1783
[HP-310] Haldimand to Ross, 05-26-1783
[HP-311] Ross to Haldimand, 07-04-1782
[HP-312] Ross to Haldimand, 07-13-1782
[HP-313] Indian Council, 04-05-1781
[HP-314] Indian Council, 04-26-1781
[HP-315] Indian Council, 12-10-1781
[HP-316] Indians to DePeyster, 04-19-1783
[HP-317] McKee to DePeyster, 04-26-1783
[HP-318] Irvine to DePeyster, 08-15-1783
[HP-319] McKee to DePeyster, 09-08-1783
[HP-320] Ross to Haldimand, 07-07-1782
[HP-321] Haldimand to Ross, 05-04-1782
[HP-322] Haldimand to Aubrey, 04-08-1779
[HP-323] Haldimand to Harris, 08-26-1779
[HP-324] Haldimand to Fraser, 07-13-1780
[HP-325] DePeyster to Haldimand, 11-12-1780
[HP-326] Powell to Haldimand, 10-09-1780
[HP-327] Butler to Haldimand, 11-03-1780
[HP-328] Pawlings to Haldimand, 06-27-1782
[HP-329] Butler to Powell, 10-01-1781
[HP-330] William Butler to Haldimand, 09-22-1781
[HP-331] Butler to Crown, 05-01-1785
[HP-332] McKee to Haldimand, 09-06-1778
[HP-333] McKee to Johns, 08-22-1783
[HP-334] LaMotte to Haldimand, 08-22-1783
[HP-335] Butler's Rangers Muster, 03-31-1781
[HP-336] St. Duskey, 1779-1781
[HP-337] Bradt's Company, 11-30-1783
[HP-338] Bradt Provisions, 03-08-1781
[HP-339] Detroit, 09-22-1773
[HP-340] Detroit, 08-05-1782
[HP-341] Rebel Commission, July 1781
[HP-342] Indian Department Roll Officers, 02-24-1783
[HP-343] Butler's Rangers Return, 03-26-1779
[HP-344] Butler's Rangers Return, 10-03-1780

[HP-345] Butler's Rangers Return, 09-30-1781
[HP-346] Butler's Rangers Return, 11-29-1780
[HP-347] Butler's Rangers Return, 11-05-1779
[HP-348] Butler's Rangers Return, 04-08-1779
[HP-349] Butler's Rangers Return, 02-03-1778
[HP-350] Return Detroit, 05-01-1782
[HP-351] Return Detroit, 06-01-1782
[HP-352] Return Detroit, 07-01-1782
[HP-353] Return Oswego, 06-01-1782
[HP-354] Return Oswego, 04-23-1782
[HP-355] Return U. Posts, 01-01-1782
[HP-356] Return U. Posts, 02-01-1782
[HP-357] Return U. Posts, 03-01-1782
[HP-358] Return U. Posts, 08-01-1782
[HP-359] Return Detroit, 08-03-1782
[HP-360] Return Detroit, 09-01-1782
[HP-361] Return Detroit, 08-01-1782
[HP-362] Butler's Rangers Return, 01-01-1779
[HP-363] Major Ross Raid, 09-29-1781
[HP-364] Indian Department, 01-11-1783
[HP-365] Prisoners to Detroit, 05-16-1782
[HP-366] Caldwell Company, 12-24-1777
[HP-367] King's Royal Regiment New York Return, 08-25-1783
[HP-368] Medicine, 06-10-1784
[HP-369] Return to Oswego, 09-09-1782
[HP-370] Ships to Ontario, 09-10-1782
[HP-371] Oswegatchie, 09-11-1782
[HP-372] Provisions to Niagara, 01-24-1778
[HP-373] Return to Indians – Niagara, 12-30-1778
[HP-374] Butler's Rangers – Requisition, 09-09-1779
[HP-375] Troops Upper Country, 10-21-1779
[HP-376] Troops Upper Country, 11-15-1779
[HP-377] Detroit Inventory, 07-13-1784
[HP-378] Return, 06-25-1784
[HP-379] Return Indian Department to Detroit, 02-24-1783
[HP-380] Loyalist Return to Detroit, 09-02-1784
[HP-381] Sinclair to DePeyster, 03-08-1780
[HP-382] DePeyster to Bolton, 03-08-1780
[HP-383] Johnson to Haldimand, 09-17-1781
[HP-384] Haldimand to Johnson, 09-20-1781

[HP-385] Haldimand to Powell, 04-21-1782
[HP-386] DePeyster to Bolton, 06-08-1780
[HP-387] Chesne to DePeyster, 08-19-1782
[HP-388] Haldimand to Maclean, 10-31-1782
[HP-389] DePeyster to Powell, 04-03-1781

Patrick Peter Fitzpatrick Sources

[PF01] National Archives Canada, Public Record Office, A.O.12, Vol. 29, pp.133-134.
[PF02] National Archives Canada, Public Record Office, A.O. 13, Vol. 12, pp. 426-428.
[PF03] British Library, Haldimand Papers, AddMss21842, Papers of Secret Intelligence, pp.143-146
[PF04] Minutes of Commissioners for Conspiracies, p.179
[PF05] Records of the Dutch Reformed Church of Caughnawaga, New York, vol. I, p.43.
[PF10] National Archives Canada, War Office 28 (MG13), Vol. 10, p.254.
[PF14] National Archives Canada, Haldimand Papers, AddMss21827, Muster rolls of loyalists and other provincial corps serving in America, 1776-1784.
[PF15] National Archives Canada, Haldimand Papers, AddMss21828, Musters of refugee loyalists and disbanded soldiers in Canada, 1784.
[PF20, 26] National Archives Canada, Haldimand Papers, AddMss21818, Letters to Haldimand from officers of the Kings Royal Regiment of New York, 1779-1783.
[PF21] National Archives Canada, Haldimand Papers, AddMss21819, Letters from Haldimand to officers of the King's Royal Regiment of New York, 1779-1783.

Secondary Sources – Book

[AF] Association, Fort Ligonier, *War for Empire in Western Pennsylvania*, Fort Ligonier Association, Fort Ligonier, Pennsylvania, 1993.
[BB] Bearor, Bob, *The Battle on Snowshoes,* Heritage Books, Inc., Bowie, Maryland, 1997.

[BC] Butterfield, C.W., *History of the Girtys*, Robert Clark and Co., Cincinnati, Ohio, Reprint by Log Cabin shop, Inc., Lodi, Ohio, 1995.

[BC2] Butterfield, C.W., *An Historical Account of the Expedition against Sandusky under Col. William Crawford in 1782*, Robert Clark and Co., Cincinnati, Ohio 1873.

[BJ] Bonin, Jolicoeur, *Travels in New France*,

[BK] Burnham, Koert and David Martin, *La Corne St. Luc- His Flame*, Highlands Press, Keeseville, New York, 1991.

[BR] Booth, Russell, *The Tuscarawas Valley in Indian Days 1750- 1797*, Gomber House Press, Cambridge, Ohio, 1994.Russell Booth

[BW] Brown, Wallace, and Hereward Senior, *Victorious in Defeat: The American Loyalists in Exile*, New York, New York, 1984

[CC] Calloway, Colin, *The Western Abenaki of Vermont, 1600-1800*, University of Oklahoma Press, 1990.

[CE1] Cruikshank, Ernest, *The Story of Butler's Rangers and the Settlement of Niagara*, Welland: Lundy's Lane Historical Society, 1893. Reprint, Richardson, Bond, and Wright Limited, Owen Sound, Ontario, Canada, 1975.

[CE2] Cruikshank, Ernest, and Gavin Watt, *The King's Royal Regiment of New York*, T.H. Best Printing Co., Toronto, Ontario, 1984.

[CJ] Cuneo, John, *Robert Rogers of the Rangers*, Fort Ticonderoga Museum, Ticonderoga, New York, 1988.

[CW] Campbell, William, *Annals of Tryon County*, J. & J. Harper, New York, 1831.

[DB] Dunnigan, B.L., *Siege- 1759, The Campaign Against Niagara*. Old Fort [AB] Niagara Association, Youngstown, New York, 1996.

[DE] Dodge, Edward, *Relief is Greatly Wanted, The Battle of Fort William Henry*, Heritage Books Inc., Bowie, Maryland, 1998.

[DF] Drimmer, Frederick, *Captured by the Indians*, Dover Publications, Inc., New York, 1961.

[DW] DeHass, Wills, *History of the Early Settlement and Indian Wars of West Virginia*, Holitzell, Wheeling, Virginia, 1851, reprinted McClain Co., Parsons West Virginia, 1995.

[EA] Eckert, Allan, *Wilderness Empire*, Bantam Books, Boston, Massachusetts, 1969.

[EA2] Eckert, Allan, *That Dark and Bloody River, Chronicles of Ohio River Valley,* Bantam Books, new York, 1996.

[FA] Foote, Allan D., with James Morrison, Joseph Robertaccio, and Alan Sterling, *Liberty March, The Battle of Oriskany,* Utica: North Country Books, Utica, New York, 1998.

[FD] Freeman, Douglas, *George Washington, A Biography, Vol. 1&2,* Charles Scribner's Sons, New York, 1948.

[FJA] Fitzpatrick, Jack Alan, *The Story of My Life,* unpublished by author, Kelowna, British Columbia, 1990.

[FJ1] Flexner, James, *Mohawk Baronet, A Biography of Sir William Johnson,* Syracuse University Press Edition, Syracuse, New York, 1989.

[FJ2] Flexner, James, *George Washington, The Forge of Experience, 1732-1735, Vol. 1,* Little, Brown and Co., Boston Massachusetts, 1965.

[FM] Fryer, Mary Beacock, *King's Men, The Soldier Founders of Ontario,* Dundurn Press, Toronto, Ontario, Canada, 1980.

[FM2] Fryer, Mary Beacock, *John Walden Meyers, Loyalist Spy,* Dundurn Press, Toronto, Ontario, Canada, 1983.

[GA] Gallup, Andrew, and Donald Shaffer, *La Marine, The French Colonial Soldier in Canada, 1745-1761.* Heritage Books, Inc., Bowie, Maryland, 1992.

[GC] Gehring, Charles and William Starna, *A Journey into Mohawk and Oneida Country, 1634 – 1635 The Journal of Harmen Meyndertsz van den Bogaert,* Syracuse University Press, Syracuse, New York, 1988.

[GJ] Graves, James, *Fatal Decision at Blue Licks,* Military History Magazine, Leesburg, Virginia, August 2002, volume 19, #3 issue.

[GR] Griffing, Robert, text by George Irvin, *The Art of Robert Griffing, His Journey into the Eastern Frontier,* East/West Visions, Gibsonia, Pennsylvania, 2000.

[HE1] Hamilton, Edward, *Adventures in the Wilderness: The American Journals of Louis Antoine de Bougainville, 1756-1760,* University of Oklahoma Press, 1964.

[HE2] Hamilton, Edward, *Fort Ticonderoga, Key to a Continent,* Fort Ticonderoga Press, Ticonderoga, New York, 1995.

[HL] Huey, Lois, and Bonnie Pulis, *Molly Brant, A Legacy of Her Own,* Old Fort Niagara Association, Youngstown, New York, 1997.

[HR] Horsman, Reginald, *Matthew Elliott, British Indian Agent,* Wayne State University Press, Detroit, Michigan, 1964.

[HW1] Hintzen, William, *The Border Wars of the Upper Ohio Valley (1769-1794),* Precision Shooting, Inc., Manchester, Connecticut, 1999.

[HW2] Hintzen William and Joseph Roxby, *The Heroic Age, Tales of Wheeling's Frontier History,* Closson Press, Apollo, Pennsylvania, 2000.

[HW3] Hintzen, William, *Rice's Fort Attacked, September 13-14th,1782,* True Wetzelian, Vol. VII,#3, Issue # 39, May-June, 2003, published by author, Freetown, Indiana.

[JJ] Johnson, Sir John, *Orderly Book of Sir John Johnson During his Campaign Against Fort Stanwix from Nov. 4th 1776 to July 30th, 1777,* Barnes and Co., New York, 1881.

[KD] Kent, Donald, *The French Invasion of Western Pennsylvania,* Pennsylvania Historical and Museum Commission, Harrisburg, Pennsylvania, 1954.

[KI] Kelsay, Isabel, *Joseph Brant, Man of Two Worlds,* Syracuse University Press, Syracuse, New York, 1984.

[KP] Kopperman, Paul, *Braddock at the Monongahela,* University of Pittsburgh Press, Pittsburgh, Pennsylvania, 1977.

[KR] Ketchum, Richard, *Saratoga, Turning Point of America's Revolutionary War,* Henry Holt and Company, New York, 1997.

[LB] Loescher, Burt Garfield, *The History of Rogers Rangers, Volume 4,* Heritage Books Inc., Bowie, Maryland, 2002.

[LT] Lewis, Thomas, *For King and Country, George Washington, The Early Years,* John Wiley and Sons, Inc., New York, 1993.

[MB] McDowell, Bart, *The Revolutionary War, America's Fight For Freedom,* National Geographic Society, Washington, D.C., 1967.

[MJ] Morrison, James, *A History of Fulton County in the Revolution,* Author, Gloversville, New York, 1977.

[MR] May, Robin, and Gerry Embleton, *The British Army in North America 1775-1783,* Osprey/Reed Books, London, England, 1997.

[NA] Niles, Anderson, *Battle of Bushy Run,* Pennsylvania Historical and Museum Association, Harrisburg, Pennsylvania, 1991.

[NL] Nelson, Larry, *A Man of Distinction Among Them, Alexander McKee and the Ohio Country Frontier, 1754-1799*. Kent State University Press, Kent, Ohio, 1999.

[OW] O'Meara, Walter, *Guns at the Forks*, University of Pittsburgh Press, Pittsburgh, Pennsylvania, 1979.

[PF] Parkman, Francis, *Montcalm and Wolfe*, Reprint by Modern Library, New York, 1999.

[PT] Pieper, Thomas and James Gidney, *Fort Laurens, 1778-1779*, Kent State University Press, Kent, Ohio 1976.

[RM] Reid, Max, *The Story of Old Fort Johnson*, G.P. Putnam and Sons, New York, 1906, reprinted by Heritage Books, Inc., Bowie, Maryland, 1998.

[SH] Swiggett, Howard, *War Out of Niagara, Walter Butler and the Tory Rangers*, Ira Friedman, Inc., Port Washington, New York, 1963.

[SJ] Smith, James, *Scoouwa: James Smith's Indian Captivity Narrative*, Ohio Historical Society, Columbus, Ohio, 1978.

[SM] Schoenfeld, Max, *Fort de la Presqu'ile*, Erie County Historical Society, Erie, Pennsylvania, 1979.

[SR] Swartz, Roger, *Fields of Honor: The Battle of Fort Freeland*, Warrior Run/ Fort Freeland Heritage Society, Turbotville, Pennsylvania, 1996.

[TE] Thomas, Earle, *Sir John Johnson, Loyalist Baronet*, Dundurn Press, Toronto, Ontario, Canada, 1986.

[SW] Sargent, Winthrop, *History of an Expedition Against Fort Du Quense*, in 1755, Wennawoods Publishing, Lewisburg, Pennsylvania, 1997.

[SWI] Shakespeare, William, *The Life and Death of Julius Caesar*, Ginn and Co., Boston, Massachusetts, 1939.

[TE] Tooker, Elizabeth, *An Ethnography of the Huron Indians, 1615 - 1649*, Syracuse University Press, Syracuse, New York, 1991.

[WGA] Waller, George, *The American Revolution in the West*, Nelson Hall, Chicago, Illinois, 1976.

[WG1] Watt, Gavin and James Morrison, *The British Campaign of 1777: The St. Leger Expedition*, Mothersill Printing, Bowmanville, Ontario, 1988.

[WG2] Watt, Gavin, *The Burning of the Valleys*, Dundurn Press, Toronto, Ontario, Canada, 1997.

[WM] Walsh, Mark, *Your Most Humble and Obedient Servant, William Caldwell,* University of Windsor, Ontario, Canada, 1984.

[WP] Wallace, Paul, *Indian Paths of Pennsylvania,* Pennsylvania Historical and Museum Commission, Harrisburg, Pennsylvania, 1998.

Index

Symbols

L

M

O

P

About the Author

Alan Howard Fitzpatrick was born in Regina, Saskatchewan and as a child lived across Canada before moving from Toronto, Ontario to the United States at the age of 15. A seventh generation descendent of a United Empire Loyalist, Alan became an American citizen after moving to Ohio and earning a degree in psychology from Kent State University. He is a founding member of Wheeling, West Virginia's premier heritage event, "Fort Henry Days," commemorating the "last battle of the American Revolution" fought at Wheeling's Fort Henry in 1782. Alan currently resides with his two sons, Nathan and Isaac, in Benwood, West Virginia, several miles below Wheeling and less than a mile from the site of Foreman's Massacre.